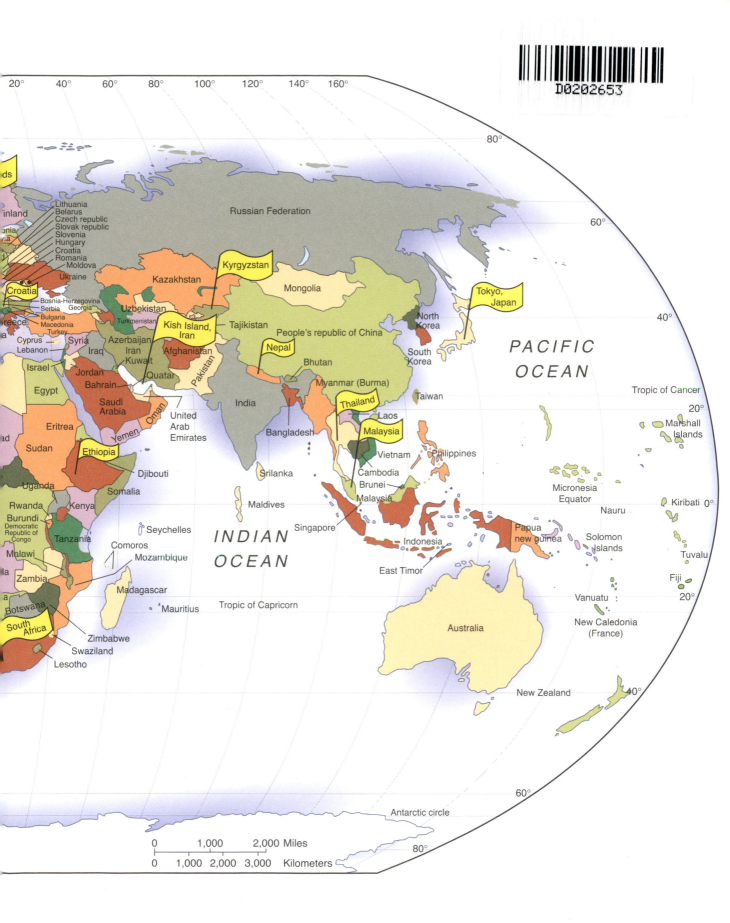

20° 40° 60° 80° 100° 120° 140° 160°

80°

60°

Russian Federation

Lithuania
Belarus
Czech republic
Slovak republic
Slovenia
Hungary
Croatia
Romania
Moldova
Ukraine

inland

Croatia

Bosnia-Herzegovina
Serbia
Bulgaria
Macedonia
Turkey

Greece

Cyprus
Lebanon

Syria

Iraq

Israel

Jordan

Egypt

Bahrain

Saudi
Arabia

Eritrea

Sudan

Ethiopia

Djibouti

Uganda

Somalia

Rwanda
Burundi
Democratic
Republic of
Congo

Kenya

Tanzania

Malawi

Zambia

Botswana

South
Africa

Zimbabwe

Swaziland

Lesotho

Kazakhstan

Kyrgyzstan

Mongolia

Uzbekistan

Turkmenistan

Kish Island,
Iran

Tajikistan

People's republic of China

Azerbaijan

Iran

Kuwait

Quatar

Afghanistan

Pakistan

Nepal

Bhutan

North
Korea

South
Korea

Tokyo,
Japan

PACIFIC
OCEAN

40°

United
Arab
Emirates

Oman

Yemen

India

Myanmar (Burma)

Taiwan

Tropic of Cancer

20°

Bangladesh

Thailand

Laos

Marshall
Islands

Malaysia

Vietnam

Philippines

Srilanka

Cambodia

Brunei

Micronesia
Equator

Maldives

Malaysia

Kiribati 0°

INDIAN
OCEAN

Singapore

Nauru

Comoros

Mozambique

Indonesia

Papua
new guinea

Solomon
Islands

Tuvalu

Madagascar

East Timor

Fiji

Mauritius

Tropic of Capricorn

Vanuatu

20°

New Caledonia
(France)

Australia

New Zealand

40°

Seychelles

60°

Antarctic circle

0   1,000   2,000 Miles

80°

0   1,000 2,000 3,000   Kilometers

Tourism

Concepts and Practices

Tourism

Concepts and Practices

John R. Walker

McKibbon Professor and Fulbright Senior Specialist
South Florida Sarasota Manatee
and

Josielyn T. Walker

Prentice Hall
Boston   Columbus   Indianapolis   New York   San Francisco   Upper Saddle River
Amsterdam   Cape Town   Dubai   London   Madrid Milan   Munich   Paris
Montreal   Toronto   Delhi   Mexico City   Sao Paulo   Sydney   Hong Kong   Seoul
Singapore   Taipei   Tokyo

Editor in Chief: Vernon Anthony
Acquisitions Editor: William Lawrensen
Developmental Editor: Sonya Kottcamp
Editorial Assistant: Lara Dimmick
Director of Marketing: David Gesell
Campaign Marketing Manager: Leigh Ann Sims
Curriculum Marketing Manager: Thomas Hayward
Senior Marketing Coordinator: Alicia Wozniak
Marketing Assistant: Les Roberts
Associate Managing Editor: Alexandrina Benedicto Wolf
Project Manager: Kris Roach
Senior Operations Supervisor: Pat Tonneman
Operations Specialist: Deidra Skahill

Senior Art Director: Diane Ernsberger
Cover Designer: Jeff Vanik
Cover Art: iStock
Manager, Cover Visual Research and Permissions: Karen Sanatar
Manager, Rights and Permissions: Zina Arabia
Interior Image Permission Coordinator: Richard Rodrigues
Image Cover Permission Coordinator: Cathy Mazzucca
Lead Media Project Manager: Michelle Churma
Full-Service Project Management: Linda Zuk, WordCraft, LLC
Composition: S4Carlisle Publishing Services
Printer/Binder: Courier/Kendallville
Cover Printer: Lehigh-Phoenix Color Hagerstown
Text Font: Sabon LT Std; 10.5/12.5

Credits and acknowledgments borrowed from other sources and reproduced, with permission, in this textbook appear on appropriate page within text or on page 537.

Library of Congress Cataloging-in-Publication Data
Walker, John R.
  Tourism: concepts and practices/John R. Walker, Josielyn T. Walker.
    p. cm.
  ISBN 0-13-814245-9 (978-0-13-814245-2)   1. Tourism.   I. Walker, Josielyn T.   II. Title.
  G155.A1W3436 2011
  910.68—dc22   2009047970

10 9 8 7 6 5 4 3 2

Prentice Hall
is an imprint of

PEARSON

www.pearsonhighered.com

ISBN-10:   0-13-814245-9
ISBN-13: 978-0-13-814245-2

To Christopher and Selina

BRIEF CONTENTS

CONTENTS

Chapter 4   Tourism Economics

Part 2   Organizing Tourism   147

Part 3   Operating Sectors 1   257

Chapter 8   Attractions and Entertainment   259

Chapter 9   Business Travel: Meetings, Conventions, and Expositions   293

Chapter 11 Cultural and Heritage Tourism   351

Part 5   Operating Sectors 2   405

Welcome to *Tourism: Concepts and Practices*. This book is intended as a comprehensive university and college level student-friendly tourism text.

Features of This Book

Student-friendly features that were well received in the Introduction to Hospitality series are also included in this *Tourism* text.

- Chapter learning objectives.
- Check Your Knowledge questions dispersed throughout all chapters.
- "Geography Spotlight" features describe locations that embody the seven reasons to travel: education, romance, adventure, ecology, culture/heritage, remote lands, and relaxation.
- "Focus On" features: Written by contributing authors who are experts in their field, these boxes offer unique personal perspectives on chapter topics.
- "Corporate Profile" features describe the practices, growth, and scope of leading corporations and organizations.
- Highlighted key words and concepts. Set boldface, with easy-to-understand definitions in the Glossary, the key words and concepts help you recall the importance of and the meaning of these important terms. Master the key words and concepts of the text and improve your test scores.
- Review questions designed to improve critical thinking skills. By answering these review questions, you will reinforce your mastery of the materials presented in the text and may improve your test scores.
- Chapter summaries highlight the most important points in the chapter. They provide a brief review of the chapter and reinforce the primary terms, concepts, and topics.
- Apply Your Knowledge: Apply the knowledge and skills learned in each chapter to real-life tourism topics.
- Interesting Websites: Surf the Net to uncover answers to specific tourism questions.
- Suggested Activities: Hone your skills on topics related to tourism.
- "Career Information" features describe the skills, challenges, and realities of various careers in the field of hospitality.
- Case Studies: Practice dealing with realistic tourism situations.
- Internet Exercises challenge students to learn more online about the industry.

Textbook Structure

Tourism: Concepts and Practice is divided into five parts:

Part 1   The Characteristics of Tourism
        Chapter 1   Introduction to Tourism
        Chapter 2   Motivation for Leisure Tourism

Part 1 of the book introduces the characteristics of the tourism concepts and systems approach that forms the foundation of the text. Tourism past and present is discussed, and tourism demand and motivation are examined. Building upon *why* people want to be tourists, we discuss the nuances of tourism marketing and economics.

Part 2 focuses on the organization of tourism. The roles of international, national, regional, and state/local tourism organizations are examined. Tourism policy, planning, and the important topics of sustainability and tourism research are also discussed, with examples of current practices.

Part 3 examines the first part of the operating sectors with an overview of the attractions and entertainment industry and the business of conventions, meetings, and expositions.

Part 4 highlights the social, cultural, heritage, and ecotourism impacts of tourism from the tourist's and host community's perspectives. Eco-tourism is discussed in detail, with numerous examples.

Part 5 looks at the second part of tourism operations. Distribution organizations are examined, and their importance in the tourism system is explained. Sea, rail, air, and auto transportation are discussed, and lodging and restaurants are reviewed. Finally, the future of tourism is introduced.

Dear Future Tourism Professional,

This textbook is written to empower you and help you on your way to becoming a future leader of this great industry. *Tourism: Concepts and Practices* will give you an overview of the world's largest and fastest growing industry groupings. Each chapter contains information about the numerous tourism segments, the many different areas of career opportunities, and career paths as well as profiles of industry practitioners and leaders.

Read the Book

Read and study the text, including the profiles, boxes, Check Your Knowledge questions, and Review Questions, and discuss and debate the Case Studies. Use the many tools throughout this textbook—including boldface key words and concepts and glossary of terms—to facilitate your reading and understanding of the concepts. You will be amazed at how much more you get out of class by preparing ahead of time.

Use the Resources Accompanying this Book

Make use of the excellent and free Companion Website (www.pearsonhighered .com/johnwalker) for this book with its sample test questions, review information, and links to tourism websites. You will improve your chances of not only success in this class but also enjoying it more than others.

Success in the Classroom

Faculty constantly say that the best students are the ones who come to class prepared. We know that as a tourism student you have many demands on your time: work, a heavy course load, family commitments, and, yes, fun—plus a lot of reading and studying for your other courses. With this in mind, we tried to make this book as visually appealing, easy and engaging to read, and as enjoyable as possible.

Wishing you success in your studies and career.
Sincerely,
John and Josielyn Walker.

Take some time to turn the page and review descriptions of all the features and tools in this book and find out how they will facilitate your reading and understanding of the concepts. Discover the exciting opportunities in the numerous and varied segments of the tourism industry.

Intricacies of Tourism

As you begin to read the book, you'll recognize this hallmark text was written by authors with years of tourism operations experience. There are numerous industry examples that illustrate the key topics. This not only makes for a more engaging read, but it also helps you understand the material presented.

Focus On. . .

This feature highlights selected tourism issues and organizations. They relate real-world responses to tourism challenges and give students insights into career choices and activities. Written by contributing expert authors, these features offer unique personal perspectives on chapter topics.

FOCUS ON

Cultural Heritage: Carnival

A great deal is revealed from the way a community celebrates. Some celebratory traditions date back hundreds of years. Most people enjoy a good party and very few festivals are bigger or more popular than Carnivals, whether it is Carnival in Rio de Janeiro, Trinidad, or Aruba; Mardi Gras in New Orleans; Caribana in Toronto; the Notting Hill Carnival in London; Barbados's Crop Over or New York City's Labor Day parade on Eastern Parkway. Carnivals are a time to dance in the streets to festive music, parade in costumed groups, and enjoy the company of friends.

The Western history of Carnival dates from medieval times when Catholics started a tradition of celebration ahead of the Lenten season. *Carnevale*, translated "putting away the meat," represents the last opportunity to be festive before the solemnity and fasting of Lent. This tradition spread from Italy around the world with Catholicism, although Eastern Orthodox religions also include a pre-Lent Carnival tradition.

There are probably thousands of carnivals worldwide, and they are an important marketing opportunity for increasing visitation and spending, as well as for showcasing the destination's culture. A challenge is that many carnivals take place at the same time, the two days before Ash Wednesday. Enjoying several carnivals during a single year is impossible except where the celebration takes place outside the traditional pre-Lent period.

McKercher and du Cross in their book *Cultural Tourism: The Partnership between Tourism and Cultural Management* (~~~~~~~ 2002) pre~~~~~~

Corporate Profiles

Learn about the practices, growth, and scope of leading corporations and organizations.

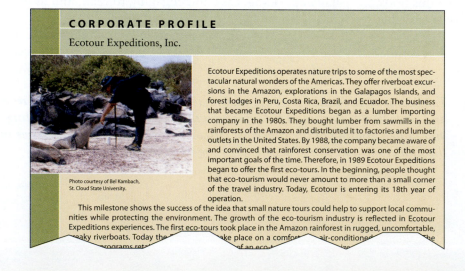

CORPORATE PROFILE

Ecotour Expeditions, Inc.

Photo courtesy of Bel Kambach, St. Cloud State University.

Ecotour Expeditions operates nature trips to some of the most spectacular natural wonders of the Americas. They offer riverboat excursions in the Amazon, explorations in the Galapagos Islands, and forest lodges in Peru, Costa Rica, Brazil, and Ecuador. The business that became Ecotour Expeditions began as a lumber importing company in the 1980s. They bought lumber from sawmills in the rainforests of the Amazon and distributed it to factories and lumber outlets in the United States. By 1988, the company became aware of and convinced that rainforest conservation was one of the most important goals of the time. Therefore, in 1989 Ecotour Expeditions began to offer the first eco-tours. In the beginning, people thought that eco-tourism would never amount to more than a small corner of the travel industry. Today, Ecotour is entering its 18th year of operation.

This milestone shows the success of the idea that small nature tours could help to support local communities while protecting the environment. The growth of the eco-tourism industry is reflected in Ecotour Expeditions experiences. The first eco-tours took place in the Amazon rainforest in rugged, uncomfortable, ~~~~~reaky riverboats. Today the ~~~~~~~~ake place on a comfor~~~~~~air-conditioned~~~~~~~~~~the ~~~~~rograms ret~~~~~~~~~~~~~of an eco-t~~~~~~~~~

Geography Spotlight

We travel for many reasons: business, family, conventions, leisure, and so forth. Contributing authors Dr. Duncan Dickson and Katie Noland have selected various locations around the world, and they take you there with various reasons for the journey. We look at seven diverse reasons to travel: educational tourism; romantic tourism; adventure tourism; eco-tourism; cultural/heritage tourism; remote tourism; and sea, sand, and sun tourism.

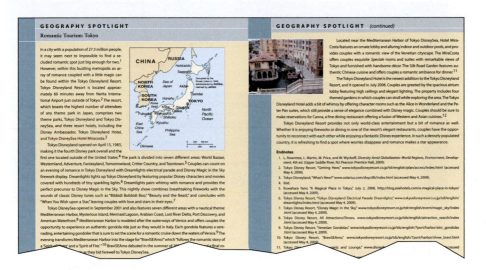

Career Information

This feature gives you more information and descriptions of career opportunities, along with a listing of related websites. Learn about skills, challenges, and realities of various careers.

CAREER INFORMATION

If you are interested in a career in tourism planning and sustainable development, you have several different options. Many people work for organizations directly involved in the field, such as the World Tourism Organization or the United Nations Environment Committee. Also, a number of smaller organizations are involved in tourism planning and development on a regional or local basis in almost every part of the world.

Another career choice with great future potential is to work within a corporation, such as a hotel or a cruise provider, and handle their environmental policies and issues. Because the demands on companies to be environmentally friendly and sustainable are increasing drastically, so will the need for people with the knowledge and interest to ha... ...ics for them.

Hone Your Critical Thinking Skills

Case Studies

Case studies in each chapter challenge you to test your skills and knowledge as you address real-world situations and recommend appropriate actions.

CASE STUDY

Double-Booked

The convention bureau in a large and popular convention destination has jurisdiction over the convention center. A seasoned convention sales manager, who has worked for the bureau for seven years and produces more sales than any other sales manager, has rebooked a 2,000-person group for a three-day exposition in the convention center. The exposition is to take place two years from the booking date.

The client has a 15-year history of holding conventions, meetings, and expositions in this convention center and has always used the bureau to contract all space and services for them. In fact, the sales manager handling the account has worked with the client for 7 of the 15 years. The bureau considers this client a "preferred customer."

The convention group meeting planner also appears in a magazine ad giving a testimony of praise for the convention bureau, this particular sales manager, and the city as a destination for conventions.

Shortly after the meeting planner rebooks this convention with the bureau, the bureau changes sales administration personnel, not once, but three times. This creates a challenge for the sales manager in terms of producing contracts, client files, and event profiles, and in the recording and distribution of information. The preferred customer who rebooked has a contract, purchase orders for vendor services, a move in and setup agenda, and an event profile from the sales manager. The sales manager has e...

Internet Exercises

Surf the 'net to uncover answers to specific tourism questions. The Internet Exercises challenge you to learn more and prepare you for a career in this fascinating industry.

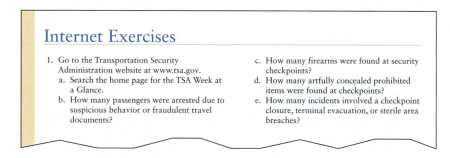

Internet Exercises

1. Go to the Transportation Security Administration website at www.tsa.gov.
   a. Search the home page for the TSA Week at a Glance.
   b. How many passengers were arrested due to suspicious behavior or fraudulent travel documents?
   c. How many firearms were found at security checkpoints?
   d. How many artfully concealed prohibited items were found at checkpoints?
   e. How many incidents involved a checkpoint closure, terminal evacuation, or sterile area breaches?

Suggested Activities

Put what you have learned to work and see how concepts discussed come to life when applied to the real world.

Suggested Activities

1. Identify which kind of hotel you would like to work at and give reasons why.

2. Think of your favorite restaurant and write down all the things you like about it. Compare your answers with the other members of your class.

Important Memory Tools

Objectives

At the beginning of each chapter, this list gives you a "heads-up" on what will be discussed and how to organize your thoughts. The objectives summarize what you need to know after studying the chapter and doing the exercises, cases, questions, and Apply Your Knowledge.

> **OBJECTIVES**
>
> After reading and studying this chapter, you should be able to:
>
> - List the major players in the amusement park industry.
> - Identify trends in the amusement and theme park industry.
> - Explain the reasons for the immense growth of the gaming entertainment industry.
> - Explain the main reasons for travel in the following areas: fairs, festivals, events, historic places/sites, and performing arts.
> - Give some examples of important festivals, fairs, and events.
> - Discuss trends in leisure travel.

Check Your Knowledge

Every few pages, the Check Your Knowledge section will help you to review and reinforce material that has just been covered.

> **▶ Check Your Knowledge**
>
> 1. List the major important eco-tourism destinations around the world.
> 2. What countries in Africa provide great safaris?
> 3. What skills and attitudes are needed to be a sustainable tourist?

Chapter Summary

The chapter summary highlights the most important points in the chapter. This summary is a brief review of the chapter that reinforces the main terms, concepts, and topics.

Key Words and Concepts

Highlighted in bold with easy-to-understand definitions in the glossary, the key words and concepts help you to recall the importance of and meaning of these terms. Master the key words and concepts of the text and improve your test scores.

Review Questions

By answering these review questions, you will reinforce your mastery of the materials presented in the text and most likely will improve your test scores.

Visuals

Color format with lively photographs, drawings, and figures will sustain your interest and provide visual aids to learning.

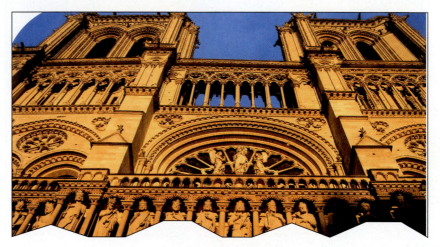

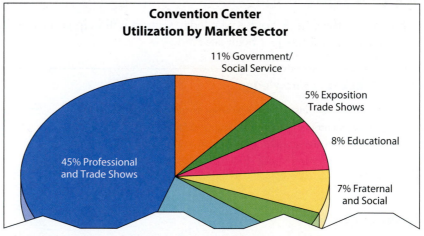

Convention Center
Utilization by Market Sector

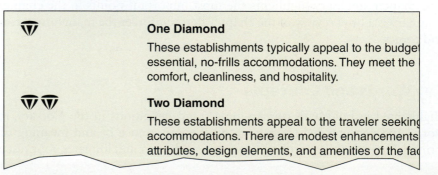

One Diamond

These establishments typically appeal to the budge
essential, no-frills accommodations. They meet the
comfort, cleanliness, and hospitality.

Two Diamond

These establishments appeal to the traveler seeking
accommodations. There are modest enhancements
attributes, design elements, and amenities of the fac

Additional Student Resources

Companion Website: www.pearsonhighered.com/ johnwalker

This online student study guide has been designed specifically to help you review, reinforce, and apply the concepts presented in the book. This interactive site features chapter-specific modules: practice exams with immediate answer assessment, and relevant Internet links.

We now invite you to join us and share the enthusiasm for tourism!

ACKNOWLEDGMENTS

This book is dedicated to the outstanding friends and colleagues listed below, who helped shape this text. We are very grateful for their help and to our twins Christopher and Selina, who seemed to know when we needed a break and pulled us off our chairs and into the pool.

Michael Scantlebury, you did an incredible job of reviewing the text and making a number of insightful suggestions for its improvement.

Greg Dunn, my colleague, thank you for your important contributions to the Tourism Marketing chapter and for your excellent review of it.

Dr. Katerina Annaraud, thank you for reviewing Chapter 4, Tourism Economics.

Brad Kamp, thank for your outstanding contribution to Chapter 4. You helped make more sense of tourism economics.

Holly Loftus and Stacy Tomas thank you for your excellent contributions to Chapter 7.

Bel Kambach, thanks for your photographs, "Focus On" features, and cases, especially the one French kissing a stingray. You helped with your enthusiasm and encouragement, and by introducing me to two amazing gentlemen. My sincere thanks to you.

Mark Green, thanks for your expert international photography.

Rick Pawlenty, thanks for your award-winning American photography.

Sonya Kottcamp, thank you for being such a sweet person to work with. You picked up on all my oversights and made sure everything was perfect for production of this text.

Bill Lawrensen, we made it! Thanks to you for your guidance and resource help during the preparation of the manuscript.

We would also like to thank the reviewers for their insightful thoughts and comments. They are:

Alan Bright, Colorado State University; Robertico Croes, Rosen College of Hospitaility Management, University of Central Florida; Linda Cropper, El Paso Community College; James H. Ferguson, CHA, Hawaii Community College; Joan Ferrante, Miami Dade College; Tadayuki Hara, Rosen College of Hospitality Management; Bel Kambach, St. Cloud State University (SCSU); Bradley Kamp, University of South Florida; Xiang (Robert) Li, Ph.D., University of South Carolina; Nancy Gard McGehee, Virginia Tech; Ingrid O'Connell, Schenectady County Community College; Jess Ponting, San Diego State University; Dr. Michael Scantlebury, UCF Rosen College of Hospitality Management; Dr. Neha Singh, California State Polytechnic University—Pomona; Dallen J. Timothy, Arizona State University; Muzzaffer Uysal, Virginia Tech; Zheng Xiang, SMHM/University of North Texas; and Jian Zhang, The Collins College California Polytechnic University—Pomona.

Contributing Authors

This text is also dedicated to the following contributing authors, who added immeasurably to the text with their knowledge and expertise.

Kathleen L. Andereck, Ph.D., *Arizona State University*

Carla Barbieri, Ph.D., *Department of Parks, Recreation and Tourism, University of Missouri*

Alan D. Bright, Ph.D., *Colorado State University*

Robertico R. Croes, Ph.D., *Rosen College of Hospitality Management, University of Central Florida*

Duncan Dickson, Ed.D., *Rosen College of Hospitality Management, University of Central Florida*

Daniel R. Fesenmaier, Ph.D., *Temple University*

Tadayuki (Tad) Hara, Ph.D., *Rosen College of Hospitality Management, University of Central Florida*

Amy Hart, *Columbus State Community College*

Belkis Kambach, Ph.D., *St. Cloud State University*

Richard C. Knopf, Ph.D., *Arizona State University*

Khoon Y Koh, Ph.D., *Central Connecticut State University*

Katie Noland, *Rosen College of Hospitality Management, University of Central Florida*

Michael Scantlebury, Ph.D., *Rosen College of Hospitality Management, University of Central Florida*

Alan Seidman, Ph.D., *The Hospitality College, Johnson & Wales University*

Neha Singh, Ph.D., *The Collins College of Hospitality Management, California State Polytechnic University (Cal Poly, Pomona)*

Wayne W. Smith, Ph.D., *College of Charleston*

Stacy R. Thomas, Ph.D., *North Carolina State University*

Alistair Williams, *Johnson & Wales University*

Florian Zach, Ph.D., *Temple University*

Janet B. Zinck, MA, CTA, *Assistant Professor of Hospitality Management, Monroe Community College*

Our sincere thanks to all who helped in the preparation of this text.

John R. Walker, D.B. A., and Josielyn T. Walker BSBA,
Fulbright Senior Specialist and McKibbon Professor
University of South Florida

Dr. John R. Walker is a Fulbright Senior Specialist and the McKibbon professor at the School of Hotel and Restaurant Management at the University of South Florida. John is the former Dean and Marshall Professor Emeritus of the School of Hospitality Management at United States International University, San Diego, California.

John's years of industry experience include management training at the Savoy Hotel London, followed by terms as food and beverage manager, assistant rooms division manager, catering manager, and general manager with Grand Metropolitan Hotels, Selsdon Park Hotel, Rank Hotels, Inter-Continental Hotels, and the Coral Reef Resort, Barbados, West Indies.

He has received the President's award for Scholarship and the Outstanding Teaching award. He has also received the President's award of Merit based on teaching excellence, scholarship, and service, each year from its inception in 1992 until 2003, when he moved to the University of South Florida. In 2004 he received the Patnuby Award for exemplary performance through teaching and authorship of tourism and hospitality publications.

John's work has been published in *The Cornell Hotel Restaurant Administration Quarterly* and, *The Hospitality Educator's Journal*. He is a member of the editorial review board of the journal *Progress in Tourism and Hospitality Research* and *The Journal of Human Resources in Hospitality and Tourism*. He is an advisory board member for Prentice Hall's Hospitality and Tourism publications, and he has been invited to teach and give seminars in a number of countries.

John is a leading author of hospitality and tourism textbooks; his texts are used at over 700 universities and colleges worldwide. He has authored the following texts, four of which have been translated into Chinese, Russian, Spanish, and Portuguese languages:

- *Introduction to Hospitality,* fifth edition, Prentice Hall (2009).
- *The Restaurant: From Concept to Operation*, fifth edition, John Wiley & Sons (2008).
- *Supervision: Human Resources Leadership in the Hospitality Industry*, sixth edition, with Jack E. Miller, John Wiley & Sons (2010).
- *Exploring the Hospitality Industry,* Prentice Hall (2007).
- *Introduction to Hospitality Management,* third edition, Prentice Hall (2009).
- Contributing author in *The Encyclopedia of Tourism*, published by Routledge (2001).

John is a past president of the Pacific chapter of the Council on Hotel, Restaurant, and Institutional Education (CHRIE). He is a Certified Hotel Administrator and a Certified Foodservice Management Professional.

John enjoys a variety of cultural, recreational, and artistic activities. He is married to Josielyn and they live in Sarasota, Florida. They are blessed with twins Christopher and Selina. John and Josielyn sponsor a number of high school and college students and volunteer presentations at Universities and Colleges.

Josielyn is a graduate of the University of the Northern Philippines and the owner-operator of Suso Beach Eco Resort.

PART I
The Characteristics of Tourism

ΑΡΕΤΗ
ΚΕΛΣΟΥ

CHAPTER 1

Introduction to Tourism

OBJECTIVES

After reading and studying this chapter, you should be able to:

- Describe the evolution of tourism.

- Define the scope and importance of tourism, both for the U.S. economy and internationally.

- Explain why tourism is described by Gunn and Leiper as a system.

- Suggest why so many governments promote tourism and why tourist revenue is so highly valued.

- Describe the types and characteristics of tourism.

GEOGRAPHY SPOTLIGHT

Educational Tourism: Ethiopia

The East African country of Ethiopia is believed to be the birthplace of humans and civilization and offers a rich historical (and prehistoric) background that tourists can experience through its archaeological sites, museums, and university.

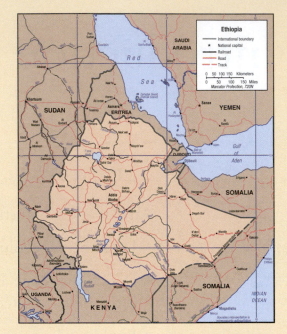

According to the British Broadcasting Company (BBC),[1] Lucy was discovered in 1974 by anthropologist Professor Donald Johanson. His team found 47 bones of a species named *Australopithecus Afarensis* that lived approximately 3.2 million years ago; this species was the first hominid to walk upright.

The Federal Democratic Republic of Ethiopia is situated in the horn of sub-Saharan Africa. Neighboring Sudan and Somalia cast the shadow of violence and poverty across Ethiopia, the oldest independent country in Africa and one of the oldest in the world.[2] The capital city, Addis Ababa, is home to a population of 2 million and is the political and educational center of the country. Addis Ababa contradicts the colonial norm in Africa by being the last of the royal capitals established by the Abyssinian Empire rather than colonized by the British Empire.[3]

Archaeological Tours is a specialized tour company based in New York City that every month offers trips to different destinations led by acclaimed scholars. Professor Ori Z. Soltes, lecturer at Georgetown and Johns Hopkins Universities, leads a 16-day tour of the archaeological wonders and historical background of Ethiopia. Acting as headquarters for the journey, Addis Ababa University also offers tours of the National Archaeological and Ethnographic Museums.[4] Near the university is the Ethiopian National Museum, which houses the remains of Lucy, "the mother of man." Travelers who really want to understand their surroundings in Ethiopia can also visit the United Nations Economic Commission for Africa headquarters, the African Union headquarters, St. Georges Cathedral, and Shengo Hall (Parliament Building), which, according to iExplore, is the world's largest prefabricated building.[5]

The educational focus point in Ethiopia is Axum, located in the northern part of the country. The Kingdom of Axum was the first royal capital and dates back to the pre-Christian era, making it one of the oldest empires in Ethiopia. It was comparable to Rome and Byzantium and was the first kingdom in sub-Saharan Africa. Axum offers travelers an archaeological experience with monolithic obelisks, royal tombs, and the ruins of ancient castles that are remnants of several Muslim wars.[6]

GEOGRAPHY SPOTLIGHT *(continued)*

"Recent reports estimate that 68% of Ethiopian children attend primary school and just 16% complete their secondary education."[7] However, with the emergence of a small middle class, the younger generations of Addis Ababa are working to improve their education levels and in turn Ethiopia's overall economic stability and future. Travelers can transform their vacation by participating in a voluntourism program. For example, Projects Abroad combines

Courtesy of Werner Forman / Art Resource, NY

travel with community service by enlisting tourists to contribute to projects in the areas of teaching, conservation and environment, medicine and health care, human rights, and journalism.[8] By engaging in the local economy rather than being consumers of it, tourists can gain a unique educational, emotional, and psychological experience that simultaneously benefits the recipients of the service.

In Ethiopia, visitors can witness a developing country that has made many efforts to further its development and position on a global scale and experience archaeology like nowhere else in the world. Travelers can have fun and learn about the history and culture of Ethiopia, and programs such as Projects Abroad enable visitors to give back time and service to the host country, yielding a definitive educational and responsible travel experience.

Endnotes

1. British Broadcasting Company, "Mother of Man—3.2 Million Years Ago," www.bbc.co.uk/sn/prehistoric_life/human/human_evolution/mother_of_man1.shtml (accessed March 27, 2009).
2. K. Shiveley, Addis Ababa, Ethiopia, website, www.macalester.edu/courses/geog61/kshively/index.html (accessed March 27, 2009).
3. Ibid.
4. Archaeological Tours, "Ethiopia," www.archaeologicaltrs.com/af_ethio.html (accessed March 27, 2009).
5. iExplore, "iExplore Ethiopia Experience," www.iexplore.com/tour/43816 (accessed March 27, 2009).
6. Shively, Addis Ababa, Ethiopia, www.macalester.edu/courses/geog61/kshively/index.html
7. Projects Abroad, "Volunteering Projects and Internships in Africa—Ethiopia," www.projects-abroad.co.uk/destinations/ethiopia/ (accessed March 27, 2009).
8. Ibid.

Source: http://unwto.org, retreived September 9, 2009. © UNTWO, 9284404409.

Welcome! As a student of tourism, you have opportunities to explore the world.

This book is divided into five parts: the characteristics of tourism, organizing tourism; operating sectors (Parts 3 and 5); and social, cultural, heritage, and eco-tourism. Part 1, Characteristics of Tourism, introduces tourism past and present; tourists' motivation: the reasons why people travel; tourism marketing; and tourism economics.

Part 2, Organizing Tourism, focuses on tourism organizations and policy; tourism planning and sustainable development; and tourism research. Parts 3 and 5, Operating Sectors I and II, look at the **industry sectors** of **attractions** and entertainment; conventions, meetings, and expositions; transportation; lodging and restaurants; and tourism distribution organizations. Part 4 looks at the social, cultural, and heritage aspects of tourism, as well as eco-tourism.

We can approach tourism from multiple viewpoints: social, cultural, economic, political, product, travel, accommodation, educational, legal, marketing, human resources, heritage, ecological, environmental, political, international relations, geographical, and sustainable development. In this book, we examine these approaches to tourism.

As shown in Figure 1–1, tourism has grown immensely during the last 50 years and is expected to continue growing in the future. In consideration of all the areas **interrelated** with tourism, it is no wonder that scholars and industry experts have recommended a **systems approach** to studying tourism. One of the important things to remember about the tourism system is that if something happens in one area, it will likely cause an effect in another area. For example, rising oil prices and the decrease in the value of the U.S. dollar are causing an increase in European and Asian travel to the United States and a decrease in U.S. citizens' visitation to places that require medium to long-haul travel such as Europe and Asia.

In February 2009, international passenger arrivals in Paris, France, declined by 8.1 percent compared to the same month the previous year. Overall, the U.S.

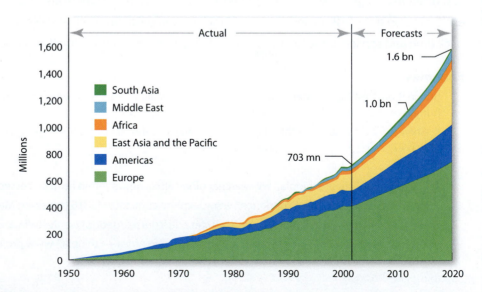

Figure 1–1 • International Tourist Arrivals, 1950–2020

Source: World Tourism Organization, *Tourism 2020 Vision*, Volume 1: *Africa.* Madrid, Spain: World Tourism Organization, www.unwto.org, (accessed May 24, 2009). © UNWTO, 9284404409.

Department of Commerce calculates that visits by Americans to Europe dropped by 7 percent in 2008.[1] Even domestic U.S. tourism has decreased as more people decide to take fewer trips. According to Destination Analysis, a San Francisco–based market research firm, the average number of trips the typical American took in the past 12 months has fallen from 7.3 to 5.1, and that organization expects to see travelers taking fewer trips and visiting destinations closer to home.[2] Next, let's consider the definition of tourism.

Definition of Tourism

The United Nations World Tourism Organization (UNWTO) states that **tourism** comprises *the activities of persons traveling to, and staying in places outside their usual environment for not more than one consecutive year for leisure, business, and other purposes.*[3] This is the definition of tourism that we use throughout this book.

Also, tourism is frequently considered in terms of the **demand side**, meaning the tourists' motivations, and the **supply side**, the sectors that satisfy tourist needs. Other important terms associated with tourism are **infrastructure**, the components that an area's residents rely on such as roads, bridges, communications networks, markets and supermarkets, and so on; and **superstructure**, facilities that have been built to accommodate the needs of tourists such as cruise terminals, airports, and convention centers (although these also support the area's residents), hotels, resorts, restaurants, and car rentals.

A Systems Approach

A systems approach to tourism is based upon *general systems theory* first suggested by Ludwig von Bertalanffy, who defined a *system* as "a set of elements standing in interrelation among themselves and with the environments."[4] Early proponents of the tourism system concept were two leading authorities on tourism: Clare Gunn of Texas A&M University, and Neil Leiper of Southern Cross University. Gunn describes the *functioning tourism system*, consisting of the supply side of attractions, services, promotion, information, and transportation.[5] Leiper suggests a model of a tourism system that has five elements:

1. *The tourist.* The people who plan and prepare for a visit to another place
2. *Three geographical regions:*
   a. *Traveler-generating region.* The feeder markets for the destination. A destination may have several traveler-generating regions, such as the island nation of Barbados, West Indies, where the traveler-generating regions are mainly the United Kingdom, United States, Canada, Venezuela, and Germany.
   b. *Transit route.* All the places a person may visit on the way to the final destination.
   c. *Tourist destination region.* The "pull" factor where demand is created and the reason why people travel. For example, a person sees a catchy

advertisement for Australia. The "in-your-face" approach (the current advertisement says, "Where the bloody hell are you, then?" meaning "why aren't you here in Australia?") plus the scenery in the advertisement may be so attractive as to cause a person to book a vacation there.

3. *An industrial element (the travel and tourism industry).* The distribution of travel via travel agents, the Internet, tour groups, discount travel companies, attractions, lodging, and restaurants.

Leiper strongly advises a holistic approach to tourism.[6] A systems approach to tourism includes local communities and residents of areas receiving tourists. It also considers the effects of an action on other parts of the tourism system. Figure 1–2 illustrates the tourism system model. Notice how it looks like a spider's web—when something occurs in one area, its effects reverberate in other areas. For example, if the price of oil goes up, it increases the price of travel; therefore, we may assume that fewer people will travel, so revenues drop in destination attractions, lodging, restaurants, entertainment, and shops. We can see now that tourism does not exist in a vacuum but is part of a larger world and is influenced by multiple factors such as the changing value of a currency or an outbreak of a serious disease.

Wall and Mathieson suggest a conceptually brilliant framework for tourism that includes three basic elements[7]:

- A dynamic element that involves travelers' decisions to travel to a selected destination or destinations and the multitude of social, economic, and institutional factors that affect these decisions
- A stay in the destination, including interaction with the economic, environmental, and social systems of the destination
- A consequential element, resulting from the two preceding components, which concerns the effects on the economic, environmental, and social subsystems with which the tourist is directly or indirectly in contact

The framework and the various interrelating variables are illustrated in Figure 1–3. Notice the three main elements: the dynamic element, the destination element, and the consequential element. Throughout this text, we examine these important elements and discuss their application in the context of tourism.

Perspectives on Tourism

We can study tourism from several perspectives. With a holistic interdisciplinary approach, we include all the elements of Figure 1–2 as well as geography; motivation; marketing; economics; political organizations and policy; agriculture; planning and sustainable development; anthropology; research; architecture; attractions and entertainment; business travel in the form of conventions, meetings, and expositions; social factors; culture and heritage; ecotourism; distribution organizations; transportation; lodging and restaurants; and the future of tourism. These various perspectives are discussed in the chapters that follow.

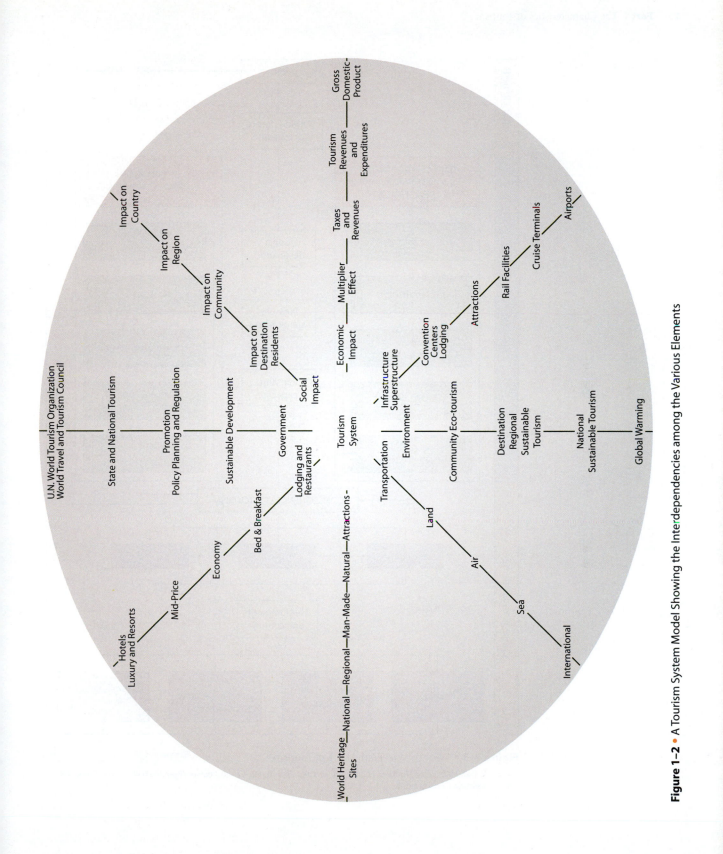

Figure 1–2 • A Tourism System Model Showing the Interdependencies among the Various Elements

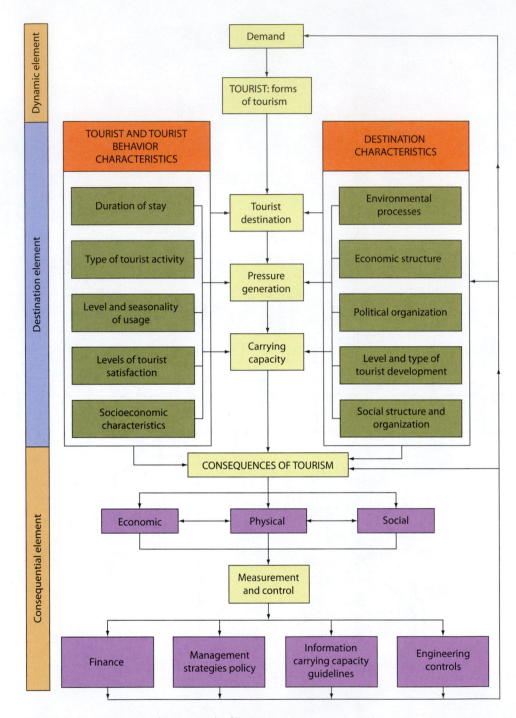

Figure 1–3 • A Conceptual Framework of Tourism

Source: Wall and Mathieson, *Tourism: Change, Impacts and Opportunities,* p. 20. Pearson/Prentice Hall. Harlow, Essex, U.K. 2006. Permission kindly granted.

The Tourism Product

In a narrow sense, the tourism product consists of what the tourist buys.[8] In a wider sense, the tourist product is a combination of what the tourist does at the destination and the services used during the stay. There are four main characteristics of a tourism product.

The first is *service*, which is **intangible** because it cannot be inspected physically. For example, a tourist cannot sample a Caribbean cruise or a European tour before purchasing one.

The second characteristic is that the tourism product is largely psychological in its attraction. It is more than airline seats or car rentals; it is the temporary use of a different environment, its culture, heritage, and experiences.

A third characteristic is that the product frequently varies in quality and standards. A tourist's hotel experience may be excellent one time and not so good at the next visit, or a beach visit may be ruined by a red tide (a form of algae that washes up on the beach and has a bad odor).

A fourth characteristic of the tourism product is that the supply of the product is fixed, for example, more hotel rooms cannot be instantly created to meet increased demand. Likewise, the number of cabins on a cruise ship are fixed, and if demand decreases, unsold cabins cannot be sold the next day or next cruise to make up for it.

Types and Characteristics of Tourism

There are four major types of tourism:

Internal tourism. Residents of a country visiting other parts of their own country

Domestic tourism. Inbound tourism plus internal tourism

International tourism. Inbound tourism, which are visits to a country or region by nonresidents

Outbound tourism. Visits by residents of a country or region to another country or region

The special characteristics of tourism make it different from other industry groupings in the following ways[9]:

1. Burkart and Medlik, and Cruz cite these characteristics of tourism:
   a. Because of its complexity, tourism is a combination of phenomena and relationships.
   b. It has two essential elements: the dynamic element—the journey, and the static element—the stay.
   c. The journey and the stay are to and from destinations outside the place of residence and work.
   d. The movement to destinations is temporary and short term with the intention to return within a few days, weeks, or months.
   e. Destinations are visited for purposes not connected with paid work, that is, not for employment purposes and not for business or vocational reasons.

2. With tourism, the consumer goes to the product; with most other industries, the product is brought to the consumer.

3. The products of tourism are *not used up*; thus, they do not exhaust countries' natural resources. In contrast, the products of other industries have a limited life and are trashed, recycled, and replaced with new ones.

4. Tourism is a *labor-intensive* phenomenon.

5. Tourism is *people-oriented*—one of the motivations of tourists is to visit other places, meet people, and see how they live.

6. Tourism is a *multidimensional phenomenon*. It is dependent on many and varied activities that are separate but interdependent.

7. Tourism can be *seasonal*. During vacation seasons, millions of tourists travel, which results in increased revenues for tourism agencies. But when vacations are over, these companies experience a big decline in dollars earned.

8. Tourism is *dynamic*. It is characterized by changing ideas and attitudes of its consumers and therefore must always be prepared and willing to adjust to these changes.

These varied characteristics of tourism indicate that it is a fascinating area of study. One way to study tourism is to examine its industry sectors.

Tourism Industry Sectors

Several interacting industries make up the tourism system, including lodging, attractions, transportation, and foodservice:

Lodging. Lodging includes all the different types of accommodations that tourists use, from camping spots and cabins in a national park, to resorts and hotels, to bed-and-breakfast inns, to all-suite properties.

Attractions. Attractions are differentiated as **natural attractions**, as in Mount Fuji, a park, or a beach, and **man-made** attractions, as in the Euro Disney theme park. Destinations are also attractions: cities such as Athens, Hong Kong, Rome, Paris, and London receive millions of tourists every year.

Transportation. Transportation is by automobile, ship, rail, or air. Personal autos, rental cars, and coaches are the most frequently used vehicles by tourists. Cruising includes exotic ports of call to add interest and on-board entertainment to add excitement for passengers. Rail travel has decreased in the United States, but in Europe and parts of Asia the train

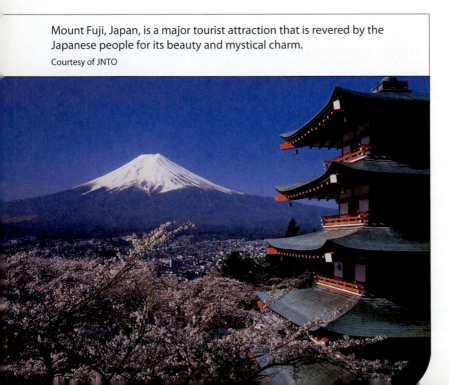

Mount Fuji, Japan, is a major tourist attraction that is revered by the Japanese people for its beauty and mystical charm.

Courtesy of JNTO

is a convenient way to sightsee and travel between major cities. Air travel has made distant locations seem much closer. By air, Europe and Asia are only a few hours away, and with the newer Airbus 380 and Boeing's Dreamliner, long-haul flights, such as New York to Singapore or Hong Kong, are now nonstop.

Foodservice. **Foodservice** relating to tourism mostly includes restaurants and cafés that cater to tourists as well as people living in the tourist area. The choice of dining available likely reflects the type of food and service that the target market wants.

It is interesting to note the interconnectivity between and among these tourism industry sectors. To an extent, the lodging sector relies on the other segments to bring guests to stay. Figure 1–4 illustrates the interrelated nature of the tourism system, in which many sectors come together to provide services to tourists, and this offers numerous employment opportunities.

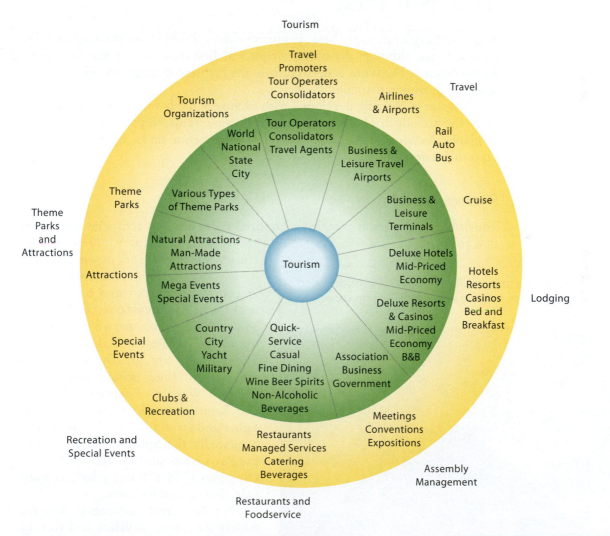

Figure 1–4 • The Interrelated Nature of the Tourism System

Source: Walker, John R., *Introduction to Hospitality Management,* 3rd., © 2010. Electronically reproduced by permission of Pearson Education, Inc., Upper Saddle River, New Jersey.

► **Check Your Knowledge**

1. How can the study of tourism be approached?
2. What are the main sectors of in the interrelated tourism system?
3. What is the World Tourism Organization's definition of tourism?

Before we continue, let's look at tourism past and present. From this perspective, we can gain an idea of what the future of tourism may hold (discussed in Chapter 16).

Tourism Past

Travel and exploration are basic to human nature. People have traveled since the earliest times, although the term *tourism* was first used only in the early nineteenth century. The word is derived from the Hebrew word *torah*, which means studying, learning, searching.[10]

Tourism in the past developed with each new mode of transportation. First came the preindustrial time, and then later came trains, ships, automobiles, and airplanes. As we shall see, each mode of transportation had a significant impact on tourism development.

Preindustrial Age

Tourism as we know it is about a hundred years old, but centuries ago a limited form of tourism was available to the very rich. About 5,000 years ago, cruises sailed up and down the Nile River and farther. Descriptions of Queen Hatshepsut's travel to Punt (believed to be on the east coast of Africa) in 1480 BCE were recorded on the walls of the temple of Deir el-Bahri at Luxor. These reliefs are greatly admired to this day for their beauty and artistic value.[11] Wealthy Egyptians, Greeks, and Romans would travel to see the sights and attractions of the old world, principally the Sphinx, the pyramids, the Parthenon, and the Acropolis. The Olympics (776 BC) and religious festivals also caused tourism.

Before Greek currency became widely accepted, travelers had to take along goods to trade for their needs. When the money of the Greek

The pyramids attracted early tourists, who, like today's tourists, marveled at the engineering feats of constructing such magnificent structures.
Courtesy of Mark Green

city-states became an international currency, travel increased. Once the wheel was invented, roads followed naturally and people could use carts to pull loads. In 2050 BCE, a King of Ur bragged that he went from Nippur to Ur, a distance of some 100 miles, and back in a day.[12] The Greeks and Romans developed an extensive network of roads across their empires, which enabled people to travel up to 100 miles a day by changing teams of horses every few miles. Romans traveled to see the pyramids, temples, and spas and baths as well as festivals, theater, and sporting events.

Early ships plied the Nile and the Mediterranean for trading purposes and carried passengers, who had to bring their own food and servants with them. A number of port cities around the Mediterranean traded various raw and finished goods with each other.

Rome was an important stop on the Grand Tour and is still on the agenda of numerous tourists to Europe
Courtesy Dan Bannister © Dorling Kindersley

The remarkable journeys of Marco Polo were for trade purposes and cannot really be counted as tourism, yet the account of his travels helped inspire others to travel. By the Middle Ages, travel for religious pilgrimages became popular. Again, those who could afford it traveled to Jerusalem, Mecca, and Rome. In England and parts of Europe, post houses (primitive lodging facilities) were spaced a few miles apart, the distance a team of horses could pull a stagecoach. At these post houses, travelers would find meals, beverages, and even straw to sleep on. About the same time in Japan travelers were accommodated in inns called *reyokans* where bathing was, and still is, the principal ritual. *Reyokans* still exist today and are a tourist attraction.

The Grand Tour was originally a sixteenth-century Elizabethan idea meant to enable elite young men to complete their education and prepare them for important positions in government by traveling with the ambassadors of the day. Later, it became the norm for wealthy young men and women to make a Grand Tour with a tutor that included several European cities, such as Paris, Rome, Florence, Milan, Venice, Vienna, Nice. In Paris, they studied the French language, fencing, dancing, and riding. In Italy, they studied music, art, and sculpture. The tour generally lasted up to three years and they returned home via Switzerland, Germany, and the Netherlands or Belgium.

Trains

The advent of steam power gave birth to rail travel, which dramatically increased the growth of tourism as hotels, resorts, entertainment facilities, and restaurants opened to cater to the needs of an increasing number of tourists. As the railways developed, travel organizers began to offer excursions. The first of these was in

England where, in 1841, Thomas Cook arranged for 570 passengers to travel round-trip between Leicester and Loughborough. The success of this venture encouraged him to arrange similar excursions using chartered trains. In 1866, he organized his first American tour. In 1874, he introduced "circular notes," which were accepted by banks, hotels, shops, and restaurants. These were in effect the first traveler's checks.[13]

One of the main factors that led to the development of railroads in the United States was the need to move goods and people from one region of the country to another. Farm goods needed to be transported to industrial areas, and people wanted a quicker way to head west, especially after the discovery of gold in California. Those who already lived at the frontier wanted the same conveniences as their neighbors in the east, such as efficient postal service. Although railroads were first used in the seventeenth century in England, it was not until the early nineteenth century that steam locomotives were considered a reliable form of transport and a worthwhile investment. In the beginning, the planning and construction of railroads were erratic as private investors as well as the federal government began to finance construction all over the continent. Short lines were built but soon abandoned because they were unprofitable. Farsighted individuals constructed longer railroads and dreamed of the day when a transcontinental railroad would cross the nation.

Just dreams? Not at all. Soon after, in 1846, the idea quickly spread and people devised solutions to the problems plaguing the continental rail, including North–South sectional politics. Wealthy merchants such as Leland Stanford decided to back the rail and made a huge profit in doing so. Also, a large influx of immigrants provided the labor necessary for the laying of tracks. In 1869, both the Union Pacific Railroad and the Central Pacific were joined at Promontory Point, Utah. The transcontinental railroad was complete.

▶ Check Your Knowledge

1. Where and when were railroads first used?
2. Where were the Union Pacific Railroad and the Central Pacific joined?

The Railroad Revolution, Its Impact, and the Decline of Rail Travel

Railroads made mass travel possible. With trains, long-distance travel became both cheaper and faster and made the horse and ship seem like overpriced snails. Enjoying rapid success, railroads set the pattern for mobility, permitted contact between distant parts of a country, and soon became the largest business after agriculture. At the end of the nineteenth century, more capital was invested in U.S. railroads than in all other manufacturing enterprises combined. Railroads were the vehicle for the huge growth of the modern American economy. Without them, western expansion would have been delayed for decades.

From a travel and tourism point of view, the train also spurred enormous growth. The vast rail networks across North America, Asia, and Europe made the train station a central part of nearly every community. Naturally, hotels and restaurants soon opened conveniently close to train stations. Seaside resorts, mountain resorts, and other tourist areas outside population centers became easily accessible by train, drawing people who were unwilling to brave a long and hard horse and carriage ride.

Railroads played a major part in the development of the United States and many other countries. From the mid-1800s onward, trains began to carry large numbers of people over long distances to resorts and cities far from their homes. The railroads opened up the country so that people could travel more easily, comfortably, and quickly to resorts. The railroads also brought changes in the lodging industry as taverns along turnpikes gave way to hotels situated near railway stations. In 1869, rail travel across America was made possible by the transcontinental connection, which enabled a traveler to complete the journey in six days.[14]

Despite its huge importance and popularity, the decline of rail travel started as early as the 1920s. Why did this happen? The two main reasons should come as no surprise: the bus and the car. In addition, the Great Depression of the 1930s certainly did not help in drawing travelers. Although World War II brought a new surge in rail passenger numbers, people seldom traveled for pleasure, and at the close of the war the decline in rail travel continued because automobiles began to be more available, and people had the money to buy them. By 1960, airplanes had taken over much of the long-distance travel market, further reducing the importance of the train. As a result of the decline, most private rail carriers began to focus on the freight transportation market rather than invest in passenger cars and facilities.

To stave off a possible collapse of passenger rail services, the U.S. Congress passed the Rail Passenger Service Act in 1970 (amended in 2001). Shortly after, the National Railroad Passenger Corporation began operation as a semipublic corporation established to operate intercity passenger trains, a move in the direction of seminationalization of U.S. railroads. The corporation today is known as Amtrak and with more than 500 stations in 45 states provides satisfaction-guaranteed service to their guests.[15] During 2006, Amtrak welcomed aboard more than 24.3 million passengers, representing the fourth straight year of record ridership when comparing the same routes. An average of more than 67,000 passengers ride on 300 Amtrak trains per day.[16]

▶ Check Your Knowledge

1. What were the major reasons for the decline in rail travel?

2. When did the use of automobiles and buses begin to replace passenger rail travel?

3. How and when did Amtrak start?

Cruising

Until 1830, travel by ship was quite primitive and mostly for discovery,

Stratford-upon-Avon, England, was among early train travelers' destinations.
Courtesy Rob Reichenfeid © Dorling Kindersley

trading, or migration purposes. The Peninsula and Orient (P&O) company was the first to offer cruises between Britain, Spain, and Portugal. By 1880, one of P&O's ships had been upgraded to the status of a cruising yacht that sailed around the world. The first American cruise ship, the *Quaker City*, sailed from New York to Europe and the Middle East in 1867. Ships such as the *Titanic* offered a new kind of luxury to entice tourism: for the rich there was first class, and for the less well-off there were other classes supplying minimal comforts. Crossings (voyages across an ocean such as the Atlantic) became popular. Some ships made the journey from England to India, a British colony at the time. Indeed, the word *posh* derives from sea voyages to India: wealthy persons traveled in cabins that were on the port side and shaded from the sun going out (outward bound = PO) and starboard home (SH). Cruising became the fashionable thing to do until air travel caused a slight decline in cruising. Then, ironically, the airplane brought more passengers to the cruise lines.

FOCUS ON

The Study of Tourism

John and
Josielyn Walker

Tourism is a fascinating subject to study because it is dynamic and can be viewed from a number of different perspectives. Among these perspectives are political, social, economic, cultural, leisure, recreation, environmentally sustainable, psychological, research, heritage, marketing, transportation, lodging, foodservice, and attractions. Each of these perspectives takes a separate view of tourism yet is a part of the tourism system of interdependent segments as shown in Figure 1–2.

Tourism can be a vital force for peace that can either help develop parts of the world by bringing tourists and socioeconomic gains to the residents. However, tourism is not a panacea; if not managed properly, it leads to degradation. The remaining chapters of this book introduce a number of tourism-related topics and issues that will hopefully stimulate your interest.

Competition for tourists is increasing as more governments realize that tourism brings in new money to destinations and that this new money employs more people and provides additional tax revenues. We can hope that all governments are concerned with the sustainability of tourism. The need to preserve the culture and heritage of destinations has never been greater. The impacts of tourism can be both positive and negative, the trick is to recognize and deal with the negative aspects before they do any damage.

Looking at tourism past and present can help indicate where tourism may be headed in the future. It is interesting to note that tourism increased with each successive mode of transportation, enabling tourists to visit ever more remote and exotic locations. From humble beginnings, tourism has become a major global force that requires responsible use to sustain resources for future generations.

Source: This feature was written by authors John and Josielyn Walker.

Automobile Travel

The internal combustion engine automobile was invented in Germany. The idea for automobiles emerged from steam engines in the late 1880s, when Karl Benz and Gottlieb Daimler built a factory for internal combustion engines, which is now Mercedes-Benz.[17] Before long, Henry Ford produced his first vehicle and invented the techniques for making automobiles on an assembly line. By 1914, Henry Ford was producing one Model-T Ford every 24 seconds.[18] The automobile quickly became America's obsession.

In 1895, there were about 300 "horseless carriages" of one kind or another in the United States—gasoline buggies, electric cars, and steam cars. Even during the Great Depression, almost two-thirds of American families had automobiles. Henry Ford's development of the assembly line and construction of good solid roads helped make the automobile the symbol of American life that it is today. By 1925, massive construction of hardtop roads began. Road building continued even during the years of deepest depression. The interstate system was made possible by legislation passed by Congress in 1956. The call of the open road lead many families to purchase an automobile and travel along routes such as the famous Route 66 from Chicago to Los Angeles. Motels and restaurants sprang up along the highways to accommodate and feed the travelers.

The auto changed the American way of life, especially in the leisure area where it both created and satisfied the urge to travel. The automobile remains the most convenient and rapid form of transportation for short and medium distances. It has made Americans the most mobile people in history and has given them options not otherwise possible. Whereas many Europeans ride their bikes or use the bus or train to get to school or work, Americans cannot seem to function without a car. In fact, it is not uncommon for an American to drive 20,000 miles a year. To put this in perspective, a road trip that starts in Seattle, goes to San Diego, crosses the south to Key West, turns north up the East Coast to Boston, and then crosses the northern part of the country back to Seattle is about 9,000 miles.

Air Travel

The Wright Brothers, who enjoyed the hobby of gliding, decided to fit an engine to one of their gliders with movable fins and wingtip controls. To find an engine light enough, they had to build their own. In 1903, they tested their 13-horsepower engine. On the first run it lifted the craft in the air for 12 seconds and covered a distance of 120 feet.[19] From then on, airplane design and construction proceeded rapidly.

In 1909, an airplane was flown across the English Channel (about 28 miles), and by 1919 scheduled air passenger service began between London and Paris. To be the first to attempt to cross the Atlantic Ocean, Charles Lindberg persuaded a group of St Louis investors to fund construction of a new airplane. The *Spirit of St. Louis* was built in 60 days. With 450 gallons of fuel on board (the tanks blocked his forward visibility), Lindberg made the first solo crossing of the Atlantic Ocean in 1927. This history-making 28-hour flight was a major turning point in aviation history and was a catalyst for massive investment in the airline industry.

In the United States, the first scheduled air service began in 1915 and traveled between San Diego and Los Angeles. Later, in 1930, the Douglas Company in California introduced the DC-2, which could carry 14 passengers and fly at a speed of 213 miles per hour. Next, the DC-3 came into service in 1936; it was the workhorse of the airline industry for decades and still about 2,000 of them are still flying.[20]

Development of Air Travel

Not until 1935 did commercial flights become feasible, and airlines were able to make a profit without government subsidy for the first time. A few years later, Pan Am scheduled the first regular transatlantic flights using a seaplane and resorting to multiple stops along the way.

World War II had a great impact on the airline industry. During the war, every available plane was pressed into military service, familiarizing thousands of service men and women with travel by air. Pilots were trained, hundreds of airports were built, and great advances were made in aircraft design. Boeing, Lockheed, and McDonnell Douglas employed large staffs and developed facilities to satisfy the increasing demand for aircraft. Since then, airplanes and facilities have become more and more sophisticated and able to carry ever-increasing passenger loads.

Commercial jet airplanes came on the market in the early 1950s with the Boeing 707, one of the first long-range planes, and the 727, a highly successful medium-range jet. Boeing's 700 series has since evolved into many different makes and models. For instance, the remarkable 747, the jumbo jet, was introduced in the late 1960s and is now the 747-400, a major long-haul plane with enormous passenger capacity and an excellent safety record. It can transport 500 passengers at a cruising speed of 600 miles per hour over distances of about 7,000 miles. The Boeing 747 has brought faraway places such as Bali, Indonesia, within reach of large numbers of tourists. Currently, Boeing's Dreamliner and the Airbus 380 can fly from New York to Singapore or Hong Kong without stopping.

Of course, the evolution of air travel does not end here. The governments of the United States and many other countries are developing supersonic planes with reduced noise and sonic boom systems to transport passengers and high-value cargo faster and more conveniently, for instance, to the Pacific Basin. Future developments of airplanes may include planes that have a capacity to carry more people, planes that are more environmentally friendly, and smaller aircrafts and airports customized for business and personal purposes.

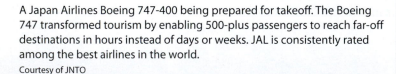

A Japan Airlines Boeing 747-400 being prepared for takeoff. The Boeing 747 transformed tourism by enabling 500-plus passengers to reach far-off destinations in hours instead of days or weeks. JAL is consistently rated among the best airlines in the world.

Courtesy of JNTO

Tourism Present

Now let's look at the scope and importance of tourism in the present day.

The Importance of Tourism

Tourism is important in both developed and developing countries. It plays an important role in the social and economic well-being of many host citizens and tourists alike. The main elements are as follows[21]:

1. *A vital force for peace.* Tourism, properly designed and developed, can help bridge the psychological and cultural distances that separate people of different races, colors, religions, and stages of social and economic development. By facilitating more genuine social relationships among individuals, tourism can help people overcome prejudices and foster international understanding and become the world's peace industry.

2. *Social importance.* Both tourists and host community citizens can gain enormous benefits from social interaction based on the experiences that tourism provides. Both the tourist and the host community citizens can learn a lot from each other.

3. *Economic importance.* Tourism makes a significant contribution to the economies of many countries. For some, tourism helps earn foreign currencies and reduce a balance of payments deficit. (This happens when a country buys more from abroad than it earns from the goods it sells abroad; hence a balance of payments deficit occurs.) Some of the countries that tourism helps with the balance of payments are Mexico, Thailand, the Philippines, Greece, and Turkey.

4. *Cultural enrichment.* Through tourism, people can appreciate the rich human and cultural diversity that the world offers and evolve a mutual trust and respect for one another and the dignity of life on earth. Tourism contributes to the preservation and development of the world's cultural heritage. It encourages governments to preserve historical sites and monuments and motivates indigenous groups to preserve their heritage in the form of dance, music, and artifacts.

5. *Employment opportunities.* Tourism provides employment opportunities and career development for millions of people.

6. *Educational significance.* Tourism enhances individuals' education in a variety of ways: via the opportunity to learn about other cultures and places; by contact with people in the host community; and by experiencing the travel and tourism phenomenon.

The real economic impact of tourism is more noticeable in places that have a comfortable climate and beautiful beaches or good conditions for skiing and winter activities and where travel and tourism are often the major sources of employment. It is the principal source of income, for example, in the Bahamas, Barbados, the Dominican Republic, the Cayman Islands, and Bermuda. In many other places, such as the Netherlands and Chile, although tourism is not the top industry, it is certainly a necessary and important source of foreign exchange. In cities such as Paris, London, and New York, tourism supplements and supports other industries. With the expected growth in the importance and impact of tourism, the opportunities for a graduate in the travel and tourism industry are virtually unlimited.

Ask any North American how their trip to Europe was. They might answer by relating an amazing tale of experiencing a variety of cultural interests including language, food, architecture, customs, arts, landscapes, and music and an increased appreciation for other countries. In this way, travel and tourism have the potential to contribute to world peace, harmony, and understanding. In addition, travel and tourism enrich culture and history by stimulating development of areas of cultural and historic interest.

Given the decline in the manufacturing and agricultural industries, tourism has become the leading global grouping of industries, particularly in many developing countries. The reasons for this are, among others, the opening up of national borders, people living longer, an increase in disposable incomes in much of the developed world and some developing nations, lower transportation costs as compared to a few years ago, and more people with the time and money as well as an interest in traveling.

In a broader perspective, travel and tourism not only provide individuals an opportunity for personal growth and development, but also contribute in a positive way to humankind's well-being. Yet, humanity is obligated to face the new challenges arising from tourism in the natural, social, and cultural realms. Travel and tourism have a significant role to play, not only in the global dialogue, but more important in implementing solutions that lead to better use of the world's limited resources.[22]

Jafar Jafari, founding editor-in-chief of the *Annals of Tourism Research*, comments:

> Actually, tourism now means different things to different people. To governments, tourism may mean sources of employment, economic activities, per capita expenditure, multiplier effects; to the industry sectors, it may suggest promotion, arrivals, length of stay, receipts; while to religious groups, it brings to mind pilgrimage, spiritual search, universal brotherhood, unacceptable forms of tourist practices. To anthropologists, tourism represents a domain of study which includes contacts between the host and the guest, culture change, commoditization of heritage, prudence. Finally, to the host destinations, tourism means American tourists, Japanese tourists, inflation, intrusion; and to the tourists themselves, tourism offers escape from the daily routines, indulgence in leisure pursuits, rest and relaxation, education.[23]

Jafar Jafari's Four Platforms

The rapid growth of tourism over many centuries eventually led to many countries realizing that, after World War II, tourism was a tool for economic development including the generation of jobs and foreign exchange earnings. Dr. Jafar Jafari calls this the *advocacy platform* because many people were advocating for tourism development.[24] In the 1970s, a *cautionary platform* represented studies and views that argued that tourism is not all benefits and, significantly, comes with many sociocultural and economic costs. Publications focused on the dark side of tourism and cautioned host communities against perceived and documented costs and unwanted consequences.

After the advocacy and cautionary voices were heard, many researchers began to examine different forms of tourism development, arguing that all are not equal and indeed some are more desirable than others. This perspective represents the *adaptancy platform*, favoring one alternative over another. The resulting writings favored such forms as agritourism, cultural tourism, ecotourism, rural tourism, and sustainable tourism. These three platforms, at times sounding simultaneously, both then and today, led to the formation of the *knowledge-based platform* in the 1990s, wherein the advocacy, cautionary, and adaptancy positions are articulated and combined to form the basis of a more holistic multidisciplinary treatment and understanding of tourism. By studying tourism as a *whole*, we can bring forth its underlying structures and functions; the resulting knowledge fosters the development of theoretical constructs and practical applications.[25]

The Scope of Travel and Tourism

Mass travel and tourism as we know them today did not begin until after the end of World War II (1945) when superhighways, commercial jets, and higher disposable income made it possible for tens of millions of people in the United States and other industrialized nations to hit the road and take to the skies. In 1950, there were a little more than 25 million international tourists. This number increased to 898 million international arrivals in 2007. Of course, a majority of U.S. citizens choose to visit Mexico or Canada when traveling internationally. Of those who travel overseas, the majority go to the European Union, to countries such as the United Kingdom, France, Spain, Italy, and Germany.

Travel flows change continuously and are dependent upon such factors as economic conditions including exchange rates, political factors, and business conditions. The most dramatic changes in travel flows have resulted from the affluence and business power of Japan and more recently China and India. Until 1980, the Japanese were not inclined to travel. By 2000, Japan was the number one country in overseas foreign arrivals to the United States, followed by the United Kingdom, Germany, and France. By 2006, Japan had slipped behind the United Kingdom. It will be interesting to see whether European and Japanese travelers will come in greater numbers to the United States as a result of the increased value of the euro against the dollar and the yen. Certainly, it is expected that fewer Americans will travel abroad until the value of the dollar improves.

Tourism is a collection of large interrelated industries that have an impact on the world's economy. Figure 1–5 shows the United Nations World Tourism Organization's report of the top 10 most visited countries.[26] As shown, countries in western Europe and North America receive most of the world's tourists, although countries such as China and India have moved up the rankings. Figure 1–6 shows the United Nations World Tourism Organization's international tourism receipts for the top 10 countries.[27]

The **World Travel and Tourism Council (WTTC)** declares that tourism is the world's largest industry. The gross output from tourism is more than $6 trillion

Rank	Country	Regional Market	International tourist arrivals (2007)[1]	International tourist arrivals (2006)[8]
1.	France	Europe	81.9 million	79.1 million
2.	Spain	Europe	59.2 million	58.5 million
3.	United States	North America	56.0 million	51.1 million
4.	China	Asia	54.7 million	49.6 million
5.	Italy	Europe	43.7 million	41.1 million
6.	United Kingdom	Europe	30.7 million	30.1 million
7.	Germany	Europe	24.4 million	23.6 million
8.	Ukraine	Europe	23.1 million	18.9 million
9.	Turkey	Europe	22.2 million	18.9 million
10.	Mexico	North America	21.4 million	21.4 million

Figure 1–5 • International Tourist Arrivals, Most Visited Countries

Source: United Nations World Tourism Organization, "International Tourist Arrivals by Country of Destination," *UNWTO World Tourism Barometer* 6, no. 2 (June 2008), www.unwto.org, (accessed August 1, 2008). © UNWTO, 9284404409.

Rank	Country	Regional Market	International Tourism Receipts (2007)[1]	International Tourism Receipts (2006)[8]
1.	United States	North America	$96.7 billion	$85.7 billion
2.	Spain	Europe	$57.8 billion	$51.1 billion
3.	France	Europe	$54.2 billion	$46.3 billion
4.	Italy	Europe	$42.7 billion	$38.1 billion
5.	China	Asia	$41.9 billion	$33.9 billion
6.	United Kingdom	Europe	$37.6 billion	$33.7 billion
7.	Germany	Europe	$36.0 billion	$32.8 billion
8.	Australia	Oceania	$22.2 billion	$17.8 billion
9.	Austria	Europe	$18.9 billion	$16.6 billion
10.	Turkey	Europe	$18.5 billion	$16.9 billion

Figure 1–6 • International Tourism Receipts, Top Tourism Earning Countries

Source: United Nations World Tourism Organization, "International Tourism Receipts," *UNWTO World Tourism Barometer* 6, no. 2 (June 2008), www.unwto.org, (accessed August 2, 2008). © UNWTO, 9284404409.

of economic activity (total demand, that is, 100 percent of world market share); this is 9.4 percent of the world's gross domestic product (GDP) and 8.7 percent of total world employment of 220 million jobs! Or 1 in every 11.5 jobs worldwide is tourism related.[28]

According to the UNWTO, there were 898 million international tourist arrivals in 2007, representing a 6.5 percent growth per year from 1950 to 2007. This is an amazing sustained growth rate. International tourism receipts totaled US$733 billion, or US$2 billion a day, in 2006.[29] Tourism represents about 35 percent of the world's exports of services and more than 70 percent in less developed countries (LDCs). This clearly illustrates so many developing countries' dependence on tourism. The UNWTO 2020 Vision forecasts that international arrivals will rise to 1 billion by 2010[30] and to 1.6 billion by 2020, which is almost double the current number of arrivals.[31]

When viewing statistics on tourism, it is important to remember that domestic tourism is larger than international tourism, so we must keep statistics for international tourism in context: it is very important but not as impactful as domestic tourism is. When both international and domestic tourism are considered, the complete picture is available.

Business Travel

International airlines, hotels, restaurants, and car rental companies all court international business travelers, and they have good reason for doing so. Consider this: the business traveler often travels on short notice and cannot take advantage of advance-purchase or discounted airline fares, hotel rates, or rental car deals. Likewise, many business travelers are first-class or business-class "frequent fliers" and are especially sought after by airlines because they, or more accurately, their companies, pay for their tickets.

Business travel has four primary components:

1. Business travel for meetings, conferences, seminars, workshops, and training sessions
2. Incentive travel, where participants enjoy the incentive they worked hard to earn usually at an all-expenses stay at a top hotel or resort
3. Normal business travel, which can also be a combination of the first two components
4. Research and teaching travel, which is business travel for research or educational purposes

At many hotels and resorts, business travelers are a high percentage of guests Monday through Friday. Additionally, business travelers can enjoy a break from routine and be exposed to new people and places. In addition to transport and accommodation, business travelers frequently eat and meet their customers or colleagues at different restaurants.

Because of the economic downturn, business travel is likely to decline slightly as companies cut back on employee travel and use more Internet communications. But one interesting aspect of business travel is that it is fairly consistent throughout the year, whereas **leisure travel** tends to peak during school vacations and holidays.

CORPORATE PROFILE

American Express

Courtesy Cindy Karp, Black Star

Today, American Express is a multi-billion-dollar holding company, but this has not always been the case. This prestigious company first began in 1850 when businessmen Henry Wells, William G. Fargo, and John Butterfield collaborated to form a small express company as a means of cooperating with each other instead of competing for the market for express services in the New York area. Through their innovativeness and competitiveness, they soon expanded into other parts of the United States. When they started the company, American Express was supposed to stay in business only for 10 years. However, when the time for ending the business came in late 1859, the company had become so successful that the founders decided to stay in business by restructuring the company and starting the new American Express.

To get business booming, the company negotiated contracts with railroads, packet boats, and steamships. The introduction of the American Express Money Order (1882) and the American Express Travelers Cheque (1891) was also a huge success. The company also introduced other creative means of making money, such as shipping fresh vegetables to northern states in the winter (a venture that turned out to be very popular among the rich). Though American Express did not provide financial services yet, it soon realized the importance of the banks as customers because bank packages were small and easy to ship and at the same time highly profitable.

In the early 1900s, American Express underwent a timely foreign expansion as well as opened a travel department, both of which helped improve the company's economic position. Because of its strong position in the market, and its provision of financial services without being classified as a bank, American Express also stood firm during the Great Depression. Later, with the boom in the international economy after World War II, the company's growth was explosive and the number of employees increased from 1,566 to 7,766 in only 10 years partly because of the introduction of the American Express Credit Card.[32]

Today the American Express Company is perhaps best known as the world's largest travel agency. Its global travel, financial, and network services (for both individuals and corporations) include charge and credit cards, Travelers Cheques, travel and related consulting services, financial planning, investment management services, brokerage services, mutual funds, international banking, accounting, tax preparation and financial education services to small businesses, pension and other employee benefit plans, and much more. Through its family of Corporate Card services, American Express helps companies and institutions manage their travel, entertainment, and purchasing expenses.[33]

American Express is also one of the nation's top places to work, according to *Fortune*, *Working Woman*, *National Black MBA Journal*, and *Latina Style*. It offers competitive salaries combined with an extensive and innovative benefits program. In addition, being the world's largest and most competitive travel agency, it offers great opportunities and awards for team members. On the company website (www.americanexpress.com) you might find an interesting career opportunity!

Source: http://home3.americanexpress.com/corp/our_story.asp

Domestic Travel and Tourism

In the United States, the economic impact of tourism is equally impressive: tourism is a $1.3 trillion industry. (If one dollar equaled one second of time, then $1.3 trillion would equal 41,000 years.)[34] The U.S. Department of Commerce International Trade Administration figures indicate that there were 55.9 million visitors to the United States in 2007 and they spent $122 billion in this country.[35] Tourism is responsible for supplying one out of eight nonfarm jobs[36] and is a leading provider of tax revenues for federal, state, and local governments.

▶ Check Your Knowledge

1. Which countries receive the most tourists per year?
2. How many people are employed within the tourism industry in the United States?

Domestic Leisure Travel

Travel for leisure is an already large and growing sector of the tourism industry. Leisure travel includes travel for recreation, visiting friends and relatives, history and culture, attractions, entertainment, cruising, and sightseeing. It also includes spring break travel. According to the **Travel Industry Association (TIA)**, domestic U.S. person-trips in 2007 totaled 1,999 million. Seventy-five percent of these trips were for leisure travel, 25 percent were for business, and approximately 9 percent of the total combined business and pleasure travel. The main mode of transport was auto/truck/RV and accounted for 85 percent; other common ways of reaching destinations were by airplane (9 percent), bus or coach (2 percent), rental car (6 percent), and train or ship (4 percent). The study also shows that the top activity for these domestic travelers was shopping, followed by attending social or family events, and outdoor activities.[37] Five of the most popular states that are visited by U.S. residents are California, Florida, Texas, Pennsylvania, and New York.

Domestic leisure travel is important not just in the United States, but in all countries. Some countries actively promote the idea of residents visiting other parts of their own country because domestic tourism keeps money inside the country and maintains employment within the country. For example, Canadians living in western Canada can visit eastern Canada, and vice versa.

Domestic Business Travel

Domestic business travel includes all forms of tourism that are work related, when people are not motivated to travel by recreational pursuits but because of their work, especially to attend meetings, incentives, conferences, and exhibitions. The acronym MICE (meetings, incentives, conferences, exhibitions) is sometimes used in business tourism to indicate these four core market areas.[38]

An art gallery in Sedona, Arizona
Courtesy of Sedona Chamber of Commerce

A variety of tourism-related businesses benefit from domestic travel and tourism such as airlines, auto rental companies, hotels and restaurants, convention centers, attractions, and retail outlets. All of these businesses have a number of suppliers, and the effects of tourism trickle up the supply chain; for example, a convention center hires companies that arrange the exhibits, provide audio visual equipment, entertainment, meals, and so forth.

Interrelated Businesses

The travel and tourism industry involves a complex set of interrelated businesses that all serve the tourist in one way or another. Because of this, growth in one area often causes growth in the businesses related to it. Let's take a closer look at this phenomenon. Obvious tourist businesses include retailers such as travel agents and tour operators. The airlines are also directly involved, as are car rental companies, railroads, bus lines, recreation or gaming entertainment facilities, hotels, and restaurants. As a group, they are called hospitality, travel, and tourism businesses.

Because of the interrelatedness of the industry, travel marketing and destination development are closely related. For example, the hotel and restaurant business in a particular area has a symbiotic relationship with the airlines that serve the area. The relationship can be obvious for destinations such as Hawaii, Tahiti, or Fiji, but is less visible for hotels such as the Days Inn and Holiday Inn in downtown Los Angeles. The relationship becomes apparent when Pacific airfares are reduced and hotel occupancy in Los Angeles rises sharply. Sales volumes for nearby restaurants also reflect the change in airfare. Similarly, when the Asian countries' economies take a downturn, attendance at Disneyland drops.

A similar connection exists for most rental car agencies, sightseeing services, ski resorts, and other travel-related businesses. Fare changes are one aspect that reflects this interdependence. For example, a reduced airfare between New York City and Denver increases the number of skiers at Steamboat Springs and Aspen. Conversely, an increased airfare between the continental United States and Hawaii reduces visits to the Polynesian Village on Oahu, the number of cars rented, and the number of condominiums and hotel rooms sold.

Other factors, of course, also affect the travel and tourism industry. These include promotion and advertising, government policy, general economic conditions, the value of a particular currency, the relations between the governments of two countries, the appeal of competing destinations, the safety of a destination, and the destination's general reputation.

▶ Check Your Knowledge

1. Give some examples that illustrate the interrelatedness of different areas of tourism.
2. Name some services provided by American Express.
3. Why is the **tourist dollar** so valuable?

Where Do Americans Travel?

There are so many possible destinations to visit and things to do, both within the United States and abroad; however, some are more popular than others, and these are presented throughout the text. Most Americans tend to think of vacation spots as beaches, mountains, and forests. However, a large number of vacations also take place in major cities. The main purpose of a vacation is sightseeing, recreation, and visiting friends and relatives followed by trips for business or conventions. If you travel, what is *your* purpose for traveling? What about your parents? Do you notice any differences in interests between the generations?

Tourism and You

According to the World Travel and Tourism Council, in the future the tourism industry is expected to grow 50 percent faster than other sectors of employment, which means that it is an excellent career option. It already is the largest of all sectors of world employment.

In the tourism industry, you can choose to work for one of an enormous number of tourism-related companies in many different positions, with any kind of working hours, benefits, and wages, and you will never be bored. With an industry that is constantly changing, growing, and challenging, what choice could possibly be better?

CAREER INFORMATION

Do you know exactly where you want to be in 5 or 10 years? The best advice is to follow your interests. Do what you love to do and success will soon follow. Often, we assess our character and personality to determine a suitable path. Some opt for the accounting, financial, and control side of the tourism business; others, perhaps with more outgoing personalities, vie for sales and marketing; still others prefer operations, which could be either in back or in front of the house. Creating your own **career path** can be both an exciting and a daunting task. However, the travel and tourism industry is generally characterized as dynamic, fun, and full of challenges and opportunities. Remember, someone has to run the national, state, and city tourism offices; Walt Disney World; Holland America Cruise lines; Marriott Hotels; eco-resorts; car rental companies; and cultural tourism attractions or be the airport manager.

The anticipated growth of tourism over the next few years offers today's students numerous career opportunities in each section of the industry, as well as increasing job stability. Every chapter in this book lists and describes some career possibilities for the specific sectors under discussion. However, we can make many generalities about a career in the tourism and hospitality industry. For example, a regular 8 to 5 job is not the norm for the tourism professional. Nearly all sectors of the industry operate up to 24 hours a day, 365 days a year—evenings, weekends, and holidays. The good news is that all sectors are experiencing growth and should continue to expand over the next few years. Also, the number of executive positions is expected to increase in the near future, which, if you do some simple calculations, puts *you* in a great position.

Having said that, how do you get to the executive level? Within every segment of the travel and tourism industry, having broad work experience in the field is an important prerequisite for any career path. As a student, you have virtually unlimited opportunities to gain valuable experience through internships and part-time work. In addition, many entry-level positions exist in the industry, which are frequently building blocks for management training.

So, what will your degree do for you? The World Travel and Tourism Council estimates that in the next few years the industry is expected to create millions of new jobs and will continue to grow at a steady rate. As the industry grows, so does the need for more and better skilled employees. If you obtain a bachelor's degree, your first career position could be with a **convention and visitors bureau (CVB)** in the sales and marketing department at a salary of $34,000 with a $2,000 signup bonus, and within a few years, your salary could easily double. Likewise, you could join the management training program of a major hotel or resort corporation at a starting salary of $32,000–$34,000. Again, after a few years, your salary has the potential to more than double. There are many other examples from each sector of the industry. For instance, a general manager with a good restaurant chain may receive a base salary of $40,000 with a substantial bonus based on performance, bringing total compensation to $70,000. However, one thing is for sure: the average salary of those with a bachelor's degree is substantially higher than the salaries of those with only a high school diploma.

So, you can work at a convention and visitors bureau or top-class hotel, amusement park or cruise line, or an airline or restaurant. The industry has experienced tremendous growth in the last 50 years that is expected to continue in the future. In most sectors, the number of executive positions is expected to increase significantly. A career in the tourism industry will most certainly offer you opportunities to use your creativity and constantly improve as well as an exciting mix of constant change and experiences that go way beyond what you get in most other workplaces.

Summary

1. Tourism is one of the largest and fastest growing, dynamic, multidisciplinary industry groupings.

2. A systems approach to tourism has been proposed by Drs. Clare Gunn and Neil Leiper, who suggest a model for the tourism system that has five elements: the tourist; geographical regions: feeder markets, transit routes, tourist destination regions; and the travel and tourism industry, including distribution, attractions, and lodging and restaurants.

3. The United Nations World Tourism Organization definition of *tourism* is the activities of persons traveling to and staying in places outside their usual environment for not more than one consecutive year for leisure, business, and other purposes.

4. Types of tourism include internal, domestic inbound plus internal, and international inbound and outbound.

5. *Tourism* is the umbrella term used to describe the socioeconomic forces that drive the interrelated industry sectors of transportation, lodging, conventions, attractions, restaurants and managed services, gaming entertainment, recreation, and leisure.

6. The history of tourism includes tourism in the preindustrial age, the development of trains and railroads, automobiles, and travel by air and ship.

7. "Tourism Present" looks at the scope and importance of tourism.

8. In the United States, tourism is a leading provider of tax revenues and a direct employer of millions of people.

9. The dramatic increase in tourism that is occurring and that will continue in the future results from the opening up of national borders, an increase in disposable income, lower transportation costs, longer life expectancy, and increased leisure time.

10. Travel and tourism comprise a complex set of interrelated businesses that serve the traveling public. For example, car rental companies, gaming entertainment facilities, and hotels all have a stake in each other's businesses.

11. Obvious travel and tourism businesses include retailers such as travel agents and tour operators. However, airlines, car rental companies, railroads, recreation and gaming facilities, bus lines, hotels, and restaurants are also directly involved.

12. Governments around the globe have begun to use tourism as an instrument to spur sluggish economies. One way governments do this is by establishing **National Tourist Offices (NTOs)**. In addition, governments allocate specific budgets to conventions and visitors bureaus.

13. Leisure travel involves travel for recreation, history, culture, entertainment, sightseeing, nature, and to visit relatives.

14. Leisure travel accounts for about 75 percent of all U.S. resident travel.

15. Travel for business purposes is necessary, and as such, is associated with many positive and negative aspects. On the positive side, travel is tax deductible. However, it can often be very stressful.

16. Most domestic trips are taken for sightseeing, recreation, and vacation purposes. Other common reasons for hitting the road include visiting friends or family, religious and ecological tours, as well as physical exercise vacations.

17. Travel flows change continuously and are dependent upon such things as exchange rates, political factors, and business conventions.

Key Words and Concepts

attractions
business travel
career path

convention and visitors bureau (CVB)
demand side

foodservice
industry sectors
infrastructure

intangible
interrelated
leisure travel
man-made
National Tourist Office (NTO)
natural attractions
superstructure

supply side
systems approach
tourism
tourist dollar
transportation
Travel Industry Association
  (TIA)

United Nations World Tourism
  Organization (UNWTO)
World Travel and Tourism
  Council (WTTC)

Review Questions

1. Why is tourism described as a system?
2. According to the World Travel and Tourism Council, what is the projected forecast for the tourism industry? What are your predictions?
3. List and describe the characteristics of tourism.
4. Discuss the tourism product.
5. What can we learn from tourism past and present that may help us project into the future of tourism?
6. What are the most popular tourist destinations in the world?
7. What are the major international tourist destinations for Americans? Why do you think there is a difference between the most popular destinations and those that Americans travel to?
8. The large majority of international travel takes place within and between North America and western Europe. Name some reasons for this phenomenon.
9. What services does American Express offer?
10. From which perspectives can we look at tourism?

Interesting Websites

Office of Travel and Tourism:
  tinet.ita.doc.gov
Travel Industry Association: www.tia.org

United Nations World Tourism Organization:
  www.unwto.org
World Travel and Tourism Council: www.wttc.org

Internet Exercises

1. Go to the website of the United Nations World Tourism Organization at www.unwto.org and look for news and events or other items of interest to discuss in class.
2. Go to the website of the Travel Industry Association at www.tia.org. What does the TIA do, and what are its main objectives?

Apply Your Knowledge

1. Give examples of major companies in the following segments of the tourism industry: transportation, lodging, conventions, attractions, restaurants and managed services, gaming entertainment, recreation, and leisure.
2. Explain the importance of tourism.

Endnotes

1. Tiffany Stecker, "Paris Tourism Feels the Economic Chill," *Business Week*, March 31, 2009, www .businessweek.com/globalbiz/content/mar2009/ gb20090331_063129.htm?campaign_id=rss_lifestyle (accessed September 1, 2009).

2. Destination Analysts, "Amidst Economic Woes, Americans Hitting the Brakes on Travel," July 15, 2008, www.destinationanalysts.com/ State%20of%20the%20American%20Traveler% 20Survey.htm (accessed September 1, 2009).

3. World Tourism Organization, www.unwto.org, August 2, 2006.

4. Ludwig von Bertalanffy, *General System Theory: Foundations, Development, Applications* (New York: G. Braziller, 1976), as cited in Robert Christie Mill and Alastair M. Morrison, *The Tourism System*, 4th ed. (Dubuque, IA: Kendall Hunt, 2002), 3.

5. Clare A. Gunn, *Tourism Planning: Basics, Concepts, Cases*, 3rd ed. (Washington, DC: Taylor and Francis), as cited in Mill and Morrison, *Tourism System*, 3.

6. Neil Leiper, *Tourism Systems: An Interdisciplinary Perspective* (Palmerston North, New Zealand: Massy University, 1990), as cited in Mill and Morrison, *Tourism System*, 3.

7. Geoffrey Wall and Alister Mathieson, *Tourism: Change, Impacts and Opportunities* (Harlow, Essex, England: Pearson Prentice Hall, 2006), 19.

8. This section draws on Zenaida L. Cruz, *Principles of Tourism: Part 1* (Manila, Philippines: Rex Book Store, 2006), 7.

9. Ibid. 2, 11.

10. Lionel Casson, *Travel in the Ancient World* (London: Allen & Unwin, 1974), 32.

11. www.touregypt.net/historicessays/hatsepsult.htm

12. Eric Friedheim, *Travel Agents: From Caravans and Clippers to the Concorde* (New York: Travel Agent Magazine Books, 1992), 25.

13. Ibid.; Cruz, *Principles of Tourism*, 19.

14. Jan Van Harssel, *Tourism: An Exploration*, 3rd ed. (Upper Saddle River, NJ: Prentice Hall, 1994), 4.

15. Amtrak, "Amtrak National Facts," www.amtrak.com/servlet/ContentServer?pagename= Amtrak/am2Copy/Title_Image_Copy_Page&c= am2Copy&cid=1081442674300&ssid=542 (accessed September 1, 2009).

16. Ibid.

17. Paul R. Dittmer and Gerald G. Griffen, *The Dimensions of the Hospitality Industry: An Introduction* (New York: Van Nostrand Reinhold, 1993), 352.

18. Ibid.

19. Van Harssel, *Tourism*, 27.

20. Ibid.

21. Cruz, *Principles of Tourism*, 11–13.

22. World Travel and Tourism Council, "Welcome," www .wttc.travel (accessed May 23, 2008).

23. Jafar Jafari, "Research and Scholarship: The Basis of Tourism Education," *Journal of Tourism Studies* 14, no. 1 (May 2003): 6.

24. This section draws on Jafar Jafari, "Tourisms Landscape of Knowledge," *ReVista*, Winter 2002, www.drclas.harvard.edu/revista/articles/view/35 (accessed September 1, 2009).

25. Jafar Jafari, "Research and Scholarship," 9.

26. United Nations World Tourism Organization, "International Tourist Arrivals by Country of Destination," *UNWTO World Tourism Barometer* 6, no. 2 (June 2008), http://unwto.org/facts/eng/pdf/ barometer/UNWTO_Barom08_2_en_LR.pdf (accessed August 1, 2008).

27. Ibid.

28. http://www.wttc.org/eng/About_WTTC/ (accessed September 9, 2009).

29. http://pub.unwto.org/WebRoot/Store/Shops/Infoshop/ Products/1324/080206_unwto_barometer_01- 08_eng_excerpt.pdf (accessed September 9, 2009).

30. World Tourism Organization "Tourism 2020 Vision," www.unwto.org/facts/eng/vision.htm (accessed September 1, 2009).

31. www.unto.org/index.php

32. American Express, "Our Story," http://home3. americanexpress.com/corp/os/history.asp (accessed September 1, 2009).

33. *Becoming American Express: 150 Years of Reinvention and Customer Service*, courtesy of American Express.

34. U.S. Travel Association, "Travel Industry Fun Facts," www.tia.org/pressmedia/fun_facts.html (accessed January 27, 2007).

35. U.S. Department of Commerce International Trade Administration, *United States Travel and Tourism Exports, Imports, and the Balance of Trade: 2007*, www.tinet.ita.doc.gov/outreachpages/download_ data_table/2007_International_Visitor_ Spending.pdf (accessed October 7, 2008).

36. Ibid.

37. Travel Industry Association of America, Domestic Research: Travel Volume and Trends," www.tia.org/ travel/tvt.asp (accessed May 23, 2008).

38. Loykie Lominé and James Edmunds, *Key Concepts in Tourism* (Basingstoke, Hampshire, UK: Palgrave Macmillan, 2007), 18.

CHAPTER 2

Motivation for Leisure Tourism

OBJECTIVES

After reading and studying this chapter, you should be able to:

- Discuss tourists' motivation for leisure travel and tourism.

- Describe Maslow's hierarchy of human needs and Epperson's push-pull model.

- Discuss Pearce's leisure ladder model and Plog's psychographic model.

- Discuss the role and importance of the National Park System.

- Outline the different groups of sports tourists as well as the major sporting events.

- Describe the typical adventure traveler.

- Name the most common destinations for religious travel.

- Discuss the fundamentals of health care tourism.

GEOGRAPHY SPOTLIGHT

Romantic Tourism: USA

Yosemite naturalist and park ranger Carl Sharsmith was once approached by a visitor to the Yosemite National Park and asked the following question: "If you had one day to spend in Yosemite, what would you do?" Ranger Sharsmith answered, "Madam, I would sit by the Merced River and cry."[1] Furthermore, Ralph Waldo Emerson once wrote about the beauty of Yosemite: "In Yosemite, the grandeur of these mountains perhaps unmatched in the world. . . ."[2] This opinion is held by the hundreds of thousands of visitors that revisit Yosemite on a regular basis. Yosemite is one of the most stunning national parks in the United States, with visitor demographics ranging from adventure enthusiasts to workaholics looking for a place to relax. More important, Yosemite provides an ideal backdrop for "popping the question" and serves as an important romantic getaway for couples in every stage of their relationship.

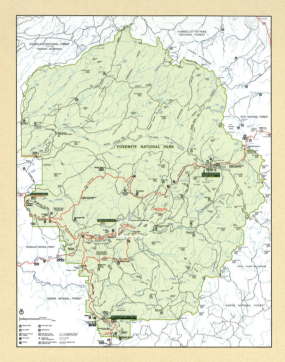

Yosemite National Park is located in central California near the Nevada border. According to the National Park Service's official website, Yosemite is nearly 1,200 square miles and is best known for its waterfalls.[3] In addition to waterfalls, visitors can find "deep valleys, grand meadows, ancient giant sequoias, a vast wilderness area, and much more."[4] Yosemite waterfalls are fed by snowmelt during May, which is the month in which a perfect romantic getaway can take place. Moreover, May marks the end of spring, which means that many flowers are blooming, wildlife is active, and a romantic couple can wear summer clothes in the picturesque valleys and bundle up when they reach the crown of the Sierra Range.

The following list outlines several of the most romantic locations in Yosemite, according to the Yosemite Resorts website[5]:

1. *Old Inspiration Point.* To get to Old Inspiration Point, couples can hike 1.3 miles in the late afternoon to catch the eastern horizon during the sunrise.[6] This is the most ideal time of day to visit this location because of the colors that dance on the mountains, creating a mystical, romantic atmosphere. This uphill hike certainly makes a hiker work to reach the top, but couples can then finish their day by giving each other foot and calf massages.

GEOGRAPHY SPOTLIGHT *(continued)*

2. *Base of Yosemite Falls.* This area is the most traveled trail in Yosemite Valley because of its magnificent views of the Yosemite Falls. For a more intimate location, couples are encouraged to hike to Yosemite Creek and view the falls from there. Not only are the views spectacular, but the sound of the babbling creek sings a natural, relaxing, intimate tune to which couples can continue their hike.

Courtesy of Rick Pawlenty

3. *Yosemite Falls Trail.* This trail leads couples to the tippy-top of Yosemite Falls and offers unparalleled views of Half Dome, North Dome, Sentinel Rock, Sentinel Dome, Lost Arrow, and Yosemite Valley. This trail is 4.7 miles long, but well worth the hike.[7] As stated on the Yosemite Resorts website, this is "a spectacular place to propose, [but] you just might have to catch your breath first."[8]

4. *Glacier Point.* This location requires couples to walk 1 mile, but it is such an easy walk, most of it is even wheelchair accessible. The views from this location inspire gasps, "oohs," and "aahs." It is one of the most popular spots in Yosemite because of the lack of incline while walking to the top. Crowds will gather, but there are plenty of views to go around. According to the Yosemite Resorts website, "It's one of those spots where you can't help but hug one another."[9]

5. *Sentinel Dome.* Sentinel Dome offers a 360-degree view of Yosemite Valley and is far more secluded than Glacier Point. Looking to the west, couples can see Yosemite Valley and the Merced River canyon. Looking to the east, they can see assorted peaks of the High Sierra. To the north, El Capitan and Yosemite Falls are also in view. This location envelopes couples in the grandeur of Yosemite.

6. *Tuolumne Meadows.* This subalpine meadow offers many romantic hideaways, such as grassy lands and beaches along the Tuolumne River. For athletic couples, this meadow is a wonderful location for a trail run. Again, this level of activity will afford couples the ability to exchange massages afterward.

(continued)

7. *The Lower Merced River.* The Lower Merced River flows from pool to pool, which creates an environ-ment dotted with beaches, secluded woodsy locations, isolated rock formations throughout the pools, and a calm atmosphere, which encourages couples to meander through the area hand in hand. Afternoon picnics or sunset watches are a great way to create memories with significant others.

After enveloping themselves in the breathtaking sights offered by Yosemite National Park, couples would be hard-pressed not to be in a romantic mood. Pairing one of the most glorious displays of nature with a pam-pering environment found in a nearby luxury resort, whispering sweet-nothings into a loved one's ear, and holding each other close become an integral part of the Yosemite experience for couples.

Endnotes

1. Yosemite Resorts, "Visiting Yosemite," www.yosemiteresorts.us//visit/index.htm (accessed September 7, 2008).
2. Official National Park Handbook, *Yosemite: A Guide to Yosemite National Park California* (Washington, DC: Division of Publications National Park Service, U.S. Department of the Interior, 1990), 8.
3. National Park Service, "Yosemite," www.nps.gov/yose/index.htm (accessed September 2, 2009).
4. Department of the Interior, "Yosemite National Park," www.nps.gov/yose/ (accessed September 5, 2008).
5. Yosemite Resorts, "Visiting Yosemite."
6. Yosemite, "Yosemite Hikes Site Map," www.yosemitehikes.com/sitemap.htm (accessed September 7, 2008).
7. Ibid.
8. Yosemite Resorts, "Visiting Yosemite."
9. Ibid.

Tourist Motivation for Leisure Travel

This chapter looks at the motivators for leisure travel, or more simply, *why* people use their free time to roam the planet. In recent years, there has been a dramatic increase in leisure travel, and indications are that the trend is likely to continue. Some people can afford to travel, and they frequently do, perhaps in part to escape the pressures of their daily lives. Leisure tourism has become an important ingredient in our quality of life. Most of us welcome an escape from our daily routines, and a few days or weeks away certainly provide such a change.

Professor Muzaffer Uysal poses an interesting question when he asks, "How does one examine motivations for pleasure travel?" He quickly adds, "To answer this question, we must begin with a definition of motivation: The term *motive* has been used to refer to internal forces and external forces and incentives that guide, direct and integrate a person's behavior, for future personal satisfaction." Therefore, motivation is an interpersonal phenomenon.[1]

Iso-Ahola classifies motivational forces, for optimal stimulation and arousal (equilibrium), into approach (seeking) and avoidance (escaping).[2] Iso-Ahola also indicates that, depending on the daily mundane stimulation and arousal level, people pursue **leisure** activities to achieve feelings of mastery and competence or to leave the routine environment. He presents the notion that there are two motivational forces that become determinants of tourism behavior[3]:

- *The desire to leave the everyday environment behind*—Escaping personal and/or interpersonal environments
- *The desire to obtain psychological or intrinsic rewards through travel in a contrasting environment*—Seeking personal and/or interpersonal intrinsic rewards

According to Dr. Uysal, not all vacations and trips can be classified on the 50-50 principle of escaping and seeking. For instance, one family may travel to Florida or Virginia to get away from it all, but another may go on safari in Kenya to appreciate a different culture and environment. Then, consider someone who visits friends and family one time and takes a cruise as the next vacation.[4]

In this chapter, we examine the different motivations and elements or *types* of leisure tourism, as illustrated in Figure 2–1. The categories are not all inclusive, however. For instance, sports tourism fits into more than one classification in that it can be commercial (Super Bowl), noncommercial (kids' soccer tournaments), or live (all live sports, whether commercial or not). This chapter begins with a description of the most common theories that apply to the motivations for leisure travel. We then move on to a discussion of some of the newest and most exciting categories of leisure travel, namely, the ones that fit under the description "recreational tourism." The motivations for business and other forms of tourism are covered in separate chapters.

Recreational	Attractions	Entertainment	Other
Travel for Natural Beauty	Amusement Parks	Fairs and Festivals	Eco-tourism
Travel for Sports	Gaming Entertainment	Performance Arts	Visiting Friends and Family
Adventure Travel	Animal Attractions	Shopping	
Religious Travel	Heritage Tourism	Events	
Health-Care Tourism	Cultural Tourism		

Figure 2–1 • Leisure Tourism Categories

The challenge for tourism marketing professionals is that motivation is an individual thing and varies considerably between similar groups of people based on their own personal motivations and cultural conditioning.[5] So, given that everyone is different as are the factors they are motivated by, how do we begin to examine tourists' motivations? The answer is to consider the main factors that motivate most tourists[6]:

- *Personality*—Whether a person is outgoing or a loner, adventurous or cautious, confident or timid influences the individual's travel decisions.
- *Lifestyle*—The concept of lifestyle is connected with the form of behavior specific to a social position. (Krysztof Przeclawski, Lifestyle, in *Encyclopedia of Tourism,* edited by Jafar Jafari, published by Routledge, London, 2000.)
- *Past experience*—Past experiences may influence a decision positively or negatively depending on the situation. For example, if a person enjoyed an experience in a certain place, that person may be more inclined to return to that place.
- *Past life*—Memories from earlier periods in a person's life might motivate him or her to revisit a place from the past, such as where he or she grew up or spent time.
- *Perceptions*—People's perceptions of their own strengths and weaknesses, whether these relate to their wealth or their skills, influence their decisions to travel and where.
- *Image*—How people wish to be viewed by other people affects travel choices.

Swarbrooke and Horner add that motivations change over time for each individual in response to changes in personal circumstances; for example[7]:

- Having a child or meeting a new partner
- An increase or reduction in income
- Changes in health
- Changing expectations or experiences as a tourist

Travel Motivators

A lot of people love traveling, but have you ever thought about *why* that is, and what they gain from it? Think of some reasons why *you* do, or would like to, travel. Over the course of history, motivations for travel have been fairly obvious: religious conviction, economic gain, war, escape, and migration. Some research reveals the reasons *why* people travel and vacation. However, because of the fact that research and an established motivation theory are generally lacking, the comments included here are necessarily subjective and are made principally to stimulate investigation.

Some surprising findings show up in consumer research. Leisure trips account for 75 percent of Americans' domestic travel. Business comes in as the second most popular reason for travel (25 percent of Americans' trips are business related), and 9 percent of trips are for leisure and business combined.[8] Some people seem to thrive on the *change* brought by travel. Others need the relaxation of a *quiet* vacation, and still others seek a pitch of *excitement* that does or does not exist in their regular lives. Many psychotherapists also acknowledge that people have a basic need for fun and freedom. Pleasure travel can certainly be a way to fulfill this need.

In their excellent text *Consumer Behavior in Tourism*, John Swarbrooke and Susan Horner suggest that there is no widely recognized way of categorizing the main motivating factors in tourism. But they do suggest that motivating factors can be split into two types[9]:

- Those that motivate a person to take a vacation
- Those that motivate a person to take a particular vacation to a specific destination at a particular time

Some of the major types of tourism motivators are illustrated in Figure 2–2.[10] Actually, according to Swarbrooke, attractions are arguably the most important component in the tourism system. They are the main motivators for tourists' trips and are the core of the tourism product. Without attractions there would be no need for other tourism services.[11] Indeed, tourism as such would cease to exist if it were not for attractions. Chapter 8 is devoted to attractions.

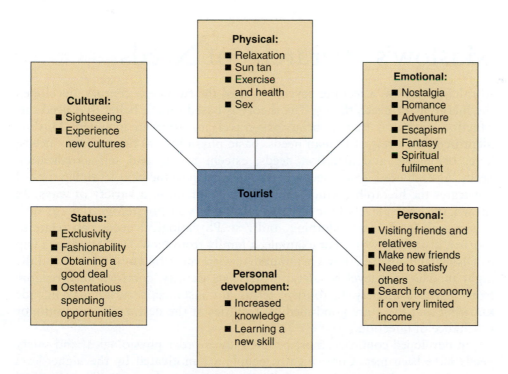

Figure 2–2 • A Typology of Motivators in Tourism
Source: John Swarbrooke and Susan Horner, *Consumer Behavior in Tourism* (Oxford, England: Elsevier Butterworth-Heinemann, 2005). With permission of Elsevier Butterworth-Heinemann.

Motivation, Needs, and Expectations

Juergen Gnoth discussed the motivation, needs, and expectations (MNEs) of tourists. He states that from the holidaymakers' perspective, tourism is a response to felt needs and acquired values within temporal, spatial, social, and economic parameters. Once needs and/or values have been activated and applied to a vacation scenario, the generated motivation constitutes a major parameter in expectation formation. Expectations, in turn, determine perceptions of performance of products and services as well as perceptions of experiences.[12]

▶ Check Your Knowledge

1. What are the main factors contributing to the immense growth in leisure travel that has and is taking place?
2. What were the most common historical travel motivators?

Now, let's take a quick look at some of the existing theories that we can use to cast light on why people travel. As mentioned, these can be interpreted in a variety of ways, and you can try to find your own examples as well.

Maslow's Hierarchy of Needs

Abraham Maslow, a leading psychologist of the twentieth century, developed the hierarchy of needs theory. The theory is based on the belief that need satisfaction motivates human behavior—travel and tourism included. Maslow identified five levels of human needs: basic physiological needs; safety needs; love, belonging, and affection needs; esteem needs; and self-actualization needs. As each need is satisfied, a person moves up to the next level. Figure 2–3 illustrates the hierarchy, which can relate to tourism in a variety of ways. As shown, the lowest level of the hierarchy includes *basic physiological needs* such as survival, food, water, clothing, and rest. Physiological needs can relate to tourism in various ways. For example, a family from New York State on a trip to Disneyland, an area they are unfamiliar with, must find a hotel to spend the night in. The next level is safety: protection, security, comfort, and freedom from fear and anxiety. In tourism terms, for instance, security may include knowing that there are good medical facilities at the destination and little or no chance of infection.

In developed countries, most people's lower-order physiological and safety needs have been met. Consequently, people are motivated by the higher-level needs that may also be met or partially met by travel and tourism. The next level in the hierarchy includes the need for belonging, love, and affection. In a tourism context, a family might travel to visit friends and family or bond with other tourists or families.

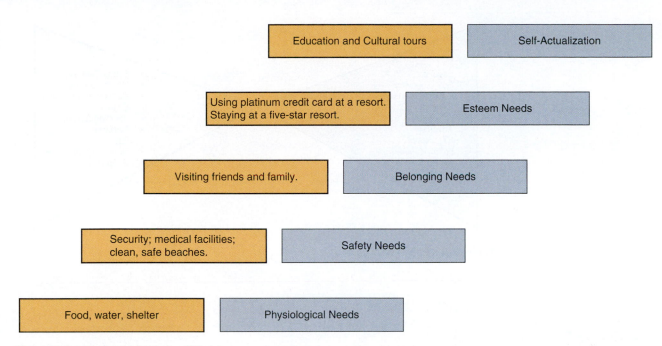

Figure 2–3 • Maslow's Hierarchy of Needs

Esteem needs—the desire for status, self-respect, and success—must be met next. The family visiting Disneyland might satisfy the need for status by using a platinum credit card, a hotel VIP card for check-ins at a special desk, or an airline frequent flyer card to obtain upgrades, additional recognition, and privileges. Self-actualization, or the desire for self-fulfillment, is the highest level of Maslow's hierarchy. In tourism terms, self-discovery may take place via educational tours, travel for cultural or heritage purposes, or by learning the language and culture of the destination before arrival.

The Push-Pull Model

An interesting way of modeling travel motivations is to divide them into factors that push and those that pull people to travel. Travel consultant Arlin Epperson's push-pull model illustrates this theory.[13] People travel because they are "pushed" into making travel decisions by internal, psychological forces, and "pulled" by the external forces of the destination's attributes.[14] In other words, the push motivators are related to the tourists' desire, whereas the pull motivators are associated with the attributes of the destination.[15]

Epperson lists push factors as the intangible desires to travel that are generated from within a person. Examples are shown in Figure 2–4. Pull factors are attractions such as Disneyland, Sea World, a museum, a **national park**, or perhaps a famous football stadium. Epperson argues that most travel is likely to be motivated to some degree by both push and pull factors. For example, a vacation in an isolated mountain cabin would allow for escape, self-discovery, and rest (push factors), while at the same time providing scenic beauty (pull factor).

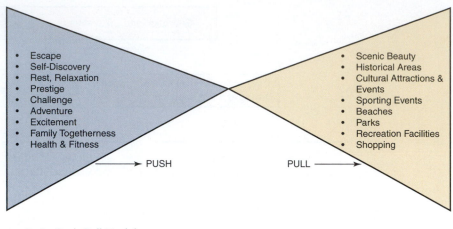

- Escape
- Self-Discovery
- Rest, Relaxation
- Prestige
- Challenge
- Adventure
- Excitement
- Family Togetherness
- Health & Fitness

PUSH →

PULL →

- Scenic Beauty
- Historical Areas
- Cultural Attractions & Events
- Sporting Events
- Beaches
- Parks
- Recreation Facilities
- Shopping

Figure 2–4 • Push-Pull Model

FOCUS ON

Push and Pull Motives

Kathleen L. Andereck

State tourism marketing organizations have generally focused their advertising and promotion efforts on out-of-state markets. Following the terrorist attacks of September 11, 2001, and the following economic downturn and reduced travel activity, however, many organizations began to develop and implement promotion campaigns targeted toward their own residents. Little research has been done to investigate differences between the travel motives of residents versus those of tourists. This kind of information has implications for promotion and advertising targeting residents. This case applies the push-pull framework to examine differences in decision making about destination choice on such trips.[1] The tourism literature is rich with discussion about the operational effects of push and pull motives in affecting product choice and travel patterns. The notion is that, in terms of individual decision making, both internal (push) and external (pull) factors influence choice.

Push factors are intrinsic to the decision maker and are commonly construed as the psychological needs or wants of the consumer. Common factors that have been identified include escape, socialization, adventure, relaxation, status enhancement, family togetherness, and achievement.[2] Such psychological needs, depending on which ones are dominant at any given time, serve to "push" the consumer toward a particular genre of environments or services. Pull factors are features, attractions, or attributes of the destination itself. The destination offers a set of tangible and intangible benefits that serve to "pull" the consumer toward that option. Common pull factors include historical features, cultural features, shopping services, nature/outdoor experiences, urban experiences, entertainment potential, sports, beaches, mountains, water resources, weather, and a myriad of other site or service attributes.[3]

The literature on the push-pull framework is at once simple and complex. At its simplest level, it gives tremendous insight on the reasons why individual travelers might be prone to prefer certain destinations over others as they scan their environments for tourism opportunities. With knowledge of individual preferences, marketing campaigns can be designed to amplify or highlight certain attributes of a destination or service that appeal to specific target markets. Toward this end, much literature has been generated to show

FOCUS ON   (continued)

how to design market campaigns in light of consumer groups carrying different push portfolios (e.g., Fodness),[4] pull portfolios (e.g., Sirakaya and McLelland),[5] or portfolios distinguished by different combinations of both push and pull factors (e.g., Turnbull and Uysal; Uysal and Jurowski).[6] The framework has been used in contexts as diverse as outdoor recreation choice,[7] ski destination choice,[8] international travel patterns,[9] and spring break travel selections.[10] At a more complex level, evidence suggests that highly interactive effects exist between push and pull features in affecting choice. Borrowing from the consumer behavior literature, Klenosky provides a meaningful glimpse into the predictive power of capturing the interactive effects of the relatively abstract psychological needs that serve as push factors and the relatively concrete destination attributes that serve as pull factors.[11] Such interactive analyses hold great promise for destination managers in developing complex market campaigns anchored in promoting appropriate "benefit bundles" to target markets.[12]

To gather information on push and pull motives, two surveys were conducted, each designed by Arizona State University researchers in collaboration with Arizona Office of Tourism officials interested in developing databases to inform the development of market campaign portfolios. The first was a survey of individuals who entered a promotion billed as the Arizona Giveaways and Getaways (AGG) Sweepstakes, which was conducted during the summer of 2003. The second was a survey of nonresidents who requested travel information in response to a promotion entitled the Target Cities Campaign (TCC) conducted during the winter of 2004. Multimedia advertisements were targeted to Chicago, Dallas, Denver, Minneapolis, Portland, and St. Louis. Arizona Office of Tourism staff and Arizona State University jointly designed an eight-page questionnaire for each survey. Although there were certain distinctions between the two instruments, each shared a common bank of sociodemographic questions, a common battery of 16 items designed to identify and measure push motives and a common battery of 14 items designed to identify and measure pull motives.

Initially, tests were conducted to determine whether demographic differences existed between the resident population and the out-of-state population used for the study. The groups did not differ significantly on five sociodemographic variables included in the questionnaires: gender, age, marital status, children in the household, and income. However, the out-of-state population had slightly higher levels of education. The tests also revealed a lower percentage of out-of-state Latinos, although the base representation in the resident population was small (5.3 percent). On the whole, the data suggest that the likelihood is low that differences emerging from database comparisons would be artifacts of sociodemographic influences.

The 16 push items were measured on a five-point Strongly Disagree/Strongly Agree scale. For residents, the highest-ranked motives were having fun, getting away from everyday life, and relaxation. For nonresidents, the highest-ranked were the same; however, analysis revealed that the two groups differed in some ways, with nonresidents being more strongly defined by the desire to experience new and different places, spend time with friends and family, experience nice weather, do many different things/activities, view scenery, and experience other cultures. There were no group differences for the 10 remaining push measures: having fun, learning about history and culture, getting away from everyday life, excitement/adventure, relaxation, experiencing nature, being physically active, seeing interesting sights, being entertained, and having an enjoyable night life.

The 14 pull items consisted of possible activities visitors desired at their destination. For residents, the most desired attributes were viewing scenery, shopping, and natural area activities. For nonresidents, the most desired activities were viewing scenery, visiting family and friends, and shopping. Analysis found that nonresidents were more likely to desire the following attributes at their destination: friends and family, the Grand Canyon, scenery, sporting events, and golf. Residents were more likely to desire natural area activities. No

(continued)

F O C U S   O N   (*continued*)

significant differences emerged for the eight remaining pull factors: cultural, arts, and heritage activities; adventure activities; shopping; sports; entertainment; resorts/spas; dude/guest ranches; or business/convention facilities.

Perhaps the most revealing insight from this analysis was the relative stability of the push and pull factor portfolios across the resident and non-state-resident populations. At the intuitive level, one would expect substantive differences in the structuring of the portfolios—sufficient to call for significant restructuring of marketing campaigns as an organization strives to capture a greater share of the resident-based travel. However, there were more similarities than differences. For the push factors, the highest-ranked motives were the same. Only 7 of 16 push items yielded significant differences, but in every case, the differences were in the same direction and ultimately valued highly by each population (nonresidents showed more intensity than residents on these items, but they were nonetheless highly valued by each). The pull items revealed a few more interesting dynamics. Shopping emerged as a highly ranked element in the portfolio of residents, yet ultimately the differences between the populations remained nonsignificant. Also, residents were more inclined to seek natural area activities, whereas nonresidents were more inclined to simply view scenery. Residents were also substantially less oriented to visiting family and friends. Differences emerged for three other items (Grand Canyon, sporting events, and golf), yet each of these attributes was valued by both populations. From a marketing perspective, the data on the whole speak to the promise of effective results by delivering a consistent message to both populations with an important exception: build "natural area activities" and "shopping opportunities" into the array of "benefit bundles" targeted to residents, and build imagery of "family and friend" relationship building into images targeted to nonresidents.

This analysis adds to the increasing body of research that has demonstrated the capacity of the push and pull motive framework to inform the development of tourism campaigns. In the case of the Arizona Office of Tourism, specific insight was offered on how to modify marketing images targeted to in-state travelers in light of the post–September 11 economic environment. Ultimately, local tourism service providers—not to mention the many businesses that are fed by the Arizona tourism industry—will be the beneficiaries of this research.

References

1. M. Uysal, and C. Jurowski, "Testing the Push and Pull Factors," *Annals of Tourism Research* 21, no. 4 (1994): 844–846.

2. G. M. S. Dann, "Anomie, Ego-Enhancement and Tourism," *Annals of Tourism Research* 4, no. 4 (1977): 184–194; D. B. Klenosky, "The 'Pull' of Tourism Destinations: A Means-End Investigation," *Journal of Travel Research* 40, no. 4 (2002): 385–395; R. C. Knopf, "Human Behavior, Cognition and Affect in the Natural Environment," in *Handbook of Environmental Psychology*, ed. D. Stokols and I. Altman (New York: John Wiley, 1987), 783–825.

3. M. Bonn, M. Uysal, and L. Furr, "A Segmentation Analysis of Peak Season and Shoulder Season Resort Visitors," in *The Tourism Connection: Linking Research and Marketing*, the 21st TTRA Annual Proceedings (1990), 61–79; Klenosky, "The 'Pull' of Tourism Destinations," 385–395.

4. D. Fodness, "Measuring Tourist Motivation," *Annals of Tourism Research* 21, no. 3 (1994): 555–581.

5. E. Sirakaya, and R. W. McLellan, "Factors Affecting Destination Choices of College Students," *Anatolla: An International Journal of Tourism and Hospitality Research* 8, no. 3 (1997): 31–44.

6. D. R. Turnbull, and M. Uysal, "An Exploratory Study of German Visitors to the Caribbean: Push and Pull Motivations," *Journal of Travel and Tourism Marketing* 4, no. 2 (1995): 85–92; Uysal, and Jurowski, "Testing the Push and Pull Factors," 844–846.

FOCUS ON (*continued*)

7. R. C. Knopf, K. L. Andereck, K. Tucker, B. Bottomly, and R. J. Virden, "Building Connections among Lands, People and Communities: A Case Study of Benefits-Based Management Plan Development for the Gunnison Gorge National Conservation Area," in Management Model in *Proceedings of the Fourth Social Aspects of Recreation Research Symposium*, ed. P. Tierney (San Francisco: San Francisco State University, 2004), 73–85.

8. D. B. Klenosky, C. E. Gengler, and M. S. Mulvey, "Understanding the Factors Influencing Ski Destination Choice: A Means-End Analytic Approach," *Journal of Leisure Research* 25, no. 4 (1993): 362–379.

9. Turnbull, and Uysal, "An Exploratory Study of German Visitors to the Caribbean," 85–92.

10. Sirakaya, and McLellan, "Factors Affecting Destination Choices," 31–44.

11. Klenosky, "The 'Pull' of Tourism Destinations," 385–395.

12. R. C. Lewis, "The Positioning Statement for Hotels," *Cornell Hotel and Restaurant Administration Quarterly* (May 1981): 51–61.

Source: Kathleen L. Andereck, PhD, and Richard C. Knopf, PhD., School of Community Resources and Development, Arizona State University

Other Theories

Pearce developed a model similar to Maslow's hierarchy of needs (physiological needs, safety needs, social needs, ego needs, need for self-fulfillment), but it goes further by providing more detailed insights into specific tourist behaviors. The leisure ladder model attempts to explain individual behaviors on the basis of stages in a tourist's life cycle. People change throughout their lives according to the life cycle stage they are in. Think of your own family: likely there are some young singles, married without kids, married or single with kids, and retired older adults. In each life stage, people have different motivations for tourism. According to Pearce, tourists move through a hierarchy (or series of steps) similar to the one developed by Maslow.[16] Once a tourist has taken care of the physiological needs, he or she then moves up to the next level.

Stanley Plog developed a model that classifies the U.S. population along a psychographic continuum that delineates personality types, ranging from the psychocentric (who prefer familiar travel destinations) at one extreme to the allocentric (who prefer adventure and more exotic destinations) at the other. Most travelers fall into a large bell-shaped

The splendor of the national parks attracts millions of visitors annually.
Courtesy of Rick Pawlenty

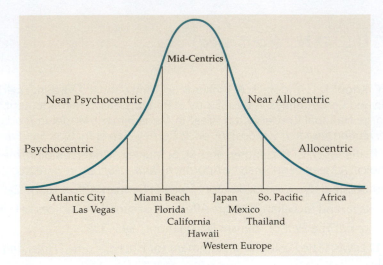

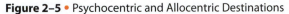

Figure 2–5 • Psychocentric and Allocentric Destinations
Source: Adapted from Stanley Plog, "Why Destination Areas Rise and Fall in Popularity" (paper presented to the Southern California Chapter of the Travel Research Association, October 10, 1972), as cited in Edward Mayo and Lance Jarvis, *The Psychology of Leisure Travel* (Boston: CBI Publishing Company, 1981), 118.

curve between the two extremes. Figure 2–5 illustrates the types of destinations that psychocentrics and allocentrics are likely to visit: psychocentrics prefer to travel to well-known destinations that have been visited by millions before; these destinations tend to be constant and predictable. Allocentric personalities tend to be more adventurous, curious, energetic, and outgoing; they are usually attracted to novel destinations such as the South Pacific, Asia, and Africa.[17]

Card and Kestel recognize three categories of motivation: curiosity, social interaction, and rejuvenation.[18] Crompton and Pearce maintain that motivation should be seen as only one of the many variables that contribute to explaining and predicting tourist behavior.[19] They also suggest that travel decisions are the result of several motives, or multimotives. Muzaffer Uysal writes[20] that "the globalization of tourism has resulted in more culturally diverse travelers with different preferences, motivations, expectations, and needs. The nature of this diversity in global tourist behavior and the reciprocal interaction between the traveler and destinations will naturally pose new challenges and create new opportunities for destinations, promoters, marketing professionals and social scientists examining tourist behavior."

▶ Check Your Knowledge

1. Name the five levels of human needs according to Maslow.

2. Give one example of how travel and tourism can be linked to self-actualization needs.

3. Give examples of push and pull factors when it comes to reasons why people travel.

Travel Values

Theories aside, several factors influence *why* people travel (or why they don't), *where* they go, and *when*. For most people, and perhaps especially for students, *value* for money and time is a major influence.

The cost of transportation, and of course the time it takes, especially when long distances are involved, is always a factor for travelers in determining if and when pleasure travel takes place. Travel prices change more rapidly than food prices do—some destinations quickly become expensive while others become relatively inexpensive, depending on government policies, exchange rates, real estate costs, labor costs, and various supply and demand factors.

From time to time, a nation devalues its currency or the political situation in a country becomes unstable—factors that bring down tourist prices. For example, the attempted coup in Thailand a few years ago was responsible for a large decrease in tourism to that country. Prices of tourist-related activities, accommodations, and meals were slashed sharply, and Thai Air flights were discounted to encourage visitors. Another example: the Mexican government's sudden devaluation of the peso in the 1980s and 1990s sharply reduced tourism prices there and consequently increased tourism.

In 2003, the United Nations World Tourism Organization (UNWTO) reported a 2 percent decrease in worldwide international tourism receipts (which are inflation-adjusted and weighted local currencies). Major factors in this decline were the continuing effects of the September 11, 2001, terrorist attacks in the United States, the Asian severe acute respiratory syndrome (SARS) outbreak, the Bali bombing, the wars in Iraq and Afghanistan, and the global economic recession. Northeast Asia, Southeast Asia, and Oceania showed the worst economic decline, but the economies in North America, Africa, and Europe were also slowed.[21] Currently, a similar drop is likely because of the current global economic crisis.

If governments would like to encourage leisure tourism, they can manipulate a number of factors to create travel bargains, such as placing ceilings on room and meal prices. This has been done in Italy, Spain, and several former communist countries. Governments can also set artificially high or low rates of exchange for foreign currencies either to reduce or accelerate tourism.

The traveler who is not restricted by time will most likely be able to find the trip that offers the best value. The situation anywhere in the world will almost certainly change within a few years, so a destination that once was prohibitive in cost may become more affordable in the future. The wise traveler with no time restraints orders trips that take advantage of conditions existing at the moment. For example, a few years ago travel to London was relatively expensive for Americans until the British government devalued the pound, making tourism more affordable in that country. Then, the American dollar dropped in value, and London became expensive once again, almost doubling in travel cost. Here is another example: following World War II, Austria was a low-cost vacation spot in Europe. As popularity and supply and demand raised the prices somewhat, budget-conscious travelers began visiting Spain and Portugal and later Greece and Turkey for affordable trips; now they go to eastern European countries.

The Professional Traveler

More people travel regularly than ever before. School teachers, college professors, students, and retirees make up a large percentage of these travelers. They crisscross the country and fan out across the world, ending up in such places as Paris, New Delhi, Rome, Athens, London, Shanghai, Sydney, Bangkok, Bali, and Cape Town. **Professional travelers** are forever planning the next trip, recounting the last one, or recouping their energies and fortunes. Travel can be a way of life. The hard-core traveler becomes a collector of countries, a fancier of distant places, and a connoisseur of exotic spots, people, and things. Like an investor keeping a portfolio of stocks, the professional traveler keeps a portfolio of travel experiences and memories, adding to them each year.

During the off-season, professional travelers take the time to gather resources for the next trip, to read, to plan, and to relish the anticipation of sallying forth again. The professional traveler, like all travelers, is interested in excellent service and will return to and recommend places where they have experienced outstanding service. Francis Noe and Muzaffer Uysal note, "The locus of satisfaction resides between the service provider and customer. It is the interaction process that transpires between these roles that creates a dissatisfied or satisfied, and in some cases delighted tourist."[22] Consider the factors that motivate the professional traveler as discussed in the following sections.

▶ Check Your Knowledge

1. Name some different reasons why it can suddenly get a lot cheaper or more expensive to travel to a certain country.
2. What is a professional traveler?

The Grand Canyon receives more than 5 million visitors a year.
Courtesy of Rick Pawlenty

Travel for Natural Beauty

Whether avid campers, hikers, or simply Sunday strollers, most people are inspired and motivated by grand vistas and experiences with nature, which often brings them to national or state parks. The mass departure from cities and suburbs to the countryside for weekend getaways is evidence of the human need to see trees, grass, streams, and the open sky. The idea of getting away to forests, mountains, and the seaside accelerated with the Romantic Movement of the 1800s, which brought a new appreciation for the beauties of nature. Nowadays, city slickers frequently dream about "escaping it all" to recharge their energies for yet another period of urban stress, traffic, and pollution.

The idea of preserving exceptional lands for public use became popular after the Civil War when America's receding wilderness left unique natural resources vulnerable to exploitation. In 1872, by establishing Yellowstone as a national park the U.S. government began what was to become a worldwide national park movement.[23] Yellowstone was the first national park in the U.S. system, which today includes 54 parks.[24]

The national parks in the United States attract more than 438 million people a year.[25] Remember the interrelated nature of travel and tourism? The parks attract businesses that provide accommodation—hotels, motels, cabins—as well as foodservice, which creates employment and brings in income for the area. Many facilities are government built, whereas concessionaires, private persons, and national/international companies run others. Regardless of their ownership, all plans and specifications for new construction must be approved in advance by the National Park Service. Near national parks, the U.S. government controls accommodation and other rates, including food prices. Advertising and sale items are also government controlled. Likewise, standards covering public health, sanitation, and visitor comfort and convenience are set and maintained under government supervision. This control even extends to wages, hours of work, and conditions of employment for people who work in and around the parks.

Camping

Camping—whether in recreational vehicles (RVs), tents, or in the open air—is sometimes overlooked as part of the travel and tourism industry. Travel to the great outdoors is a multi-billion-dollar business and is competitive with hotels, motels, and restaurants. Campers travel millions of miles a year in the United States, Canada, and Europe. Statistics in dollars and numbers of campers show that camping is an enormous business with vast expenditures for RVs and other camping equipment. Millions of RVs are in operation. The demographics of campers may cut across social and economic lines, but most are families and semiretired or retired persons.

Parks

There are various types of parks at many levels throughout the world. For instance, the immensely popular Hyde Park in London, England, is one example of an urban park. Other types of parks are classified according to county, state, or federal level. Nevertheless, all parks, whatever the level, must achieve a balance between meeting the needs of visitors and maintaining the parks' preserves. This is not an easy task.

▶ Check Your Knowledge

1. During which historical era was the appreciation of the beauty of nature reborn?

2. How many U.S. national parks are there?

3. What groups of people are most likely to go camping?

State Parks

Cuts in state general funding are forcing many state park managers to look for alternative sources of income. Increasing user fees, flexible pricing, central reservation systems for camping, corporate sponsorships, volunteers, "friends" groups, and allowing bids on commercial use permits and concessions are just some of the means managers have used to solve the problem. To illustrate this point, let's take a closer look at a couple of state parks and what they have done to improve their situation.

Ohio provides a great example of how parks can successfully use alternative revenue sources to both their own and their visitors' satisfaction. In Ohio, campers unwilling to buy or haul their own gear into the wild can choose between a wide variety of rental options, such as Rent-a-Camp and Camper Cabins, Rent-an-RV, Rent-a-Tepee, Rent-a-Yurt, Cedar Cabins, and houseboat rental. The various options fit every budget and ensure that everyone, from the experienced camper to the novice, can have a great time. For the corporate market, selected parks offer meeting rooms and conference planning services as well as golfing.[26]

Since 1991, New Hampshire's park system has been required (by state law) to finance its operating budget through internally generated funds. As a result, the system has become a pioneer in self-sufficient park operation. Some of the key measures ensuring their success have been adjusting user fees, including the introduction of the per-person entrance fee and the annual pass, an extensive donor program, a wide use of volunteers, and a growing system of partnerships with companies. For example, the park system came to a recent agreement with PepsiCo through a competitive bid process for five years' exclusive beverage sales rights. PepsiCo secured the contract by committing to fund an education and awareness program for the state parks that would have been unaffordable without the partnership. And if the guests prefer Coke? Too bad—but hopefully the benefits gained will outweigh the suffering.

It appears inevitable that most state parks will become more like enterprises in their revenue and fund-raising activities. In Ohio and New Hampshire, the efforts appear to be working.

National Parks

The U.S. National Park Service was founded in 1916 by Congress to conserve scenery, wildlife, and natural and historic resources as well as provide for their use by the public so that future generations could enjoy, learn from, and be inspired by them. The system comprises 384 areas covering more than 83 million acres in 49 states, the District of Columbia, American Samoa, Guam, Puerto Rico,

Saipan, and the U.S. Virgin Islands. Because of their rich diversity these areas are of such national significance as to justify special recognition and protection in accordance with various acts of Congress.[27]

The numerous designations within the National Park System were either created by Congress or by the president, who can proclaim national monuments under the Antiquities Act of 1906. The names of many park areas are descriptive of the areas they encompass—lakeshores, seashores, battlefields, and so forth— but others cannot be neatly categorized because of the diversity of resources in them. However, all units of the system have equal standing in the national system, as decided by Congress in 1970.[28]

▶ Check Your Knowledge

1. List some measures state park managers can do to improve a park's financial situation.

2. In how many states are there national parks?

The National Park Service (NPS) manages a diversity of areas. In addition to the better-known *parks* such as Yellowstone and Yosemite, the NPS also manages many other heritage attractions, including the Freedom Trail in Boston, Independence Hall in Philadelphia, the Antietam National Battlefield in Sharpsburg, Maryland, and the *U.S.S. Arizona* Memorial at Pearl Harbor in Hawaii, among others. It also cares for a myriad of cultural artifacts, including ancient pottery, sailing vessels, colonial period clothing, and Civil War documents.

The ever-expanding mandate of the National Park Service calls for understanding and preserving the vitality of each park's ecosystem and the protection of unique or endangered plant and animal species. The NPS monitors various ecosystems, from the Arctic tundra to coral atolls, researches the air and water quality around the nation, and observes biological diversity. The following sections describe some of the most extraordinary parks in the system. Figure 2–6 shows the 10 most visited national parks in the United States.

The Great Smoky Mountains National Park

Great Smoky Mountains National Park is America's most visited national park,[29] and for good reason. Believed by scientists to have formed more than 1 billion years ago, the Smoky Mountains, where the park is situated, are the highest peaks in the Appalachian Mountain range. Easy access and a well-developed road system make it easy for visitors to enjoy this park's stunning views, rich wildlife and flora, tumbling streams, weathered historic buildings, and forests that reach as far as the eyes can see.

In 1000 BC, the Cherokee Indians took up residence in the Smoky Mountains. They were virtually isolated until the Spanish conquistadors arrived in 1540, and, more than two hundred years later, other immigrants from the Old World began to settle, first in small groups, and then increasingly in overwhelming numbers. The two groups of people, indigenous and immigrants, lived side by side with

10 Most Visited National Parks (2007)	
Park Unit	**Recreational Visits**
1. Great Smoky Mountains NP	9,372,253
2. Grand Canyon NP	4,413,668
3. Yosemite NP	3,503,428
4. Yellowstone NP	3,151,343
5. Olympic NP	2,988,686
6. Rocky Mountain NP	2,895,383
7. Zion NP	2,657,281
8. Grand Teton NP	2,588,574
9. Cuyahoga Valley NP	2,486,656
10. Acadia NP	2,202,228

National Park System, Recreation Visits by Year							
1916	358,006	**1940**	16,755,251	**1964**	111,385,700	**1988**	282,451,441
1917	490,705	**1941**	21,236,947	**1965**	121,312,000	**1989**	269,399,837
1918	454,841	**1942**	9,370,969	**1966**	133,081,100	**1990**	255,581,467
1919	811,516	**1943**	6,828,420	**1967**	139,675,600	**1991**	267,840,999
1920	1,058,455	**1944**	6,339,775	**1968**	150,835,600	**1992**	274,694,549
1921	1,171,797	**1945**	11,713,852	**1969**	163,990,000	**1993**	273,120,925
1922	1,216,497	**1946**	21,752,315	**1970**	172,004,600	**1994**	268,636,169
1923	1,493,792	**1947**	25,534,188	**1971**	153,693,000	**1995**	269,564,307
1924	1,607,498	**1948**	29,858,828	**1972**	165,653,523	**1996**	265,796,163
1925	2,054,562	**1949**	31,736,402	**1973**	168,923,083	**1997**	275,236,335
1926	2,314,995	**1950**	33,252,589	**1974**	171,054,779	**1998**	286,739,115
1927	2,797,840	**1951**	37,106,440	**1975**	190,390,827	**1999**	287,130,879

Figure 2–6 • The 10 Most Visited Parks in the United States

Source: Courtesy of National Park Service

only occasional quarreling. In 1838, however, more than 13,000 Cherokee were forced to leave their native lands. Only a few rebellious natives remained along with their Caucasian counterparts.

As the years progressed, more and more people settled in the Smoky Mountains. Around 1900, logging concerns discovered the Smoky Mountains, and many poor farmers found work with these companies. During the next 30 years, 67 percent of the future park was clear-cut. Logging brought employment and hard currency to the mountain communities, but destroyed the environment. With each and every technological advance more trees began to fall until almost the entire southern Appalachian forest was eliminated. Activists such as Horace Kephart and the National Park Service actively began to promote the idea of preservation of the Smoky Mountains. Soon others joined the movement.[30] In 1926, President Calvin Coolidge signed a bill that provided for the establishment of a national park in the Smoky Mountains.

The state governments of Tennessee and North Carolina as well as countless citizens responded by giving millions of dollars to purchase parkland from the farmers and lumber companies. This, however, proved to be a very difficult task to accomplish. The Great Smokies were owned by hundreds of small farmers and a handful of timber and paper companies. The farmers did not want to leave their family homesteads, and neither did the large companies want to abandon their huge forests of timber, many miles of railroad track, extensive systems of logging equipment, and whole villages of employee housing.[31] Ironically, those most dedicated to the formation of a national park were not conservationists but rather motorists interested in scenic beauty.

After much effort, the Great Smoky Mountains National Park was officially established on June 15, 1934. President Franklin Roosevelt formally dedicated the park in September 1940. In addition to its history, the following are other factors that make the park unique:

- It is one of the largest protected areas east of the Rocky Mountains.
- It has more than 50,000 acres of forest and more than 800 miles of trails.
- It is designated by the United Nations as an international biosphere.
- It is home to more than 5,500 species of plants.
- The park contains approximately 60 native mammals, more than 200 species of birds, 38 species of reptiles, 40 amphibian species, and 58 species of fish, not to mention an abundant number of land snails, insects, and spiders.[32]

The park offers a number of activities for guests including nature walks, camping, hiking, fishing, horseback riding, swimming, tubing, picnicking, biking, special programs for children and adults, and, of course, accommodations. The Great Smoky Mountains National Park has 10 campgrounds and, although they are primitive, all campgrounds come equipped with cold running water and flush toilets. Otherwise, park guests can stay at Le Conte Lodge. No restaurants or food facilities are located in the park.[33]

As mentioned, with tourism come a number of negative impacts on the environment. The main goal of the Great Smoky Mountains National Park is to protect the park's natural environment for future generations. One of the ways the park is trying to accomplish this is to reintroduce native species, such as the river otter, to the area.

Within the park, rangers play a very active role in the community. Besides providing maintenance, first aid, and security, the rangers also are involved in elementary education and developing public awareness on issues of park values, preservation, critical resources, management, and so on.

▶ Check Your Knowledge

1. Name a few of the famous heritage attractions managed by the National Park Service.

2. When was the Great Smoky Mountains National Park established?

3. What features make the Great Smoky Mountains National Park unique?

Yosemite National Park

Yosemite formed more than 500 million years ago when the region it covers today, the Sierra Nevada, was submerged in the sea. Through the years, many geographical changes have taken place. Molten rock cooled beneath thick layers of sediment rock and formed granite. Erosion, water, glaciers, and continuous weathering over time have carved Yosemite into what it is today. It is most widely known for its waterfalls, cliffs, and unusual rock formations.

Populated by Native Americans for around 8,000 years, the area became flooded with gold seekers in the 1850s, causing numerous conflicts between the two groups. Others soon followed, as writers, artists, and photographers spread the word about the Incomparable Valley throughout the world. The entrepreneur James Hutchings saw the great potential of this emerging tourism and soon began constructing hotels and residences, fencing livestock areas, and planting orchards and more—damaging Yosemite Valley's ecosystem as a result.

After an appeal by conservationists to the senator of California in 1864, the U.S. government realized the adverse ecological impact of private exploitation of the Yosemite area. As a result, Yosemite National Park was established October 1, 1890, to preserve a portion of the Central Sierra Nevada in eastern California.

Yellowstone National Park

Yellowstone, the first and oldest national park in the world, was "dedicated and set apart as a public park or pleasuring ground for the benefit and enjoyment of the people" in 1872[34] and "for the preservation, from injury or spoliation, of all timber, mineral deposits, natural curiosities, or wonders . . . and their retention in the natural condition."[35] In the 1970s, the park was also recognized internationally by the designations World Heritage Site and International Biosphere Reserve.[36]

Yellowstone is an excellent place to view wildlife, and the fact that the park is one of the most successful wildlife reserves in the country makes it a popular tourist destination. On a typical day, visitors can view bison, moose, elk, mule deer, bighorn sheep, and much more. But they must beware of bears and wolves! For those interested in history, the park contains cultural sites dating back 12,000 years. However, Yellowstone is perhaps better known for the dependable geyser eruptions of Old Faithful: every 45 to 75 minutes, the famous geyser expels 5,000 to 8,000 gallons of water, a truly spectacular sight.[37]

Ninety-nine percent of the park's 3,400 square miles remains undeveloped, providing a wide range of habitats and supporting one of the continent's largest and most varied mammal populations. Yellowstone is a true wilderness, one of the few large, natural areas remaining in the lower 48 states of the United States. Here, visitors meet nature on *its* terms, not *theirs*.[38] The scenery in Yellowstone is truly awesome. Long before any recorded human history in Yellowstone, a massive volcanic eruption spewed an immense volume of ash that covered all of the western United States, much of the Midwest, northern Mexico, and some areas of the eastern Pacific. The eruption dwarfed that of Mount Saint Helens in 1980 and left a caldera 30 miles wide by 45 miles long. That climatic event occurred approximately 640,000 years ago and was one of many processes that shaped Yellowstone National Park.[39]

Yellowstone boasts a marvelous list of sights, attractions, and facilities: a large freshwater lake, the highest in the nation; a waterfall almost twice as high as Niagara; a dramatic, 1,200-foot-deep river canyon; and the world's most famous geyser, Old Faithful.

▶ Check Your Knowledge

1. What is the motivation of most visitors to visit Yosemite Valley?
2. What is considered by many to be the most interesting sight in Yellowstone National Park?
3. What animals can visitors expect to see in Yellowstone National Park?

Travel for Sports

What role do sports play in your life? Are you one of those who would travel miles and miles to see your favorite team play or spend a small fortune to ski in an awesome Swiss resort or catch the perfect wave at a secluded Hawaiian beach? Sports give millions of people something in common, a kind of separate life divorced from the workaday world, a life in which identification with a team or a sports hero sometimes overrides logic. People from many walks of life suddenly become united in their feelings of identification with a sports team or an outstanding athlete. Travel for sports includes traveling to attend spectator sports and/or participate in individual sporting activities such as soccer, basketball, football, baseball, hockey, golf, rock climbing, and skiing. The Olympic Games is a hallmark sporting event, attracting hoards of people to the host city. Millions of tickets were sold for the 2008 Olympics in Beijing. That is a lot of people who travel, stay in hotels, eat in restaurants, as well as check out the area's attractions. Even though the Olympics attracts more people than any other sporting event, it is easy to see why sports tourism plays an important role in the tourism industry. According to a report prepared for the First World Conference on Sport and Tourism jointly organized by the International Olympic Committee (IOC) and World Trade Organization (WTO), sports and tourism have a major socioeconomic impact on an area that is appreciated in most societies and increasingly recognized by governments.[40] Sporting events are an effective way to promote and encourage tourism. Some examples of famous sporting events that people travel to attend include the following:

- The World Cup featuring the best soccer teams in the world
- The Australian Open, French Open, U.S. Open, and Wimbledon, prestigious tennis tournaments held annually
- The Super Bowl, the annual competition between the two best American football teams
- The World Series, the final fight for the title of best U.S. baseball team
- America's Cup, perhaps the most famous yachting race
- The Masters Golf Tournament, a gathering of the world's best golf players
- NASCAR auto racing held in various locations

Texas Motor Speedway
Courtesy of Fort Worth Convention and Visitors Bureau

Although major sporting events in the world are big moneymakers and attract many people, sports tourism also includes local-level games and competitions. Small communities embrace even small sporting events because of their positive effects on the local economy.

The concept of health through physical activities for all ages has sparked renewed interest and participation in a variety of sports.[41] Interactions between sport and tourism, such as the role of sports in promoting domestic, national, and international friendship and understanding among people and communities, have prompted government leaders to foster and enhance specific sporting activities.

As mentioned, sports activities have tremendous economic impacts. Billions are spent on theme parks and attraction attendance yearly." As proven by the Travel Association of America, sports and travel indeed go together. Every year, two out of five U.S. adults (38 percent) attend an organized sports event, competition, or tournament as either a spectator or participant while traveling.[42]

Businesses and entrepreneurs are becoming more sensitive to the sports tourists' needs by promoting tours, events, and destinations. Cruise lines are creating specialized sports cruises, enabling spectators and participants to enhance their skills, to meet professional athletes, to attend major events, and to simply immerse themselves in their favorite sports. The same goes for hotels and resorts.

These days, people have a heightened awareness of healthy living and the benefits of being physically fit. Many people realize the need for a vacation and often include relaxation and exercise in their itineraries. Thus, many cities adapt to this recreational need for sporting activities, facilities, and events. Some sports activities often practiced in a leisure environment include hiking, tennis, bicycle riding, golf, sailing, inline skating, skiing, and swimming. Of course, a lot of adventure tourism (discussed next) also fits into the sports tourism category.

▶ Check Your Knowledge

1. What is a main motivator for travelers to attend sports events?

2. Name some famous sports events that draw lots of visitors from other areas.

3. What are the main reasons why sports tourism has become so popular?

Adventure Travel

Looking for some action? Want to see something different from bars, clubs, and quiet museums? Not a problem! There are plenty of adventure tours around, ranging from off-road bike tours, to whitewater rafting, African safaris and wildlife tours, rainforest canopy tours, and bungee jumping, to name just a few. Adventure travel is an important segment of the travel and tourism industry and is growing at a fast pace as people increasingly seek active and challenging activities to add something extra to their vacation.

Actually, as many as one-half of U.S. adults, or 98 million people, took an adventure trip in the last few years, and 31 million adults engaged in hard adventure activities such as whitewater rafting, scuba diving, and mountain biking. **Adventure travelers** are more likely to be young, single, and employed compared to all U.S. adults.[43]

One adventure travel company in Hawaii, known as Hawaii—Land of Aloha, offers a three-island adventure. The tropical adventure holiday begins on Kauai, the oldest and lushest of all the islands. Visitors spend three incredible days on the "Garden Isle" hiking the plunging sea cliffs of the Na Pali Coast, swimming in Ke'e Lagoon, ascending Waimea Canyon, and enjoying exquisite views along the rigorous trails of Kokee Park. On the fourth day, the tour visits Maui, the "Valley Isle." The day is devoted to flora study and photography as participants trek into the lush tropical forests of the west main mountains. After rising with the sun, visitors hike through the Haleakala Crater, which descends into the jaws of the world's largest caldera. Then, they follow the ancient Hawaiian footpaths to the panoramic summit of Pun Olai, ending up at Maneka Beach, where they snorkel prior to catching the evening's flight to Hilo, "the Big Island." The fifth day begins with a presentation on volcanology followed by a hike across the steaming floor of Kilauea Iki, the world's most active volcano. Participants explore the botanical and geological wonders of the park, stroll through the towering bamboo forests to a waterfall deep inside Waipio Valley, soak up the sun on the powdery sands of Hapuna, and eat at an authentic family luau.[44]

Religious Travel

Special and personal interests play an important role in why people travel to certain destinations—or even travel at all. Perhaps one of the less talked about reasons for travel is travel for religious purposes. **Religious travel**, which is often referred to as **pilgrimage**, has been practiced for hundreds of years and is still fairly common today. Such travels can be broken down into two main categories: first, satisfying one's religious convictions; and second, fulfilling one's curiosity about a particular faith or practice.

Thousands of sites (including holy lands, churches, temples, and mosques) throughout the world attract millions of tourists each year. They partake, either as participants or as spectators, in a wide variety of activities that express their respect and devotion to the religion. For instance, thousands of Buddhists make pilgrimages to the four holy mountains of Buddhism and pay homage to Buddha at the several temples, some of which are still in daily use today.

CORPORATE PROFILE

G.A.P Adventures

Courtesy of Mark Green

When people are tired of the one-week-in-the-Florida-sun vacation and want to do something exciting and off the beaten path, G.A.P Adventures is the perfect company to turn to. This company provides more than 600 different itineraries in more than 100 countries and has during the last few years given more than 20,000 travelers the adventure of their lifetime. This year, approximately 1.5 million people are expected to visit the company's website—for some, it will change their lives forever.

G.A.P's CEO Bruce Poon Tip is one out of only three finalists nominated for the Entrepreneur of the Year award, sponsored by NASDAQ, Ernst & Young, and the *National Post*.

The company has practiced its corporate philosophy "The freedom of independent travel with the security of a group" since the start. G.A.P respects its travelers as individuals, and there is no requirement for travelers to be athletic to embark on one of the trips. The only thing travelers need to have is a spirit of adventure and the desire to experience a world totally different from what they are accustomed to.

The concept of responsible tourism is very important to G.A.P Adventures. It has helped to improve the conditions in the many countries it brings tourists to visit—groups come and go, interact with the local populations, and leave behind only footprints. The company's commitment is to support local people and communities and to protect the environment their groups travel in.

G.A.P hires people in six different areas, namely, tour leaders, operations (mainly locals in the category), sales and marketing, travel services, accounting and administration, and air department. There is no specific job description, but the most important thing is that employees fit into the company culture and live by the company core values. Although G.A.P employees might not personally change the world, at least they get to see it!

Maybe the most obvious choice is the position as a G.A.P tour leader. In this position, your main task is to make people's holiday dreams come true and make sure all passengers have a fun and safe time. Most of the time, the local hostel where you spend the night is your home, and your office is your backpack. On your way to work, you might have to walk up the Inca Trail or canoe down the Amazon. If you are interested in meeting and really interacting with people from different cultures and like to show your passion to passengers of different backgrounds, ages, and interests, this is the perfect job for you.

Some of the requirements to work as a G.A.P tour leader include fluency in English and Spanish, a love for Latin America (which is the main area of operations), and excellent people skills. No matter what happens and how bad your day is, you always have to be the happy and helpful leader. Additional skills needed include awareness of, and commitment to, sustainable tourism, both environmentally and culturally, as well as commitment because the job contracts are 12 to 18 months at a time.

It takes time to become the perfect adventure tour leader, and once you have learned it G.A.P wants you to stay for a while. You also need to be resourceful, which means being able to solve any kind of problem that might arise, expected or unexpected. Because of the nature of the work you also need to have good health, first aid certification, and a certain level of computer literacy (Internet/e-mail/Microsoft Word/Microsoft Excel). If you have seen the world or want to see it in a truly interactive way, and you have leader skills and are adventurous and brave, this might be the perfect challenge for you. Why not give it a try?

Source: This feature draws on G.A.P Adventures' website: www.gapadventures.com

For Muslims, the pilgrimage to Mecca—the Hajj—is the peak of their religious life. The Hajj, meaning "visit to the revered place," is the fifth pillar of Islam and the most significant manifestation of Islamic faith. For Muslims who are mentally, physically, and financially able to make the faithful journey to Mecca, performing this ritual affirms their faith. Many rituals are performed during this pilgrimage, which must be undertaken at least once during a Muslim's lifetime.[45]

For those of the Catholic faith, the Vatican is a holy land of sorts. It is home to the Pope, and millions travel to the Vatican hoping to attend mass and catch a glimpse of the pontiff. In actuality, some Catholics travel to wherever the Pope visits.

Other religious sites include Oberammergau, Germany; the Angkor Temples in Cambodia; the Ganges River in Bengal; the Holy Land in Israel; and Lourdes in France. For those who are interested in ancient religions and groups, some popular destinations are the ancient and mysterious pyramids of Egypt, Rome in Italy, the Inca capital of Machu Picchu in Peru, as well as the many ruins in Mexico, Guatemala, Honduras, Belize, and El Salvador.

A Buddhist Temple
Courtesy JNTO

Interestingly, it has been suggested that the masses of people traveling to the many Disney parks also can be classified as pilgrims. Vuconic, among others, claims that religion and tourism are intertwined, as "the activity of one creates the conditions for the activity of the other."[46] Indeed, several authors have suggested that Disney has become the equivalent of a religion with its theme parks being the "holy land" and Mickey Mouse being an "omnipresent demigod."[47]

For hundreds of years, hospitality and travel professionals and entrepreneurs have sought out the potential business brought by religious travelers. The impact such tourists have on the host town or area is significant. As any other tourists, pilgrims look for appropriate accommodations, transportation, restaurants, and recreational or heritage attractions. Thus, we can see the interrelated nature of travel, tourism, and hospitality even within this relatively small component of the industry.

▶ Check Your Knowledge

1. Who is the typical adventure traveler?

2. What are the two categories of religious travel?

3. Where are the major holy lands for Buddhists, Muslims, and Catholics?

Medical and Health Tourism

Stressed out? Need some rest? Want to be pampered and regain your energies? There are plenty of opportunities out there, and more and more people take advantage of the numerous options that exist in medical and health tourism. Inspired by push factors, these tourists look for escape, self-discovery, rest, and beautiful scenery among other things.[48]

The term *medical and health tourism* may be new, but the phenomenon has existed for some time. Goodrich and Goodrich define health tourism as the attempts of tourist facilities such as hotels, resorts, and destinations to attract tourists by deliberately promoting their health care services and features in addition to regular tourist amenities.[49] Health care services might include but are not limited to the following:

- Hydrotherapy treatments
- Beauty treatments
- Relaxation techniques
- Cellulite treatment
- Medical examinations
- Operations of all kinds
- Special exercise, diet, and nutritional advice
- Medical treatments for specific diseases such as arthritis
- Alternative therapies
- Body massages

The search for health and longevity has created a frenzy for going to spas and bathing in the sea. Spa vacations have long been popular in Europe, but new resort hotels everywhere are likely to include a spa and a wide range of facilities related to wellness and health improvement. Well-known health tourism destinations in Europe include Baden, Lausanne, St. Moritz, and Interlaken in Switzerland as well as Baden-Baden and Wiesbaden in Germany. In the United States, popular destination resorts and spas can be found in California, for example, the famous Pritikin Longevity Center, as well as in Colorado and Arizona.

Vacationing is often considered an investment in health, but how can travelers get the most out of their time away? Many physicians urge people not to take one "all-out" vacation once every year, but rather a series of smaller vacations as a means of recouping one's energies, interests, and enthusiasm for the job. Three 1-week vacations are likely to be more healthful than one 3-week vacation. Similarly, spacing vacations over summer, fall, and winter can be more satisfying to the vacationer (and to tour operators) as well. Increasingly, people include a visit to the spa as part of a longer break, or simply as a weekend trip.

Medical tourism is on the increase as more places internationally offer less expensive services as compared to those in the United States. Dentists and surgeons in Southeast Asia, India, and eastern Europe offer a complete range of medical procedures at a fraction of the cost in the United States.

Other Motivations for Leisure Travel

Several additional motivations for tourists are discussed in Chapter 8, Attractions and Entertainment. Among them are amusement parks, gaming entertainment, fairs and festivals, shopping, performing arts, and historic sites. Chapter 11 describes social, cultural, and heritage tourism, and Chapter 12 presents an overview of ecotourism. The topics of these chapters have direct influences on motivation for leisure travel and tourism.

San Diego Museum of Art
Courtesy of San Diego Convention and Visitors Bureau

Trends in Motivation for Leisure Tourism

Not only is tourism facing immense growth, but a new form of tourism is emerging as well: more sustainable, environmentally and socially responsible, and characterized by flexibility and choice. A new type of consumer is driving it: more educated, experienced, independent, conservation-minded, respectful of cultures, and insistent on value for money. To remain competitive, tourism destinations and industry players alike must adapt by reinventing tourism.

CAREER INFORMATION

You can choose from a wide variety of career options if you want to work in the recreational field of leisure travel. One option is to work for the National Park Service as a park ranger or in one of the many other positions offered, for example, photographers, park police, museum staff, and managerial and financial administrative personnel. For more information about employment within the NPS, visit the website at www.nps.gov and look at training and employment opportunities.

Another exciting career alternative is being a tour leader with an adventure travel company. Depending on what company you decide to join, you can hike your way through the Amazon, jeep across southern Australia, or teach your clients to ride elephants in the mountains of northern India. If you want to join the health care discipline, you might consider working in a spa, giving luxury treatments and serving health food to stressed out celebrities. And you do not need to be an athlete to make money from sports tourism; if you have ever been to a sporting event, you have probably seen that those events are made possible through a vast number of event personnel.

Just think: someone has to manage the Field Museum in Chicago, Sea World in Orlando, safari tours in Africa, and all other leisure tourism activities. Try an internship in an area you like and see where it leads you.

Another important trend is the increasing importance of the Internet in the industry, both as a source of travel-related information for the consumers, and as a means of actually booking trips. A third trend is that more and more state and national parks have to finance themselves, that is, come up with money to pay for employees, maintenance, and so forth on their own. This has lead to several parks starting to charge entrance fees, but also to many parks finding new and creative ways of supporting themselves. Finally, women are emerging as powerful consumers with a strong impact on travel worldwide, which brings new challenges for both commercial and noncommercial industry players.

CASE STUDY

As the research manager for a state tourism office, you have been given the job of finding what motivates these prospective visitors to travel. You decide to do a survey of people in states close to yours who asked for travel information. Some of the people who requested information actually did visit, while others did not. You decide to look at the data on those who did not visit to gain insight into how you might attract them to your state. The results indicate a fairly large percentage of the people in this group are interested in cultural, arts, and heritage experiences; driving to view scenery; shopping; and attending festivals. They also report that they travel to have fun, to see interesting sights, to view scenery, and to experience new and different places.

You need to provide some advice to the director of the tourism office and to the advertising department on how to best reach these people and increase numbers of visitors. What advice will you give them?

Source: Courtesy Kathleen Andereck, Arizona State University

Summary

1. Leisure travel has increased dramatically in recent years. This indicates people's need to escape daily routines and improve their quality of life. The growth on leisure travel has been encouraged by an increase in disposable income, values and lifestyle changes, greater variety in leisure travel and tourism options, increased awareness in travel and tourism, demographic influences, and increased leisure time.

2. Abraham Maslow developed a hierarchy of needs theory based on the belief that need satisfaction motivates human behavior. His hierarchy includes psychological needs, safety needs, need for belonging and love, esteem needs, and self-actualization needs. These levels of needs are useful when determining travel and tourism motivators. Pearce suggests a leisure ladder model, and Plog's psychographic model classifies the U.S. population along a psychographic continuum delineating their personality types, ranging from psychocentric at one extreme to allocentric at the other.

3. Arlin Epperson suggests the push-pull model for explaining tourist motivation. Factors that pull include attractions and those that push include personal needs and desires.

4. Cost and time play large roles in determining if and when pleasure travel takes place, as do political factors, safety, and government intervention.

5. The idea of preserving exceptional lands for public use in the United States arose after the Civil War when America's receding wilderness left unique natural resources vulnerable to exploitation. In 1872, the U.S. government began what was to become a grand-scale park system by establishing Yellowstone as a national park. Yellowstone was the first national park in the system, which today includes 54 parks.

6. Dwindling budgets and increasing needs for maintenance are forcing state parks to look for innovative sources of revenue.

7. The National Park System of the United States comprises 384 units covering more than 83 million acres in 49 states, the District of Columbia, American Samoa, Guam, Puerto Rico, Saipan, and the U.S. Virgin Islands.

8. The National Park System units include national parks, national monuments, national preserves, national historic sites, national historic parks, national memorials, national battlefields, national cemeteries, national recreation areas, national seashores, national lakeshores, national rivers, national parkways, and national trails.

9. Travel for sports include both spectator sports and individual sporting activities. The reasons for the surge in sports tourism include popular sporting events such as the Olympics, focus on healthy lifestyles, increased interaction between sports and tourism, and a new tendency to break up vacations into smaller but more frequent blocks of time throughout the year.

10. Adventure travel is growing at a fast pace as people increasingly seek active and challenging activities to add something extra to their vacation.

11. Religious travel, often referred to as pilgrimage, has been practiced for hundreds of years and is still fairly common today. There are two reasons for religious travel: satisfying one's religious convictions, and fulfilling one's own curiosity about a particular faith or practice.

12. The search for health and longevity, as well as the added pressures of people's lives, has caused many tourists to look for escape, self-discovery, rest, and so on when going on vacation.

13. Some current trends in leisure travel are shorter and more frequent vacations, increasing use of the Internet, a "reinvention" of tourism to accommodate the demands of the new consumer, and greater female impact on the industry.

Key Words and Concepts

adventure travelers	national park	professional traveler
leisure	pilgrimage	religious travel

Review Questions

1. What factors can you identify as reasons for the increase in leisure travel?

2. Summarize the concepts discussed in Maslow's hierarchy of needs theory.

3. Give examples of vacations that push versus those that pull (three each). Are there some destinations that could serve as both? How? Be sure to thoroughly explain your reasoning.

4. Explain the role of government policies in the leisure travel and tourism industry. What can governments do to increase or decrease the number of visitors to their country?

5. Why has the interest in adventure travel seen such an amazing growth?

6. What are the most romantic locations in Yosemite?

Interesting Websites

G.A.P Adventures: www.gapadventures.com

National Park Service: www.nps.gov

Sportsline: www.sportsline.com

Sports Tourism International Council: www.sptourism.net

Internet Exercises

1. Go to the website of the National Park Service. Which is the newest national park and what is the reason it was declared so?

2. On the Internet find three companies that offer adventure travel and describe some of the interesting packages they offer.

Apply Your Knowledge

1. Plan a visit to a national park.

2. Show how the major push and pull factors worked for a vacation you have had or one you would like to take.

Suggested Activity

Ask 10 different people what their motivation was for their last vacation. Compare their answers with the motivations discussed in this chapter and be prepared to discuss your findings in class.

Endnotes

1. Muzaffer Uysal and Lee Ann R. Hagan, "Motivation of Pleasure Travel and Tourism," in *VNR's Encyclopedia of Hospitality and Tourism*, ed. Mahmood A. Khan, Michael D. Olsen, and Turgut Var (New York: Van Nostrand Reinhold, 1993), 798.

2. Iso-Ahola, as cited in Uysal and Hagan, "Motivation of Pleasure Travel and Tourism," 799.

3. Ibid.

4. Uysal and Hagan, "Motivation of Pleasure Travel and Tourism," 799.

5. Ibid.

6. John Swarbrooke and Susan Horner, *Consumer Behavior in Tourism* (Oxford, England: Elsevier Butterworth-Heinemann, 2005), 55.

7. Ibid.

8. Travel Industry Association of America, "U.S. Travel Market Overview-Travel Volumes and Trends," April 30, 2007, www.tia.org/researchpubs/us_overview_volumes_trends.html (accessed September 2, 2009).

9. Swarbrooke and Horner, *Consumer Behavior in Tourism*, 53.

10. Ibid., 54.

11. Swarbrooke and Horner, *Consumer Behavior in Tourism*, as cited in Michael Scantlebury, "Heritage Tourism, Keeping the Right Balance: Economic Progress and Sustainable Tourism," workshop presented at the 8th Sustainable Tourism Conference, Caribbean Tourism Organization, Puerto Rico, April 23–25, 2006.

12. Juergen Gnoth, "Tourism Motivation and Expectations Formation," *Annals of Tourism Research* 24, no. 2 (1997): 283–304.

13. Arlin Epperson, "Why People Travel," *Leisure Today*, April 1983, 54.

14. J. L. Crompton, "Motivations of Pleasure Vacation," *Annals of Tourism Research* 6 (1979): 408, 424; M. Uysal and C. Jurowski, "Testing the Push and Pull Factors," *Annals of Tourism Research* 21, no. 4 (1994): 884–846, as cited in Yooshik Yoon and Muzaffer Uysal, "An Examination of the Effects of Motivation and Satisfaction on Destination Loyalty: A Structured Model," *Tourism Management* 26 (2005): 45–56.

15. S. Cha, K. McCleary, and M. Uysal, "Travel Motivation of Japanese Overseas Travelers: A Factor-Cluster Segmentation Approach," *Journal of Travel Research* 34, no. 1 (1995): 33, 39; H. C. Oh, M. Uysal, and P. Weaver, "Product Bundles and Market Segments Based on Travel Motivations: A Canonical Correlation Approach," *International Journal of Hospitality Management* 14, no. 2 (1995): 123, 137, as cited in Yoon and Uysal, "An Examination of the Effects of Motivation," 45–56.

16. Roy A. Cook, Laura J. Yale, and Joseph J. Marqua, *Tourism: The Business of Travel* (Upper Saddle River, NJ: Prentice Hall, 2002), 37.

17. John R. Walker, *Introduction to Hospitality Management*, 3rd ed. (Upper Saddle River, NJ: Prentice Hall, 2010), 73.

18. J. A. Card and C. Kestel, "Motivational Factors and Demographic Characteristics of Travelers to and from Germany," *Society and Leisure* 11, no. 1 (1988): 49–58, as cited in *Tourism Principles and Practice*, 3rd ed., ed. Chris Cooper, John Fletcher, Alan Fyall, David Gilbert, and Stephen Wanhill (Harlow, Essex, UK: Pearson Education Limited, 2005), 56.

19. Crompton, "Motivations of Pleasure Vacation," 408–424, as cited in Uysal and Hagan, "Motivation of Pleasure Travel and Tourism," 807.

20. Muzaffer Uysal, *Global Tourist Behavior* (New York: International Business Press, 1994), 1.

21. Bryan Wilson, "Travel Industry Trends and Predictions, 2004," August 2004, www.metropolitantour.com/919356-Travel-Industry-Trends-and-Predictions-2004.html (accessed September 2, 2009).

22. Francis P. Noe and Muzaffer Uysal, "Social Interaction Linkages in the Service Satisfaction Model," *Journal of Quality Assurance in Hospitality and Tourism* 4, no. 3–4 (2003): 7–22.

23. National Park Service, "The National Park System Caring for the American Legacy," www.nps.gov/legacy/mission.html (accessed September 2, 2009).

24. Ibid.

25. National Park Service Public Use Statistics Office, "NPS Stats," www2.nature.nps.gov/stats/ (accessed September 2, 2009).

26. Ohio State Parks, "Get Outdoors and Have Fun at Your Beautiful Ohio State Parks!" www.dnr.state.oh.us/tabid/80/default.aspx (accessed September 2, 2009).

27. National Park Service, "The National Park System Caring for the American Legacy."

28. Ibid.

29. Ibid.

30. Zero-Cut, "Logging Our National Forests: Clearcut or Zero-Cut Now?" www.forestcouncil.org/learn/features/zerocut/zerocut.html#top (accessed September 2, 2009).

31. Gatlinburg Chamber of Commerce International, "Great Smoky Mountains National Park," www.gatlinburg.com/national-park/ (accessed September 2, 2009).

32. John William Uhler, "Great Smoky Mountains National Park Information Page," www.great.smoky.mountains.national-park.com/info.htm (accessed September 2, 2009).

33. Ibid.

34. http://www.nps.gov/yell/index.htm retrieved September 9, 2009.

35. Ibid.

36. National Park Service, Yellowstone National Park information page, www.nps.gov/yell/index.htm (accessed September 2, 2009).

37. Ibid.

38. Ibid.

39. AreaParks.com, Yellowstone National Park, http://yellowstone.areaparks.com/ (accessed September 2, 2009).

40. World Tourism Organization, "Sport and Tourism—Introductory Report," August 2002. www.world-tourism.org/cgi-bin/infoshop.storefront/EN/product/1265-1 (accessed September 2, 2009).

41. John Douvis, Aminuddin Yusof, and Stavros Douvis, "An Examination of Demographic and Psychographic Profiles of the Sport Tourist," *Cyber Journal of Sport Marketing*, www.ausport.gov.au/fulltext/1998/cjsm/v2n4/douvisyusof24.htm (accessed September 2, 2009).

42. Travel Industry Association, "Domestic Travel Fast Facts—Travel Trends from 'A to Z,'" www.tia.org/travel/TravelTrends.asp (accessed September 2, 2009).

43. Ibid.

44. Hawaii–Land of Aloha. www.sni.net/trips/hi/hawaii.html, March 3, 2001.

45. Haidar Moukdad, "The Hajj: The Muslim Pilgrimage to Mecca and the Holy Places," April 30, 1995, www.encyclopedia.com/doc/1P1-2328622.html (accessed September 2, 2009).

46. B. Vuconic, *Tourism and Religion* (Oxford, England: Elsevier Science, 1996), 188.

47. S. M. Fjellmann, *Vinyl Leaves—Walt Disney World and America* (Boulder, CO: Westview Press, 1992); Nichola Toda Krause, "There's a Mouse in the House: A Vacation-Time Reflection on Disney and the True Faith," *Orthodox Family Life*, 1997, www.theologic.com/oflweb/secular/disney2.htm (accessed September 2, 2009); E. E. Tamm, "Is Big Brother Wearing Mouse Ears? An Epic Struggle against the Cultural Hegemony of Walt Disney," 1996, www.usc.edu/dept/gjsa/reflex/mick.html (accessed September 2, 2009).

48. John R. Walker, *Introduction to Hospitality*, 5th ed. (Upper Saddle River, NJ: Prentice Hall, 2009), 231.

49. Jonathan N. Goodrich and Grace E. Goodrich, in *Managing Tourism*, ed. S. Medlik (Oxford, England: Butterworth Heinemann, 1991), 107.

CHAPTER 3

Tourism Marketing

OBJECTIVES

After reading and studying this chapter you should be able to:

- Describe the steps in the marketing system and explain why marketing is important for companies in the tourism industry.

- Understand the role of a market situation analysis and name the four aspects of the SWOT analysis and how they can be used for strategic planning.

- Identify the different steps in the marketing segmentation process.

- Name and describe the Ps of tourism marketing.

- Outline the most significant trends taking place within the field of tourism marketing.

- Explain how sales are conducted and managed in the tourism business.

GEOGRAPHY SPOTLIGHT

Romantic Tourism: Thailand

Romantic surroundings of lush lily pad gardens line open-air villas, a stone's throw from pristine palm tree beaches. Hua Hin, Thailand, discovered and developed as a resort destination for the Thai royal family in the 1920s, stands today as one of the few resort destinations that attracts both native Thais and foreigners. With its beauty and modern luxury offerings, its charming five-star resorts, and cultural history, Hua Hin is among Thailand's most popular getaway and romance vacation destinations.[1]

Hua Hin is located about 140 miles from Bangkok in the narrowest section of the long geographical stretch of the country. After 70 years, development continues in Hua Hin, including the completion of several five-star hotels, private residences, and golf courses. Among these developments, Six Senses Resorts and Spas has introduced visitors to a getaway that is incomparable to any other in the area. The Six Senses Hideaway Hua Hin is located 15 miles from the Hua Hin village center. The development company began in 1995 and has developed six brands of accommodations representing 17 properties across the Maldives, Vietnam, Oman, Fiji, Jordan, and Spain. The luxury boutique resort company's purpose is "to create innovative and enlightening experiences that rejuvenate our guests' love of SLOW LIFE."[2] This concept is expanded into "Sustainable, Local, Organic, Wholesome, Learning, Inspiring, Fun, Experiences." Six Senses positions itself as the "leader in providing sustainable tourism options for consumers,

GEOGRAPHY SPOTLIGHT *(continued)*

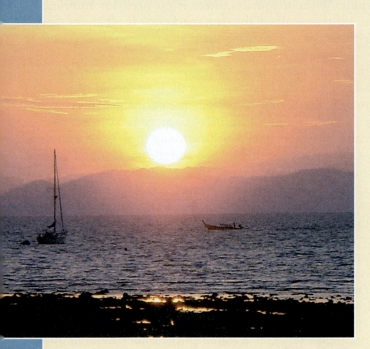

Courtesy of Mark Green

suppliers and partners."[3] All of its properties utilize environmentally friendly building materials and food sources. The core focus is on encouraging and educating their guests, employees, and vendors. The Six Senses Hideaway strives to bring attention to the reality of the destination as the primary goal of the experience.

The resort in Hua Hin is designed to separate the welcome center and reception area from the guest villas. The guest villas are interconnected by pathways that wander through lily pad lagoons, palm trees, exotic gardens, and wildlife areas. Each of the 55 luxurious and spacious guest villas has its own pool with a landscaped garden. All of the villas have an indoor/outdoor shower, steam room, outdoor bathtub, and a treatment area where a spa attendant can be hired to perform services. In this unique outdoor ambiance, guests can relax in their outdoor living room with sofas and satellite TV. The Six Senses Hideaway also provides an extensive list of services for weddings and honeymoons. Guests can enjoy the food and beverages provided at the resort in the public areas or in the comfort of their own villa. Meals can be custom made from any cuisine and contain fresh, local ingredients from the resort's own organic herb and vegetable garden.[4]

Hua Hin offers visitors a wide variety of activities, stimulating or relaxing. Local Thai culture has been preserved by the few local people that reside in the region, minimizing the impact made by tourism and economic development. Doing their part by incorporating environmental sustainability and social responsibility into their way of business, Six Senses Resorts has dedicated its finances, research, and innovation to providing guests with an unmatched luxury experience. With its seemingly endless growth potential, Hua Hin, Thailand, continues to provide the Thai people a local vacation resort getaway and foreign travelers an all-encompassing experience that should not be missed.

Endnotes

1. Hua Hin, Thailand, "Welcome to Hua Hin, Thailand's, Royal Beach Resort," www.hua-hin.com (accessed March 30, 2009).
2. Six Senses Hideaway Hua Hin, "Six Senses Hideaway Hua Hin, Thailand," www.huahin.bangkok.com/sixsenses-huahin (accessed March 30, 2009).
3. Six Senses Hideaway Hua Hin, "Six Senses Hideaway Hua Hin, Thailand."
4. Six Senses Hideaway Hua Hin, "Six Senses Hideaway Hua Hin, Thailand."

In this chapter, we look at the marketing of tourism, its main terms and concepts, types of marketing, and how it can be used to increase revenues and profits for companies in the tourism industry. Marketing is critically important to the success of tourism organizations. Without tourists, there is no need for frontline employees—or anyone else for that matter! Tourism marketing is all about discovering tourists' needs and wants and providing them at a reasonable cost and profit.

Marketing begins with a corporate philosophy, vision, and mission statement. These should not just hang on the boss's office wall; they should be practiced every day. Peter Drucker, the highly respected management expert and scholar, said that the only valid definition of business purpose is to create customers. With tourism, we can easily change the word *customer* to *guest*—because this implies that we will take better care of them—and add the phrase "and keep them coming back again and again."

Creating great guest experiences means finding a product or service that a number of people need or want. For example, Ted Arison and later his son Micky pioneered the fun cruises that are the hallmark of Carnival Cruise Lines. Because they had older and slower ships (all they could afford at the time), the Arisons realized early on that it would be too difficult to compete head on with the more established cruise companies. So, they devised the idea of making cruising affordable and letting entertainment be a key ingredient. Passengers loved the idea of cruising on the "fun ships," and Carnival has become the largest and most successful cruise line in history because it fulfills a need that many people had: providing a quality, fun cruising experience at a value price. Understanding and fulfilling needs are fundamental to the discipline of marketing.

The American Marketing Association's definition of **marketing** is this: "Marketing is the activity, set of institutions, and processes for creating, communicating, delivering, and exchanging offerings that have value for customers, clients, partners, and society at large."[1] A more simplistic way of describing marketing is to find a guest need and provide exceptional product and service at a fair price that keeps guests recommending and returning and that yields a reasonable profit. Many people believe that marketing is the same as sales. Actually, sales is considered one of the tools of marketing and is used to promote and build business.

A **marketing orientation** is the philosophy of understanding what guests want and need, developing products and services that best meet their needs, and communicating with them to generate awareness, interest, and purchase. Often, this entails giving guests great value and exceptional service. Marketing orientation spans from when a guest picks up the phone or goes online to make a reservation to bidding them a fond farewell and inviting them to return soon (with friends). A sales orientation is when a company develops products and services that it thinks customers would like and then sells the services to them. Unless there are no other comparable products in the market, customers may or may not like what a company sells and may or may not buy it. By having a marketing orientation and listening to customers rather than having a sales orientation and dictating to customers, companies can ensure that customers will like and buy their products.

There is a direct correlation between having satisfied guests who become loyal to a business and the success of the business. For instance, the organizational needs of the business include the need to make a profit. If guests are satisfied, they most likely will return, spend more with the business, and provide the company the opportunity to make more money and profit. The key to marketing is to keep guests delighted and give them a reason to come back. In turn, they may tell others about the experience and help a business attract new customers.

The Marketing System

Businesses must do marketing on a continual basis. This means that they cannot do just one marketing campaign to ensure sales for the following years. They should view marketing as a systematic and continuing activity for which they must be constantly involved in all steps of the tourist purchase process by offering different products and services in ways that are meaningful and relevant to tourists. Both large corporations and small independent tourism businesses adopt marketing systems to increase market penetration of new and existing markets with existing products, exploit new **market opportunities** with new products, and increase overall **market share**. In a simplified view, the marketing system consists of these steps, as shown in Figure 3–1: planning/identifying needs, developing marketing strategies and suitable campaigns, implementing and following through, following up and marketing research.

The Importance of Marketing

Marketing is everything. It is about attracting the right guests, delivering superior service, quality, and value, exceeding guest expectations, and establishing a relationship that ensures **continuous loyalty**. We say that marketing makes the

Figure 3–1 • The Marketing System

business world go around because without marketing, we would not have tourists. Without tourists, we would not need the other disciplines in the industry. Everyone from the corporate executive to the line employee is—or should be—involved in marketing. Whereas most tourists never see executives or managers, they do meet and interact with many front-line associates.

Guest loyalty is a very important concept in tourism and can be measured in several ways. Loyal guests or tourists typically use/visit the same business more frequently, spend more there, and recommend the business to others. Therefore, all decisions and actions in a business should improve guest service (which will result in improved profitability); for example, a cruise line can concentrate on reducing the check-in time for passengers and an amusement park can focus on providing options for guests to engage in during waiting periods. Disney is an expert at handling waiting times. It provides baggage holding services, park passes, food and beverage and tour options, and even locker rooms for guests to change in while waiting for check-in. Guests become instantly engaged in the Disney enterprise, which increases guest satisfaction, and they spend money in the hotels and parks in the process. Disney also provides TV screens, live characters, music, and lighting to make the waiting time for its park rides appear to go faster. For world-class hospitality and entertainment companies such as Disney, an enhanced guest experience and high levels of guest satisfaction lead to greater customer loyalty and profit.

We need to remember that the guest pays the salaries of tourism employees, so the guest is really our boss. This is best exemplified by the story of an

Great food, beverages, and service at reasonable prices help ensure guest loyalty.
Courtesy Sedona Convention and Visitors Bureau

American consultant who was in Japan talking to a group of Japanese employees at a major tourism corporation. He said, "In my business the guest is king." At that moment, a gentleman ran down from the rear of the hall and grabbed the microphone and said, "In my business, the guest is God." He was the company president.

If we look at things through our guests' eyes, we have a better chance of making the right decisions on how to improve the guest experience. American Airlines did it with "More room in coach." It listened to its passengers, who told the airline that they could do with a little more leg room in coach. American was then able to advertise that it was the only airline to offer more leg room in coach. Similarly, Southwest Airlines found that passengers wanted everyday low fares and did not necessarily care for assigned seats, so it initiated low fares between cities, no change fees, open seating, and a fun, relaxed atmosphere. Southwest has historically been one of the most profitable airlines and, not surprisingly, a recipient of annual quality and passenger satisfaction awards.

The leading tourism corporations of excellence all have a strong marketing orientation because, as the expression goes, "without heads in beds and butts in seats, you ain't got anything in the bank." A marketing orientation is a philosophy of providing value and exceptional service for guests. A company can realize the importance of marketing when, for example, regular guests who usually visit a restaurant once a month go twice instead, doubling the sales of the restaurant. In tourism, we need to think long term and build relationships with our tourists so that they become brand loyal to our companies: approximately 80 percent of our business comes from 20 percent of our guests.

Marketing is important for any business that wishes to sell a product or service to tourists, other businesses, or both. Marketing not only serves as a way to find out what tourists actually want, but also to inform potential tourists that a product or service is available and encourage them to use it. Marketing is also a way of explaining a product's or service's advantages and distinct characteristics. It also makes the market work better because guests can know all of the new products entering the market and improvements that have been made, which makes them able to get the best value for their budgets and preferences. For example, a resort in a tropical climate can stress "cool" new quiet air-conditioned rooms.

Marketing also makes it easier for consumers and sellers to get together to exchange products, services, and money. With marketing, consumers know what products are available and where they can be found. The power of the Internet has revolutionized how we get together to exchange products, services, and money. Twenty-four hours a day, every day, from virtually anywhere in the world, travelers can look for and book a room, airline seat, cruise, vacation package, or train ticket. In just a few clicks, tourists can review destinations and prices, purchase an air ticket, select a hotel, book a tour, reserve a rental car, and confirm a golf tee time or spa treatment appointment. They can compare prices for individual parts or the whole vacation package in real time. Before the Internet, it would take hours if not days and the assistance of travel agents, reservationists, operators, and guidebooks to navigate the tourism marketing system and exchange with travel suppliers.

Tourism's Unique Product

The tourism product is different from traditional goods in that it can be characterized as perishable, intangible, and variable in nature, and because the tourism product is different, marketing and sales can be more difficult. Tourism products such as destinations; transportation in the form of airline seats, cruise line cabins, motor coach seats, or train seats; overnight accommodations in the form of hotel rooms or resort cabins; and food in the form of restaurant meals are perishable—if they are not sold today, they can never be sold. A hotel can't sell tomorrow a room that went unoccupied, and a cruise line cannot sell a cruise cabin that left port empty yesterday. (Perhaps one exception is that a restaurant could sell an unsold meal tomorrow as a special.) Tourism products and services have no shelf life: they cannot be stored for sale at a later date. The perishability of the product brings additional challenges in marketing and sales. For instance, a resort may have to use unique promotions and pricing to ensure that all rooms are sold before the end of the day. It may offer specials, packages, group rates, and holiday events to entice and encourage guests to book rooms in advance, and then offer last-minute deals to those who wait to book closer to the day of arrival. Airlines encourage patrons to purchase tickets weeks in advance by offering lower fares for flights that are more than two weeks out. This way, they can better manage demand and supply. Because of perishability, tourism organizations use various marketing tactics to ensure that their product does not go unsold, or in other words, perish.

Tourism products and services are basically intangible: tourists cannot experience a destination such as the Seychelles Islands in the Indian Ocean until they arrive and stay a while. Contrast this with test driving an automobile before buying one—prior to purchase the driver can feel the leather seats, the power of the engine, the way the car hugs the road. In tourism, for the most part, the product is simultaneously produced and consumed. The exotic destination experience is unknown until tried. Tourists cannot taste or smell the gourmet restaurant meal in advance because the chef prepares the meal right when ordered. The airline experience is unknown—passengers don't know how comfortable the first-class seat is or if they have extra leg room in coach—until they have paid for it, boarded the plane, and sat down. The amusement park experience is unknown until tourists arrive and start riding the rides. A visitor really doesn't know how comfortable the "X" bed is at a Westin resort until he or she has paid for the room and checked in.

Marketers have strategies to deal with intangibility. Some product can be viewed, felt, and sampled prior to purchase. For instance, marketers try to exploit the tangible aspects of the tourism experience. Atmospherics (e.g., light, music, scent, plants, décor, quality of furnishings and finishes, uniforms, entrances, signs) are used to signify, in a tangible way, the quality of the experience provided by a business. Another tactic is to involve the tourist in co-production of the product and experience. For instance, in Bali, Indonesia, tourists are invited to participate in the dancing at a kind of luau. In this way, tourists share in developing their own experience.

This beluga whale encounter cannot be experienced in advance, yet marketing aims to make it tangible by using a website and promotional videos.
Courtesy of Dr. Belkis Kambach

One additional characteristic of tourism is that the product is variable in nature. Because of the heavy human element in delivering the tourism product, the service quality and output are subject to extreme variability. The quality of the experience is dependent on the quality and training of the employees, the employee–tourist interaction, and the tourist–tourist interaction. Even when standards are set, policies are in place, and training has been undertaken, the best tourism and hospitality companies still find it difficult to deliver a consistent experience every time in every location. On the other hand, goods can be checked for defects before they leave the factory and hit the shelves for sale. With tourism, that luxury is not available. The tourism product is a service product, which makes it more difficult to manage, market, and sell.

Strategic Planning for Marketing and Sales

Sound strategy starts with sound research. In today's increasingly competitive and ever-changing marketing environment, the more successful tourism entities continually scan for new market opportunities and emerging threats as well as both internal and competitive environments. Some call this process a *market situation analysis*, which typically entails the analysis of four distinct categories of information: the industry in which business is conducted; the macroenvironmental factors that may influence the business (e.g., sociocultural, economic, technological, and political-legal factors); the competition; and the internal business environment.

Market Situation Analysis

The purpose of a market situation analysis is to answer the following questions: Is the market attractive? Is pursuing a strategy in this market a good idea? Is it a good idea to enter the marketplace? Companies can make conclusions about the market situation by determining the opportunities and threats that exist in the marketplace. By understanding what is happening in the environment, tourism entities can better map a strategy moving forward and use this knowledge and insight to achieve a competitive advantage. One tool companies can use to make determinations is the **SWOT analysis**, which stands for strengths, weaknesses, opportunities, and threats.

The SWOT Analysis

Strengths and weaknesses are factors to consider within the organization, whereas opportunities and threats relate to external factors. Also, the four categories can be distinguished because strengths and opportunities affect an entity in a positive way, and weaknesses and threats have a negative impact. The ownership/management can control, at least in the long term, internal factors, namely, strengths and weaknesses, whereas opportunities and threats occur out of the ownership/management's control, and the best way to handle these is for the company to have an approach where all employees actively scan the environment for opportunities and threats so that the company can take action in time. (See Figure 3–2.)

Strengths

Strengths are positive internal characteristics of the entity. Common examples of strengths are good employees, a favorable work climate, a good reputation as a

Figure 3–2 • Strengths, Weaknesses, Opportunities, and Threats (SWOT) Analysis

destination, modern facilities, financial strength, and experienced management. What mainly makes strengths different from opportunities is that strengths are internal to the entity, so to a large extent are controllable by the entity. When strengths are good and plenty, it is usually an indicator that the entity is heading in the right direction.

Weaknesses

Like strengths, weaknesses are also internal factors, that is, factors that are within the entity's control. Weaknesses are never good, so it is important to realize that most of the time they are within the control of the ownership/management. Although it may require massive inputs of money, time, and other resources, the entity can usually find a way to come to terms with weaknesses. The same criteria by which an entity evaluates its strengths may also be used for weaknesses. Typically, companies evaluate a list of factors both on an internal basis and on a competitive basis. Is the entity in a weak location whereas competitors are in strong locations? Is the entity weak in service quality whereas competitors have better service quality and better-trained employees?

Opportunities

Opportunities are positive possibilities for an entity that originate in the outside environment. An opportunity can be, for example, a strong economy with high demand, positive consumer trends, and changes in the social landscape that favor the business the company is in. For example, tourist requests for more outdoor/adventure, volunteer, or cultural experiences are opportunities for a company to develop new tourism products to meet the new demand and tourist preferences. A good management team makes sure that they, as a well as all employees, look for opportunities and bring them to the management's attention so that the company can adapt and take advantage of them quickly. Seizing opportunities and acting fast can be seen as closely related to the concept of strategic planning discussed earlier.

Threats

Negative factors in the outside environment that affect the entity's sales or overall performance are referred to as threats. Threats are similar to opportunities in that they are out of the management's control, and an entity needs to make sure that all its employees scan the environment for threats so that the entity can have a chance to act and prevent losses that otherwise might be taking place. Threats can take many different forms, from a competing car rental company opening up across the street from the existing one, to wars and political instability. For instance, threats of high gas prices or of a recession can really negatively affect the tourism entity.

Competitive Analysis

A competitive analysis is done utilizing the information from the strengths and weaknesses of the SWOT analysis. This is usually a more detailed analysis of the key competitors and leads to an action plan of how to increase market share. For instance, a destination such as Hawaii might consider its major strengths to be a rich culture, excellent year-round climate, natural beauty, and sporting and recreational opportunities, yet, compared to some other destinations, it is farther away and more costly (its weaknesses). The outcome of a competitive analysis in this situation would be the realization that a Hawaiian resort should market to tourists who want cultural, beach, and sporting activities in the United States.

Market Potential

Another very important aspect of market research is the estimation of the potential market in terms of **market size** as expressed in monetary terms and market share. Market potential should be viewed as the total available demand for a hospitality product within a particular geographic market at a given price.[2] When we think about the cruise market, we quickly realize how much potential there is and therefore why several more large ships are being built. The number of people who say they want to go on a cruise compared with the number who have already been on a cruise is positive for the cruise industry.

Marketing Tourism in a Recession

The marketing of tourism in a recession becomes even more complex as nations, states, destinations, and attractions vie for a shrinking market. A generalization is that people will take shorter, less costly vacations and travel to destinations that are closer to home. For example, a family decides to visit Disney World because they received a promotion for free entrance on a family member's birthday. Instead of staying at a four-star property, they opt for an economy Disney resort or stay at a nearby hotel and take a bus into the park. They will likely spend less on food and beverages and souvenirs than they would when there is no recession.

So, how do marketers attract visitors in a recession? They offer greater value for the money because this is what tourists are looking for. Airlines do it with special offers and promotions packages to cities that they fly to and offers for hotel accommodation and car hire. Destinations do it by pairing, offering a special deal with hotels and attractions included. If the value of the euro is higher against the dollar, then advertising in Europe and places where Europeans will see the advertising can pay off. (See the Ypartnership marketing in action feature later in this chapter.) Hotels offer special promotions of stay two nights, get the third night free. Cruise lines offer all-inclusive beverage service and other on-board amenities included in the price of the cruise.

Many tourism entities aim to drive potential business to their own websites instead of to intermediaries. Airlines, cruise lines, and lodging companies say they offer the lowest price, but sometimes they are undercut by discount offers from consolidators or bulk ticket agencies that obtain large volume discounts. In a recession, tourism entities increasingly attempt to cut out the intermediary by offering value-added products and special offers.

Marketing Segmentation, Targeting, and Positioning

Now we segment the market, target specific segments in the market, and develop a positioning platform that resonates with potential and existing customers. In segmenting the market, we essentially slice the market into groups of potential tourists with like characteristics such as geographic origin, demographic profile, psychographic orientation, and behavioral preference. The intention is for tourism entities to better understand the different groups of people in the marketplace.

The process of **market segmentation** is simple. First, the tourism entity divides the market into different groups that have similar characteristics. Then, the tourism entity creates a profile of each of these segments. Finally, the entity analyzes which segments it should and should not target based on the size, profit potential, accessibility, and desire of each group.

In geographic segmentation, we focus on segmenting the market based on where people live or are from (e.g., Rio de Janeiro, Brazil, or Lima, Peru). This is often done by segmenting the market by postal zip code. Geographic segmentation is relatively easy and inexpensive to do, but the downside is that not all people who live in a certain zip code are alike in their preferences for tourism goods and services.

Another commonly employed market segmentation technique is that of demographic segmentation whereby the market is sliced into groups of people who exhibit similar demographic characteristics such as age, income, gender, household composition, ethnicity, and educational level. Again, demographic segmentation is relatively inexpensive as compared to alternative methods yet is still susceptible to the same mistake in assuming that people of the same age, income, or ethnicity, for example, enjoy the same activities, have the same lifestyles, or prefer the same types of tourism products. Not everyone 65 years old loves to go cruising just as not everyone 20 years old likes to backpack around Europe.

A third market segmentation technique is psychographic segmentation where the focus is on the attitudes of consumers in terms of their social values and lifestyles. For instance, the market is segmented based on people's attitudes toward technology, risk, or even family values. Increasingly, tourism entities are lining up to better understand and develop a profile of consumers that are technology savvy—those who are regular users of new technologies such as cell phones, PDAs, video games, the Internet, and even social networking sites such as MySpace. Alternatively, the market may be segmented by people's values in terms of the importance of family or their drive to experience life. If a tourism entity knows that there is a segment of people who place a high value on spending time with their family or who enjoy new experiences, it can develop tourism products that meet those needs and preferences such as family getaways or adventure trips.

The last method of segmenting the market is behavioral segmentation, which slices the market into groups of people with similar consumption behavior such as regular versus first-time visitors, those who purchase a trip for a special occasion versus those who just want to get away, or business travelers versus leisure travelers. In sum, there are many ways to segment a market and most

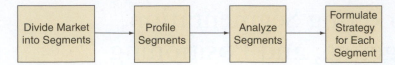

Figure 3–3 • The Marketing Segmentation Process

tourism entities use a combination of methods and criteria. The steps of market segmentation are illustrated in Figure 3–3 and are discussed in more depth in the following subsections.

Identifying Target Markets

Once a segmentation of the market is completed, the next step is to look at the different segments and see which groups are most attractive and may be most profitable to market to. First, the segments are reviewed regarding their attractiveness in terms of size and value. This review is highly dependent on what type of product or service is being marketed. For example, a **target market** for most major airlines is business travelers, people with generally higher incomes who have occupations that require them to travel a lot for work. On the other hand, for many amusement parks, such as Disney World, families with children are the main target market segment. There are several markets to consider:

People who are visiting friends and family, domestic and international

Leisure travelers, domestic and international

Business travelers, domestic and international

Group tours travelers, domestic and international

Within each of these major groupings are several subgroups; for example, in the leisure travelers group there are subgroups of those who prefer to travel for cultural, sports, medical, nature, volunteer, education, or relaxation reasons. Plus, more and more people combine trips with part business (attend a meeting) and pleasure (go with their spouse and relax for the weekend). There may be a dual purpose for the trip, meaning that the trip may be prompted by more than one reason, such as a business trip with a leisure component added.

Who will be the target market for the Fort Worth Zoo?
Courtesy of the Fort Worth Convention and Visitors Bureau

Market Positioning

Once the target market is established, the next step is **market positioning**. Most companies look to position their product in the minds of consumers ahead of the competition. Good marketers under-stand that their tourism product must have a lead position in the minds of consumers normally based on one or two key attributes that differentiate the product from competitors. For instance, Costa Rica is positioned as a premier eco-tourism destination. Hotels and restaurants are often evaluated on two dimensions: service quality and price. Hyatt Hotels is positioned as a high-quality, higher-priced, business-class hotel company. Ritz Carlton is positioned as a luxury resort and high-priced product. Ruth's Chris Steakhouse and Morton's the Steakhouse are positioned as high-quality steak restaurants whereas McDonalds is positioned as a quick service restaurant with good quality food and facilities. Carnival is positioned as the "fun" cruise line with moderate prices.

Paris, France, positions itself as the City of Love.
Courtesy of Mark Green

Positioning determines and influences the target customers' perception of the product or service marketed. Positioning can be done in several ways; some of the most important ways are as follows:

- *Better than the Competition*—The **better than the competition approach** is a common approach used when the product marketed is similar to the products of the competition, for example, "It's Better in the Bahamas." *Better* can be defined in many ways, including having a lower price, such as a low-cost trip to Cancun, Mexico.

- *Different from the Competition*—The **different from the competition approach** is when an entity introduces a product or service to the target market that is different from all current offerings. For example, Eva Air offers Evergreen Deluxe Class seating that is a class between economy and business. For a couple of hundred dollars more on an 18-hour trans-Pacific flight, paying for this seating class is well worth it to some travelers.

- *Opposite of the Competition*— One of the most interesting ways of positioning a product or service, opposite of the competition means selling and marketing a product as being unlike competing products. Palawan, one of the Philippine islands, is a good example of the opposite of the competition approach: the island is promoted as the "last frontier."

Market positioning is about creating an image for the product that will make people desire it and hopefully buy it. Marketing positioning is closely linked to **marketing management** described later, where pricing strategies, products, distribution channels, and promotional activities are coordinated to ensure the best image and sales of a product.

Brands and Brand Marketing

Brands are defined as unique elements that identify a product and set it apart from the products of other producers or service providers. Today, brands are becoming a more and more important part of a company's marketing strategy, mostly because having a well-known brand tends to create so-called **brand identity**. The four pillars of brands are that they are unique, relevant, esteemed, and well known. The most important considerations when developing a brand and its visual identity (logo and tagline) are the following:

- It must be easy to remember.
- It must have a positive connotation.
- It must be graphically shaped in a way that it can be easily recognized on different kinds of packages and in different sizes.
- It should look good both in color and black and white.
- It must be easily seen so that it will catch customers' eyes wherever it is.
- It must be usable, positive, and inoffensive in all the markets where it is to be used.

Brands often signify certain attributes about a product or company. Consumers may associate food quality, price, atmosphere, and service level with a brand. For instance, the Disney brand is recognized as providing a high-quality experience across its many subbrands. The state of Texas brands itself as "a whole other country." The Southwest Airlines brand is known for its low-cost tickets and reputation for fun flying. Hotels, restaurants, chefs, and even destinations and countries can be branded.

Brands are developed through a very thorough process. Sometimes new brands are created because of opportunities in the marketplace and sometimes destinations or tourism entities are rebranded because the original brand may be faltering and or was incorrectly developed and positioned in the first place.

People identify with brands, and strong brand identity helps consumers make purchasing decisions. For example, a resident of Manhattan seeking a quick weekend getaway might consider a trip to a nearby city or town such as Springfield, Massachusetts, birthplace of basketball and home of the Basketball Hall of Fame; or perhaps somewhere on the coast, such as Cape May or Ocean City, New Jersey. Identifying with a particular brand causes the consumer to think and feel a certain way about a destination or resort and helps with the decision-making process.

If a tourist has a good experience with a brand, that increases the probability of the tourist returning or using the brand again in the future and may lead to what is called **brand loyalty** where the consumer becomes loyal to the brand of interest and has a positive attitude toward the brand that may result in the person spreading positive word of mouth or making repeated purchases of the brand. In tourism, we call this the "same time next year." For example, a large number of tourists return to Barbados, an island in the West Indies, and many other destinations year after year.

Brand loyalty is very important because it has been shown that an increase of just 5 percent in retaining current loyal tourists can translate into a 25 percent increase in profitability because it is less expensive to retain tourists than it is to get new ones, and loyal tourists typically spend more.

Tourism entities try to make brand loyalty stronger in many ways. One well-known example is the airlines' frequency or affinity programs that intend to reward passengers for their loyal patronage. Frequent flier bonus programs typically award passengers mileage or points each time they fly with a particular airline, stay in a particular hotel, rent a car from a particular agency, or use a credit card affiliated with the airline, and passengers can accumulate miles or points to put toward a free flight. Bonus programs like this provide incentives for passengers to choose certain airlines over another and have proven very efficient at fulfilling this purpose. This practice has also spread to hotel chains and car rental companies.

FOCUS ON

Tourism Marketing

Khoon Y. Koh

Achieving the 3 Rs with 10 RPs

A community pursuing tourism development needs its touristic enterprises (Type 1 and Type 2) to achieve the three Rs of marketing: R1 = recruitment (acquiring customers), R2 = retention (keeping customers), and R3 = referral (promoting customers to spread positive word of mouth). Whether we call travel consumers customers, visitors, or tourists, if a significant number of touristic enterprises are successful in achieving their three Rs, collectively, they are branding their community. On the other hand, if most of them are unable to achieve the three Rs, they are unlikely to be sustainable—a diminishing tourist industry contributes little to a community's socioeconomic health.

How could touristic enterprises achieve their three Rs? If they follow the traditional marketing mix framework, they need to plan and execute the four RPs strategically. This author suggests the addition of six more RPs to enhance their likelihood of success based on the concept of exchange maximization (maximization of buyers' value and sellers' yield).

RP 1: Right Purchasers

Without a minimal inflow of customers, touristic enterprises are unsustainable. Customers are thus the foci of all marketing activities. And because enterprises have limited resources and not all travel consumers have the same need, want, and/or expectation, touristic enterprises, therefore, should practice target marketing. This means that they need to practice concepts such as market segmentation, market segment profile, and market segment analysis to identify their right purchaser mix.

RP 2: Right Products

Touristic enterprises' offerings must genuinely meet target market's needs and wants; otherwise, consumers are unlikely to buy even if they are offered favorable deals. This means touristic enterprises need to practice concepts such as product innovation and development, product differentiation, product positioning, and product life cycle to formulate their right product mix.

RP 3: Right Promotion

Enterprises need to build in their target markets a favorable share of mind, share of heart, and share of pocket if they hope consumers will buy repeatedly from them. Touristic enterprises thus need to employ a variety of

(continued)

FOCUS ON   (*continued*)

communication tools including the concept of integrated marketing communications to comprise their right promotion mix.

RP 4: Right Place

Touristic enterprises need to make their offerings easily and conveniently accessible so that consumers who are interested in checking out/buying could do so with minimum effort. They thus need to address concepts such as location, supply chain, channel integration, logistics, and operational hours (day/time) to establish their right place mix.

RP 5: Right Price

Touristic enterprises need to price their products innovatively to induce trials and purchases and maximize yields. Thus, they should not hesitate to experiment with different pricing practices in accordance with their selected purchaser mix, product mix, promotional mix, and place mix to determine their right price mix.

RP 6: Right Performer

If employees' appearance and behavior could significantly help or hurt any enterprise, then touristic enterprises must view employees as another marketing resource. This means they need to practice internal marketing involving concepts such as selection, training, empowerment, motivation, support, shaping, evaluation, reinforcement, and/or rectification.

RP 7: Right Purchase-scape

If attractive stores are more likely to attract consumers than unattractive ones are, and if consumers in attractive stores tend to linger longer, be more likely to return, and suggest the store to others, then touristic enterprises need to creatively design and keep up their physical and cyberspace presences to increase the likelihood of becoming customers' third living space. This means they need to practice concepts such as aesthetics, functionality, safety and security, and ambiance (physiological and psychological comfort).

RP 8: Right Process

If consumers prefer all transactional experiences to be as hassle-free as possible (instead of tolerating hassle-laden experiences), then touristic enterprises need to conscientiously ensure that all travel consumer transactional phases (before purchase, during purchase, after purchase phases) are smooth as soap. This means they need to practice concepts such as service mapping, service standards and scripts, service recovery, incremental technology, queue management, and service audits.

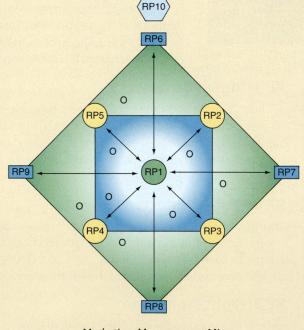

Marketing Mix

Marketing-Management Mix

FOCUS ON (*continued*)

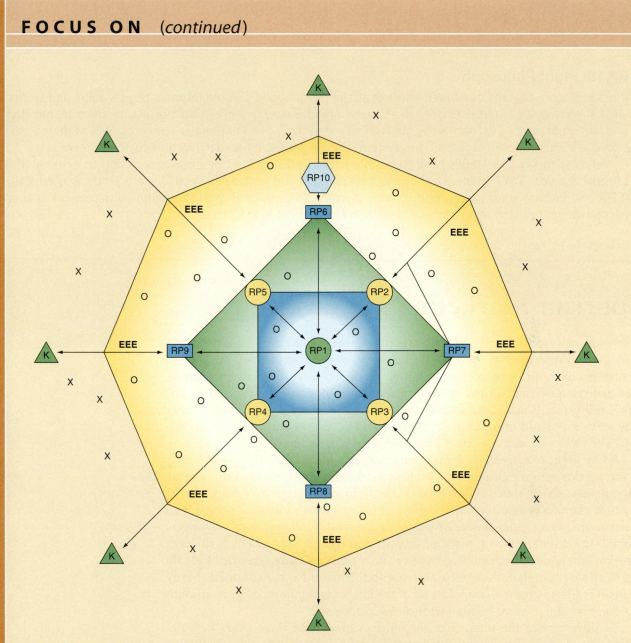

Integrated Marketing-Management Web Model.

RP 9: Right Psyche

If consumers like to be treated as special/valued customers rather than just another consumer, then touristic enterprises need to express their appreciation and understanding of travel consumers' individual and collective expectations continuously to minimize customer defections. This means they need to address concepts such as service surprise, customization-personalization, guarantees, loyalty programs, referral reward incentives, ancillary services, and consumerism.

(*continued*)

FOCUS ON (continued)

RP 10: Right Philosophy

If readers agree that the combined effect of all the preceding RPs would improve buyers' value and sellers' yield, then touristic enterprises need to embrace a modus operandi of holistic hospitality: the total thinking and feeling of treating consumers as guests! This means they need to practice concepts such as shared mission and vision, learning organizations, systems thinking, integrity, leadership, and customer research.

Needless to say, the 10 RPs have to be integrated and sustained by entities adapting to external and internal realities (SWOT analysis). They must be planned and executed effectively, efficiently, and ethically (EEE) and include continuous improvement (Kaizen). This comprehensive operational framework is thus named Integrated Marketing-Management Web Model (IMM-Web Model).

Courtesy of Khoon Y. Koh, Ph.D., Central Connecticut State University

Tourism Marketing Management

Marketers use specific tools and processes to sell their products and achieve company goals. Professor Neil Borden of Harvard University developed the six elements: product, price, place, promotion, servicing, and marketing research. McCarthy later reduced these to four elements: product, price, place (distribution), and promotion.[3] These four Ps focus on the marketing of products rather than services, so additional Ps were added: process, physical attributes, and people.[4] The following subsections discuss each P in more detail.

A key point to remember is that marketers can manipulate (play with) each of the marketing mix elements to achieve marketing goals, such as to increase sales, market share, tourist/guest mix. As the following paragraphs point out, at any time changes can be made to the product (rooms versus suites for people who prefer more space), price (lower or higher to attract different types of passengers looking for different fares), place of distribution (online versus selling through travel agents), and promotion mix (offer short-term getaway fares or "kids fly free" sales to stimulate short-term interest and demand for the product). Many tourism entities strive to manipulate all of the elements simultaneously to smooth out demand and achieve higher yields on what they sell.

To differentiate the uniqueness of tourism marketing three other key elements were added: intangibility, inseparability of production and consumption, and the difference that can occur in the service delivery resulting from the nature of the person providing the service.[5] To show the difference between goods and services the term *hospitality marketing mix*, developed by Renaghan, is used.[6]

Product

The items sold by companies in the tourism and hospitality industries are mainly services, which makes the product aspect of tourism marketing a bit different. Before purchase, purchasers cannot evaluate services the same way they can evaluate products—by their size, weight, smell, taste, and so forth (physical attributes). Products such as tourism destinations and attractions, hotels, resorts, and restaurants are high in what is called experiential attributes, meaning that consumers cannot judge quality until they are using or have used the product. Guests' expectations and the ability to meet, and preferably exceed them, become the central factor. This is obviously harder to do than is creating a standardized product because expectations are highly subjective and therefore likely to be different with every customer. Surveys and other follow-ups with guests then become a central part of the product aspect because they enable companies to find out how well they did in comparison with the tourists' expectations, as well as where improvements can be made to do even better in the future.

Destinations, regions, and countries interested in tourism identify their attributes as natural or man-made. They can list both types and compare their offerings with the various market needs and wants to see which target markets to aim for. For example, if the natural beauty of a destination lends itself to nature tourism or adventure tourism, then a destination can develop these two target markets. Likewise, if the same destination has beautiful old buildings and a thriving arts community, then cultural tourists can also be a target market.

Because tourists will want to judge before purchasing the quality of service, tourism entities must pay particular attention to attributes consumers could use such as brand reputation and appeal, and ease of access, service, quality of resorts/hotels, attractions, and restaurants. In other words, is the destination considered user-friendly?

Product Life Cycle

Tourism destinations go through a product life cycle that includes four phases: introduction, growth, maturity, and decline. The concept is that a destination is "introduced" to the market and that it grows in time to maturity and then, if not carefully managed or promoted, may decline. Each stage in the life cycle takes several years. Figure 3–4 shows a destination's product life cycle.

Introduction—A destination is introduced when it becomes readily accessible to tourists and they begin to go there. It takes time for the number of tourists to build up to the point where the destination becomes popular. Believe it or not, there are still some relatively undiscovered destinations out there. As more tourists visit the destination, it begins to enter the growth phase of the life cycle.

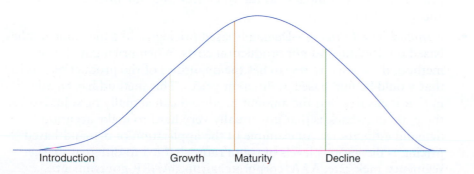

Figure 3–4 • A Destination's Product Life Cycle

Growth—Growth is when the destination grows in popularity. The economic gains are clearly visible and profits should be made by those involved with tourism to the destination.

Maturity—It can take years for a destination to reach maturity or it may happen quickly, depending on a number of circumstances including the economy, fuel prices, and whether the product is refreshed or revitalized. In maturity, the number of tourists levels off and growth and market share flatten.

Decline—The decline stage of the life cycle is when the number of tourists visiting a destination declines as well as use of the tourism-related businesses such as attractions, lodging, and restaurants.

Price

The second P is price, which has a tremendous impact on the success or failure of a tourism product. Very few people are so wealthy that they can buy things without first finding out how much they cost. Usually a lower price has a positive effect on the demand for a product. In basic economics, there are two components of price: the first is the monetary component and the second is an informational component usually represented as $P = Q$, or price equity relationship: the higher the price, the greater the quality (and parenthetically, the greater the customer's expectations). Consider the cost of a room at a hotel: the cost is $69 a night at one hotel and $169 a night at another hotel. What is the difference between them? $100.

Companies use different methods for pricing their products and services; some emphasize customer demand, others, price, competition, or customer needs. Some pricing methods are popular for introducing new products and services. Following are the most frequently used pricing methods:

- *Cost-plus Pricing*—Cost-plus pricing simply means that the company calculates what the fixed and variable costs are for one unit of the product or service. Then, the desired profit is added to this number, and the new sum is the price the unit is sold for.

- *Price-floor Pricing*—Price-floor pricing is used in certain situations where the economy is going bad or when for some other reason demand is low. It is a good idea to sell some units of the product or service at a price lower than the target price, a price so low that it only covers the marginal cost of producing the extra unit, to keep occupancy high. Price-floor pricing helps the company decide when lowering the price is a good idea and when it isn't.

- *Demand-based Pricing*—Demand-based pricing is, like the name implies, based on demand and not production costs. When pricing with this method, the company researches the quantities of the product or service that would be purchased at different prices. This method has an advantage in that it ensures that the amount produced can actually be sold. However, the main drawback is that it is usually very hard to make accurate demand estimations. An example of the application of demand-based pricing is the various levels of room rates charged to different market segments: rack rate, AAA, corporate, airline, AARP, government, conference, and so forth.

Some common pricing tactics include the following:

- *Penetration Pricing*—Here, a low price is charged from the beginning, encouraging as many people as possible to buy and start using the product. For example, a steakhouse or brewpub opens in a highly competitive market and uses price to gain market share.
- *Trial Pricing*—Trial pricing is similar to penetration pricing, where a low price is set initially to encourage many people to try the product or service. The difference is that soon the price is raised to a much higher level after customers have tried the product, and then stays there.
- *Parity Pricing or Price Matching*—Price is also based on competition, but here the company is not the first one to set prices. Instead, when using parity pricing, the company follows the pricing of the competitors and tries to stay as close to their prices as possible, thereby reducing the impact of price differences on customer decisions. The airline industry uses parity pricing: if American drops its price on a particular route, then other carriers frequently follow by adjusting (lowering) their prices.
- *Value Pricing*—Value pricing focuses on how much consumers value the product. This makes sure that the price charged makes the product or service the best possible value for the guests.
- *Negotiated Pricing*—Negotiated pricing is common. The method simply means that the price is open for negotiation and is not fixed. For example, in catering, the caterer says that they can provide 500 dinners at $50 each, and the event organizer says that they can afford only $30 a dinner. After further discussion, the parties agree to some menu modifications and an agreeable price.
- *Quantity Discounts*—Quantity discounts are frequently offered. When a customer purchases a large amount of a product or service, a discount is given. Group rates on airplanes and tours are illustrative of this pricing concept.
- *Cash Discounts*—If a consumer (or retailer) pays for a product or service in cash, the seller gives a discount, usually a couple of percentage points of the total price. This strategy is possible because if paid in cash, the seller can use the money to invest and make money, something they miss out on when allowing creditors a longer time to pay. Suppliers frequently offer a cash discount to hospitality and tourism operators for prompt payment of invoices.
- *Seasonal Discounts*—Seasonal discounts are used by many resorts, airlines, and other tourism entities to fill up during times when the demand is low. For example, off-season rates are offered in resort areas.
- *Two-part Pricing*—Two-part pricing is when there are two different components of the total price. One good example of this is gym memberships, which usually consist of an entrance fee as well as a monthly fee.
- *Pricing by Priority*—This pricing strategy implies that the customers who pay the most have first priority. There are many examples of this pricing strategy, including cruises and airline seats, where prices are often initially high but get lower at the end, selling the remaining places to bargain-hunting travelers.

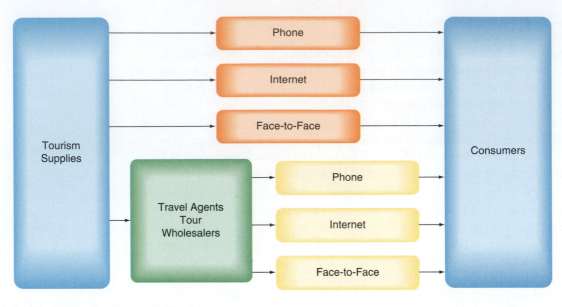

Figure 3–5 • The Distribution System for Tourism

- *Price Bundling*—Two different products or services are sold together as a package. For example, visit Orlando and the price of the trip includes airfare, hotel, and admittance to an attraction. The total is less than if each item is purchased separately.

Place/Location/Distribution

In the hospitality and tourism contexts, place should be approached in two ways: availability and location. Availability in the traditional marketing sense means that the market can access the product. In tourism, place is often discussed as location. For instance, a beach in Florida is easier for someone in Ohio to reach than a beach in Europe is. This is referred to as feeder cities and catchment areas. The expression "Location, location, location" can be critical for a tourism entity's success. It's one thing to have an exotic destination, but if people cannot easily get to it, then it will be less frequented. Similarly, amusement parks need to be located within driving or flying range of their target markets. Few, if any, people will drive two thousand miles just to visit a water park. Figure 3–5 illustrates how tourists connect with tourism providers in the distribution system for tourism.

Although beautiful, this Polynesian island is somewhat remote, which precludes large numbers of tourists visiting.
Peter Bush © Dorling Kindersley

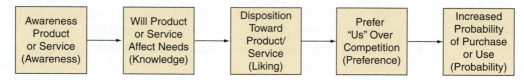

Figure 3–6 • The Effect That Promotion Has on the Buying Process

Promotion

Figure 3–6 shows the effect that promotion has on the buying process. First, before a guest can buy something, she must be *aware that the product or service exists*. Second, she also needs to know *how the product or service will affect her needs* (knowledge). Third, she *forms a positive disposition toward the product or service* (liking). Fourth, she *must prefer one brand over other brands of the same product* (preference). Fifth, if all of this is accomplished, *the probability has increased that* the guest will use or buy the product or service.

Having an excellent product, at a good price and in the right place is not enough. Sales goals will not be obtained unless the consumer is aware of the product's existence. There are several ways of promoting; which is the best way depends on the product, the target market, and other factors. Some frequently used tools for promotion are the following communication tools:

- *Sales Promotion*—**Sales promotion** includes any activity aimed at giving consumers or retailers an extra incentive to buy the product or service. Some examples are coupons that give a discount and competitions where buying the product or more of the product in one way or another gives purchasers the chance to win an exciting prize. The most important advantage with sales promotion is that it is usually effective in creating excitement about the product among potential tourists. An important disadvantage is that the effect is short term, and many companies might be doing this kind of promotion, which makes it hard for a company to get the message through to the tourists.

- *Advertising*—**Advertising** is the most familiar of the promotional elements in use. Advertising is communicating about the product in different media, such as newspapers, TV, radio, magazines, and on the Internet. The tourism entity pays for this communication, and it is nonpersonal. Examples of advertising for companies in the tourism industry are commercials for countries, states, airlines, and tour packages offered by tour operators or travel agencies. The best thing about advertising is that the company has complete control over what is said in the message and what image is created, while whereas the most important drawbacks are the cost as well as sometimes low credibility.

- *Magazines*—Promotions can appear in magazines, particularly travel and leisure magazines.

- *Personal Selling*—**Personal selling** occurs when there is a direct contact between the consumer and a sales representative from the tourism company. This usually happens either face to face or over the phone, although e-mail is gaining more and more importance. Personal selling is used frequently when the sales are business-to-business, and they have the advantage that the representative can adapt the message to sell to each individual. The main drawback is that it can be very costly for the company because this medium is very labor intensive.

- *Public Relations (PR)*—**Public relations** is a common term for all activities aimed at creating a positive image of the tourism entity or destination among potential and actual tourists and the community. Many destinations employ professional public relations agencies or large advertising agencies that have PR specialists on staff. PR includes the writing of press releases about the destination; sponsoring events, like Cinco de Mayo or Mardi Gras festivities; and damage control and spinoffs of positive facts if negative news occurs. Using public relations gives the promotion both high credibility and a low price. However, it is hard to control these messages and whether they really reach the target audience, and it is even harder to track and analyze the results. Ronald McDonald House is a good example of a company gaining positive public relations from its charitable works. The coveted prize of having a *New York Times* travel section write-up on a destination can really enhance a destination's marketing campaign, and because it is not paid for by the destination, it becomes more believable to the potential market. Several other newspapers have travel sections that write about various destinations for free.

- *Direct Mail*—Tourism entities can purchase names of individuals or blanket certain zip codes in the hope of reaching people interested in the tourism destination or service being offered. Provided the mailing is well prepared, it may interest people and results can be tracked by requesting people respond to a particular address or call a specific number.

- *E-mail*—Once a database of names and addresses has been developed, it is easy to e-mail potential guests about topics they might be interested in. Airlines do this with their frequent flyer passengers and so does Marriott with their millions of guests.

- *Websites*—A good website is very helpful in providing information to prospective tourists. Websites are an excellent way for a small or medium-sized company to compete with larger ones because they can share a presence on the Web. A good site can have a profound effect on prospective tourists because tourists can see color images of the destination and view attractions, hotel rooms, and restaurants, which can help overcome some uncertainties. Being able to book travel arrangements and vacations online is a convenience to guests and an increasing number of tourists are availing themselves of online tools to do this.

- *Television*—Television is a good but expensive way of getting a message across to millions of potential tourists. TV is used mostly by countries, states, or cities with enough money to purchase this kind of advertising. The TV market can be selected along with the channel to target potential tourists. The Travel Channel is a good example of selective advertising that is less costly than advertising on NBC, CBS, or ABC.

- *Radio*—Radio can be a good way to draw attention to a destination, but it is more challenging to create an advertisement for the travel market. Radio can easily target certain geographic markets but cannot so easily target specific segments. Tourism entities can use stations likely to be heard by some in the demographic category presumed to include their target market.

FOCUS ON

St. Petersburg/Clearwater, Florida

Courtesy of Peter
Yesawich and
Ypartnership

The St. Petersburg/Clearwater area ranks among the most popular destinations in the state of Florida. It also ranks as the fifth largest convention and visitors bureau defined by total tourism receipts and resort tax collections.

St. Petersburg

Although the county has numerous attractions and recreational amenities of interest to visitors, consumer research reveals that the single most important factor visitors seek is a great beach experience. Fortunately, the destination has multiple top-rated beaches (according to an annual evaluation by Dr. Stephen Leatherman—aka Dr. Beach). The county was looking for its tourism agency to develop and implement an integrated marketing program to achieve the goal of increasing overnight visitation to the destination. Here is an overview of the promotion project:

Objectives. The objectives of the program include: (1) increase qualified inquiries from prospective visitors by a minimum of 5 percent year-over-year, (2) grow resort bed tax collections—the primary source of funding for the convention and visitors bureau (CVB)—by a minimum of 2 percent annually, and (3) boost the occupancy and average daily rate realized by local hotels and resorts.

Strategy. Ypartnership's strategy has been to establish St. Petersburg/Clearwater as the premier beach vacation destination—or Florida's Beach—in a state chock full of beach destinations. The rationale for this strategy derives from the growing collection of awards bestowed on the area over the past several years by such respected sources as TripAdvisor and Dr. Beach. This beach focus has been fortified and expanded in recent years to include many other wonderful recreational offers the destination affords to its visitors.

With a depressed U.S. economy and weak dollar, significantly more Europeans are flocking to the United States to take advantage of the exchange rate and incredible values. Consequently, the number of European visitors to Orlando is growing with a large charter proportion landing at the Orlando–Sanford International Airport. In fact, European visitors to St. Petersburg/Clearwater (SPC) spent just shy of a billion dollars during 2007 alone.

According to statistics prepared by Research Data Services, U.K. visitors typically spend two weeks on their Florida vacation, but only plan the first five to seven days. Although landlocked in Orlando, they long for the true Florida beach experience that St. Petersburg/Clearwater delivers. So, Ypartnership created the first "attraction" visitor experience upon arrival in the Orlando area.

Execution. Ypartnership developed and evolved a fully integrated marketing communications program that celebrates St. Petersburg/Clearwater's core attributes, effectively leveraging the unique strengths of each chosen medium while taking advantage of an in-depth understanding of the target market's seasonal visitation trends. The campaign—consisting of cable television, radio, lifestyle magazines, newspapers, interactive cross-channel cooperative advertising, and promotional marketing—was written to drive qualified visitors to the destination website: FloridasBeach.com (now VisitStPeteClearwater.com).

Specifically to attract U.K. visitors, Ypartnership created the first attraction visitor experience upon arrival in the Orlando area at the Orlando–Sanford International Airport. Location of this attraction was key, so the agency carefully chose a placement where 100 percent of arriving charter international travelers would see,

(continued)

FOCUS ON (*continued*)

hear, and spend time with the message. As travelers wind through arrival hallways working their way toward Customs, they're led to a large room featuring a 35-foot custom-wrapped wall with six 50-inch plasma screens playing a dynamic, high-definition program—with specially scored original soundtrack—that follows visitors through their day in St. Petersburg/Clearwater, from sunrise to sunset. The opposite wall offers a beach photo opportunity.

To further increase exposure, on the escalator to Customs, walls come alive with projected images of the destination. Finally, while in line at Customs, four flat screens loop a destination slideshow highlighting key beaches, proximity to Orlando, and directions to the nearby brochure rack for a free visitor guide.

Results. The results of this campaign have been striking. It has delivered sustained growth year after year across all key metrics. Since 2004, unique visitors to the website (FloridasBeach.com) grew an average number of 52.5 percent year-over-year and a total of 132 percent between 2004 and 2007. Finally, the average daily rate in lodging establishments jumped 8.6 percent year-over-year and spiked 28 percent from 2004 to year-end 2007.

Because the airport video installation was completed in only July 2008, it is still too early to see an incremental influx of international visitors to St. Petersburg/Clearwater from the Orlando area. Effectiveness over the coming months—and, indeed, years because this is a three-year commitment—will be realized through significant spikes in international visitors reported through intercept interviews gathered in market by Research Data Services.

Canyon Ranch

The ownership of Canyon Ranch retained Ypartnership to assist with the rebranding and repositioning of this legendary spa resort. Specifically, after 25 years of leadership in the spa category, the brand found itself in a position where numerous competitors were beginning to replicate its unique product/service formula and, accordingly, apply competitive pressure to its highly successful business.

Strategy. Extensive customer research preceded the agency's creation of the advertising campaign and revealed that Canyon Ranch's targeted customers had grown even more interested in the wellness aspect of spa going (beyond just pampering). Furthermore, a comprehensive review of competitors in the category revealed very little differentiation in the messages being delivered by other emerging brands. Ypartnership initiated two critical steps as a result: (1) the agency revised the property's graphic signature (no small task after 25 years) and appended a new slogan (The Power of Possibility), and (2) repositioned the brand in new perceptual space: life enhancement. These initiatives resulted in a new positioning strategy for the brand: Canyon Ranch, the world's only life-enhancement resort.

F O C U S   O N *(continued)*

Execution. The advertising campaign that was developed to introduce this concept was called Reflections and included a series of executions that revealed guests of the ranch reflecting on one of their more memorable experiences while visiting. All units ran as half-page, color spreads, thereby dominating the signatures on which they ran. The campaign concept was then adapted to all collateral, direct marketing, and on-property merchandizing materials. It was subsequently adapted to the website, and the color palettes were, in turn, adapted to employee uniforms and, eventually, the design of the vans used to pick up people at the Tucson and Hartford airports.

Results. The campaign enabled Canyon Ranch to gain even more prominence with affluent travelers and support the growth of its successful new real estate development business (Canyon Ranch Living).

Courtesy of Ypartnership

Understanding Markets

Even though a product may be the best product available on the market, or the one that gives the guests the best value for their money, there is no guarantee that they will buy it. In addition, a product or service that is immensely popular in one area, city, or country may not raise much interest in another area. This is simply because people have different interests and preferences. Successful marketers understand these differences as well as the need for proper research before the introduction of a new product to an area.

A tourism-related example is the Walt Disney Corporation's introduction of Euro Disneyland in France, Europe. The Disney parks in the United States have been successful and are very popular. However, when opening one in Europe, the corporation incurred huge losses because it had not taken into consideration the differences in vacation habits between Europeans and Americans. For Americans, with their two or three weeks of vacation per year, a day in Disneyland is the perfect activity to do with family. They spend a lot of money but also squeeze in a lot of fun in just one day. However, Europeans, accustomed to almost four times the amount of vacation time that Americans get, did not want to spend their whole budget in one day, but spread their money over a longer period of time. The location of the park, just outside Paris, is another reason for its early lack of success. The climate in northern France does not lend itself to outdoor attractions during the winter. This is just an example of how differences in demand are important to consider when making marketing decisions.

Destination Marketing

The business of marketing a country, state, or city is still marketing. That is, the basic principles of creating value for the consumer still apply. For instance, it is still a must to determine what a consumer or group of consumers deem important; then, to develop an offering that comes as close as possible to meeting those needs. This applies for individual leisure travelers as well as business/fraternal organizations. Is the leisure traveler seeking adventure, knowledge, or excitement, and does he adhere to "green tourism"?

The all-important four Ps of marketing apply to destinations:

Product—For example, compare two island cities, New York and Honolulu. One offers excitement, dazzling nightlife, Broadway, incredible restaurants, and museums and monuments of national significance and pride. The other offers tropical air, blue water, relaxation, and rest.

Price—Price refers to the total cost to the target market (individual or group) to attain the package offered. Total cost may be the cost of traveling, lodging, fees/admissions, and so forth to attain what the target market values. As in the world of branded goods, this variable can be and often is adjusted to attract the segment of the market that is of greatest value to the marketer.

Place—The place element in this scenario may refer to the accessibility of the destination and ease of entry and exit. Assume for a moment that Walt Disney World (WDW) in Orlando, undoubtedly one of the most visited cities in the world, did not assist in or insist on or develop for itself the infrastructure necessary for tourists to access its offerings: no major highway, no major road widening or extensions, no airport capable of handling jumbo jets or the volume of air traffic that it currently enjoys. How successful would WDW be? Making a destination accessible is mandatory. Does that mean big airports and eight-lane highways? No, it means having regularly scheduled or on-call shuttle vehicles available to transport the target consumer from the entrance point to the unique destination.

Promotion—The element of promotion is often thought by many to be the key to success. If there is nothing of value to the consumer, then no kind of promotion will ensure success. Perhaps, it may attract a few, but after an unfulfilling experience, the word will spread that the destination's promises are empty, thus ensuring failure. Promotion is the use of a compilation of marketing tools (advertising, sales promotion, public relations, and personal selling) that can be powerful in making a destination's existence known, offering the place as unique from other destinations, and inducing travel by offering incentives. Those who act as gatekeepers, agents, and consolidators must be "influenced" to promote the destination.

When using advertising in destination promotion, tourism entities are not advertising only the destination but, more important, what the place has to offer. A city by any other name is still a city. In today's shrinking world, New York City, Tokyo, or Madrid all resemble each other, other than the language of signage. So, what makes NYC different from Tokyo or Madrid, St. Louis or Los Angeles? Differentiation is the focus of the promotions effort. That uniqueness is what is central to promotion.

Consider, for example, should we promote all of Texas to everybody? The answer is a resounding no. Texas is a state, not a destination. The Alamo is a destination, the Panhandle is a destination, west Texas with its Wild West feeling is a destination, the border is a destination. All of these destinations are in Texas, but all of them are not equally attractive to all potential visitors.

FOCUS ON

Tourism Marketing

Alistair Williams

Tourism has become a major economic activity as expectations with regard to the use of our leisure time have evolved, attributing greater meaning to our free time. However, studying the behavior of consumers has become increasingly complex, with tourism operators offering a multitude of venues in which people can consume. Bars, restaurants, hotels, theme parks, casinos, and cruise ships all operate as "cathedrals of consumption," offering increasingly complex consumption opportunities to increasingly complex consumers.

Experiential marketing, arguably tourism marketing's most contemporary orientation, was first introduced by Pine and Gilmore (1998) who described it as "when a person buys a service, he purchases a set of intangible activities carried out on his behalf. But when he buys an experience, he pays to spend time enjoying a series of memorable events that a company stages to engage him in a personal way."* Experiential marketing is about taking the essence of a product and amplifying it into a set of tangible, physical, interactive experiences that reinforce the offer. Rather than seeing the offer in a traditional manner, through advertising media such as commercials, print, or electronic messaging, consumers "feel" it by being part of it. Experiential marketing describes marketing initiatives that give consumers in-depth, tangible experiences to provide them with sufficient information to make a purchase decision. It is widely argued that as the science of marketing evolves, experiential marketing will become the dominant marketing tool of the future.

The Four Dimensions of the Tourism Experience

Experience marketing requires us to think about experiences across the bipolar constructs of customer participation (ranging from active to passive) and connection (ranging from absorption to immersion). These two constructs divide experiences into four realms; namely, education, entertainment, escapist, and esthetic. The best tourism experiences combine these realms to secure a "sweet spot" wherein the event is truly experienced. To achieve this, we exploit a series of six design principles when staging experiences, namely, the following:

1. Developing a cohesive theme for the experience, which involves establishing a cohesive set of images and meanings for the experience.

2. Harmonizing impressions with positive cues, which refers to the creation of memorable sensory stimuli, or the "takeaways" of the experience.

3. Eliminating negative cues by removing anything that diminishes, contradicts, or distracts from the unity of the theme.

4. Mixing in memorabilia, which refers to the fact that tourism consumers have always purchased mementos of their vacations, whether these are postcards, logoed T-shirts, or caps.

*B. J. Pine and J. H. Gilmore, "Welcome to the Experience Economy," *Harvard Business Review*, July/August 1998, 97–105.

(continued)

FOCUS ON *(continued)*

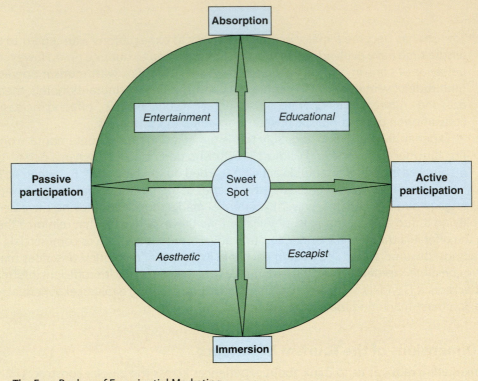

The Four Realms of Experiential Marketing
Adapted from Pine and Gilmore, 1998

5. Engaging all five senses, which is important because the more sensory an experience, the more memorable it will be. Most tourism and hospitality offerings have a range of sensory elements, such as sounds, sights, smells, touch, and taste.

6. Soliciting feedback, which is critical if experiential marketing is to be effective. Although many tourism businesses seek feedback through such mechanisms as guest questionnaires, experiential marketing requires more innovative and creative solutions.

It is becoming clear that the next competitive battlefield for tourism businesses will lie in staging experiences. Innovative experience design will become an increasingly important component of a tourism firm's core capabilities. Those who go beyond service excellence to market experientially will lead the creation of value in this sector.

Courtesy of Alistair Williams, Johnson & Wales University.

Marketing Action Plan

The previously discussed four Ps (product, price, place, and promotion) are tools that a marketer uses to achieve the tourism entity's goals. The marketing action plan is simply an extension of how each tool will be used to construct a strategy to achieve goals. Once all the essential elements are in place, a market situation analysis allows the determination of the following factors:

- Who competitors are
- How the entity fares in the marketplace
- In the case of a new entity, how it can be expected to fare in comparison to the competition once it knows what the market is like, which companies are currently serving the market, and the respective share of entities

Additional analysis can provide a picture of the target market(s) and to some degree how it is currently being served by others. Big or small, large market share or little market share, every tourism entity has available to it the four Ps. The major differences in marketing will be the amount of money available for marketing and perhaps a slightly different target segment.

Once the target market is identified, an entity can decide what is to be accomplished by marketing (for example, the goal: to achieve a 30 percent market share of all those who desire to engage in adventure tourism in the area). Next, the questions flow and the action plan provides the answers. For instance, to achieve a 30 percent share of the target market several things must be done. What is it about the product (Phuket, Thailand, say) that will attract the designated target market? Such elements as service, convenience, availability, comfort, access to location, price, amenities, and food and beverage offerings will determine the market share received. An outline for a marketing action plan follows:

Overall Marketing Objective—To gain X percent of market share

Target Market Description—Be as precise as feasible

Strategic Actions

Product—Stress all attributes of the product, especially any competitive advantages

Price—Establish and package pricing strategy that accents the value of the product

Promotion—Theme: availability, affordability, deliverance of a quality experience

Headings for a Marketing Plan

A marketing plan should contain the following sections[7]:

1. Executive Summary
2. Corporate Connection
3. Positioning Statement

4. Environmental Analysis and Forecasting

5. Segmentation and Targeting

6. Next Year's Goals

7. Action Plans: Strategies and Tactics

8. Resources Needed to Support Strategies and Meet Goals

9. Marketing Control

10. Presenting and Selling the Plan

11. Preparing for the Future

Marketing plans are done for large and small tourism entities alike.

Sales

Sales are an important part of marketing. The difference between marketing and sales is that with marketing, the focus is on the guest. With sales, the focus is on the product or service for sale. The sales department, whether of a city's convention and visitors bureau, an attraction, or a lodging facility, is responsible for making sales to tourists in the target market to increase market share. Sales can be to new accounts or existing ones.

Many countries, states, and cities have tourism offices in other countries to attract tourists. National tourism offices also represent their countries at the major conventions and expositions; Pow Wow is one of the major trade shows. Each sales department is organized in a way that best suits the organization. On a city level, some convention and visitors bureaus have national or international sales offices in addition to unit sales departments. The sales team may then be split up according to the various target markets: leisure, association, corporate, incentive, and so on, and by region: Northeast, Midwest, West, Southeast and so on. The sales team maintains account files with follow-up ticklers. It also prospects for new business by making cold calls to potential clients (usually by telephone).

Trends in Tourism Marketing

The world of tourism marketing is ever changing, and new trends and developments are always in progress. Following is a discussion of some of the most widespread and important ones going on at this time.

First, there will likely be a strong potential for growth in terms of tourism marketing as a consequence of the pent up demand for tourism and hospitality resulting from the economic downturn. When the economy improves, there will be an increase in tourism and hospitality services use. With the economic downturn, the amount of traditional marketing has increased and many new, creative ways of marketing, advertising, and positioning have been developed.

Second, the tourism and hospitality market is becoming increasingly more global. This means issues such as cultural diversity and ethical responsibility become more important.

Third, more tourism entities are realizing the true importance of retaining guests, thus companies are marketing heavily to current and previous guests. The frequent flier mileage programs used by airlines are one example of this; the Starwood Preferred Guest frequent stay program used by Starwood Hotels is another example.

There will continue to be tremendous growth in tourism and hospitality marketing and sales over the Internet. Not only are the major companies in the industry using the Internet, but more and more small and medium-sized hospitality and tourism companies are creating their own websites, allowing their guests to learn about them, their products and services, as well as book and purchase tourism products online.

CAREER INFORMATION

Tourism organizations need good marketing and salespeople to do both marketing and sales management and management planning by figuring out the best product, pricing, distribution, and promotion and sales strategies. They need to develop exciting advertising campaigns that catch the attention of the consumer and deliver offers of extraordinary value for the guests' money while at the same time being profitable and creating and maintaining relationships with guests. If this area interests you: Congratulations! You may begin in a line position in the area of your interest because you need to know the product you are marketing or selling before you can market or sell it. Graduates can acquire an overview of a company by working in various departments before specializing in the marketing and sales areas. Thousands of marketing and sales positions are available across the spectrum of tourism and hospitality. Someone has to market and sell all the countries of the world, the national parks, Disney World, Carnival Cruises, hotels, resorts, and restaurants and cities.

CASE STUDY

Marketing Events

Two students at my university plan to start a company: AA Event Master, LLC. They plan to stage a two-night hip-hop musical event in an indoor stadium in the City of Bristol, Connecticut, sometime during the last week of December 20XX. The stadium seats a maximum of 500 people. AA Event Master estimates that it needs to sell 250 tickets each night of the event to break even. Each ticket will cost $55, but if tickets are purchased for two nights, the cost is $100. AA Event Master believes it will be a successful event because residents in Bristol and its surrounding communities (such as Burlington, Plainville, Southington, Terryville, Thomaston, and Wolcott) want recreational opportunities during the month of December.

The name of the proposed event will be "Winter Hip-Hop Soiree." All attendees will be presented with a free T-shirt upon entrance. Night 1 activities will include a buffet dinner followed by a short presentation on the historical development of hip-hop music, including exhibits of personal memorabilia of famous regional/national hip-hop singers and an hour of nonstop hip-hop singing by various regional singers. As for night 2, a 45-minute sit-down dinner will be followed by two hours of nonstop hip-hop singing by various local/regional singers with dancing permitted. The second night will close with a 15-minute outdoor pyrotechnic display.

To promote the event, AA Event Master plans to buy newspaper ads in the *Hartford Courant* (a regional newspaper): twice a week during the months of September and October; and thrice a week during November and December. And beginning in December (once a week), they will hire students to place flyers under the windshield wipers of cars parked in the targeted communities' high schools, colleges, universities, malls, grocery stores, and hotels/motels. They will also send weekly e-mails to all accessible e-mail addresses in the targeted communities. In addition, they will try to secure the students' radio station at Central Connecticut State University to provide live coverage for each night in exchange for 10 free admission tickets. Finally, they hope to canvass ESPN (located in Bristol) as a possible sponsor of the event and to video record the event for later broadcasting.

Questions

1. Using Maslow's hierarchy of needs (refer to Chapter 2), what types of needs is this event seeking to satisfy?
2. Is the approach planned by AA Event Master accurately described as a marketing approach?
3. Do you feel their promotion mix is effective (and ethical)?
4. Do you think they will succeed in getting at least 250 attendees each night?
5. What suggestions would you offer AA Event Master to improve the likelihood of success?

Courtesy of Khoon Y. Koh, Central Connecticut State University.

CASE STUDY

Experiential Marketing, Taj Hotels Resort and Palaces

Taj Hotels Resorts and Palaces is one of Asia's largest hotel companies, having been incorporated in 1903. It now comprises more than 75 luxury, premium, midmarket, and value hotels across India, Malaysia, the United Kingdom, the United States, Bhutan, Sri Lanka, Africa, the Middle East, and Australia.

Taj recently created a number of exceptional tourism experiences including the Baghvan at Pench National Park and Banjaar Tola, in Madhya Pradesh. These experience-based accommodations seek to re-create the mobile palaces used by the Mughal emperors of the sixteenth and seventeenth centuries. The main lodges are typically built around fragrant courtyards, outfitted with rattan day beds and ebony chests set under black glass chandeliers, creating an eclectic, post-Colonial look. Bedroom accommodation is in tented pavilions, featuring rooftop platforms covered in pillows; bamboo floors strewn with hand-woven carpets; royal pennants; love swings made from salvaged wood; and traditional artwork. Pavilions typically offer solar-powered heated pools and outdoor showers, which lead directly to a forest of dense teak trees, rocky hills, and streams that appear to be drawn from the set of *The Jungle Book*. This tradition is counterpointed by the hotels' spa, which showcases disciplines such as yoga, meditation, Ayurveda healing, and massage and which features double spa suite tents that "capture the essence of royal Indian traditions through blending ancient Indian wisdom with contemporary therapies in order to introduce secret rejuvenation experiences from the splendor of regal India."

During guests' stay, they also have the opportunity to experience traditional royal entertainment, where the campfire is the focal point of the entertainment program and rhythms of the Thar music can be heard as well dancing, magic shows, puppet shows, jugglers, flaming torches, and camel parades. At these pavilions, Taj chefs have studied the cuisines of the royal houses of India to further evoke images of royalty. Finally, other Taj experiences allow guests to sail on a reproduction ceremonial imperial barge to re-create the splendor of a state cruise.

Questions

1. Apply Pine and Gilmore's model to the Taj pavilion experience, identifying examples drawn from each of the four realms.
2. How does Taj establish a cohesive set of images and meanings for the pavilion experience?
3. What memorabilia do you think Taj could develop and retail to ensure that guests truly experience Taj Pavilions?

Courtesy of Alistair Williams, Johnson & Wales University.

Summary

1. The definition of marketing is "the process of planning and executing the conception, pricing, promotion, and distribution of ideas, goods, and services to create exchanges that satisfy individual and organizational objectives." The goal of marketing is to satisfy consumers' or guests' needs, either existing ones or ones that are created by the company in question.

2. Marketing and sales should be done on a continual basis and with a systematic approach.

3. One commonly used tool in marketing is the SWOT analysis, where strengths, weaknesses, opportunities, and threats are identified.

4. The process of market segmentation consists of dividing the market into groups, profiling the groups, analyzing the segments, and formulating strategy for each segment.
5. Brand marketing is increasing in importance as a way of creating guest loyalty.
6. Marketing management consists of four tools, commonly known as the four Ps: product, price, place, and promotion.
7. The most visible trends currently taking place in the field of hospitality and tourism marketing and sales are strong potential growth in hospitality and tourism products and services and thereby their marketing, increasing globalization, a focus on returning guests and guest loyalty, and a more frequent use of the Internet for tourism marketing.

Key Words and Concepts

advertising
better than the competition
   approach
brand
brand identity
brand loyalty
continuous loyalty
different from the competition
   approach

geographic concentration
market opportunities
market positioning
market segmentation
market share
market size
marketing
marketing management
marketing orientation

personal selling
public relations
sales promotion
SWOT analysis
target market

Review Questions

1. What is the general definition of marketing? Does it differ from any definitions of marketing that you have heard before?
2. Describe the marketing system.
3. Give examples of market positioning strategies.
4. Name some of the factors that make business-to-business marketing different from traditional marketing (directed toward consumers).
5. List and describe the four Ps of marketing management.
6. What are the four components of the SWOT analysis? What is this analysis used for?
7. How would you describe experiential marketing?

Interesting Websites

U.S. Government website for travel and recreation: www.usa.gov/citizen/topics/travel/recreation.shtml

Virginia's Tourism: website www.virginia.org

Florida's Tourism: website www.visitflorida.com

Indiana's Tourism: website www.in.gov/tourism/marketing

Hawaii's Tourism: website www.hawaiitourismauthority.org

Australia's Tourism: website www.tourismaustralia.com

Washington State Tourism Marketing Plan 2009/2010; www.experiencewa.com/images/pdf/m_2008-03-28%20final%20marketing%20plan.pdf

Internet Exercises

1. Go online and find the website for England, Australia, and Canada and identify which is the best for a potential tourist and why.
2. Find and then compare and contrast examples from the Internet on how different companies market themselves in the hospitality and tourism industries. Go to the following sites: Carnival Cruise Lines, Walt Disney World, Florida, Virginia, and your state.

Apply Your Knowledge

1. Give examples of factors that must be considered when marketing a destination such as your state and Florida.
2. Give examples of companies in the tourism industries that use the different pricing strategies.
3. Give examples of companies or organizations that use any of the marketing strategies discussed in this chapter.

Suggested Activity

Create the outline for a tourism marketing plan for a country, state/province, or county/city.

Endnotes

1. American Marketing Association, http://www .marketingpower.com/ResourceLibrary/MarketingNews/ Pages/2008/42/1/MN1508Keefe.aspx?sq=definition+of +marketing, retrieved September 19, 2009.
2. Philip Kotler, John T. Bowen, and James C. Makens, *Marketing for Hospitality and Tourism*, 4th ed. (Upper Saddle River, NJ: Pearson Prentice Hall, 2006), 773.
3. N. Boden, "The Concept of the Marketing Mix," *Journal of Advertising Research* 4 (June 1964): 2–7, as cited in Stowe Shoemaker and Margaret Shaw, *Marketing Essentials in Hospitality and Tourism: Foundations and Practices* (Upper Saddle River, NJ: Prentice Hall, 2008), 58.
4. Stowe Shoemaker, Robert C. Lewis, and Peter C. Yesawich, *Marketing Leadership in Hospitality and Tourism: Strategies and Tactics for Competitive Advantage* (Upper Saddle River, NJ: Pearson Prentice Hall, 2007), 62.
5. Stowe Shoemaker and Margaret Shaw, *Marketing Essentials in Hospitality and Tourism: Foundations and Practices* (Upper Saddle River, NJ: Prentice Hall, 2008), 58.
6. L. M. Renaghan, "A New Marketing Mix for the Hospitality Industry," *Cornell Hotel and Restaurant Administration Quarterly*, April 1981, 31–35.
7. Kotler, Bowen, and Makens, *Marketing for Hospitality and Tourism*, 767.

CHAPTER 4

Tourism Economics

OBJECTIVES

After reading and studying this chapter you should be able to:

- Explain the relationship between tourism and economics, taking into account the theories of micro- and macroeconomics.

- Describe the law of demand and law of supply of tourism services, the variables affecting these factors, and the concept of equilibrium.

- Discuss pricing of tourism services.

- List and describe the costs and benefits of tourism for a host community.

- Explain the concept of input–output analysis, and other means of assessing the economic impact of travel and tourism.

- Briefly discuss the economic impact of travel and tourism on the United States.

GEOGRAPHY SPOTLIGHT

St. Lucia, a Caribbean Island Nation

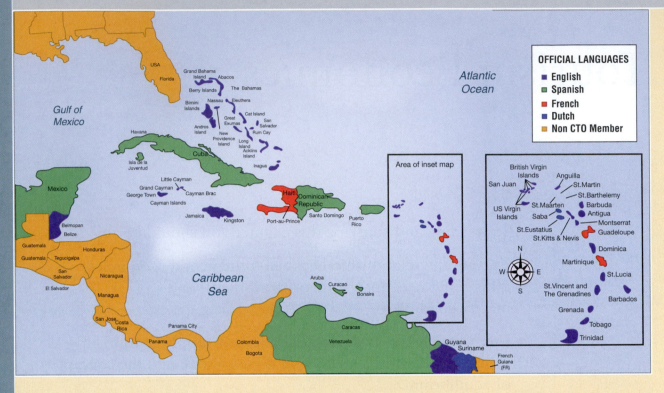

For many people, some of the most romantic times of their lives includes their wedding and honeymoon. "St. Lucia may be *the* most popular island in all of the Caribbean for weddings and honeymoons."[1] Romance is in the air on this Caribbean island with lush forests, beautiful beaches, picturesque waters, and highly recognized Twin Pitons. The small island's 160,000 residents welcome guests from around the world to celebrate love and romance on their home island. Through the 1980s and into the 1990s, tourism gained popularity and today, "Tourism [is] St. Lucia's main source of income and the industry is the island's biggest employer."[2] Presently, the island's focus on tourism, luxury resorts, romantic hideaways, beaches and foliage, activities, and more all make it the perfect destination for romantic tourism.

"A honeymoon in St. Lucia tends to be a quieter, more low-key experience than it is in some of the other Caribbean islands."[3] The island is home to the Diamond Botanical Gardens where "waterfalls gush from the mouth of [volcanoes]" and where "hot springs . . . feed the historical mineral baths."[4] Another romantic destination to visit on the island is the Balenbouche Estate. The former sugar plantation is now an eco-lodge, organic farm, and heritage site where tourists can enjoy the culture of the island.[5]

In addition to low-key experiences, St. Lucia offers a wide variety of activities for more adventurous couples. The Treetop Adventure Park in Dennery provides activities such as a rope challenge course,

GEOGRAPHY SPOTLIGHT *(continued)*

ziplining, cycling, hiking, kayaking, and snorkeling. Rain Forest Trams offers guests a slightly less adventurous option to explore the island. Guests can get an aerial view of the island during a 75-minute gondola ride through the treetops in an open-air gondola. In addition to the gondola flights, guests can also bird watch and hike around Rain Forest Trams property.[6]

Nigel Hicks © Dorling Kindersley

One of the island's most luxurious, and romantic, hotels is Ladera, "a small, lush, tropical gem that is world acclaimed yet still relatively unknown."[7] Ladera is an adults-only resort that features 6 villa suites and 25 suites. Each suite has an "open wall," which allows couples to enjoy the breathtaking scenery and sounds of the rainforest, as well as a private plunge pool and villa pool to relax in. Guests can enjoy activities including daily tours, market tours, mixology classes, an art exhibition, and more. Guests can also relax in the resort's spa with a variety of treatments; in-room couple's massages are available as well. Set in the lush landscape of St. Lucia, Ladera is a leading romantic destination with its unique open-wall suites and private pools, relaxing spa, and wedding and honeymoon packages.

From gondola rides through the treetops to mineral baths to beach weddings, St. Lucia offers a variety of activities that make the small island a top romantic tourist destination. St. Lucia's tropical climate, attractive landscape, beaches, and wide range of activities attract couples from around the world. Whether they seek a relaxing vacation or an adventurous getaway, St. Lucia offers visitors the opportunity to experience a destination focused on love and romance.

Endnotes

1. D. Stallings, A. Collins, D. Leto, and M. Sullivan, *Fodor's Caribbean 2009* (New York: Fodor's Travel Publications, 2009).
2. Central Intelligence Agency, "Saint Lucia," in *World Factbook* https://www.cia.gov/library/publications/the-world-factbook/geos/st.html (accessed February 8, 2009).
3. Cynthia Blair, "Romantic Activities in St. Lucia," About.com, http://honeymoons.about.com/od/stlucia/tp/activities.htm (accessed February 3, 2009).
4. Diamond Botanical Gardens, Waterfall, Mineral Baths, Nature Trail, and Old Mill, home page, www.diamondstlucia.com/index.htm (accessed February 3, 2009).
5. Balenbouche Estate, St. Lucia, home page, www.balenbouche.com (accessed February 8, 2009).
6. Rain Forest Aerial Trams, "St. Lucia—Introduction," www.rainforestrams.com/stluciaintro.html (accessed February 3, 2009).
7. Ladera Above and Beyond, home page, www.ladera.com (accessed February 3, 2009).

This chapter examines economics as related to tourism, using examples and exercises to help readers enjoy and better absorb the material. Modern economic thought began with Adam Smith and his book *The Wealth of Nations* (1776). He presented the concepts of aggregate supply and demand, the increased productivity resulting from specialization, and the invisible hand that guides resources to where they have the highest value.[1]

All economic questions arise because we want more than we get. We want a peaceful and secure world. We want clean air, lakes, and rivers. We want long and healthy lives. We want good schools, colleges, and universities. We want spacious and comfortable homes. We want time to hang out with our friends, to enjoy sports, music, travel, and so on.[2] What each one of us gets is limited by time, the incomes we earn, and by the prices we must pay. Let's say we wanted to take a vacation: we would be limited by our budget (how much we can afford) and time, so this leaves some unsatisfied wants—not enough money or time or both.

The inability to satisfy all our wants is called **scarcity**. We all face scarcity, rich and poor alike. For example, we may want to visit friends in Boston or Virginia, but we only have $100 to spend—not enough to fly there, but maybe enough to go by bus. When a wealthy person wants to take a cruise but also wants to attend a business convention scheduled at the same time, he is also facing scarcity. As a society, we also face scarcity: health care for all, computers in every classroom, no pollution, and so forth. We need to make choices based on the available information and resources and may find an **incentive**—a reward that encourages—or a penalty that discourages an action.[3]

Economics is a social science that examines how society chooses to allocate scarce resources. The study of travel and tourism economics is based on human beings' wants and decisions to travel as well as how they and tourism entities make the best possible use of resources.

The economics of tourism can be studied at both the microeconomic and macroeconomic levels. **Microeconomics** is concerned with individual consumers, firms, and industries. In tourism, studies of individual sectors such as restaurants, airlines, cruise lines, hotels, motels, attractions, gaming, opportunity costs, competition, and cross elasticity of demand are considered the interface of tourism and a microeconomic approach.[4] **Macroeconomics**, on the other hand, is concerned with all of the economic activity of a specific nation or region. A macroeconomic approach to tourism would examine tourism's effect on national or regional employment and income and attempt to capture the direct and indirect income from tourism via the multiplier effect, leakage, balance of payments, and foreign exchange.[5]

Tourism economics is frequently used to examine the economic impacts of tourism. Nickerson and Wilton state that "While measures related to economic impact assessment are conceptually simple, the actual collection of such information is extremely difficult."[6] What might distort any findings is the possible bias that economic researchers and tourism planners could have given that they are under pressure from policymakers, politicians, and special interest groups to prove their points of view.

Returns from any economic activity are, of course, heterogeneous; they differ across groups. Hence, optimum returns in real-world applications depend on one's point of view. For example, corporations may seek to maximize profits; residents may seek to maximize jobs or local quality of life; local governments may seek to increase tax revenues.[7]

Tourism Demand and Supply

Economics is concerned with which goods and services should be produced, how they should be produced, and who should eventually gain use of the products. **Demand** and **supply** are the most fundamental and powerful of all economic tools. An understanding of these is important to learning tourism economics. This chapter relies on graphs and examples of demand and supply to help you develop an understanding of the economics of tourism.

The demand side of the market is concerned with how buyers act. It is important to make the distinction between the *quantity demanded* and the *demand*. The quantity demanded of a good or service is how much buyers want to buy at the current price (for example, $99 for a one-day pass to Walt Disney World). The demand indicates the different quantities demanded at different prices, holding all other variables constant. When only the price changes, the quantity demanded changes. The **law of demand** states that price and quantity demanded are inversely related: as price increases, quantity demanded decreases, and the opposite case also holds. (If Disney World one-day passes were priced at $125, demand would decrease.) This relationship is illustrated in Figure 4–1, which shows the total quantity of hotel rooms demanded in a particular location at different prices. The *y* (vertical) axis indicates the price of rooms in dollars, and the *x* (horizontal) axis indicates the quantity of hotel rooms demanded. As we follow the curve from A to B (moving along the curve), the curve slopes downward. With the decrease in price from $90 (point A) to $60 (point B), quantity demanded increases from 20 rooms (point A) to 40 rooms (point B)—thus the inverse relationship between price and quantity demanded! The same is true if you go the other way, from B to A (with an increase in price, demand decreases).

Demand curves or schedules show the different quantities demanded at the different prices, holding other relevant variables constant. If one of these variables that affects demand changes, the entire demand curve moves. For tourism demand, variables capable of shifting the entire demand curve include the following:

- Prices of rooms in other locations
- The season
- The amount of disposable income available to the traveler

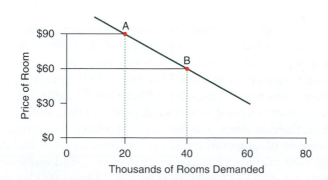

Figure 4–1 • The Relationship of Supply and Demand

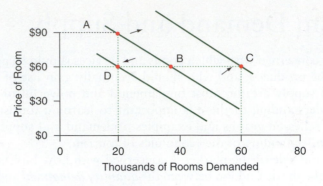

Figure 4–2 • An Increase in Tourism Demand

- Transportation to the destination (price, ease)
- Exchange rates
- The popularity of the location as a destination spot
- The population's confidence about the future in general

An example of an increase in demand is given in Figure 4–2, where a nearby hotel raises its prices by 20 percent. This causes an outward (to the right) shift in the demand curve for the first hotel from point B to point C. After the competitor increases its price (and the first hotel doesn't), more customers visit the first hotel, increasing the number of rooms occupied from 40 (point B) to 60 (point C).[8] After the increase in demand, the hotel increases its rental revenue from 40 rooms × $60 = $2,400 to 60 rooms × $60 = $3,600, an increase of $1,200. There are two ways, both correct, of describing the effects of an increase in demand. After an increase, for any given price, demanders wish to buy a larger quantity. Or, after an increase in demand, demanders are willing to pay more for the same quantity.

A leftward or inward shift of the demand curve represents a decrease in demand. This may be caused by an increase in the price of airfares. Because of the increased costs associated with traveling to the destination, demand for the destination hotel will decrease because certain customers cannot afford the trip anymore. As with an increase, there are two ways to think of the effects of a decrease in demand. After a decrease, at any given price, buyers wish to buy less. For sellers to sell the same amount after a decrease in demand, they must lower the price.

Because fewer people will travel to the destination, the hotel's demand curve will shift inward (to the left) from point B to point D, resulting in only 20 rooms occupied (point D) at the same average room price of $60; hence, the hotel experiences a decrease in income from 40 rooms × $60 = $2,400 to 20 rooms × $60 = $1,200, or a decrease of $2,400 − $1,200 = $1,200.

Demand for a tourism good or service depends on the number of consumers, their preferences, their incomes, and the prices of related tourism goods and services. As the number of potential consumers grows, so does the demand for a product. Population growth, new roads or air service, and more widespread information about a particular tourist destination all increase the number of potential tourists and, therefore, demand.

Elasticities of Demand		Income Elasticities	
Foreign Travel[a]	−1.8	Hotel Rooms[c]	0.44
Restaurant Meals[a]	−2.3	Restaurant Meals[d]	1.48
Air Travel (leisure)[b]	−1.52	Live Theater[d]	1.98
Air Travel (business)[b]	−1.15	Wine[d]	1.40

Cross-Price Elasticities	
French Tourists' Destination: UK/Spain[e]	0.745
Restaurants with Waiter Service/Fast Food Restaurants[f]	0.148
Hotel Rooms/Competing Hotels in Same City[c]	0.12
Gasoline/Rail Travel[g]	0.12

Figure 4-3 • The Elastics of Demand, Income Elasticities, and Cross-Price Elasticities

Sources: [a]*Principles of Economics*. By Arthur O'Sullivan and Steven Sheffrin, Prentice Hall, 2002.

[b]"A survey of recent estimates of price elasticities of demand for transport." By Jong Say Yong, W. G. Waters, and Tae H. Oum; The World Bank, Policy Research Working Paper Series: 359, 1990.

[c]"Lodging Demand for Urban Hotels in Major Metropolitan Markets." By Linda Canina and Steven Carvell, *Journal of Hospitality & Tourism Research* 2005; 29.

[d]*Recreation Economic Decisions,* 2nd edition. By John Loomis and Richard Walsh, Venture, 1997.

[e]"Long-Run Structural Tourism Demand Modeling: An Application to France." By Ramesh Durbarry, University of Nottingham TTRI Working Paper, 2002.

[f]"The Restaurant and Fast Food Race: Who's Winning?" By Douglas M. Brown, *Southern Economic Journal*, 1990; 56.

[g]National Transport Model- Working Paper 3, UK Department for Transport.

Related goods are classified as either substitutes or complements. Two goods are substitutes when, if the price of one increases (decreases), the demand for the other good increases (decreases). The preceding example of competing hotels illustrates substitute goods. Other substitutes in tourism include air travel and rail travel; theme parks and cruises; and neighboring restaurants in a resort area. Complementary goods are usually consumed together. When the price of a good increases (decreases), demand for its complements decreases (increases). Transportation and hotels are complementary goods. Other examples of complementary goods in tourism include hotels and neighboring golf courses; lift tickets and ski lodges; and wine and entrees in a restaurant.

Disposable income plays an important role in tourism demand. Nearly all tourist services are normal goods. A normal good's demand increases (decreases) when income increases (decreases). Normal goods with demand that changes by more than income changes are called luxury goods, while if demand changes by less than income, the good is called a necessity. Cross-country bus service in the United States is an example of an inferior good. The demand for inferior goods decreases as income increases.

When people's preferences change, demand changes. Preferences change as the seasons change, as the reputation of a firm changes, as people's expectations of the overall future of the economy change, and so forth. The major goal of a marketing agency is to change consumer's preferences about the product. Figure 4–3 shows the elastics of demand, income elasticities, and cross-price elasticities.

When producers contemplate a price change, it is critical they know how sensitive quantity demanded is to changes in prices. Just looking at the slope or steepness of the demand curve is not enough because if the units of measurement change, so does the slope, even though demand itself is unchanged. To determine sensitivity to price changes, economists use a measure called elasticity.

The elasticity is the ratio of the percentage change in the quantity (Q) divided by the percentage change in the price (P). In symbols, the elasticity formula is written $E_d = \%\Delta Q / \%\Delta P$, where Δ stands for "change in."

When quantity changes by more than price, the demand is said to be elastic. The bigger the percentage change in quantity relative to the percentage change in price, the more elastic is demand. For example, with elastic demand, a 5 percent increase in price lowers quantity by more than 5 percent. Likewise, a 10 percent price cut would increase quantity by more than 10 percent. When quantity doesn't change by as much as price, demand is inelastic. For example, with inelastic demand, a 20 percent increase in price would reduce quantity by less than 20 percent. Using more familiar language, we can say the more sensitive quantity is to price changes, the more elastic is demand. Similarly, the less sensitive quantity is to price changes, the more inelastic is demand.

Elasticity of Demand

There are three main determinants of the elasticity of demand. Probably the most important is the availability of substitutes. When there are more close substitutes available for a good/service, or there is more time to find substitutes, the more elastic is demand. Likewise, the harder it is to substitute for a good/service, or the shorter the time frame, the more inelastic (i.e., less elastic) is demand. An example in tourism is the demand for air travel. Travelers who plan far in advance (usually vacation travelers) have many substitutes for any particular flight: flights at different times that day, flights on nearby dates, flights on all of the other airlines, and alternative forms of travel. Thus, vacation travelers have very elastic demand.

Business travelers often need to be at a specific place at a specific time and date, often with little advanced notice. In addition, because business travelers tend to fly more, they are more likely to belong to frequent flier clubs. When looking at a specific flight from a business traveler's point of view, flights at different times or dates, or on different airlines, are not very good substitutes. It follows that business travelers have inelastic demand.

The other determinants of the elasticity of demand involve income. The more sensitive demand is to changes in income, the more elastic is demand. Thus, luxury goods have a more elastic demand than do necessities. In addition, the elasticity of demand depends on the fraction of income spent on the good. The larger this fraction, the more elastic is demand. Returning to the vacation versus business travelers, air travel is a luxury for vacationers but a necessity in business. Likewise, as a share of a family's budget, a vacation flight will be larger than one business trip's share of an entire firm's costs. Compound these effects with the substitution effect mentioned previously and it is clear that demand for leisure travel is much more elastic than the demand for business travel.

In summary, the major determinants of price elasticity are the following:

- Availability and quality of substitute products
- Status of the product (is it regarded as a necessity or a luxury?)
- Share of income spent on the product
- Amount of time available to consumers to adjust to the price change

It is crucial for suppliers to have a good estimate of the price elasticity to make informed decisions on pricing. The elasticity is related to total revenue (which equals the price of the good or service times the quantity of the good or service sold). If demand is elastic, lowering price will increase revenue. If a supplier lowers price when demand is inelastic, total revenue will actually decrease. In addition, the markup suppliers can charge above cost is related to the elasticity.* The more elastic is demand, the smaller the markup suppliers can charge. Likewise, the less elastic (i.e., more inelastic) is demand, the larger the markup suppliers can charge. This explains why business travelers pay a higher fare than vacationers do for seats in the same flight and class.

The Cruising Industry as a Unit for Microeconomics
Courtesy of San Diego Convention and Visitors Bureau

Any variable that affects demand has a corresponding elasticity. The two most commonly estimated elasticities are the cross-price and the income elasticities. The cross-price elasticity measures how sensitive demand for one good or service is to changes in the price of a related good or service. For substitute goods, the cross-price elasticity is positive. As a rule, the higher the cross-price elasticity, the better substitute is the other good or service. Complementary goods have negative cross-price elasticities. The income elasticity measures how sensitive demand is to changes in income. Luxuries have an income elasticity greater than one, necessities between zero and one, and inferior goods have negative income elasticities.

▶ Check Your Knowledge

1. What two theories are tourism economics built upon?
2. What does the law of demand imply?
3. Explain the concept of price elasticity.

Supply

The quantity supplied is the amount that sellers wish to sell at a given price. Supply (just like demand) is the various quantities supplied at all of the different prices, holding all other relevant variables constant. In economics, the **law of supply** states that the quantity of a good supplies (that is, the amount that owners

---

*When maximizing profits, firms set marginal revenue (the increase in revenue from selling the last one) equal to marginal cost (the increase in cost from producing the last one). The optimal difference between price and marginal cost as a percentage of price is equal to -1 / E_d. It follows that the less elastic is demand, the higher suppliers can mark up the price.

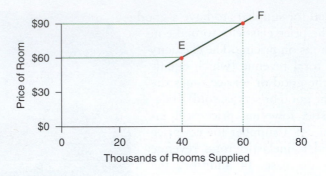

Figure 4–4 • Tourism Supply Curve

or producers offer for sale) rises as the market price rises, and falls as the price falls.[9] As a rule, **supply curves** are upward sloping—as price increases, so does the quantity supplied. Why? The opportunity to earn more money, of course!

The following example demonstrates the total supply of hotel rooms at various prices. In Figure 4–4, the y (vertical) axis indicates the prices of rooms in dollars, and the x (horizontal) axis indicates the quantity of hotel rooms supplied. Point E indicates that at an average rate of $60 per room, the quantity supplied is 40 rooms. At point F, however, an average room rate of $90 results in 60 rooms supplied. As shown, a change in the price of a room results in the change of the quantity supplied, other variables kept constant. Hopefully, the math works out!

$60 × 40 rooms = $2,400

$90 × 60 rooms = $5,400

The increased supply of rooms at a higher price increases revenues by $3,000 ($5,400 − $2,400).

Equilibrium Price

Like demand, an increase in supply is a shift out to the right. After an increase in supply, sellers are willing to sell more at any given price or are willing to accept a lower price for the same output. A decrease in supply is a shift back to the left. When supply decreases, sellers need to be paid more to produce the same output level or are willing to produce a smaller quantity at any given price. If only the price changes, quantity supplied changes. But what causes supply itself to change? The market supply of a product depends chiefly on two things: the cost of making the product or service, and the number and size of the producers making it. Anything that causes the cost of making a product or service to change changes supply. If costs increase, supply decreases. Similarly, if costs decrease, supply increases.

What causes costs to change? Changes in the way a product or service is made or offered, or changes in the prices of the inputs used to make the product. As new technologies are adopted, if they lower cost, a technological improvement can increase supply. For example, improvements in building and air-conditioning design led to an increase in supply of large resort hotels in Las Vegas. When an input price increases (decreases), supply decreases (increases). Inputs are products used to make something else. Examples of inputs in the production of tourism services include labor, building materials, restaurant supplies, insurance, jet fuel, and electricity. For example, the recent large increase in property insurance rates in Florida has led to a decrease in the supply of smaller "Mom and Pop" beach resorts. Lower interest rates lead to an increase in supply across all sectors of the tourism industry. Local governments often increase the supply in the tourism sector by offering tax breaks or selling public land at a discount. The increased supply of new sports stadiums and arenas provides an illustration.

The other determinant of supply is the number and size of producers. If companies enter or expand, supply increases. If firms exit or downsize, supply deceases. It is often said that demand creates its own supply, and in one sense, this is true. If companies believe that demand will increase, or that a recent increase is permanent, then supply will increase as more companies enter the growing market. Of course, if companies forecast a shrinking demand, exit and contraction will occur. It is also important to note that although demand can change dramatically in a very short time, supply often takes time to change. For example, a new resort hotel might take five years to go from an idea to opening its doors. This example illustrates another difference between demand and supply: supply decisions are usually made based on expectations about the future. For example, Southwest Airlines purchased jet fuel months in advance, saving millions of dollars when the prices peaked in the summer of 2008.

The price at which quantity demanded equals quantity supplied is called the **equilibrium**. In other words, this is the price at which the demands/expectations of buyers and sellers balance. Figure 4–5 shows the graphical example. At point G, both the quantity supplied and demanded meet at 40 rooms at an average room price of $60. The equilibrium of supply and demand is stable in the sense that once the equilibrium price is reached, it stays the same as long as neither supply nor demand changes.[10] When initially setting prices, it is not unusual for a firm to choose a price that is different from the equilibrium price. If the price is below equilibrium, the quantity demanded exceeds the quantity supplied and there is a shortage in the market. For example, if the price is $30 instead of $60, then quantity supplied is around 30 rooms instead of 40 rooms because fewer suppliers are willing to rent their rooms at cheaper prices. At the same time, quantity

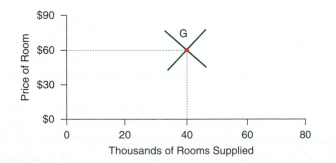

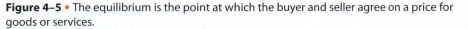

Figure 4–5 • The equilibrium is the point at which the buyer and seller agree on a price for goods or services.

demanded increases from 40 to 50 rooms as the price decreases from $60 to $30. Hence, there is a gap between the quantity supplied and the quantity demanded at a price of $30. A gap between quantity supplied and quantity demanded also occurs at a price above the equilibrium point, such as $70, where the quantity supplied exceeds the quantity demanded. Naturally, this is because at higher prices, more hotels are willing to offer rooms, but fewer consumers are willing to purchase rooms. When quantity supplied is larger than quantity demanded, economists say there is a surplus in the market.

The **law of supply and demand** states that if prices are allowed to adjust, they move toward the equilibrium. When there is a surplus of hotel rooms in Las Vegas in the summer, the casino hotels and resorts lower their prices. Likewise when a city hosts the Super Bowl, there is a shortage of hotel rooms, so the prices are increased. Outside of textbooks, markets are not usually in equilibrium. But the law of supply and demand guarantees that markets are always moving toward the equilibrium.

When a change in supply or demand knocks a market out of equilibrium, we would like to know what will happen to price and output in the new equilibrium. By looking at simple supply and demand graphs, we can determine the movement of price and output. There are four possible combinations to examine:

- Only demand changes.
- Only supply changes.
- Both supply and demand change in the same direction.
- Supply and demand change in opposite directions.

When only demand increases, like when a competitor raises its price, both the equilibrium price and output level increase. After a decrease in demand (with supply unchanged) the opposite occurs: both price and quantity drop. When supply is the only one to change, price and quantity move in opposite directions. An increase in supply causes equilibrium output to rise, but equilibrium price to fall. Likewise, a decrease in supply raises price but reduces quantity. Figure 4–6 shows the effects of price and quantity from a supply or demand shift.

Things are a bit more complicated when both supply and demand change at the same time. First let's look at what happens when both increase. Say, for example, that a new Florida beach resort opens at the beginning of the spring break season. At that time, there will be more buyers and sellers in the market, so we know for a fact that the quantity sold will increase. However, we are not sure what happens to price—that will depend on the relative elasticities of supply and demand as well as which one increases more. So, when both supply and demand increase (or decrease) we know what always happens to quantity (increase with an increase in both, decrease with a decrease in both), but we won't know ahead of time what will happen to price.

What if supply and demand move in opposite directions? Suppose that a new island resort opens just as airfares dramatically increase (this is an increase in supply and a decrease in demand). When supply increases, we know that sellers are willing to take a lower price. When demand decreases, we know that for any given quantity, demanders are willing to pay less than before. It is clear then that if

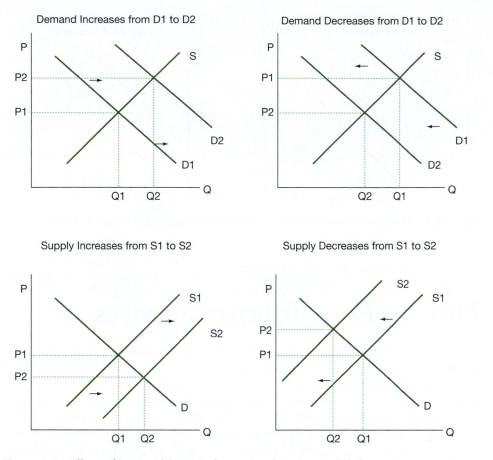

Figure 4–6 • Effects of Price and Quantity from a Supply or Demand Shift

supply increases while at the same time demand decreases, the price in the market will go down. What happens to the amount sold is unclear—it could go either way. Thus, when both supply and demand move in opposite directions, we always know what happens to price (it moves in the same direction as the demand), but we can't tell in advance what will happen to quantity. The effects of supply and demand changes on prices and output are summarized in Figure 4–7.

▶ Check Your Knowledge

1. Describe the fundamentals of the supply curve.
2. What is the equilibrium point?
3. Explain why gaps sometimes occur between supply and demand.
4. What happens to price and quantity when supply, demand, or both change?

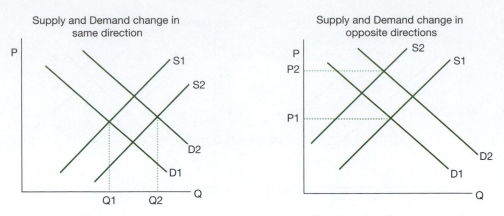

Figure 4–7 • Effects on Price and Output of a Simultaneous Change in Supply and Demand

How to Price Tourism Services

In general, tourism businesses appear to be in a highly competitive industry with limited flexibility to set prices. Either they sell at or below the established market price or see a rapid drop in sales. Yet, even with limited flexibility, tourism owners and operators are able to formulate their pricing based on elements such as product attributes, location, natural environment, facilities offered, relationships with guests and real and perceived differences in the quality of products and services.[11]

With pricing, the concept of demand means that consumers will purchase more of a good or service at a low price than they will at a high price. So, if a hotel sells 150 rooms for $120 but the same hotel sells 300 rooms for $80, then the hotel would maximize sales revenue by establishing a price of $80. This is all quite straightforward and correct providing the $80 covers all costs, including mortgage, and leaves a reasonable profit (about 20 percent).

Demand-Based Pricing

Demand-based pricing is based upon demand and not production costs. So, if demand increases, then up goes the price. Ever tried to fly home for Thanksgiving or Christmas? Well, the airlines use concepts called **yield management** and **revenue management** to price their seats to maximize revenue. Amazingly, airline seat prices change hundreds of times a day—even while travelers are trying to enter their information. Computers use complicated formulas to consider all the information available on a given route on a particular day. The demand for business travel is often heavy in the early morning and will drop for travel midday. Again, because of heavier demand for travel on Mondays, Tuesdays, and Fridays, prices tend to be higher on those days. Similarly, when demand is lower, in midweek and on the weekend, prices may be lower.

The lodging industry borrowed yield management and revenue management from the airlines for the pricing of its rooms. Generally, a hotel will sell some rooms a few months out for a slightly lower price, and as the date approaches the price will increase providing the demand is there—the rationale is that people want to stay, so up go the prices. Prices also tend to increase as holidays and high season approach because at these times demand increases.

Restaurants are quick to add up the cost of ingredients and add on other costs by determining a pricing structure of, say, food cost of 28 percent. So, once the cost of ingredients is known they determine the cost of the menu item and then look at their competitors to see what their prices are and adjust the ingredients or pricing or both. Restaurateurs strategically place items that give good contribution margins (the contribution margin is the difference between the cost and sale of an item), for example, if one menu item costs $5 to produce and sells for $25, then the contribution margin is $20. If, however, another item costs $3 to produce and sells for $14, the contribution margin is $11. Restaurants would obviously prefer to sell more of the $25 item, so they place it in a prominent position on the menu.

Break-Even Point

Break-even point is another interesting element of pricing. It is the point at which sales just cover costs; no profit or loss is made, but as sales increase, profit is made. Break-even point costs include both fixed and variable costs. Fixed costs include rent/mortgage, insurance, and managerial costs. It is interesting to note that the per unit fixed cost burden declines as the sales increase. Doubling sales would reduce fixed costs per unit by half. Variable costs include wages, food, beverages and all other supplies, music and entertainment, marketing, utilities, training, uniforms, licenses, china, glassware, cutlery, and linen.

Many tourists plan their trips in advance, allowing them time to compare prices and facilities of numerous tourist destinations, all the while searching for the best perceived value for their money. The development of the Internet as a shopping tool has only increased this competition among tourist destinations. Price plays a critical role in a tourist's purchasing decision. The ability to correctly price its products is fundamental to the success of a tourism-related business or organization.

Approaches to Pricing

Pricing in the tourism industry is difficult for two reasons. First, some companies in the industry have at least some **market power**. Market power is the ability to influence price. In addition, for most companies, pricing decisions must be made while thinking about how rival firms will react. It is this component that doesn't allow us to use the simple pricing rules put forth in introductory economics texts.

Typically, price is determined by some combination of the **comparative approach** and the **cost-plus approach**. The comparative approach assesses what prices similar operations are charging for the same or similar services/products. Cost-plus pricing sets price as some fraction above the

The break-even number of passengers on this airplane is around 80 percent.
Courtesy of Rick Pawlenty

production costs. In a world with limited or no competition, we saw earlier that the "plus" part of the cost-plus price depends on the elasticity of demand. However, how rivals react to a firm's pricing decision limits how much the company can charge, thus the reliance on the comparative approach as well. When setting a price, companies in the tourism industry need to keep in mind the following points:

- Tourism marketing organizations traditionally require a margin or payment for their services, usually in the form of commissions or as an add-on service charge.
- When pricing, all costs should be considered, not just expenses.
- There are implications to undercutting other operators, such as reduced profit margins, negative perceptions of quality, or the possibility of starting a price war.
- It is essential to assess what others are charging for similar products or services. This is one of the best methods to estimate consumer demand.

Because of market power and the interactions among competitors, pricing in the tourism industry is complex enough to warrant an entire book. However, the supply and demand tools discussed at the beginning of this chapter provide a solid foundation. If a successful marketing program increases demand, tourism entities can either raise their prices and sell the same amount, or leave their prices the same and sell more. Likewise, if a new competitor opens nearby, this increase in supply means the supplier must lower the price to sell the same amount as before, or expect to sell less. Information about current industry supply and demand as well as forecasts of the future can be obtained from accounting records, past experience, consumer surveys, industry trade publications, and memberships in trade associations. Successful pricing requires knowledge of costs and industry supply and demand.

Balance of Payments (BOP)

A nation's balance of payments (BOP) is the record of all economic transactions between its residents and the rest of the world.[12] The BOP is an indicator of economic and political stability in a country and helps investors decide whether to invest in a particular country. Usually, the BOP is calculated every quarter and every calendar year.[13] All money going in and out of a country is accounted for in the calculation of the BOP. Included in those totals are imports and exports of goods and services; payments and liabilities to foreign countries, or debts; credits received from foreign countries, reflected as credits; and financial capital and transfers.

The balance of payments comprises the *current account*, the *capital account*, and the *financial account*:

- The current account transactions are dominated by the trade in *goods and services account*, the primary income account, and secondary income account.
- The financial account records transactions that involve financial assets and liabilities that take place between residents and nonresidents.
- The capital account transactions focus on the changes in ownership of real and financial assets.[14]

Naturally, countries want to at least have a balance of payments that is equal or hopefully better than equal, meaning that a nation takes in as much money (credit) as it gives out to other countries (debit). The balance of payments is one of the major indicators of a country's status in international trade. But having a negative balance is not all bad. For example, although a country might have a deficit in merchandise trade (indicating that it is importing more than it is exporting), it may show a surplus in another area, such as its investment and tourism-related income. The International Monetary Fund (IMF) uses the balance of payments accounts to make decisions when considering a country for a loan. For many countries, tourism has a positive effect on the balance of payments with revenues coming into the country for transportation, accommodation, meals, entertainment, attractions, and shopping.

Tourism has a huge impact on the balance of payments for many countries. If, for example, a U.S. citizen were to fly to Europe on a European airline, stay in hotels, eat in restaurants, sightsee, attend events, and go shopping, these would all be money flowing out of the United States. Of course, it can get more complicated: what if the European airline was using a Boeing 747-400 manufactured in the United States? Then, an allowance for an appropriate amount would have to be made. However, if the traveler flew on a U.S. airline, then at least some of the money would be counted as spent in the United States. If travelers from European or other nations visit the United States, then the United States realizes exports, meaning the foreign travelers' money would be coming into the United States. Naturally, it is to the balance of payments advantage of the United States to have more tourists visiting the United States than to have U.S. tourists going abroad. Governments like the concept of tourism exports because of their positive effect on the gross domestic product and the balance of payments.

The balance of payments is affected by the value of the U.S. dollar compared to other currencies. When the value of the U.S. dollar declines compared to other currencies, then, all other things being equal, more tourists will visit the United States. However, during times when the value of the U.S. dollar is higher compared to other currencies, more U.S. citizens are likely to travel abroad than are foreign tourists to visit the United States. This has a positive or negative effect on the balance of payments depending on which is the dominant factor—a stronger or weaker U.S. dollar.

Gross Domestic Product (GDP)

The gross domestic product (GDP) is the total value of goods and services produced in a nation. GDP may be calculated three ways: by adding up the value of all the goods and services produced, by adding up the expenditure on goods and services at the time of sale, or by adding up producers' incomes from the sale of goods or services. However, it is difficult to measure GDP precisely because every country has an unofficial economy consisting of transactions not reported to the government.[15]

   GDP = Consumption = Consumer Spending

   + Investment = The sum of all the country's businesses spending on captial

+ Government Purchases = The sum of government spending

+ Net Exports = The nation's total net exports, calculated as total exports minus total imports

Consumption is the largest component of the GDP. In the United States, the largest and most stable component of consumption is services and that includes tourism. GDP is commonly used as an indicator of the economic health of a country, as well as to gauge a country's standard of living.[16]

Costs and Benefits of Tourism

We all know that tourism affects the economy of a destination area. Large cities such as Las Vegas and Orlando depend extensively on tourism. However, the benefits of a large tourism sector are debatable. Using resources to build a tourism sector means fewer resources for other sectors. These costs must be included when estimating tourism's effect on a city, region, state, or nation.

One method to determine the net effects of the tourism sector is called a **cost-benefit analysis**. The basic questions asked in a cost-benefit analysis are, "Do the short-term economic benefits of providing this service outweigh the economic costs?" and "What are the effects on long-term growth?" Much research in tourism is related to the estimation of tourism's contribution to regional income. The statistical analyses used to measure economic impact are sometimes complicated, and results are disputed among the experts. Although there tends to be more agreement when measuring costs, the net benefit of an action in the tourism sector is often subject to debate.

It is clear that income from tourism is huge for most states in the United States, provinces in Canada, other industrialized nations, and an increasing number of developing countries. The amounts, however, are subject to definitions and to reliability and interpretation of the data collected. In this section, we look at some ways to measure the costs and benefits of tourism, how to increase income, and we attempt to discover who benefits and by how much. Research suggests that there is a strong link between tourism development and poverty reduction in developing countries. This is confirmed by Drs. Roberto Croes and Manuel Vanegas,[17] who conclude that enthusiastic tourism development policies as a means of economic expansion may be fully effective in that tourism development leads to poverty reduction, rather than the other way around. This may suggest redirecting appropriate resources in support of tourism development and marketing policies.

Tourism Taxes as Tangible Benefits

Tourism generates tax revenue, some of which is directly collected and some of which is indirectly imputed. Many countries have a departure tax on travelers; other countries have what is called an admission tax. Large cities sometimes impose a hotel room tax or **transient occupancy tax** (**TOT**), otherwise known as the bed tax. These are all examples of directly collected taxes.

Many governments raise a significant fraction of their tax income from import duties, which for political reasons are much easier to collect than income taxes. The travelers then pay the taxes indirectly by buying food, beverages, and other goods that have been imported and by staying in hotels and other facilities that in turn have imported building materials and other inputs used in their operations. Generally, most nonincome tax revenue comes from sales or value-added taxes paid by visitors and residents alike. Usually, a part of these taxes goes into the city's general fund. Some cities have chosen to reinvest much of the tax revenue directly collected from tourists into tourism development and promotion, including marketing, convention centers, and cultural programs.

This hotel contributes more than $4 million in transient occupancy taxes.
Courtesy of San Diego Convention and Visitors Bureau

Impact on Quality of Life

Tourism may impose significant costs on a destination if it reduces quality of life. This sometimes happens when a destination is not prepared for a large number of visitors. Some of these negative effects include traffic congestion, increased crime rates, noise and air pollution, vandalism, excessive demand on public facilities and water supplies, as well as overcrowding of beaches, forests, and parks that results in the destruction of plants and wildlife and reduction in visitor and resident enjoyment.

Yet quality of life is a highly subjective matter. It can be viewed from many perspectives—number of entertainment options available to residents, ease of movement in and around the area, presence or absence of smog and advertising signs, availability and crowding of public transportation, road congestion, and so on. Great differences exist in what people like and dislike. Many New Yorkers' eyes light up when they think of returning there, whereas others cringe at the thought of going to New York City. Some visitors to Bangkok may enjoy the crowds, while others complain about the traffic congestion or waiting lines that these crowds cause.

Opportunity Cost and Tourism

When calculating the costs of tourism, it is important to include the **opportunity cost**. The opportunity cost of a resource is its value in its next best use. If you have two uses for a resource, and you can only choose one, the opportunity cost is the value of the resource in its second use, the one you did not choose. To give an easy example, you either have the option to go to class tomorrow morning or to sleep in. If you choose to go to class, you do so at the expense of forgone sleep. If you choose to sleep in, then your opportunity forgone is learning something in class.

Does tourism give the economy more than it takes? Are benefits evenly distributed or do they go to a relatively small minority? Do the increases in government revenue generated by tourism pay for the added government services? Could more benefits be generated by investing in other sectors of the economy? Dollars brought into an economy by tourism stimulate certain sectors of the economy, often increasing the costs of certain goods. In some cases, inflation causes the economy to become overheated. Landowners and developers may become rich, but the cost to the average citizen usually multiplies because of the increased cost of living. Within a community, the costs and benefits of tourism are not evenly distributed. What may benefit one group may harm or be a disadvantage to another group. Hotel and restaurant operators may benefit from tourism, but, as mentioned earlier, permanent residents may suffer in terms of crowding, pollution, noise, and in some cases a changed way of life.

Having said that, most communities would probably prefer a "smokeless," nonindustrial economic base like tourism or other service industries. But in many areas it is not a question of whether tourism is beneficial or not because the area may have no other options. Tourism development may be a necessary choice for areas that have natural beauty, a pleasant climate, and yet are remote from skilled labor markets and raw materials needed for manufacturing. Bermuda, the island nation in the Atlantic situated 600 miles from the East Coast of the United States, was once a small agricultural producer. Tourism was an obvious choice to improve the island's economy. Today, services are by far the major industry, comprising an overwhelming 89 percent of the country's gross domestic product.[18]

Opportunity cost is one of the most important concepts in economics, yet it is often overlooked when "running the numbers" because it is not an expense. Whenever developments in tourism areas are planned, it is critical that governments determine what the opportunity cost of the best alternative forgone is. For example, a better alternative to building a hotel at an ocean site could be constructing a wilderness refuge dedicated to protecting endangered bird species. The best alternative could also be to build the hotel because of the possibility of significantly increased revenues, tax income, and employment opportunities that benefit the local community. Many factors need to be taken into consideration to decide which alternative is the best.

Two other questions that should be asked to discern whether tourism development is the right alternative for a country or community are: "Are the residents of a destination fully employed?" and "Would they produce more for the economy in jobs other than those connected with tourism?" For example, the Bahamas and most of the smaller Caribbean Islands can barely subsist as agricultural economies. They are also too remote from industrial centers to be competitive as small manufacturers, so they turn to tourism to improve economic development. The Bahamas has tried producing pineapples, cotton, fishing, and even rum running, none of which were particularly successful. Thus, resources devoted to tourism have low opportunity costs, and the Bahamian economy has become substantially tourism based.

FOCUS ON

Tourism Satellite Accounts

Tadayuki Hara

Tourism satellite accounts (TSAs) is a set of rules to measure the economic contributions of tourism as an industry. Unlike some misperceptions, it is not a modeling technique but rather close to "accounting rules." Why does it include the word *satellite*, and what is the earth to a satellite? The framework to measure the industries was developed in the first part of the twentieth century when coal was the main source to power the heavy industries, such as steel. So, the main industrial sectors were considered to include agriculture, mining, construction, transportation and public utilities, manufacturing, wholesale trade, retail trade, FIRE (finance, insurance, and real estate), and services. With lists of those major industrial sectors, the earth was formed. Tourism as an industry was not significant enough when the steel industry was the backbone of the power of the nations in the 1930s and 1940s. The earth framework became a foundation for the important global framework to measure nations' economic activities such as gross domestic product (GDP), and the framework has been known as the **System of National Accounts (SNA),** which had a major revision in 1993 by the United Nations, the Commission of the European Communities, the International Monetary Fund, the Organisation for Economic Co-operation and Development, and the World Bank. (The work is under way to incorporate updates to the SNA to the 2008 version.)

When tourism started to emerge as a significant economic activity as a result of the surge of travelers in the 1970s and 1980s, the framework of industrial sectors has been used for decades, so tourism could not squeeze into the established club of industrial sectors. Therefore, just like a satellite moves around the earth, tourism orbits the established industries of the SNA. The concept of measuring tourism as a satellite industry enables its effects to be observed and estimated.

The following sites contain further details: the United Nations Statistics Division "About the System of National Accounts 1993" page at http://unstats.un.org/unsd/sna1993/introduction.asp and the United Nations World Tourism Organization Statistics and Tourism Satellite Account page at www.unwto.org/statistics/index.htm.

If you are interested in learning how the TSA works, you must have a basic understanding of how the input–output (I-O) and social accounting matrix (SAM) work because TSA is based on I-O modeling.[1] Dr. Wassily Leontief was awarded the Nobel Prize in Economics for I-O modeling in 1973, and Sir Richard Stone was awarded the Nobel Prize in Economics for SAM in 1984. I-O and SAM can be major hurdles for tourism students and even for some faculty members to learn TSA. Two books explain the concepts:

R. Miller and P. Blair, *Input-Output Analysis: Foundations and Extensions* (Upper Saddle River, NJ: Prentice Hall, 1985)

T. Hara, *Quantitative Tourism Industry Analysis: Introduction to Input-Output, Social Accounting Matrix Modeling and Tourism Satellite Accounts* (Oxford, England: Butterworth-Heinemann-Elsevier, 2008)

Endnotes

1. S. Okubo and M. Planting, "U.S. Travel and Tourism Satellite Accounts for 1992," *Survey of Current Business* 78 (1998): 8–22.

Source: Courtesy of Tadayuki (Tad) Hara, PhD, Rosen College of Hospitality Management, University of Central Florida.

Tourism represents a high percentage of gross domestic product (GDP) for many developing countries, in this case the Caribbean island of Barbados.

Martin Richardson, Rough Guides/Dorling Kindersley

The Mixed Economy

Tourism is not necessarily an "either-or" proposition; it often blends well with other businesses. Puerto Rico and Barbados are both examples of mixed economies. Today they are both dependent on their agriculture as well as tourism. Cape Cod is an example of an area forced to rely to a large extent on tourism. Originally an agricultural and fishing community, by the 1930s these industries were no longer competitive and the gap was filled by tourism. Nantucket Island and Martha's Vineyard were once whaling centers; now tourism and construction are the principal industries.

The largest concentrations of hotel rooms in the United States are in Las Vegas (Nevada), New York (New York), and Orlando (Florida), where tourism forms a sizable part of the cities' economies. London is often thought of as a huge financial and industrial center, but it is also a major tourist center: nearly 95 percent of all American visitors to England spend some time in London. Shanghai, China; New Delhi, India; Heidelberg, Germany; Florence, Italy; and Boston are other examples of cities that combine various industries with tourism. Florida's mixed economy rests upon four legs: tourism, government spending, agriculture, and industry.

Even small rural communities can become involved with tourism economics via agritourism, particularly organic farming. Organic farming is likely to attract nature-oriented tourists, and by using a social accounting matrix model, Drs. Tadayuki Hara and Yuri Mansury found that a successful campaign to promote organic agriculture not only is expected to deliver higher production output, but also generate a more egalitarian distribution.[19]

► Check Your Knowledge

1. What are the two main approaches to pricing in the tourism industry?

2. In what way can tourism bring tax income to an area?

3. What is meant by opportunity cost?

Who Benefits from Tourism and by How Much?

Should tourism be encouraged and expanded? What amount of public funds should be used to market and advertise tourism? What is the power per dollar of advertising? And, perhaps more important, who benefits from this development?

Nations and communities in today's interdependent world must import goods from other areas. Tourism can bring in substantial amounts of money that offset the cost of a country's imports. Some self-sufficient nations still need the foreign exchange brought by tourism.

The first people to benefit from tourism are likely to be the land developers, the landowners, and those entrepreneurs who provide transport, accommodations, food and beverages, sightseeing, and other entertainment for the traveler. But what benefits accrue to the rest of the population of the tourist destination area? Do the 70 million-plus travelers to Florida each year benefit areas other than south Florida and Orlando? Does the citizen living in Jacksonville benefit from the tourist industry 200 or 300 miles away to the south? What good is the tourist industry to the retired person living in Florida? In what way does tourism affect the schoolteacher who lives in Boracay, Philippines?

The critics of tourism are quick to point out that in most of the less developed countries, capital goods such as those needed to build a hotel or restaurant, including cement, steel, fixtures, air-conditioning units, and so forth, are not available locally and must be imported. Much of the food consumed by the visitor, such as steaks, hamburgers, white flour, and similar items, must be imported. The country involved, therefore, does not reap as many benefits from the tourist dollar as it might seem. Tiny Gambia in West Africa is a good example. Gambia's government borrowed heavily to build tourist facilities, gave foreign investors years of income tax exemptions, as well as the freedom to export capital and profits, so many of the revenues from tourism are diminished by the high purchasing costs of imported goods.

A good example of just how much a community can benefit from tourism is given by Dr. Robertico Croes, who recently developed a master plan for the preservation of the people of Guayas Province in Ecuador. The plan calls for a doubling of the number of tourists and, in turn, creates 30,000 more jobs and generates money for an impoverished community. The benefit to the community will create many opportunities for people and bring in money for the government to give back in health care and education. The plan includes everything from improving local signage to launching an international marketing campaign to training hundreds of service workers. The master plan should increase arrivals by half a million and boost tourism spending from about $380 million to $912 million by 2018. A novel way of starting the plan occurred in May 2008 when more than 50,000 people including residents, visitors, and city officials gathered on Guayaquil's famed boardwalk, El Malecon, to simultaneously send a text message—"UR GNG 2 LV IT"—via mobile phones to friends and family outside the country, inviting them to experience Guayas firsthand.[20]

Those concerned with developing a visitor industry, whether a government or private person, will want to know the likely extent of economic and other impacts on the area. A cost-benefit analysis attempts to quantify and compare the pros and cons of tourism. Pros can be such things as increased tax revenues, job generation, improved social services, and an increase in restaurants and entertainment options. Negative impacts include change or loss of indigenous identity and values resulting from standardization, loss of authenticity, staged authenticity, and adaptation to tourist demands. Culture clashes may arise because of economic inequality and irritation caused by tourist behavior. Physical influences causing social stress must also be addressed. But can you see a small

Money spent by tourists in this market store in Indonesia is counted as an export.

Courtesy of Dr. Belkis Kambach

problem here? The tricky part of a cost-benefit analysis is actually quantifying the impacts of tourism. As we all know, what some residents may regard as positive developments, others may consider negative, so it is difficult to determine which factors need to be measured and how to measure them so that they can be compared to yield significant results.

The Multiplier Effect

In this section, we discuss how or by what process tourist revenues affect the economy. The **multiplier effect**, also referred to as the ripple effect, tries to measure the total impact of "fresh" or new dollars that enter an economy. For example, when Carmen in Honduras, gets her paycheck she may choose to invest part of it, she may also spend some on a new hairstyle, pay to put gas in her car, or buy a restaurant meal or some necessities. The money that is invested or used for purchases is referred to as the first round of spending. Part of what is spent in the first round is re-spent for a second round of spending. The second round of spending occurs when the gas station owner receives income (from Carmen's purchase of gas), and then spends this income on something else, such as the paychecks for the employees of the gas station. And then theses paychecks are spent, and so on. Carmen's paycheck has been divided up and turned into income for several other people. So, a new dollar of spending creates more than a dollar of economic activity. The entire process is illustrated in Figure 4–8 (a further explanation of the ripple effect in terms of tourism).

When a dollar (or other currency) enters a community and is then spent outside the community, its benefit is felt only once. If the same dollar is re-spent within the community, its benefit is multiplied: it adds more value, pays more wages, finances more investments, and ultimately creates more jobs. Thanks to this multiplier effect, each additional transaction in which the dollar is involved creates just as much wealth as a new dollar from the outside, but relies on local decisions made by people who care about the community.[21] The tourist may pay $40 to take a tour. The tour operator pays local drivers, makes a personal profit, and will spend some or most of that profit within the economy. Some leaks occur, such as the purchase of gasoline—a good imported to the area. The next day, the tourist rents a boat to go sailing. If the boat was built within the destination area, much of the purchase price will remain in that economy. The boat owner's profit remains in that economy, and the owner in turn spends most of that profit.

The illustration can go on and on, but it is easy to see that rounds of spending are kicked off by the injection of tourist dollars into a destination economy. As a general rule of thumb, the greater the percentage of the tourist dollar that

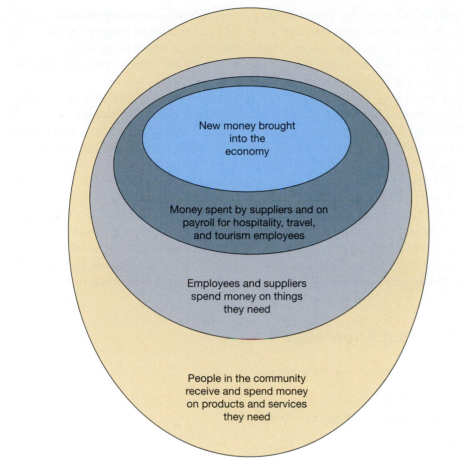

Figure 4–8 • The Ripple Effect

remains in the area and the faster it is re-spent, the greater its effect in "heating" the economy of an area. Leaks of dollars from the ripple effect occur when money leaves the economy for purchases of imported goods and services from outside the community. Other leaks occur when profits leave an area, for example, when hotels are owned by foreign companies. Of course, not every dollar spent on a vacation to another region goes to that region. For example, if an American citizen decides to spend his or her vacation in Brazil, much of the cost of the vacation will be spent in the United States. An American travel agency or an American airline might benefit from the citizen traveling abroad, while some of the goods and services consumed in Brazil might be provided by U.S.-based firms.

Import Propensity

To establish how much of the tourist dollar remains at the destination, it is necessary to find out where it is spent and how much of it is sent out of the destination area. The **import propensity** is the percentage of the tourist dollar that is sent to another area. This represents a leak from a destination area. For example, in Hungary the tourist dollar is broken down according to where it was spent—hotel, restaurant, store, and so on. The percentage of the expenditure that leaves Hungary is figured as its import propensity. Knowledge of the import propensity is necessary to determine the multiplier effect correctly. Import propensities vary across destinations.

Did you know that in economics, tourism services are viewed as exports? This concept may be somewhat difficult to grasp because services are not tangible like, for example, machinery or wheat. Nevertheless, offering services to tourists produces income for the tourist destination area in the same way that tangible goods shipped from the area do. Put simply, when a foreign tourist comes to the United States and buys goods and services at the destination, the United States exports to the tourist, even though the transactions take place within the United States. Likewise, when a U.S. citizen travels to another country and buys the country's goods and services, these figure as imports to the United States. The Travel Industry Association of America reports that both domestic and international visitors spent $730 billion in 2008, including international passenger fares. That is $2 billion a day or $84.5 million an hour.[22]

▶ Check Your Knowledge

1. What is the cost-benefit ratio?
2. Explain the ripple effect.
3. What is meant by import propensity?

Cost of Public Services

A growing tourism sector increases the demand for various public services. The costs of providing these services vary widely between an undeveloped area such as the island of Grenada and a highly sophisticated city such as Honolulu. Increased tourism increases the costs of public services such as highways, airports, police and fire protection, sewage, and local parks and recreation. Again, it is important to ensure that benefits from tourism outweigh the costs. The bottom line should be "Will the community benefit?"

Public Costs of Immigrant Workers

Some tourist areas already have full employment or the residents choose not to work in some tourist-related jobs, as is the case in the Bahamas and the U.S. Virgin Islands. If workers must be brought in, the initial cost to the community is high. Additional public services of all kinds may be needed. Much hotel employment is of an unskilled or semiskilled nature, work that requires a minimum amount of education or training. Such unskilled or semiskilled employees are usually paid at the bottom of the wage scale and make the smallest tax contributions, which might not always be enough to offset costs of the increase in public services required.

Guidelines for Assessing the Economic Impact of Travel and Tourism

To estimate the economic impacts of travel, recreation, and tourism, we must begin with an estimate of visitor spending. This spending is often analyzed via visitor surveys. Changes in visitor spending can be utilized to estimate multiplier effects or to convert spending changes to associated changes in income and employment. There are three kinds of spending that generate impacts:

- Spending by visitors, for example, on lodging, food, transportation, recreation, and retail purchases
- Durable goods purchased by visitors and households in the area
- Government or organizational spending (construction and development, and operations and maintenance)

Each kind of spending often is measured individually, and in many cases, only one type may be of interest in a given situation. Trip spending is most easily gathered in conjunction with on-site visitor surveys; durable goods purchases are best measured through household surveys or secondary sources; and construction and government or organizational purchases are generally acquired from internal records of the organization.

Tourism Satellite Accounts

Although most industries are measured by counting what is produced, tourism is defined by what visitors buy. Measuring tourism is difficult. Unlike other sectors in the economy, tourism cannot be measured using standard economic accounting methods. As such, tourism is a demand activity that touches many industries, and the key is to separate the level of industry activity made by visitors from that which is contributed by residents.[23]

Given the difficulty in collecting reliable data for assessing the relative significance of tourism to an economy coupled with the fact that tourism is a collection of various industries under an umbrella of convenience, the United Nations and the World Tourism Organization adopted **tourism satellite accounts** to measure the significance of tourism's economic impacts on national economies on an annual basis.

Tourism satellite accounting is the international (UNWTO, Organisation for Economic Co-operation and Development [OECD]) standard for measuring the contribution of tourism to an economy. By using this standard, each tourism satellite account (TSA) is able to be compared, one with another. So, we can tell the contribution of a sector of tourism in, say, Canada and compare it to that of, say, Australia or Barbados.

The purpose of TSAs is to provide answers to key questions such as the following[24]:

- How much of each tourism dollar is retained in the country?
- How does government support compare to tax revenues generated by tourism?
- Are current levels of capital investment sufficient to sustain tourism growth?
- Do tourism growth rates reflect the growth rates in the manufacturing sector?
- What is tourism's contribution to the gross domestic product (GDP)?
- What is tourism's impact on the other industry sectors?
- How does tourism compare with other industries?
- How many people are directly and indirectly employed in tourism?
- What impact does tourism have on the balance of payments?

With results from a TSA, governments and tourism industry sectors can assess the importance of tourism and make informed decisions relating to tourism such as investment, marketing, and policy.

The recommended methodological framework takes the form of a basic system of concepts, classifications, definitions, and tables that is compatible with international and national accounting guidelines and that allows for comparisons between regions, countries, or groups of countries.[25] The concept of tourism satellites is based on the need for a framework that will provide consistency over time and between countries and compatibility between industries when calculating the significance of tourism to the economy.[26]

TSA Economic Concepts

The travel and tourism satellite account is based on a demand-side concept of economic activity because the industry does not produce or supply a homogeneous product or service like traditional industries (agriculture, electronics, steel, etc.) do. Instead, travel and tourism is an industrial activity defined by the diverse collection of products (durables and nondurables) and services (transportation, accommodations, food and beverage, entertainment, government services, etc.) that are delivered to visitors. There are two basic aggregates of demand in the TSA[27]:

1. *Travel and tourism consumption* represents the value of products and services that has been consumed by visitors. It is the basic demand-side aggregate used to construct an explicitly defined production-side "industry" equivalent for comparison to other industries.

   Travel and tourism consumption includes the following:

   Personal travel and tourism

   Business travel

Government expenditures for visitor services such as cultural (art museums), recreational (national park), or clearance (immigration/customs) to individual visitors; visitor exports, which includes spending by international visitors on goods and services[28]

2. *Travel and tourism demand* builds on travel and tourism consumption to include travel and tourism products and services associated with residual components of final demand. It is used to construct a broader economy-wide impact of travel and tourism. The residual elements of travel and tourism are as follows[29]:

   Government Expenditures—Collective expenditures made by agencies and departments associated with travel and tourism, but generally made on behalf of the community-at-large, such as tourism promotion, aviation administration, security services, and sanitation services

   Capital Investment—Investment by travel and tourism providers (the private sector) and government agencies (the public sector) to provide facilities, equipment, and infrastructure to visitors

   Exports (nonvisitor)—Consumer goods sent out of state for ultimate sale to visitors (such as clothing, electronics, or gasoline) or capital goods sent out of state for use by industry service providers such as aircraft or cruise ships

   Taxation—Taxes paid by both individuals and companies involved with tourism

   T&T Industries Employment—Travel and tourism industry employment plus those faceless jobs associated with industry suppliers (airline caters, laundry services, food suppliers, wholesalers, accounting firms, etc.), government agencies, manufacturing and construction of capital goods, and exported goods used in travel and tourism

The benefits of a TSA are well described by Global Insights when they liken the tourism industry to an iceberg, where only the direct effect is above the surface and the larger indirect effect is below the surface.[30] Following are questions a community or destination can ask to begin to quantify the effects of tourism on its economy:

1. How can we communicate the full value of tourism to policymakers, businesses, and citizens?
   Quantify the contribution that tourism makes to GDP, jobs, wages, and taxes, as well as how it benefits other economic sectors.
2. Are we spending enough on tourism promotion and infrastructure?
   Compare government support of the tourism sector with government revenue generated by tourism.
3. Which are our best economic development targets and are candidate industry–requested concessions worth it?
   Allow policymakers to compare the size and growth of tourism to other industrial sectors.

4. What is the return on investment of public tourism investment?
   Enable analysts to assess long-term health of the tourism sector vis-à-vis capital investment and government support.

5. How can we benchmark ourselves against our destination competition?
   Provide an accepted international standard for benchmarking.

▶ Check Your Knowledge

1. List some social costs usually connected to tourism.

2. What are the three main types of tourism spending?

3. Give examples of spending categories for tourism.

Region, Origin of Visitors, Number and Types of Visitors

A region may be defined by a map or as a given radius from a destination site (e.g., report all spending that occurred within 20 miles of this site). Identifying a region of interest and measuring spending that occurs within this region are often difficult, particularly when visitors are on extended trips and stop in many places. Only the portion of trip spending that occurs within the region itself generates local economic impact. In some situations it may also be desirable to separate spending at the particular site (be it a hotel, marina, or state park) from spending off-site within the surrounding region.

To identify regional flows of dollars, it is important to separate residents of the designated region from nonresidents (tourists or visitors). In a strict economic impact analysis, only nonresident spending in an area is treated as "new dollars" to the region. The spending by local residents may not represent new spending if it otherwise would be spent somewhere else in the community. Separating residents from nonresidents can also be argued for based on significant differences in their spending patterns in the area.

The accuracy of the estimate of spending depends on the accuracy of the data the estimate is based on. Because total spending is generally estimated by multiplying a per visitor average by the number of visitors, we cannot have an accurate estimate without a good estimate of the number of visitors. The numbers we have should match the unit of analysis for which we want to estimate spending.

Because spending can vary significantly between different types of visitors, it is recommended that we estimate spending within narrowly defined visitor types or segments. Segments can be defined in several distinct ways, but for determining spending profiles of visitors, it is suggested that segments be defined based on the following categories:

Residents and nonresidents

Overnight visitors and day visitors

Type of lodging used

Visitors should also be segmented by type of transportation. For example, visitors arriving by air will have spending patterns quite different from auto travelers. After taking these segmentation variables into account, we may further segment by recreation activity subgroups (e.g., boaters, anglers, hunters, downhill skiers, sightseers) or **socioeconomic groups**. In a segmented analysis the total spending must be divided into the segments for which spending is estimated.

Units of Analysis

The units of analysis in travel and tourism studies vary in terms of the number of individuals in the particular group or party and the time period covered. Let's begin with the number of people in the group as the basic unit of spending analysis. In many cases, per day estimates will be derived from per party trip estimates, divided by the length of stay in the area. Visitor hours or visitor days, if accumulated across parties, are not good units for examining spending. Eight visitors staying one hour at a park would have very different spending patterns from one visitor staying eight hours in the park. Operationally, the *party* is generally defined as all persons arriving in the same vehicle or staying in the same room or at the same campsite. A *trip* encompasses the time from when the party leaves their permanent home, or in some cases some other temporary residence (seasonal home), until the time they return or otherwise terminate the given trip.

Tourism Arrivals and Projections

In 2007, international tourist arrivals grew by an estimated 6 percent to reach a new record figure of nearly 900 million.[31] This represents a growth of more than 100 million in two years, almost 52 million more than the arrivals in 2006. The United States alone welcomed a total of 55.9 million international visitors in 2007.[32] World gross domestic product (GDP) has experienced its longest period of sustained growth for 25 years, with figures around or above 5 percent since 2004.

Economies worldwide have shown increased volatility and although the recession may have 'bottomed out' it will likely take two or three years for confidence to grow again. UNWTO's *Tourism 2020 Vision* forecasts that international arrivals are expected to reach nearly 1.6 billion by the year 2020; 1.2 billion will be intraregional and 378 million will be long-haul travelers.[33] The total tourist arrivals by region shows that by 2020 the top three receiving regions will be Europe (717 million tourists), East Asia and the Pacific (397 million), and the Americas (282 million), followed by Africa, the Middle East, and South Asia.[34]

Trends and the Economic Impact of Travel and Tourism on the United States

After examining the international perspective, it is interesting to look a bit further into the economic impact of tourism on the United States in particular. Research conducted by the Travel Industry Association of America confirms that travel and tourism continues to be big business for the United States. The reason the travel and tourism industry has thrived is the prolonged growth of the U.S. and the world's economy, but now because of the decline in the value of the U.S. dollar, there will likely be fewer U.S. citizens visiting other countries and many more travelers visiting the United States.

With the huge sums of money spent on tourism and related goods and services, it does not take a college degree to figure out that the taxes generated as a result must be proportionate. As domestic and international travel in the United States has continued to increase, so have tax revenues for federal, state, and local governments.

▶ Check Your Knowledge

1. Why is it important to define regions when measuring tourism spending?
2. Into which groups are tourists usually divided when calculating tourism spending?
3. List some of the problems often associated with measuring tourism spending.

CAREER INFORMATION

Careers in the area of tourism economics may be limited, but they are interesting and well rewarded. Most nations, states, and some larger cities have economists who work on economic impacts, cost-benefit analysis, and the tourism multiplier. A bachelor's degree is a necessity and an advanced degree is often required.

CASE STUDY

Tourism Satellite Accounts for the United States

The United States, the largest economy in the world, does not have a central governmental organization that deals with tourism exclusively, whereas many other nations in the world have a Ministry of Tourism or the equivalent. Does it indicate that relative importance of tourism as an industry is insignificant in the United States? Can we know how many people are employed in tourism as an industry? What is the percentage of international visitors among the total tourism expenditures in the United States?

These are the questions that those in the tourism industry truly wish to answer. Tourism satellite accounts (TSAs; in the United States, which may be referred to as TTSAs—travel and tourism satellite accounts) is the accounting method used to answer these tough but important questions. You can answer some questions by yourself:

1. Go to www.bea.gov/industry/index.htm.
2. Scroll down the page to the Satellite Accounts section.
3. Under the "Survey of Current Business" heading, click the U.S. Travel and Tourism Satellite Accounts for 2005–2008 link. You need Adobe Acrobat Reader, which is a free download, to view this document. You can download Acrobat Reader by clicking the link in the right column of the Web page.

Questions

1. Which has been larger for the U.S. economy, the cash inflow from inbound travel and tourism (foreign visitors coming to visit the United States) or the cash outflow from outbound travel and tourism (American visitors visiting other nations)? (Hint: See Table G.)

2. What is the percentage of international visitors among the total tourism expenditures in the United States? (Hint: See Table H.)

3. In terms of expenditures, the amounts spent by business travelers are about twice as large as those of household (individual) travelers in the United States from 2000 to 2006. True or false? (Hint: See Table J.)

4. What is the total numbers of jobs in existence that are attributable to tourism as an industry in 2007? (Hint: See Table M.)

5. Who has been responsible for creating the TTSA for the United States?

Source: Eric S. Griffith and Steven L. Zemanek, *U.S. Travel and Tourism Satellite Accounts for 2005–2008*, Survey of Current Business, Bureau of Economic Analysis, June 2009, www.bea.gov/scb/pdf/2009/06%20June/0609_travel-text.pdf (accessed September 15, 2009).

Summary

1. Economics deals with the efficient utilization including consumption, distribution, and production of scarce resources (goods and services) to satisfy human wants. The study of travel and tourism economics is based on human beings' wants and decisions to travel and how they make the best possible use of resources. Tourism economics is built upon two theories: microeconomics and macroeconomics.

2. The law of demand indicates that if the price of one good or service increases while other prices stay the same, consumers have a tendency to substitute that good or service with a cheaper one.

3. Several other variables also affect demand, including prices in other locations, disposable income, popularity of the location or product, and the population's confidence about the future in general. These aspects contribute to the product's perceived value.

4. The demand for a good or service may be affected by a change in consumers' available incomes. A normal good or service will have an increased demand because of an increase in consumer income, whereas the demand for an inferior good or service will decrease.

5. The law of supply suggests that if the price of a good or service increases while other prices stay the same, producers tend to produce a greater quantity of that good or service. Other variables besides price can influence the quantity of a good or service supplied. For example, a government reduction in taxes paid by hotel owners will often result in an increase in supply.

6. The price at which quantity demanded equals the quantity supplied is called the equilibrium point—the price at which the demands/expectations of buyers and sellers balance.

7. Most consumers are highly price sensitive, which makes it important to consider the perceived value of a product/service. There are two common ways of pricing tourism services: the comparative approach (fitting expenses and profit margin within a predetermined price), and the cost-plus approach (costs are accounted for and an amount for profit is allocated before a selling price is determined).

8. Though impact from tourism is huge for most industrialized nations, its real costs and benefits are hard to measure. Some common ways of measuring and defining the impact of tourism are through direct and indirect tax income, impact on quality of life, opportunity costs, economic mix, cost-benefit ratio, the multiplier (ripple) effect, import propensity, distribution of tourism spending, cost of public services, public cost of immigrant workers, and social costs.

9. The three types of visitor spending are trip spending by visitors, durable goods purchased by visitors and households in the area, and government or organizational spending (construction and development/operations and maintenance). Spending should be further subcategorized to provide a correct and more complete estimate, and to identify the kinds of spending that are relevant and should be reported.

10. Tourism satellite accounts measure the significance of tourism's economic impact on national economies on an annual basis.

11. Expenditures from domestic and international travelers have grown to more than $550 billion. Tourism is the United States' largest services export industry, one of the country's largest employers, and the third largest retail sales industry.

Key Words and Concepts

comparative approach
cost-benefit analysis
cost-plus approach
demand
economics
equilibrium
import propensity
incentive
law of demand

law of supply
law of supply and demand
macroeconomics
market power
microeconomics
multiplier effect
opportunity cost
revenue management
scarcity

socioeconomic groups
supply
supply curve
System of National Accounts
  (SNA)
tourism satellite accounts
Transient Occupancy Tax (TOT)
yield management

Review Questions

1. What is the equilibrium point? Explain in your own words and use examples related to travel/tourism.
2. Differentiate between macroeconomics and microeconomics.
3. Which factors cause the demand curve to shift, and which cause movements along the demand curve?
4. Explain the difference between normal and inferior goods or services and name an example of each.
5. How would you define opportunity cost? Give an example of an opportunity cost you have experienced recently when you had to make a choice.
6. What aim does the cost-benefit ratio serve? What is the major problem concerning the cost-benefit ratio analysis?
7. Which would be your favorite activity in St. Lucia?
8. Explain the concept of tourism satellite accounts.

Interesting Websites

Asia-Pacific Economic Cooperation: www.apec.org/

Bureau of Economic Analysis: www.bea.gov/

Economist Intelligence Unit: www.eiu.com

International Labour Organization: www.ilo.org

Organization for Economic Co-operation and Development: www.oecd.org

Travel Industry Association of America: www.tia.org

World Tourism Organization: www.world-tourism.org

World Travel and Tourism Council: www.wttc.org

Internet Exercises

1. What is the current impact of the tourism and travel industry on the U.S. economy? In this context, find out current figures for tax revenues generated from this industry, and for the expenditures of domestic and international tourists in the United States. Compare with

past years to discern the current trend. (Hint: You can find these figures by browsing through Travel Industry Association's website at www.tia.org.)

2. What is the composition of tourists in the United States (domestic versus international)?

Which countries are the main generators for tourism and travel–related income to the United States? (Hint: At the website www.tia .org you can find useful links under Press Room and Research.)

Apply Your Knowledge

1. Explain in your own words the concepts of supply and demand. Give travel/tourism-related examples of each. Construct supply and demand curves to go with your examples.

2. Explain what the multiplier effect is and what stages it consists of by using the example of a tourist paying two room nights at the Marriott in Honolulu.

Suggested Activity

Give an example of how tourism demand and supply affects a tourism area or entity you are familiar with.

Endnotes

1. D. E. Lundberg, M. H. Stavenga, and M. Krishnamoorthy, *Tourism Economics* (Hoboken, NJ: John Wiley and Sons, 1995), 26.
2. Michael Parkin, *Microeconomics*, 7th ed. (Boston: Pearson Addison Wesley, 2005), 2.
3. Ibid.
4. David Begg, Stanley Fisher, and Rudiger Dornbusch, *Economics*, 8th ed. (Maidenhead, Kent, England: McGraw-Hill, 2005); John Tribe, *Economics of Leisure and Tourism* (Oxford, England: Butterworth-Heinemann, 1999), as cited in Loykie Lomine and James Edmunds, *Key Concepts in Tourism* New York: Macmillan, 2007), 60.
5. Ibid.
6. Nickerson and Wilton as cited in Timothy J. Terrell and Robert J. Johnson, "The Economic Impacts of Tourism: A Special Issue," *Journal of Travel Research* 45 (August 2006): 3–7.
7. Terrell and Johnson, "Economic Impacts of Tourism," 3–7.
8. Lundberg, Stavenga, and Krishnamoorthy, *Tourism Economics*, 29–30.

9. Al Ehnrbar, "Supply," *Concise Encyclopedia of Economics*, Library of Economics and Liberty, www.econlib.org/library/enc/Supply.html (accessed June 13, 2008).
10. Ibid.
11. This section draws upon: Donald Holecek, *Pricing Tourism Products and Services* (East Lansing: Michigan State University Extension, 1999). The author acknowledges with thanks the kind professional courtesy of Dr. Donald Holecek.
12. William A. McEachern, *Macroeconomics: A Contemporary Introduction*, 7th ed. (Mason, OH: Thomson, 2006), 60.
13. James D. Gwartney, Richard L. Strop, Russell S. Sobel, and David A. Macpherson, *Macroeconomics: Private and Public Choice*, 11th ed. (Mason, OH: Thomson–South-Western, 2006), 403.
14. Gwartney, Strop, Sobel, and Macpherson, *Macroeconomics*, 405.
15. Irvin B. Tucker, *Macro Economics for Today*, 4th ed. (Mason, OH: Thomson, 2005), 107.

16. QuickMBA.com, "Gross Domestic Product (GDP)," www.quickmba.com/econ/macro/gdp/ (accessed October 14, 2008).

17. Roberto Croes and Manual Vanegas Sr., "Cointegration and Causality between Tourism and Poverty Reduction," *Journal of Travel Research* 47 (2008): 94–105.

18. Central Intelligence Agency, "Bermuda," *CIA World Fact Book 2007*, https://www.cia.gov/library/publications/the-world-factbook/geos/bd.html (accessed September 12, 2009).

19. Yuri Mansury and Tadayuki Hara, "Impacts of Organic Food Agritourism on a Small Rural Economy: A Social Accounting Matrix Approach," *Journal of Regional Analysis and Policy* 37, no. 3 (2007): 213–222.

20. Christine Dellert, " 'UR GNG 2 LVE IT': Rosen College Professor Helps Attract Tourists to Ecuador," UCF Newsroom, May 28, 2008, http://news.ucf.edu/UCFnews/index?page=article&id=0024004106f02ced5011a120324f30350a (accessed September 12, 2009).

21. Michael Kinsley, "RMI's Economic Renewal Program: An Introduction," in *Economic Renewal Guide*, 3rd ed. (Snowmass, CO: Rocky Mountain Institute, 1997), www.rmi.org/images/other/EconRenew/ER97-02_EconRenewIntro.pdf (accessed September 12, 2006).

22. Travel Industry Association, www.tia.org/pressmedia/fun.facts.html (accessed September 23, 2009).

23. HIS Global Insight, "Tourism Satellite Accounts," http://globalinsight.com/ProductsServices/ProductDetail847.htm (accessed October 15, 2008).

24. Ibid.

25. United Nations World Tourism Organization, "Statistics and Measurement of Tourism," http://secnet041.un.org/unsd/EconStatKB/KnowledgebaseArticle10050.aspx accessed September 23, 2009.

26. Chris Cooper, John Fletcher, Alan Fyall, David Gilbert, and Stephen Wanhill, *Tourism: Principles and Practice*, 3rd ed. (Harlow, Essex, England: Pearson Education, 2005), 160.

27. This section draws on: http://www.indiandata.com/travel/economic_concepts.html (accessed September 23, 2009).

28. Ibid.

29. Ibid.

30. IHS Global Insight, "Tourism Satellite Accounts."

31. United Nations World Tourism Organization, World Tourist arrivals: From 800 million to 900 million in two years, *World Tourism Barometer* 6, no. 1 (January 2008), http://unwto.org/facts/eng/pdf/barometer/UNWTO_Barom08_1_excerpt_en.pdf (accessed September 12, 2009).

32. U.S. Department of Commerce, International Trade Administration, *United States Travel and Tourism Exports, Imports, and Balance of Trade: 2007*, www.tinet.ita.doc.gov/outreachpages/download_data_table/2007_International_Visitor_Spending.pdf (accessed October 7, 2008).

33. United Nations World Tourism Organization, "Tourism 2020 Vision," http://unwto.org/facts/eng/vision.htm (accessed September 12, 2009).

34. Ibid.

PART 2

Organizing Tourism

CHAPTER 5

Tourism Policy and Organizations

OBJECTIVES

After reading and studying this chapter you should be able to:

- Define tourism policy and list the reasons for tourism policy in a development context.

- Explain the purpose of tourism policy in its main areas of concern.

- Recall current issues and events in the main areas of concern of tourism policy.

- Describe the roles and operations of major tourism organizations.

GEOGRAPHY SPOTLIGHT

Eco-tourism: Morocco

Following suit with the green movement gripping the globe, the country of Morocco has grown into one of the largest and most established tourism destinations in its region—with every effort made to reduce environmental and cultural impact. Eco-tourism is the wave of the future in tourism development, and the country of Morocco has recognized this and created a niche in this area among the North African nations.

When the Global Code of Ethics for Tourism was written in 2001, the World Trade Organization (WTO) inspired all member nations to adopt, incorporate, and develop sustainable tourism practices.[1] As a result, a newly created committee of the government wrote the Moroccan Charter of Responsible Tourism.[2] This charter outlines

GEOGRAPHY SPOTLIGHT   *(continued)*

Courtesy of Luis Viega--
Getty Images/Image Bank

sustainable economic benefits and development. It also pledges to respect values by promoting and preserving the country's culture and heritage, respecting the environment to conserve for future generations, and avoiding exploitation of the people.

Eco-tourism/responsible tourism is often misinterpreted and misrepresented by many travelers and destinations as being an adventure travel experience. Although engaging with natural landscapes, geographical wonders, and flourishing ecosystems is a quality that adventure and eco-travel have in common, the latter goes beyond and considers the sustainability of the travel activity and the well-being of the local culture, and strives to form a harmonious relationship with the natural and sociocultural environment.[3]

Since 1996, Naturally Morocco Holidays, a "responsible tourism operator," has worked hard to reach the goal of connecting travelers with local people so that they can achieve understanding of local, cultural, and environmental issues.[4] This U.K.-based company strives to be entirely sustainable by considering the impact all of their staff, suppliers, clients, buildings, food and beverage, transportation, and tour activities have on the local environment. They work hard to minimize negative environmental, social, and cultural impacts, and at the same time to generate economic benefits for locals and host communities.[5]

Before a trip, tourists are provided with sustainable preparation guidelines in their tour packets. Information on the social and the political situation along with suggestions of ways to minimize impact on local cultures by considering dress codes, eating etiquette, alcohol taboos, photography code, and religious traditions are included. Those who are traveling by air are encouraged to offset the damage done to the atmosphere by the airplane by donating to Climate Care, a company that provides carbon-neutralizing offsets for the air transport by tree planting, providing financial support for renewable energy, and other methods.[6]

Clients of Naturally Morocco arrive in Agadir and are transported to their home base of Taroudant. Located about 225 kilometers south of Marrakesh, Taroudant has suffered a loss in tourism with the growth of Agadir. Naturally Morocco noticed this struggle and developed a home base and guesthouse in Taroudant, which also houses the offices of the Centre Environnemental et Culturel Marocain (CECM). This organization assists the local community in development projects and promotes conservation education for both locals and travelers. The food offered at the guesthouse is mostly vegan/vegetarian, gluten free, and derived from local products and cuisines. The four-story building's sustainable infrastructure includes solar panels for water heating, water conservation systems, and window/ceiling design to allow for ample ventilation.[7]

The company offers several different tour options based out of Taroudant that range from 5 to 16 days. Environmental impact is reduced through travel on foot or by horse with stops at either primitive camping sites or small environmentally friendly guesthouses. Visitors can experience the Anti Atlas Mountains, overnight desert excursions, the Dades Gorge, the Chefchaouen Mountains, Ouzoud Waterfalls, and Mogador Islands—one of the only places in the world to view the flight of the Eleonora's falcon.[8]

(continued)

GEOGRAPHY SPOTLIGHT *(continued)*

The Moroccan government and Naturally Morocco have completely embraced the principal values and practices of eco-tourism. Along with the governmental initiatives toward responsible tourism, a plan has been established to lessen the impact of the common traveler and motivate visitors to help minimize their impact on the natural and cultural environments.

Endnotes

1. World Tourism Organization, "Ethics in tourism: Background," www.world-tourism.org/code_ethics/eng/global.htm (accessed March 21, 2009).

2. Visit Morocco, "The Moroccan National Tourist Office," www.visitmorocco.com/index.php/eng/Footer/Qui-sommes-nous (accessed March 20, 2009).

3. International Ecotourism Society, home page, www.ecotourism.org/site/c.orLQKXPCLmF/b.4835241/k.D3B1/About_TIES__The_International_Ecotourism_Society.htm (accessed March 21, 2009).

4. Naturally Morocco Holidays, "Naturally Morocco Holidays: Experience the real Morocco," www.naturallymorocco.co.uk/morocco_inter_map_full.htm# (accessed March 21, 2009).

5. Ibid.

6. Ibid.

7. Ibid.

8. Ibid.

Source: Courtesy of The International Ecotourism Society (TIES), www.ecotourism.org.

Tourism policy, as defined in the *Dictionary of Hospitality, Travel and Tourism*, is plans, strategy, and actions of a decision-making body calculated to achieve identified, specific goals related to tourism.[1] The purpose of tourism policy is to provide structure and framework for tourism development by establishing goals and setting the guidelines for how certain goals should be met. For example, if the goal is to increase sustainable tourism in an economically depressed area, then the policy will give priority to development in the area. This might include providing low-interest development loans, providing temporary tax relief for businesses moving into the area, spending public money on agreed-on projects, actively promoting the tourism area, and coordinating the efforts of public and private organizations to achieve common goals of sustainable tourism development. The term *policy* is used to reflect a broader understanding of the political, societal, and human context of public sector–led decision making.[2] Figure 5–1 illustrates a framework model for tourism policy.

Stakeholder Input

With tourism policy formulation there are a number of stakeholders. In government at all levels, many agencies such as land use, zoning, waste management, transportation, port districts, and city planning offices, are stakeholders.

Tourism industries are represented by transport, lodging, restaurants, destination management, attractions, and events. Social, cultural, and environmental groups; residents of the community; and international and domestic tourists are also stakeholders. These various groups all have a stake in the development of tourism and need to be involved in policy formation to ensure success.

Vision, Mission, and Ecologically Sustainable Development

Someone or some group of community members, businesses, and government officials develops a vision and mission for tourism and tourism development for the nation, state, region, city, or community. For example, some years ago, the government of Mexico had a vision of several ideal locations for tourism development. Mexico applied for and received World Bank Development funding, and infrastructure was developed to support tourism development in Cancun, Ixtapa, Mazatlan, and Ziwataneo. These developments were planned as a national policy for tourism development. Acapulco, on the other hand, was not well planed; it just developed with shanty houses for staff on the hills around luxury hotels. Problems of pollution, overcrowding, water and waste management still continue to plague Acapulco.

Asset Evaluation

The purpose of asset evaluation is to examine and inventory the existing and potential assets of a destination. These assets would include infrastructure to attractions and entertainment, climate, and natural beauty. Elements that lend themselves to sustainable or eco-tourism development are assessed and prioritized for policy enactment.

Tourism Policy Goals

Once a tourism organization, whether it is a nation, state, region, county, city, or destination, has assessed its current circumstances, as in its strengths, weaknesses, opportunities, and threats (using a SWOT analysis), it can then determine where it wants to go by setting goals. With stakeholder input (see Figure 5–1), tourism policy can help move the organization toward goal accomplishment. Edward Inskeep, a former World Tourism Organization consultant and author, explains that policies usually evolve from surveys and analyses of present tourism development patterns and infrastructure, tourist attractions and activities, and the tourist markets.[3]

Inskeep suggests that governments should take the leading role in determining tourism policy because the policy developed will affect the entire country and its communities and must balance economic, environmental, and social concerns.[4] However, private industry and all community stakeholders should also be a part of the process for the policy to be successful. Inskeep adds that tourism policy can

Figure 5–1 • A Framework Model for Tourism Policy

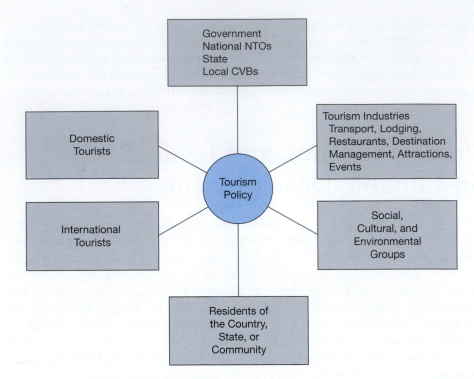

Figure 5–2 • Tourism Policy Stakeholders

take many forms and be developed for many different reasons, including economic, infrastructural, or social reasons, or for growth or **sustainable development**.

Tourism policy can be a catalyst for bringing together all the various stakeholders. Figure 5–2 shows the stakeholders interested in tourism policy. One important goal for tourism policy should include sustainable or green tourism, which is discussed in the section on the World Travel and Tourism Council (WTTC) later in this chapter and also in Chapter 6, "Tourism Planning and Sustainable Development."

One broadly conceptual scheme for considering the implications of policy change and development pressures in human endeavor is the ecologically sustainable development (ESD) framework as espoused in the *Brundtland Report*.[5] The principles and ideas set out in the *Brundtland Report* have been translated into national goals, policies, and more detailed principles. The ideas of ESD have also permeated the planning and policy documents of many countries.[6] Here are some examples of policy goals and characteristics of ecologically sustainable tourism[7]:

Goals

To improve the material and nonmaterial well-being of communities

To preserve intergenerational and intragenerational equity

To protect biological diversity and maintain ecological systems

To ensure the cultural integrity and social cohesion of communities

Characteristics

Tourism that is concerned with the equality of experiences

Tourism that has social equity and community involvement

Tourism that operates within the limits of the resource—including minimization of impacts and use of energy and the use of effective waste management and recycling techniques

Tourism that maintains the full range of recreational, educational, and cultural opportunities within and across generations

Tourism that is based on activities or designs that reflect the character of a region

Tourism that allows the guest to gain an understanding of the region visited and encourages guests to be concerned about, and protective of, the host community and environment

Tourism that does not compromise the capacity of other industries or activities to be sustainable

Tourism that is integrated into local, regional, and national plans

For example, say a country wants to increase the number of international visitors. It might establish tourism policies that improve or extend its airport's operations to allow for jumbo jets to land. If the government does not have the money necessary for the improvements, it may apply for a World Bank Development Loan. Likewise, if a country or state wants to build a cruise terminal or a convention center, it must bring all interested stakeholders together, establish a policy, and if necessary have a referendum to see whether local residents will allow taxpayer money to be used for such a facility.

A few years ago when Lego wanted to build a theme park called Legoland in Carlsbad, California, some residents were for the development, others against it. Those against Legoland were worried about increased congestion, noise, pollution, and so on. In the end, a majority of residents were in favor of a Legoland park as an additional attraction, an enhancement to the economy, and a contributor of tax revenues. Other examples of tourism policy are the United Nations Millennium Development and the Global Code of Ethics for Tourism Goals (both discussed later in this and other chapters).

There are also examples of tourism policy that did not work well. When only one entity in the tourism system is focused on rather than the whole tourism system, policy usually does not succeed. For example, Disneyland in California has a multilayered subsystem that developed around the huge Disney enterprise, including a slew of motels. Some places are more seedy than others; they were allowed to appear as a result of inadequate tourism policy and planning. Another example occurred in Africa, where, in some areas, hotels were established inside national parks and reserves without consideration of the ecological consequences and infrastructure needs that accompany development.[8] Sustainability has suffered, and now many of those parks and reserves are threatened, not only from an ecological point of view but also from the perspective of local, human needs. Both these cases illustrate that development that is considered from only a single perspective fails to take account of the strains inflicted on other areas of the system of which it forms a part.[9]

Tourism policy in cities can take many forms. For example, creating a special area of tourism interest such as an "Intermuros" like the one in Manila, Philippines, or a pedestrian way where no cars or bikes are allowed like the one in Munich, Germany. In Vigan, Philippines, an old Spanish-built World Heritage city, traffic is banned from one of the main plazas on the weekends so that tourists can enjoy the city as it used to be with *kalesa* (a horse-drawn carriage) rides around the old city on cobbled streets.

Impact Analysis

The impact analysis assesses the impact of the potential development from several key points of view, including the perspectives of access, transportation, infrastructure, social and cultural, employment, and especially environmental. Forecasting models are now available and being improved upon at the major universities to help with impact analysis. These models predict the extent of the various impacts that tourism could have on a destination.

Policy Enactment

Assuming all the parts fall into place and are agreed on by the stakeholders, then the policy can be enacted. Licenses and permits can be granted and the development can begin.

Government Initiatives and National Tourism Organizations Involved with Tourism Policy

Tourism policy development, as we know it, began after World War II. In 1945, Europe was in economic shambles as a result of the devastation and destruction caused by war. Governments quickly realized that tourism could be a catalyst for **economic development** by earning badly needed foreign exchange. Fortunately, many of Europe's historic treasures survived the war. Because Europe was able to develop its tourism more quickly than it could develop production industries, Americans who had the economic capability to travel there did, and in droves.[10] The U.S. government encouraged Americans to travel to Europe, and it wasn't until the mid-1950s that the U.S. government realized that a substantial deficit in tourism revenue had developed. American tourists were spending substantially more money in Europe than European tourists were spending in the United States. To solve this problem, President Eisenhower directed that a study of the barriers to international travel to the United States and ways of promoting such travel be undertaken in 1957.

In 1961, the International Travel Act founded the United States Travel Service (USTS) and stipulated that USTS seek to "stimulate and encourage travel to the United States by foreigners for the purpose of study, culture, recreation, business, and other activities as means of promoting friendly understanding and good will among peoples of foreign countries and the United States."[11] In the 1970s, a National Tourism Policy Study was undertaken by the Senate Commerce Committee, which by 1978 issued three reports. The first included an overview of legislation affecting tourism and problems associated with the federal role in tourism policy at the time. In 1979, the USTS was eliminated as a result of budget reductions.

When the **National Tourism Policy Act of 1981** became law, the act redefined the national interest in tourism and created the United States Travel and Tourism

Administration (USTTA), which replaced the United States Travel Service as the nation's government tourism office. The mission of the USTTA was this:[12]

- To reduce the nation's travel deficit
- To develop, plan, and carry out a comprehensive program to promote friendly understanding of the United States abroad and stimulate travel to the United States from abroad
- To encourage the development of tourist facilities, package tours, and other arrangements to meet the requirements of foreign visitors to the United States
- To encourage the simplification, reduction, or elimination of barriers to travel and the facilitation of international travel generally
- To collect, publish, and provide for the exchange of statistics, schedules of meetings and fairs, and information on other attractions that relate to international travel and tourism
- To consult with foreign governments on travel and tourism matters and represent U.S. tourism interests at international and intergovernmental meetings
- To develop and administer comprehensive programs relating to travel industry information, data service, training and education, and technical assistance
- To encourage travel to and from the United States on U.S. carriers
- To cooperate with the Department of Commerce to efficiently carry out the national tourism policy

Implementation of this act resulted not only in the development of a coherent tourism policy with the main purpose to promote tourism, but also emphasized the benefits that could be realized from tourism as a driving force that would stimulate economic, social, and political activities.

Policy Instruments

Bill Bramwell suggests four types of instruments for implementing tourism policy:[13]

- *Government encouragement* through information, education, and general persuasion directed at operators or communities in tourism areas.
- *Government financial incentives* that alter the prices facing businesses, tourists, or host communities. They may be taxes or subsidies intended to make some resources more or less expensive than others so that activities change in consequence. Examples are fees for entry to sites and attractions

Tourism policy made Route 66 an attraction for lovers of nostalgia.
Courtesy of Rick Pawlenty

and tourist taxes—also called transient occupancy or bed taxes—collected by lodging entities.

- *Government expenditure* on actions taken directly by government or state-owned agencies, such as spending on public transport, land purchase, and conservation measures in national parks, and on community development initiatives and waste management.
- *Government regulations* that prohibit or require particular courses of action and are backed up by the law. An example is land-use zoning in a tourist area.

U.S. Travel Association and Office of Travel and Tourism Industries

Strange as it may seem, the United States is the only industrialized nation in the world without a national tourism office—because the federal government decided to let private industry and the states promote tourism. Facing a lack of funding from the federal government, the tourism and travel industry realized that it had to act on its own to stimulate international travel to the United States. The Travel Industry Association (TIA; in January 2009, this organization changed its name to U.S. Travel Association) and the Tourism Industries/International Trade Administration at the U.S. Department of Commerce came together in a private–public partnership to promote tourism to the United States.

Because most countries maintain a National Tourism Office, the Office of Travel and Tourism Industries (OTTI) fulfills this inherent federal role of expanding travel and tourism business opportunities for employment and economic growth. The office is housed in the International Trade Administration, Manufacturing, and Services Bureau, Services Division of the Department of Commerce.

Based on Section 10 of Public Law 104-288, known as the National Tourism Organization Act of 1996, the Secretary of Commerce is responsible for performing critical tourism functions such as collecting and publishing comprehensive international travel and tourism statistics and other marketing information, facilitating the reduction of barriers to travel, representing the United States international travel and tourism interests to foreign governments, and maintaining the U.S. participation in international travel and tourism trade shows, as well as developing and implementing a comprehensive tourism policy and plan.

The primary functions of OTTI are as follows[14]:

- Management of the travel and tourism statistical system for assessing the economic contribution of the industry and providing the sole source for characteristic statistics on international travel to and from the United States
- Design and administration of an international promotion program and export expansion activities
- Development and management of tourism policy, strategy, and advocacy
- Provision of technical assistance for expanding this key export (international in-bound tourism) and assisting in domestic economic development

OTTI plays an active role in domestic and international policy issues as they relate to the U.S. travel and tourism industry. From a domestic policy perspective, OTTI serves as the Secretariat for the Tourism Policy Council. The Tourism Policy Council (TPC) is an interagency committee established by law for the purpose of ensuring that the nation's tourism interests are considered in federal decision making. Its major function is to coordinate national policies and programs relating to international travel and tourism, recreation, and national heritage resources that involve federal agencies. The TPC, originally established in 1981, was reauthorized by the U.S. National Tourism Organization Act of 1996 (22 U.S.C. 2124) and began to hold meetings from that point forward.

Today, within the federal government, there is a renewed sense of the importance of the travel and tourism industry to the U.S. economy. With the expanded charter of the Travel and Tourism Advisory Board to submit a national tourism strategy for the United States to the Department of Commerce secretary, the Tourism Policy Council is deemed to be the center for assessing the recommendations and implementation. The Assistant Secretary for Manufacturing and Services chairs the council on behalf of the secretary. Representatives from 17 federal agencies and departments are identified as members and formally invited to participate.

OTTI participates in the activities of global tourism development in multiple international intergovernmental organizations. Serving as the National Tourism Office for the U.S. government, OTTI is the representative to the Asia-Pacific Economic Cooperation (APEC) Tourism Working Group. The APEC Tourism Working Group promotes sustainable economic development through tourism and encourages investment and development throughout the Asia-Pacific region. The APEC Tourism Charter reflects a commitment to improve the economic, cultural, social, and environmental well-being of APEC member economies through tourism (www.apec.org).[15]

OTTI is also the U.S. government representative to the Organisation for Economic Co-operation and Development (OECD) Tourism Committee. The OECD Tourism Committee serves as a forum of exchange for monitoring policies and structural changes affecting the development of international tourism. The committee promotes sustainable economic growth through tourism initiatives. The committee serves to further statistical policy through its working group, in which the United States participates. Tourism is an important economic activity and issue of public policy in the majority of OECD member nations.

▶ Check Your Knowledge

1. Define tourism policy and explain its importance.

2. Who should assume the lead role in developing tourism policies? Why?

3. What caused the substantial deficit in tourism revenues for the United States in the 1950s?

4. Which legislative acts and institutions were introduced in an attempt to reduce this deficit?

Homeland Security, Visitor Facilitation, and Visitor Safety and Security

The Department of Homeland Security, Customs and Border Protection, issues travel news, travel alerts, advice for U.S. citizens and international visitors. International visitors to the United States from visa waiver countries are now required to apply for travel authorization online through the Electronic System for Travel Authorization (ESTA). Trusted Traveler programs provide expedited travel for preapproved, low-risk travelers through dedicated lanes and kiosks.

However, Homeland Security makes it harder for visitors from several non–Visa Waiver Program (VWP) countries to obtain a visa; therefore, fewer tourists are coming. This is because some people will not bother to go through all the hassles to get a visa (finger-printing all 10 fingers after paying $100 and queuing for hours at an American embassy). This has adversely affected inbound tourism and the associated spending within the United States by several billion, which also translates to thousands of lost jobs.

Visitor Facilitation

Visitor facilitation aims to improve the visitor's experience of gaining access to and arriving in the United States by reducing barriers to entry, continuing and expanding the Visa Waiver Program, and improving customer services at international ports of entry. This is important because the process by which an international visitor gains access to the United States provides that person with his or her first impression of the country. Therefore, it is utterly important to adopt technologies that can process visitors more quickly, as well as improve the operations of the inspection agencies.

In 1986, Congress created the **Visa Waiver Program (VWP)**, which provides access for international visitors from, currently, 34 low-risk countries to come to the United States for up to 90 days without having to obtain a visa. Participating countries in the VWP include the following:

Andorra	Italy
Austria	Japan
Australia	Liechtenstein
Belgium	Luxembourg
Brunei	Monaco
Denmark	The Netherlands
Finland	New Zealand
France	Norway
Germany	Portugal
Iceland	San Marino
Ireland	Singapore

Slovenia	Switzerland
Spain	United Kingdom
Sweden	Uruguay

Recent additions to the list include the Czech Republic, Estonia, Hungary, Latvia, Lithuania, the Republic of Korea, and the Slovak Republic. The VWP is important for the economy for three main reasons:

- It stimulates business by facilitating access of foreign visitors to the United States, who in turn spend more than $94 billion annually on hotel rooms, food and beverages, car rentals, and group tours.

- It keeps the United States competitive in the international travel market because it makes it easier for foreign visitors to enter the country. In some non–visa waiver countries, it can take months for a tourist to obtain a U.S. tourist visa from the U.S. Embassy or Consulate. Travelers from countries that participate in the VWP can come to the United States with just a valid passport and a return plane ticket.

- Because of its reciprocal nature, member countries are required to drop their visa requirements among each other. For example, Americans do not need a visa to visit Australia, France, or any other country in the program, which greatly facilitates travel among these countries.

Ensuring the permanency of the VWP demonstrates U.S. hospitality toward international visitors and is vitally important for enhancing the nation's competitiveness in this industry. One of the most important acts passed in the United States was the **Americans with Disabilities Act of 1990,** which addresses access for people with disabilities throughout most or all aspects of life, including employment and government services, among others. The travel industry was significantly affected by the Americans with Disabilities Act (ADA). With this act, the travel industry has made great strides in reducing physical barriers that inhibit or prevent the delivery of services to the traveling public with disabilities, which in the United States alone constitutes about 40 million people.[16] According to Title II of the act, public services cannot deny participation in programs or activities to people with disabilities when those services are available to people without disabilities. Public transportation systems, such as public transit buses, must also be accessible to individuals with disabilities. Title III of the act concerns public accommodations including restaurants, hotels, stores, and privately owned transportation systems, which must be built or made accessible to individuals with disabilities.

▶ Check Your Knowledge

1. Which is the fastest-growing segment in the tourism industry?
2. What is the purpose of visitor facilitation policies?

The objective of policies in **visitor safety and security** is to mobilize the industry to respond to concerns about traveler safety and security through community partnerships and disaster preparedness programs. Although many travelers might select a destination because of its physical or cultural environment, there are some who choose one destination over another for security reasons. The terrorist attacks on the World Trade Center in New York on September 11, 2001, and several other incidents of crime against international visitors in recent years have received international media attention that in turn has affected visitor destination choices in some key generating markets. Real and perceived threats to personal safety and security have a significant impact on the number of arrivals at destination cities. Perceptions of U.S. destinations as unsafe also have an obvious negative effect on travelers' comfort levels as well as their enjoyment of the destinations and attractions available.

To enhance security at U.S. borders and improve inspections, new policies have been drawn up in response to the attacks on September 11, including the Border Security Act of 2002, which requires U.S. visas, passports, and other travel documents issued after October 2004 to be fraud- and tamper- resistant and to contain biometric data. Additional safeguards were added to the Visa Waiver Program, including a review of all member countries no less than every five years to determine their eligibility for the program, the requirement for all VWP travelers

FOCUS ON

Tourism Management: The Elkhart County, Indiana, Convention and Visitors Bureau (ECCVB)

Daniel R. Fesenmaier

Located in northern Indiana, Elkhart County is one of the most vibrant tourism destinations in Midwest USA. As the leading organization charged with marketing the destination, the Elkhart County Convention and Visitors Bureau (ECCVB) is responsible for this success. Over the past two decades, the ECCVB has grown two brands to make tourism one of the most important industries in an area that is otherwise dominated by manufacturing and distribution centers. The most important brand is "Amish Country," which builds upon the fourth largest Amish community in the United States and presents the destination as a country-life destination. The second brand is "The RV Capital of the World" and is based on the recreational vehicle (RV) industry in the Elkhart County area, which produces more than 50 percent of all RVs in the United States. Today, this marketing program generates more than 380,000 room-nights sold in Elkhart County (in 2008) and $244 million in visitor spending (in 2007).

Today, ECCVB's policies are geared toward improving its competitive advantage. Marketing used to be the most important vehicle used by destination marketing organizations to promote the destination. However, over the past few years the operational goal of ECCVB shifted away from marketing to make it a leader in destination management. For example, ECCVB has become a co-creator of new tourism products including new festivals, events, the Quilt Gardens Tour, and recreational trails. Importantly, because many of these "products" are visited by local residents of Elkhart and surrounding counties, ECCVB has been recognized for helping increase the quality of life of the residents of Elkhart County. Additionally, ECCVB has changed dramatically the structure of the organization to include a number of "new tasks" such as community development, Internet marketing, direct marketing, and partnership development. For example, the position of technology marketing manager was developed as a response to the increasing importance of the Internet. Besides creating and updating the website (www.amishcountry.org), this position is responsible for the placement of ads on the Internet (e.g., Google adwords) and the implementation of to possess a machine-readable passport, as well as enhancements of the authority of the Attorney General so that, in consultation with the Secretary of State, he or she can temporarily remove a country from the program for emergency reasons, such as a breakdown in law and order, government overthrow, war, severe economic breakdown, or any other event that is a threat to U.S. security. These new regulations have helped VWP stimulate the U.S. economy.

Technology links all the departments and facilitates homeland security and communication. Some recent examples of technology are described in the next section.

Technology

Policies in **technology** are used for several different reasons, such as to increase use of new and emerging technologies that will enhance the visitor experience and dramatically change the way the travel and tourism industry does business.

Rapid developments in technology often result in significant changes in consumer behavior, which in turn constantly create a need for new business strategies,

---

FOCUS ON (*continued*)

Florian Zach

customer relationship technologies (e.g., leads management). A second newly created position was that of the destination development manager. This position focuses on creating new development projects in the area in cooperation with local organizations to drive visitor spending and economic impact. Restructuring the organization revealed that only three out of eight positions involve marketing tasks, whereas the remaining positions revolve around the development of new tourism products for the area. Thus, ECCVB moved from a traditional destination marketing organization toward a destination management organization that is actively involved in the development of the destination for the benefit of both tourists and local residents.

ECCVB's success as a destination management organization is based upon two key strategies. First, it was important to identify the nature of the market base for the two brands. Specifically, ECCVB purchased an efficient customer contact management system to better work through the many leads. Additionally, ECCVB collaborated with the National Laboratory for Tourism and eCommerce (NLTeC) at Temple University to develop a marketing information system (called SMART) to assist in conducting and managing visitor surveys. The main goal of the survey effort is to learn about visitors to the area in terms of satisfaction, demographics, the awareness of marketing efforts, and factors affecting their decision to visit the area. Over the past five years ECCVB has conducted studies at 21 festivals and 5 hotel properties and has shared the findings with festival organizers and managers of accommodation businesses to provide advice for future festivals or business.

Second, and most important, ECCVB utilizes the survey system as a tool for partnership development. Because ECCVB does not own accommodation properties or attractions, it depends upon the support of local (tourism) businesses and nonprofit organizations (e.g., chambers of commerce) as well as local and regional governments. These relationships are essential for the ECCVB to support the tourism industry in developing new projects. Hence, the relationships between ECCVB and its partners create win-win-win situations; not only between the ECCVB and its partner, but between the partners themselves, because those are the businesses where money is spent and agencies where taxes are paid. Finally, local residents are winners in that jobs are created and investments in attractions and the countryside increase the quality of life for residents.

Source: Courtesy of Daniel R. Fesenmaier and Florian Zach, Temple University.

marketing programs, and delivery systems. For example, travel and tourism businesses must today be prepared to market to customers who are better informed, better educated, and more sophisticated. Today's young generations of consumers grow up with computers, fax machines, cellular telephones, and electronic mail. This requires businesses in the travel and tourism industry to adopt new approaches to product development, sales, marketing, and ultimately, the delivery of visitor experiences.

New technologies provide an opportunity to universally enhance the overall travel experience. Some examples include the following:

- *Smart Cards*—A smart card is a plastic card embedded with a computer chip that stores and transacts value and/or information data between users. Smart cards are used in the health care, banking, transportation, and entertainment industries for anything from buying groceries, to going to the movies, using a pay phone, and visiting the library.

- *Electronic Ticketing*—Electronic tickets have replaced paper ticketing and greatly speed check-ins at airports. The traveler simply goes to the airport with the record number of the reservation, checks in, shows proper identification documents, and then receives the boarding pass for the plane. No documents are lost, last-minute changes and reservations can be made quickly, and the traveler can transfer to another carrier without his ticket needing to be reissued.

- *Automated Highway System (AHS)*—Specially equipped highway lanes guide vehicles automatically by controlling steering, braking, and throttling via sensors, computers, and communication devices on the lanes and in the vehicles. The system has great potential to eliminate driver error, enhance road safety, and reduce congestion, fuel consumption, and emissions. There are also automated toll payment options across the systems of states.

- *Airline Innovations*—New technological developments in the airline industry include new passenger jets such as the Airbus 380, which can fly 8,200 nautical miles nonstop, and fly from New York to Hong Kong with 853 passengers (if they are all in economy seating) or 525 passengers in three classes of seating.[17] The Boeing 787, a family of three different aircraft, also known as the Dreamliner, carries between 210 and 330 passengers up to 3,050 nautical miles depending on which aircraft is used.[18] Both Airbus's and Boeing's latest aircraft are about 20 percent more fuel efficient and are less noisy than their predecessors.

- *Electronic Information Kiosks*—These kiosks are freestanding or desktop appliances with sensitive touch screens. They are set up in public places to provide real-time traffic and transit status reports and other useful information for travel planning and decision making. Handheld personal digital assistants (PDAs) also can give the same information.

- *Intelligent Transportation Systems*—Intelligent transport systems work hand in hand with traveler information systems to provide travelers with pertinent information about the transportation system, such as schedules of public transportation, travel time between point A and point B, carpools, and the availability of parking spaces in certain areas. Travelers can access this information via the phone, television, radio, pagers, the Internet, handheld electronic devices, and electronic signs.

- *CARS-511 (Condition Acquisition and Reporting System)*—CARS-511 is a system put in place by a multistate agreement in North America that provides immediate access to nationwide real-time travel information on road conditions, public transportation, and traffic simply by dialing 5-1-1.

Technological advances like these expedite and ease travel by giving visitors more time to participate in activities at destinations. The speed at which many of these new technologies are adopted has a direct impact on the future of the U.S. travel and tourism industry. It is essential that leaders in the industry develop strategies to adopt new technologies at all levels of the industry through new awareness and educational programs.

Research and Statistics

The objective of **research and statistics** about tourism is to develop a reliable economic analysis system of the tourism industry that uses uniform public and private sector data collection and reporting methods. These data will help better represent the tourism industry in government accounting systems, which is one area of tourism research and statistics.

Measuring the travel and tourism industry is very difficult because economic activity of tourism is not as easily identifiable as that of other industries producing more tangible products, such as manufacturing and retail. Unlike most industries, tourism industries are made up of many different sectors that sell different products and services, such as the hotel industry, the passenger airline industry, and the food and beverage industry. Expenditures from the travel and tourism industry cut across different segments that do not fit into a single product SIC (Standard Industrial Classification) code or NAICS (North American Industry Classification System) code, by which most economic sectors are measured.

Therefore, tourism satellite accounts (TSAs) were developed to measure travelers' purchases of different products and services, such as airfares, lodging, food and beverages, shopping, and other travel expenditures. TSAs clearly separate and show the major components of tourism in the U.S. economy, including the production of tourism commodities (goods and services purchased), the supply and consumption of tourism commodities, tourism (purchasing) demand by type of commodity and type of visitor, tourism gross domestic product, and tourism employment. The information gathered and obtained is of great importance to policymakers, investors, employers, and employees in the industry. TSAs are described in more detail in Chapter 4.

In the coming years, more U.S. travel companies are expected to make positive economic impacts on the U.S. economy through overseas operations. As U.S. companies strive to become a major force in all viable international tourism markets, it is crucial that the research and data that guides decision making is consistent throughout the industry and compatible with internationally accepted data collection and reporting methods, which greatly enhances accuracy, comparability, and understanding of the economic importance of travel and tourism as the industry moves through the new century. Organizations working in this area include the **Travel and Tourism Research Association (TTRA)**, which is an international network of more than 800 travel and tourism research and marketing professionals who advocate standards, quality research, and marketing information to the industry. TTRA has become the recognized source for providing current data on the travel and tourism industry to businesses and governments to develop tourism policies and marketing strategies. Other organizations providing research data about the travel and tourism industry in the United States and worldwide include TIA, the World Tourism Organization, Pacific Asia Travel Association (PATA), the International Association of Convention and Visitors Bureaus (IACVB), as well as various research and statistical publications, such as *The National Travel Monitor* published by Ypartnership/Yankelovich Inc.

Travel research is important because it can help identify problems and their causes; trends or market changes; new markets, products, and services and uses for products and services. It aids in sales promotion by finding out what customers' attitudes and preferences are and can also create goodwill because customers feel that the company or destination cares about them. Finally, research may help reduce waste by identifying inefficient operational methods that can then be improved.

Education and Training

Education and training is vital in the industry to increase awareness of travel and tourism's contribution to job creation, and improved public and private sector coordination of education and training initiatives enhance career and employment opportunities and worker skills.

Employment in the tourism industry has three specific characteristics:

- *Seasonal*—**Seasonality** arises because visitor demand is not spread evenly throughout the year. A good example is the winter tourism industry in Lake Tahoe in California attracting many visitors around Christmas or Easter time, which at the same time increases the demand for employees in the region, such as skiing instructors and staff for hotels.

- *Labor Intensive*—**Labor intensity** occurs in the major tourism industries, meaning it takes more employees per customer to deliver the tourism product or service than, for example, it takes in the manufacturing industry, where automated production lines enable one person to produce thousands of units easily. In this respect, tourism increases employment and supports local economies.

- *Higher Employment Growth*—There is higher **employment growth** in the travel and tourism industry as compared to the total economy because of the demand for tourism by an increasing number of people.

To ensure that the visitor's or guest's experience will be outstanding and of highest quality, managers and human resource professionals are increasingly creating learning organizations, which are dedicated to the continuous improvement of the service process to obtain excellence. The process begins at recruitment and continues through actual service delivery to its evaluation and improvement, if needed, to better tailor it to the client's expectations. Managers need to select the right employees, who not only are qualified for the job, but also have a personable attitude and motivation. To let employees know how they're doing, supervisors must provide feedback, such as suggestions, support, or training to enhance knowledge and skills, as well as give incentives to employees to keep them motivated. Incentives can include giving employees more responsibility on the job or transferring them to higher positions; giving more pay, vacation days, or other bonuses; and, of course, compliments or organizational recogni-

Training is a vital part of delivering exceptional guest service.
Courtesy of John Coletti, Allyn & Bacon

tion when individuals accomplish a project or meet and exceed objectives and standards. On the whole, a workplace environment needs to be created that facilitates motivation and excellence.

With the continued expansion of travel and tourism, increasingly demanding consumers, changing technologies, and specific customer preferences and needs, the demand for well-educated and professionally trained personnel is increasing. A qualified employee in the travel and tourism industry is expected to have the necessary operational skills for the job: knowing certain computer programs, for example, reservation systems in hotels and airlines. In addition, the employee should also have excellent communication skills and a positive work attitude; be self-motivated and sensitive to and respectful of cross-cultural differences; speak at least one language other than English; and greatly increase his or her chances of getting a job by demonstrating study or work experience in other countries.

Key corporations and organizations of the travel and tourism industry encourage and facilitate the expansion of training standards, certification, and opportunities to support enrollment of **school-to-work programs** and career paths for students interested in pursuing a profession in travel and tourism. These organizations include the Travel Industry Association of America (TIA), the American Hotel and Lodging Association (AH&LA), the National Restaurant Association (NRA), the International Council on Hotel, Restaurant Institutional Education (I-CHRIE), the International Association of Convention and Visitor Bureaus (now the DMAI), the Academy of Travel and Tourism, the U.S. Chamber of Commerce, the Hotel Employees and Restaurant Employees International Union, the Department of Labor, the Department of Education, and private companies such as Marriott International and McDonald's Corporation.

Environment

Environmental policies are developed to preserve natural, historic, and cultural resources for future generations, and to expand urban and rural economic development opportunities through a national strategy for fostering environmental and cultural travel and tourism.

The U.S. national parks are among the country's most powerful magnets for both international and domestic travelers, and public lands generally are the core of the U.S. national tourism resource base. Adequate funding, balanced management, and responsible development of federal and state public lands and cultural resources are all critical to continued tourism growth.

Balanced development of travel and tourism has a direct impact on the quality of life of residents, local economies, and visitors' experiences. For example, the tranquility and beauty of many public lands attract visitors, but overcrowding and/or lack of adequate infrastructure to support visitor populations can degrade enjoyment. Preventing littering of the natural environment and cities and controlling and reducing pollution from car exhaust fumes and waste oil from ships are necessary to maintain clean water for recreation, fauna and flora of wetlands, seas and lakes; these are all areas of critical concern to the quality of life of local residents, the protection of the environment and cultural heritage of the people, as well as the health of the tourism industry. Therefore, everyone having an impact on the environment, including locals, tourists, and employees in the industry, must be educated about ecosystems and cultural sensitivities. Diplomatically stated do's and don'ts are frequently part of visitor orientation at environmentally fragile and culturally sensitive tourism destinations. The community-wide economic benefits generated by visitors provide local communities with jobs and stimulated economies and provide museums, historic sites, and cultural and natural attractions with funds crucial to maintaining and expanding their product offering.

Last, consumer and trade surveys indicate a growing interest in rural tourism, multicultural tourism, eco-tourism, and other alternatives to mass tourism. Cultural organizations are excellent resources for the tourism industry in providing quality visitor experiences. They can ensure accurate interpretation of local history and quality arts experiences while ensuring the continued vitality of community life for residents and visitors alike.

▶ Check Your Knowledge

1. Give examples of new technologies that may enhance the tourist's experience.

This diver is careful not to disturb the environment—including the sharks!

Courtesy Mark Green

2. Why is it so difficult to develop reliable statistics for the tourism industry as compared to other industries?

3. Which are the special characteristics of employment in the tourism industry?

Transportation Infrastructure

The **transportation infrastructure** is the system that includes the facilities, roads, bridges, equipment, and organizations needed to make transportation functional and available to the traveling public. This system encompasses cars, limousines, taxis, buses, trains, aerial tramways, subways, airplanes, ships and cruise lines, and all other means of transportation available to travelers.

The transportation system of the United States today comprises about 3.9 million miles of public roads, 120,000 miles of major railroads, more than 25,000 miles of commercially navigable waterways, and more than 5,000 public-use airports. The transportation system also counts more than 500 major urban public transit operators and more than 300 ports on the coasts, inland waterways, and the Great Lakes.[19] Over the last century, the development and refinement of transportation technologies increased dramatically. Infrastructure transportation systems have been developed for land, sea, and air domains and have made it possible for us to have increasingly fast and efficient access to all parts of the world. The objective of tourism policy in this important and ever-expanding domain is to ensure appropriate funding for the U.S. transportation and natural resources infrastructure, which is essential to keep pace with the increasing numbers of tourists and changing travel patterns, and the need for more efficient transportation in terms of cost and time. U.S. policy influences transportation in several ways: funding for air, road, rail, and sea passenger facilities and operational activities. U.S. policy includes the granting of visas; for example, Chinese group tours are now arriving in numbers, a remarkable change over a few years ago.

Highway Travel Issues

Congestion has become a major issue on the U.S. public road system. Travel in the United States is increasing and with it more congestion on the nation's highways and airways, which costs billions of dollars each year in wasted fuel and lost time. Congestion is in fact a growing threat to quality of life and the economy of the nation, and it affects the traveler's or tourist's experience negatively. Sound policies are needed in the areas of, for example, support for and extension of the public transportation system.

Diverging viewpoints still exist about solutions to the problem of increasing road traffic considering the fact that the population of the nation is growing constantly. Some people favor expansion of existing roadways; others believe that funds should rather be invested in improving the public transportation system, including, among others, buses and railways. The task of policymakers in regard to this issue is to take into consideration several alternatives and weigh their benefits and costs, as well as their adaptability to local and regional areas and need.

International Tourism Organizations

Travel and tourism is recognized and facilitated by a wide variety of organizations large and small, international and local, private and governmental. These organizations exist to help tourism entities and make it easier and more enjoyable for tourists to experience their destinations. The following subsections of this chapter present these organizations.

Tourism, like everything else, needs some form of organization and structure to prosper. In tourism, some large organizations maintain a global presence such as the United Nations World Tourism Organization (UNWTO), a specialized agency of the United Nations, and the World Travel and Tourism Council (WTTC). Others focus on regional interests such as the Pacific Asia Travel Association (PATA), or national interests, such as the national tourism offices (NTOs) of various countries. State or provincial interests also exist and are represented accordingly. Each of these organizations is important because it strives to enhance the tourism experience for both tourists and citizens. Examples of how these organizations help shape tourism policy are also given in the following sections.

The United Nations World Tourism Organization

The leading intergovernmental tourism organization is the United Nations World Tourism Organization (UNWTO). Formed in 1975 and headquartered in Madrid, Spain, it represents official countries and territories, national promotion, and development. The UNWTO is recognized as a specialized agency of the United Nations Economic and Social Council because of the vital information it gathers and publishes on world tourism trends, marketing approaches, and the protection of natural and cultural resources.

The UNWTO's mission is to develop tourism as a significant force for fostering international peace and respect for human rights, as well as economic prosperity, job creation, and international trade. The UNWTO also aims to provide incentives for protecting the environment and cultural heritage. Its members include 160 countries and territories and some 350 affiliate members representing transport companies, tourism development agencies, educational institutions, local governments, and private sector companies such as tour operators, airlines, and hotel groups.[20] The UNWTO provides a vital forum for governments and industries to meet and address issues of common interest and concern.

The UNWTO believes that governments have a vital role to play in tourism. The organization exists to help nations throughout the world maximize the positive impacts of tourism, such as job creation, new infrastructure, and foreign exchange earnings, while at the same time minimizing negative environmental or social impacts. The UNWTO also serves as a mediator in the event of a tourism-related dispute between nations.

Overall, the UNWTO works to increase the awareness of and appreciation for tourism. One of its ways of doing this was the establishment of World Tourism Day, a day dedicated to fostering international awareness of the importance of tourism and its social, cultural, political, and economic values. Since 1980, World Tourism Day is commemorated on September 27 each year, which is the anniversary of the adoption of the UNWTO Statutes. This day also signifies the end of the high season in the Northern Hemisphere and the beginning of the season in the Southern Hemisphere, when tourism should be of interest to hundreds and thousands of people worldwide.

In its core activities, the UNWTO assists governments with tourism issues such as feasibility studies, technology transfer, and marketing projects, as well as provides a growing network of training and education centers. By participating in sustainable development forums, such as the Earth Summits in Rio and Johannesburg, and the Globe seminars in Canada, the UNWTO attempts to help translate environmental concerns into practical measures. Furthermore, the UNWTO acts as an information resource center to its members on trends and statistics in the global tourism environment and is strongly engaged in facilitating and improving the quality of international travel by promoting **trade liberalization**, as well as the standardization of travel documents, safety, security, and technical standards.

St. Petersburg, Russia, a UNESCO World Heritage Site
Courtesy of Mark Green

An example of tourism organizations linking with tourism policy is the second annual United Nations World Tourism Organization Ministers' Summit where tourism ministers debated the challenges of the global economic downturn, climate change, and poverty reduction targets. UNWTO Secretary-General Francisco Frangialli said: "A new and more demanding economic scenario has emerged. While factoring this into the international tourism agenda, we must not lose sight of the challenges of climate change and the fight against poverty.[21]

UNWTO Regional Activities

The UNWTO has regional offices and programs throughout the world; some examples of their activities include:

- *Regional Support*—The UNWTO has a representative in each region of the world (Africa, Americas, East Asia and the Pacific, Europe, Middle East, and South Asia), who meet with the top tourism officials of these regions to analyze problems and find solutions, create specific development projects, and hold national seminars on particular problems of a country, for example, eco-tourism in Kyrgyzstan.

- *Regional Promotion Projects*—In cooperation with the United Nations Educational, Scientific and Cultural Organization (UNESCO), the UNWTO carries out special projects that promote tourism to a group of member countries. For example, in 1994, the UNWTO launched the Silk Road project aimed at revitalizing through tourism the ancient highways used by Marco Polo and the caravan traders who came after him. Sixteen Silk Road countries have joined together for the project and joint promotional activities include a brochure and video, familiarization trips, and special events at major tourism trade fairs.

The UNWTO and Ethical Issues

The UNWTO has adopted a code of ethics, an overview of which is as follows:

- *Adoption of the Global Code of Ethic*—In 1999, at a UNWTO general assembly meeting in Santiago, the principles of the Global Code of Ethics were adopted. The code affirms, for example, the right to tourism and the freedom of tourism movements, tourism's contribution to the mutual understanding and respect between peoples and societies, and tourism as a factor of sustainable development and as a user and contributor to the cultural heritage of humankind. Francesco Frangialli, former secretary-general of the United Nations World Tourism Organization, says this about the code:

  > The Global Code of Ethics for Tourism sets a frame of reference for the responsible and sustainable development of world tourism. It draws inspiration from many similar declarations and industry codes that have come before and it adds new thinking that reflects our changing society at the beginning of the 21st century.
  >
  > With international tourism forecast to nearly triple in volume over the next 20 years, members of the World Tourism Organization believe that the Global Code of Ethics for Tourism is needed to help minimize the negative impacts of tourism on the environment and on cultural heritage while maximizing the benefits for residents of tourism destinations.
  >
  > The Global Code of Ethics for Tourism is intended to be a living document. Read it. Circulate it widely. Participate in its implementation. Only with your cooperation can we safeguard the future of the tourism industry and expand the sector's contribution to economic prosperity, peace and understanding among all the nations of the world.[22]

- *Statement on the Prevention of Organized Sex Tourism*—In 1997, the UNWTO established the Task Force to Protect Children from Sexual Exploitation in Tourism, a global action platform of tourism-related key players from the government and tourism industry sectors, international organizations, nongovernmental organizations, and media associations whose aim is to prevent, uncover, isolate, and eradicate the sexual exploitation of children in tourism. Such exploitation takes place in several countries such as Thailand and Brazil.

International Labour Organization

The International Labour Organization (ILO) is a UN specialized agency that promotes social justice and internationally recognized human and labor rights. The ILO was created under the Treaty of Versailles in 1919 together with the League of Nations and outlived that body to become the first specialized agency associated with the United Nations in 1946. Its original membership of 45 nations has now grown to 173.

The ILO formulates international labor standards and sets minimum standards of basic labor rights, such as the right to organize, to form associations, to bargain collectively, to equality of opportunity and treatment, and to not be forced into labor. The methods by which the ILO achieves its goals include formulating international policy standards and programs, supervising their observance, extending technical cooperation in the field to member states, and conducting research, training, and education to help advance all these efforts.

The ILO views the tourism industry sector as one of vital importance to most countries. For many developing nations, tourism is a valued contributor to foreign exchange and employs far more people than manufacturing industries do. Tourism, therefore, can positively contribute to the social, economic, and cultural well-being of a developing community. The ILO assists member countries by means of technical cooperation activities, which are designed to meet the specific needs of each individual country. These may take the form of field studies and preparatory work that usually precede large-scale projects. An example is planning and organizing of training for jobs in the tourism industry, particularly hotels and restaurants.

ORGANIZATIONAL PROFILE

World Travel and Tourism Council

Courtesy of Mark Green

The World Travel and Tourism Council (WTTC) is the global business leader's forum for travel and tourism. Its members are chief executives from all sectors of the travel and tourism industry, including accommodation, restaurants, foodservice, catering, cruises, entertainment, recreation, transportation, and other travel-related services.

The WTTC's primary goal is to offer information on current issues and trends for the industry players as well as to governments involved, and to provide effective solutions in good human resource practices in the global travel and tourism industry. The following seven strategic priorities of the WTTC focus on the potential for the travel and tourism industry to generate millions of new jobs.

- Envision the future for travel and tourism and make it "everybody's future."
- Measure and communicate travel and tourism's strategic and sustainable economic contribution.
- Promote the positive image of travel and tourism as a provider of jobs and career opportunities.
- Encourage free access, open markets and open skies, and the removal of barriers to growth.
- Match infrastructure and customer demand.
- Develop access to capital resources and technological advancement.
- Promote responsibility in natural, social, and cultural environments.

(continued)

ORGANIZATIONAL PROFILE *(continued)*

The WTTC also works with governments to make them realize the full economic importance of the world's largest generator of wealth and jobs, and seeks to engage all governments in the creation of new jobs across the world economy during the coming years. The concept of FAST—Future Automated Screening for Travelers, which uses biometric identification, computerized processing, and automated entry to expedite border crossing while enhancing security—gives governments the opportunity to achieve a uniform standard for future automated border clearance arrangements. Furthermore, the WTTC also provides information on the travel and tourism industry, its issues, and policies in a number of categories. The organization established the WTTC Human Resource Center, which provides information and tools on the global travel and tourism sector, advisory and consulting services, product marketing and distribution, as well as a collection of case studies and good practices from travel and tourism businesses around the world.

The WTTC and the Green Globe Program

One of the fundamental beliefs of the WTTC is that the travel and tourism industry and governments worldwide have a shared stake in the protection of the environment. Clean air and water as well as attractive scenery are at the heart of the product. Growth, and the jobs it will create, is highly dependent on building a sound environmental framework for tomorrow's development. Therefore, the WTTC created the Green Globe program, which also plays an important role in ensuring market responsiveness to the environmental imperative.

Green Globe, which counts membership of almost a thousand companies in more than a hundred countries,[23] encourages companies to enter a continuing cycle of improvement, with guidance and support services to help adapt corporate culture and practice. The Green Globe program asks its tourism businesses and destinations members to make a commitment to, within an agreed timeframe, achievement of sustainable tourism practices. More specifically, these practices include to reduce greenhouse gases, improve energy efficiency, protect air quality, control noise, manage waste water, develop better community relations, respect cultural heritage, enhance social performance, conserve nature and wildlife, practice good land management, and conserve ecosystems.[24] By improving environmental performance, companies and communities not only limit pollution or waste, but can reduce costs, engage workers, and attract positive local interest and goodwill. Ultimately, Green Globe's objective is to provide consumers with an assurance that its members are striving toward improving the future of travel and tourism.

Today, Green Globe 21 is the world's only truly global travel and tourism certification program, which arose from Agenda 21's principles for sustainable development and was endorsed by 182 heads of state at the 1992 United Nations Earth Summit in Rio de Janeiro. The program is managed by several joint venture partners—Green Globe Ltd. (London), Green Globe Asia Pacific (Canberra), the Caribbean Alliance for Sustainable Tourism in Puerto Rico, and the Entrepreneurship Academy in Africa. Furthermore, it has also formed strategic alliances that include the Société Générale de Surveillance, Anglo Japanese American Registrars USA, the Tourism Industry Association of New Zealand, and the Ecotourism Association of Australia. All these partners and alliances make it possible for Green Globe to operate on a global scale, which is crucial for the purpose of the organization, if it is to achieve environmental, social, and cultural improvements on the global, national, and local scales.

► Check Your Knowledge

1. What is the mission of the World Tourism Organization?
2. What activities is ILO involved in?
3. Describe tourism satellite accounts.

International Air Transport Association (IATA)

The modern IATA was founded in Havana, Cuba, in April 1945 and is the successor to the International Air Traffic Association, which was founded in the Hague in 1919, marking the year of the world's first international scheduled services. IATA today unites approximately 280 airlines and is regarded as the global organization for international air carriers. With the mission to serve and represent the airline industry, IATA coordinates the transportation of passengers, freight, and mail in its global airline network, as well as ensures that its member airlines operate in a safe, secure, reliable, efficient, and economical manner.

Today the airline industry is more than 100 times larger than it was 50 years ago, and it is currently undergoing what can be the greatest upheaval of its history. With globalization and the merging of international markets, rising fuel and labor costs resulting in several airline bankruptcies, cultural diversity, changing technologies, rapidly changing consumer preferences, increased levels of competition, liberalization, and privatization and global alliances, IATA constantly needs to adapt to meet the demands of its members and extend its range of services to help members improve the management of their businesses. So far, IATA has significantly contributed to facilitating the expansion of this industry.[25] It provides information to the aviation industry on safety and operations, financial management, distribution systems, passenger and cargo sales, training, publications, market research and statistics, legal services, governments, and other international relations. IATA's standards, practices, and procedures have a multitude of benefits for those participating in the airline industry, including the following[26]:

- Consumers benefit from cheaper airline tickets and one-stop shopping because IATA's interairline cooperation greatly simplifies the shipping and travel process. For example, a passenger can purchase a single airplane ticket for connecting flights to different countries on different airline companies with one phone call, and he or she can pay for the ticket in one currency.

- Third parties, such as passenger and cargo agents, are represented to the airline industry through IATA and can thereby benefit from the industry's professional skills and agency service standards.

- IATA links airlines from different countries, which benefit from joint resources despite country differences including language, currency, culture, and customs. The joint resources provide the airlines with more opportunities, less costs, and innovative problem-solving approaches, which allows them to work more efficiently.

- IATA develops aviation industry working standards, such as for safety and efficiency, that appeal to most governments, which can benefit from the organization's experience and expertise in the aviation industry.

Besides developing standards and procedures for the airline industry to enhance customer service continuously, IATA is also involved with environmental and consumer issues, legal and industry support, corporate communications, scheduling, and facilitation. The organization is also a valuable information source on the world airline industry. Its Airline Product Database and annual World Air Transport Statistics publication are valuable sources of international airline data, helping consumers and industry members compare airline carriers and measure their performance.

International Civil Aviation Organization (ICAO)

Truly international air navigation requires uniformity of numerous factors on a worldwide scale for safety in operating procedures. This is why, in November 1944, 32 states set up the ICAO by signing the Convention on International Civil Aviation with the goal to secure international cooperation to unify regulations, standards, and procedures regarding civil aviation matters. At the same time, the Chicago Conference accomplished very important work in the technical field by laying the foundation for a set of rules and regulations regarding safety in flying, which paved the way for the application of a common air navigation system throughout the world.[27]

ICAO has since acted as the central agency to unify rules and regulations concerning training and licensing of aeronautical personnel both in the air and on the ground, rules for air traffic control systems and practices, communication systems and procedures, registration and airworthiness requirements of aircraft in international air navigation, as well as aeronautical meteorology, maps, and charts. The organization, which is headquartered in Montreal and currently consists of 190 nations,[28] works by dividing the world into different regions, such as the North Atlantic region and the European-Mediterranean region, and establishing regional offices. These regional offices assist states in solving specific air navigation problems and make sure that regional activities, even though they may vary because of differences in economic, technical, and social environments, are in sync with international air transportation.

Recently, the ICAO reinforced its global aviation security strategy as a response and long-term safeguard against possible terrorist activities in the airline industry. Within days of the attacks on the World Trade Center, the ICAO-contracted states reviewed existing security regulations and tightened security measures, particularly at airports. Many new standards were adopted, such as reinforced cockpit doors, to restore consumer confidence in air transportation. On a long-term basis, ICAO's security strategy focuses on the detection of threats to airline security so that proactive measures can be taken in time, continual monitoring of and upgrades to existing security processes, and expediting the clearance of passengers while maintaining the highest level of security, which can be accomplished in part through new technology such as machine-readable travel documents and biometric identification.[29]

▶ Check Your Knowledge

1. How many countries are members of the Green Globe program?

2. In what way does IATA bring benefits to the players in the airline industry?

3. When was ICAO started?

Regional International Organizations

Many important tourism organizations operate on a regional level. The most important ones, namely, the Organisation for Economic Co-operation and Development (OECD), the Pacific Asia Travel Association (PATA), the Caribbean Tourism Organization (CTO), and the European Travel Commission (ETC), are described in the following subsections.

Organization for Economic Co-operation and Development (OECD)

The OECD was set up under a convention in Paris in 1960 and is today known as an international organization assisting governments in the domains of economic, social, and governance challenges of a globalized economy, such as democratic governance and the market economy. Its governing body, the council, consists of representatives of member countries, who meet to discuss, develop, and refine policies by comparing experiences, seeking answers to common problems, and working to coordinate domestic and international policies to deal with the increasingly globalized world. Members can establish either legally binding agreements, for example, codes for the free flow of capital and services between countries, or nonbinding or so-called soft-laws on difficult issues, such as guidelines for multinational enterprises. Besides agreements, OECD members also discuss national policies and their impact on the international community. The OECD has a secretariat in Paris, which monitors trends, analyzes and forecasts developments, and is regarded as one of the world's most reliable sources on statistical, economic, and social data.

Original OECD members included several European and North American countries, which have over time been joined by Japan, Australia, New Zealand, Mexico, Korea, Finland, and four former communist states in Europe, namely, Hungary, Poland, the Slovak Republic, and the Czech Republic. Today, its 30 members account for two-thirds of the world's production in goods and services[30] and contribute to about 70 percent of world tourism trade[31]; however, the OECD proposes that membership is not exclusive and only limited by a country's commitment to a market economy and democracy. Nonmembers are invited to subscribe to OECD agreements and treaties, and the organization is now involved in work with 70 nonmember countries from Brazil, China, and Russia to least developed countries in Africa and elsewhere.

The OECD Tourism Committee is the only global forum for the discussion and coordination of tourism policies and actions among industrialized countries.

Once a year, the Tourism Committee unites senior policymakers to discuss policies and major developments in the tourism industry. For this purpose, OECD members receive information on tourism issues once a year from OECD's Statistical Working Party of the Committee for Industry and Business Environment. The committee also cooperates with the World Tourism Organization, the European Union, and the International Labour Organization in regard to policies and required actions in the tourism industry.

Pacific Asia Travel Association (PATA)

PATA is a nonprofit travel trade association that was created with the mission to serve government tourist offices, hotels, airlines, and other travel-related companies throughout the Pacific Asia region to enhance the growth, value, and quality of Pacific Asia travel and tourism for the benefit of its membership.[32]

The visionary achievements of the Pacific Asia Travel Association began in 1951. At this time, Pacific travel needed a pioneer to connect nations, with travel being the common bond. Governments became involved together with representatives from a variety of travel organizations. PATA has been a sponsor of the development of tourism within the Pacific region. To achieve its mission, PATA provides its members with development, education, training, and marketing services in addition to critical leadership in preserving the area's unique environmental and cultural resources.

Travel to PATA member countries has grown enormously in the past decade from 25 million visitors a year to more than 90 million today, and the number is still growing.[33] Recognizing the impact on destinations that this dramatic increase in travel may have, and believing that the present and future success of Pacific Asia's travel industry depends on sustainable environmental and sociocultural preservation, PATA offers destination-planning assistance to member countries in the form of advisory groups. In 1992, it created the Green Leaf Program aimed at encouraging travel industry organizations to show commitment to the PATA Code for Environmentally Responsible Tourism. The Green Leaf Program further intends to bring commercial advantages to tourism businesses meeting the program's criteria by actively encouraging consumer support of these businesses. Participating PATA member countries were awarded from one to three "green leaves" according to the level of environmentally friendly criteria they met. The higher the leaf count, the more prestige the country gained on the tourism market for environmentally conscious travelers. The Green Leaf Program has now merged with WTTC's Green Globe 21. The major reasons for this integration were Green Globe's certification program, audit and verification

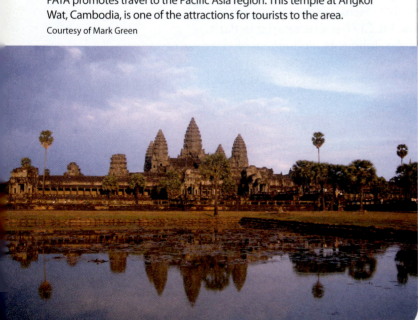

PATA promotes travel to the Pacific Asia region. This temple at Angkor Wat, Cambodia, is one of the attractions for tourists to the area.

Courtesy of Mark Green

system, and its continued monitoring plan, which PATA members can access. PATA is the recognized authority on Pacific Asia travel and tourism and provides links and a vast array of travel information about the Pacific Asia region to its members, the industry, and travelers.

Caribbean Tourism Organization (CTO)

The Caribbean Tourism Organization (CTO) provides leadership for tourism organizations in the Caribbean region. With headquarters in Barbados and marketing operations in New York, London, and Toronto, it is the Caribbean's tourism development agency and comprises 32 member governments and a myriad of private sector organizations and companies. The CTO's mission is to provide, to and through its members, the services and information needed for the development of sustainable tourism for the economic and social benefit of the Caribbean people. The organization provides specialized support and technical assistance to member countries in the areas of marketing, human resources development, research, information management, and sustainable development.[34]

European Travel Commission (ETC)

The ETC is responsible for the worldwide promotion overseas of Europe as a tourist destination. Members are national tourism organizations from 34 European Union countries. Established in 1948, its goal is to attract overseas customers to the European market.

The ETC's policy and principles are that it "should increase the level of tourism from other parts of the world to Europe as a result of its marketing activities. It should provide a forum for individual members to exchange ideas and experiences for the benefit of each member and the whole group."[35]

The ETC's mission is "To work together to build the value of tourism to all the beautiful and diverse countries of Europe through, in particular, cooperating in areas of sharing best practices, marketing intelligence and promotion."[36] The mission is accomplished by meeting the following main objectives of the ETC:

- Promote Europe as an attractive tourist destination
- Assist member national tourist offices (NTOs) to exchange knowledge and work collaboratively
- Provide industry partners and other interested parties with easy access to material and statistics regarding inbound tourism to Europe

  Activities and events of the ETC include the following:

- Public relations
- Consumer advertising in selected overseas markets
- Trade promotions
- Market research
- Professional development for members (seminars, information exchange)
- Liaison with other relevant agencies (e.g., the European Commission's Tourism Unit [Directorate General for Enterprise], the United Nations World Tourism Organization [UNWTO], and the Organisation for Economic Co-Operation and Development [OECD])

The organization also provides a forum for the directors of the European national tourism organizations to meet regularly, exchange advice, and take measures against actions that are considered detrimental to tourism.

▶ Check Your Knowledge

1. What is the purpose of the OECD?
2. Why was PATA founded?
3. What is the responsibility of the ETC?

Tourism at the National Level

Governments decide on the status, functions, and structure of national tourism organizations. Some countries have recognized the importance of tourism and elevated it to cabinet level, which means that there is a minister of tourism, who makes recommendations on issues involving tourism to the cabinet, which includes the prime minister or president. In other countries, such as the United States, Canada, and Australia, the government, to save money, has found it necessary to reduce its support of tourism. Instead, the government forms a public–private organization to represent travel and tourism, such as the Travel Industry Association in the United States.

Travel Industry Association (TIA)

TIA came into existence in 1941 as a private, nonprofit association and is today recognized as the nation's leader in promoting and facilitating increased travel to and within the United States. TIA defines its role on behalf of the tourism and travel industry as to "represent and speak for the common interests and concerns of all components" and to "increase the understanding of tourism's impact and its importance to the economic, social, and cultural life of the United States."[37] TIA is based in Washington, D.C., and it represents and speaks for the common interests and concerns of the entire $740 billion U.S. travel and tourism industry and has 2,600 member organizations, including hotels, airlines, car rental companies, cruise lines, convention and visitors bureaus, state tourism offices, attractions, and theme parks.[38]

TIA's goal is to promote and increase travel to and within the United States to make the country the world's number one tourism destination. The association also aims to protect the industry from governmental initiatives that would impede travel by discriminating against the traveler and the travel industry. Being the authoritative and recognized source of research, analysis, and forecasting for the entire tourism and travel industry of the United States, TIA's yearly agenda stresses the distribution of marketing and research publications as well as marketing programs to the industry. Its work can hence be summarized as taking place in three key areas:

- *Government Affairs*—TIA pursues the establishment of efficient policies concerning, for example, the Border Security Bill, Immigration and

Naturalization Service Visa Regulations, and the Visa Waiver Program. TIA hopes to achieve a major partnership with the U.S. travel industry and the federal government to attain sophisticated branding, positioning, and promotion of the United States to reach potential visitors around the world and compete with other countries that invest major sums in promotional campaigns each year. The organization also partners with the National Park Service and the U.S. Forest Service to encourage travelers to purchase park and forest passes so that the visibility of America's natural and historic sites among travelers is increased.

- *Marketing*—TIA supports three major marketing programs, including the annual International Pow Wow, which is the world's international travel trade show; the annual Marketing Outlook Forum, which is a gathering of travel industry leaders for an intensive three-day series of information sessions on the global economic, social, political, and marketing trends that will affect travel; and finally, the Annual National Tourism Week, which celebrates tourism and raises tourism awareness.

- *Research*—TIA lobbies the Department of Commerce (DOC) for additional federal funding for two research projects: the Travel and Tourism Satellite Account (TTSA), which provides tourism organizations with official statistics for the planning of competitive strategies in the global marketplace; and the In-Flight Survey, which is a monthly survey of international air travelers that the government uses to calculate the balance of trade.

That TIA effectively combines marketing, research, and governmental activities can be seen clearly in the action plan it developed as a response to the September 11 tragedy. The post-9/11 six-month recovery plan was intended to enhance safety and ensure the ongoing economic vitality of the industry. It consisted of these three components, namely, research, marketing, and partnership with the government.

Federal Aviation Administration (FAA) and the Department of Transportation (DOT)

The FAA has its origins in the passage of the Federal Aviation Act in 1958, which was prompted by a series of midair collisions and the introduction of jet travel in the United States. The purpose of this act was to establish safety rulemaking in the airline industry and to develop and maintain a common civil-military system of air navigation and air traffic control.

In 1966, a cabinet department was created, named the Department of Transportation (DOT), which was to combine major federal transportation responsibilities. The DOT began its operations on April 1, 1967, and it incorporated the Federal Aviation Administration. FAA's prime responsibilities still center around aviation security issues and policies, noise standards, safety certification of airports, and airport navigation aids, as well as programs such as Free Flight, which enhances data sharing and optimization of all phases of flight among the aviation industry, from planning and surface transportation to direct flight paths.

Today, the DOT works to ensure that the national transportation system is accessible, safe, and convenient and that it enhances peoples' quality of life. DOT closely monitors industry practices and policies and functions like a portal for the different transportation sectors in the United States. On its website (www.bts .gov/virtualib/gov.html) are links to federal, international, regional planning, and state organizations in the transportation industry.

National Transportation Safety Board (NTSB)

The NTSB is an independent federal agency charged by Congress with investigating every civilian aviation accident in the United States. The NTSB maintains a database of accidents and serves as a "court of appeals" for certification safety matters.

Tourism Industries (TI)

TI is an office that has been in service in the Department of Commerce since the elimination of the USTTA. Its mission is to foster an environment that encourages and allows the U.S. travel and tourism industry to generate revenues and jobs through tourism exports. The office is organized in three groups that each take care of distinct responsibilities. The first is the Deputy Assistant Secretary for TI who serves as the principal contact person between the U.S. government and the U.S. tourism industry on policy issues, technical assistance, and research. The second, the Tourism Development Group, provides travel data to and from the United States, forecasts the economic impact of international travel to the nation, and provides technical assistance to communities and businesses to enhance their visibility on the tourism market. Finally, the Tourism Policy Council coordinates national policies and programs concerning tourism, recreation, and national heritage issues and works to ensure that national interests are fully considered in federal decision making affecting tourism development. Figure 5–3 shows an organization chart for a national or state tourism department.

Tourism at the State and Regional Levels

Tourism organizations at the state level include those that are at the territorial and provincial levels. Each of the 50 states of the United States has a government agency responsible for the promotion of travel and tourism within and to its boundaries. Domestic travel promotion is the foremost objective of state tourism organizations, including promotion to residents and the residents of nearby states. Nowadays with the increasing popularity and worldwide accessibility of the Internet, states increasingly focus on promoting their destinations to foreign visitors through websites. Other popular promotion channels include information kiosks, toll-free phone numbers, fax-on-demand services, and mail brochures. Many of these organizations also operate travel information and welcome centers and even set up marketing offices in other parts of the country or overseas. Because tourism

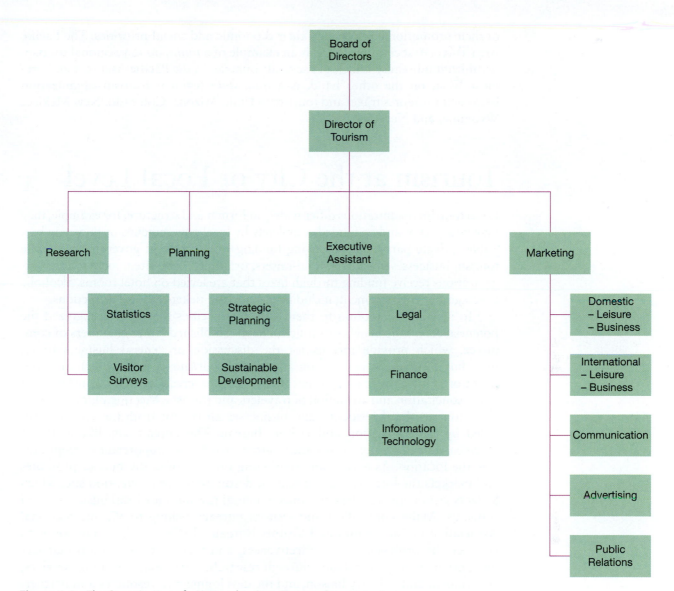

Figure 5–3 • The Organization of a National or State Tourism Department

is not a tangible product, but rather a service or experience, many state tourism organizations offer familiarization trips to travel writers, tour wholesalers, and travel agents so that these professionals can experience the travel and tourism services of the particular state and then promote it in the market. This type of promotion is very effective because renowned writers and agents can credibly provide a realistic insight on what the traveler should expect, which helps make the tourism experience a little more predictable.

The objective of regional tourism organizations (RTOs) is to attract tourists to their specific geographic region. Very often, RTOs have nonprofit status and receive funding from their membership of private tourism businesses or from state or provincial grants. The United States has a large number of regional tourism organizations, which can be of different types depending on the geographic extent of their promotional efforts and their economic and social priorities. The Pacific Area Travel Association (PATA) is an example of a *multicountry* regional tourism organization because it includes several countries in the Pacific Asia region. Foremost West, on the other hand, is a *multistate* regional tourism organization because it promotes travel and tourism in Utah, Arizona, Colorado, New Mexico, Wyoming, and Nevada.

Tourism at the City or Local Level

Local tourism organizations differ widely in format and structure; for example, they may be a part of and be funded completely by local governments, or they may be a public–private partnership receiving funding from the local government, private tourism businesses, members, fund-raisers, or grants. Very often, local tourism organizations receive funding through taxes that are levied on hotel rooms, alcoholic beverages, or entertainment, including casinos and tickets to local attractions.

To increase promotion to their area, major cities that have recognized the potential economic benefits of tourism have established either **chambers of commerce**, which provide forums for the discussion of general business topics including tourism, or convention and visitors bureaus (CVBs), which are nonprofit organizations that represent the common interests of a city or urban area in the solicitation and attraction of travelers and tourists. Meeting planners, travelers, tourists, local residents, and businesses all benefit from the services provided by the convention and visitors bureau. The bureau acts like a liaison between residential businesses and visitors or business opportunities from outside the location. As a sales and marketing organization, the bureau promotes and markets the local area as a vacation destination and convention site, which attracts visitors or travelers and thus potential revenues for local businesses and residents. Many convention and visitors bureaus belong to the **International Association of Convention and Visitors Bureaus (IACVB)**, whose mission is to enhance the professionalism, effectiveness, and image of destination management organizations worldwide through research, education, consulting services, government and industry liaison, and the development of resources and partnerships. The organization was founded in 1914 and has its seat in Washington, D.C. Over the years, it has developed the Convention Industry Network (CINET), which is today the world's leading meetings and conventions database and provides marketing and sales information to its members through its large collection of meeting profiles of different associations and corporations worldwide.

▶ **Check Your Knowledge**

1. Which organization is today's recognized leader in tourism promotion to and within the United States? What are its three key functional areas of operation?

2. Which promotional channels are becoming increasingly popular on the state and local levels?

CAREER INFORMATION

Several different employment opportunities relate to policy issues in tourism. Good entry positions are with chambers of commerce or convention and visitors bureaus, where you could, for example, develop marketing programs for local areas. Policy issues are addressed whenever geographical areas need to be restructured; therefore, numerous government and public/private organizations exist that specialize in planning and implementing restructuring programs for city parks, zoos, the transportation infrastructure including landscaping, as well as programs enhancing public safety issues. For basically every tourism aspect discussed in this chapter, there are employment opportunities. These could be in relation to the environment, tourism education and training, or improving and conducting tourism and travel-related research and producing and evaluating statistics and data valuable for the entire industry. In the technology sector, you could develop new technologies that reduce emissions or use alternative energies and enhance a traveler's or visitor's experience of the country. Work opportunities exist in tourist offices and information centers, in governmental organizations such as the FAA, and in international organizations such as the UNWTO and International Labor Office (ILO).

Tourism policy is in fact a bottomless well of changes and need for continuous innovation because demands of consumers, the population, economy, and industry evolve over time and policy issues need to be adapted or put into place to accommodate these developments. The bottom line is that every one of us faces policies every day, and you should be actively involved in this area when you feel that something needs to be changed or can be improved.

▶ Check Your Knowledge

1. What are the major current trends in tourism policy and organizations?
2. List some possible career paths within the segment.

CASE STUDY

Governance and Pro-Poor Tourism: The Case of Marikina City in the Philippines

(Because of space constraints, this case has been reduced; however, you may contact Dr. Rodriguez for the full version.)

Come and visit the city of Marikina, in the National Capital Region of the Philippines, to examine the incredible example of how a city can successfully adopt a governance and pro-poor tourism program.

Pro-poor tourism was chosen as a major theme for this case because of the following:

- As tourism takes center stage in developing countries, the tourism sector is increasingly perceived as being able to contribute to the proliferation of economic activities, which if managed in a specific way, can address poverty alleviation issues.
- Ashley asserts that community-based tourism projects are not necessarily pro poor because the revenues derived from tourism activities can be confined to serve the interests of relatively well-off stakeholders.[1]

The proliferation of books and articles related to pro-poor tourism makes it an interesting topic especially for the academe and the poor. The presentation and exchange of data on the planning and implementation of pro-poor tourism especially in Asian countries can help inform many stakeholders who are interested in understanding the contribution of tourism development in poverty alleviation.

Marikina City as a Tourism Site

Twenty years ago, Marikina was an unremarkable town littered with trash and where sidewalk vendors ruled the streets. Marikina now wants to be known as "the shoe capital of the Philippines." Located near the city of Manila, it is believed to be where the shoe industry in metro Manila started. Many residential villages within the municipality were formerly farms used for agricultural crops until these were converted to provide housing for migrants from other provinces seeking work in the metropolis.

Marikina in the late 1980s was not considered a popular tourism destination. An election in the early 1990s catapulted a local executive who introduced radical changes in governance. This led to the emergence of Marikina as a model city. To date, many visitors are pleasantly surprised to see thoroughfares free of clutter and vendors and a municipal hall that enforces its own definition of order. As a result of these changes, Marikina has garnered and continues to garner many awards that generated interest among other cities' executives eager to learn from its experience. This started the ball rolling for domestic tourism despite the fact that Marikina has few tourism assets. Marikina has no beach resorts and no first-class hotels and places of interests are limited to the city proper.

Now, however, Marikina is hailed as a model city for tourism development, and the interesting thing is that many of the tourists are other cities' municipal officials who have come to see for themselves just how a city should be governed. Tourists, along with the other municipalities' officials, enjoy the city's attractions:

Sentrong Pangkultura: Built in 1887, this historical edifice, which was the actual home of Kapitan Moy, the recognized father of the shoe industry, takes tourist's down memory lane of rustic Spanish villas and airy capiz windows.

Teatro Marikina: The city's commitment to the arts is manifest in the modern arts facility for plays, concerts, shows, seminars, exhibits, and conventions.

World of Butterflies: A 2000-meter expanse of lush gardens that is home to 20 species of butterflies.

CASE STUDY *(continued)*

The Marikina River Park: The Marikina River Park is a 10-kilometer-long riverside park of 220 hectares. The river park is for all citizens and tourists to enjoy as a sports and recreational park—even for fishing in the river.

The Shoe Museum and Shoe Industry: Former First Lady Imelda Marcos's 4,000 pairs of shoes had to be housed somewhere, so why not the shoe capital of the Philippines? Shoes of other notables are also on display. The shoe industry in Marikina has long been unable to compete with imported Chinese shoes, but has discovered a captive market niche of tourists and excursionists. Individuals and groups go on field trips to Marikina and are brought to small shoe factories to watch how shoes are produced using labor-intensive methods and are encouraged to buy finished products.

How It Happened

In three words: leadership and governance. Take, for example, the mayor's presentation to the Asian Development Bank: "Our targets and goals are clear; our performances are properly measured. We are challenged and motivated to continuously meet our productivity and excellence. Public order and safety are excellent; the police force is cited as the most outstanding in the region. Taxes due are collected—something that does not often happen in the Philippines—this facilitates the budgeting process and avails the city of funds for the many social programs that citizens and tourists can enjoy."

World Bank executives were so impressed after touring the city and its Marikina River Park, Homeowners Drive Settlements site, Marikina Public Market, and bikeways. The bikeways network is a recipient of a US$1.3 billion grant from the Global Environment Facility of the World Bank. Additionally, the World Bank named Marikina City one of the model cities in the world.

Poverty Alleviation

The city's approach to poverty alleviation is multipronged, addressing the health, housing, education and livelihood, and values of our people. Tourism helps poverty alleviation by providing employment opportunities; by bringing new money into the city for the "multiplier effect" to happen; by producing tax revenues for community services, infrastructure, and education. In fact, the city is so well run that many other cities are sending officials to see how they do it, resulting in a boost to tourism.

Ashley emphasizes the value of supply chains, enterprise linkages, nonfinancial partnerships, and capability building and translates these into specific activities that can be planned and implemented at the level of local government officials.[2] An investigation of the Marikina government unit in this study focuses on the context of tourism development as an alternative source of livelihood and the manner in which the tourism office is managed, including the leadership style of the local executive directly responsible for the promotion of tourism. The problems were as follows:

1. What are the tourism-related programs, projects and activities that are being done at the level of Marikina's local government units?

2. What insights on governance can be generated from the investigation of tourism-related portfolios of this local government unit to link tourism to pro-poor concerns?

Data obtained given the variables enumerated by Ashley are shown in Table 5–1.

The data presented in Table 5–1 are not exhaustive in the sense that there may be other programs/projects that are operating but that were not observed and sourced using secondary documents. A comparison of data shows the diversity of what can be considered pro-poor projects in Marikina. Many of these

(continued)

C A S E   S T U D Y   (*continued*)

Table 5–1 Comparative Data on Marikina Using Ashley's Matrix

Is there government to:	City of Marikina
Boost local inputs into the tourism supply chain? This question addresses the presence of leakages of tourism earnings. It emphasizes the importance of local sourcing that opens more opportunities for marginalized groups.	Local government unit (LGU) manages tours that showcase local cuisine and manufactured products. It manages museums, one of which displays the famous "shoes of Imelda Marcos." Conscious efforts are also exerted to source materials and local manpower for festivals sponsored by the local government unit. (Source: MCTTIPO brochure)
Support micro/small/community tourism entrepreneurs? Lack of financing and training in developing countries are often cited as reasons why marginalized sectors are unable to benefit from tourism development. Support craft makers and vendors? Provide a market space for tourist craft sales?	The LGU has a micro lending project. In addition, it manages a "Manpower House Livelihood Skills Training and Productivity Center" to encourage businesses in the food trade, cosmetology, dressmaking, spa/massage, reflexology. (Source: Marikina City, 2007, Annual Report) It has an investment promotions plan that gives incentives to "local . . . micro, small scale enterprises." (Source: Marikina Chamber of Commerce and Industry Information Kit). It also supports a shoe caravan composed of small shoe manufacturers that go to the countryside. Several areas are designated by the LGU to provide support for groups of entrepreneurs. The LGU has a "cooperatives month" to support micro entrepreneurs.
Accredit a "local guide" category? Employment of local guides provides opportunities to common folks.	Employees of the LGU, particularly MCTTIPO, are hired as guides in the tours that it manages.
Apply levy or rebate to tourism-related businesses?	No data
Apply a minimum wage?	No data
Stimulate partnerships between the private sector and communities?	The LGU does not depend on a privately controlled tourism association. MCTTIPO, an office attached to the office of the city mayor, manages tourism. The LGU has linkages with 62 local sister cities and 12 foreign sister cities. (Source: MCTTIPO brochure)
Influence private sector behavior via concessions, licensing, or codes?	No data
Catalyze destination linkages among stakeholders?	The LGU plans and implements several festival projects every year. Examples of these are *Ka Angkan* (Our Ancestors); *Ilog- Nayon* (River-Countryside); *Sapatos* (Shoe); Christmas; *Rehiyon –Rehiyon* (Regional Festivals).

C A S E   S T U D Y   (*continued*)

Is there government to:	City of Marikina
Share poverty alleviation revenues with communities?	The LGU leases spaces for local artists (*Teatro* Marikina), for gatherings of groups (Sentrong Pangkultura); it has a program to help senior citizens have access to Medicare (Privilege card). (Source: Marikina City 2007 Annual Report)
Channel donations from tourists to communities?	No data
Address social, cultural costs of tourism?	No data
Address environmental, physical costs of tourism?	Traffic because of busloads of visitors is a problem identified as a result of tourism. The absence of sidewalk vendors probably minimizes the inconvenience.
Involve poor in plans and policy making?	There is diverse representation of stakeholders in policy formulation.
Make strategic choices based on evidence for pro-poor impact?	No data

projects have direct links with tourism development even if their effects on poverty alleviation cannot be directly established.

The material by Ashley is the only one that details the connection between governance and pro-poor tourism. The material is impressive because it contains data obtained from collaborative work of SNV Netherlands Development Organization with "ministries of tourism, tourism boards, hotel associations, community based tourism organizations as well as associations of tour operators"[3.] and contains information in tourism sites in Asia (Lao PDR) and Africa (Ethiopia, Tunisia, Gambia, Kenya, Mozambique, Rwanda, Tanzania, and Uganda).

Insights from Marikina City

1. **On the Value of a Tourism Council as a Vehicle for Tourism Development.** Marikina does not rely on an active tourism council with heavy participation of the private sector. It has an office—Marikina Culture, Tourism, Trade, Investment Promotions Office (MCTTIPO)—that operates under the office of the city mayor. This office manages tour packages like *Lakbay Aral* (educational trips) with students as its market segment. These trips are designed to showcase shoe factories, a hat factory, a shoe museum, and a miniature museum among others.

MCTTIPO collects statistics of tours it manages. The data on types of tours, number of visitors, and dates of visit are used to identify markets served by the touristic offerings.

As the city mayor was provided data on tourism revenues, the decision to invest in related tourism assets became more justified. This could be one of the reasons why the city is offering diverse tourism attractions. It has publicly owned museums, shopping malls, a new convention center, and a hotel. In addition, it manages a number of festivals regularly. The *Ka Angkan* (Our Ancestors) festival has developed to be a well-attended activity of original families who settled in Marikina when it was still an agricultural municipality. The festival

(continued)

CASE STUDY *(continued)*

has evolved to a level where interpretive materials on family monikers are shared in an exhibit that is part and parcel of the festival. The *Rehiyon-Rehiyon* (regional) festival has also reached a spectacular combination of street dancing and performance where constituent *barangays* (villages) are represented in performances.

In the last *Rehiyon-Rehiyon* (regional) festival (December 2008), MCTTIPO said costumes of the *barangay* (village) performers were farmed out to local dressmakers. Skills training, job fairs, promotion of local products, and provision of financing (microfinance) under the office of the city mayor provide the linkage with diverse stakeholders who stand to benefit from tourismic activities.

Given the example of Marikina, one can ask whether a centrally managed tourism organization can be a more effective vehicle for tourism to be pro poor. The desire to involve diverse tourism stakeholders cognitively should lead to more equalized sharing of the benefits of tourism, and this is widely accepted in Marikina. The active control of the management of a tourism office by the city mayor provides the wherewithal to address issues related to managing supply chains, diversifying touristic offerings, and providing the infrastructure and the linkages needed by marginalized members of the community.

2. **On the Role of Leadership Styles in Pro-Poor Tourism.** MCTTIPO's role in maximizing tourismic revenues can also be attributed to the style of leadership of the city mayor. MCTTIPO is managed like an investment center where "return on investments" is included as part of the control system. The supervisor of MCTTIPO regularly reports on performance of the office and is "rewarded" or "punished" depending on how the office operates to produce results. This style of leadership makes the supervisor of MCTTIPO conscious of the need to aggressively promote the tourismic packages and be on the constant lookout for new tourismic offerings.

3. **On the Context of Tourism Development as It Relates to the Propensity to Be Pro Poor.** Tourism development in Marikina came at a point when the city had proven itself to be competent in the many areas of governance. Marikina received local as well as international recognition for efficient and effective delivery of public services. The infrastructure to include diverse stakeholders to participate in tourism development was in place before tourism was recognized as a sector worth investing in. This is an interesting phenomenon in the management of tourism councils. Could it be possible to put up pro-poor projects and struggle to develop tourism at the same time? If the council is composed of only private business interests, how great will the propensity be to include pro-poor projects in the development of tourism? How decisive is the role of the local executive in this scenario?

4. **On Impact Studies of Tourism on Marginalized Sector.** Last but not least, Cattarinich mentions the complex nature of the phenomenon of poverty.[4.] Is it economic, social, cultural, or political? How can local government units minimize poverty if they do not attempt to define poverty given its unique context? This could also be the reason why "addressing cultural, social and physical impacts" was mentioned by Ashley as one of the tools for local government units to be pro poor. How can pro-poor tourism projects be evaluated to address the concern of Ashley, that is, net benefits of tourism projects in relation to costs? Tourism development has unintended results, and the brunt of the negative effects are said to be heavier on disadvantaged groups. Tourism that is led by private capital is said to be insensitive to these concerns.[5.] Using an economic definition of poverty, one may ask if beneficiaries earned more as a result of pro-poor tourism.

Conclusion

For this case, the tools prescribed by Ashley regarding pro-poor tourism were used to examine Marikina City in the National Capital Region. The programs, projects, activities in the site of investigation were enumerated and analyzed. The insights from the analysis of data show areas of concern that can be used as inputs in making tourism development more sensitive to the needs of marginalized sectors.

CASE STUDY (continued)

Questions

1. Do you think poverty alleviation can be seriously addressed as tourism develops? What examples can you give based on what you have seen in your own country regarding tourism development and poverty alleviation?

2. Identify concrete activities local government units can initiate and support to address poverty alleviation through tourism development.

3. Identify paradoxes and problems that must be negotiated as poverty alleviation and tourism development are considered. How can these paradoxes and problems be managed and converted into opportunities to ensure that marginalized individuals get the support they need?

Endnotes

1. Caroline Ashley, *How Can Governments Boost the Local Economic Impacts of Tourism? Options and Tools*. SNV East and Southern Africa, November 2006, www.propoortourism.org.uk/toolbox091106.pdf.

2. Ibid.

3. Ibid.

4. Xavier Cattarinich, "Pro Poor Tourism Initiatives in Developing Countries. Analysis of Secondary Case Studies," April 2001, www.propoortourism.org.uk/ppt_pubs_working papers.html.

5. Michael C. Hall, ed., *Pro-Poor Tourism: Who Benefits? Perspectives on Tourism and Poverty Reduction* Cleveden, UK: Channel View Publication, 2007.

Additional Readings

Arsenio Balicasan, "Poverty Reduction: What We Know and Don't," University of the Philippines' Centennial Lecture Series, January 31, 2008.

Mickey Castano, "Breathe Easy in Marikina," *Space. Explorations in Modern Living* 3, no. 1 (2008): 32–35.

Marikina City Planning and Development Office, *Data on Poverty in Marikina*, 2008.

Marikina Cultural, Tourism, Trade and Investments Promotions Office, *Data on Tourism Projects and Revenues*, 2008.

"Eco Savers Wins Galing Pook Award," *Marikina River Digest* 8, no. 1 (January–March 2008).

Marikina Chamber of Commerce, *Marikina: A Model City of Competitiveness*, 2007.

Marikina City, *Annual Report. Our City's Transformation Continues, Marikina River Digest*, vol. 8 no. 1, January–March, 2008 pp. 1, 7.)

Marikina Valley Chamber of Commerce and Industry, *It's Time to Invest in Marikina City*, 2008.

Office of the Municipal Agriculturist's Project List for CY 2008, *Municipal Social Work Development Office Highlights of Accomplishments Reports*, 2008.

Source: Courtesy of Corazon P. Rodriguez, Ph. D. Dean, Asian Institute of Tourism, University of the Philippines.

Summary

1. Policy and planning are essential factors in successful tourism development. Reasons for developing tourism are economic, infrastructural, or social; **extent of tourism growth** and sustainability must also be considered.

2. Because of the lack of a national tourism office in the United States, many states have created their own tourism offices. Realizing that the United States could greatly enhance its promotional impact overseas by creating a brand name unifying all of its states, public–private cooperative marketing efforts, such as those conducted through TIA's efforts, have been established. New marketing concepts promoting the United States in terms of a "brand-name" destination, that is, "See America," and efforts of these organizations have since focused on promoting the importance of the travel and tourism industry for the United States to its government and other industry sectors.

3. Factors that need to be considered in the travel and tourism industry's policy include rapid increases of new technologies that are constantly aiming at improving product or service quality and enhancing energy efficiency, the need to conduct and gather reliable research and statistics, as well as the need to educate and train travel and tourism industry workers. Transportation is key to generating and enabling economic growth and maintaining a high quality of life. A top priority in the transportation system, particularly in the aftermath of September 11, remains to ensure the safety and security of the traveling public through, for example, border regulations, as well as improving access for all Americans and visitors. In light of the scarcity of natural resources worldwide, the conservation of the natural environment is another top priority, as well as maintaining and striving toward sustainable environmental development and preserving historical and cultural resources for future generations.

4. Tourism organizations exist at all levels of government and serve to promote travel and tourism to their respective destinations by analyzing the factors necessary to consider when planning tourism policies. These organizations also take into account political and economic considerations as well.

5. On the international level, the largest and perhaps best known travel and tourism organization is the World Tourism Organization, which is affiliated with the United Nations. Other organizations include the International Labour Organization (ILO), the World Travel and Tourism Council (WTTC), the International Air Transport Association (IATA), and the International Civil Aviation Organization (ICAO). Regional international organizations include the Organisation for Economic Co-operation and Development (OECD), the Pacific Asia Travel Association (PATA), the Caribbean Tourism Commission (CTC), and the European Travel Commission (ETC). On the national level, the Travel Industry Association (TIA) promotes the United States to both domestic and international visitors, and other organizations include the Federal Aviation Administration (FAA), the Department of Transportation (DOT), the Department of State (DOS), and the Department of Homeland Security (DHS).

6. Tourism organizations at the state, regional, and city or local levels are often managed through limited funds with little assistance from the national government. Promotions may be directed by the local governments or by a combination of public and private forces.

Key Words and Concepts

Americans with Disabilities
   Act of 1990
chambers of commerce
economic development
education and training
employment growth
environmental policy
extent of tourism growth
International Association of
   Convention and Visitors
   Bureaus (IACVB)

labor intensity
learning organizations
National Tourism Policy Act
   of 1981
research and statistics
school-to-work programs
seasonality
sustainable development
technology
tourism policy

trade liberalization
transportation infrastructure
Travel and Tourism Research
   Association (TTRA)
Visa Waiver Program (VWP)
visitor facilitation
visitor safety and security

Review Questions

1. What is the ultimate purpose of tourism policy? Which might be specific reasons for tourism policy development?
2. What are the methods of policy development?
3. Why is the Visa Waiver Program so important for the U.S. economy? To what extent has it recently been amended as a result of national security issues?
4. What are the characteristics of tourism employment?
5. What is the importance of research and statistics for the tourism and travel industry?
6. What is the role of the United Nations World Tourism Organization?

7. Choose two regional organizations that either directly or indirectly promote travel and tourism. What are their main functions, and what effects do these organizations have on the industry?
8. What has the Moroccan "responsible tourism operation" done to promote sustainable tourism in Morocco?
9. Do you think that Elkhart County CVB is correct in promoting two brands in its tourism promotion, and if so, why? What other strategies could it use?

Interesting Websites

American Hotel and Lodging Association: www .ahla.com/

Amtrak: www.amtrak.com

Council of Hospitality and Restaurant Institute Educators: www.chrie.org

Department of Education: www.ed.gov

Department of Labor: www.dol.gov

Department of Transportation: www.dot.gov

European Travel Commission: www .etc-europe-travel.org

Federal Aviation Association: www.faa.gov

International Air Transport Association: www .iata.org

International Association of Convention and Visitors Bureaus: www.iacvb.org

International Civil Aviation Association: www .icao.org

International Labour Organization: www.ilo.org

International Society of Travel and Tourism Educators: www.istte.org/

National Council of State Tourism Directories: www.tourstates.com

Organisation for Economic Co-operation and Development: www.oecd.org

Pacific Asia Travel Association: www.pata.org

Texas Transportation Institute: http://tti.tamu.edu/

Tourism Industries: www.tinet.ita.doc.gov/

Travel Industry Association: www.tia.org

Travel and Tourism Research Association: www.ttra.com

U.S. Chamber of Commerce: www.uschamber.com

World Tourism Organization: www.world-tourism.org

World Travel and Tourism Council: www.wttc.org

Internet Exercises

1. Look on the United Nations World Tourism Organization's website and find information related to tourism policy.
2. Research the "Green Facts" section of the Green Globe 21 program (at www.greenglobe.org) on current environmental issues. What can you do to help the environment in these areas?
3. Find out what the specific program benefits for the Green Globe 21 members are.

Apply Your Knowledge

1. What are the benefits of the tourism and travel industry for the United States? Which areas might be of concern?
2. What is the purpose of tourism organizations in general? Why and how should tourism organizations cooperate?

Suggested Activity

Create a tourism policy for one aspect of tourism in your area.

Endnotes

1. Charles J. Metelka, *The Dictionary of Hospitality, Travel and Tourism*, 3rd ed. (Albany, NY: Delmar, 1990), 155.
2. Nancy Stevenson, David Avery, and Graham Miller, "Tourism Policy Making: The Policymakers' Perspectives," *Annals of Tourism Research* 35, no. 3 (July 2008): 732–750.
3. Personal conversation with Edward Inskeep, March 4, 2008.
4. Edward Inskeep, *Tourism Planning: An Integrated and Sustainable Development Approach* (New York: Van Nostrand Reinhold, 1991), 29.
5. G. H. Brundtland, *The Brundtland Report. Our Common Future.* World Commission on Environment and Development (Oxford, England: Oxford University Press, 1987), as cited in Philip L. Pearce, Ginna Moscardo, and Glen F. Ross, *Tourism*

Community Relationships (Oxford, England: Pergamon, 1996), 6.

6. J. J. Pigram, "Sustainable Tourism Policy Considerations," *Journal of Tourism Studies* 1, no. 2 (1990): 2–9; T. Sofield, "Sustainable Ethnic Tourism in the South Pacific: Some Principles," *Journal of Tourism Studies* 2, no. 1 (1991): 56–72, as cited in Pearce, Moscardo, and Ross, *Tourism Community Relationships*, 6.

7. Pearce, Moscardo, and Ross, *Tourism Community Relationships*, 7.

8. Donald G. Reid, *Tourism Globalization and Development: Responsible Tourism Planning* (London: Pluto Press, 2003), 73.

9. Ibid.

10. David L. Edgell Sr., *International Tourism Policy* (New York: Van Nostrand Reinhold, 1990), 43.

11. International Travel Act of 1961, Chapter 31, Section 2122, p. 158, as cited in Edgell, *International Tourism Policy*, 10.

12. Ibid.

13. Bill Bramwell, *Interventions and Policy Instruments for Sustainable Tourism in Global Tourism*, 3rd ed., ed. William F. Theobald (Oxford, England: Elsevier, 2005), 410.

14. Office of Travel and Tourism Industries, "About OTTI," http://tinet.ita.doc.gov/about/index.html#TD (accessed April 3, 2008).

15. http://tinet.ita.doc.gov/about/tourism_policy.html

16. Roy A. Cook, Laura J. Yale, Joseph J. Marqua, *Tourism: The Business of Travel*, 2nd ed. (Upper Saddle River, NJ: Prentice-Hall, 2002), 339.

17. Airbus, "Aircraft Families: A380 Family," www.airbus.com/en/aircraftfamilies/a380/ (accessed March 28, 2008).

18. www.newairplane.com (accessed September 24, 2009). 21. U.S. Department of Transportation, home page, www.dot.gov/about_dot.html (accessed March 28, 2008).

19. U.S. Department of Transportation, home page, www.dot.gov/about_dot.html (accessed March 28, 2008).

20. www.unto.org/aboutwto/index.php (accessed September 24, 2009).

21. "UN Meets at WTM to Tackle Problems," *Travel Trade Gazette*, July 18, 2008.

22. http://unwto.org/ethics/index.php (accessed September 24, 2009). 27. www.greenglobe21.com/index_cn.html (accessed September 11, 2002).

23. www.greenglobe21.com/index_cn.html (accessed September 11, 2002).

24. www.wttc.org/bin/pdf/original_pdf_file/progresspriorities01.pdf (accessed September24, 2009). This is not a PATA endnote30. International Air Transport Association, "History—Part 1," www1.iata.org/about/history.htm (accessed September 12, 2008).

25. International Air Transport Association, "History—Part 1," www.iata.org/about/history.htm (accessed September 12, 2008).

26. International Air Transport Association, "About Us," www1.iata.org/about/index, (accessed September 12, 2008).

27. www.icao.int/cgi/goto_m.pl?icao/en/hist/history02.htm (accessed September 24, 2009).33. www.icao.int/cgi/statesDB4.pl?en (accessed September 24, 2009). 34. www.icao.int/icao/en/strategic_objectives.htm (accessed September 24, 2009).35. www.oecd.org/pages/0,3417,en_36734052_36734103_1_1_1_1_1,00.html (accessed September 24, 2009). 36. Ibid. 37. Pacific Asia Travel Association, "About PATA," www.pata.org/patasite/index.php?id=5 (accessed April 10, 2009).

28. www.icao.int/cgi/statesDB4.pl?en (accessed September 24, 2009).

29. www.icao.int/icao/en/strategic_objectives.htm (accessed September 24, 2009).

30. www.oecd.org/pages/0,3417,en_36734052_36734103_1_1_1_1_1,00.html (accessed September 24, 2009).

31. Ibid.

32. Pacific Asia Travel Association, "About PATA," www.pata.org/patasite/index.php?id=5 (accessed April 10, 2009).

33. Pacific Asia Travel Association, www.pata.org/frame.cfm?pageid=8 (accessed September 9, 2008).

34. Caribbean Tourism Association, *Caribbean Sustainable Tourism Policy Framework*, www.onecaribbean.org/content/files/CbbnSustainableTourismPolicyFramework.pdf (accessed April, 11, 2009).

35. European Travel Commission, "Welcome to the European travel Commission," www.etc-corporate.org/modules.php?name=Content&pa-showpage&pid=16&ac=2 (accessed April 11, 2009).

36. Ibid.

37. U.S. Travel Association, "About," www.tia.org/About/ (accessed September 16, 2002).

38. U.S. Travel Association, www.tia.org/about/what_we_do.html (accessed September 25, 2009).

CHAPTER 6

Tourism Planning and Sustainable Development

After reading and studying this chapter you should be able to:

- Explain the life cycle of tourism.

- Differentiate between the various approaches to tourism planning.

- Discuss the role of governments in tourism planning.

- Explain the purpose of and reasons for tourism policy.

- Explain what sustainable development is and how tourism is tied to it.

GEOGRAPHY SPOTLIGHT

Cultural Heritage Tourism: Nepal, Central Asia

As the birthplace of Buddhist religion and culture, the home of Mount Everest, and with archaeological remains 10,000 years old, the Federal Democratic Republic of Nepal is a cultural haven of South Central Asia.[1] The culture of Nepal is based on Hinduism and the teachings of the Buddha, and the country is filled with beautiful architecture, art, festivals, music, and ample temples and shrines. Today, most of the societies of the great Himalayas have primitive infrastructure or live in Buddhist monasteries.

Kathmandu, the capital city of Nepal, is home to about half of the country's population. Kathmandu and its surrounding areas are also the location of the highest concentration of temples, shrines, museums, palaces, and other significant pilgrimage sites. Each temple and shrine is attached to a legend or belief that represents and commemorates the powers and accomplishments of a specific god or the Buddha. Approximately 50 temples and palaces stand within walking distance at Kathmandu Durbar Square. The square is a great starting point for a cultural and heritage experience of Nepal. Nearby are the Krishna Temple, Bhimsen Temple, the Golden Temple of Hiranya Varna Mahavira, and Sundari Chowk, priority religious sites for Hindus. A few kilometers from the city center stands the stupa of Swoyambhunath. This dome-shaped monument is believed to be the site of the first Nepalese settlement. Painted on the stupa (Sanskrit meaning "heap," a mound-like formation that holds Buddhist relics) is the largest image of the Sakyamuni Buddha in Nepal. All of these sites are United Nations Educational, Scientific and Culture Organization (UNESCO) World Heritage sites.[2]

Apart from the religious sites to be visited, Bhaktapur Durbar Square also offers visitors some of the arts and architecture developed in Nepalese medieval times. The artwork of Nepal is heavily influenced by religious beliefs. The majority is wood and stone sculptures and different uses of precious metals in architecture and jewelry. Paintings are limited to religious depictions and storytelling of the Buddha and Hindu gods.

GEOGRAPHY SPOTLIGHT *(continued)*

Visitors can also visit 13 museums and libraries. The Lumbini Museum, National Art Gallery, International Mountain Museum, and Natural History Museum are among the more popular.[3]

Most of the festivals and holidays in Nepal are based on religious figures or events that honor a certain god or goddess. Historical festivals are celebrated to maintain heritage and commemorate significant events. Agricultural events mark the different seasons of harvesting and planting but are different from the seasonal festivals, which are celebrated to mark the beginning of special seasons.[4]

Located right outside Kathmandu, the Kopan Monastery has established itself as a thriving monastery of 360 monks and provides a spiritual and cultural learning experience to dedicated followers, casual visitors, and those on retreat. "Discovering Buddhism" is a 7- or 10-day introductory course to meditation and culture. All accommodations, meals, and necessary materials are included. The general accommodations are dormitory style, but participants can upgrade to a private room with private facilities. All meals are, of course, vegetarian, but plentiful. Travelers are expected to embrace the monastic lifestyle completely, which requires that they adhere to certain additional restrictions.[5] This course at the Kopan Monastery can be a prequel or sequel to a Nepalese historical adventure, and travelers can have an incomparable experience.

Courtesy of Mark Green

Although adventure tourists visit Nepal because of its great peaks, the country offers a rich cultural experience. Even those traveling for the sole purpose of mountain climbing find many towns offer authentic cultural experiences along with breathtaking views of Mount Everest.[6]

Endnotes

1. Encarta Encyclopedia, "Nepal," http://encarta.msn.com/encyclopedia_761562648/Nepal.html#s1 (accessed April 2, 2009).
2. Nepal Tourism Board, "Naturally Nepal: Once Is Not Enough," www.welcomenepal.com/promotional/aboutus-introduction.php (accessed April 3, 2009).
3. Ibid.
4. Ibid.
5. Kopan Monastery, "Kopan Monastery," www.kopanmonastery.com (accessed April 2, 2009).
6. Nepal Tourism Board, "Naturally Nepal."

Planning involves selecting the various goals that an organization wants to achieve and the **strategies** (actions) to be taken to ensure that those **goals** are accomplished. In organizations, executives determine where the organization is and where it wants to go. Goals are established for each of the key operating areas (see Figure 6–1).[1]

- Organizational structures, such as government tourism offices and private sector tourism associations working cooperatively together
- Tourism-related legislation and regulations such as standards and licensing requirements
- Education and training programs and training institutions to prepare persons to work effectively in tourism
- Availability of financial capital to develop tourist attractions, facilities, services and infrastructure, and mechanisms to attract capital investment
- Marketing strategies and promotion programs to inform tourists about country or region and induce them to visit it, and tourist information facilities, and services in the destination areas
- Travel facilitation of immigration (including visa arrangements), customs, and other facilities and services at the entry and exit points of tourists

Figure 6–1 • Elements of Efficient and Effective Tourism Development

Planning may be done over the short term (**tactical or operational planning**) or long term (**strategic planning**). Tourism planning begins with strategic planning (creating long-term plans) such as a **tourism master plan**. Tourism master plans begin with an environmental scan that assesses social-cultural, technological, economic, educational, political, and legal factors.

Sustainable development is defined as development that meets the needs of the present without compromising the ability of future generations to meet their own needs.[2] At a minimum, sustainable development requires maintaining ecological integrity and diversity, meeting basic human needs, keeping options open for future generations, reducing injustice, and increasing self-determination. There is a definite link between tourism planning and sustainable development. In fact, all tourism development should be planned to be sustainable.

Effective **tourism planning** follows on from tourism policy and is necessary to develop regions and destinations in such a way as to harmonize with the surrounding countryside, culture, and social and economical activity. Most tourism locations and attractions have a **life cycle** that proceeds from introduction, to growth, through maturity and decline.

Good planning helps ensure that fair and sustainable policies are enacted, whereas an absence of proper planning likely contributes to negative perceptions of a place and adverse impacts. Similarly, good planning can help ensure that the location or attraction avoids decline by prolonging its maturity phase. Managing sustainable tourism requires that the public sector (that is, government bodies such as city planners and transportation departments) and the private sector (tourism entities and residents) interact.[3]

Without proper tourism planning destinations encounter problems. For example, an area may become overdeveloped when it receives more tourists than it can handle. Or pollution may become so bad that the area receives negative media coverage, as was the case with Boracay, a popular tourist destination island in the Philippines. Successive governments in that location failed to resolve the sewage disposal problem adequately. Eventually, people noticed untreated sewage in the water while they were swimming. Needless to say, this and other similar incidents led to a dramatic decrease in the number of tourists to the island, which forced the authorities to "clean up their act." Other examples of challenges for tourism planners can be found in many locations, from popular cities such as London and Paris to over-crowded U.S. national parks. For example, after the recent global economic recession, tourism organizations were forced to quickly change plans because of the deteriorating global economy. For example, airlines had to handle high fuel and labor costs and fewer passengers.

A host of factors such as pollution reduction, green tourism, and new technology all affect tourism planning for large and small entities. Environmental scanning is an analytical process that allows investors and executives to anticipate future trends and allocate their human and economic resources accordingly.[4]

The sustainable planning process can be lengthy and frustrating. Community participation in the tourism planning process is advocated as a new way of implementing sustainable tourism. Yet, despite good intentions and the model of a

Consider the tourism planning that is required to prepare for this ship's arrival, passengers' stay, and their departure.
Courtesy of Mark Green

"ladder of citizen participation," it remains difficult to get everyone in agreement on just how community tourism should be developed.[5] Given tourism's substantial social, economic, and environmental impacts—positive and negative—planners can no longer afford to dismiss tourism as tangential to other planning functions.[6]

Tourism Planning as Part of a System

Edward Inskeep, a United Nations World Tourism Organization (UNWTO) tourism planning expert with years of UNWTO service and author of several master plans, explains that tourism planning should be thought of as an integrated system of supply and demand factors. The demand is created by international and domestic use of attractions, facilities, and services. The supply factors include transportation and other infrastructure (airports, roads, rail, cruise terminals, etc.), water, electric, sewage disposal, attractions, accommodations and foodservice, other tourist facilities and services, and industrial elements. For efficient and effective tourism development, Inskeep suggests tourism planners ensure that the elements shown in Figure 6–1 are in place. When these elements are planned, organized, managed, and harmonized, everyone benefits from a social, cultural, economical, and sustainable tourism perspective. Sustainable tourism implies that the environment is conserved for the future as well as enjoyed now.[7]

Tourism planning is similar to planning for any business activity: it begins with the terms of reference, which sets the parameters of the planning activity. After the terms of reference are determined, the planning process follows the model framework illustrated in Figure 6–2. Planning is a continuous process; after step 7, the process begins all over again.

- **Step 1:** Formulate the goals and objectives of the tourism development plan.
- **Step 2:** Determine the current situation of attaining primary and secondary data. Develop a tourism inventory. This could be of attractions, accommodations, etc.
- **Step 3:** Analyze the existing situation and determine what needs to be done to meet the set goals and objectives.
- **Step 4:** Develop action plans for each element.
- **Step 5:** Formulate recommendations for each element based on the action plans.
- **Step 6:** Implement the plan and assign responsibilities to individuals/organizations to ensure successful and timely completion.
- **Step 7:** Monitor results and make adjustments as necessary.

Figure 6–2 • A Tourism Planning Framework

There are various approaches to tourism planning. These approaches depend on the particular situation, but may include the following:

- *Community-Focused Approach*—This approach is a part of a sustainable approach and incorporates community opinions at each step in the process.
- *Sustainable Approach*—This approach plans to avoid environmental and sociocultural degradation. Projects and regions are developed and operated in accordance with strict environmental and sociocultural guidelines so as to sustain the resources for future generations. Associated with this approach is planning and controlling visitation volume.
- *Systems Approach*—In this approach, tourism is viewed as a complete and integrated system. For example, vacationers need to be influenced to go to a particular destination. Travelers must first book their air tickets, travel to the airport, check in, fly, arrive at the destination, take ground transportation to the hotel, check in at the hotel, visit attractions and restaurants, and so forth. Each component that the traveler interacts with is part of the system.
- *Governmental Approach*—Governments need to be involved with several aspects of tourism from keeping track of the number of tourist visits and expenditures to bilateral agreements for airlines.

Planning Premises

Many international planning premises are derived from the various World Tourism Conferences. For example, the Manila Declaration of the United Nations World Tourism Organization lays a foundation for recognizing the importance of natural and cultural resources in tourism and emphasizes the following points:

- The need for total fulfillment of the human being
- An increasing contribution to education
- Equality of destiny of nations

- The liberation of humans in a spirit of respect for identity and dignity
- The affirmation of the originality of cultures and respect for the moral heritage of peoples
- Conservation of resources for the benefit of both tourists and the residents of the tourism area.[8]

The Joint Declaration of the United Nations World Tourism Organization and the United Nations Environment Program (UNEP) formalized interagency coordination on tourism and the environment. UNEP's mission states that the protection, enhancement, and improvement of various components of the environment are among the fundamental conditions for the harmonious development of tourism.

Regional planning provides probably the best opportunity for achieving environmental protection goals through the use of zoning strategies and regulations. It can be used to encourage concentration of tourist activity in some areas and/or dispersion in other areas so that the extreme pressures are restricted to resilient environments and fragile environments can be given the most rigid protection measures.

▶ Check Your Knowledge

1. What are the names of the stages in the life cycle of tourism destinations and attractions?
2. What elements does Inskeep suggest be considered for efficient and effective tourism development?
3. What are the steps in the tourism planning process?

Guiding Principles for Tourism Development

Additional guiding principles were suggested at the Hague Declaration on Tourism cosponsored by the Inter-Parliamentary Union and the World Tourism Organization; the declaration continues to emphasize protection of the environment and made the word *sustainable* part of the tourism vocabulary.[9] The idea that tourism planning and development should be sustainable makes sense because, otherwise, areas would simply deteriorate rapidly and become uninteresting or unsuitable as tourist destinations or attractions.

Clare Gunn and Turgut Var, professors emeriti at Texas A&M University, suggest the following goals for tourism planning:[10]

- Enhanced visitor satisfaction
- Developing all infrastructures and providing recreation facilities for visitors and residents alike
- Improved economy and business success

Edward Inskeep suggests the following for specific goals for a tourism plan:

- Tourism development goals that include political, environmental, social, economic factors.

- A survey of the historical, environmental, sociocultural, economic, and land use factors and resources—man made and natural—that may have some bearing on the plan.

- An assessment of the present and potential activities and attractions.

- Transportation capabilities and infrastructure available to the area and within the area.

- An inventory of lodging-hotels, resorts, motels, bed and breakfast inns.

- An analysis of the markets currently served and a determination of future target market's needs.

- A determination of the carrying capacity of the country or area, including an assessment of the impact on the environment, social, cultural, and economic life of the country or community.

- The development of an integrated tourism policy.

- Development of a comprehensive tourism plan which includes participation by all the stakeholders. Environmental, government, social, cultural, economic as well as the key tourism businesses: airlines, cruise lines, motorcoach, automobile, car rental, lodging, restaurant, attractions etc.,

- Draft of plan is presented and input given.

- Plan is modified.

- Evaluation procedures for the plan are established.

- Procedures for ongoing updates are agreed.

Figure 6–3 • Inskeep's Goals for a Tourism Plan

- Sustainable resource use
- Community and area integration

The goals for a tourism plan are shown in Figure 6–3.

Tourism planning takes place simultaneously at various levels. As mentioned, on the international level, UNWTO and UNEP are involved in interagency coordination on tourism and the environment. They encourage governments and tourism officials to think strategically and tactically about protection, enhancement, and improvement for the harmonious development of tourism. Other international organizations include the International Civil Aviation Organization (ICAO), the International Air Transport Association (IATA), the Organisation for Economic Co-operation and Development (OECD), and several regional organizations such as the Pacific Asia Travel Association (PATA), and the Caribbean Tourism Organization (CTO).

Gaining the approval and cooperation of about 200 countries is a major task, particularly when developed and developing nations may have different views on topics such as environmental protection. However, there are some examples of successful international cooperation, for example, the development of the Mayan Route, which is a 1,500-mile route that joins Mayan archaeological sites in the five Central American countries of Mexico, Guatemala, Belize, El Salvador, and Honduras. This cooperative effort promotes tourism in Central America.

Government Involvement in Tourism Planning and Development

Government involvement is necessary in tourism planning and development in several areas, including the following:

- Policy
- Regulations
- Obtaining finances
- Issuing/monitoring loans
- Resource management
- Superstructure (primarily construction, facilities, and equipment to service the needs of tourists in a region including tourist information, lodging, attractions, restaurants, transportation, and events)
- Infrastructure (primarily residents' facilities and equipment required for living including water, electricity, sewage system, fire and police departments, education system, and libraries)
- Transportation
- International treaties
- Recording and publishing information
- Human resource development
- Training
- Health care
- Sanitation

Tourism Planning at the National Level

At the national level, tourism development corporations (TDCs) are a frequently used government mechanism for assisting tourism development. They are usually quasi-government agencies that generally are involved with development plans, proposals, and human resource planning, training, or even operation of tourism facilities. TDCs can also facilitate government loans for small business tourism development.

Edward Inskeep recommends that the national level of tourism planning focus on the following several elements:[11]

- Tourism policy
- A physical structure plan including identification of major tourist attractions, designation of tourism development regions, international access points, and the internal transportation network of facilities and services

- Other major infrastructure considerations:

  The general amount, types, and quality level of accommodation at different star levels and other tourist facilities and services

  The major tourist routes in the country and their regional connections

- Tourism organizational structures, legislation, and investment policies
- Overall tourism marketing strategies and promotion programs
- Education and training programs
- Facility development and design standards
- Sociocultural, environmental, and economic considerations and impact analyses
- National-level implementation techniques, including staging of development and short-term development strategy and project programming

Inskeep also includes land use planning as a critical component of tourism management and development. Land use planning includes planning for access, water, power, sewage, and telecommunications. Land is zoned for specific uses by elected officials (e.g., the planning subcommittee of a city council). Once the subcommittee makes a recommendation, the city council then votes on it. Requests for land use are frequently subjected to an environmental study to determine the impact of the proposed project on the environment. Other factors related to land use are the nature of the land; its location, climate, topography, wildlife, coastal and marine areas; ecological systems; natural resource areas; and historic interests.

A major planning effort by the U.S. travel industry aims to provide funding for the promotion of a more user-friendly travel system in the United States. Time will tell whether this effort is successful. Not only are international travelers frustrated by delays, fingerprinting, cancelations, and hassles at airports including lost luggage and long security lines, Americans have also turned massively away from air travel, a recent poll showed. "The survey results show that air travelers avoided 41 million trips in the last 12 months . . . because of the hassle of flying." Roger Dow, president of the Travel Industry Association, which commissioned the poll, says, "That's 100,000 trips a day and the cost impact to the U.S. economy is 26.5 billion dollars."[12] Now add in travelers' fears of swine flu and expect further decreases.

On a positive note, U.S. travel and tourism exports reached historic highs in 2008, when visitors spent $142.1 billion on travel and tourism-related activities within the United States, an increase of 16 percent over the previous year.[13]

Elements Necessary for Regional Tourism Development

Professor Claire Gunn suggests 12 elements are necessary for successful regional development:[14]

- Natural resources
- Cultural resources

- Viable service communities
- Access
- Markets
- Favorable development image
- Local acceptance of tourism
- Favorable government controls
- Available land for development
- Availability of entrepreneurs and managers
- Availability of labor
- Availability of finances

Regional tourism development entities must exercise great care to obtain a positive outcome. If a tourism region has all of the preceding elements, it is likely to experience successful tourism development. Should one or more of the 12 elements be missing, success of tourism development will most likely diminish. However, just having the elements in place does not automatically guarantee success, which is why there is a great need for tourism planning to coordinate the elements into a cohesive plan.

▶ Check Your Knowledge

1. Name some of the organizations involved in tourism planning.
2. List some areas where government involvement is recommended or necessary at a national level.
3. According to Claire Gunn, what are the 12 elements necessary for successful regional development?

Unsuccessful Tourism Development

Tourism development can turn ugly if something goes awry. The following letter, addressed to *Condé Nast Traveler* magazine, describes a resident's reaction to hotel development on the big island of Hawaii.[15]

> The people of the Big Island, Hawaii, were given a chance to vote on whether a new resort should be built on the then pristine Haupana Beach. Unfortunately, the wording on the ballot was confusing, and as a result, Haupana will never be the same. Your photograph does not show the huge cranes and mountains of earth blocking the view of the Kohala Mountains, and it cannot describe the noise pollution by heavy trucks and other equipment. The construction of this hotel has also caused pollution of the water at the northern end of the beach. Haupana used to be my favorite beach in the world, but now it literally brings tears to my eyes to drive by.

Many nations have regarded tourism as a panacea to provide an economic quick fix to ease a loss of production, employment, or revenues. As a result, some many destinations have become overtourised, glutted with congestion and overburdened facilities. Even though scenery and other natural resources are touted in promotions, visitors often experience more ugly commercialism than beautiful scenery.[16] The result is generally the overbuilding of hotels, polluted beaches, cultural conflict, and dissatisfied tourists. Stephen Smith, a professor of recreation and leisure studies at the University of Waterloo, suggests that the typical evolution of unplanned tropical beach resorts has eight stages:

1. Some local settlement; no significant tourism.
2. First tourism; second home strip development.
3. First hotel; high-budget visitors; new jobs.
4. More hotels; strip intensified; houses displaced.
5. More lodging; cultural disruptions; beach congestion/pollution.
6. More hotels; flood and erosion damage; tourism dominates.
7. Resort government fails; urbanized resort.
8. Serious pollution; lateral spread; fully urbanized.[17]

This model can also be applied to other types of tourism development.

Several early examples of tourism development belong in the "how not to" file. Here are a few: In the early 1900s, wealthy British and other Europeans were attracted to then British East Africa (now Kenya and Tanzania) for big game hunting. Within a few decades of the Europeans arriving, the blaubok (a large antelope) and quagga (a zebra) were eliminated, both of whom had survived 3 million years of contact with indigenous people. Men boasted of killing 200 elephants on safari.[18] One notable example of the carnage caused through hunting was an expedition led by then President Theodore Roosevelt and his son, in which 5,000 animals of 70 different species were killed, including nine of East Africa's white rhinos.[19]

In the early 1960s, many of the quiet and peaceful fishing villages of the Costa Brava and Costa del Sol regions in Spain were inundated with swarms of less than desirable tourists mostly from northern Europe. These quaint villages were marred by huge signs advertising English tea, hot dogs, and German beer, which some could not keep from "throughing up." What followed was uncontrolled development of high-rise hotels, condos, and rooms for rent that over a short time transformed the villages into mass tourism destinations in their worst form. This resulted in environmental decay. A poor image combined with overcrowding, low safety and hygiene standards, and cheaper forms of accommodation and catering reduced the perceived attractiveness of the region.[20]

Another example of how tourism can have a negative impact can be seen in the center of Paris in the once beautiful park known as the Bois de Bologna. For a while, the park looked more like a refugee camp when many former eastern European citizens "squatted" in the park in a massive campsite that included dilapidated trailers, laundry hanging on makeshift clotheslines, and pets along for the "vacation."

Tourism has polluted the famous beaches in the south of France. For years, the Cote d'Azur has been a popular haunt of the rich and famous. Cities such as Nice, St. Tropez, Cannes, and Juez le Pain became celebrity hangouts after their discovery in the 1950s and 1960s. Now, at the height of the season, public beaches are wall-to-wall people. On private beaches, visitors can rent a parasol and a 6 foot by 4 foot plot for the day for approximately $50.00.

The effects of too many tourists have necessitated that the famous Cathedral of Notre Dame restrict its number of visitors to 400 per day, down from several thousand. The prehistoric cave paintings at Lascaux in southwest France were closed in 1964 to prevent further deterioration of the paintings. Human breath, which gives off carbon dioxide, proved harmful to the paint. Now, this famous site's replica, Lascaux II, which was built to allow visitors a chance to experience the caves, is in trouble for the same reason. The challenge for tourism officials is to "manage" these precious resources given the expected increase in the number of tourists.

Those in academic circles have voiced concerns about the effects of tourism. In the publication *The Golden Hordes* by Turner and Ash, the whole process of tourism development is questioned.[21]

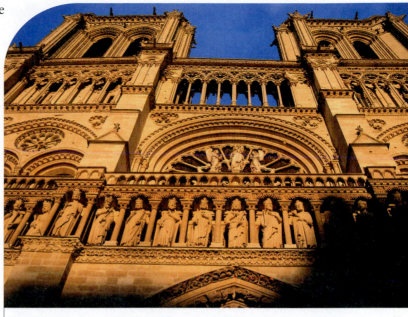

Notre Dame Cathedral, Paris, France. The life span of this tourist attraction has been extended by tourism planning.
Courtesy of Mark Green

These examples might give the false impression that all tourism is destructive. That is not the case. The point here is that tourism development should be sustainable and needs to be planned.

FOCUS ON

Tourism Planning and Sustainable Development: The Dance of the Sun, Sand, and Sea (SSS) Tourism Model with Sustainability

Robertico Croes

For quite some time, commentators have been concerned and hesitant about the existing sustainable opportunities for small island destinations in the world. The concern, apprehension, and sometimes outright negative attitude toward these opportunities seem to stem from the limitations of small-scale, misguided ambitions and limited managerial capacity. Doubt regarding the survival chances of these small island destinations is predominantly related to the **carrying capacity** of the destination.

Carrying capacity refers to a destination's recommended developmental limits to maintain ecological balance while supporting the tourism industry. A destination that has gone beyond its carrying capacity often appears to attract mass tourism and is perceived to have reached the final stage of decline in the product life cycle.[1]

Despite the apprehension expressed in the literature about the survival chances of small island destinations, the Sun, Sand, and Sea (SSS) tourism model has persisted; and small island destinations seem to reap rapid development fruits. Indeed, a new stream in the literature posits

(continued)

FOCUS ON (*continued*)

that not only are more tourism-intensive countries small in size, but they have grown more and faster than larger countries.[2] Some small tourist destinations display comparable high income per capita when compared to that of larger, more developed countries, thereby indicating a capacity for smaller destinations to overcome the pitfalls of size constraints.

There is evidence that the rise in per capita income may be linked to an improved natural environment. Thus, the additional income of developing countries may be logically reallocated to further improve the natural environment.[3] Currently, it appears that small island destinations have successfully defied the narrow definition of sustainability as measured by past research. This past research placed more importance on environmental destruction than primarily on population poverty and unemployment, which seem to be the main areas of development concern for small island destinations. As a result, small tourist destinations have increased their income. Therefore, they are more inclined to assign resources to improve their environment, which then continues to increase their sustainability.

Typically, small island destinations have found ways to balance their dependence on natural environmental resources and economic development. Their ability to accomplish this balance seems to arise from their understanding of how quickly to adjust, tweak, and manage tourist demand, and then alter the product accordingly.[4] This ability may also stem from understanding that as their destination's attractiveness increases, issues relating to the presence of excessive tourists may also occur. Their management capability is reflected in their efforts to constantly restructure the market through product specialization, market segmentation, innovative marketing processes, renovation of the existing infrastructure, and, finally, focus on quality demand and thus higher revenues per capita.

An example of this approach has been the character of the destinations of the Caribbean region. Dubbed the most tourism-dependent area in the world, the Caribbean has consistently entertained a world-class tourism infrastructure and service. The Caribbean continues to be engaged in a sustainable restructuring process manifested not only in the quality of the hotels and services, but also in investments in the local infrastructure and in efforts to minimize the potential negative impact on the environment. There is a strong incentive to live in concord with nature because the survival and prosperity of the population hinge upon the quality of its natural resources.

The island of Aruba interpreted the restructuring of sustainable tourism as a conscientious effort to preserve the balance between tourism demand and ecological life. Since 1996, 20 percent of its land mass has been designated as protected conservation areas to offset impending conflicts and challenges among residents, developers, and tourists. Such conflicts and challenges were anticipated as a result of the challenges of the globalization process of tourism.

Therefore, more attention was given to the actual and potential impact of tourism on ecological forces from both the local residents and visitors alike. As a result of Aruba's sustainable tourism restructuring efforts, the Arikok Park maintains support from the local residents as well as tourists. Perhaps this is one reason why Aruba has been able to consistently attract relatively high-spending tourists over the years.[5]

Arikok Park is located at the northwestern coastal side of Aruba and stretches over almost half of the coastline. The park is the habitat of unique flora and fauna species such as the rattle snake (*Crolatus unicolor*), the burrowing owl, and some endemic plants. In addition, the park hosts one of the largest Arawak cave painting collections in the Caribbean. It covers some beautiful natural scenery and hosts the highest mountain on the island.

The park covers four distinct zones. The central zone is the tourist's main attraction, providing access to a wide variety of cultural and historical landmarks, such as Quandirikiri, Huliba and Baranca Sunu Caves, the beaches, the old agricultural sites such as Fontein, and the goldmines. The North and South Zones are highly

FOCUS ON *(continued)*

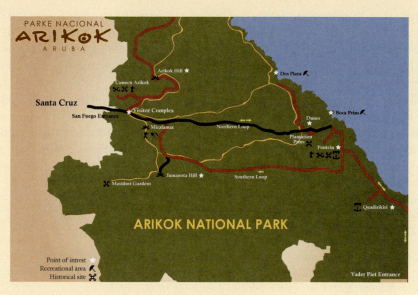

Courtesy of Fundacion Parke Nacional Arikok

sensitive ecological areas and have been designated as research and educational areas. These areas display a great deal of the local biodiversity largely made up of inedible plant and animal species where farming has proven intractable.

The fourth zone, the transition zone, is a zone on the outskirts of the other three areas. This buffer area adheres to strict guidelines aimed at minimizing the impact of any development within a one-kilometer radius of the park. The buffer zone touches the only Ramsar site (preserved wetlands) in Aruba, namely, the Spaans Lagoen area.

Protection of endemic fauna, flora, and the ecological system, as well as the preservation of heritage sites are important but are not the only goals of the park. What is really unique to this park is its strategy of using environmentally friendly design, building materials, and green energy to create the physical infrastructure of the park. The buildings in the park have been designed from the ground up as green buildings (which is a rarity in the region and in Aruba). This is in keeping with the mission statement of the park, which is as follows:

Mission Statement Arikok National Park:
We are dedicated to the conservation and education of Arikok National Park's natural environment and cultural heritage to both citizens and guests, allowing ecologically sustainable use for the benefit of future generations.

The design of the buildings includes the optimal use of wind and water to cool the heat triggered by the tropical weather. For example, the foundation of one building is built over a basin that is naturally filled with water and is intended to cool rooms from beneath the floor via ventilation openings. The combination of the basin's water, wind, and the ventilation system creates a more pleasant room temperature without the use of air-conditioning units. In addition, the park has incorporated a big windmill and two big solar panel grids to power the office building and the visitors' complex. Investments in the park during the past 10 years have exceeded US$15 million in building the legal infrastructure, business organization, and the physical infrastructure such as road systems, the visitors' complex, and so on.

(continued)

FOCUS ON (*continued*)

As Aruba continues to grow economically, it allocates more resources to preserve the delicate balance between ecology and its way of life. Located adjacent to the park is another example of sustainable efforts. Recently, Aruba invested more than US$100 million in creating the Vader Piet renewable energy field. This field will have a capacity of generating about 18 percent of the island's total energy consumption. Making use of its constant and pleasant breeze, Aruba is becoming one of the leaders in the region in renewable energy. It is expected that by 2010 about 18 percent of its energy consumption will be derived from renewable energy sources, thereby lessening its dependence on oil consumption.

The combination of a precise awareness of the developmental role of tourism, the tradition of reinventing the tourist product, and the use of technology bodes well in this case for a sustainable future of the SSS product. It is as if the Caribbean destinations understand the rhythm of nature and have been dancing eternally in a creative catharsis reflective of the bond between a people, their natural resources, and their perpetual pursuit for sustainable prosperity.

Endnotes

1. Y. Apostolopoulos and D. J. Gayle, eds., *Island Tourism and Sustainable Development: Caribbean, Pacific, and Mediterranean Experiences* (Westport, CT: Praeger, 2002); L. Briguglio, B. Archer, J. Jafari, and G. Wall, *Sustainable Tourism in Islands & Small States: Issues and Policies* (London: Pinter, 1996).

2. R. Brau, P. Lanza, and F. Pigliaru, "How Fast Are the Tourism Countries Growing? Cross-Country Evidence," FEEM Working Paper No. 85.2003, http://papers.ssrn.com/sol3/papers.cfm?abstract_id=453340 (accessed May 29, 2009).

3. G. Grossman, (2003). "Trade and the Environment: Friends or Foes?" In *Economic Directions* 13, no. 3 (2003).

4. R. Croes, "A Paradigm Shift to a New Strategy for Small Island Economies: Embracing Demand Side Economics for Value Enhancement and Long Term Economic Stability," *Tourism Management* 27, no. 3 (2006): 453–465; E. Aguilo, J. Alegre, and M. Sard, "The Persistence of the Sun, Sun and Sand Tourism Model," *Tourism Management* 26, no. 2 (2005): 219–231.

5. M. Vanegas and R. Croes, "Growth, Development and Tourism in a Small Economy: Evidence from Aruba," *International Journal of Tourism Research* 5 (2003): 315–330.

Source: Courtesy of Dr. Robertico Croes, PhD, Rosen College of Hospitality Management, University of Central Florida

Sustainable Tourism Development

For many years, concerns about the environment, particularly in developing countries and overdeveloped cities, and the future well-being of the world's communities have become more prevalent. The fear of losing natural and cultural resources to disruptive activities has sparked a keen interest on preventing, or even reversing, further damage and chaos. Dr. David Edgell, a leading tourism authority, says it all with his succinct statement: "The environment is the tourism industry's most important resource."[22]

Although such concerns are not new, it was not until the 1970s that issues about the well-being of the world and its inhabitants became a top priority. The United Nations first coined the term *sustainable development* in 1972 and used it to stress responsible actions in development projects. The key concepts of tourism sustainability include meeting the needs of both visitors and host communities and protecting and enhancing the tourism attraction for the future as part of a national economic resource. The relationship between tourists, host communities, businesses, attractions, and the environment is complex, interactive, and symbolic. Basically, tourism must improve the quality of life of the host population.[23]

Sustainable development is usually credited to the *Brundtland Report*, officially the report of the World Commission on Environment and Development. The report was based on an inquiry into the state of the earth's environment led by Gro Harlem Brundtland, the Norwegian prime minister, at the request of the General Assembly of the United Nations (UN).[24] The key environmental concerns of the UN were the high levels of unsustainable resource usage associated with development and the resulting pollution and major environmental problems such as global warming and depletion of the ozone layer, which threaten human well-being.[25]

Many governments, businesses, and communities have realized the importance of conserving and protecting their natural surroundings. Depending on the specific situation, needs, and capabilities, all parties and organizations have the same goal of being able to save the fragile earth and today's lifestyles and conserving them for future generations to enjoy.

Two key factors of sustainable tourism are *community-based tourism* and *quality tourism*. Community-based tourism "focuses on community involvement in the planning and development process, and developing the types of tourism which generate benefits to local communities." This ensures that a majority of the benefits go to locals and not to outsiders. Quality tourism basically offers tourists "good value for money." It does not necessarily mean that it is expensive. This also serves as a protection of local (natural) resources and as an attraction to the kinds of tourists who will respect the local environment and society. To accommodate the desires of tourists, several types of sustainable tourism exist, such as social, cultural heritage, and eco-tourism.

As pointed out by the United Nations World Tourism Organization, at many destinations traditional tourism management practices have caused undesirable social and environmental impacts.[26] Some of these impacts may significantly reduce the economic viability of the local tourism industry. On an even larger scale, this can in turn reduce the prosperity of the industry as a whole. Particularly at risk are tourist destinations with sensitive cultures or fragile ecosystems, as well as those that are highly economically dependent on the tourism industry.

The situation has been most acute in nations and regions that have experienced rapid growth in the tourism sector. In Mexico and parts of the Mediterranean, for example, tourist demands have led to an often disorderly urbanization of large stretches of the coastline. World-famous Cancun started out with the intention of developing a sustainable resort, but what became of that notion? It is a prime example of *un*sustainability and one of the worlds's most congested charter mega-destinations. Yes, tourism development in Cancun has attracted a lot of money to the area. However, who benefits most—the local economy, or giant corporations? On the other hand, who has to suffer the social and environmental consequences of this developmental "explosion"? Obviously, there is a need for present and future leaders in the tourism industry to be aware of and educated enough to secure the survival of their businesses or destinations, not only in the present, but also for the future.

► Check Your Knowledge

1. List the stages of evolution of unplanned tropical beach resorts.
2. Give examples of negative results of unplanned tourism development.
3. Define sustainable development.

UNWTO Indicators of Sustainable Tourism

As mentioned earlier, tourism is highly dependent on the environment.[27] The United Nations World Tourism Organization Environment Committee recognizes the consequences of not taking proper care of the world's environment. According to Collin, the environment is anything outside an organism in which the organism lives.[28] It can be a geographical region, a certain climate condition, or the pollutants or noise that surrounds an organism. The human environment can include a country or region or town or house or room in which a person lives. From this definition, it is evident that the environment of tourism can be viewed as possessing social, cultural, economic, and political dimensions in addition to the physical one.[29]

Thus, the UNWTO Tourism and Environment Task Force developed a set of internationally accepted indicators of sustainability for the tourism industry. The indicators function as management and planning tools for tourism development. Also, they provide information enabling developers to better understand the impact of tourism and links between tourism and the natural and cultural environments in which the industry operates, and also largely depends on. Although these indicators were developed a few years ago, they are still in use, and at this time the UNWTO is putting extra resources into a task force that is to produce a revised guide on how to use the measures.

The indicators can be used for both small-scale and large-scale tourism development projects; by national, regional, or local governments and planners; by resort owners, park managers, and even members of local communities concerned with and involved in tourism and its impact. In the jungle of information surrounding the world's largest industry, it is often difficult to extract the *relevant* facts pertaining to economy and environment. At the same time, the reality for many managers is that they must make decisions without adequate information. The UNWTO indicators provide such relevant information that can contribute to better decision making and, consequently, a more sustainable future for the tourism industry. There are two sets of indicators that managers can use and that we look at further in this chapter:

- General **core indicators** of sustainable tourism that can be applied to all destinations
- **Destination-specific indicators** that can be applied to particular ecosystems or types of tourism at a particular site, location, or destination.

These indicators can be further broken down into the two subcategories of supplementary **ecosystem-specific indicators** (for example, for coastal areas, parks and protected areas, or mountainous areas) and **site-specific indicators** (these are developed for one specific site). What are the real benefits of and reasons for using these indicators and how is it done? Well, managers that identify and measure these indicators are able to see specific cause-and-effect relationships between tourism and the environment. This includes being better able to

- Identify emerging issues and prevent or mitigate them
- Identify impacts early enough to act before they become problematic
- Support sustainable tourism development while identifying limits and opportunities
- Promote management accountability, and develop responsible decision making built on knowledge

This is not the only set of indicators available to tourism managers. Numerous international efforts have resulted in long lists of sector-specific indicators and measures of biological integrity and system stability. Economic indicators such as multiplier effect are used worldwide to measure how income from the tourism industry affects the local economy. (The topic of tourism economics is discussed in further detail in Chapter 4.) In contrast, the UNWTO approach is one of the first tools aimed specifically at measuring and supporting sustainable tourism.

This brings us to the question of how these indicators were developed. In short, they were initiated by the UNWTO and based on work done in Canada, Mexico, the Netherlands, and the United States. The core indicators discussed here were selected because they provide basic but sufficient information about key human–environment interactions resulting from tourism. Thus, they enable sustainable tourism management at virtually any destination. Before we go into more detail, look at Figure 6–4 for a quick overview of the core indicators and what they measure.

▶ Check Your Knowledge

1. What are the indicators of sustainability for the tourism industry used for?
2. What are the two different sets of indicators?

Site Protection

The site protection indicator simply measures the level of protection at the site, in accordance with categories developed by the International Union for Conservation of Nature and Natural Resources (IUCN).[30] Although each of the

INDICATORS	SPECIFIC MEASURES
Site Protection	Category of site protection to International Union for Conservation of Nature and Natural Resoures (IUCN) index
Stress	Tourist numbers visiting site (per annum/peak month)
Use Intensity	Intensity of use in peak period (persons/hectare)
Social Impact	Ratio of tourists to locals (peak period and over time)
Development Control	Existence of environmental review procedure or formal controls over development of site and use densities
Waste Management	Percentage of sewage from site receiving treatment
Planning Process	Existence of organized regional plan for tourist destination region (including tourism component)
Critical Ecosystems	Number of rare/endangered species
Consumer Satisfaction	Level of satisfaction by visitors (questionnaire-based)
Local Satisfaction	Level of satisfaction by locals (questionnaire-based)
Tourism	Proportion of total economic activity generated by tourism only
Contribution to Local Economy	

Figure 6–4 • The Core Indicators of Sustainable Tourism

Source: United Nations World Tourism Organization, *What Tourism Managers Need to Know* (Madrid, Spain: UNWTO, 2004), 11–21. © UNWTO. 9284404409.

following categories has specific management objectives, the actual level of protection may vary depending on the circumstances of the site in question:

• Category 1 represents *strict protection*, such as strict nature reserves or wilderness areas.

• Category 2 represents *ecosystem conservation and recreation areas*, such as national parks.

• Category 3 represents *areas for conservation of natural features*, such as natural monuments.

• Category 4 represents *conservation through active management*, such as habitat or species management areas.

• Category 5 represents *landscape or seascape conservation and recreation areas*.

• Category 6 represents *sustainable use of natural ecosystems*, such as managed resource-protected areas.

Stress

The number of tourists entering a site is often indicative of the amount of stress the site is under. Monitoring visitors is therefore a good way of obtaining information. Entrance statistics can be used to estimate stress for managed sites, such as national parks and wildlife reserves. For sites and areas that are not directly managed, other information sources can be utilized, for example, road traffic counts.

A typical example of a site under stress is Peru's famous Inca Trail. The Inca Trail is located in the Andes, stretching from the city of Cuzco to the former capital of the Inca Empire, the ancient city of Machu Picchu. Ever since the discovery of Machu Picchu, curious visitors have flocked to the area, which can presently be reached either by train and a short hike, or by the Inca Trail, a strenuous 4-day hike from Cuzco. The trail, taking hikers through the amazing views and mystical ruins of the Sacred Valley of the Incas, has become so popular that the Peruvian government fears the negative impacts of its constant "traffic." And rightly so: lately, the Inca Trail has earned and proven a reputation for being overcrowded, as thousands of adventurous tourists cross off yet another "must-do"

Machu Picchu and the Inca Trail
Courtesy of Mark Green

item on their list. So, what has been done about it? Admission fees have been doubled, hikers' fees have tripled, and a restriction has been put on the numbers of hikers allowed on the trail at any given time.[31]

The following categories of environmental impact highlight the types of risks associated with unsustainable tourism practices:

- Stressing the capacity of infrastructure by overcrowding
- Polluting air, water, and soil
- Overuse of natural resources
- Creation of noise and disruption
- Changing of the cultural character of host communities

In addition, there may be effects upon tourism from the activities of other economic sectors, including these:

- Removing land from its potential use as a tourism attribute (urban renewal activities, designation of resource development zones, exclusive forest extraction areas)
- Changing the quality of environmental attributes and, consequently, of experiences obtained by tourists (deforestation; river and coastal pollution; elimination of animal, fish, and plant species of interest to tourists)

With an effective means of understanding both the limits and opportunities afforded by the environment for tourism, and by providing a way to measure the effects of its actions, the tourism industry can best ensure its future viability. As such, properly planned tourism development, combined with protection of the environment, supports the concept of sustainable tourism. In working to achieve sustainable tourism, the goal is to ensure that tourism practices meet the needs of both present and future generations at the location concerned.

Use Intensity or Density Indicators

The **use intensity indicator** or **density indicator** measures potential levels of over-use of the natural resource in question. For managed sites, such as the Inca Trail in the previous example, information and numbers can be obtained easily and transformed into meaningful information. This indicator, which is a simple mathematical ratio, shows the number of people at the site divided by its area. For areas and sites that don't directly collect statistics, first they must identify the boundaries of the destination, and then gather numbers from different sources including transportation statistics and tourist counts.

Social Impact

We cannot measure sustainable tourism without including the social and cultural effects of tourism development, which is why this indicator is important. To measure potential social impact, the ratio of tourists to locals (at peak period) is used. This can be done by simply dividing the number of tourists by the population of the site. Again, for organized tourism, numbers are easily obtained. Say, for example, that a cruise ship enters a port, bringing 2,000 tourists into a port whose population is 500. This makes the ratio of tourists to locals 4:1. (In some cases, the host communities may be able to absorb the number of visitors, but in others the number of visitors may be overwhelming for the host community.) If tourism at a particular destination is less organized, statistics are more difficult to compile (such as with the stress indicator earlier). In this case, it might be better to develop specific measures for tourism impact on a certain district or community, rather than for the region as a whole.

Development Control

The development control indicator determines the extent to which projects receive a prior environmental review according to existing national, regional, or local legislation. Survey responses are ranked from 1 to 5, where 1 indicates no development control and progressively higher ranks are given for increased degrees and effectiveness of control. In addition, often it is useful for managers to monitor the level of enforcement or completeness of the review process. This may sound simplistic, and it can be at a site level. At the regional and national levels, progress can be measured in regard to the establishment of review procedures protecting key environmental assets.

Waste Management

When assessing waste management, the key indicator used is the percentage of sewage that receives treatment. Again, the process is fairly simple and can be calculated by dividing the amount of sewage treated by the total amount produced at the site. For intensively managed sites, this can usually be estimated by looking at sewage and water authority records. In some locations, septic and cesspool systems are the norm. For many sites, unfortunately, the amount of sewage receiving treatment may be close to zero. Again, because of the stress factor discussed earlier, this indicator is more important at sites accommodating a large number of people.

▶ Check Your Knowledge

1. What are the six categories of site protection?
2. What are the types of risks associated with unsustainable tourism practices?
3. How is the tourist to locals ratio calculated?

Planning Process

As with the development control indicator, this indicator is based on a ranking of 1 to 5. The ranking may be done by a team of consultants and host stakeholders. A score of 1 indicates that tourism development and activity were not formally planned. As before, successively higher rankings indicate increased usage and efficacy of the process. The basis of the concept is that most of the resources used by tourists are managed by other sectors. Thus, the values central to successful and sustainable tourism can be identified and protected only by a comprehensive planning process. In addition, it may be useful for managers to identify clearly the degree to which this planning process respects all the values important to tourism.

Critical Ecosystems

The basis for the critical ecosystems indicator is the theory that the rarer a species is, the more tourists will be interested in seeing it; therefore, it will also be more vulnerable. When this situation occurs it becomes essential to monitor the critical ecosystems and species, to protect them as well as to protect the tourism industry that depends on them. The indicator is based on the number of known species at risk, which can be classified as endangered, vulnerable, or threatened. If the number of species at risk changes, it means that one or more species have been eradicated, saved, or stressed.

Consumer Satisfaction

How do we obtain information about and rate consumer satisfaction? The good old questionnaire and sampling approaches work well. Here, visitors are asked two questions, of which one is mandatory and the other optional.

The optional question is asked if the first question proves to be inadequate or inappropriate. The mandatory question measures the perceived quality of the tourist's experience and therefore reflects many of the changing conditions at the destination as well as the tourists' changing expectations.

To make it a bit more clear, let's take a look at the questions asked. The mandatory question goes:

"In your last (current) visit to _____, which best describes your experience?" The respondent is then asked to rate the answer on a scale from 1 to 5, where a score of 5 equals Very Happy, and 1 equals Very Unhappy. Afterward, if needed, the questioner may ask the following supplementary question, which is: *"Would you recommend this tourist destination to your friends?"*

To further clarify the tourist's experiences, the questioner may also ask an additional open-ended question to find out why the tourist chose a particular rating. This information can help managers of individual sites better interpret the responses to the questionnaire. To get a large enough random sample for analysis (which is usually more than 100 people) and to ensure validity of the research, those administering the questionnaire must follow appropriate sampling methods. If the tourism market has several distinctly different segments, for example, summer visitors versus skiers, or hotel visitors versus campers, tourism entities may need to sample them separately. In addition, they must make sure that each of these segments is represented proportionately in the survey. Obviously, the segments will have different comments and concerns, and improper sampling methods may fail to reveal the true satisfaction of all visitors who visit the destination. If and when tourism entities conduct repeat monitoring, it is important for validity and comparison reasons that they continue to use the original sampling method.

Resident Satisfaction

As we all know, residents at a destination are affected by the tourism industry, either positively or negatively. The level of satisfaction or dissatisfaction can be measured by asking two questions of residents, one mandatory and one optional. Again, the optional question is asked if the first proves to be inadequate or inappropriate.

The first question is: *"What is your opinion of the tourism industry in your community?"*

The resident is asked to rate the response using a scale from 1 to 5, where a score of 5 equals Very Happy, and 1 equals Very Unhappy.

The supplementary question is: *"All things being equal, would you like to see:*

a) *More tourism?*

b) *The same level of tourism?*

c) *Less tourism?"*

If the community consists of clearly different segments, such as, for example, different ethnic groups, castes, or tourist sector workers, they may have to be sampled separately from each other. To reveal the most accurate level of resident satisfaction, each segment needs to be represented proportionately in the survey, and the original sampling method must be used when conducting future surveys.

Proportional Contribution of Tourism to the Local Economy

This last core indicator measures how dependent the local economy is on tourism. Obviously, the more dependent a destination is, the more at risk the economy is if it experiences fluctuations in tourism activity—as in an economic downturn or an outbreak of an infectious disease such as swine flu. The same can be said for the environment, in that pressure for development may be ill conceived by residents, and therefore would be greater if the destination has a high dependency on tourism.

For example, consider the problems faced by many remote islands. Islands such as the Bahamas and Bermuda have little choice but to depend on tourism for employment and income generation. For islands with, for example, approximately 90 percent of their GDP generated from tourism, how does a recession affect the economy?

"Residents" of this tourism destination seem unperturbed by their visitor.
Courtesy of Mark Green

▶ Check Your Knowledge

1. Describe the critical ecosystems.
2. What are the two questions used when measuring local satisfaction?

Composite Indices

The composite indices of sustainable tourism (see Figure 6–5) are made up of core indicators and ecosystem-specific indicators, which are combined into a single measure of sustainability that can be monitored over time. However, because of the large differences between sites, composite indices must be uniquely tailored to each site.

Carrying Capacity

Carrying capacity is defined as the amount of tourist activity that can be accommodated in a site, such as a beach, a village, or a region, without incurring serious damage.[32] Carrying capacity can be divided into sociocultural carrying capacity,

Carrying Capacity	Composite early warning measure or key factors affecting the ability of the site to support different levels of tourism
Site Stress	Composite measure of levels of impact on the site (its natural and cultural attributes) due to tourism and other sector cumulative stresses
Attractiveness	Qualitative measure of those site attributes that make it attractive to tourism and can change over time

Figure 6–5 • Composite Indices for Sustainable Tourism
Source: United Nations World Tourism Organization. www.UNWTO.org, © UNWTO. 9284404409.

environmental carrying capacity, and economic carrying capacity. It is usually expressed as a threshold (for example, in terms of maximum number of visitors per day).[33]

Carrying capacity as an indicator measures how fragile the site is, as well as changes in its ability to support various tourism activities. Usually, the carrying capacity indicator is a combined measurement of the quality, quantity, and sensitivity of a site's environmental assets, such as forest cover or quantity of natural areas, and the capacity of its structures.

Carrying capacity is used to get an idea of how many tourists, doing the most common range of activities, the site can handle. This number or limit can usually be raised by good management and planning. Conversely, degradation caused by mismanagement can lower the limit. Think back to our discussion of national and regional parks, and park management. How can popular national parks raise their carrying capacity? For example, how can they reduce crowding and overuse of the most popular areas?

Site Stress and Site Attraction

The **site stress** and site attraction indicator can be made up of several different measures of use intensity that are relevant to the site or "hot spot" in question. Examples are number of tourists, type of activity, frequency of activity, or intensity/concentration of use. A large number of measures used/created indicate that the site is under pressure from a wider range of activities. Of course, if the number rises, stress on the system has most likely risen, which means that the environment and/or tourism activities on the site may be adversely affected.

Site attraction is measured by factors such as landscape variety, cultural variety, uniqueness, level of maintenance, level of unrest/political stability/security, ease of access, cleanliness, and so forth. It is used to measure changes in the destination's desirability from the perspective of the tourist. A significant reduction of aesthetic appeal, for example, would negatively affect the site attraction index. On the other hand, good management and site rehabilitation can have profound positive effects on the index. However, it is important to note that the site attraction index cannot be used to measure differences between sites. This is because each and every site has a mix of attractions and attributes that is unique.

Supplementary (Destination-Specific) Indicators

Whereas the core indicators are great for a large number of destinations, some areas and sites are so unique that they need special consideration in the form of destination-specific indicators. Under this heading, two different classes have been developed. The first class is ecosystem-specific indicators, which is further split into eight different ecosystem categories/groups:

- Coastal zones (see Figure 6–6 for an example)
- Mountain regions
- Managed wildlife parks
- Unique ecological sites
- Urban environments
- Cultural sites (heritage)
- Cultural sites (traditional communities)
- Small islands

The second class, called site-specific management indicators, is uniquely designed for application at one *specific* site.

ISSUE	INDICATORS	SUGGESTED MEASURES
Ecological destruction	Amount degraded	Percentage in degraded condition
Beach degradation	Level of erosion	Percentage of beach eroded
Fish stocks depletion	Reduction in catch	Effort to catch fish Fish counts for key species
Overcrowding	Use intensity	Persons per meter of accessible beach Number of species
Disruption of fauna (e.g., whales)	Species count	Change in species mix Number of key species sightings
Diminished water quality	Pollution levels	Fecal coliform and heavy metal counts
Lack of safety	Crime levels	Number of crimes reported (theft, assault)
	Accident levels	Water-related accidents as a percentage of tourist population

Figure 6–6 • Ecosystem-Specific Indicator—Coastal Zones
Source: United Nations World Tourism Organization. © UNWTO. 9284404409.

La Jolla Shores, California. Is this an example of sustainable tourism?
Courtesy of San Diego CVB

To provide a more quantitative approach toward tourism sustainability and resilience, Drs. Tyrell and Johnson, tourism experts, have developed a model for assessing tourism's dynamic resilience, or the ability of social, economic, or ecological systems to recover from tourism-induced stress. Their model suggests that the long-term as well as the short-term operational benefits and costs of tourism be considered.[34]

▶ Check Your Knowledge

1. What are the composite indices measured?
2. How are they made up?
3. Give examples of ecosystem-specific indicators.

As the world's largest industry, affecting much of the world, the travel and tourism industry has the opportunity to really make a difference in the sustainable development of the communities and countries in which it operates. Of course, cooperation between developers, businesses, governments, nongovernmental organizations (NGOs), and the resident population is needed. This is where **Agenda 21** for the travel and tourism industry helps in defining priority areas for action, complete with objectives and suggested steps to achieve them. The strategic and economic importance of travel and tourism is also analyzed, and the enormous benefits in a sustainable tourism industry are clearly demonstrated.[35] There are enormous benefits in the sustainable tourism industry. So, what does sustainability include? Take a look at the following guiding principles for the travel and tourism industry:[36]

- Travel and tourism should assist people in leading healthy and productive lives in harmony with nature.
- Travel and tourism should contribute to the conservation, protection, and restoration of the earth's ecosystem.
- Travel and tourism should be based on sustainable patterns of production and consumption.
- Travel and tourism, peace, development, and environmental protection are interdependent.
- Protectionism in trade in travel and tourism services should be halted or reversed.
- Environmental protection should constitute an integral part of the tourism development process.

- Tourism development issues should be handled with the participation of concerned citizens, with planning decisions being adopted at local levels.

- Nations shall warn one another of natural disasters that could affect tourists or tourist areas.

- Travel and tourism should use its capacity to create employment for women and indigenous peoples to the fullest extent.

- Tourism development should recognize and support the identity, culture, and interests of indigenous peoples.

- International laws protecting the environment should be respected by the travel and tourism industry.

According to the UNWTO, the travel and tourism industry faces a considerable challenge as well as a need for fundamental reorientation to implement Agenda 21. However, the cost of inaction will outweigh the cost of action, and the very future of tourism may be dependent on the sustainable actions taken today.[37]

Strategic Environment Assessment

In partnership with both public and private sector representatives, the **Green Globe** Programme evaluates the current level of environmental performance of a tourism entity by using a strategic environmental assessment. Results normally include the following information:

- Cataloguing and documenting of positive and negative environmental impacts currently affecting the destination

- Identifying critical environmental performance gaps that exist between the current state of the destination and its environmental vision for the future

- Identifying opportunities for remedial action through both public and private initiatives

- An environmental policy for the tourism sector

- A detailed report on the current situation

- Identifying specific sustainable development recommendations for the destination

Action, Planning, Prioritizing, and Monitoring

Once the strategic environmental assessment has been made, Green Globe can work with the destination or tourism entity to set environmental improvement priorities and implementation timetables, as well as research sources of funding.

Sustainability indicators with which all parties can monitor and review their achievements are also introduced. These are established separately for each destination, but are based on the priority areas identified in Agenda 21 for the travel and tourism industry.

Climate Change

The 1992 UN Conference on the Environment and Development (UNCD Earth Summit) in Rio de Janeiro attempted to address a controversial agenda designed to protect the earth's environment and to foster less destructive industrialization and development. Unfortunately, the outcomes have been limited. The World Summit on Sustainable Development held in Johannesburg in 2002 noted that "progress in implementing sustainable development has been extremely disappointing since the 1992 Earth Summit.[38]

The second International Conference on Climate Change and Tourism (Davos, Switzerland, October 2007) underscored the need for the tourism sector to rapidly respond to climate change if it is to develop in a sustainable manner. This requires actions to mitigate greenhouse gasses from the tourism sector, derived especially from transportation and accommodation activities; adapt tourism businesses and destinations to changing climate conditions; apply existing and new technologies to improve energy efficiency; and secure financial resources to assist regions and countries in need.[39] These measures represent a vital element in poverty reduction efforts and for the achievement of the UN Millennium Development Goals.[40]

Increasingly, climate change, also referred to as global warming, is of great concern to tourism planners, governments, and citizens. When the earth's temperature rises and the ice melts in Greenland and other areas of the Arctic and Antarctica, the very existence of the Maldives, other islands, and coastal areas is threatened. The Great Barrier Reef and the Florida Everglades are both being threatened by global warming. As a result, people are beginning to measure their carbon footprint and reduce the pollution they cause that contributes to climate change.

In response to mounting concerns about climate change, the Kyoto Protocol adopted in 1977 formalized the commitment to cut greenhouse gas emissions by 5 percent by 2012. However, these emissions have only increased since 1997. Moreover, there is a consensus on the inadequacy of the targets set in the Kyoto Protocol (still not ratified by the United States and several other countries), together with the signing of and implementation of other agreements with greater environmental impact.[41] The seriousness of the problem has prompted policy and management intervention. At the international level, in 2003, the World Tourism Organization issued the *Djerba Declaration on Tourism and Climate Change*, urging governments to do the following:[42]

1. Adopt the Kyoto Protocol on greenhouse gas emissions
2. Research and collaborate on climate change
3. Move tourism up the agenda in the climate change discussion
4. Implement sustainable water use practices and the ecological management of sensitive areas
5. Raise consumer awareness of the issue

Tourism planners, sustainable development experts, some government officials, environmentalists, and many tourists realize that tourism has an impact on global climate change and that we need to act now to avoid further pollution, including the erosion of the ozone layer. Transportation, in particular, air and motor vehicle travel, are sources of tourism pollution, so should we avoid long-haul travel to be more environmentally responsible? There are many challenges and opportunities, such as the following:[43]

- Making it clear that protecting the environment is not incompatible with economic development, and that sustainable development clearly benefits both the economy and the environment
- Connecting environmental sustainability to the fight to eradicate poverty and to eradicate hunger in the world—the first and seventh, respectively, of the UNWTO's Development Goals

It is our responsibility to do whatever we can to ensure that we and others translate the goals into actions that meet or exceed the goals of responsible and sustainable tourism development and management.

An interesting example of tourism and climate change is Cambodia, which is one of the highly vulnerable countries in the Mekong region that is susceptible to the impact of changing climate. Tourism and especially eco-tourism are highly climatic sensitive sectors. Tourists love good weather—if the weather is too hot or too cold, tourists find it very hard to travel. The recent climate changes have brought extreme weather hazards to Cambodia such as storms, floods, droughts, and the resultant devastation. This hits a developing country like Cambodia harder than it would a developed country. A central part of the country's eco-tourism policy states that eco-tourism development must strive to protect and conserve natural resources on which it largely depends. It also seeks to reduce carbon emissions by using local resources where it is appropriate, saving energy and recycling. Another part of the policy introduces incentives by providing a "Green Label," which is a highly recognized award given to those who follow eco-friendly practices. Eco-tourism is a good way to promote environmental education and awareness to both hosts and guests.[44]

CAREER INFORMATION

If you are interested in a career in tourism planning and sustainable development, you have several different options. Many people work for organizations directly involved in the field, such as the World Tourism Organization or the United Nations Environment Committee. Also, a number of smaller organizations are involved in tourism planning and development on a regional or local basis in almost every part of the world.

Another career choice with great future potential is to work within a corporation, such as a hotel or a cruise provider, and handle their environmental policies and issues. Because the demands on companies to be environmentally friendly and sustainable are increasing drastically, so will the need for people with the knowledge and interest to handle these topics for them.

CASE STUDY

To Develop or Not? The Case of the Neyaashiinigmiing Alvars

Identified by the United Nations Educational, Scientific and Cultural Organization and Biosphere Program (UNESCO MAB) as part of the World Biosphere Reserve, the Neyaashiinigmiing Indian Reserve (known on the map as Cape Croker) boasts four alvars, a rare and extremely fragile ecosystem.

> Alvars are natural communities of humid and sub-humid climates, centered around areas of glaciated horizontal limestone/dolomite (dolostone) bedrock pavement with a discontinuous thin soil mantle. These communities are characterized by distinctive flora and fauna with less than 60% tree cover that is maintained by associated geologic, hydrologic, and other landscape processes. Alvar communities occur in an ecological matrix with similar bedrock and hydrologically influenced communities.[1]

Alvars cover only about approximately 0.2 percent of the globe and contain some of the most globally rare flora and fauna. They are also easily damaged. Given the small soil cover on top of the bedrock, these environments are extremely sensitive to soil erosion either caused by wind or inappropriate human interaction. For instance, one vehicle driven on the land could cause irreparable damage by spinning its tires, which would cause all of the soil to the bedrock to be displaced.

Community Background

Neyaashiinigmiing has a distinct culture that makes this location a perfect ecocultural tourism destination. Neyaashiinigmiing offers an opportunity to experience an authentic and fascinating ecocultural tourism experience. Cape Croker Park (the reserve's primary attraction) connects beautifully to the Bruce Trail (a world-famous trail that travels for hundreds of miles along the Niagara Escarpment) and contains wildlife, flora, and fauna that are unmistakably distinct and rare (like the Pink Lady Slipper Orchid). The Chippewas of Nawash, a First Nations people, also display a rich culture and heritage that are attractive to many visitors.

The primary strength of the tourism industry in Neyaashiinigmiing is its incredible natural environment combined with a flourishing cultural landscape that is distinct and authentic. This was shown to be true when more than 90 percent of visitors cited the natural environment or the unique culture of the community as the primary reason for coming to Neyaashiinigmiing.[2] There is also the traditional Pow Wow, which brings in between 3,000 and 5,000 visitors yearly and is one of the largest in Ontario. Cape Croker Park also is a strong attraction with several paths that link to the Bruce Trail. Opened in 1967, Cape Croker Park draws approximately 15,000 visitors annually into the community with a population of approximately 500.

The community needs strong economic development. The community has a significant unemployment rate because of its remote location and seasonal nature of the industries that are present (tourism, fisheries, and forestry).

The Neyaashiinigmiing Alvars

In 1998, the Neyaashiinigmiing alvars were evaluated by the Nature Conservancy.[3] It found that all four alvars in Neyaashiinigmiing were conservation priority rank 1 areas. This means that all four alvars were: (1) found to contain rare or endangered plant species; (2) in good to excellent condition at the time of the evaluation; and (3) of a significant size to make preservation efforts achievable.

The Neyaashiinigmiing sites also represent four varying types of alvars: (1) a tufted hairgrass wet alvar grassland; (2) a little bluestem alvar grassland; (3) juniper alvar shrubland; and (4) a creeping juniper—shrubby cinquefoil alvar pavement. The alvars found on Neyaashiinigmiing are very sensitive and could easily move from being relatively pristine to heavily damaged, if not managed properly.

CASE STUDY *(continued)*

Development Issues

The alvars could be a major attraction for eco-tourists. The challenge, however, is that if trails are developed, soil erosion along the trail will occur quickly; thus, if the alvars are to be developed, a puncheon would need to be built. A puncheon is a raised trail on wood planks where fragile soil exists. They are extremely expensive to build and require substantial maintenance and frequent replacement.

There is also a question of how much this development would enhance the overall fiscal situation. Although some guides could be hired and a fee for the tours could be charged, these jobs would be seasonal in nature and would not be well paid. Given the expense to develop the sites with appropriate parking, signage, bathroom facilities, and trail protection, cost recovery is not certain for a community that needs all of the resources it currently has available to it.

Questions

1. Are the Neyaashiinigmiing alvars a suitable place to develop an eco-tourism product? Why or why not?
2. If the Neyaashiinigmiing alvars were to be developed for eco-tourism purposes, what protections would need to be put into place to ensure their conservation?

Endnotes

1. Carol Reschke, Ron Reid, Judith Jones, Tom Feeney, and Heather Potter, *Conserving the Great Lakes Alvars: Final Technical Report of the International Alvar Conservation Initiative* (Chicago: Nature Conservancy, March 1999), www.epa.gov/ecopage/shore/alvars/alvar.pdf (accessed April 28, 2009).
2. W. W. Smith, *Cape Croker Park Visitor Study* (Neyaashiinigmiing, Ontario, 2002).
3. Reschke, Reid, Jones, Feeney, and Potter, *Conserving the Great Lakes Alvars.*

Source: Courtesy of Wayne Smith, College of Charleston

Summary

1. Planning is an essential factor in sustainable development and should include both supply and demand factors. Supply factors include such industries as transportation, accommodations, and attractions, as well as sewage system, electricity, and other such necessities. Demand must come from the use of the supply factors.

2. Edward Inskeep developed a method for development that calls for the creation of organizational structures, education and training programs, availability of capital, marketing strategies, and ease of entry and exit for all international travelers. He believes that if all of the elements are carefully planned, sustainable development can easily be implemented.

3. Complete tourism planning involves seven fundamental steps, including formulating goals and objectives, developing a tourism inventory, analyzing the existing situation, formulating recommendations, developing action plans, implementing these plans, and monitoring results and making necessary adjustments. Tourism planning is a continuous process.

4. Four approaches to planning include the community-focused approach, the sustainable approach, the systems approach, and the governmental approach. When planning, it is important to take into consideration the premises of UNEP and the UNWTO and other organizations as well as state and national regulations.

5. The UNWTO Environment Committee developed a set of indicators of sustainability for the tourism industry that can be divided into general core indicators and destination-specific indicators. They are used as management and planning tools for tourism development.

6. Planning for sustainable development entails raising the standard of living for the host people, developing recreational facilities, ensuring that development within the destination meets with the approval of the host people, and finally, establishing programs consistent with the people's cultural, social, and economic philosophy while at the same time optimizing visitor satisfaction.

7. Agenda 21 includes issues such as combating poverty, planning and managing land resources, managing ecosystems, and strengthening the role of women and youth and their communities, among others. More summits were scheduled to deal with these issues, resulting in charters and treaties. A special part of Agenda 21 provides solutions for the tourism industry. Other interesting policies and organizations dedicated to the topic include Green Globe and the UNWTO's Global Code of Ethics for Tourism.

8. Community-based tourism and quality-based tourism both have roles to play in sustainable tourism. A delicate balance must be maintained between the two. Other elements of sustainable tourism include special interest tourism, adventure tourism, village tourism, agritourism, walking or cycling tours, community assistance, and eco-tourism.

Key Words and Concepts

Agenda 21
carrying capacity
core indicators
density indicator
destination-specific indicators
ecosystem-specific indicators

goals
Green Globe
planning
life cycle
site stress
site-specific indicators

strategies
strategic planning
tactical or operational planning
tourism master plan
tourism planning
use intensity indicator

Review Questions

1. What are the indicators of sustainable tourism and how can they aid the travel and tourism professional in developing and maintaining a plan for sustainable tourism development?
2. Following are some of the issues that face many tourism developers. What would you do to overcome these issues?
   a. Overcrowding and pollution at beaches
   b. Overcrowding in cities
   c. High crime rates
   d. Depletion of fish stocks
   e. Endangered species (both plant and animal)
   f. Water pollution
   g. Defamation of cultural and ecological tourist sites

3. Why is tourism planning so important? What elements should be considered for development?
4. What is sustainable tourism? How does this definition differ from that of eco-tourism? Tourism in general?
5. What is Agenda 21 and what role has it played in sustainable tourism development?
6. List the different types of tourism that can be classified under sustainable tourism. Describe them in detail and explain what role they play in the tourism industry.
7. Describe some of the experiences tourists might enjoy in Nepal.
8. Explain the concept of the SSS tourism model.

Interesting Websites

Green Globe: www.ec3global.com

International Union for Conservation of Nature and Natural Resources: www.iucn.org

Organisation for Economic Co-operation and Development: www.oecd.org

United Nations: www.un.org

World Travel and Tourism Council: www.wttc.org

Internet Exercises

1. Go online and find companies that provide some of the categories of sustainable tourism mentioned in this chapter. Which one would you chose to do your trip with and why?

2. Look through the websites of the United Nations Environment Programme, World Tourism Organization, and other international organizations, and find the current environmental issues for tourism.

Apply Your Knowledge

1. Give at least three examples of destinations where the tourism planning has been successful, as well as three destinations where uncontrolled tourism growth has taken place.

2. If you were to plan the development of a tourism destination or attraction, what factors would you place the most weight on? Which ones do you think would matter less?

Suggested Activity

Create a tourism policy for one aspect of tourism in your area.

Endnotes

1. John R. Walker, *Introduction to Hospitality Management*, 3rd ed. (Upper Saddle River, NJ: Pearson Education, 2010), 494.
2. Geoffrey Wall, "Sustainable Development," in *Encyclopedia of Tourism*, ed. Jafar Jafari (London: Routledge, 2000), 567.
3. Seldjan Timur and Donald Getz, "A Network Perspective on Managing Stakeholders for Sustainable Urban Tourism," *International Journal of Contemporary Hospitality Management* 20, no. 4 (2008): 445–461.
4. Sandro Formica and Tanvi H. Kotheri, "Strategic Destination Planning: Analyzing the Future of Tourism," *Journal of Travel Research* 46, no. 4 (2008); 355–367.
5. Etsuko Okazaki, "A Community-Based Tourism Model: Its Conception and Use," *Journal of sustainable Tourism* 16, no. 5 (2008): 511–529.
6. Rich Harmill and Thomas D. Potts, "Tourism Planning in Historic Districts: Attitudes toward Tourism Development in Charleston," *Journal of the American Planning Association* 69, no. 3 (2003): 233.
7. Edward Inskeep, *National and Regional Tourism Planning: Methodologies and Case Studies*. World Tourism Organization. London: Routledge, 1994), 5–7.
8. World Tourism Organization, *Manila Declaration* (Madrid: World Tourism Organization, 1980), as cited in Clare A. Gunn and Turgut Var, *Tourism Planning: Basics, Concepts, Cases*, 4th ed. (London: Routledge, 2002), 15.
9. World Tourism Organization, *The Hague Declaration on Tourism* (Madrid: World Tourism Organization, 1989).
10. Gunn and Var, *Tourism Planning*, 15.
11. Edward Inskeep, *Tourism Planning: An Integrated and Sustainable Development Approach* (New York: Van Nostrand Reinhold, 1991), 35.
12. Jennifer Michels, "The Profession: A New Day at TIA," *Travel Agent,* April 25, 2005.
13. http://tinet.ita.doc.govtinews/archive/tinews2009 (retrieved April 28, 2009).
14. As cited in William C. Gartner, *Tourism Development: Principles, Process, and Policies* (New York: Van Nostrand Reinhold, 1996), 238.
15. *Conde Nast Traveler*, www.cntraveller.com, February 2008.
16. Gunn and Var, *Tourism Planning*, 2002.
17. Stephen Smith, *Tourism Analysis: A Handbook* (Upper Saddle River, NJ: Prentice Hall, 1996).
18. G. Monbiot, "No Man's Land," *Tourism in Focus* 15: 10–11, London: Tourism Concern, as cited in Andrew Holden, *Environment and Tourism* (London: Routledge, 2000), 32.
19. Ibid.
20. M. Brake and L. A. France, "The Costa del Sol," in *Tourism in Spain: Critical Issues*, ed. M. Brake, J. Towner, and M. T. Newton (Wallingford: CAB International, 1966), 302, Chapter 11, 265–308, as cited in Andrew Holden, *Environment and Tourism* (London: Routledge, 2000), 67.
21. L. Turner and J. Ash, *The Golden Hordes: International Tourism and the Pleasure Periphery* (London: Constable, 1975).
22. David L. Edgell, Sr., *Managing Sustainable Tourism: A Legacy for the Future* (New York: Haworth Hospitality Press, 2006), 6.
23. Ibid., 15.
24. Holden, *Environment and Tourism*, World Commission on Environment and Development, 1987, 162.
25. Ibid.
26. World Tourism Organization, *What Tourism Managers Need to Know: A Practical Guide to the Development and Use of Indicators of Sustainable Tourism* (Madrid, Spain: World Tourism Organization, 2004).
27. This section is based on the World Tourism Organization, *What Tourism Managers Need to Know.*
28. P. H. Collin, *Dictionary of Ecology and Environment*, 3rd ed. (Teddington, England: Peter Collin Publishing), as cited in Holden, *Environment and Tourism*, 24.
29. Ibid.
30. International Union for Conservation of Nature and Natural Resources, "2007 IUCN Red List," www.iucnredlist.org (accessed September 18, 2009).

31. InfoPeru.com, Machu Picchu Travel Guide, www
   .infoperu.com/peru/eng/cusco/machu1.html (accessed
   September 18, 2009).
32. Loykie Lomine and James Edmunds, *Key Concepts in
   Tourism* (Basingstoke, Hampshire, England: Palgrave
   Macmillan, 2007), 22.
33. Ibid.
34. Timothy J. Tyrrell and Robert J. Johnston, "Tourism
   Sustainability, Resiliency and Dynamics: Towards a More
   Comprehensive Perspective," *Tourism and Hospitality
   Research* 8, no. 1 (2008): 14–21. Palgrave Macmillan.
35. Ibid.
36. Focus on Tobago's Environment, "Sustainable
   Tourism," www.scsoft.de/et/et2.nsf/KAP2View/
   37CD1E91D9EAD34D052568C1004D44F9?
   OpenDocument (accessed September 18, 2009).
37. United Nations Environment Programme, "The
   Environment in the News," November 30, 2007,
   www.unep.org/cpi/briefs/2007Nov30.doc (accessed
   September 18, 2009).
38. Peter E. Murphy and Garry G. Price, "Tourism and
   Sustainable Development," in *Global Tourism*, 3rd ed.,
   ed. William F. Teobald (Oxford, England: Elsevier
   Butterworth Heinemann, 2005), 167.
39. World Tourism Organization, foreword, in *Climate
   Change and Tourism: Responding to Global
   Challenges* (Madrid, Spain: World Tourism
   Organization, 2008).
40. Ibid.
41. Mario Lubetkin, Climate Change: We Need a
   Proactive Media. http://www.ispnews.net/columns
   .asp?idnews=42465
42. Chris Cooper, John Fletcher, Alan Fyall, David Gilbert,
   and Stephen Wanhill, *Tourism Principles and Practice*,
   3rd ed. (Harlow, Essex, England: Pearson Education,
   2005), 755.
43. Lubetkin, Climate Change.
44. Sonya Yin, "National Tourism Policy: Responding to
   Climate Change," *In Focus, Contours: The Ecumenical
   Coalition on Tourism*, June–July 2008, 5–7.

CHAPTER 7

Tourism Research

OBJECTIVES

After reading and studying this chapter, you should be able to:

- Understand why tourism research is necessary.
- Realize the importance of research goals.
- Explain the types of research.
- Describe the research process.
- Design a questionnaire.

GEOGRAPHY SPOTLIGHT

Sea, Sand, and Sun: Kish Island, Iran

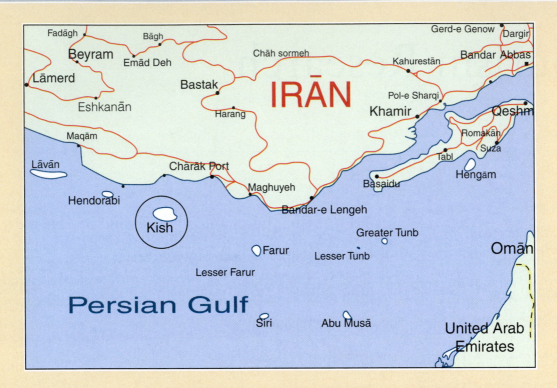

Usually, tourists hold the assumption that Dubai, United Arab Emirates, is the best and only option for sea, sand, and sun travel in the Middle East. The travel industry has put Dubai on a pedestal because of its glamour, architecture, and exclusivity. However, Dubai has overshadowed several similar development projects that have followed its example. One such location is the Islamic Republic of Iran, Kish Island, the alternative to Dubai.

Iran, formerly Persia, in known as being one of the world's oldest areas of civilization, spanning all the way back to 1500 BCE.[1] This holy land has been overlooked by the Western travel industry because of political unrest, religious war, and negative relations with the U.S. government. However, there is much more to experience in Iran than what is perceived in the West, and Kish Island is a great example of what Iranian tourism has to offer.

This Persian Gulf resort, located about 18 kilometers off the southern coast of Iran, was once a major trading center during the Ghaznavid, Seljuki, Kharazm Shahid, and Mongol eras. In 1970, the founding of the Kish Development Organization designated the island as a free trade zone and "as a geographically strategic spot for international trade and tourism."[2] This sparked economic development, increased trade, and transformed Kish into a desirable destination for travel.

The beaches are desirable because of their pristine sand, which is said to have a special glow, outstanding marine life, and clear waters.[3] The scuba diving and snorkeling is among the best in the world because of the abundance of reefs and species.[4] The Kish Diving Center provides visitors with an array of classes, certifications,

GEOGRAPHY SPOTLIGHT *(continued)*

en.wikipedia.org/wiki/File: Jhcfjuhfuvfjhyf.jpg

and great guided tours. At the same time, visitors can enjoy all other sea/sand/sun-related activities such as jet-skiing, boating, fishing, water ski-ing, and parasailing in the safety of shark-free waters. Tourists can benefit from the year-round warm and humid temperatures (77°F average), much like the weather of the Caribbean but without the hurricanes.[5]

Like more well-known destinations, Kish has breathtaking hotels, a spice of history and culture, and great shopping because of its free trade zone priv-ileges. As a part of the Sabet Park and Resort, a 70-hectare lush green park, guests also have access to the top attractions on the island, including Dolphin Park. This marine life amusement park and museum offers visitors a first-of-its-kind experience in the Middle East.[6]

In addition, tourists can also visit an array of historical attractions including the ancient town of Harireh, the Unknown Greek Ship, the underground town of Kariz, and the Marjaan Beach Park. Visitors can shop at one of the 14 duty-free supermalls, which contain a plethora of items drastically cheaper than on the mainland.[7]

The Kish Trade Promotion Center speaks of the Kish Development Plan, highlighting the developments in industrial and touristic operations.[8] There is no limitation on investment in any of the economic sectors. The only condition is that any activity shall not pollute the environment and cause threat to the destination as a whole. The overall plan has brought more than 110 industrial companies ranging from automobile pro-duction to textiles. Further, the Flower of the East development project is a $1.7 billion tourism complex that will include a 7-star hotel, two 5-star hotels, three residential complexes, malls, sports facilities, and a marina.[9]

The future of Kish Island looks optimistic, and this destination will, with a bit of luck, become more visible to the international tourism industry. Despite the political disagreements between the United States and Iran, this is an opportunity and destination that tourists cannot miss.

Endnotes

1. MSN Encarta, "Persia," http://encarta.msn.com/encyclopedia_761564512/Persia.html (accessed September 18, 2009).
2. Dariush Grand Hotel-Sabet Hotel Group, "Ultimate Relaxation in Dariush Grand Hotel," www.dariushhotel.com/F-SP-ENG.htm (accessed March 17, 2009).
3. Kish Trade Promotion Center, "Kish: Gem of the Persian Gulf," www.kishtpc.com/ktpc_kish_over_view.htm (accessed September 18, 2009).
4. Dariush Grand Hotel-Sabet Hotel Group, "Ultimate Relaxation in Dariush Grand Hotel."
5. Ibid.
6. Kish Free Zone Organization, Kish portal, www.kish.ir/HomePage.aspx?TabID=0&Site=DouranPortal&Lang=en-US (accessed September 18, 2009).
7. Ibid.
8. Kish Trade Promotion Center, "Kish: Gem of the Persian Gulf."
9. Ibid.

Imagine you want to open a resort in a popular tourist area. You must consider several items before you do. This type of endeavor will surely require a great deal of research to open and operate. Some questions to ask include these:

- Where would you open the resort?
- Is the location seasonal?
- What type of resort will it be?
- Will the resort have a theme or concept to build on?
- Who will potential guests be?
- How would you reach potential guests?
- Who will be your competition?
- Where are they located?

Tourism research aids tourism entities in the journey to finding the answers to these questions, as well as the many other questions that are sure to arise. The purpose of this chapter is to give a general overview of why tourism research is necessary, research goals, types of research conducted, as well as the general concepts involved in conducting tourism research.

Why Is Tourism Research Necessary?

The World Tourism Organization reports that tourism has become a major source of foreign exchange in many countries.[1] International tourism has grown rapidly in recent decades and ranks second only to oil in world trade.[2] Tourism research provides both businesses and consumers with a wealth of information. Most important, it provides information, which facilitates the decision-making process. Tourism research is now supported by more than 40 academic journals; many conferences such as the Council for Australian University Tourism and Hospitality Education (CAUTHE) are held annually and others are convened on an ad hoc basis; and many international organizations such as the Travel and Tourism Research Association (TTRA), the Association for Tourism and Leisure Education (ATLAS), and the Asia Pacific Tourism Association (APTA) focus on tourism as an industry.[3]

Research Goals

Although each individual tourism research project differs in its goals, this type of research seeks some general goals. For businesses, tourism research helps to identify trends in the markets. For example, if there are more consumers than sellers, the result is higher pricing and more demand, leading to less availability. If there are more sellers than buyers, the result is lower pricing caused by surplus, and less demand. By identifying trends, businesses can make better-informed decisions when developing promotions and planning for the future.

Tourism research also helps to unveil the economic impact of tourism in given areas, occupancy trends (most important to the lodging and dining sectors), and general consumer behavior. Market research assists businesses in ascertaining the need for new products that may better serve consumer needs and wants. It also aids in creating additional sources of possible profits and uncovers preexisting sources (currently in use) that are not profitable, reducing wasteful spending.

In addition, tourism research may examine the performance of certain areas in an operation, monitor guest satisfaction, and assist in drawing attention to potential problems. To succeed in the tourism market of the twenty-first century, operators have to know their market and know their consumers so as to offer them distinctive products and travel experiences.[4]

For the consumer, tourism research also aids in the decision-making process. Many consumers rely on ratings systems to guide them in their travels. For instance, the **American Automobile Association (AAA)** offers travel books to members that include diamond ratings for businesses (such as lodging and restaurants). AAA's professional evaluators assign each approved hotel and restaurant a rating of one to five diamonds, describing the level of complexity in service, décor, and amenities (simple to luxurious).[5] To be considered for approval and rating by AAA, hotels and restaurants must first apply for an evaluation to determine whether they meet requirements for comfort, cleanliness, and hospitality. If approved by AAA, a professional evaluator visits the establishment for an evaluation. All evaluations are unannounced to ensure that AAA's professionals experience a hotel or restaurant just as a consumer would.[6]

Categories of Research

Research can be broken down into four categories: descriptive, analytical, predictive, and normative. **Descriptive research** is also commonly referred to as **statistical research**. It aims to answer the questions who, what, where, when, and why? It is used when researchers want to describe the characteristics of a population or phenomenon. Descriptive research often focuses on a particular variable. It is accurate, but does not aim to uncover the **causation**. It is used to gain a better understanding without influencing (or manipulating) variables. For example, descriptive research is used in market studies, when researchers examine customer habits.

Analytical research is also commonly referred to as **explanatory research**. It builds upon descriptive research by seeking to uncover causation. Once a phenomenon or pattern has been uncovered, a hypothesis may be derived and influencing factors are examined further. This type of research is generally not generalizable to the population, but is specific to the circumstance.

Predictive research aims to make a prediction about an occurrence of something happening in the future. It is often based on past behaviors, attitudes, demographics, and other generalized phenomena. **Normative research** is also known as **applied research**. It not only aims to uncover the facts, but also seeks to provide recommendations for future improvements. Normative research is less concrete because it requires a subjective point of view.

Eric Cohen suggests four principal issue areas that were tapped for the early study of tourism: characteristics of the tourists, relations between tourists and locals, the structure and functioning of the tourist system, and the consequences of tourism.[7] Which category do you think research about each of these issues would fall into?

Types of Research

Qualitative Research

Qualitative methods[8] use subjective or humanistic research techniques distinctly different from "formal" or mathematical models known as **quantitative methods**.[9] Both qualitative and quantitative research methods have a role to play in tourism research. One of the main differences between the two is that qualitative research is much quicker to conduct than quantitative research is. Tourism leaders and researchers utilize qualitative research tools such as the **focus group** because these tools can provide findings that quantitative techniques cannot deliver. In a focus group, subjects are brought together to discuss an issue. Led by a facilitator, the group brainstorms topics and frequently comes up with findings that the researchers could not have discovered using more formal methods. Often, in such cases, open-ended questions are asked, allowing participants to respond freely.

Much tourism research lends itself to qualitative techniques. Researchers, for example, often seek to evaluate how a tourism opportunity will affect the host community of a region. Quantitative techniques may not take the unique feelings of specific people into account whereas humanistic-oriented qualitative research does more effectively in such circumstances. Tourism research embraces various qualitative techniques, such as those that derive from sociocultural anthropology, and the results have been impressive.

Quantitative Research

The sciences and business have tended to favor quantitative methods where, in statistical analysis, the researcher gathers data and evaluates them to locate trends or correlations.[10] The researcher begins with a null hypothesis, which presupposes that no patterns exist. In a simplistic example, the researcher may want to know whether having live music in a hotel or beach bar leads to higher profit. The researcher could compare the profits from a random sample of nights when there was entertainment and when no entertainment was available. All variables except entertainment should be held constant. Using situational analysis, the researcher could point to a possible relationship between entertainment and profits. But the researcher would have to demonstrate that the two samples were truly representative. Thus, if the weather was bad on every night when live entertainment was presented, the public may have stayed away because of the weather and thus the results of the statistical analysis would not reflect reality.

Both quantitative and qualitative research methods are significant and legitimate; however, on many occasions quantitative research techniques are indeed the method of choice.[11]

The Survey Method

The **survey method** is the most frequent type of tourism research conducted. Its purpose is to gather information about human populations by asking questions of respondents. When using this method, it is important for the interviewer to interview a **representative sample** of the group being studied. The representative sample should reflect the characteristics of the population to be studied at large. The survey research sector can be divided into two categories: questionnaires and interviews.

Surveys/Questionnaires

Surveys or questionnaires can be broken down into several types. They may be based on opinion (opinion surveys); interpretative; or based on facts (factual surveys).

Opinion surveys ask respondents questions regarding what they think about particular topics. Answers are based on personal opinion. Therefore, the answers are not necessarily right or wrong. An opinion survey may ask respondents to evaluate a certain topic or express their attitudes and beliefs.

Interpretative surveys ask respondents to answer why they chose a particular course. For example, a hotel may ask its guests why they chose to stay at the hotel; an airline may ask why passengers chose to fly with them.

Factual surveys can be thought of as being more concrete in the questions they ask. For example, they may ask travelers what recreational activities they participated in while they were traveling. The answers are based on fact alone, no interpretation or opinion is expressed.

Survey Administration

Surveys can be administered through the mail, through electronic devices, during interviews, or over the telephone.

Mail Surveys

Mail surveys are a low-cost way of administering surveys to a large, broad group of people. They involve simply mailing the questionnaire to a representative sample and asking respondents to answer the questions and return the completed survey. These surveys are also convenient in that the respondents are free to complete the questionnaire at their leisure. This type of administration also eliminates the chances of interviewer–interviewee bias because there is no contact made between them.

Some of the main disadvantages of mail surveys are low response rate compared to other administration methods and the fact that the language and structure of the questions can influence the outcome. Many people will not even look at the survey before it goes into the recycling bin! By using the mail survey method, researchers also assume that the respondents have a high enough literacy level to complete the survey, the survey is in the respondents' primary language (or they are fluent enough to understand the language of the survey), and they do not have other conditions that may inhibit them for completing the survey (e.g., dyslexia).

Electronic Devices

Electronic devices are expanding in popularity with the continued growth of the Internet. Electronic surveys are administered in a number of ways. They may be transmitted via e-mail messages, posted as forms on Internet websites, distributed on public computers (e.g., in high-traffic areas such as libraries, hotel lobbies), or even come preloaded on computers. Electronic surveys are fast, low in cost, and provide respondents with anonymity (which results in more honesty when providing answers).

However, electronic surveys also have some disadvantages. Because of the nature of electronic device administration, obtaining a representative sample is not possible, unless researchers are targeting a specific population. For instance, if a survey appears on a website, anyone visiting that website is free to respond. This proves problematic because the responders may not reflect the population as a whole. However, it would not be problematic if the target were to survey people who use computers or that specific site.

Interviews

For the purpose of this chapter, we break down interviews into five categories: structured, semistructured, unstructured, telephone, and focus group.

Structured interviews are the least flexible of the interview category. They are very orderly and include prearranged interview questions. In addition, they often have codes for responses. These interviews are often used in market research. Questions used in a structured interview are often **close ended**. They include **dichotomous** (yes/no), scaled (excellent, good, fair, poor), or multiple choice questions.

The limitation of a structured interview is that it restricts what the interviewer is allowed to ask and what the interviewee is allowed to respond with. Sometimes, if time allows, the interviewer may ask a broad question concerning any additional information the interviewee would like to provide at the close of the interview, but the scope of follow-up questions during the structured interview is confined. However, they do not come without benefits. These interviews are quick to administer (which allows a lot of data to be collected in a short time frame) and are very easy to analyze. Such analysis is usually done with computer programs.

Semistructured interviews allow the interviewer to adapt follow-up questions according to the respondent's answers. There is a schedule to be followed, but this is simply to ensure that all topics of interest are covered. The order of questions and the manner in which they are asked is left up to the interviewer during the interview. This allows for a more conversational and communicative approach. Semistructured interviews are more time consuming to conduct and analyze than structured interviews are. However, they are less limiting to the interviewer and allow more exploration.

Unstructured interviews (also called nondirectional) have no prearranged format. The interviewer may have a general set of probe topics to include, but is not confined to or required to ask about them. Generally, the questions asked during an unstructured interview are **open ended**, which allow respondents to provide responses of their own free will. These interviews are primarily used in sociological contexts.

Telephone surveys could fall under either the questionnaire or interview category of survey research. They are included in this section because they involve both an interviewer and an interviewee taking part in an interview. This method involves the interviewer (or computer) simply reading questions over the telephone to the respondent from a questionnaire and recording the respondent's answers into a computer database as they are provided.

These surveys are conducted much faster than any of the personal interview approaches and are also less costly. There are several disadvantages, however, to telephone interviews. People may have unlisted phone numbers or no telephone. Some respondents may skew their answers because they feel like they have been imposed or intruded on. These surveys must also be brief and conducted in a short manner or the number of respondents will be limited.

Focus groups gather together around 6 to 12 prescreened respondents. The prescreening ensures relevancy to the target market (or **market segment**) to be studied. The interviewer then asks focused questions about the topic being investigated. This type of research is qualitative; the purpose is to develop a broad and deep understanding rather than a quantitative summary.[12] A focus group session usually takes between one to two hours. Focus groups in tourism research are often used to provide a basis for further research and/or to uncover traveler motivations.

▶ Check Your Knowledge

1. Define market trend.

2. What is a representative sample and why is it important?

The Experimental Method

The **experimental method** examines cause-and-effect relationships under controlled conditions. This involves the researcher setting up a test, or experiment, to simulate what happens in the real world. It involves two variables: the **independent variable (IV)** and the **dependent variable (DV)**. The researcher in some way manipulates the independent variable. The dependent variable is then measured to see if there is a change. One major factor in experimental methods is the issue of **validity**, that the experiment truly measures the construct of interest (or what it is supposed to measure). To have a valid experiment, all variables that are not of interest must be eliminated to ensure that the researcher is measuring the effect of only the IV on the DV. **Confounding** or **extraneous variables** are variables in experimental studies that are hard to separate from the IV

FOCUS ON

Tourism Research

Stacy R. Tomas

Any tourism business owner will say that smart business decisions are usually based on research. Research helps businesses, destinations, and tourists make wise decisions. Tourism research can help destinations make informed decisions about development and marketing. Tourism research can also help destinations, businesses, and communities understand the impacts of tourism, both good and bad. Without accurate information (obtained from sound research), it can be difficult to make informed decisions.

Often, when tourism increases in a destination, the host community experiences benefits from the economic impact of tourists spending money in the local community. However, being able to accurately quantify the true economic impact of tourism on a community is not a simple task. As decision makers weigh options about whether to allow or curb more tourism development, or to continue or discontinue tourism-related activities, reliable information is needed.

For example, there is a large annual sport fishing tournament on the East Coast that has been in existence for more than 50 years. This tournament brings many anglers and spectators each year to a relatively small city. The city has always felt that the tournament was good for local businesses but did not know exactly what the tournament meant to the economy of the area. Likewise, tournament organizers thought that the competition annually brought valuable tourist dollars to the area but had no way to quantify the economic value of the tournament. As such, the tournament board of directors decided to commission an economic impact analysis to determine the economic contribution of tourist spending as a result of the tournament on the host city.

Survey research was employed to ascertain tourists' and tournament participants' spending in the local area during the tournament. The survey instrument asked respondents to provide their expenditures in several categories, length of stay, and number of persons in their traveling party, as well as other questions. Once the data were collected, they were analyzed using economic modeling software and results were achieved. Although the results of the study are not absolutely verifiable (as most survey results are not), the study was able to provide research-based answers to several questions, including the economic impact of the tournament on the local community. For the first time, the tournament and the city were able to understand, in terms of dollars, what the tournament meant to the local community.

A tournament of this magnitude is expensive to produce and requires significant human and financial resources. Annually, the tournament seeks sponsorships to support the event. The results of the economic impact analysis are useful in helping the tournament to calculate its return on investment. In addition, the economic impact analysis allows the tournament to explain how sponsors' donations were leveraged to create a significant impact on the local community.

Additionally, although the tournament is hosted by the board of directors, the local community still bears associated costs. While the tournament is occurring, the city must provide extra city services, and local residents must endure crowds and traffic congestion. The tournament makes considerably large donations within the city to support charities and worthy community projects in efforts to be a good steward of the city and to promote and preserve the natural and cultural resources of the area. In addition to this, the data derived from the economic impact analysis provided more information to demonstrate to the city the numerous other economic contributions that are made to the city as a result of the tournament.

Without results of the economic impact analysis, which was based on sound research and research methods, the tournament board of directors and the city's decision makers could only speculate on the economic contribution of the tournament. This research has allowed the tournament and the city to better understand what the event means to the local economy, and to quantify that contribution.

Once you graduate and become employed in the tourism industry as a practitioner, you will be asked to make decisions that could be costly for your employer or the community. However, if you can made these decisions with the assistance of research, either conducted by you or gathered from a secondary source, you will be able to make more informed decisions about how to proceed. Accurate and reliable information gathered from sound research will allow you to make effective and prudent decisions.

Source: Courtesy of Stacy R. Tomas, North Carolina State University

and DV. They can have influences on the variables of interest that the experimenter has not accounted for. For this reason, the experimental method is rarely used in tourism research.

The Observational Method

The **observational method**, also called naturalistic observation, involves examining the constructs of interest in real-world conditions. The key here is that the researcher simply observes and acts like a shadow. Researchers must be careful not to interfere with the variables being studied. Observations that do interfere with the variables of interest are termed *reactive* and are no longer valid. For example, an amusement park researcher may observe the concessionaires and their patrons during the lunch hour to determine whether the process is efficient and convenient for the patrons. Based on the observations, he or she may then recommend hiring more servers, opening more vending lines, or providing more dining tables in an effort to provide a more enjoyable experience for the patrons.

The observational method is more objective and accurate than the other methods described in this chapter. It eliminates the chance of interviewer biases occurring during the study. The observational method also allows researchers to examine spontaneous behaviors, which may not happen when conducting other types of research. However, it has limitations. It cannot answer *why* certain things may have occurred in the study. It can also be costly and the circumstances under which it may be used are somewhat limited.

▶ Check Your Knowledge

1. What is the goal when using the experimental method?

2. What are confounding variables?

3. What does the observational method consist of?

Research Process

Although there is no standard way of conducting tourism research, it is imperative that researchers follow some basic steps to ensure they obtain accurate and meaningful results. Effective tourism research follows the steps in the research process, paying specific attention to conducting a thorough demand (i.e., situational) analysis. The following describes the primary steps in the research process:

1. *Problem identification.* The first step in the research process is to identify the problem or area in which there is a need for further research. During this step the topic is selected.

2. *Demand or situational analysis.* The second step in the research process is to start gathering all pertinent information, or to conduct a demand analysis (also called a situational analysis). This step is critical to the researcher. A demand analysis does exactly what you would expect: it analyzes the demand for research on the selected topic. It ensures that the research will yield the new idea, not a replica of research already conducted. The researcher should have a good grasp on all relevant background information on the topic before developing the hypothesis (discussed in more detail next).

3. *Informal investigation.* During an informal investigation, the researcher furthers her or his knowledge on the research to be conducted. This may include going to the local library, conducting Internet searches, and talking informally with people of interest to the research design. During this step, the researcher also starts informally developing the hypothesis. A **hypothesis** is a prediction about future behaviors that is derived from observations and theories.[13] Hypotheses are often based on theories. A **theory** is an explanation of a phenomenon based on careful and precise observations.[14] Therefore, a theory has been tested and proved through scientific methods; a hypothesis has not been tested yet.

4. *Research design.* When the previous steps have been completed, the researcher starts to determine the research design. This includes the identification of relevant variables of interest, the data that need to be obtained, and the procedures that will be carried out to obtain these data. In addition, the hypothesis is put into more concrete, formal terms.

   Two types of data may be used in the research process: **primary data** and **secondary data**. Primary data are the original data that have been collected for a specific purpose. They are collected by and for the research design at hand. Secondary data are previously collected data that may be of interest. They are data that have not been collected by or for the researcher. An example of secondary data in tourism research may be a government report that includes total industry sales for the previous year. This type of information can be gathered quickly through library records or on the Internet. Primary data are generally collected over a long time period as a part of the research project.

   Other major sources of secondary data include the following:

   - *U.S. Bureau of the Census.* Data include 200 years of population information (e.g., housing, labor, agriculture).

- *Bureau of Labor Statistics.* Includes employment data.
- *Integrated Public Use Microdata Series.* Includes U.S. Census samples.
- *International Data Sources.* Data are primarily focused on economics and politics.

    The research must address some concerns if using secondary data in a research study. The researcher should ask the following questions:

- Who conducted the research study, and who is the authority under which those data were collected?
- What was the original purpose of the study?
- Was the study conducted through a reliable source?
- Does the data appear to be free from biases? For example, did the researcher have ulterior motives?
- Are the data really relevant to the current research variables?
- Are the data accurate and well organized?
- Have good **operational definitions** been used? An operational definition is clear, concise, and completely detailed.
- When was the study conducted, and is it still relevant to the present day?

5. *Data collection.* Once the type of research design has been determined, it is time to collect data. If the research design enables the use of secondary sources, then data collection should be just a matter of obtaining and organizing them. If using primary data, this step depends on the research design. It may consist of conducting surveys or observational studies or using the experimental method.

6. *Data analysis and interpretation.* Once the data have been collected, they must then be coded, tabulated, and analyzed. Today, this step is usually completed by entering the data into a computer program, such as the Statistical Package for the Social Sciences (SPSS). The first stage is often merely establishing counts or frequencies of response, often expressed in percentages.[15] This is followed by a cross-tabulation of the variables, in which the responses to one question are matched with responses to another.[16] This may reveal associations between the variables of interest.

7. *Research findings.* The cross-tabulation can reveal statistical data. The researcher is then left with several reports containing the conclusions to the study. The data are then interpreted and written up in a report. It is important that the results be written in a comprehensive and clear manner. The report should include relevant background information, the research methodology used, a detailed analysis of findings, recommendations, and copies of the forms used (usually included in the appendices). In addition, many

A customer satisfaction survey being completed
Courtesy of www.istockphoto.com

researchers use tables and/or diagrams to lay out the information in a clear manner. A summary of the objectives, findings, and recommendations should also be provided for the reader at the beginning; this is sometimes referred to as an abstract.

▶ Check Your Knowledge

1. What is a hypothesis?
2. What is a theory?
3. What should be included in the research findings?

Designing Questionnaires

Although they are the most used tool in the research process, effective questionnaires are somewhat difficult to construct. Before starting to design a questionnaire, the researcher must clearly define and clarify the research goals. Several considerations must be taken into account. The length of the questionnaire, its complexity, and question sensitivity must be weighed before determining the collection mode. For example, long questionnaires may not work well on the telephone, complex questions may require an interviewer to be sure that they are understood, and sensitive questions may be best given in a self-administered format.[17]

According to Dr. Laura Colosi of Cornell University, researchers should keep the following key points in mind when developing a questionnaire:

- What type of information is needed both to capture the important objectives of the research and to fulfill its purpose?
- What type of question(s) and response(s) will best capture the information sought?
- In what format should the questionnaire be designed to make it user-friendly and to also capture the breadth of information needed?[18]

Following are the steps a researcher should take when designing a questionnaire:

1. Based on the research objectives, plan what to measure.
2. Formulate a selection of questions and choose the best to include in the questionnaire.
3. Decide on the layout and the order in which the questions will appear.
4. Run a pilot test.
5. Correct any problems and run a retest if necessary.[19]

There are also some general guidelines to follow:

- Arrange the questions in a logical order (simple first).
- Keep the questions short, clear, and unambiguous.
- Avoid bias (if in doubt, discard the question).

- Do not use questions that ask the participant to recall information.
- Include instructions.
- Do not use leading questions (which make one response more attractive over the others).
- Do not use double-barreled questions (those that address more than one issue).
- Keep questions nonintrusive and provide broad answer choices when possible.

Selecting the Answer Format

As discussed previously, open-ended questions do not provide a concrete set of answers for respondents to choose from and therefore cannot be assigned values as easily as closed-ended questions. Close-ended questions are used more often in tourism research because they have concrete answers from which respondents can choose. Following are the main types of questions and answers used in questionnaires.

Multiple Choice

The respondents are asked to pick the best answer or answers from among all the possible options to answer the given question. This type of question and answer format is used when there are a fixed number of options to select from.

Likert Scale

The respondents are asked to indicate how closely their feelings match the question or statement on a rating scale. The number at one end of the scale represents least agreement (usually worded as "Strongly Disagree") and the number at the other end of the scale represents most agreement (usually worded as "Strongly Agree"). This type of question and answer format is used to assess respondents' feelings.

Ordinal

The respondents are asked to rank order the provided statements (e.g., put a 1 next to the item that is most important to them and put a 5 next to the item that is least important to them). This type of question and answer format is used when the researcher wants to see how respondents will rate items in relation to other items.

Categorical

The respondents are simply asked to put themselves into one of the provided categories (e.g., male or female). This type of question and answer format is used when the respondents must only be able to belong to one of the categories.

Numerical

The respondents are asked to provide a numerical value (e.g., How old are you?). This type of question and answer format is used only when a real number is needed.

▶ **Check Your Knowledge**

1. What should a researcher do before starting to design a questionnaire?
2. When is an ordinal answer format used?
3. When is a Likert scale answer format used?

CORPORATE PROFILE

Visit Florida

Barry E. Pitegoff

Marketing research is the application of independent, objective, scientific-method-based intelligence gathering to enhance the power of your marketing decisions. You hire marketing professionals to develop strategies and tactics that have a fairly good chance of success on their own. You enhance that probability of success with good marketing research. It might cost you a million dollars to make a television commercial with a 50-50 chance of increasing sales by $10 million. Therefore, the expected outcome of running that commercial is 50 percent of $10 million, or $5 million. If I invest $100,000 in some research to test three versions of the commercial and wind up with a commercial with a 70-30 chance of success, I just increased my expected outcome to $7 million, or an increase of $2 million for an investment of $100,000. Not bad.

Visit Florida is the private–public company that serves as the tourism marketing agency for Florida. We are the custodians of the state's image and we are entrusted with the growth of the state's largest industry. More than 80 million people visit Florida every year. More than $65 billion is spent in the Tourism and Recreation category in Florida each year.

At Visit Florida, we apply marketing research at several critical points, fairly similarly to how a packaged goods company might do it. Most important, we try to use research ahead of big marketing decisions to improve those decisions. Sometimes this means pretesting advertising concepts with qualitative and quantitative research. Sometimes it means testing new logo concepts and designs before switching. Sometimes we look at how to approach a new market of potential visitors to us. Sometimes that new market is defined geographically, such as China. Sometimes it is defined demographically, such as younger people or older people. Sometimes it is defined psychographically, such as gay and lesbian travelers, wedding-related travel, honeymoons or destination weddings, or the effect of having children in the travel party.

We also use market research to measure the impact of a program we did, such as a specific television campaign, to measure satisfaction with our programs or to test our website's usability. Sometimes we use research to strategize against a new competitive factor, such as continually watching attitudes of Americans toward opening travel with Cuba and how to respond to any threats to market share. Sometimes we track attitudes.

beSatisfied has been a great research supplier to Visit Florida for two ongoing projects that we can talk about. (Even at Visit Florida, some research is confidential.) Every month, beSatisfied telephones Floridians to ask about where they went on vacation in the past month. These surveys are conducted in English and Spanish, depending on the preferred language of the respondent. At the same time, we ask Floridians about their attitudes toward tourism in Florida and how important tourism is to them. In tourism, our residents are hosting more than 80 million guests a year. If these visitors feel that our residents do not want them here, then surely they will go elsewhere.

Recommendations for Further Research

The Travel and Tourism Research Association (TTRA) provides researchers with sources of information through publications, conferences, and networking. It provides members with employment opportunities in the tourism field, interactive forums, as well as educational opportunities.[20]

CORPORATE PROFILE (*continued*)

beSatisfied also does annual surveys for us of the satisfaction of our key partners. When we do that, Visit Florida operates as a business-to-business researcher. There are more than 3,500 tourism companies in Florida that have become partners with Visit Florida, ranging from the major theme parks to small bed–and–breakfast facilities. How pleased are they with our programs? How can we improve them? This is important to research and to respond to in order to keep our business alliances strong. Similarly, Visit Florida, like many private businesses, has a board of directors setting the policy and direction for Visit Florida. In our case, there are just more than 50 members of the board. Through the team at beSatisfied, these board members are polled annually on how satisfied they are with the performance of the managers at Visit Florida.

This type of surveying done for Visit Florida in these examples requires the most professional of interviewers. Instead of calling consumers at random and not needing their names, these interviewers are calling our board members and industry partners who know us by name. If the respondent feels upset by the interviewer, we will surely hear about it and our professional relationship with the respondent will be in jeopardy. We brief the interviewers in person, we monitor the initial days of interviewing, and we follow up if one of these types of respondents has an additional question as a result of the surveys.

It is very important to stay on top of how this field changes. That is why we are active in the Marketing Research Association. . . . Sometimes technology changes, such as when we went from paper surveys to electronic surveys, meaning you can tabulate as you go along. Sometimes it is dealing with the challenge of random digit phone surveys when almost one-fifth of the country does not have land lines and you cannot automatically dial cell phones for surveys. There are ways to handle this. In our case, we are dealing with known samples with known names and known phone numbers. Sometimes, you change surveys because of how people change. Twenty years ago, we used to ask, "When you go on vacation, do you take along children under the age of 18?" Now we ask, "When you go on vacation, do you take along children or grandchildren under the age of 16?" This is related to the sociology factor of KGUY, or Kids Grow Up Younger, meaning there is a shifting down of age-appropriate and age-specific behavior.

Finally, and related to that, only put questions in surveys where you can apply and use the information from them. My favorite example is the traditional demographic classifying question: SMWD, check one. Are you single, married, widowed, or divorced? First, really see whether the responses to this correlate in any way to other questions. How does the box you check in that question reflect how you answer the other questions? In my case, I try to check all four boxes but the survey usually does not let me. Today I am officially single. My first wife died, so I will always be widowed. My second marriage ended in divorce, so I will always be divorced. I have a dating relationship which is "all but married." Give me a really good reason to use that question before putting it in a survey.

Good luck in your career.

Source: Courtesy of Barry E. Pitegoff, Former Vice President of Research at Visit Florida.

The United Nations World Tourism Organization (UNWTO) is a specialized agency of the United Nations. It is the leading international organization in the field of tourism. It serves as a global forum for tourism policy issues and a practical source of tourism know-how. WTO membership includes 160 countries and territories and more than 350 affiliate members representing the private sector, educational institutions, tourism associations, and local tourism authorities.[21] The UNWTO also conducts research on various aspects of tourism.

Tourism Industries, U.S. Department of Commerce Office of Travel and Tourism Industries (OTTI) collects, analyzes, and disseminates international travel and tourism statistics for the U.S. travel and tourism statistical system.[22] The department's primary functions are as follows:

- Management of the travel and tourism statistical system for assessing the economic contribution of the industry and providing the sole source for characteristic statistics on international travel to and from the United States

- Design and administration of an international promotion program and export expansion activities

- Development and management of tourism policy, strategy, and advocacy, and technical assistance for expanding this key export (international inbound tourism) and assisting in domestic economic development.[23]

The **U.S. Travel Data Center (USTDC)** is the research division of the Travel Industry Association (TIA). The Travel Industry Association is a nonprofit trade organization that represents and speaks for the common interests of the $740 billion U.S. travel industry.[24] The center's main objectives are as follows:

- Conduct statistical, economic, and market research concerning travel

- Encourage standardized travel research terminology and techniques

- Monitor trends in travel activity and the travel industry

- Measure the economic impact of travel on geographic areas and the cost of travel in the United States

- Evaluate the effect of government programs on travel and the travel industry

- Forecast travel activity and expenditures

Conclusion

Tourism research is a vital asset to the industry. For businesses, tourism research assists in the identification of **market trends**, helps to unveil the economic impact of tourism, occupancy trends, and general consumer behavior. Market research assists businesses in ascertaining the need for new products, aids in creating additional sources of possible profits, and uncovers preexisting sources that are not profitable. For the consumer, tourism research aids in the decision-making process. Effective tourism research is dependent on clearly defined research goals, a thorough demand analysis, and a well-developed research design.

Trends in Tourism Research

- Tourism will continue to be a fast growing sector in research.
- With less time to travel, there will be an increase in travelers taking shorter vacations (e.g., long weekends); tourism research will examine this trend.
- There will be an increased research focus on travelers using the Internet for their traveling needs.
- Research will focus on the increased traveler demand for destinations that protect the authenticity and geographic character of destinations.
- There will be more research concentrating on the baby boomer generation as they enter retirement, including traits, destinations, and activities.
- There will be more research concentrating on Generation X as they enter their peak earning years.
- With fluctuations in the economy come fluctuations in business travel; research will continue to examine this association.
- With more Generation Y consumers and employees, additional research becomes advantageous as organizations may want to learn more about their lifestyle preferences.
- As with business travel, consumer confidence has also led to swings in the travel sector; research will continue to inspect this relationship.

CASE STUDY

Conducting Tourism Research

You are the research director of a large zoo located in the southern United States. The zoo has a national reputation and is the only zoo in the state. The zoo has experienced much success over the years and is a popular tourism attraction for the state. Over the past few years, there has been a noticeable increase in the number of Hispanic visitors to the zoo. The zoo director approaches you and asks you to find out more about the zoo's Hispanic visitors and whether the zoo is effectively meeting the needs of this market segment. How do you proceed?

Questions

1. What types of research methods might you use to conduct your research? Why?
2. What types of information would be useful to know?
3. Many of the visitors do not speak English as their first language. How might you gather information from these visitors?
4. Is there any secondary data the zoo could use to learn more about the Hispanic travel market in general?

Source: Courtesy of Stacy R. Tomas, North Carolina State University.

Summary

1. Tourism research provides both businesses and consumers with a wealth of information. Most important, it provides information that facilitates the decision-making process.
2. Although each individual tourism research project differs in its goals, there are some general goals that this type of research seeks to uncover or explain.
3. The survey method is the most frequent type of tourism research conducted. Its purpose is to gather information about human populations by asking questions of respondents.
4. Surveys may be based on opinion (opinion surveys); interpretative; or based on facts (factual surveys).
5. Surveys may be administered through the mail, through electronic devices, during interviews, or over the telephone.
6. The experimental method examines cause-and-effect relationships under controlled conditions.
7. The observational method, also called naturalistic observation, involves examining the constructs of interest in real-world conditions.
8. Effective tourism research follows the steps in the research process, paying specific attention to conducting a thorough demand (i.e., situational) analysis.
9. Effective questionnaires are somewhat difficult to construct.
10. Before starting to design a questionnaire, the research goals must be clearly defined and clarified.
11. For businesses, tourism research assists in the identification of market trends, helps to unveil the economic impact of tourism, occupancy trends, and general consumer behavior.

Key Words and Concepts

American Automobile Association (AAA)
analytical research
applied research
causation
close-ended question
confounding
dependent variable (DV)
descriptive research
dichotomous
experimental method
exploratory research
extraneous variables
factual surveys
focus groups

hypothesis
independent variable (IV)
interpretative surveys
market segment
market trends
normative research
observational method
open-ended question
operational definition
opinion surveys
predictive research
primary data
qualitative methods
quantitative methods
representative sample

secondary data
semistructured interview
statistical research
structured interview
survey method
telephone survey
theory
Tourism Industries, U.S. Department of Commerce Office of Travel and Tourism Industries (OTTI)
unstructured interview
U.S. Travel Data Center (USTDC)
validity

Review Questions

1. What is a focus group?
2. Discuss the relationship between the independent variable and a dependent variable.
3. Discuss the benefits and drawbacks of surveys administered through the mail.
4. Discuss the benefits and drawbacks of surveys administered over the telephone.
5. Discuss the difference between structured, semistructured, and unstructured interviews.

Interesting Websites

American Association for Public Opinion Research (AAPOR): www.aapor.org

American Statistical Association: www.amstat.org

Council of American Survey Research Organizations: www.casro.org

Integrated Public Use Microdata Series International: https://international.ipums.org/international

U.S. Census Bureau: www.census.gov

U.S. Department of Labor Bureau of Labor Statistics: www.bls.gov

Internet Exercises

1. Go to the U.S. Department of Labor Bureau of Labor Statistics website at www.bls.gov. Follow the Spending and Time Use link. Answer the following questions:
   a. What are the two consumer expenditure surveys used to collect data?
   b. According to the tables provided, what is the average income for all consumers before taxes? What is the average age of the referenced person(s)?
   c. What is the average annual expenditure on entertainment?
2. Go to the Travel Industry Association (TIA) website at www.tia.org. Click on the link to research and publications. What is the latest just-released research information?

Apply Your Knowledge

1. Provide some reasons why tourism research is important for businesses.
2. How have you made use of tourism research in your own life?
3. What is the difference between primary data and secondary data?
4. What is the difference between qualitative research and quantitative research?
5. What are the steps in the research process?

Suggested Activity

Develop two survey questionnaires, one for tourist satisfaction in your community and the other to enable community residents to determine their level of satisfaction with tourism.

Endnotes

1. As cited in W. Wu, S. Hsiao, and C. Tsai, "Forecasting and Evaluating the Tourist Hotel Industry Performance in Taiwan Based on Grey Theory," *Tourism and Hospitality Research* 8, no. 2 (2008): 137, www.palgrave-journals.com/thr/journal/v8/n2/abs/thr200817a.html (accessed September 19, 2009).

2. F. L. Chu, "Forecasting Tourism Demand: A Cubic Polynomial Approach," *Tourism Management* 25, no. 2(2004): 209–218.

3. Eric Laws, review of: *Tourism Research Methods: Integrating Theory with Practice*, by Brent W. Ritchie, Peter Burns, and Catherine Palmer, *Asia Pacific Journal of Tourism Research* 12, no. 1 (March 2007): 67–69.

4. Canadian Tourism Commission, "The American Tourism Market: Evolution 2010,"www.corporate.canada.travel/en/ca/index.html (accessed November 13, 2008).

5. AAA Newsroom, "AAA's Diamond Rating Process," www.aaanewsroom.net/Main/Default.asp?CategoryID=9&SubCategoryID=22&ContentID=86 (accessed October 27, 2008).

6. Ibid.

7. Eric Cohen, "The Sociology of Tourism: Approaches, Issues, and Findings," *Annual Review of Sociology* 20 (1984): 373–392.

8. This section draws on: Alf H. Walle, "Qualitative Research," in *The Encyclopedia of Tourism*, ed. Jafar Jafari (London: Routledge, 2000), 478.

9. Walle, "Qualitative Research," 478.

10. This section draws on: Walle, "Qualitative Research," 483–484.

11. Ibid., 478.

12. Program Development and Evaluation, *Focus Group Interviews, Quick Tips #5*, University of Wisconsin-Extension, Madison, WI, www.uwex.edu/ces/pdande/resources/pdf/Tipsheet5.pdf (accessed November 3, 2008).

13. S. Davis and J. Palladino, *Psychology*, 5th ed. (Upper Saddle River, NJ: Prentice Hall, 2006), 11.

14. Ibid.

15. C. Cooper, J. Fletcher, A. Fyall, D. Gilbert, and S. Wanhill, *Tourism: Principles and Practice* (Essex, England: Pearson Education, 2005), 103.

16. Ibid.

17. Linda Stinson, *Designing a Questionnaire: Section on Survey Research Methods* (Alexandria, VA: American Statistical Association, 2000).

18. Laura Colosi, *Designing an Effective Questionnaire* (Ithaca, NY: Cornell University Cooperative Extension, 2006).

19. Cooper, Fletcher, Fyall, Gilbert, and Wanhill, *Tourism*, 103.

20. Travel and Tourism Research Association, "About TTRA," www.ttra.com/about.php (accessed November 13, 2008).

21. World Tourism Organization, "About UNWTO," www.unwto.org/aboutwto/index.php (accessed November 13, 2008).

22. Office of Travel and Tourism Industries, "Travel and Tourism Research Programs," http://tinet.ita.doc.gov/research/index.html (accessed November 13, 2008).

23. Office of Travel and Tourism Industries, "About OTTI," http://tinet.ita.doc.gov/about/index.html (accessed November 13, 2008).

24. Travel Industry Association, "About," www.tia.org/about/what_we_do.html (accessed November 13, 2008).

PART 3

Operating Sectors 1

CHAPTER 8

Attractions and Entertainment

OBJECTIVES

After reading and studying this chapter, you should be able to:

- List the major players in the amusement park industry.

- Identify trends in the amusement and theme park industry.

- Explain the reasons for the immense growth of the gaming entertainment industry.

- Explain the main reasons for travel in the following areas: fairs, festivals, events, historic places/sites, and performing arts.

- Give some examples of important festivals, fairs, and events.

- Discuss trends in leisure travel.

GEOGRAPHY SPOTLIGHT

Romantic Tourism: Tokyo

In a city with a population of 27.5 million people, it may seem next to impossible to find a secluded romantic spot just big enough for two.[1] However, within this bustling metropolis an array of romance coupled with a little magic can be found within the Tokyo Disneyland Resort. Tokyo Disneyland Resort is located approximately 60 minutes away from Narita International Airport just outside of Tokyo.[2] The resort, which boasts the highest number of attendees of any theme park in Japan, comprises two theme parks, Tokyo Disneyland and Tokyo DisneySea, and three resort hotels, including the Disney Ambassador, Tokyo Disneyland Hotel, and Tokyo DisneySea Hotel Miracosta.[3]

Tokyo Disneyland opened on April 15, 1983, making it the fourth Disney park overall and the first one located outside of the United States.[4] The park is divided into seven different areas: World Bazaar, Westernland, Adventure, Fantasyland, Tomorrowland, Critter Country, and Toontown.[5] Couples can count on an evening of romance in Tokyo Disneyland with Dreamlights electrical parade and Disney Magic in the Sky firework display. Dreamlights lights up Tokyo Disneyland by featuring popular Disney characters and movies covered with hundreds of tiny sparkling lights.[6] Dreamlights pairs whimsy with romance and provides the perfect precursor to Disney Magic in the Sky. This nightly show combines breathtaking fireworks with the sounds of classic Disney tunes such as "Bibbidi Bobbidi Boo," "Beauty and the Beast," and concludes with "When You Wish upon a Star," leaving couples with love and stars in their eyes.[7]

Tokyo DisneySea opened in September 2001 and also features seven different areas with a nautical theme: Mediterranean Harbor, Mysterious Island, Mermaid Lagoon, Arabian Coast, Lost River Delta, Port Discovery, and American Waterfront.[8] Mediterranean Harbor is modeled after the waterways of Venice and offers couples the opportunity to experience an authentic gondola ride just as they would in Italy. Each gondola features a serenading, entertaining gondolier that is sure to set the scene for a romantic cruise down the waters of Venice.[9] The evening transforms Mediterranean Harbor into the stage for "BraviSEAmo!" which "follows the romantic story of a 'Spirit of Water' and a 'Spirit of Fire.' "[10] BraviSEAmo debuted in the summer of 2009 and will extend a final romantic offering to guests as they bid farewell to Tokyo DisneySea.

GEOGRAPHY SPOTLIGHT *(continued)*

en.wikipedia.org/wiki/File:
Tokyo_DisneySea_Venice.jpg

Located near the Mediterranean Harbor of Tokyo DisneySea, Hotel Mira-Costa features an ornate lobby and alluring indoor and outdoor pools, and provides couples with a romantic view of the Venetian cityscape. The MiraCosta offers couples exquisite *Speciale* rooms and suites with remarkable views of Tokyo and furnished with handsome décor. The Silk Road Garden features authentic Chinese cuisine and offers couples a romantic ambiance for dinner.[11]

The Tokyo Disneyland Hotel is the newest addition to the Tokyo Disneyland Resort, and it opened in July 2008. Couples are greeted by the spacious atrium lobby featuring high ceilings and elegant lighting. The property includes four themed gardens in which couples can stroll while exploring the area. The Tokyo Disneyland Hotel adds a bit of whimsy by offering character rooms such as the Alice in Wonderland and the Peter Pan suites, which still provide a sense of elegance combined with Disney magic. Couples should be sure to make reservations for Canna, a fine dining restaurant offering a fusion of Western and Asian cuisines.[12]

Tokyo Disneyland Resort provides not only world-class entertainment but a bit of romance as well. Whether it is enjoying fireworks or dining in one of the resort's elegant restaurants, couples have the opportunity to reconnect with each other while enjoying a fantastic Disney experience. In such a densely populated country, it is refreshing to find a spot where worries disappear and romance makes a star appearance.

Endnotes

1. L. Rowntree, L. Martin, M. Price, and W. Wyckoff, *Diversity Amid Globalization: World Regions, Environment, Development*, 4th ed. (Upper Saddle River, NJ: Pearson Prentice Hall, 2009).
2. Tokyo Disney Resort, "Getting Here," www.tokyodisneyresort.co.jp/tdr/english/plan/access/index.html (accessed May 4, 2009).
3. Tokyo Disneyland, "What's New?" www.solarius.com/dvp/dlt/index.html (accessed May 4, 2009).
4. Ibid.
5. Kuwahara Yami, "A Magical Place in Tokyo," July 2, 2008, http://blog.asiahotels.com/a-magical-place-in-tokyo/ (accessed May 4, 2009).
6. Tokyo Disney Resort, "Tokyo Disneyland Electrical Parade *Dreamlights*," www.tokyodisneyresort.co.jp/tdl/english/dreamlights/index.html (accessed May 4, 2009).
7. Tokyo Disney Resort, "Disney Magic in the Sky," www.tokyodisneyresort.co.jp/tdr/english/event/magic_sky/index.html (accessed May 4, 2009).
8. Tokyo Disney Resort, All Attractions/Shows, www.tokyodisneyresort.co.jp/tds/english/attraction_search/index.html (accessed May 4, 2009).
9. Tokyo Disney Resort, "Venetian Gondolas," www.tokyodisneyresort.co.jp/tds/english/7port/harbor/atrc_gondolas.html (accessed May 4, 2009).
10. Tokyo Disney Resort, "BraviSEAmo," www.tokyodisneyresort.co.jp/tds/english/7port/harbor/show_bravi.html (accessed May 4, 2009).
11. Tokyo Disney Resort, "Restaurants and Lounge," www.disneyhotels.jp/dhm/english/rest/index.html (accessed May 4, 2009).
12. Tokyo Disney Resort, "Tokyo Disneyland Hotel," www.tokyodisneyresort.co.jp/index_e.html (accessed May 4, 2009).

This chapter looks at one of the most interesting and exciting parts of tourism—attractions and entertainment. The chapter presents amusement parks, gaming entertainment, animal attractions, fairs, festivals, events, as well as performance arts. Other forms of attractions are covered in separate chapters, including cultural and heritage tourism, leisure tourism, and eco-tourism. For each segment, the major players in the industry are listed, together with trends. Visitors to these parks are inspired by the pull factors described in Chapter 2. The interrelated nature of travel, tourism, and hospitality combines to facilitate the overall guest experience.

Definition and Typology of an Attraction

Alan Lew writes that attractions are more than just a site or an event; they are an integral part of a larger tourism system that also consists of tourists and markets. Attraction typologies vary considerably depending on whether they are being used for marketing or planning purposes.[1]

The system that creates and supports an attraction must have three major components to exist: an object or event located at a site, a tourist or consumer, and a marker, an image that tells the tourist why the object or event is of interest. It is around these three basic elements that the entire tourism industry is constructed.[2] Most attractions, including events, have some kind of nucleus that epitomizes the experience, and how this is presented is important to tourists in their selection of attractions to visit. Most major destinations consist of a collection of attraction nuclei, the most important of which are considered primary and the less important are secondary. In some destinations, several attractions are clustered, presenting a logistical challenge of access to and transportation among the attractions. Figure 8–1 shows the categories of attractions and entertainment.

Attractions are either natural or made. Some attractions are the landscape in national and state parks; the countryside; specific flora and fauna; the Napa Valley; buildings such as the Parthenon in Athens; bridges, such as the Sunshine

	Natural ———————→ Built Environment		
NATURAL	**CULTURAL**	**RECREATIONAL**	**ENTERTAINMENT**
City Parks	Architectural	Auto Racing	Amusement Arcades
Climate	Archaeological	Biking	Amusement Parks
Coastal Areas	Arts	Birding	Gaming
Countryside	Ballet	Canoeing	Mega Events
Fauna	Broadway	Football	Movies
Flora	Concerts	Golf	Theme Parks
Islands	Cuisine	Health	
National Parks	Ethnic	Hiking	
Scenery	Festivals	Spas	
State Parks	Handicrafts		
Wildlife	Historic Sites		
	Museums		
	Pageants		
	Religious		
	Theater		

Figure 8–1 • The Categories of Attractions and Entertainment

Bridge near Tampa, Florida; monuments, such as the Vietnam Veterans Memorial; and theme parks, such as Walt Disney World. An attraction may also be an event that is significant enough to elevate it to the status of an attraction. When we think of an attraction often amusement and theme parks come to mind first.

Amusement and Theme Parks

Amusement park is the generic term for a collection of usually rides or other forms of entertainment attractions for the purpose of entertaining large groups of people. Today, the terms *amusement parks* and *theme parks* are often used interchangeably. In the United States, the nation's estimated 400 amusement parks are packed with approximately 335 million people, bringing in an estimated $11.5 billion.[3] These visitors enjoyed more than 1.5 billion "rides"! However, seasonal changes and weather affect attendance rates. In most places, with the exception of the warm, southern park locations, the number of visitors decreases considerably in the wintertime. In some cases, visitation may be so slow that certain parks have to shut down or reduce their hours.

The attractions business is highly competitive with other travel and tourism markets. Theme parks can be compared with a roller coaster. They require continuous improvement and expertise to keep guests safe, happy, and entertained.

The International Association of Amusement Parks and Attractions (IAAPA) was founded in 1918. It is the largest international trade association for permanently situated amusement facilities worldwide. The organization represents more than 4,500 facility, supplier, and individual members from more than 90 countries.[4] With attendance figures reaching record numbers, the future looks bright. According to IAAPA, attendance at the top 50 U.S. theme parks is increasing annually.[5] Competitors try to outdo each other by breaking records on the different rides and attractions. The parks that continue to introduce new attractions and promote themselves as tourist destinations generally increase their market share.

There are literally thousands of attractions throughout North America. There are more than 400 amusement parks and traditional attractions in the United States alone. According to a recent statistical survey conducted by IAAPA, Magic Kingdom at Walt Disney World in Florida was the most visited amusement park in the world. The most visited amusement park outside of the United States was Tokyo Disneyland.[6] The following subsections look at some of the main attractions, which include Knott's Berry Farm, Worlds of Discovery, Six Flags, the Walt Disney Corporation, and Universal Studios.

Knott's Berry Farm

It all began in the 1920s in Buena Park, California, with a small berry farm and tearoom. As Knott's restaurant business grew, different attractions were added to the site to keep waiting customers amused. After a gradual expansion, more than 80 years after its humble beginnings, Knott's Berry Farm became the largest independent theme park in the United States. although they are now owned and operated by Cedar Fair Entertainment. Today, Knott's Berry Farm is 150 acres of rides, attractions, live entertainment, historical exhibits, dining, and specialty shops. The park features six themes: Ghost Town, Indian Trails, Fiesta Village, the Boardwalk, Wild Water Wilderness, and Camp Snoopy, which is the official home of Snoopy and the Peanuts characters.

Knott's Berry Farm has truly been a great influence on the American theme park industry. Hundreds of parks, both independent and corporate owned, started to develop following the birth of Knott's. Creator Walter Knott may have figured out why amusement parks became so popular so quickly. He was quoted as saying, "The more complex the world becomes, the more people turn to the past and the simple things in life. We [as in the amusement park operators] try to give them some of those things."[7] Even with the ever-increasing competition, Knott's continues to attract guests with its authentic historical artifacts, relaxed atmosphere, emphasis on learning, famous food, varied entertainment, innovative rides, and specialty shopping.[8]

▶ Check Your Knowledge

1. How many amusement parks are there in the United States, and how many visitors do they have every year in total?

2. Who are the major players in the theme park business?

Worlds of Discovery: Anheuser-Busch InBev Companies

Anheuser-Busch Companies is a St. Louis–based corporation that agreed to be purchased by the Belgo-Brazilian beverage company InBev in July 2008. Anheuser-Busch has subsidiaries that include the world's largest brewing company and the second largest U.S. manufacturer of aluminum beverage containers. It is also the largest corporate-owned theme/animal park company in the United States. Currently, the Worlds of Discovery operate the following parks in the United States[9]:

- *SeaWorld*—The three SeaWorld parks are located in California, Florida, and Texas. Each park has various themes, marine and animal attractions, shows, rides, and educational exhibits. SeaWorld is based on the creatures of the sea. Guests can pet dolphins and other fish, watch shows featuring Shamu, the famous killer whale, and learn all about the mysteries of the sea. Several rides are also available at SeaWorld, and countless exhibits feature everything from stingrays to penguins. The Orlando park is introducing a new roller coaster ride. The flying coaster takes riders on a manta-themed journey that will include a new ray habitat filled with at least 300 of these underwater creatures.[10] In addition, there is also talk of the attraction being set in a fantasy type village.

- *Aquatica*—SeaWorld recently opened a new water park, Aquatica. Located just across the street from SeaWorld Orlando, Aquatica features 36 slides, six rivers and lagoons, and more than 80,000 square feet of sparkling white, sandy beaches. Aquatica's South Seas–inspired flora features more than 100 species of trees and 250 species of shrubs, grasses, vines, and flowers. In total, 60,000 plants cover the grounds of the park.[11] In addition, the park amenities include private cabanas available for rent, dining, and 3.3 million gallons of 84° water![12]

- *Busch Gardens*—These theme parks feature both exciting thrill rides and attractions in addition to large zoos and safari parks. Busch Gardens, located in both Tampa, Florida, and Williamsburg, Virginia, is perhaps the most well known of the animal-themed parks. Busch Gardens is like a zoo with a twist. It features equal numbers of thrill rides and animal attractions. Guests can take a train ride through the Serengeti Plains, where zebras and antelope run wild, hop aboard a giant tube ride through the Congo River rapids, or ride on one of the parks' many world-record-holding roller coasters. The theme for the Williamsburg Park is that of the "Old Country." It re-creates the seventeenth century charm of the Old World European atmosphere with a journey through nine authentically detailed European hamlets. "The Dark Continent" in Tampa has a distinctly African theme. The Williamsburg, Virginia, location is also rolling out a series of Sesame Street–themed attractions. These include a new kid's area composed of a minicoaster, mini log flume, and a wet/dry play area filled with Big Bird, the Cookie Monster, and others characters such as Elmo.[13]

Thrill seekers can enjoy this ride at Busch Gardens.
Dave King © Dorling Kindersley

- *Adventure Island*—Adventure Island is also located in Tampa and is the only water park in the Tampa Bay area. It is also the only water theme park on Florida's west coast featuring several unique water play areas and thrilling splash rides. The water park comprises more than 25 acres of fun-filled water rides, cafes, and shops.

- *Water Country USA*—Anheuser-Busch's other water theme park is located in Williamsburg, Virginia. It is "the mid-Atlantic's largest water park, featuring more than 30 water rides and attractions, live entertainment, shopping, and restaurants." Like Adventure Island, Water Country has an educational atmosphere to help guests, especially children, learn water safety techniques. Everything in the park is set to the theme of the 1950s surfing era.

- *Sesame Place*—This 14-acre park is located in Langhorne, Pennsylvania, and is dedicated totally to a Sesame Street theme. It was designed with the goal of stimulating children's natural curiosity to learn and explore, while building self-confidence as they interact with other children.

- *Discovery Cove*—Adjacent to SeaWorld in Orlando, Florida, Busch's newest addition Discovery Cove is an exclusive, reservations-only tropical paradise, offering up-close encounters with dolphins and other exotic sea life. Guests can swim with dolphins and snorkel through a coral reef, tropical river, waterfalls, and an amazing freshwater lagoon, among other things.

▶ Check Your Knowledge

1. Name some of the Six Flags theme park locations.
2. What are three theme parks operated by Worlds of Discovery?

CORPORATE PROFILE

Six Flags Theme Parks, Inc.

Bill Aron, PhotoEdit Inc.

Six Flags is a world-renowned theme park corporation.[14] The company owns and operates 20 different parks spread out over North America, Latin America, and Europe. Locations include Mexico City, Belgium, France, Spain, Germany, and most major metropolitan areas in the United States. In fact, 74 percent of the continental United States parks are located within a six-hour drive. Six Flags has earned the title of the world's largest regional theme park company. Annually, more than 25 million visitors are reported to entertain themselves at Six Flags theme parks worldwide, 90 percent of which reported a desire to return!

Now who is behind this huge success? The founder of the first theme park was a man named Angus Wynne. He was a Texas oil baron with a vision. His vision was to create a family entertainment park that was fun as well as affordable and, most important, within reachable distance from where people lived. A simple amusement park was transformed into a theme park by Wynne by adding innovative rides with theme presentations. His first park opened in Texas in 1961. The transformation proved to be a huge success with the public; visitors were drawn in crowds to the newly opened theme park.

The park was named after the six different flags that flew over Texas at one time, representing the six different countries that governed Texas through history. The theme park was divided into six different regions, each modeled after the country it represented. Visitors could marvel at Spanish haciendas or French bistros, all the while in the company of Southern belles and pirates.

Today, Six Flags has a licensing agreement with DC Comics and Warner Bros. This means characters such as Batman, Superman, and Bugs Bunny and the gang can be found wandering around the parks and having their pictures taken with park visitors. With fantastic rides and show-stopping entertainment, the parks have become one of the first-choice amusement parks for entertainment-seeking families and individuals.

Funding for expansion of the company was drawn primarily from the profits made from the first successful parks opened, including the first one in Texas. In 1996, Six Flags went public for the first time, meaning it allowed the public to purchase its stock as opposed to handpicked private investors. The shares were sold at $18 each, and their purchase totaled nearly $70 million. Only one year later, the company had raised $200 million with its public offering. With these kinds of funds, Six Flags continued purchasing land or old amusement parks and turning them into Six Flags theme parks, rapidly expanding their reach. The parks became so successful and had such a high income that large corporations, including AOL, Kodak, and Univision, signed major sponsorship deals with Six Flags. Perrier and Pringles also joined the sponsorship team.

The current management team has been in effect since 1994. President Gary Story serves simultaneously as the chief operating officer and director. He was the company's executive vice president before his promotion to president. The CEO of the company is Kieran E. Burke, former president of Six Flags from 1989 to 1994. He also serves as director and chair of the board. With the management team going strong and further expansion planned, the future success of Six Flags looks bright.

Six Flags now offers "print and go tickets" from home, making it easier for guests to enjoy the park experience by avoiding entrance lines. New rides include Tornado, which emulates the experience of being sucked through the eye of a giant tornado. There are seven new interactive simulation adventure rides at various parks; among them are Stargate 3000, Ragin' Cajun, and Mardi Gras thrills ride.

CORPORATE PROFILE *(continued)*

If you are looking for a job in the theme park business, you might be interested in knowing that Six Flags employs more than 50,000 seasonal workers and 5,000 full-time employees. They are committed to providing a fun and challenging experience for their employees, and they offer competitive wages as well as benefits. Six Flags also offers exciting internships for those still in college. They provide flexible work hours at several positions and employ a wide diversity of people, including high school and college students. You can apply for seasonal jobs online at www.sixflags.com/jobs.

The Walt Disney Corporation

Unlike many other entertainment corporations, Disney and its characteristic logo, the mouse ears, is widely known over the world. Over the years, the corporation has expanded from cartoons and movies to include many different aspects of the tourism and entertainment industry, such as theme parks, resorts, cruise lines, hotels, and even television broadcasting. The first Disney theme park, Disneyland, located in Anaheim, California, opened in the spring of 1955. Walt Disney had a dream of opening another park, Disney World, and he developed the master plan, but unfortunately, he died before his dream could be realized. His brother Roy helped to open Disney World in Orlando, Florida, in 1971.

Each park has certain features that remain constant. For instance, each park has its own Main Street USA, Frontierland, Fantasyland, Tomorrowland, and Toontown. The Magic Kingdom in Florida has all these features. However, Walt Disney World is composed of four major theme parks: Magic Kingdom, Epcot, Disney's Animal Kingdom, and Disney's Hollywood Studios, with more than 100 attractions, 22 resort hotels themed to faraway lands, spectacular nighttime entertainment, and vast shopping, dining, and recreation facilities that cover thousands of acres in this tropical paradise.[15]

Walt Disney World includes 25 lighted tennis courts, 99 holes of championship golf, marinas, swimming pools, jogging and bike trails, water skiing, and motor boating. The resort also offers a unique zoological park and bird sanctuary on Discovery Island in the middle of Bay Lake; 226 restaurants, lounges, and food courts; a nightclub metropolis to please nearly any musical palate; a starry-eyed tribute to 1930s Hollywood; and even bass fishing. In 2009, Walt Disney World introduced a new centerpiece, an "American Idol" theme show. Reports indicate that guests will participate in a daily competition that eventually crowns a new American Idol (or, at least, a Disney-ified version).[16] New attractions for the Disneyland park are not scheduled to open until 2010 and beyond, but massive construction is planned and under way. Construction includes a new lagoon show, a Little Mermaid–themed dark ride, and a thrill ride based on Pixar's *Cars* movie.

Disney hotels are architecturally exciting and more affordable than ever. The fun-filled Disney's All-Star Sports Resort and Disney's colorful All-Star Music

Resort are categorized as value-class hotels. Disney's Wilderness Lodge is one of the park's jewels, with its impressive tall-timber atrium lobby and rooms built around a Rocky Mountain geyser pool.

For nighttime fun, there are numerous restaurants and nightclubs near Pleasure Island. In all, the park has a cast of 37,000 hosts, hostesses, and entertainers famous for their warm smiles and commitment to making every night an especially good one for Disney guests.

There is more to enjoy than ever in ExtraTERRORestrial Alien Encounter, developed in collaboration with George Lucas, and Transportarium in New Tomorrowland. Already open are Fantasyland's Legend of the Lion King; Epcot's INNOVENTIONS; the mind-blowing 3-D adventure, Honey, I Shrunk the Audience, in Future World; and, at the Disney-MGM Studios, the ultimate thriller, The Twilight Zone Tower of Terror.

Magic Kingdom

The heart of Walt Disney World and its first famous theme park is the Magic Kingdom, the "happiest land on earth," where "age relives fond memories" and "youth may savor the challenge and promise of the future." It is a giant theatrical stage where guests become part of exciting Disney adventures. It is also the home of Mickey Mouse, Snow White, Peter Pan, Tom Sawyer, Davy Crockett, and the Swiss Family Robinson.

More than 40 major shows and ride-through attractions, not to mention shops and unique dining facilities, fill its seven lands of imagination. Each land carries out its theme in fascinating detail—architecture, transportation, music, costumes, dining, shopping, and entertainment are designed to create a total atmosphere where guests can leave the ordinary world behind. The seven lands include the following:[17]

- *Main Street USA*—Turn-of-the-century charm with horse-drawn streetcars, horseless carriages, a penny arcade, and grand-circle tour on Walt Disney World Steam Railroad

- *Adventureland*—Explore Pirates of the Caribbean, wild animal Jungle Cruise, Swiss Family Treehouse, and Tropical Serenade by birds, flowers, and tikis

- *Frontierland*—Thrills on Splash Mountain and Big Thunder Mountain Railroad, musical fun in Country Bear Jamboree, Shooting Gallery, Tom Sawyer Island caves and raft rides

- *Liberty Square*—Steamboating on the Rivers of America, mystery in the Haunted Mansion, whooping it up in Diamond Horseshoe Saloon, viewing the impressive Hall of Presidents with the addition of President Bill Clinton in a speaking role

- *Fantasyland*—Cinderella Castle is the gateway to the new Legend of the Lion King plus Peter Pan's Flight, Snow White's Adventure, Mr. Toad's Wild Ride, Dumbo the Flying Elephant, Alice's Mad Tea Party, musical cruise with doll-like dancers in It's a Small World, Cinderella's Golden Carousel, and Skyway cable car to Tomorrowland

- *Mickey's Toontown Fair*—Mickey's House, Grandma Duck's Farm, Mickey's Treehouse playground, and private photo session in Mickey's Dressing Room

- *Tomorrowland*—Sci-Fi city of the future, new frightening Alien Encounter, Transportarium time machine travels in Circle-Vision 360, new whirling Astro-Orbiter, Space Mountain, new production of Carousel of Progress, Grand Prix Raceway, elevated Transit tour, new Disney Character show on Tomorrowland Stage[18]

Epcot

Epcot is a unique, permanent, and ever-changing World's Fair with two major themes: Future World and World Showcase. Highlights include Illumi-Nations, a nightly spectacle of fireworks, fountains, lasers, and classical music.

Future World shows an amazing exposition of technology for the near future, home, work, and play. The newest consumer products are continually added. Major pavilions exploring past, present, and future are shown in the Spaceship Earth story of communications. The Universe of Energy giant dinosaurs help explain the origin and future of energy. There are also the Wonders of Life with spectacular Body Wars, Cranium Command and other medical health subjects, the World of Motion, Journey into Imagination, The Land with spectacular agricultural research and environmental growing areas, and The Living Seas, the world's largest indoor ocean with thousands of tropical sea creatures.

Around the World Showcase Lagoon are pavilions where guests can see world-famous landmarks and sample the native foods, entertainment, and culture of 11 nations:[19]

Disney Characters Making a Memorable Moment
Peter Wilson © Dorling Kindersley

- *Mexico*—Mexico's fiesta plaza and boat trip on El Rio Del Tiempo plus San Angel Inn for authentic Mexican cuisine
- *Norway*—Thrilling Viking boat journey and Restaurant Akershus
- *China*—Wonders of China Circle-Vision 360 film tour from the Great Wall to the Yangtze River plus Nine Dragons Restaurant
- *Germany*—Authentic Biergarten restaurant
- *Italy*—St. Mark's Square street players and L'Originale Alfredo di Roma Ristorante
- *United States*—The American Adventure's stirring historical drama
- *Japan*—Re-creating an Imperial Palace plus Teppanyaki Dining Rooms
- *Morocco*—Morocco's palatial Restaurant Marrakesh
- *France*—Impressions de France film tour of the French countryside, Chefs de France
- *United Kingdom*—Shakespearean street players plus Rose & Crown Pub
- *Canada*—Halifax to Vancouver Circle-Vision 360 tour

Each showcase has additional snack facilities and a variety of shops featuring arts, crafts, and merchandise from each nation.

Disney's Hollywood Studios

With 50 major shows, shops, restaurants, ride-through adventures, and back-stage tours, Disney's Hollywood Studios combines real working motion picture, animation, and television studios with exciting movie attractions.[20] The newest adventure in the Sunset Boulevard theater district is the Twilight Zone Tower of Terror, with a stunning 13-story elevator fall. The famous Chinese Theater on Hollywood Boulevard houses the Great Movie Ride.

Other major attractions include a Backstage Studio Tour of production facilities, Catastrophe Canyon, and New York Street; a tour of Walt Disney Animation Studios, Florida; exciting shows at Indiana Jones Epic Stunt Spectacular and Jim Henson's Muppet Vision 3-D; plus a thrilling space flight on Star Tours.

Especially entertaining for movie and TV fans are the SuperStar Television and Monster Sound Show, where audience members take part in performances. Favorite Disney films become entertaining stage presentations in the Voyage of the Little Mermaid theater and in Beauty and the Beast, a live, 25-minute musical revue at Theater of the Stars. The best restaurants include the Hollywood Brown Derby, 1950s Prime Time Cafe, Sci-Fi Dine-In Theater, Mama Melrose's Ristorante Italiano, and the Studio Commissary.

All this and much more are what help make Walt Disney World Resort the most popular destination resort in the world. Since its opening in 1971, more than 500 million guests, including kings, queens, and celebrities from around the world and all U.S. presidents in office since the opening, have visited one of the parks. What causes the most comment from guests is the cleanliness, the friendliness of its cast, and the unbelievable attention to detail—a blend of showmanship and imagination that provides an endless variety of adventure and enjoyment.

Animal Kingdom focuses on nature and the animal world around us. Guests can go on time-traveling rides and come face to face with animals from the pre-historic past to the present. Shows are put on featuring Disney's most popular animal-based films, such as *Lion King* and *A Bug's Life*. Safari tours that bring guests up close and personal with live giraffes, elephants, and hippopotamuses are also offered at Animal Kingdom.

Walt Disney World Resort's two water parks are Blizzard Beach and Typhoon Lagoon. Blizzard Beach has a unique ski resort theme, while Typhoon Lagoon is based on the legend that a powerful storm swept through, leaving pools and rapids in its wake. Both parks offer a variety of slides, tube rides, pools, and moving rivers that drift throughout the parks.

Disney Tokyo

The Tokyo Disney Resort is located just outside of Central Tokyo in Urayasu City. It features two theme parks (Disneyland and DisneySea), unique dining, a variety of shops, and accommodations including the Disney Hotels.[21] The Disneyland Park opened April 15, 1983, and was the first Disney park to open outside the United States. The Oriental Land Company owns Disneyland and DisneySea. They are the only Disney parks not (at least partially) owned by the Walt Disney Company.

Disney Paris

Disneyland Resort Paris is located in Marne-la-Vallée, in the eastern suburbs of Paris, France. On April 12, 1992, it opened to the public and was the second Disney resort to open outside the United States (the first was Disney Tokyo). The resort includes two theme parks, a retail, dining, and entertainment district, and seven Disney-owned hotels. It is owned by Euro Disney S.C.A. (more than 39 percent of its stock is held by the Walt Disney Company). The resort also includes both a Disneyland Park and a Walt Disney Studios Park.[22]

Disney Hong Kong

Hong Kong Disneyland is located on Lantau Island, about 20 minutes from Hong Kong International Airport. The original Disneyland in California inspired the park's design. The whole resort is 310 acres and includes a theme park with four lands and two themed hotels.[23] The theme park is owned by Hong Kong International Theme Parks, which is an incorporated company, jointly owned by the Walt Disney Company and the Government of Hong Kong. It is the smallest of the Disneyland Parks, with a capacity of 34,000 visitors per day.

▶ Check Your Knowledge

1. What is the name of the first Disney park ever and where is it located?
2. What features are present in all Disney parks?

Universal Studios

Universal Studios has been giving guided tours on its famous movie sets for more than 30 years, and tens of thousands of people visit Universal every day.[24] Since its founding, Universal Studios has become the most formidable competitor facing the Disney Corporation.

In Orlando, Florida, Universal Studios has enjoyed huge success, despite encroaching on the "kingdom" of Disney. In addition to its Hollywood and Orlando parks, Universal has since expanded into Japan. Why has it been so successful? One reason for Universal's success is its adaptation of movies into thrill rides. Another is its commitment to guest participation. Guests get to help make sound effects and can participate in "stunts," making Universal Studios more than just a "look behind the scenes."

Universal Studios is also a good example of what is predicted to occur in the future in regard to amusement and theme parks. It is offering more realistic thrill rides by combining new technologies and state-of-the-art equipment. Universal Orlando has introduced its newest addition, the Hollywood Rip, Ride, Rockit roller coaster. At 165 feet tall, the coaster will claim the title of world's highest vertical lift, in addition to having one of the tallest loops in the world.[25] Universal is touting the coaster as one on which riders can customize the on-board lighting and sound to give the ride a personalized experience.[26]

The company has realized that visitors tend to go to theme parks just because they happen to be in the area. By greatly expanding the experience, NBC Universal is hoping that its improvements will make travelers want to

Universal Studios offers great rides and fun for the whole family.
Stephen Whitehorn © Dorling Kindersley

visit Universal Studios as a one-stop destination. Following are the Universal theme parks:[27]

- *Universal Studios Hollywood*—This was the first Universal park and boasts the title of the world's largest movie studio and theme park. As part of its new studio tour, visitors are taken into the tomb of the Mummy, feel the hot breath of King Kong, experience a major earthquake, and are right in the middle of a Hollywood movie shoot. Afterward, they can "chill" at the Universal City Walk, a street that claims to offer the best in food, nightlife, shopping, and entertainment.
- *Universal Orlando*—This park is a destination in itself, with two theme parks, several themed resorts, and a bustling City Walk. In Universal Studios, like in the Hollywood park, visitors can explore the exciting world of movie making. Its newest and most exciting park, Islands of Adventure, gives visitors the best in roller coasters and thrill rides, whereas Wet'n Wild offers the opportunity to enjoy a range of cool waterslides, among other things. If visitors are not already exhausted by the mere thought of it, they can check out City Walk for some food, shopping, and a taste of the hottest nightlife in town. Myriads of venues, popular with tourists and locals alike, offer an amazing variety of cool bars, hot clubs, and live music.
- *Universal Studios Japan*—This park features 18 rides and shows, some brand new and others old favorites, plus great dining and shopping.

Other Theme Parks

Other important parks include Cedar Point, Morey's Piers, and Hersheypark. Cedar Point, located in Sandusky, Ohio, has been voted the best amusement park in the world by *Amusement Today* readers. The park boasts an unheard of 17, yes, 17 roller coasters (more than any other park in the world)! The lineup includes three of the top 10 steel roller coasters in the world.[28] Cedar Fair Kings Island (near Cincinnati, Ohio) is introducing a $22 million, 230-foot tall, 80-mile per hour Diamondback coaster. When complete, the nearly mile long Diamondback ride will represent the park's largest ever investment.[29]

Morey's Piers, located on the boardwalk in Wildwood, New Jersey, next to historic Cape May, New Jersey, and not far from both Ocean City and Atlantic City, offers around 100 exciting amusement park rides and attractions, including two large beachfront water parks, kiddie rides, roller coasters, and more.[30] Hersheypark, located in Hershey, Pennsylvania, features 90 acres of clean, green fun, all adjacent to the famous Hershey's Chocolate factory. It features more than 60 rides and attractions, as well as live entertainment, food, and games.[31]

▶ Check Your Knowledge

1. What are the main reasons why Universal Studios parks have become so popular?
2. Where are the Universal Studios parks located?
3. What are the features of Cedar Point, Morey's Piers, and Hersheypark?

FOCUS ON

Attractions and Entertainment

John and
Josielyn Walker

Attractions and entertainment are an integral part of the tourism system, accounting for much of the rationale for tourism by "pulling" people to them. Many of the components of the tourist trip—for example, transport and accommodation—are demands derived from the consumer's desire to enjoy what a destination has to offer in terms of things to see and do.[32]

Attractions are first categorized as natural or built environment (see Figure 8-1), and then by ownership—public or private. Historically, certain attractions became popular, among them the original Seven Wonders of the World, as declared by Philon of Byzantium in 200 BCE: the Hanging Gardens of Babylon, the Great Pyramid of Egypt, the Statue of Zeus at Olympia, the Temple of Artemis at Ephesus, the Mausoleum at Halicarnassus, the Colossus of Rhodes, and the Lighthouse at Alexandria.

More recent lists, of which there are many, include hundreds of so-called Wonders of the World. Among the more popular are the Great Wall of China, the Taj Mahal, the Serengeti migration, the Galapagos Islands, the Grand Canyon, Bali, the Amazon rain forest, and the Great Barrier Reef. It is interesting to note the difference between the original Seven Wonders of the World and the more recent popular wonders in that the originals were mostly of the built environment compared to the more recent that are more natural.

Entertainment includes attractions such as amusement and theme parks, festivals, fairs, gaming, movies, amusement arcades, and mega or hallmark events such as the Running of the Bulls in Pamplona, Spain, Carnival in Rio de Janeiro, Brazil, the Super Bowl, and the Olympics.

The management of attractions presents several challenges and opportunities for tourism officials. These challenges and opportunities include infrastructure (water, waste management, utilities, communications, roads), services usually provided by the government; and superstructure (rail, auto, and bus transportation, hotels, resorts, restaurants, entertainment places, shopping centers, museums), services usually provided by corporations or privately. Other issues include overcrowding, seasonality, and sustaining the site for the future enjoyment of tourists. For example, one of the biggest challenges for the planners of the Super Bowl is where to park the hundreds of corporate jets that fly in.

Restricting the flow and number of tourists visiting an attraction can be a challenge. Consider how many tour buses can be parked in Oxford, England, or in one of the beautiful squares in Paris—at times they seem to overwhelm the very places that tourists want to see. To reduce traffic many attractions have instituted a park-and-ride approach to better control the flow of visitors. The travel and tourism distribution chain also helps by offering special deals on off-peak travel to selected destinations.

Attractions have the same product life cycle as any product. The mature stage is prolonged by introducing new elements to appeal to changing demographics and tastes in the target market. We have only to look at

(continued)

FOCUS ON (*continued*)

the theme parks to see innovative new things for people to enjoy. Cities also want to attract tourists, so they create areas that appeal to some tourists, such as San Francisco's Fisherman's Warf, Chicago's Navy Pier, San Diego's Old Town or Gas Lamp District. Consider zoos with interesting exhibits like the birth of a baby panda bear to see how an attraction's life can be extended.

Some attractions are so alluring that they draw people in great numbers, as with Walt Disney World and the other Disney parks. Most need an assortment of tourist-related services such as transportation, accommodation, and foodservice. The management of the attractions and related services also offer a number of interesting career possibilities.

Animal Attractions

Another sector that has been growing substantially is the one of animal attractions. Although they are usually not the main reason people visit a state or city, zoos, aquariums, and wild animal parks attract millions of visitors every year.

Zoos

Every kid's dream, and just as much fun for parents, zoos are one of those things that just don't seem to go out of style. They are forms of tourist attractions that people may visit when in a destination city such as New York, Chicago, or San Diego. Approximately 150 million people visit a U.S. zoo every year.[33] The first zoo in the United States was the Philadelphia Zoo, built in 1859. Even today, zoos are extremely popular in the United States and Canada, and almost every major city has one. In fact, the popularity of zoos was proven when the Walt Disney Corporation unveiled its Animal Kingdom as one way to combine the effects of visiting a zoo with that of any other theme park. Busch Gardens and SeaWorld also have similar parks.

Following are examples of two of the most popular and noteworthy American zoos.

Wild Animal Park, San Diego, features many exciting animal species from around the world in a natural setting.
Courtesy of San Diego Convention and Visitors Bureau

San Diego Zoo, California

The San Diego Zoo attracts many tourists from across the country for a variety of reasons. It may be in part because of the favorable climate that allows the zoo to operate all year round. Also, the zoo has a large collection of animals, interactive programs, and educational programs for children.

The world-famous San Diego Zoo is located in historic Balboa Park in downtown San Diego, California. Founded in 1916 by Dr. Henry Wegeworth, the zoo's original collection totaled 50 animals. Today, it is home to 4,000 animals of more than 800 different species. The zoo also features a prominent botanical collection with more than 700,000 exotic plants.[34] The zoo's breeding programs help not only to enhance the zoo, but also provide hope for the survival of many endangered animals. The first baby panda ever born in captivity, Hua Mei, was born at the San Diego Zoo.[35]

The National Zoo

The National Zoological Park in Washington, D.C., is part of the respected Smithsonian Institution. More than 2,000 animals from nearly 400 species make their home in this zoo.[36] Among the rare animals featured at the National Zoo are a giant panda, komodo dragons, rare Sumatran tigers, and Asian elephants.

The National Zoo is located in a quiet residential area only minutes away from other Smithsonian museums, the Capitol, and the White House. It is not only a place to observe the behavior of certain animals, but also a place that works actively to educate visitors on conservation issues and the various interactions among living organisms. The National Zoo breeds endangered species and reintroduces the animals into their natural habitats. The zoo also participates in other visitor education programs and biological research.[37]

Aquariums

Aquariums are attractions that provide thrilling educational experiences to millions of tourists each year. They are also multi-million-dollar showpieces displaying creatures vastly different from us who dwell on land. For example, each year, 1.6 million visitors pass through the doors of the National Aquarium in Baltimore.[38] This impressive aquarium seeks to stimulate public interest in and knowledge about the aquatic world, focusing on the beauty of these species in their natural environments. It uses only the most modern interpretative techniques to engage and get an emotional response from visitors. In fact, many visitors walk out with a desire to become more environmentally responsible.[39]

▶ ## Check Your Knowledge

1. What zoo is the oldest in the United States?

2. Name some rare animals you can find at the National Zoo.

Fairs, Festivals, and Events

Believe it or not, Woodstock, Gay Pride, the Olympic Games, and the local harvest festival have something in common: they all come under the umbrella of **event tourism**. This is a relatively new term that can be defined as the systematic planning, development, and marketing of **festivals** and special events as tourist attractions, development catalysts, and image builders for attractions and destination areas.

However, it is important to note that events often fall under more than one category, for example, event/sports tourism and event/heritage tourism.

In each case, travel, accommodations, and restaurant meals become a part of the travel and tourism experience. Indeed, over the past few years, event tourism has been a rapidly growing segment of the tourism industry. **Fairs**, festivals, and events are public celebrations that are staged the world over, although it is often difficult to tell the difference among the three categories. In general, however, fairs are usually larger and extend over a longer period of time. Event tourism may range from local street festivals and fairs through county, state, or provincial fairs all the way up to the World Fairs. All these are important because they enrich our lives and provide interesting career opportunities in such fields as event management.

Each festival or special event has a high degree of uniqueness, which distinguishes it from permanent attractions. Some festivals and events appear to be staged purely to attract tourists. Many cities in the United States are well known for their festivals, which bring in droves of vacationers year after year. The following subsections examine some of the more notable festivals and events.

Oktoberfest in Munich, Germany

Rivers of beer and rowdy people, Oktoberfest has taken on a life of its own. The first Oktoberfest was held on October 17, 1810, in honor of the marriage of Crown Prince Ludwig of Bavaria to Princess Therese Von Saxe-Hildburghausen. These days, the festival has become, above all, a celebration of German beer. The Lord Mayor of Munich opens the first barrel, and the 16-day festival begins. Both citizens and tourists flock to this event, which is marked by folk costume parades in which brewery horses draw floats and decorated beer wagons through the streets. Oktoberfest celebrations also take place in a number of North American cities. The Munich Oktoberfest—known by the locals as the "Wiesn"—is the biggest public festival in the world. Each year, around 6 million visitors attending Oktoberfest drink 6.9 million liters of "beer."[40] Approximately 104 oxen are grilled and souvenir hunters try to steal almost 200,000 glass steins![41]

Carnival in Rio de Janeiro, Brazil

The world's most famous Carnival is Rio's main event, and it happens at the peak of the Brazilian summer. This four-day celebration attracts hundreds of thousands of people from all corners of the world, starting on a Saturday and ending on Fat Tuesday (Mardi Gras—*gras* is the French word for fat, and *Mardi* is French for Tuesday; Mardi Gras occurs before Ash Wednesday). The concept originated as a pagan celebration in ancient Rome or Greece and was imported from Italy in the late nineteenth century. During its Golden Age in the 1930s, the famous Samba Parade was added—now the main attraction of the Carnival. The whole city participates in this free event.[42]

Reggae on the River in California

Music festivals are held in virtually every state and province in the United States and Canada, each one attracting thousands of people. Some festivals are larger than others and travel from place to place, making it easier for leisure travelers to come to the event, such as the Horde Festival, and some are smaller such as California's Reggae on the River; all festivals are considerably important in the area of leisure travel.

Reggae on the River's success is reflective of what is happening in the leisure travel industry. Leisure travel is beginning to encompass a larger market because more events, festivals, and other activities have sprung up to meet a variety of personal interests. For instance, in 1984 when the Reggae festival first began, it attracted only 1,200 visitors. Today, however, the festival is known as the best Reggae and World Music Festival in the United States. The festival's 10,000 tickets are always sold out in advance. The event takes more than six months to plan and requires the help of 1,000 volunteers.[43]

Carnival in Rio is an incredible experience.
Antonio Ribeiro, ZUMA Press - Gamma

Mardi Gras in New Orleans, Louisiana

Mardi Gras began more than 100 years ago as a carnival and has evolved into a world-renowned party. This festival in New Orleans is arguably the most flamboyant of all festivals and takes place in January, February, and March. Festivities begin on January 6, with a series of private balls. The days leading up to Fat Tuesday are filled with wild parades, costume contests, concerts, and overall partying. The famous Bourbon Street is home to most of the party-going crowd, and it is often too crowded to even walk down. Beads are big at Mardi Gras, and thousands are given out each year. The culture of New Orleans greatly adds to the festivity of Mardi Gras, as traditional jazz and blues can always be heard on most street corners. The tempo picks up in the last two weeks of the Carnival season, when streets are filled with some 30 separate parades. The parades consist of marching jazz bands and lavishly decorated two-story floats carrying people dressed in costume throwing beads out to the crowd. Each of the 20 or so floats in the parades is decorated to express a particular theme. The largest and most elaborate parades, the Krewe of Endymion and Bacchus parades, take place on the weekend before Mardi Gras, designated the "Day of Un-Rule."[44]

▶ Check Your Knowledge

1. Define event tourism.
2. Where does the major Mardi Gras celebration take place?
3. What is the world's most famous carnival?

The Gaming Entertainment Industry

Dreaming of winning big bucks in Vegas? You're not the only one. Gaming, or **gambling**, was first legalized in Nevada in 1931. In 1964, New Hampshire introduced the first state lottery. Since then, travel for gaming has grown in importance. The industry includes both land-based and riverboat casinos, card rooms, charitable games, lottery-operated games, and greyhound and horse races. The gaming industry as a whole is larger than most people can believe. Billions of dollars are wagered, or bet, on games or races every year.

The gaming industry has a tremendous impact on the various segments of the travel and tourism industry. Las Vegas is able to provide thousands of career opportunities to college graduates. For instance: hotels, the convention and expositions industry, ground transportation, and various other segments offer numerous and diversified careers related to the gaming entertainment industry.

The gaming entertainment industry has experienced substantial growth in the United States and Canada. Out of the 50 U.S. states, more than 30 have casinos (commercial or tribal) and almost every state has legalized some form of gambling.[45] Today there is a casino within about half an hour of almost all U.S. residents. A number of Native American tribes as well as several economically depressed areas have used gaming entertainment as a means of improving their economies. Other reasons for the explosion of interest in gaming entertainment include the following:

- Gaming has become accepted by the majority of society.
- It is viewed as a voluntary tax.
- People gamble and call it a night on the town.
- More retirees gamble for entertainment purposes.
- The availability of gaming entertainment has expanded considerably.

A few years ago it took only a few slot machines and a blackjack table to draw gamblers. Today, however, competition from so many new places forces casinos to provide a better product, known as gaming entertainment. Serving as a base for "social gamblers" is just one part of the total package, which includes hotel facilities, attractions and operations, entertainment and shows, lavish buffets and gourmet restaurants, retail shops, and recreational activities. In Las Vegas, entertainment "megastores" with a few thousand rooms offer striking exteriors, often with entertainment at specified hours. Tourists are given a variety of options. The Las Vegas Visitors Profile indicates that the average visitor budgets $555 for gambling and spends $108 per night on hotels, $254 on food and beverages, $62 on local transportation, $114 on shopping, and $47 on shows.[46]

Today, there are two industry giants: MGM Mirage and Harrah's. Changes in the industry happen in the wink of an eye. They both have diverse property portfolios, solid business practices, and are well respected by Wall Street. MGM Mirage, one of the world's leading and most respected hotel and gaming companies, owns several casino resorts in Nevada, New Jersey, Illinois, Mississippi, Michigan, and Australia. Recently, it bought out Mandalay Resorts Group (which owned Mandalay Bay, Luxor, Excalibur, Monte Carlo, and Circus Circus). The acquisition of Mandalay Resorts Group makes MGM Mirage one of the largest operators in Las Vegas. It now controls half of the Las Vegas strip. MGM Mirage has an impressive portfolio of properties, which include the Bellagio, MGM Grand Las Vegas, the Mirage, Treasure Island, New York–New York Boardwalk Hotel and Casino, and several others.[48]

MGM Mirage prides itself on operating the world's largest hotel/casino. The MGM Grand Hotel, located on 113 acres along the Las Vegas strip, has more than 5,034 rooms and a 171,500-square-foot casino with some 3,700 slot machines, about 160 table games, some 50 shops, a theme park, and a special events center featuring superstar acts. Across the strip is the MGM Mirage's 2,000-room New York–New York Hotel and Casino. The New York–New York Hotel and Casino includes an 84,000-square-foot casino, with more than 80 gaming tables and more than 2,000 slot machines. The Bellagio's lobby ceiling contains a breathtaking display of 2,000 hand-blown glass flowers created by world-renowned artist Dale Chihuly. A water ballet in front of the resort offers viewers a musical and visual spectacle performed by Bellagio's acclaimed water fountains. MGM Grand also runs a hotel/casino in northern Australia that caters to Asian gamblers.

MGM Mirage anticipates the opening of Project City Center Hotel and Casino. Project City Center will include 4,000 rooms in addition to three 400-room boutique hotels. It will be located in the heart of the Las Vegas Strip between the Bellagio and the Monte Carlo. In addition to the hotels and casino, the center will include 650 condominium-hotel units and 550,000 square feet of retail, dining, and entertainment space.[48]

Harrah's Entertainment and Caesars Entertainment have paired up to dominate the gaming industry. They are now the world's biggest casino operator. Harrah's Entertainment operates 40 casinos in three countries, under the Harrah's, Caesars, and Horseshoe brand names. Harrah's Entertainment, Inc., is the premier name in casino entertainment. The Harrah's brand was born in Reno, Nevada, in the late 1930s and has since grown to become the largest casino entertainment company in North America. Harrah's history is a rich combination of casino expertise and quality, launched in northern Nevada and expanded across the continent. Harrah's also owns the London Clubs International family of casinos and the World Series of Poker.[49] On January 28, 2008, Harrah's Entertainment was acquired by affiliates of private-equity firms TPG Capital and Apollo Global Management.[50]

Other gaming entertainment centers of note include Boyd Gaming, Seminole Hard Rock Casino, and Foxwoods. Boyd Gaming Corporation's impressive roster includes 16 casino entertainment properties with operations in Nevada, New Jersey, Mississippi, Louisiana, Indiana, and Illinois.[51] The Seminole Hard Rock Hotels and Casinos, located in Tampa and Hollywood, Florida, are collaborations between the Seminole tribe of Florida and Hard Rock International. The Seminole tribe has purchased the Global Hard Rock Brand.[52] Foxwoods Resort Casino in Connecticut is just an hour's drive from New York City; it is one of the largest gaming entertainment centers in the world. Owned and managed by the Mashantucket Pequot Tribal nation, it has two full-service hotels, restaurants, retail outlets, lounges, amusement rides, a museum, and a research center supporting the Pequot community.

▶ Check Your Knowledge

1. Approximately what percentage of the U.S. population visits casinos every year?
2. Where was gambling first legalized?
3. List the major casinos on the market as well as their main features.

Historic Places/Sites

Travelers and tourists have visited historic sites for thousands of years. The first sites visited in recorded history were the Seven Wonders of the ancient world, which included the Great Pyramid of Giza (Egypt), the Hanging Gardens of Babylon (Iraq), the statue of Zeus at Olympia (Greece), the Temple of Artemis at Ephesus (Turkey), the mausoleum at Halicarnassus (Turkey), the Colossus of Rhodes (Greece), and the lighthouse of Alexandria (Egypt). Historic places, sites, and museums are a part of what is now called **heritage** tourism. Heritage tourism has gained prominence in recent years, particularly with baby boomers and older adults. These groups are less likely to engage in adventure tourism and usually prefer more passive activities. Tourists visiting historic places/sites and museums are interested in our national culture. The various historic attractions appeal to a broad spectrum of the community because they are diverse and located throughout the nation.

The National Park Service maintains properties listed in the Register of Historic Places. The **National Register of Historic Places** is the United States' official list of districts, sites, buildings, structures, and objects worthy of preservation. The more than 80,000 listings represent significant icons of American culture, history, engineering, and architecture.[53] Historic sites include buildings that have been restored and that are now being used as private houses as well as hotels, inns, churches, libraries, galleries, and museums.

Because of declining funds, galleries, museums, and heritage sites have had to become creative in raising money. They have not only had to cover operating costs, but also cater to an increasing number of visitors. To self-generate revenues, they have had to become more entrepreneurial while continuing to meet their heritage preservation and educational goals. Revenue generation has often been achieved through an increased concentration on partnerships, promotions, and packages in which they team up with other operators in the tourism industry, such as tour companies, hotels, restaurants, and car rental companies.

Heritage tourism is discussed more in depth in Chapters 10 and 11, but consider

The Freedom Trail Plaque in Boston, Massachusetts
John Coletti © Dorling Kindersley

the following for a look at a few of the most important U.S. historical attractions:

- Monticello was the home of the famous statesman Thomas Jefferson, author of the Declaration of Independence, architect of American ideals as well as noble buildings, and father of the University of Virginia. The domed mansion of Monticello is set in the beautiful Virginia countryside and is well worth a visit.

- Alamo is a small town in Texas with a rich historical background. During Texas's struggle for independence from Mexico, a vicious battle took place in this town. One hundred eighty-seven Texans held out for 13 days in a group of fortified mission buildings against Santa Anna's army of 4,000 soldiers. The battle resulted in a tragic Texan defeat. Not long after that, Texans everywhere united in a rallying cry: "Remember the Alamo!" And people still do!

- The French Quarter in New Orleans is an original part of the city, full of life and history. Unlike historic districts in many other cities, it is still growing and evolving, regardless of the recent natural disasters. Locals constantly wrestle with the issue of balancing evolutionary changes with the need to preserve history. Visitors can have a great time when they visit during Mardi Gras.

- The Martin Luther King, Jr., National Historic Site is located in the residential section of "Sweet Auburn," Atlanta. Two blocks west of the home is Ebenezer Baptist Church, the pastorate of King's grandfather and father. It was in these surroundings of home, church, and neighborhood that "M. L." experienced his childhood. Here, he learned about family and Christian love, segregation in the days of "Jim Crow" laws, diligence, and tolerance. This important site is a reminder of King's significant contribution to the civil rights movement.

- The Grand Ole Opry in Nashville, Tennessee, is a live radio show in which country music guests are featured. Started more than 75 years ago, The Grand Ole Opry is what made Nashville "Music City." Since the Opry's start, Nashville has created a theme park, Opryland, and a hotel, the Opryland Resort. Famous musicians come from all over the world to showcase their talents, and tourists flock from everywhere to hear the sounds of the Opry and see the sites that Nashville has to offer. [54]

- The Freedom Trail is a walking tour through downtown Boston that passes 16 points of interest, plus other exhibits, monuments, and shrines just off the trail, some of which are a part of the Boston National Park. This interesting walk through a part of U.S. history includes both the State House and the Old South Meeting House. This was the site of many important town meetings concerning the British colonial rule, including those that sparked the Boston Tea Party. Today, there is a multimedia exhibition that depicts the area's 300-year history. The building and two other restored structures today house a bustling marketplace of more than 100 specialty shops, restaurants, and bars. Paul Revere's house is the only seventeenth-century structure left in downtown Boston. It was from this house that the silversmith left for his historic ride on April 18, 1775. Another site on the Freedom Trail is the Bunker Hill Monument.

- The Liberty Bell is housed on Market Street in Philadelphia. The bell's inscription reads, "Proclaim liberty throughout all the land unto all the inhabitants thereof," which in fact is taken from the Bible, Leviticus 25:10. For many years, it was only known as the old State House bell. Its popularity rose when a group of abolitionists, remembering its inscription, adopted the bell as a symbol of their cause; they nicknamed it their liberty bell. In the late 1800s, the bell went on tour around the United States. This trip was an effort to show the war-torn country that there had been a time in history when they had fought and died for a common cause. In 1915, when the tour ended, the Liberty Bell, as it was then known, went home to Philadelphia where it remains to this day. Throughout American history, the Liberty Bell has served as a simple reminder, a symbol of freedom, independence, and liberty, not just in the United States, but also all over the world.

▶ Check Your Knowledge

1. What were the first historic sites visited in recorded history?
2. Name some important U.S. historical attractions.

Museums

Some experts have speculated that people visit museums because of some innate fascination with the past and with diverse cultures. Who knows, but it is a fact that the number of museums in the United States has more than quadrupled since 1950. There are many types of museums, including general, art, science and technology, natural history, history, and military. Someone has to manage these operations, and the more people that travel to experience them, the more career opportunities are provided in the travel, hotel, and restaurant industries. Here are a couple of the big names in the museum sector.

The Smithsonian Institution

Established in 1846 by a man who never visited the United States, this well-known institution now holds more than 140 million artifacts and specimens. It is composed of the following museums: the Anacostia Community Museum; the Cooper-Hewitt, National Design Museum; the Hirshhorn Museum and Sculpture Garden; the National Air and Space Museum; the National Museum of African Art; the National Museum of American History; the National Museum of Natural History; the National Museum of the American Indian; the National Postal Museum; Smithsonian American Art Museum and its Renwick Gallery, and 9 research facilities in the United States and abroad, 156 affiliate museums, as well as the National Zoo.[55] The goal of the institution is to increase and diffuse knowledge, and it is also dedicated to public education, national service, and scholarship in the arts, sciences, and history.[56] Smithsonian museums attract approximately 24.2 million visitors annually and entrance is free. The National Zoo attracts about 2.6 million visitors annually.[57] In addition to its museums and research facilities, parts of the Smithsonian collection can be viewed online at http://www.si.edu.

The Field Museum, Chicago

The Field Museum is a "unique institution of public learning that utilizes its collections, researchers, exhibits, and educational programs to increase public knowledge . . . of the world."[58] The museum, located in Chicago, Illinois, takes on two issues that it reiterates time and time again in all of its exhibits and programs. These two issues are "balancing growth with responsible environmental stewardship" and the creation of "mutual respect and understanding among cultures."[59]

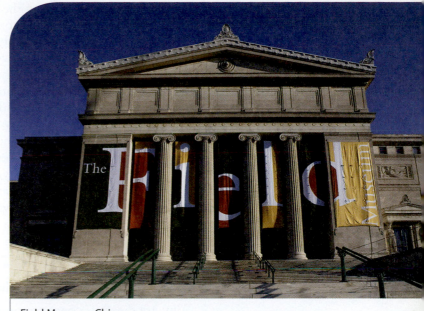

Field Museum, Chicago
Walter Bibikow, Photolibrary.com

The museum was originally founded in 1893 as a place to house biological and anthropological collections for a world exposition. These types of objects continue to form the basis of the museum's collections. In addition, the museum conducts research in the areas of geology, paleontology, archaeology, and ethnography. Furthermore, the museum houses a world-class library collection consisting of more than 20 million items.[60]

Permanent exhibits at the Field Museum range from dinosaurs to minerals and gems, plants, animals, and cultural exhibits. Temporary exhibits are also displayed from time to time. One example of this is a program entitled "The Art of the Motorcycle." This exhibit discusses the motorcycle as a cultural icon and also its technological design.

Performance Arts

Have you ever wished that you could just take off and follow your favorite band on tour? Although some people do, most of us do not have the money or time to do so. However, that does not stop us from enjoying an occasional concert, musical, theater production, comedy show, and so on when we are at home or on the road. These shows and productions are usually not, however, the primary purpose of leisure travel, although in some circumstances they are. In Orlando or Las Vegas, for example, certain shows have taken up permanent residence. The public knows this and therefore may take a trip to Orlando or Las Vegas at their convenience so that they may see a certain production. In places like New York City and London, stopping off to see a Broadway production or a concert may be an unplanned bonus.

Theaters once were immensely important. In a time before people had access to modern inventions like radio or television, books and theater were the only entertainment available. During the industrial era of the early 1900s, the importance of theaters began to wane somewhat as people became too busy juggling work and spending time with family. In addition, many people could not afford such luxuries. In modern times, however, the theater is again gaining importance. Old theaters from the vaudeville days are now being resurrected and reopened to the public—and the public is responding. Increasing numbers of people visit the theater or opera on weekends, holidays, or just for an evening out on the town. Theater is no longer attractive only to the upper classes; affordable prices make it reasonable entertainment for almost anyone.

Concerts, musicals, and comedy shows are also becoming increasingly affordable and are included in many people's vacations schedules. As we move up the hierarchy of needs, self-actualization becomes a greater motivation, and more and more people satisfy that need with a dose of culture and performing arts.

▶ Check Your Knowledge

1. What are the goals of the Smithsonian Institution?
2. Why are theaters, concerts, musicals, and comedy shows regaining importance?

Destinations

Destinations are major attractions in themselves. For example, a trip to Europe might include visits to cities such as London, Paris, Rome, Athens, and Madrid or just focus on one country, where visitors enjoy not only the city but also the countryside as well. The following subsections describe some of the world's most popular destinations.

Athens, Greece

Athens, the capital city of Greece, is one of the world's oldest cities—the cradle of Western civilization and the birthplace of democracy. Classical Athens was a powerful city-state, a center for the arts, learning, and philosophy, and home of Plato's Academy and Aristotle's Lyceum.[61] History abounds as is evidenced by the Parthenon—a temple to the Greek goddess Athena built in the fifth century BCE on the Acropolis, a flat rock above the city. Today, Athens is a bustling city of about 5 million—all of whom seem to be on the move, hence the congestion.[62]

Of the millions of tourists who go to Greece, many, after visiting Athens, take a ferry boat ride to the famed Greek Islands in the Aegean Sea. Crete, the largest island, is rugged and mountainous with beautiful beaches and a reconstruction of King Minos's Palace, which is the oldest European throne, dating back 3,500 years. Santorini, the strikingly beautiful island, is a remaining part of the cone of an extinct volcano that erupted some 3,500 years ago. Some of the picturesque white buildings cling to the rim of the volcano and are among the most photographed in the world. The best way up to the town on top of the hill is by a donkey ride. Mikonos is a trendy island with its famed windmills and fabulous beaches, some of them nude beaches. Other often-visited islands include Rhodes, with plenty of ruins, good beaches, and nightlife; Corfu, off the west coast, is greener than the other islands because of higher rainfall, and it has excellent beaches, a museum, nightlife including a casino, and is favored by package tour groups.

London, England

London was once the center of an empire that included approximately one-quarter of the globe. The name suggests history, pageantry, royalty, theater, shopping, museums, music, fashion, and now even food. London has several interesting areas such as Chelsea and the River Thames, and Hampstead on the hill with its quaint pubs and row houses. Trafalgar Square, named after the battle of Trafalgar in which Nelson defeated the French, is where a statue of Lord Nelson stands atop a tall column. Four large lions that guard the statue reputedly were made from the cannons of the French fleet. Nearby is Piccadilly Circus, the core of the theater and nightlife district, along with neighboring Soho, a former royal park and favorite hunting ground of King Henry VIII. Actually, in old English, the word *So* means wild boar or pig, and *Ho* means there. There are many other fascinating areas such as London's East End home of the Cockneys; the impressive buildings of the Houses of Parliament with Big Ben, the clock tower, and of course, Buckingham Palace, the queen's London residence.

Outside London's popular tourist spots are Oxford, where travelers can visit the famous university; Stratford-upon-Avon, the birthplace of William Shakespeare; travelers can even visit the house he was born in in 1564; Ann Hathaway's cottage, where she lived before her marriage to Shakespeare; Bath; and Stonehenge. Bath is England's most elegant city known for its Georgian architecture and, of course, its baths that date back to Roman times and that are reputed to ease the pain of arthritis. Many visitors enjoy the English countryside with quaint villages and narrow winding roads and roundabouts. And visitors can always enjoy the British pubs.

Paris, France

Paris is a city of beautiful buildings, boulevards, parks, markets, and restaurants and cafes. Paris has excitement. So, for tourists, what to see first is the often-asked question over morning coffee and croissant. There are city tours, but the best way to see the real Paris is on foot, especially if people want to avoid the hordes of other tourists! A tour could begin at the Eiffel Tower or the Cathedral of Notre Dame, the Louvre or the Musée d'Orsay, the Ile de la Cite, or simply with a stroll down the Champs-Elysées.

Paris began as a small island called Ile de la Cité, in the middle of the river Seine. In time, Paris grew onto the Left Bank (Rive Gauche) where the University of the Sorbonne was founded. The university provided instruction in Latin, so it became known as the Quartier Latin, or Latin Quarter. The Latin Quarter has a Bohemian intellectual character with lots of small cafes and wine bars similar to Greenwich Village and Soho in New York. Nearby is Montparnasse, an area that is popular with today's artists and painters. On the Right Bank (Rive Droit) of the river Seine are many attractions; one favorite is the area of Montmartre, with the domes of Sacré-Coeur and the Place du Tertre. Just walking along the winding streets up to Sacré-Coeur gives visitors a feel of the special nature of Paris. To savor the sights of the little markets with an array of fresh fruits, vegetables, and flowers; catch the aromas wafting from the cafes; and see couples walking arm in arm in a way that only lovers do in Paris add to the ambiance that captivates all who go there and provide wonderful memories.

Rome, Italy

They say, "All roads lead to Rome." Rome, the Eternal City, also called the "Cradle of Civilization," is built on seven hills beside the Tiber River, with centuries of history that seem to exude from every building. Among the most visited sites are the Colosseum, the Pantheon, the Spanish Steps, Vatican City, and the Forum. The Colosseum is the ancient stadium where gladiators fought, Christians were martyred, other sports and games were played, and thousands of men fought with ferocious animals to amuse the crowds. The Pantheon, originally built in 27 BC as a temple to all the gods of ancient Rome, was destroyed by fire in AD 80, rebuilt in 126, and is likely the best preserved building of its era. The Spanish Steps, the longest and widest steps in Europe, are situated between the Piazza di Spagna (Plaza of Spain) and the Piazza Trinita die Monti (The Holy See), the Episcopal jurisdiction of the Bishop of Rome, better known as the Pope. They are a popular hangout for tourists and residents. Vatican City is the smallest state in the world, with only 110 acres and a population of around 900.[63] In this tiny area are St. Peter's Basilica, the Vatican Museum, and Michelangelo's *Creation*, painted on the ceiling of the Sistine Chapel, and his *Last Judgment*, on the wall. The Forum Romanum was the center of political, social, and economic life in imperial Rome, with temples, basilicas, and triumphal arches; it is the place where the senate and democratic government began. Several other interesting cities to visit in Italy include Venice, Naples, and Florence, along with the Tuscan countryside.[64]

Costa Rica

Costa Rica is a country in Central America where Christopher Columbus arrived in 1502. Costa Rica is widely regarded as a leader in eco-tourism, with its natural beauty, rich heritage and culture, and friendly, well-educated people. Costa Rica is slightly smaller than West Virginia with a population of about 4 million and a predominant influence from Spain, which is evident in the official language of Spanish, religion of Roman Catholicism, and the architecture of the buildings. The World Heritage Committee has designated the Cocos Island National Park a World Heritage site; it is located 550 kilometers off the Pacific Coast of Costa Rica and is the only island in the eastern Pacific with a tropical rainforest. The underwater world of the park has become famous because of the attraction it holds for divers and for the fact that large pelagic species such as sharks, rays, tuna, and dolphins can be seen. Another World Heritage site is the Area de Conservacion Guanacaste, which has important natural habitats for the conservation of biological diversity, including outstanding dry forest habitats for endangered or rare plant and animal species.[65] With a coastline on both the Atlantic and Pacific Oceans, Costa Rica has many beautiful beaches where surfing is popular in the warm waters and diving is among the best in the world.

Costa Rica has become a popular destination for eco-tourists, who can visit an active volcano or a rainforest with its abundant and diverse known and yet-to-be-discovered life forms. The tropical rainforests of Costa Rica are among the most biodiverse on the planet; for example, there are 850 different species of birds in the country. Visitors can have extraordinary experiences in this country, some that are best appreciated with a guide.

CAREER INFORMATION

Remember, someone has to run the Smithsonian museum and the national parks and Walt Disney World. All of these attractions have several departments all with management ladders that can be climbed at varying speeds. Apart from the main attractions, there are careers in accounting, marketing, maintenance, and service; in addition to professional positions for entertainers, historians, and curators.

Gaming, like other industries, is currently experiencing a downturn. But future career prospects look good, as the gaming industry is popular with a large segment of the population. Careers are available in the gaming, lodging, food and beverage, marketing, and sales areas of the gaming industry. Although this industry makes most of its profit from gambling, excellent hotels and resorts are needed to attract gamers, and outstanding food and beverage offerings and service are needed as part of the total package. There is a tremendous repeat gaming business, so a heavy emphasis is placed on providing exceptional service to guests. College graduates with lodging or food and beverage experience can begin to climb the management ladder, first as a supervisor or assistant manager once the appropriate experience has been gained.

CASE STUDY

Disneyland Resort Paris

Disneyland Resort Paris was formerly Euro Disney, a subsidiary of Walt Disney Company. The world's number two media conglomerate opened its Euro Disney in 1992 near Paris, France. Following the success of its parks in California, Florida, and Japan, it was assumed that the same success would follow in Europe.

The early bidding process, where countries were invited to "bid" on what special incentives they would offer Disney to select their country for development of the park involved several European countries. Eventually, France and Spain became the finalists. The governments of both France and Spain offered extensive "help" to Disney for site location. Spain offered tax and labor incentives and up to 20,000 acres of land. France offered a similar package plus a way to improve the transportation infrastructure.

Factors that influenced Disney's decision were that Spain had a better climate, but France had a larger population—30 million within a day's drive—and the site was close to Paris, itself a popular tourist destination. Additionally, some 50 million tourists visit France each year and the opening of the Channel Tunnel would make the British market accessible in about four hours.

At a cost of US$4.4 billion, the park opened and had a break-even attendance of between 11.7 and 17.8 million attendees. The Disney planners assumed that with a location near Paris and with 30 million people within a day's drive there would be 50 percent French visitors to the park.

Some of the challenges associated with the opening of the park were as follows:

- The park was perceived by some as "cultural imperialism," and a backlash of things American occurred.
- Some cast members felt they were being "Disney-tized" (the French are not known to naturally smile or constantly be polite); they were not all willing to conform to Disney's strict dress code.

(continued)

CASE STUDY *(continued)*

- Visitors were not sure whether, when the park was more Europeanized, it was too American or too European.
- Admission, food and beverage, and concession prices were perceived by guests as being too high.
- The hectic pace and long hours caused high cast turnover.
- Disney's tradition of not offering wine was carried over to Euro Disney. Now wine to the French is like apple pie to Americans.
- French character was too individualistic and private to really appreciate the standardized and crowded theme park experience.
- In 1993 and 1994, Euro Disney reported substantial losses, resulting in a drop in the value of shares from FFr 68 just before the opening of the park to FFr 6 in October 1994.
- Disney planners treated Europe as a single country and imported marketing methods that had worked in the United States.
- The design of the accommodation and food and beverage service offered was considered too small for the European market. For example, whereas at other Disney parks, the guests tend to snack as they go around the park, Europeans want to sit down for a full luncheon at 1 p.m. This causes long lines and numerous complaints.
- Disney characters were even accused of polluting the French culture.
- The majority of visitors were from France (40 percent), Britain (21 percent), and Germany (7 percent).

To initiate a turnaround, Disney brought in French senior management who made the following changes:

1. Renamed the park Disneyland Resort Paris.
2. Instituted a product reassessment and reduced the number of souvenirs and menu items by half.
3. Changed marketing strategy messages to make parents and grandparents sympathetic to their children's emotional pleasure while emphasizing the adventure element for adults.
4. Adjusted pricing policies and offered reduced entrance prices for evenings.
5. Offered job flexibility and customer care programs, and instituted other efficiency measures.
6. Improved hotel occupancy from 55 percent in 1993 to 68 percent in 1995.

The park continues to offer the Disney experience with a European flair, but because of the downturn in the economy it may take years to make an acceptable return on investment.

Congratulations! You have just been appointed to the board of directors for Disneyland Resort Paris.

Questions

1. What would you have done differently from the beginning of Euro Disney?
2. What strategies and tactics will you use going forward?

Sources: From: Future Business Leaders of America National Leadership Conference materials, Anaheim, CA, 2009; College of Charleston, "Case Study of Euro Disney," http://stu.cofc.edu/~wecapps/disney.htm (accessed June 29, 2009); and Chris Cooper, John Fletcher, Alan Fyall, David Gilbert, and Stephen Wanhill, *Tourism Principles and Practice* (Harlow, Essex, England: Pearson Education, 2005), 637.

Summary

1. More than 300 million travelers visit theme parks and amusement parks each year.
2. Since the opening of the initial park in California, Disney theme parks have expanded throughout the world, and with great success. This may be in part because Disney appeals to the whole family, providing fun, magic, and novel experiences.
3. Since its founding, Universal Studios has become the most formidable competitor the Disney Corporation faces. One reason for Universal's success is its adaptation of movies into thrill rides. Another is its commitment to guest participation.
4. Gambling was first legalized in Nevada in 1931. In 1964, New Hampshire introduced the first state lottery. Since then, travel for gambling has grown in importance.
5. Reasons for the explosion of gaming entertainment in the United States include the following: gaming has become accepted by the majority of society; it is viewed as a voluntary tax; people gamble and call it a night on the town; more retirees gamble for entertainment purposes; and the availability of gaming entertainment has expanded considerably.
6. *Event tourism* is a relatively new term. It can be defined as the systematic planning, development, and marketing of festivals and special events as tourist attractions, development catalysts, and image builders for attractions and destination areas. Event tourism is a rapidly growing segment of the tourism industry, encompassing one-fifth of adult travelers.
7. Heritage tourism has gained prominence in recent years, particularly with reenactments that the baby boomers and older adults enjoy.
8. Increasing numbers of people visit the theater or operas on weekends, holidays, or just for an evening out on the town. It is usually not, however, the main reason for a trip. More affordable prices make performance arts reasonable entertainment for almost anyone.
9. Some current trends in leisure travel are shorter and more frequent vacations, increasing use of the Internet, a "reinvention" of tourism to accommodate the demands of the new consumer, and all-inclusive packages offered by the theme park corporations.

Key Words and Concepts

event tourism
fair
festival

gambling
heritage

National Register of Historic Places

Review Questions

1. What are some reasons why the gaming entertainment industry has experienced explosive growth in recent years?
2. Why do you think zoos and aquariums have remained popular?
3. What is event tourism?
4. Characterize heritage tourism.
5. Why have performance arts become popular again?
6. Which of Tokyo's attractions is of most interest to you and why?
7. What is different about Tokyo Disneyland compared to Disneyland in California?
8. How do the original and the more recent lists of the Wonders of the World differ?
9. What strategies has Six Flags used in its development?

Interesting Websites

Association of Zoos and Aquariums: www.aza.org
Aquatica: www.aquaticabyseaworld.com
Disney Corporation: www.disney.go.com

Knott's Berry Farm: www.knotts.com
Six Flags, Inc.: www.sixflags.com

Internet Exercises

1. Check the websites of at least two of the theme park corporations mentioned in this chapter. What news is coming up? Can you identify any current trends?

2. Go to the websites of one of the corporations mentioned in this chapter. Identify different career paths within the company.

Apply Your Knowledge

1. Plan visits to two different theme parks and select rides in order of priority.

2. Create a new theme park, zoo, museum, or attraction for an existing theme park.

Suggested Activity

Make a list of the different types of attractions, and then ask 20 different people which they would prefer to go to and why.

Endnotes

1. Alan A. Lew, "Attraction," in *The Encyclopedia of Tourism*, ed. Jafar Jafari (London: Routledge, 2000), 35–36.
2. Ibid.
3. International Association of Amusement Parks and Attractions, "Amusement Park Attendance and Revenue History," www.iaapa.org/pressroom/Amusement_Park_Attendance_Revenue_History.asp (accessed September 19, 2009).
4. International Association of Amusement Parks and Attractions, "About Us," www.iaapa.org/aboutus/index.asp (accessed September 19, 2009).
5. International Association of Amusement Parks and Attractions, "Amusement Park Attendance and Revenue History."
6. International Association of Amusement Parks and Attractions, "Amusement Park and Attractions Industry Statistics," www.iaapa.org/pressroom/Amusement_Park_Industry_Statistics.asp (accessed September 19, 2009).
7. Personal correspondence with Knott's Berry Farm, April 2008.
8. www.knotts.com/coinfo/history/index.shtml

9. Worlds of Discovery, website, www.worldsofdiscovery.com/worldsofdiscovery/index.html (accessed September 19, 2009).
10. Chad Emerson, "The Latest News on 2009 Attractions," *Tourist Attractions and Parks* 38, no. 7 (November 2008): 28–32.
11. SeaWorld Orlando Communications, Aqautica press kit, www.aquaticabyseaworld.com/Site/cms/assets/PressKit/Aquatica_Fact_Sheet_presskitv2.pdf (accessed September 19, 2009).
12. Ibid.
13. Emerson, "Latest News on 2009 Attractions," 28–32.
14. Six Flags, website, www.sixflags.com/national/media networks/index.html (accessed September 19, 2009).
15. Walt Disney World, "Company Overview," http://corporate.disney.go.com/corporate/overview.html (accessed September 19, 2009).
16. Emerson, "Latest News on 2009 Attractions," 28–32.
17. Walt Disney World, "Magic Kingdom Park Overview," http://disneyworld.disney.go.com/wdw/parks/parkLanding?id=MKLandingPage (accessed September 19, 2009).

18. Ibid.

19. Ibid.

20. Ibid.

21. Tokyo Disney Resort, website, www.tokyodisneyresort .co.jp/tdr/english/about/index.html (accessed September 19, 2009).

22. Disneyland Paris, website, http://us.parks.disneyland paris.com/index.xhtml (accessed June 10, 2009).

23. Hong Kong Disneyland, "About the Park," http:// park.hongkongdisneyland.com/hkdl/en_US/help/listing? name=FAQParkGeneralPage (accessed June 10, 2009).

24. Universal Studios, website, http://themeparks .universalstudios.com/themeparks_flash.html (accessed September 19, 2009).

25. Emerson, "Latest News on 2009 Attractions," 28–32.

26. Ibid.

27. Universal Studios, website, http://themeparks .universalstudios.com/themeparks_flash.html (accessed September 19, 2009).

28. Cedar Point, "Rides," www.cedarpoint.com/public/ park/rides/index.cfm (accessed September 19, 2009).

29. Emerson, "Latest News on 2009 Attractions," 28–32.

30. Morey's Piers, website, http://www.moreyspiers.com/ (accessed September 19, 2009).

31. Hershey Entertainment and Resorts, "About Hershey: Our Proud History," www.hersheypa.com/ town_of_hershey/mission_statement.html (accessed September 19, 2009).

32. Chris Cooper, John Fletcher, Alan Fyall, David Gilbert, and Stephen Wanhill, *Tourism Principles and Practice*, 3rd ed. (Harlow, Essex, England: Pearson Education, 2005), 346.

33. American Zoo and Aquarium Association, website, www.aza.org.

34. Zoological Society of San Diego, "About the San Diego Zoo," www.sandiegozoo.org/disclaimers/ aboutus.html (accessed September 19, 2009).

35. Zoological Society of San Diego, "Panda Baby Named in Zoo Ceremony," www.sandiegozoo.org/news/ panda_naming.html (accessed September 19, 2009).

36. Smithsonian National Zoological Park, "About Us," http://nationalzoo.si.edu/aboutus/ (accessed September 19, 2009).

37. Ibid.

38. National Aquarium Baltimore, "Community Affairs," www.aqua.org/communityaffairs.html (accessed September 19, 2009).

39. Ibid.

40. Oktoberfest Website, website, www.oktoberfest.de/en/ (accessed September 19, 2009).

41. Ibid.

42. Ipacom Travel, "All About Carnival in Rio," www.ipanema.com/carnival/allaboutcarnival.htm (accessed September 19, 2009).

43. Reggae on the River, website, www.reggaeontheriver .com (accessed September 19, 2009).

44. MardiGras.com, "Mardi Gras in New Orleans," www.mardigras.com (accessed September 19, 2009).

45. American Gaming Association, "Industry Information," www.americangaming.org/Industry/ factsheets/general_info_detail.cfv?id=15 (accessed September 19, 2009).

46. Las Vegas Convention and Visitors Authority, *2008 Las Vegas Visitor Profile Study*, www.lvcva.com/ getfile/VPS-2007%20Las%20Vegas.pdf?fileID=107 (accessed September 19, 2009).

47. MGM Mirage, website, www.mgmmirage.com (accessed September 19, 2009).

48. City Center Las Vegas, website, www.citycenter.com (accessed September 19, 2009).

49. Harrah's Entertainment, "Harrah's Company Home," www.harrahs.com/harrahs-corporate/index.html (accessed September 19, 2009).

50. Ibid.

51. Boyd Gaming, "Company History," www.boydgaming .com/about-boyd/mission-and-history (accessed September 19, 2009).

52. Seminole Hard Rock Hotel and Casino, "Company Profile," www.seminolehardrock.com/ company_profile/ (accessed September 19, 2009).

53. National Register of Historic Places, "National Register of Historic Places Program: About Us," www .nps.gov/nr/about.htm (accessed September 19, 2009).

54. Opry.com, "Venue Information: Opry Entertainment Complex," www.opry.com/EntertainmentComplex/ default.aspx (accessed September 19, 2009).

55. Smithsonian Institution, "About the Smithsonian," www.si.edu/about/ (accessed September 19, 2009).

56. Ibid.

57. Ibid.

58. Field Museum, "Museum Information: Mission Statement," www.fieldmuseum.org/museum_info/ mission_statement.htm (accessed September 19, 2009).

59. Ibid.

60. Ibid.

61. Hellenic Ministry of Culture, "The Unification of the Archaeological Sites of Athens," www.yppo.gr/4/ e40.jsp?obj_id==90 (accessed January 20, 2009).

62. Encyclopaedia Britannica, "Athens," www.britannica .com/EBchecked/topic/40773/Athens (accessed January 20, 2009).

63. CIAThe World Factbook https://www.cia.gov/library/ publications/the-world-factbook/geos/vt.html (accessed January 19, 2009).

64. Ibid.

65. Central Intelligence Agency, "The World Factbook: Costa Rica" https://www.cia.gov/library/publications/ the-world-factbook/geos/cs.html (accessed September 19, 2009).

CHAPTER 9

Business Travel: Meetings, Conventions, and Expositions

GEOGRAPHY SPOTLIGHT

Cultural Heritage Tourism: New York City

Cole Porter once sang, "I happen to like New York," and with so many cultural and heritage attractions in New York City, it is easy to understand why so many people are drawn to the city.[1] In 2007, more than 46 million people traveled to New York to see popular attractions including the Statue of Liberty, Ellis Island Immigration Museum, and the Metropolitan Museum of Art.[2] Many of New York City's famous tourist destinations have existed for more than a century and have contributed to the city's unique cultural background.

During the nineteenth and twentieth centuries, New York millionaires gave gifts that today make up some of New York's most famous establishments. Andrew Carnegie donated money to construct Carnegie Hall, which opened in 1891. Commodore Cornelius Vanderbilt, an "icon of philanthropy," built Grand Central Station, and in the late 1800s the Vanderbilt mansions were built.[3] J. P. Morgan, a banking tycoon, built the Morgan Library, which "houses a treasure of rare books and manuscripts."[4] In 1854, the Astor family founded the first public library in New York City. The Astors also contributed to the city by building the Waldorf-Astoria hotel. In 1946, John D. Rockefeller provided funding for the United Nations building. Today, flags of the United Nations member countries are displayed in Rockefeller Plaza. By generously giving money, art and book collections, and more these early New York City millionaires contributed to the rich cultural history that makes the city so unique.

One of New York City's most prominent symbols is the Statue of Liberty. Inaugurated in 1886, the statue is "a symbol of hope."[5] "No other monument embodies the nation's—and the world's—notion of political freedom and economic potential more than Lady Liberty."[6] Tourists can visit the monument, visit the Statue of Liberty Exhibit, take a ranger-guided tour, or view the New York City skyline from the 10th-floor viewing area.

GEOGRAPHY SPOTLIGHT *(continued)*

Courtesy of EMG Education Management

Across the bay from the Statue of Liberty is the Ellis Island Immigration Museum. More than 12 million immigrants came to the United States through Ellis Island, which opened on January 1, 1892, as a federal immigration station.[7] Ellis Island operated until 1954 and was opened as a museum on September 10, 1990. Almost half of all Americans today can trace their descendants through Ellis Island, and tourists are able to investigate their family history and genealogy at the museum. While visiting the island, guests can explore self-guided exhibits, the American Family Immigration History Center, and the Wall of Honor and see a show at the Living Theater.

"New Yorkers are an eclectic group"; this is evident in the variety of museums in New York City.[8] Tourists can visit museums such as the Whitney Museum of American Art, the Metropolitan Museum of Art, the American Museum of Natural History, the Museum of Modern Art, the USS *Intrepid* Sea, Air, Space Museum, the American Folk Art Museum, the Museum of the City of New York, and more. Each has interesting exhibits that display different aspects of American culture.

"Communities throughout the U.S. have developed successful programs linking the arts, humanities, history and tourism."[9] New York City is an example of one such community that has reaped the benefits of cultural and heritage tourism. Many destinations related to cultural and heritage tourism, such as the Statue of Liberty and Ellis Island, attempt to provide experiences that are unique only to that community. Attraction planners in the city help tourists to experience New York's vibrant culture and history through exhibits, museums, and monuments. To have continued success in the future, New York City tourism planners and destinations will need to ensure that they maintain the authenticity of the attractions and manage guests appropriately so as not to destroy the destination. New York City, with so many cultural and heritage destinations, seems prepared for success in the future because of expected growth rates in cultural and heritage tourism and increasing number of tourists to New York City.

Endnotes

1. *New York: First City of the World*, VHS (Sarasota, FL: V.I.E.W., Inc., 1997).
2. B. Silverman, *Frommer's New York City 2009* (Hoboken, NJ: Wiley, 2008).
3. *New York: First City of the World*.
4. Ibid.
5. Ibid.
6. Silverman, *Frommer's New York City*.
7. National Park Service, Ellis Island National Monument, www.nps.gov/elis (accessed January 24, 2009).
8. *New York: First City of the World*.
9. K. Craine, *A Position Paper on Cultural and Heritage Tourism*, 2005, www.pcah.gov/pdf/05WhitePaperCultHeritTourism .pdf (accessed January 27, 2009).

Development of the Meetings, Conventions, and Expositions Industry

Meetings, incentive travel, conventions, and exhibitions (MICE) represent a segment of the tourism industry that has grown in recent years. The MICE segment is very profitable. Industry statistics point to the fact that the average MICE tourist spends about twice the amount of money that other tourists spend.

People have gathered to attend **meetings, conventions,** and **expositions** since the ancient times, mainly for social, sporting, political, or religious purposes. As cities became regional centers, the size and frequency of such activities increased, and various groups and associations set up regular expositions.

Size and Scope of the Industry

Today, according to the American Society of Association Executives (ASAE), which operates in the United States with 23,000 members, about 6,000 associations operate at the national level, and a hundred thousand more function at the regional, state, and local levels. The association business is big business. Associations spend billions holding thousands of meetings and conventions that attract millions of attendees.

The hospitality and tourism industry itself consists of a number of associations, including the following:

- The American Hotel and Lodging Association
- The National Restaurant Association
- The American Culinary Federation
- The International Association of Convention and Visitors Bureaus
- Hotel Sales and Marketing Association International
- Meeting Planners Association
- Club Managers Association of America
- Professional Convention Management Association

Associations are the main independent political force for industries like hospitality, offering the following benefits:

- Governmental/political voice
- Marketing avenues
- Education
- Member services
- Networking

Thousands of associations hold annual conventions at various locations across North America and the rest of the world. Some associations alternate their venues from east to central to west; others meet at fixed locations, such as the National Restaurant Association (NRA) show in Chicago or the American Hotel and Lodging Association (AH&LA) convention and show in New York.

Key Players in the Industry

The need to hold face-to-face meetings and attend conventions has grown into a multi-billion-dollar industry. Many major and some smaller cities have convention centers with nearby hotels and restaurants. The major players in the convention industry are convention and visitors bureaus (CVBs), meeting planners and their clients, the convention centers, specialized services, and exhibitions. The pie chart in Figure 9–1 shows the number of different people and organizations involved with meetings, conventions, and expositions.

Convention and Visitors Bureaus

Convention and visitors bureaus are major participants in the meetings, conventions, and expositions market. The International Association of Conventions and Visitors Bureaus (IACVB) describes a CVB as a not-for-profit umbrella organization that represents an urban area that tries to solicit business-or

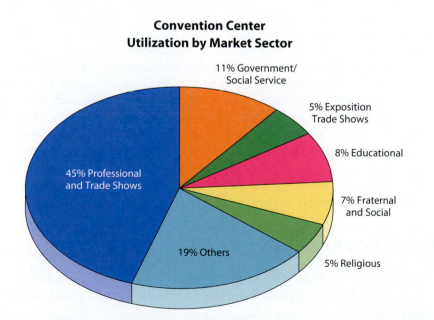

**Convention Center
Utilization by Market Sector**

11% Government/
Social Service

5% Exposition
Trade Shows

8% Educational

7% Fraternal
and Social

5% Religious

19% Others

45% Professional
and Trade Shows

Figure 9–1 • Major Players in the Convention Industry

Source: Walker, John R., *Introduction to Hospitality Management*, 3rd, © 2010. Electronically reproduced with permission of Pearson Education, Inc., Upper Saddle River, New Jersey.

pleasure-seeking visitors. The convention and visitors bureau comprises a number of visitor industry organizations representing the various industry sectors:

- Transportation
- Hotels and motels
- Restaurants
- Attractions
- Suppliers

The bureau represents these local businesses by acting as the sales team for the city. A bureau has five primary responsibilities:

1. To enhance the image of tourism in the local/city area.
2. To market the area and encourage people to visit and stay longer.
3. To target and encourage selected associations and others to hold meetings, conventions, and expositions in the city.
4. To assist associations and others with convention preparations and to give support during the convention.
5. To encourage tourists to partake of the historic, cultural, and recreational opportunities the city or area has to offer.

The outcome of these five responsibilities is for the cities' tourist industry to increase revenues.

Bureaus compete for business at trade shows, where interested visitor industry groups gather to do business. For example, a tour wholesaler who is promoting a tour will need to link up with hotels, restaurants, and attractions to package a vacation. Similarly, meeting planners are able to consider several locations and hotels by visiting a trade show. Bureaus generate leads (prospective clients) from a variety of sources. One source, associations, have national/international offices in Washington, D.C. (so that they can lobby the government), and Chicago.

A number of bureaus have offices or representatives or a sales team in these cities who will make follow-up visits to the leads generated at trade shows. Alternatively, they will make cold calls on potential prospects, such as major associations, corporations, and incentive houses. The sales manager will invite the meeting, convention, or exposition organizer to make a **familiarization (FAM) trip** to do a site inspection. The bureau assesses the needs of the client and organizes transportation, hotel accommodations, restaurants, and attractions accordingly. The bureau then lets the individual properties and other organizations make their own proposals to the client.

▶ Check Your Knowledge

1. According to the American Society of Association Executives (ASAE), in the United States how many associations operate at the national level?
2. What are the five primary responsibilities of a CVB?
3. What is the purpose of a familiarization (FAM) trip?

Destination Management Companies

A destination management company (DMC) is a service organization within the visitor industry that offers a host of programs and services to meet clients' needs. Initially, a destination management sales manager concentrates on selling the destination to meeting planners and performance improvement companies (incentive houses). The needs of such groups may be as simple as an airport pickup or as involved as an international sales convention with theme parties.

DMCs work closely with hotels; sometimes DMCs book rooms, and other times hotels request the DMC's know-how on organizing theme parties. Patricia Roscoe, chairperson of Patti Roscoe and Associates (PRA), says that meeting planners often have a choice of several destinations and might ask, "Why should I pick your destination?" The answer is that a DMC does everything, including airport greetings, transportation to the hotel, VIP check-in, theme parties, sponsoring programs, organizing competitive sports events, and so on, depending on budget. Sales managers associated with DMCs obtain leads, which are potential clients, from the following sources:

- Hotels
- Trade shows
- Convention and visitors bureaus
- Cold calls
- Incentive houses
- Meeting planners

Each sales manager has a staff or team that would include the following people:

- Special events manager, who will have expertise in sound, lighting, staging, and so on
- Accounts manager, who is an assistant to the sales manager
- A theme-events creative director
- Audiovisual specialist
- Operations manager, who coordinates everything, especially on-site arrangements, to ensure that what is sold actually happens

For example, Patti Roscoe's destination management company organized meetings, accommodations, meals, beverages, and theme parties for 2,000 Ford Motor Company dealers in nine groups over three days for each group. Roscoe also works closely with incentive houses, such as Carlson Marketing and Maritz Travel. These incentive houses approach a company and offer to set up incentive plans for companies' employees, including whatever it takes to motivate them. Once approved, Carlson contacts a destination management company and asks for a program.

Meeting Planners

Meeting planners may be independent contractors who contract out their services to both associations and corporations as the need arises, or they may be full-time employees of corporations or associations. In either case, meeting planners have interesting careers. According to the International Convention Management Association (ICMA), about 212,000 full- and part-time meeting planners work in the United States.

The professional meeting planner not only makes hotel and meeting bookings but also plans the meeting down to the last minute, always remembering to check to ensure that the services contracted for have been delivered. In recent years, the technical aspects of audiovisual and simultaneous translation equipment have added to the complexity of meeting planning. The meeting planner's role varies from meeting to meeting, but may include some or all of the following activities:

Pre-meeting Activities
- Estimate attendance
- Plan meeting agenda
- Establish meeting objectives
- Set meeting budget
- Select city location and hotel/convention site
- Negotiate contracts
- Plan exhibition
- Prepare exhibitor correspondence and packet
- Create marketing plan
- Plan travel to and from site
- Arrange ground transportation
- Organize shipping
- Organize audiovisual needs

On-Site Activities
- Conduct pre-event briefings
- Prepare VIP plan
- Facilitate people movement
- Approve expenditures

Post-meeting Activities
- Debrief
- Evaluate
- Give recognition and appreciation
- Plan for next year

As you can see, this is quite a long list of activities that meeting planners handle for clients.

Thousands of companies and associations hold meetings and conventions all over the country. Many of these organizations use the services of professional meeting planners, who in turn seek out suitable destinations for the meetings and conventions.

Service Contractors

Service contractors, *exposition service contractors*, *general contractors*, and *decorators* are all terms that have at one time or another referred to the individual responsible for providing all of the services needed to run the facilities for a trade show. Just as a meeting planner is able to multitask and satisfy all the demands in meeting planning, a general exposition contractor must be multitalented and equipped to serve all exhibit requirements and creative ideas.

The service contractor is hired by the exposition show manager or association meeting planner. The service contractor is a part of the facilities management team and, in order to use the facility, the sponsor must use the facility's service contractor. In other situations, the facility may have an exclusive contract with an outside contractor and may require all expositions to deal with this contractor. Today there are Internet service companies that can take reservations, prepare lists, and provide all kinds of services via the Internet for meeting planners.

▶ Check Your Knowledge

1. What is a destination management company?
2. What are the primary responsibilities of professional meeting planners?

Participants are leaving the convention center and likely are on their way to a bar or restaurant.
Courtesy of San Diego CVB

Associations

Today's **associations** find their roots in historical times, dating back to before the Middle Ages. Ancient Roman and Oriental craftspeople formed associations for the betterment of their trade. Medieval times found associations in the form of guilds, which were created to ensure proper wages and to maintain work standards. Associations began in the United States at the beginning of the eighteenth century, when Rhode Island candle makers organized themselves. Associations used to be viewed as groups that held annual meetings and conventions with speeches, entertainment, an educational program, and social events.

Types of Associations

An association is an organized body that exhibits some variety of volunteer leadership structure and that may concern an activity or purpose that members share in common. The association is generally organized to promote and enhance that common interest, activity, or purpose. The association industry is significant in many respects—total employees, payroll, and membership—but in one area it is the undisputed leader: it's the big spender when it comes to conventions and meetings. The following are different types of associations that participate in meetings, conventions, and expositions.

Trade Associations

A trade association is an industry trade group that is generally a public relations organization founded and funded by corporations that operate in a specific industry. Its purpose is generally to promote that industry through public relations (PR) activities such as advertising, political donation, political pressure, and education. Associations are the largest source of post-graduate professional development for America's workforce. Associations are involved in setting product safety standards and creating codes of ethics for entire professions.[1]

Professional Associations

A professional association is a professional body or organization, usually nonprofit, that exists to further a particular profession, to protect both the public interest and the interests of professionals.[2]

Medical and Scientific Associations

These associations are professional organizations for medical and scientific professionals. They are often based on a specific specialty and are usually national, often with subnational or regional affiliates. These associations usually offer conferences and continuing education. They often serve in capacities similar to trade unions and take public policy stances on issues.

Religious Organizations

Religious organizations include those groups of individuals that are part of churches, mosques, synagogues, and other spiritual or religious congregations. Religion takes many forms in various cultures and for individuals. These groups may come together in meeting places to further develop their faith, to become more aware of others who have the same faith, to organize and plan activities, to recognize their leaders, to raise funds, and for a number of other reasons.

Government Organizations

There are thousands of government organizations in the United States made up of numerous public bodies and agencies. These types of organizations can be federal, state, and local organizations. Three of them are general-purpose governments; the remaining two include special-purpose local governments that fall into the category of school district governments and special district governments.

Types of Meetings, Conventions, and Expositions

Meetings

Meetings are conferences, workshops, seminars, or other events designed to bring people together for the purpose of exchanging information. Meetings can take any one of the following formats:

Clinic—A workshop-type educational experience in which attendees learn by doing. A clinic usually involves small groups interacting with each other on an individual basis.

Forum—An assembly for the discussion of common concerns. Usually experts in a given field take opposite sides of an issue in a panel discussion, with liberal opportunity for audience participation.

Seminar—A lecture and a dialogue that allow participants to share experiences in a particular field. A seminar is guided by an expert discussion leader, and usually 30 or fewer persons participate.

Symposium—An event at which a particular subject is discussed by experts and opinions are gathered.

Workshop—A small group led by a facilitator or trainer. It generally includes exercises to enhance skills or develop knowledge in a specific topic.

The reason for having a meeting can range from the presentation of a new sales plan to a total quality management workshop. The purpose of meetings is to affect behavior. For example, as a result of attending a meeting, a person should know or be able to do certain things. Some outcomes are very specific; others may be less so. For instance, if a meeting were called to brainstorm new ideas, the outcome might be less concrete than for other types of meetings. The number of people attending a meeting can vary. Successful meetings require a great deal of careful planning and organization.

Meetings are set up according to the wishes of the client. The three main types of meeting setups are theater style, classroom style, and boardroom style:

- Theater style generally is intended for a large audience that does not need to make a lot of notes or refer to documents. This style usually consists of a raised platform and a lectern from which a presenter addresses the audience.
- Classroom setups are used when the meeting format is more instructional and participants need to take detailed notes or refer to documents. A workshop-type meeting often uses this format.
- Boardroom setups are made for small numbers of people. The meeting takes place around one block rectangular table.

Types of Meetings

There are different types of meetings and purposes for having a meeting. Some of the types of meetings are annual meetings that are held by private or public companies, board and committee meetings, fund-raisers, and professional and technical meetings. The following are some of the more popular types of meetings.

Annual Meetings

Annual meetings are meetings that are generally held every year by corporations or associations to inform their members of previous and future activities. In organizations run by volunteers or a paid committee, the annual meeting is generally the forum for the election of officers or representatives for the organization.

Board Meetings, Committee Meetings, Seminars and Workshops, Professional and Technical Meetings

Board meetings for corporations must be held annually, and most corporations hold meetings monthly or four times a year. Of course, not all are held in hotels, but some are, and that brings in additional revenue. Committee meetings are generally held at the place of business and only occasionally are held in hotels. Seminars are frequently held in hotels, as are workshops and technical meetings. To meet these needs hotels and convention centers have convention and meeting managers who go over the requirements and prepare proposals and event orders and budgets.

Corporate Meetings, Conventions, and Expositions

Meetings are mostly held by either the corporate or nonprofit industries. Both association and corporate meeting expenditures are in the billions of dollars each year. Corporations in various industries hold lots of meetings mostly for reasons of educating, training, decision making, research, sales, team building, the introduction of new products, organization or reorganization, problem solving, and strategic planning. Corporate meetings may be held for the employees or for the general public. For employees of a company, a corporate meeting is a command performance. The major objective of corporate meeting planners is to ensure that the meetings are successful.

SMERF

Many meetings are organized by either an association, a corporation, or **social, military, educational, religious, and fraternal groups (SMERF)**. Often these groups are price conscious because the majority of functions sponsored by these organizations are paid for by the individual, and sometimes the fees are not tax deductible. However, SMERF groups are flexible to ensure that their spending falls within the limits of their budgets; they are a good filler business during off-peak times.

An exhibition at a convention center
Courtesy of Rick Pawlenty

Incentive Meetings

The **incentive market** of MICE continues to experience rapid growth as meeting planners and travel agents organize incentive travel programs for corporate employees to reward them for reaching specific targets. Incentive trips generally vary from three to six days in length and can range from a moderate trip to an extremely lavish vacation for the employee and his or her partner. The most popular destination for incentive trips is Europe, followed closely by the Caribbean, Hawaii, Florida, and California. Because incentive travel serves as the reward for a unique subset of corporate group business, participants must perceive the destination and the hotel as something special. Climate, recreational facilities, and sightseeing opportunities are high on an incentive meeting planner's list of attributes to look for.

Association Meetings

Every year thousands of associations spend millions of dollars sponsoring many types of meetings, including regional, special interest, educational, and board meetings. The destination's availability of hotel and facilities, ease of transportation, distance from attendees, transportation costs, and food and beverage costs are important factors in planning association meetings. Association members attend association meetings voluntarily, so the hotel should work with meeting planners to make the destination seem as appealing as possible.

▶ Check Your Knowledge

1. What are three different types of meetings described in this chapter and what is their purpose?
2. What is SMERF?

A convention center ballroom set for a delegates function
Courtesy of the Fort Worth CVB

Conventions and Expositions

Conventions are generally larger meetings with some form of exposition or trade show included. A number of associations have one or more conventions per year. These conventions raise a large part of the association's budget. In a major convention city, convention delegates spend approximately $423 per day, almost twice that of vacation travelers. Figure 9–2 shows the average expenditure per delegate per stay by the convention type. Figure 9–3 shows convention delegates' spending in a convention city.

A typical convention follows a format like this:

1. Welcome/registration
2. Introduction of president
3. President's welcome speech, opening the convention
4. First keynote address by a featured speaker
5. Exposition booths open (equipment manufacturers and trade suppliers)
6. Several workshops or presentations on specific topics

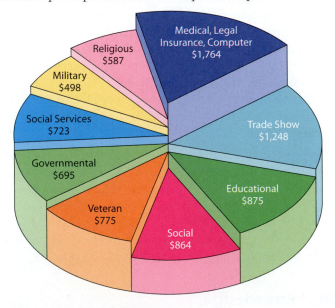

Average length of stay is 3.50 days

Figure 9–2 • Average Expenditure per Delegate per Stay by the Convention Type. The significance of these amounts is that given an attendance of several hundred to thousands of guests the economic impact quickly adds up and benefits the community in a variety of ways.

Source: Walker, John R., *Introduction to Hospitality Management,* 3rd, © 2010. Electronically reproduced with permission of Pearson Education, Inc., Upper Saddle River, New Jersey.

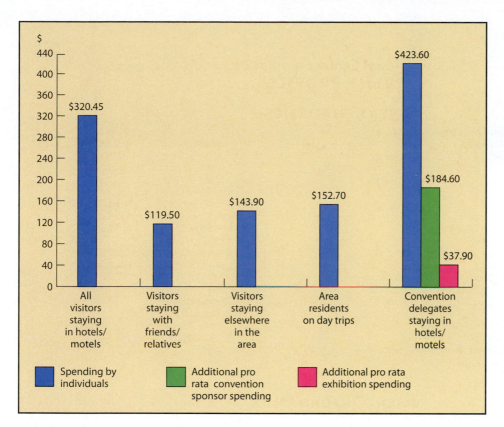

Figure 9–3 • Convention Delegates' Spending in Convention City San Francisco
Source: Walker, John R., *Introduction to Hospitality Management*, 3rd, © 2010. Electronically reproduced with permission of Pearson Education, Inc., Upper Saddle River, New Jersey.

7. Luncheon

8. More workshops and presentations

9. Demonstrations of special topics (e.g., culinary arts for a hospitality convention)

10. Vendors' private receptions

11. Dinner

12. Convention center closes

Figure 9–4 shows a convention event profile for a trade show.

Conventions are not always held in convention centers; in fact, the majority are held in large hotels over a three- to five-day period. The headquarters hotel is usually the one in which most of the activity takes place. Function space is allocated for registration, the convention, expositions, meals, and so on.

Expositions are events that bring together sellers of products and services at a location (usually a convention center) where they can show their products and services to a group of attendees at a convention or trade show. Exhibitors are an essential component of the industry because they pay to exhibit their products to the attendees. Exhibitors interact with attendees with the intention of making sales or establishing contacts and leads for follow-up. Expositions can take up several hundred thousand square feet of space, divided into booths for individual manufacturers or their representatives. In the hospitality industry, the two

16:15:28

Convention Center Corporation
EVENT PROFILE

EVENT STATISTICS

Event Name:	Apartment Association Trade Show	ID:	9506059
Sales Person:	David Ploskonka	Initial Contact:	8/3/2005
Event Manager:	Kris Roach	Move In Date:	6/22/2009
ConVis Contact:		Move In Day:	Wednesday
Food Person:		Move In Time:	6:01 am
Event Tech.:		First Event Date:	6/23/2009
Event Attend.:		First Event Day:	Thursday
Nature of Event:	LT Local Trade Show	Start Show Time:	6:01 am
Event Parameter:	Convention Center	End Show Time:	11:59 pm
Business Type 1:	41 Association	# of Event Days:	1
Business Type 2:	91 LOCAL	Move Out Date:	6/23/2009
Booking Status:	D Definite	Move Out Day:	Thursday
Rate Schedule:	III Public Show, Meetings and Location	Out Time:	11:59 pm
Open to Public:	No	Date Confirmed:	8/3/2005
Number Sessions:	1	Attend per Sesn:	3000
Event Sold By:	Facility	Tot Room Nights:	15
Abbrev. Name:	/6/Apartment Assn	Public Release:	Yes
Est Bill Amount:	Rent - 6,060.00 Equip –	0.00 Food –	0.00
Last Changed On:	8/20/05 in: Comment Maintenance	By – Alex Gohr	

This Event has been in the facility before

CLIENT INFORMATION

Company: Apartment Assn, a non-profit Corporation
          Contact Name: Dory Grieve, Sales and Marketing Coord.   ID: SDAA

     Alt Contact Name: Ms. Corrina Schultz, Finance & Operations Director

EVENT LOCATIONS

ROOM	MOVE IN	IN USE	ED	MOVE OUT	BS	SEAT	RATE	EST. RENT	ATTEND
A	6/22/09 6:01 am	6/23/09	1	6/23/09 11:59 pm	D	E	III	6,060.00	5000
AS	6/22/09 6:01 am	6/23/09	1	6/23/09 11:59 pm	D	E	III	0.00	10
R01	6/22/09 6:01 am	6/23/09	1	6/23/09 11:59 pm	D	T	III	0.00	450
R02	6/22/09 6:01 am	6/23/09	1	6/23/09 11:59 pm	D	T	III	0.00	350
R03	6/22/09 6:01 am	6/23/09	1	6/23/09 11:59 pm	D	T	III	0.00	280
R04	6/22/09 6:01 am	6/23/09	1	6/23/09 11:59 pm	D	T	III	0.00	280
R05	6/22/09 6:01 am	6/23/09	1	6/23/09 11:59 pm	D	T	III	0.00	460

FOOD SERVICES

ROOM	DATE	TIME	BS ATTEND	EST. COST FOOD SERVICE
There are No Food Services booked for this event

Figure 9–4 • Convention Event Profile for a Trade Show

Source: Courtesy the San Diego Convention Center Corporation

largest expositions are the American Hotel & Lodging Association's conference held in conjunction with the International Hotel/Motel & Restaurant Show (IHMRS) (held annually in November at the Jacob K. Javits Convention Center in New York) and the National Restaurant Association's annual exposition held every May in Chicago. Both events are well worth attending.

INTRODUCING

Jill Moran, CSEP, Principal and Owner, JS Moran, Special Event Planning & Management

Jill Moran

In my life, there is no typical day. As the owner of a special event company, I provide a variety of services to corporate, nonprofit, and social clients. I must be able to communicate successfully with a client at one moment, a vendor at the next, and a prospect at another. My job also involves managing the growth of my company, hiring the right staff and vendors for projects, and getting each job done from start to finish in a professional and timely manner.

As a business owner, I am required to keep my eye on many facets of the company almost daily. Some areas are a must to attend to such as billing, scheduling, and marketing. The squeakiest wheel that gets the most grease, though, is the actual ongoing projects. Once a project is secured, the contracting, planning, and execution stages quickly follow after the initial handshake. These components of meeting and event planning can be time and energy consuming as the details are planned out and put into motion. Event details may involve researching, attending meetings, generating event documents, developing creative concepts and themes, securing vendors to satisfy event details, or executing an event. In the planning of any given event or conference, I may be required to attend off-site visits with vendors, venues, or clients as well as use the computer or telephone to facilitate the planning process. Visits to art supply, furniture, and fabric stores, or store rooms of linen or décor vendors are also key elements as theme and design elements are worked on. Review of entertainment or speakers, planning of room layouts or trade show and exhibition space, or discussion with graphic artists also fit into the necessary details covered during the planning phase of an event.

A typical day may involve early computer time to work on production schedules, timelines, e-mails to vendors or clients, follow-up on contracts, or focused time spent on a new proposal. I find early morning (before 9 A.M.) or evening (after 8 P.M.) to be the best time for these activities. This is when I get the least telephone interruptions and it is before or after scheduled appointments that would require my time out of the office. During the typical business day, phone calls, planning activities, and appointments occupy most of the day. If I am working on an international project, there is more flexibility with this because of the time differences.

While the execution phase of projects and events keeps me busy moment by moment, the strategic planning and business management of my company also demands attention as well. The challenge for me as the owner of a small business is to carve out time for the marketing and sales arm of the business, taking time to prospect for new business at the same time that I am in the execution phase of events, so when one project comes to an end, another will be waiting in the wings. I do this by developing fresh marketing materials using photos or components of recent meetings and events, creating video or DVD-style materials to post on my website or to send to clients, making calls to colleagues, prospects, or venues to say "hello" or touch base, and attending luncheons or visits with past clients to keep in touch. I also try to spend time getting a pulse on new markets to explore or niche areas to develop in my business. I typically subscribe to a wide variety of industry and professional magazines and try to end my day flipping through and tearing out articles that may be useful.

(continued)

INTRODUCING   (*continued*)

One thing I feel strongly about is keeping an eye on the future. I have owned a home-based business since 1988 and have seen the special events industry grow and change in many ways over the years. Passionate about the industry, I made a commitment to share my experience with those starting out, serving as a mentor, speaker, author, and industry leader. I continually examine the direction events and meetings are taking, gaps in the industry that need professional attention, ways to improve the processes or offer new and better services to those who honor the value of events as vehicles for communication, education, or celebration. Whenever possible, I try to attend meetings and conferences, either in my local area or throughout the United States and internationally to get a pulse on new directions and changes in the industry. These meetings also give me ideas and feed my creative juices to approach new projects with a fresh eye. I have met colleagues who are similar to me and share my challenges and who are not at all like me and help me to consider different approaches to events. Many times, these gatherings offer terrific networking opportunities and ways to meet potential vendors or new clients.

Sometimes I feel I eat, sleep, and live special events, and in many ways I do. But work doesn't take up every moment of my life. As a mother and wife, I still try to create a fun, loving home for my family by cooking dinner almost every night and by walking daily with my husband and two dogs. These breaks during the day give me downtime and a chance to regroup. I am also active in the music ministry at my local church as a youth choir director, which offers me spiritual and community involvement. I also belong to a book group, which I often attend without completing the story. There are only so many hours in the day, and I seem to use them up very quickly. But at the end of each day, I am always looking forward to the next!

Source: Courtesy of Jill Moran.

FOCUS ON

Industry Trends: Planning Green Events

Courtesy Belkis Kambach

A Native American proverb suggests that all we do today must be done with the next seven generations in mind. This principle must be applied to the environment most importantly. Everywhere we turn there is talk about being "green," in most cases literally greenwashing us because green sells. But what does it really mean to be "green" in the MICE industry?

Trying to Define Green Events

Can we plan green events and stay within budget? The truth is that planning a green event may take a little more time and effort, but the rewards surpass the financial considerations. These events are about being mindful of not just how we leave our world for the next generation but essentially about how we touch those people and places that are involved in the event we create.

F O C U S   O N   (*continued*)

Standard event planning today results in unnecessary physical waste, including by-products such as pesticides, carbon dioxide emissions, garbage, plastics, and underpaid labor. Most events leave large, unfriendly footprints. We can all minimize the amount of negative effects that these events have on our world by amending our practices to become more sustainable ones. The steps you take to safeguard our environment and community will last for generations. With creative planning and research, we are all able to develop practices and products.

I see the downside whenever I attend annual industry conferences: beverages in individual, non-biodegradable plastic bottles; exhibitors handing out yet more foam and plastic along with nonrecyclable keepsakes that we'll never use; disposable containers creating heaps of waste; and not enough volunteers to monitor trash being stuffed into the recycle-only bins. At any event I have attended in the past years, someone is always pushing a disposable item or things packaged in plastic. Although there are strict (and legal) rules guiding exhibitors about no alcohol and no firearms on the premises, I have yet to attend an event where organizers specify, in the name of the environment, "earth-friendly trinkets only."

Factors Involved in Not-So-Green Pitfalls

One criticism of the event industry is its tendency to create more waste. The main issue is the physical components of big gatherings: food waste, drink packaging, and giveaway items, to name a few. From meetings, conferences, trade shows, expos, fairs, parades, baby showers, christenings, weddings, to even funerals, green event planning can help turn any occasion into a loving, caring, and sustainable activity.

So, What Makes an Event Green?

With information bombarding us from all directions, green planning can be overwhelming for many of us. With the ever-growing urgency to make changes and embrace methods to reduce our carbon footprint, it can feel like our sometimes seemingly small efforts are futile. However, nothing could be further from the truth. Every little change counts. Change begins with awareness. There is no argument that "going green" for events is easier in some parts of world than others, but every step you take when planning an event makes a difference.

For starters, by following some simple rules we can make our events greener while quite often even lowering the costs. Green events should aim to focus on each component of event planning and implementation, including but not limited to the following:

- *Choose a green hotel*—Before you select a hotel for your event, take the time to understand the hotel's commitment to the environment. Point out the details to guests.

- *Eat green*—Look for a green caterer when planning your event. They specialize in providing locally grown, certified organic and sustainable event food. Lately, there is more interest from clients in exploring organics. Reference such items on the menu, even naming the originating farm or dairy.

- *Save trees*—Go digital. One of the most expensive, and environmentally impactful, pieces of an event is the printed stack of handouts that organizers and presenters prepare for attendees. Use eco-friendly procedures such as electronic registration, transmission of news releases, and booking information.

- *Reuse and recycle*—When choosing materials for your conferences and meetings, focus on using materials that can be reused or recycled. For things that need to be printed, use 100 percent postconsumer recycled, chlorine-free or handmade, fair trade paper.

(*continued*)

FOCUS ON (*continued*)

- *Avoid bottled water*—Practice filling water glasses only when asked instead of pouring for every guest, which often results in water waste.
- *Use fair trade items*—Use only fair trade coffee and gift items, which promote a safe and healthy work environment, pay the producer a fair price, and regulate environmental standards.
- *Conserve energy*—Mitigate the energy consumption related to guest travel to the event by using carbon offsets.
- *Use more environmentally friendly transportation*—Biodiesel car rentals and EcoBuses are more enjoyable for everyone and will not affect future generations as negatively as regular transportation means do.
- *Use reusable bags*—Promote reusable bags.
- *Use real dinnerware*—Advocate for the use of real china, glasses, and utensils or promote the virtues of biodegradable disposables such as plates made from corn starch or bamboo.
- *Donate unused food*—Donate unserved food to local food banks or shelters.
- *Compost food scraps*—Composting reduces both financial and environmental costs. Most cities in the United States now have a composting program available to caterers and planners. Keeping 98 percent of the waste of a weekend event out of landfills should be the goal.

And the list goes on!

Pass the message on. The best way to guarantee a greener event is to share your knowledge with others in the industry. In eco-tourism and the environment, the key component is education. Make sure your clients, participants, vendors, exhibitors, presenters, and staff all know what they can do to reduce their environmental impact. There is so much we can accomplish to care for our planet if we all do our share to make improvements in this industry we love. Sometimes the hardest part of effecting change is change itself and taking the first step. It's a matter of having the will and the desire to educate our clients, and under those circumstances, anything is possible.

Organizations sponsoring conferences, meetings, and other events often strive to reduce the environmental impacts of those events. Following are links to a wide range of resources to help accomplish that goal:

- Eco Speakers–www.ecospeakers.com/green-travel-meetings/greenevents/index.html
- Green Meeting Industry Council–www.greenmeetings.info
- BlueGreen Meetings–www.bluegreenmeetings.org
- Cleaner and Greener Event Certification–www.cleanerandgreener.org/eventcertification/index.htm
- Whole Foods Market–www.wholefoodsmarket.com
- Convene Green Alliance–www.convenegreen.com
- EPA: Green Meetings–www.epa.gov/oppt/greenmeetings
- Positive Impact–www.positiveimpactevents.co.uk
- Sustainable Events–www.eventsustainability.com
- Seven-Star, Inc.–www.sevenstarevents.com
- National Recycling Coalition: Green Meetings Policy–www.nrc-recycle.org/greenmeetingsp.aspx

(*continued*)

Green Event Planners

- dkk events–www.dkkevents.com
- Green Carpet–www.greencarpetevent.com
- GreenFernEvents, LLC–www.greenfernevents.com
- Green Lily Events–www.greenlilyevents.com
- Organise This–www.organisethis.co.uk
- Pulse Staging and Events–www.pulsestaging.com

And the list goes on!

Source: Photo and text courtesy of Bel Kambach, St. Cloud State University, Minnesota.

Meeting Planning

Meeting planning includes not only the planning but also the successful holding of the meeting and the postmeeting evaluations. As we shall see, there are a number of topics and lots of details to consider.

Needs Analysis

Before meeting planners can start planning a meeting, they complete a *needs analysis* to determine the purpose and desired outcome of the meeting. Once the necessity of the meeting has been established, the meeting planner can then work with the party to maximize the productivity of the meeting. The key to a productive meeting is a meeting agenda. The meeting agenda may not always fall under the responsibility of the meeting planner, but it is essential for the meeting planner to be closely involved with the written agenda and also with the core purpose of the agenda, which may be different from what is stated. For example, a nonprofit organization may hold a function to promote awareness of its objectives through a fun activity, but its hidden agenda is to raise funds for the organization.

The meeting agenda provides the framework for making *meeting objectives*. The meeting planner must know what the organization is trying to accomplish so as to be successful in the management of their meeting or conference. It is helpful for the meeting planner, regardless of what role he or she plays to plan the meeting with the meeting objectives in mind. The meeting's objectives provide the framework from which the meeting planner will set the budget, select the site and facility, and plan the overall meeting or convention.

Budget

Understanding clients and knowing their needs are both extremely important, however, the budget carries the most weight. Setting the budget for the meeting is more successful if the meeting planner is involved in the budget planning throughout and before making a final decision on how much to spend in each area. Setting the budget for the meeting is not a simple task. Knowing how much there is available to spend will help the meeting planner to better guide clients with parameters by which the event is designed.

Budgets are planned for various activities and the amount of the budget needed fluctuates for different sites. Therefore, a working budget is necessary to be used as a guideline for making decisions for necessary changes. When changes in the budget are made, these changes must be communicated to the meeting planner so that he or she can plan activities within budgetary constraints. Revenue and expenditure estimates must be accurate and be as thorough as possible to make certain that all possible expenditures are included in the budget prior to the event.

Income for a meeting, convention, or exposition comes from grants or contributions, event sponsor contributions, registration fees, exhibitor fees, company or organization sponsoring, advertising, and the sale of educational materials.

Expenses for a meeting, convention, or exposition could include the following but are not limited to rental fees, meeting planner fees, marketing expenses, printing and copying expenses, support supplies, such as office supplies and mailing, on-site and support staff, audiovisual equipment, speakers, signage, entertainment and recreational expenses, mementos for guests and attendees, tours, ground transportation, spousal programs, food and beverage, and on-site personnel.

Request for Proposal and Site Inspection and Selection

No matter how large or small a meeting, it is essential that clear meeting specifications are developed in the form of a written request for proposal/quote (RFQ), rather than contacting hotels by telephone to get a quote. Many larger hotels and convention centers now have online submission forms available.

Several factors are evaluated when selecting a meeting site, including location and level of service, accessibility, hotel room availability, conference room availability, price, city, restaurant service and quality, personal safety, and local attractions. Convention centers and hotels provide meeting space and accommodations as well as food and beverage facilities and service. The convention center and a hotel team from each hotel capable of handling the meeting will attempt to impress the meeting planner. The hotel sales executive will send particulars of the hotel's meeting space and a selection of banquet menus and invite the meeting planner for a site inspection. During the site inspection, the meeting planner is shown all facets of the hotel, including the meeting rooms, guest sleeping rooms, the food and beverage outlets, and any special facility that may interest the planner or the client.

Negotiation with the Convention Center or Hotel

The meeting planner has several critical interactions with hotels, including negotiating the room blocks and rates. Escorting clients on site inspections gives the hotel an opportunity to show its level of facilities and service. The most important interaction is normally with the catering/banquet/conference department associates, especially the services manager, maître d', and captains; these frontline associates can make or break a meeting. For example, meeting planners often send boxes of meeting materials to hotels, expecting the hotel to automatically know which meeting they are for. On more than one occasion, they have ended up in the hotel's main storeroom, much to the consternation of the meeting planner. Fortunately for most meeting planners, once they have taken care of a meeting one year, subsequent years typically are very similar.

Contracts

Once the meeting planner and the hotel or conference facility have agreed on all the requirements and costs, a contract is prepared and signed by the planner, the organization, and the hotel or convention center. The contract is a legal document that binds two or more parties. In the case of meetings, conventions, and expositions, a contract binds an association or organization and the hotel or convention center. The components that make up an enforceable contract include the following[3]:

1. *An offer.* The offer simply states, in as precise a manner as possible, exactly what the offering party is willing to do, and what he or she expects in return. The offer may include specific instructions for how, where, when, and to whom the offer is made.
2. *Consideration.* The payment exchanged for the promise(s) contained in a contract. For a contract to be valid, consideration must flow both ways. For example, the consideration is for a convention center to provide services and use of its facilities in exchange for a consideration of a stated amount to be paid by the organization or host.
3. *Acceptance.* The unconditional agreement to the precise terms and conditions of an offer. The acceptance must mirror exactly the terms of the offer for it to make the contract valid. The best way to indicate acceptance of an offer is by agreeing to the offer in writing.

Most important, to be considered legally enforceable, a contract must be made by parties who are legally able to contract, and the activities specified in the contract must not be in violation of the law. Contracts should include clauses on "attrition and performance," meaning that the contract has a clause to protect the hotel or convention facility in the event that the organizer's numbers drop below an acceptable level. Because the space reserved is supposed to produce a certain amount of money, if the numbers drop, so does the money; unless there is a clause that says something like "there will be a guaranteed revenue of $$$ for the use of the room/space." The performance part of the clause means that a certain amount of food and beverage revenue will be charged for regardless of whether it is consumed or not.

Organizing and Preconference Meetings

The average lead time required for organizing a small meeting is about three to six months, larger meetings and conferences take much longer and are booked years in advance. Some meetings and conventions choose the same location each year, and others move from city to city, usually from the East Coast to the Midwest or West Coast.

Conference Event Order

A conference event order has all the information necessary for all department employees to be able to refer to for details of the setup (times and layout) and the conference itself (arrival, meal times and what food and beverages are to be served, and the cost of items so that the billing can be done). An example of a conference event order is given in Figure 9–5.

EVENT DOCUMENT
REVISED COPY

/6/SAN DIEGO INTERNATIONAL BOAT SHOW
Thursday, January 7, 2010–Sunday, January 10, 2010

SPACE: Combined Exhibit Halls AB, Hall A - How Manager's Office, Box Office by Hall A, Hall B –
Show Manager's Office, Mezzanine Room 12, Mezzanine Room 13, Mezzanine Rooms 14 A&B, AND
Mezzanine Rooms 15 A&B

CONTACT: Mr. Jeff Hancock
National Marine Manufacturers Association, Inc.
4901 Morena Blvd.
Suite 901
San Diego, CA 92117
Telephone Number: (619) 274-9924
Fax Number: (619) 274-6760
Decorator Co.:   Greyhound Exposition Services
Sales Person: Denise Simenstad
Event Manager: Jane Krause
Event Tech.:   Sylvia A. Harrison

SCHEDULE OF EVENTS:

Monday, January 4, 2010   5:00 am–6:00 pm   Combined Exhibit Halls AB
Service contractor move in GES,
Andy Quintena

Tuesday, January 5, 2010   8:00 am–6:00 pm   Combined Exhibit Halls AB
Service contractor move in GES,
Andy Quintena
12:00 pm–6:00 pm
Combined Exhibit Halls AB
Exhibitor move in

Wednesday, January 6, 2010   8:00 am–6:00 pm   Combined Exhibit Halls AB
Exhibitor move in
Est. attendance: 300

Thursday, January 7, 2010   8:00 am–12:00 pm   Combined Exhibit Halls AB
Exhibitor final move in
11:30 am–8:30 pm   Box Office by Hall A
OPEN: Ticket prices, Adults $6, Children 12 & under $3

Figure 9–5 • Convention Event Profile

Source: Courtesy the San Diego Convention Center Corporation

Postevent Meeting

A postevent meeting is held to evaluate the event—what went well and what should be improved for next time. Larger conferences have staff from the hotel or convention center where the event will be held the following year, so they can better prepare for the event when it is held at their facility.

Venues for Meetings, Conventions, and Expositions

Most of the time meetings and functions are held in hotels, convention centers, city centers, conference centers, universities, corporate offices, or resorts, but more and more we find meetings housed in unique venues such as cruise ships and historical sites.

City Centers

City centers are good venues for some conferences because they are convenient to reach by air and ground transportation. There is plenty of action in a major city center: attractions range from cultural to scenic beauty. Most cities have a convention center and several hotels to accommodate guests.

Convention Centers

Convention centers throughout the world compete to host the largest exhibitions, which can be responsible for adding several million dollars in revenue to the local economy. Convention centers are huge facilities with parking, information services, business centers, and food and beverage facilities included in the centers. Usually, convention centers are corporations owned by county, city, or state governments and operated by a board of appointed representatives from the various groups having a vested interest in the successful operation of the center. The board appoints a president or general manager to run the center according to a predetermined mission, and goals and objectives.

Convention centers have a variety of exposition and meeting rooms to accommodate both large and small events. The centers generate revenue from the rental of space, which frequently is divided into booths (one booth is about 100 square feet). Large exhibits may take several booths' space. Additional revenue is generated by the sale of food and beverages, concession stand rentals, and vending machines. Many centers also have their own subcontractors to handle staging, construction, lighting, audiovisual, electrical, and communications.

In addition to the megaconvention centers, a number of prominent centers also contribute to the local, state, and national economies. One good example is the Rhode Island Convention Center. The $82 million center, representing the

San Diego convention center
Courtesy of San Diego CVB

second largest public works project in the state's history, is located in the heart of downtown Providence, adjacent to the 14,500-seat Providence Civic Center. The 365,000-square-foot center offers a 100,000-square-foot main exhibit hall, a 20,000-square-foot ballroom, 18 meeting rooms, and a full-service kitchen that can produce 5,000 meals per day. The exhibit hall divides into four separate halls, and the facility features its own telephone system, allowing individualized billing. A special rotunda function room at the front of the building features glass walls that offer a panoramic view of downtown Providence for receptions of up to 365 people. Extensive use of glass on the façade of the center provides ample natural light throughout the entrance and prefunction areas.

Conference Centers

A conference center is a specially designed learning environment dedicated to hosting and supporting small- to medium-sized meetings, typically including between 20 and 50 people.[4] The nature of a conference meeting is a distraction-free learning environment. Conference centers are designed to encourage sharing of information in an inviting, comfortable atmosphere and to focus sharply on meetings and what makes them effective. Although the groups that hold meetings in conference centers are typically small in terms of attendees, there are thousands of small meetings held every month. Increasingly, hotels are now going after executive meetings where expense is not a major issue.

Hotels and Resorts

Hotels and resorts offer a variety of locations from city center to destination resorts. Many hotels have ballrooms and other meeting rooms designed to accommodate groups of various sizes. Today, they all have websites and offer the services of meeting planners to help with the planning and organizing of conferences and meetings. Once the word gets out that a meeting planner is seeking a venue for a conference, there is plenty of competition among hotels to get the business.

Cruise Ships

Meeting in a nontraditional facility can provide a unique and memorable experience for the meeting attendee. However, many of the challenges faced in traditional venues such as hotels and convention centers are also applicable to these facilities. In some cases, planning must begin much earlier with alternative meeting environments than with traditional facilities. A thorough understanding of goals and objectives, budget, and attendee profile of the meeting is essential to negotiate the best package possible. A cruise ship meeting is uniquely different from the regular meeting setting and offers a number of advantages to the attendees such as discounts, complimentary meals, less outside distraction while at sea, entertainment, and visiting more than one destination while unpacking only once![5]

Colleges and Universities

Colleges, universities, and their campuses are being used as alternative venues for meeting places. The paramount consideration in contemplating use of campus-based facilities is to know the nature of the target audience.[6] The relative cost of campus-based meetings is most of the time less expensive than a medium-priced hotel.

CAREER INFORMATION

Meetings, incentive travel, conventions, and expositions (the MICE segment) offer a broad range of career paths. Successful meeting planners are detail-oriented, organized people who not only plan and organize meetings, but also negotiate hotel rooms and meeting space in hotels and convention centers.

Incentive travel includes aspects of organizing high-end travel, hotels, restaurants, attractions, and entertainment. Because of the big budgets involved, this can be an exciting career for those interested in a combination of travel and hotels in exotic locations.

Conventions and convention centers have several career paths from assistants to sales managers, sales managers for a special type of account (e.g., associations), or for a territory. Senior sales managers are expected to book large conventions and expositions—yes, everyone has their quota. Event managers plan and organize the function/event with the client once the contract has been signed. Salaries range from $35,000 to $70,000 for assistants up to sales or event managers.

Careers are also possible in the companies that service the MICE segment. Someone has to equip the convention center and ready it for an exposition. Someone has to supply all the food and beverage items, and so on. Off-premise catering and special events also offer careers for creative people who like to create concepts and orchestrate themes around which an event or function may be planned. For all the career paths, it is critical to gain experience in the areas of your interest. Request a person you respect to be your mentor and ask questions. By showing your enthusiasm, people will respond with more help and advice.

Figure 9–6 shows an event manager's job description at a convention center.

(continued)

SAN DIEGO CONVENTION CENTER

EVENT MANAGER

DEFINITION

Under moderate direction from the services manager, plans, directs, and supervises assigned events and represents services manager on assigned shifts.

KEY RESPONSIBILITIES

- Plans, coordinates, and supervises all phases of the events to include set ups, move ins and outs, and the activities themselves
- Prepares and disseminates set-up information to the proper departments well in advance of the activity, and ensures complete readiness of the facilities
- Responsible for arranging for all services needed by the tenant
- Coordinates facility staffing needs with appropriate departments
- Acts as a consultant to tenants and the liaison between in-house contractors and tenants
- Preserves facility's physical plant and ensures a safe environment by reviewing tenants plans; requests and makes certain they comply with facility, state, county, and city rules and regulations
- Prepares accounting paperwork of tenant charges, approves final billings, and assists with collection of same
- Resolves complaints, including operational problems and difficulties
- Assists in conducting surveys, gathering statistical information, and working on special projects as assigned by services manager
- Conducts tours of the facilities

MINIMUM REQUIREMENTS

- Bachelor's degree in hospitality management, business, or recreational management from a fully accredited university or college, plus two (2) years of experience in coordinating major conventions and trade shows
- Combination of related education/training and additional experience may substitute for bachelor's degree
- An excellent ability to manage both fiscal and human resources
- Knowledge in public relations; oral and written communications
- Experienced with audiovisual equipment

225 Broadway, Suite 710 • San Diego, CA 92102 • (619) 239-1989
FAX (619) 239-2030
Operated by the San Diego Convention Center Corporation

Figure 9–6 • An Event Manager's Job Description
Source: Courtesy the San Diego Convention Center Corporation

CASE STUDY

Double-Booked

The convention bureau in a large and popular convention destination has jurisdiction over the convention center. A seasoned convention sales manager, who has worked for the bureau for seven years and produces more sales than any other sales manager, has rebooked a 2,000-person group for a three-day exposition in the convention center. The exposition is to take place two years from the booking date.

The client has a 15-year history of holding conventions, meetings, and expositions in this convention center and has always used the bureau to contract all space and services for them. In fact, the sales manager handling the account has worked with the client for 7 of the 15 years. The bureau considers this client a "preferred customer."

The convention group meeting planner also appears in a magazine ad giving a testimony of praise for the convention bureau, this particular sales manager, and the city as a destination for conventions.

Shortly after the meeting planner rebooks this convention with the bureau, the bureau changes sales administration personnel, not once, but three times. This creates a challenge for the sales manager in terms of producing contracts, client files, and event profiles, and in the recording and distribution of information. The preferred customer who rebooked has a contract, purchase orders for vendor services, a move in and setup agenda, and an event profile, all supplied by the sales manager. The sales manager has copies of these documents as well. The two hotels where the group will be staying also have contracts for the VIP group.

As is the nature of this particular bureau, other sales managers have been booking and contracting space for the same time period as the group that rebooked. In fact, the exhibit hall has been double-booked, as have the break-out rooms for seminars, workshops, and food and beverage service. The groups that were contracted later are all first-time users of the facility.

This situation remains undetected until 10 days prior to the groups' arrival. It is brought to the attention of the bureau and convention center only when the sales manager distributes a memo to schedule a preconvention meeting with the meeting planner and all convention center staff.

Because of the administrative personnel changes, necessary information was not disseminated to key departments and key personnel. The convention center was never notified that space had been contracted for the preferred customer. The preferred customer has been told about this potentially catastrophic situation. Now there is a major problem to rectify.

Questions

1. Ultimately, who is responsible for decision making with regard to this situation?
2. What steps should be taken to remedy this situation?
3. Are there fair and ethical procedures to follow to provide space for the preferred customer? If so, what are they?
4. What measures, if any, should be taken in handling the seasoned sales manager?
5. What leverage does the meeting planner have to secure this and future business with the bureau?
6. What might the preferred customer do if they are denied space and usage of the convention center?
7. How can this situation be avoided in the future?

Summary

1. Conventions, meetings, and expositions serve social, political, sporting, or religious purposes. Associations offer benefits such as a political voice, education, marketing avenues, member services, and networking.
2. Meetings are events designed to bring people together for the purpose of exchanging information. Typical forms of meetings are conference, workshops, seminars, forums, and symposia.
3. Expositions bring together purveyors of products, equipment, and services in an environment in which they can demonstrate their products. Conventions are meetings that include some form of exposition or trade show.
4. Meeting planners contract out their services to associations and corporations. Their responsibilities include pre-meeting, on-site, and post-meeting activities.
5. The convention and visitors bureaus are nonprofit organizations that assess the needs of the client and organize transportation, hotel accommodations, restaurants, and attractions.
6. Convention centers are huge facilities, usually owned by the government, where meetings and expositions are held. Events at convention centers require a lot of planning ahead and careful event management. A contract that is based on the event profile and an event document is part of effective management.

Key Words and Concepts

associations
convention
convention center
exposition
familiarization (FAM) trip
incentive market

meeting
meeting planner
meetings, incentive travel, conventions, and exhibitions (MICE)

social, military, educational, religious, and fraternal groups (SMERF)

Review Questions

1. What are associations and what is their purpose?
2. List the number of different people and organizations involved with meetings, conventions, and expositions.
3. List the primary sources of revenue and expenses involved in holding a meeting, a convention, and an exposition.
4. Describe the main types of meeting setups.
5. Explain the difference between an exposition and a convention.
6. List the duties of CVBs.
7. Describe the topics a meeting planner needs to deal with before, during, and after a meeting.
8. How can we "green" events?
9. Describe Jill Moran's job.
10. Which of New York's museums or cultural heritage sites is of most interest to you and why?

Interesting Websites

American Society of Association Executives:
www.asaecenter.org

Association of Meeting Professionals:
www.ampsweb.org

International Special Events Society: www.ises.com

Meeting Professionals International:
www.mpiweb.org

Professional Convention Management
Association: www.pcma.org

Internet Exercises

1. Organization: Best of Boston website:
www.bestboston.com Summary: Best of Boston
is an event planning company that specializes
in putting together packages for different
events, such as conventions, corporate events,
private parties, and weddings.
   a. On their website, find and then list the
   various types of events they can organize.
   b. By simply browsing through the website,
   discuss the importance of networking in
   the meetings, conventions, and expositions
   industry.

2. Organization: M & C Online website:
www.meetings-conventions.com Summary:
This excellent website offers in-depth
information on meetings and conventions
from different perspectives, ranging from legal
issues to unique themes and concepts. What is
the breaking news listed under the Breaking
News heading?

Apply Your Knowledge

Make a master plan with all the steps necessary for holding a meeting or seminar on careers in
hospitality management.

Suggested Activity

Contact meeting planners in your area and, with permission of your professor, invite them to speak to
the class about their work and how they do it. Prepare questions in advance so that they may be given
to the speaker ahead of time.

Endnotes

1. www.asaecenter.org/AdvocacyOutreach/content.cfm?
   ItemNumber=17519&navItemNumber=17537
   (accessed September 27, 2009). http://en.wikipedia
   .org/wiki/Trade_association (accessed September 19,
   2009).

2. Wikipedia, "Professional Association," http://en.
   wikipedia.org/wiki/Professional_association (accessed
   September 19, 2009).

3. Stephen Barth, *Hospitality Law: Managing Issues in
   the Hospitality Industry* (Hoboken, NJ: Wiley, 2006),
   26–29.

4. Barbara Connell, *Professional Meeting Management*,
   4th ed. (Chicago: Professional Convention
   Management Association, 2004), 557–561.

5. Ibid., 564–565.

6. Connell, *Professional Meeting Management*, 552.

PART 4
Social, Cultural, Heritage, and Eco-tourism

CHAPTER 10

Social Aspects of Tourism

OBJECTIVES

After reading and studying this chapter, you should be able to:

- Describe social aspects of tourism.
- List Cohen's social-cultural impacts of tourism.
- Discuss the typologies of tourism.
- Examine the positive and negative social impacts of tourism.
- Identify governments role in social tourism.

GEOGRAPHY SPOTLIGHT

Culture and Heritage Tourism: The Netherlands

Recognized for its iconic windmills and tulips, the western European country of the Netherlands is equally known for its Red Light District, prostitution, and marijuana use. The liberal country also has many museums, theater productions, and art exhibits, which makes "the Dutch neither the clog-wearing windmill-dwellers of popular folklore, nor the drug-dealing pornographers which they have been made out to be in recent years."[1] Instead, the open-minded nature of the Dutch people, combined with provocative and unique attractions, creates an appealing destination for travelers to experience the Netherlands's culture and heritage.

The country has become known for its unique cultural attractions and Amsterdam, the capital, is "one of the world's great cultural centers."[2] In the late 1800s, the Museum Quarter of Amsterdam, an "area of art and culture and plans, was conceived for constructing Amsterdam's great cultural monuments."[3] There are numerous attractions including the Stedelijk Museum, the Coster Diamond Factory, the Van Gogh

GEOGRAPHY SPOTLIGHT *(continued)*

Courtesy of Mark Green

Museum, and Rijksmuseum. The Anne Frank Huis, where the Frank family hid during World War II, and the Science Center NEMO are also located in Amsterdam.

In addition to the traditional museums of Amsterdam, the city is also known for darker tourism attractions found throughout the Red Light District. The area, which is known for prostitution, dates back to the thirteenth century. Attempts were made to control the problem, but "by the mid-17th century prostitution was openly tolerated" and by the mid-1800s, more than two hundred brothels existed.[4] While in the Red Light District, tourists can also visit the Hash Marijuana Hemp Museum, which features displays about the history of marijuana. Marijuana can be purchased in coffee shops throughout Amsterdam. However, "the sale of soft drugs in so-called coffee shops is not legal but is tolerated" by the police.[5] The perception of the Dutch people being laid-back and tolerant is evident throughout the Red Light District with its tolerance of prostitution and marijuana. The Netherlands provide for an area where a darker side of tourism is more readily accepted and creates a destination where travelers from around the world come to experience the country's interesting cultural tolerance of what is traditionally viewed as too risqué for mainstream tourism.

The Netherlands has been a constitutional monarchy since its first king in 1813 and "the clearest example of national symbolism is the Dutch royal family."[6] The most popular celebration of the monarchy is Queens Day (also called Orange Day and *Koninginnedag* in Dutch), which celebrates the former queen's birthday. Cars are not allowed in the city on Queen's Day because "up to one million visitors join the 750,000 locals in the world's largest street party."[7] Many people utilize boats in the canals as both transportation and as a way to continue the festivities. Those attending the celebration typically wear orange, which is the national color. "Orange is the color of the Dutch Royal Family . . . today it symbolizes a broader pride in the country and in being Dutch."[8]

As the most densely populated country in Europe, "the Netherlands has for centuries provided a safe haven for ethnic minorities fleeing from discrimination and persecution, with each minority influencing Dutch culture in its own way."[9] Because of this, the Dutch have emphasized "the country's cultural diversity, tolerance of difference, and receptiveness to foreign influences."[10] These ideas are expressed in the many cultural attractions of the country including various museums, theaters, art exhibits, and the Red Light District. While visiting the Netherlands, travelers are sure to experience a culture unlike their own, which provides for a fascinating tourist experience as they explore the country's unique tourist establishments.

(continued)

GEOGRAPHY SPOTLIGHT *(continued)*

Endnotes

1. C. Chapman, "Dutch Culture," Holland Ring website, www.thehollandring.com/dutchculture.shtml (accessed April 20, 2009).

2. G. M. L. Hammons, *The Netherlands* (New York: DK Publishing, 2008), 10.

3. Hammons, *Netherlands*, 117.

4. Hammons, *Netherlands*, 74.

5. D. Mares and A. Robben, "Culture of the Netherlands," Countries and Their Cultures, www.everyculture.com/Ma-Ni/The-Netherlands.html (accessed April 19, 2009).

6. Mares and Robben, "Culture of the Netherlands."

7. World Events Guide, "Queen's Day," www.worldeventsguide.com/event/130/Amsterdam-Netherlands/Queens-Day .html (accessed April 21, 2009).

8. S. McAllister, "The Dutch and the Color Orange," About.com, http://goamsterdam.about.com/od/planatrip/a/color_orange.htm (accessed April 21, 2009).

9. Mares and Robben, "Culture of the Netherlands."

10. Mares and Robben, "Culture of the Netherlands."

Tourists Then and Now

International tourism became a major modern mass phenomenon after 1945 when it came to embrace practically all social classes in industrialized Western societies.[1] This expansion was made possible by rising standards of living and shortening of the work year, which were accompanied by longer paid vacations in the industrialized Western countries and a rapid improvement in the means of transportation.[2]

Tourism at its most simplistic level involves a spatial separation between "home" and "away" and travel between two zones. The **social aspects of tourism** are the motivations, roles and social relations of tourists, the structure and dynamics of the tourism system and of touristic institutions, the nature of attractions and their representations, and the impact of tourism on host societies.[3] This chapter reviews the **sociology of tourism** and examines both the positive and negative impacts that tourism may have on a community. The implications of these impacts are considered and suggestions made to improve the experience both for the host community and the tourist.

Authors such as Cohen have studied the sociocultural impacts of tourism from four different but overlapping viewpoints:

1. Tourism impact studies
2. Host–guest interactions
3. Tourist systems
4. Tourists and their behavior

These four areas cover not only existing tourism but also tourism development.

The social and cultural aspects of tourism comprise the relationships between society, institutions, tourists, and host communities. Some sociocultural interactions between tourists and host communities are tangible while others are less so. The degree of tangibility varies according to the destination and community. Popular destinations may, for example, become overcrowded during the high season, resulting in very tangible and often negative outcomes, such as pollution, noise, crime, and disruption of the local culture. Social and cultural aspects of tourism are hard to separate. As with many aspects of tourism they tend to be integrated.

Some authors like Wearing are critical of tourism operations.[4] Tourism in a free market economy can exploit natural resources as a means of profit accumulation, and consequently has been described as the commercialization of the human need to travel. The notion of unlimited gain has led to the exploitation of host communities, their cultures, and environments. As with most things, many agree and many disagree.

Donald Reid, author and tourism expert, comments, "What has been lost in the discussion of tourism planning, and problem-solving process generally, is the plethora of everyday issues such as social relations, local institutions, and the condition of the environment—that are central to the lives of individuals and communities."[5] Reid adds that the crucial areas of social development and global environmental change—which continue to plague the development promises made by those promoting tourism and other forms of development—are just as important to the discussion.[6]

In an attempt to address such issues, the United Nations Millennium Summit issued a declaration, the key features of which were the emphasis on caring for the vulnerable and enabling participation by all citizens. This was the first time that world leaders have committed themselves to a time-bound series of targets and benchmarks by 2015.[7] Following on this, the United Nations World Tourism Organization (UNWTO) issued a declaration entitled **Harnessing Tourism for the Millennium Development Goals**. This declaration recognizes the economic benefits to the providers and recreational and educational benefits to the consumers; it also states that tourism has the potential to be destructive of human rights, social and cultural values, and local environments without necessarily benefitting those suffering most.[8]

The eight goals of the declaration highlight issues that have a particular effect on children: poverty, hunger, poor health, lack of education, and poor access to clean water, sanitation, and shelter. The world leaders also noted that tourism affects vast numbers as either travelers or hosts and has great potential for bringing people together, improving living conditions or despoiling them.[9]

Typologies of Tourists

Tourist typologies reflect the diversity of individual motivations, styles, interests, and values of tourists. Through time, tourists have been described as pilgrims.[10] Typologies based on age and economy were introduced by Cohen, who suggests tourist roles can be as drifters, explorers, and individual and organized mass tourists.[11]

Smith describes the demographic aspects of tourism in seven levels as numbers of tourists increased from explorers to mass and charter tourists and highlights their impacts on the host culture and local perceptions of tourism.[12] Smith also defines five destination interests and motivations: ethnic, cultural, historical, environmental, and recreational.[13] Other elements of typologies include pleasure-seeking tourists; those who seek an authentic experience; and alternative and lifestyle tourists. The categorization of tourists into typologies is now accepted as an orthodox tool in the study of sociocultural impacts.[14]

Tourist–Host Interactions

Do you prepare yourself before going off on vacation? When you travel, have you thought of the fact that you and the host probably have completely different opinions about tourism/tourists in that area? What about when tourists come to *your* area? What do you think of them, and how do you treat them? The reason why these questions are asked is that the harmony between guests and hosts and their communities can be destroyed if both are unprepared for the encounter. Conscientious tourists may enjoy learning about the destination and host community they are about to visit. This helps avoid potentially awkward or embarrassing situations. Behavior and body language common to Americans may very well be rude and unacceptable elsewhere. On the other hand, if the hosts do not deliver the services expected by the tourist, then disappointment sets in. A tourist, who is expecting air conditioning, comfortable mattresses, and CNN, will not enjoy the trip despite its other qualities, wonderful as they may otherwise be.

We can all probably recall times when we have experienced tourists behaving in what we consider an inappropriate manner, such as being loud. But what about a Muslim country that finds itself host to tourists that sunbathe topless, or people who smoke at the next table in a restaurant in Japan? Just how far should hosts go to accommodate the tourist?

Authors such as Doxey have explored the changing relationship between tourists and hosts. Values and attitudes change with time. Doxey developed the **index of tourist irritation** (see Figure 10–1) to describe how communities react to increasing levels of tourism. His **irridex** covers four main stages: euphoria, apathy, irritation, and antagonism. Beyond this is the "final stage," in which the environment is destroyed and cultural values lost.[15]

Tourist–Host Encounters

Tourists experience a variety of encounters with host communities. These encounters can range from excellent to downright scary. An early tourism scholar, de Kadt states that tourist–host encounters occur in three main contexts: where the tourist is purchasing some good or service from the host; where the tourist and the host find themselves side by side, for example, on a sandy beach or at a night club performance; and where two parties come face to face with the object of exchanging information and ideas.[16] More research has been done on the sociology of mass tourism and the United Nations Educational, Scientific and Cultural Organization (UNESCO) names four characteristics of tourist–host relationships:[17]

1. Its transitory nature
2. Temporal and spatial constraints

1. Euphoria	Visitors are welcome; there are opportunities for local people, and new money flows in—but there is little planning.
2. Apathy	Visitors are taken for granted; they become targets for profit-making, and contact becomes more formal.
3. Annoyance	Saturation is approached, with too many people visiting the destination for it to remain enjoyable—especially in the peak season. This causes the local residents to begin to have doubts about tourism. Planners try to resolve this problem by increasing infrastructure rather than by limiting growth.
4. Antagonism	Open irritation appears (including sometimes strong levels of dislike), yet planning is remedial. Promotion is increased to offset the deteriorating reputation of the destination. Tourists are now being (and are probably feeling) cheated, yet are also being blamed for increased crime and taxes, and for all sorts of everyday problems.
5. Acceptance	The place has changed permanently. Change is now accepted by residents. They have forgotten what the area was like before the first tourists arrived.

Figure 10–1 • Doxey's Irridex of Tourist Irritation
Source: Adapted from Doxey GV

3. Lack of spontaneity

4. Unequal and unbalanced experiences

The tourist encounter is transitory because tourists only stay for a few days, and during that time tourists may find the hosts fascinating because of their different social norms and culture. Alternatively, the hosts may find the tourists pesky and tolerate them for their money. Another aspect is that tourists generally visit a location only once, and then go to another one the following vacation. Those who make repeat visits are likely to enjoy a more meaningful relationship with residents of the host community.

Second, temporal and spatial constraints influence the duration and intensity of the relationship. Tourists mostly catch only a glimpse of the host community's richness of social and cultural life. Yet, because they are on vacation, tourists may have more time to relax and converse with members of the host community. A beach bar may be a gathering place for tourists and residents alike, but it offers only a superficial view of the others' life. Sometimes tourists are somewhat of a captive clientele, meaning they may be staying at a luxury resort but they have little chance of venturing outside of the resort grounds. In these situations, the extent of tourist–host encounters is very superficial. Ask any tourist who has visited Jamaica.

Third, many tourist–host encounters lack sincerity and have become too reliant upon money as a motivation, thereby unfortunately diminishing genuine hospitality. Wall and Mathieson call this a trade-off that tourists who go on package tours and other organized tourist experiences make for reasons such as convenience, risk reduction, cost benefits, and so on.[18] Unfortunately, the trade-off is for a loss of spontaneity that often makes for memorable moments in a tourist experience.

Fourth, the tourist–host encounter may be one in which two very different socioeconomic groups collide, meaning that wealthy tourists can appear to be flaunting their wealth and in so doing antagonize residents of the host community. When someone earning a few dollars a day meets someone spending hundreds of dollars a day, some resentment may occur and cause the host to try and take advantage of the situation to extort more dollars from the tourist.

Social encounters between tourists and hosts can have both positive (as in socioeconomic gains) and negative effects (as in a dilution of social values and norms) on hosts. How to maintain a harmony between tourists and hosts is a challenge. Inskeep suggests the scope and depth of the encounters include the following aspects:[19]

- Basic value and logic system
- Religious beliefs
- Traditions
- Customs
- Lifestyles
- Behavioral patterns
- Dress codes
- Sense of time budgeting
- Attitude toward strangers

Each of these elements can influence the relationship between the tourist and the host.

FOCUS ON

The Social Benefits and Costs of Mountain Tourism

Alan Bright

It is commonly understood that tourism has been and continues to be among the fastest growing and wide-ranging activities in the world. The acceptance of this phenomenon has enhanced the dialogue among practitioners, policymakers, scientists, and other tourism stakeholders regarding what impacts of this tourism growth will be realized as the twenty-first century rolls on. Nature-based tourism has received a significant amount of attention from these groups. Nature-based tourism can be further broken down into tourism in natural settings (adventure tourism), tourism that focuses on specific components of the natural environment (wildlife tourism, marine tourism, mountain tourism), and tourism developed with a goal of protecting natural areas (eco-tourism).

Much of the initial dialogue on the growth of nature-based tourism has focused primarily on the physical impacts of travel to ecologically sensitive locations, and to a similar degree, the economic impacts on a tourism region. However, in addition to the impacts of nature-based global travel on the biosphere and local and regional economies, there is a growing amount of discussion on the impacts of nature-based tourism on the cultures and societies of people, not only those who live in the

FOCUS ON (*continued*)

tourist areas, but on the traveler as well, topics that drive much of the discussions surrounding the sociology of tourism. One type of nature-based tourism that has been explored regarding its social impacts is tourism and development in mountain regions, or mountain tourism.

As a tourist destination, mountains may be the second most popular type of geographic destination in the world, next to coastal areas.[1] The sociocultural impacts of mountain tourism on tourists and residents of the mountain destination can be briefly addressed by asking two questions: Why do people go to the mountains? And why do mountain destinations want to attract tourists?

One of the most common reasons that people travel to the mountains, regardless of the activity they engage in, is to gain a sense of renewal and spiritual well-being. Mountains have long represented a romantic idealism, where pristine and unspoiled beauty found there can revitalize an individual. A second motivation for mountain tourism is escapism. With the explosion of lowland populations and overcrowding of cities, mountain retreats become a place to get away from urban problems such noise, crime, overcrowding, and pollution. A third common motivation for mountain tourism is to seek adventure through an increasing diversity of outdoor recreational sports. Activities such as skiing, hiking, backpacking, snowshoeing, mountaineering and rock climbing, mountain biking, among others are often done to not only allow tourists to test their skills, but to combine such activities with the first two motivations: renewal in a natural pristine place and escape from the hustle and bustle of city life.

In addition to the tourist's motivation for engaging in mountain tourism, there are benefits that accrue to the mountain destination. The most prominent of these are economic. Tourism to a destination holds the possibility of increased economic activity in the region as tourists purchase souvenirs, food, lodging, and take advantage of other amenities. This increased economic activity can increase the number and quality of jobs for local residents. This is especially true in mountain areas that have traditionally depended upon subsistence agriculture and other primitive existences, where tourism can result in an increase in per capita income of a local resident over that which is earned by traditional means as well as increased revenues for the local, regional, and national governments. However, the benefits to the region may go beyond economics to include societal benefits as well. One example centers around the development of tourism based on teaching traditional Japanese weaving skills in the Japanese Alps. Creighton found that the primary motivation for this type of tourism was less for economic reasons than for the residents to escape the hectic pace of corporate life in urban areas below the mountains.[2] Mountain tourism may also provide opportunities for residents to strengthen and legitimize cultures and traditions that are indigenous to the area, such as the development of community museums in the Sierra Madres of Mexico.[3] Providing services to mountain tourists may also build on social traditions of providing hospitality to travelers for some cultures, such as "tea-house trekking" found in Nepal.[4]

Negative social impacts may also arise as a result of mountain tourism. For example, when tourists from developed countries visit mountain regions in a developing country, the local residents may, over time, imitate the activities, behaviors, values, and material wants of the tourists, often with negative results. Called the "demonstration effect," this may result in not only a weakening of local cultural customs and traditions, but also an increase in crime, family disruption, and other negative changes in the values and customs of the local people. In addition to this demonstration effect, many people living in mountain areas lack sufficient skills and resources to invest in and benefit from tourism. This is due to marginalization as a result of ethnic and politically discriminatory attitudes, practices, and laws. Furthermore, young people living in these areas tire of the negatives of mountain tourism to their region and leave the area for the city, resulting in greater overcrowding and population in these urban areas.

(*continued*)

F O C U S   O N   (*continued*)

A phenomenon with significant social effects on areas that depend on mountain tourism is *amenity migration*, or long-term movement to mountain regions (or other areas of scenic beauty that draw tourists) that often results in an increase in second home development. This phenomenon, especially in the United States, is driven by a desire by people to make their enjoyment of recreational amenities in these areas, such as hiking, skiing, and scenery/surroundings a more integral part of their daily life as well as for real estate investment with the hopes of an appreciation in value of their property or for the purpose of earning rental income.[5] The economic impacts of this phenomenon are many. The construction, marketing, financing, and maintenance of second homes generate jobs and income throughout the mountain region. However, there are a number of other social impacts that must be considered as a result of amenity migration to mountain regions. First, the domination of second home development in these areas often limits the housing stock available to local workers because they are unable to afford housing in the immediate amenity region. As a result, although the construction of second homes generates increased employment, the resulting rise in property values, taxes, and other costs makes it difficult for local workers to live near where they work. In addition, the growth in second homes resulting from amenity migration places stress on the social services system in the region, whereby without proper planning, may limit the extent to which these services are readily available to all. Finally, depending on the cultural differences between long-time local residents and more recent second home owners, what starts out as a positive economic boon to a region may eventually morph into a social environment of mutual mistrust and dislike between the two groups as a result of different held values and expectations of appropriate planning within the region.

Endnotes

1. P. M. Godde, M. F. Price, and F. M. Zimmerman, "Tourism and Development in Mountain Regions: Moving Forward into the New Millennium," in *Tourism and Development in Mountain Regions*, ed. P. M. Godde, M. F. Price, and F. M. Zimmerman (New York: CABI Publishing, 2000).

2. M. R. Creighton, "Japanese Craft Tourism: Liberating the Crane Wife," *Annals of Tourism Research* 20 (1995): 463–478.

3. T. Morales, "CBMT: A Case of Community-Based Tourism in Oaxaca," contribution to Community-Based Mountain Tourism Electronic Conference, Mountain Forum, 1998.

4. M. J. Odell and W. B. Lama, "Tea House Trekking in Nepal: The Case for Environmentally Friendly Indigenous Tourism," In *Sustainability in Mountain Tourism: Perspectives for the Himalayan Countries*, ed. P. East, K. Luger, and K. Inman (Delhi: Book Faith India, 1998), 191–205.

5. L. Venturoni, P. Long, and R. Perdue, "The Economic and Social Impacts of Second Homes in Four Mountain Resort Counties of Colorado," paper presented at the 2005 Annual Meeting of the Association of American Geographers, Denver, CO, April 7, 2005.

Source: Courtesy of Alan Bright, PhD, Department of Human Dimensions of Natural Resources, Colorado State University.

Too Much Tourism?

Here is an example of what too much tourism can do in sensitive areas. An influx of tourists to Peru's famed Inca citadel of Machu Picchu may prompt UNESCO to add the jungle-shrouded ruins to its list of endangered World Heritage sites. Yearly visits to Machu Picchu, Peru's top tourist destination, have more than doubled since 1998 to 800,000 people, and conservationists advising UNESCO's World Heritage Committee warn that landslides, fires, and creeping development threaten the site. Yet the number of visitors may double again to 5,000 per day since its inclusion on the new list of the world's wonders.[20]

UNESCO officials may add Machu Picchu to its list of endangered sites that are now threatened by unregulated growth. A boom in hotel and restaurant construction in the nearby mountain town of Aguas Calientes is putting pressure on erosion-prone riverbanks and could undermine the site. Additionally, the current onslaught is contributing to destabilization of the structures separating stones, and water damage is clearly visible at the misty site. Landslides and fires are threats and in 2000 a crew filming a beer commercial damaged the iconic Intiwatana, a ceremonial stone. And the Inca Trail, a 30-mile path to the ruins, has suffered from litter, muggings, and crowding.[21]

Another example of too much tourism is from the 1970s, when the Greek Orthodox Church recommended this prayer:

> Lord Jesus Christ, Son of God, have mercy on the cities, the islands and the villages of this Orthodox Fatherland, as well as the holy monasteries which are scourged by the worldly touristic wave. Grace us with a solution to this dramatic problem and protect our brethren who are sorely tried by the modernistic spirit of these contemporary Western invaders.

Tourism and Social Change

We all know that society changes all the time, but have you considered why these changes take place? Have you thought about how you might influence the societies that you visit when traveling? It cannot be denied that tourism certainly brings change—change welcomed by some segments of society and causing debates among others. In small, close-knit societies, the effects of tourism are easily noticeable and obvious. Visitors bring change just as the Peace Corps, volunteer tourists, missionaries, and new businesses bring change. Visitors, bringing with them personal and usually middle-class values, consciously or unconsciously spread those values as they travel. Dress codes, as an example, vary around the world, and although the visitor's way of dressing and behaving influences many people, some also resent outsiders violating their codes. Figure 10–2 shows some costs and benefits of tourism to a community.

Different observers may see the same tourist attraction differently. Some believe that tourism commercializes history, ethnic identity, and culture—packaging the cultural soul of the people for sale along with their other resources—and thereby forces cultural change on people already facing problems from industrialization, urbanization, and inflation.

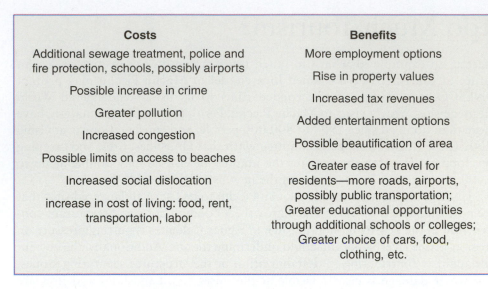

Costs	Benefits
Additional sewage treatment, police and fire protection, schools, possibly airports	More employment options
Possible increase in crime	Rise in property values
Greater pollution	Increased tax revenues
Increased congestion	Added entertainment options
Possible limits on access to beaches	Possible beautification of area
Increased social dislocation	Greater ease of travel for residents—more roads, airports, possibly public transportation; Greater educational opportunities through additional schools or colleges; Greater choice of cars, food, clothing, etc.
increase in cost of living: food, rent, transportation, labor	

Figure 10–2 • Some Costs and Benefits of Tourism to a Community

An example of such commercialization is a public ritual in Fuenterrabia, a Spanish walled town near the French border. The ritual celebrates the Alarde, Fuenterrabia's victory over the French in a famous siege in 1638. The Alarde is a re-creation of the event by large numbers of the public, a parade with martial music, and endless drumming. The ceremony was originally a statement of the courage and equality of all the people in town, affirming their existence and identity. When the Spanish Ministry of Tourism promoted the event as a tourist-attracting festival, few Spaniards wanted to participate in it. Consequently, the Alarde lost its authenticity and its meaning for the people.[22]

The **demonstration effect** on host people is well known in the tourism industry. It is defined as the phenomenon of local residents adopting the styles and manners they have observed in visiting tourists.[23] The visitor, especially the visitor from the industrialized world to a less developed country, is often seen as someone to copy. For example, if the visitor wears blue jeans, blue jeans suddenly become popular among the young people of the host country. If the visitor prefers Scotch whisky, Scotch whisky becomes the premium drink to serve at home or order at a bar. If the visitor displays a laid-back manner, laid-back behavior becomes popular. Likewise, the host community is expected to provide the comforts a tourist would find at home, which often increases the desire of the locals to acquire more of the materialistic aspects of the tourists' culture. However, sometimes the opposite is true, especially nowadays, when developing nations are trying to get out from underneath the shadow of the industrialized world. As a result, a minority sentiment of anti-West can be found in certain places.[24]

However, tourism is not always to blame for diluting culture. Mass communications have also greatly contributed to it. Also, although it is common to label tourism as a diluter of culture and a source of tension among the residents of a destination area, we must not generalize. Cosmopolitan centers such as New York and London and countries such as Switzerland, Denmark, and France all have cultures that seem to suffer little as a consequence of a large influx of tourists. This is because the visitor and the residents usually are of similar economic, educational, and cultural backgrounds. Consequently, where there are sharp differences in culture and economic status between visitor and resident, more social change can be expected.[25]

Do *you* think that cultures can withstand the "tourist invasion" of today? Keep in mind, however, that many of the kinds of cultural exchanges that tourism helps create are very positive and contribute to the enhancement of global intercultural understanding and cooperation.

Social Impact of Tourism on Quality of Life

Because we are all affected by tourism in one way or another, an important question to ask is: Does tourism reduce the **quality of life** at a destination? The answer is obviously yes when a destination is not prepared for a large number of visitors. Some of the negatives are obvious: traffic

The luau has certainly been able to withstand the tourist attention received.

Courtesy Joanne Di Bona and San Diego CVB

congestion, increased crime, noise and air pollution, vandalism, excessive demand on public facilities and water supplies, and overcrowding of beaches, forests, and parks. Yet quality of life is a highly subjective matter. It can be viewed from many perspectives—number of entertainment options available to residents, ease of movement in and around the area, presence or absence of smog and advertising signs, availability and crowding of public transportation, road congestion, and so on. As we all know, what appeals to some people may not appeal to everyone else in the community.

Tourism can contribute in many positive ways. It has the potential to promote social development through employment creation, income redistribution, and poverty alleviation. These positive consequences of tourism can arise only when tourism is practiced and developed in a sustainable and appropriate way.[26] It is also important to involve the local communities. If the community is involved in the planning of tourism, they will be more supportive. This gives tourism a better chance to thrive in the area. But does that necessarily mean that the quality of life at the destination has been affected only in a positive way?

Tourism critics usually concentrate on what happens to developing nations when tourists arrive in large numbers. Tourism, they say, is nothing but a new form of colonialism, controlled by profit-seeking corporations from the industrialized nations. The inhabitants are relegated to inferior, menial positions. Tourism, say these critics, is divisive, pitting the rich against the poor, possibly disruptive of long-term development, and involves nothing less than rewriting the economic and political geography of the world. For example, when a new resort is planned the financial backing may come from abroad and a foreign corporation or perhaps a chain operator who will use top management from their own country to manage the resort. All that is left for the local people, who may be mostly unskilled, are hourly paid positions as line employees. But does this *reduce* the residents' quality of life, or does it simply change their economy and employment structure? And has anyone asked the residents themselves what they think?

Advocates of tourism counter the previous arguments by pointing out that most tourism takes place within and between countries of the industrialized world—North America, Europe, and more recently Japan and Southeast Asia. Although there are some exceptions, relatively few tourists visit Africa, South America, or South Asia. Tourism advocates agree that tourism changes the economies of the host countries. However, they argue that it usually offers better career opportunities for the residents than their other choices, which are often limited (i.e., agriculture, textile production, and manufacturing). These advocates claim that tourism causes social change that comes about through choice, and that, given the option of cutting sugarcanes for about $3 a day in a hot, humid climate or working for about $12 a day as a housekeeper in an air-conditioned hotel, the choice is easy.

There are several other **social impacts** such as these:

- Tourism sometimes helps to revive art, dance, and crafts in host communities.

- When arts and crafts are made outside the host community, this results not only in a loss of jobs but also a loss of revenue because the arts and crafts must then be purchased from outside the community.

- In some cases, tourism can encourage crime, ranging from petty crimes such as purse snatching to more serious kidnapping and even murder (as happened in New Orleans when some tourists inadvertently wandered a few blocks off the beaten path).

- Tourism can increase prostitution—it likely existed before the destination became popular, but may have grown as a result of tourism.

- Tourists can slow residents' way of life. It takes longer to drive to work and to get a table in a restaurant in Florida when the "snowbirds" are visiting.

- Tourists unduly influence the culture of the host community and vice versa.

- Sometimes the host community resents tourists.

Most of the negative aspects of tourist impact can be overcome by better planning and management of the tourist destination, yet that is sometimes easier said than done. For example, it has taken years for some destinations to overcome the problem of raw sewage on the otherwise pristine beaches. Sometimes there are too many bureaucratic and other (corruption) hurdles in the way of something being done about it.

What impact will tourism have on this young person as she grows up?
Courtesy of Mark Green

▶ Check Your Knowledge

1. According to the advocates of tourism, among which nations does most tourism take place?

2. What is the demonstration effect?

3. How can a potentially awkward or embarrassing situation, be avoided by the tourist?

Tourists Also Change

Have you traveled to another country or spent time in a culture different from your own? Do you feel that it affected you? It is fairly obvious that visitors to foreign cultures are affected differently by what they experience. The visitor seeking relaxation or pleasure is often only minimally interested in the history and culture of the hosts. Bars and swimming pools are pretty much the same all over the world, and the tourist is therefore not in close contact with the "real" culture of the place. Other visitors actively search for and examine the host culture, compare it with their own, and perhaps experience change in their attitudes about the host people and themselves.

A study assessing tourist attitude changes toward a host people was conducted among British tourists to Greece and others visiting Morocco. The visitors were there for recreation and pleasure, yet their attitudes toward the host peoples changed as a result of the two- to three-week tours of those countries. The tourists to Greece found the Greeks less suave, more religious, and less affluent than they originally believed. Attitudes toward Moroccans also changed. Moroccans came to be seen as poorer, more conservative, more talkative, more musical, tenser, and more mercenary than before the trip. Fellow countrymen were seen, post trip, as more affluent and less tense.[27]

But how do we know that the tourists surveyed understood the real culture of their hosts, and vice versa? Generalizations about attitudinal and other changes brought on by travel, of course, should be made very carefully. People with strong prejudices about ethnic groups may only strengthen their prejudices as a result of travel because they selectively see what they feel is important. The basically generous and open person sees the good, whereas the person who needs to protect a certain view perceives what is necessary to maintain that self-image. But how can the negative influences be reduced and the positive be encouraged?

Social Tourism

Social tourism is an extremely diverse and complex phenomenon, and its meaning varies depending on the time periods and countries under discussion. Social tourism is usually defined in terms of the objectives pursued, the methods employed for achieving them, and the outcomes of participation.[28] Cazes suggests the following as important premises of social tourism:[29]

- The recognition of the basic right of all, irrespective of their social, financial, or geographical situation, to have leave from work and to have vacations

- Acknowledgment of the importance of leisure and holidays as exceptional occasions in the physical and cultural development of individuals, promoting their social natures and their integration into their community of workers as well as the broader society

- Reflection of the concern of proponents that social tourism should be an instrument of economic development, a means of managing and enhancing the natural and human environments of destination regions

Social tourism, though not very well defined, implies that the government supplies at least a partial subsidy for travel or for the destination experience. The most obvious examples of social tourism were the government-owned and -operated tourist businesses in former communist countries. There, the tourism industry was a government monopoly; trains, airlines, and destination facilities were owned and operated by the state or by agencies of the state, including state-run unions. To put it in simple terms, social tourism is subsidized tourism for people with low incomes.

In Europe, subsidized vacations take a number of forms. Employees may draw upon holiday funds set up jointly by a trade union and the employer. For example, in Germany, the Netherlands, and the United Kingdom, an employer may provide holiday bonuses. In Belgium, employers sometimes grant cash benefits for travel; and in New Zealand, state employees receive price reductions in hotels.[30]

A number of European governments subsidize and otherwise encourage tourism. Germany, Belgium, Spain, France, Ireland, Norway, the Netherlands, Sweden, and Switzerland all invest heavily in tourism. The range of aid or subsidy can be great. Belgium grants subsidies for the modernization and construction of family hotels. Spain has provided money for water and winter sports, camping sites, and rural and mountain recreational facilities. The state even owns a chain of approximately 80 inns, the *Paradores*. In France, assistance is provided for holiday villages and camping grounds: loans and grants are made for rural lodgings rented to tourists for at least three months a year for a minimum of 10 years. In Norway, loans and grants are made for the less expensive accommodations and campsites. Swedish states subsidize and make loans for investments by the private sector for lower-cost accommodations in the mountain areas of northern Sweden.[31]

An Example of Social Tourism in France

Social tourism has been practiced in Europe for years. In France, for example, Pierre Combes, former mayor of the town of Nyons, a country town in the Drome department between Rhone and Geneva, has long been active in the promotion of "social tourism." He headed VAL, a nonprofit organization combating desertification in rural areas and promoting social policies to create tourism infrastructures that benefit the local population. Mr. Combes is also active in National Open-Air Tourism (UNAT), which brings together 58 nonprofit organizations in France, representing 242,000 beds, of which 160,000 are in villages de vacances—vacation villages.

UNAT was set up in 1945, and its original goals have changed very little since. The first goal is to offer a quality tourism experience at affordable prices to as many people as possible. The second goal is to promote authentic tourist locations and to organize vacations that focus on social, learning, cultural, and sports components. Social tourism has been key to the development of some isolated regions. Some corporations support social tourism with coupons or vouchers, which enables employees to go on vacation at a very reasonable cost.

Tourism Concern and Pro-Poor Tourism Partnership

Tourism Concern is an independent charity based in the United Kingdom. Their goal is to fight tourism exploitation. They strive to ensure that tourism benefits the local people in destination communities. Currently, their membership is approximately 900, with partners in more than 20 destinations. Tourism Concern is based on five principles:

- Independence
- Listening
- Shared values and vision
- Inclusivity
- Ethical practices[32]

The vision statement is: "A world free from exploitation in which all parties involved in tourism benefit equally and in which relationships between industry, tourists and host communities are based on trust and respect."[33]

The Pro-Poor Tourism Partnership is a collaborative research project between the International Centre for Responsible Tourism (ICRT), the International Institute for Environment and Development (IIED), and the Overseas Development Institute (ODI). Pro-poor tourism, or PPT, is an approach to tourism that results in increased net benefits for poor people. There are many types of pro-poor tourism strategies, ranging from increasing local employment to building mechanisms for consultation.[34] The type of tourism or company involved does not matter, as long as it can increase the net benefits that go to the poor. Here are just a few strategies for making tourism more pro poor:

- *Increasing Economic Benefit*—Expanding business and employment opportunities
- *Enhancing Noneconomic Benefits*—Training, empowerment, and addressing tourism impacts
- *Policy Reform*—Building a more supportive framework[35]

The pro-poor tourism goals are to unlock opportunities and provide benefits to the poor from tourism in their community and to minimize the negative impacts of tourism.

Social Tourism in the United States

Contrary to popular belief, social tourism in the United States does exist. The camper in a state or federal park may sometimes be charged only a small percentage of the true cost of camping there, while the remaining cost is borne by the government—or rather taxpayers. Church camps, YMCA and YWCA camps, as well as Boy Scout and Girl Scout camps are all included under the label of social tourism if the concept is to be defined as subsidized vacationing.

Social tourism usually implies that a government or other organization subsidizes a vacation or a vacation facility for a person, usually of low social-economic

FOCUS ON

Government Involvement in Social Tourism

Courtesy of Tomasz Mysluk © Dorling Kindersley

The European Commission has a Social Tourism Division that focuses on supporting and building local communities through tourism services. Through bringing volunteers into local communities and partnering with locally arranged accommodations and nonprofits they provide a different perspective of tourism to host communities. The Social Tourism Division also aims to raise awareness of issues facing communities and populations through socially based activities and leadership development for groups and organizations while they travel.[36]

Social tourism promotes access for groups for whom going on vacation has progressively become more difficult. Social tourism strengthens the tourism industry's revenue generation potential by developing off-season tourism. Social tourism encourages the creation of longer-lasting employment opportunities in the tourism sector by making it possible to extend such jobs beyond the peak season.[37] The European Commission has successfully built up an excellent working relationship with major European stakeholders in social tourism issues. A series of conferences and workshops has been organized to enable the commission to draw on the assistance and expertise of tourism and community leaders: "Tourism for All: State of Play and Existing Practices in the EU" and the "European Year of Equal Opportunities for All" and a workshop and conference for stakeholders on senior citizens and youths entitled "Social Tourism in the EU: Youths and Senior Citizens."[38]

Social tourism provides participants the opportunity to see and learn about another side of a destination while making a difference in the local community. The Social Tourism Division uses the acronym SOCIAL:[39]

- S—Social change
- O—Open dialogue
- C—Community impact
- I—Immersion experiences
- A—Awareness building of cultural, local, and global issues
- L—Learning and leadership development

There are dual beneficiaries from a program like SOCIAL: the host communities that receive the service and the volunteers and tourists who visit the communities to provide the service. These weekend and weeklong tours include educational activities, service in local communities, training and learning of local issues, and time for reflection.[40]

standing. Many of the lodging facilities built in U.S. state parks since 1965 have, however, been first class, and the rates charged so high that they are not likely to be used by low-income families or individuals. The high room rates and first-class hotel facilities of the new tourism might be called social tourism for the middle class, but hardly for the poor. Nevertheless, it still is subsidized tourism.[41]

In addition to federally subsidized tourist areas, state-subsidized attractions are also being developed. Funded either by bond issue or massive support by the federal government, several states have moved into the resort business. Some of the facilities are spectacularly beautiful and economically very successful. For example, the state of Kentucky led the way in constructing lodge restaurant facilities, which are indeed first class. Kentucky's resort parks represent a new concept for state parks because they are complete resorts, including a range of facilities such as lodges, beaches, pools, and tennis courts.[42]

▶ Check Your Knowledge

1. What term implies at least a partial subsidy of travel?
2. What type of business have several states in the United States adopted for their tourism?

Is Social Tourism Desirable in the United States?

The answer to the question of whether social tourism is desirable in the United States must be yes. With an increased population who has increased leisure time, the day may come when the state parks are as crowded as some of the federal parks. Steps must be taken to ration their use, as well as to control the environment and avoid pollution.

Most of the federal parks are located in the western states, far away from the great population centers of the east. They represent social tourism—but social tourism primarily for those who can afford to travel considerable distances. State resort parks can make recreational experiences available to vast new numbers of people, presumably at prices they can afford. For the less affluent, the facilities and accommodations in such parks could be made available at reduced rates or at no charge at all.

Because of differences in capabilities and circumstances, some individuals and their families receive more benefits from society than others do. Included in these benefits have been the wherewithal to travel, the ownership of sites of natural beauty, and the time to enjoy nature. Social tourism is an attempt to redress the disparities in distribution of goods, making it possible for large segments of society to enjoy many of the pleasures until now experienced by a few. Why should this be done? The people of the United States own state and federal lands. Why shouldn't everyone be able to enjoy them?

CASE STUDY

Tourist Typologies

As noted in this chapter, the use of tourist typologies is a common approach to understanding the sociocultural components and impacts of travel. One tourist typology that has been cited widely and for several decades was proposed by Plog.[1] (1974) Plog suggested that people fall along a psychocentric-allocentric continuum based on the characteristics of the destinations they are drawn to. People high on allocentrism prefer unstructured vacations in exotic destinations away from what they are accustomed to at home. Psychocentric people prefer visiting destinations similar to their home with many tourist amenities, such as highly organized package tours and familiar destinations.

Believing that tourist typologies would be most effective if they are based on how people experience tourist settings, Cohen (1974) proposed four classes of tourists: the *organized mass tourist* who is dependent on all-inclusive tours or packages; *the individual mass tourist* who is likely to travel alone or with very few people; *the explorer* who seeks novel experiences but occasionally opts for familiar and comfortable accommodations; and *the drifter* who avoids tourist establishments.[2]

Furthermore, Cohen (1979) provides a theoretical and conceptual classification of visitors based on their experiences, identifying five distinct forms of experience including *recreational*, *diversional*, *experiential*, *experimental*, and *existential*.[3] Based on Cohen's experience domains, Elands and Lengkeek (2000) identify five modes of experiences with specific experiential and motivational characteristics.[4] These include (1) *amusement* (fun, familiar environment of short duration), (2) *change* (escape from boredom and everyday life, relaxation, and recovery), (3) *interest* (search for interesting vistas and stories, variation, and stimulation of the imagination), (4) *rapture* (self-discovery, unexpectedness, and discovery of physical boundaries), and (5) *dedication* (authenticity, devotion, and timelessness).

Understanding different types of destinations and the diversity of tourists that may visit each one has important implications for managers of resorts, tourism activity providers, and other travel professionals in the marketing of their resort, including aspects of product/service development and provision, pricing, and promotion.

Questions

1. What is a basic difference between Plog's approach to tourist typologies and those suggested by Cohen and others?

2. Think about any type of tourist resort (a mountain, beach, or other resort) that you have visited or are otherwise familiar with. How would you describe this resort within the context of Plog's typology? That is, what aspects of that resort might be attractive to psychocentric travelers? Allocentric travelers?

3. Describe the resort you considered in question 2 from the perspective of Cohen's typology and experience domains.

4. How did the two approaches described differ? Do you think one is better than the other?

5. How might the manager of such a resort use tourist typology information in developing and providing his or her product or service to the public?

C A S E   S T U D Y *(continued)*

Endnotes

1. Plog, S.C., "Why Destination Areas Rise and Fall in Popularity," *Cornell Hotel and Restaurant Quarterly 14*(4) (1974): 55–58.

2. Cohen, E., "Who Is a Tourist? A Conceptual Classification," *Sociological Review 22* (1974): 527–555.

3. Cohen, E. "A Phenomenology of Tourist Experiences," *The Journal of the British Sociological Association 13* (1979): 179–201.

4. Elands, B.H.M., & Lengkeek, J., *Typical Tourists: Research Into the Theoretical and Methodological Foundations of a Typology of Tourism and Recreation Experiences.* (Leiden: Backhuys Publishers, 2000).

Source: Courtesy of Alan D. Bright, Colorado State University

Summary

1. Tourism brings about social change. Tourists often unconsciously influence the community they visit, especially if there is a large gap in living standards between the two. This is also known as the demonstration effect. Similarly, tourists who take an active interest in their host community may well end up changing their own views and attitudes.

2. Doxey's irridex shows how host communities can be expected to react to tourism, from the initial euphoria, through apathy, annoyance and, finally, antagonism.

3. The term *social tourism* implies that at least part of the travel and/or destination experience is subsidized. This includes such different things as employer holiday bonuses, government-owned transportation and/or accommodations, and government-subsidized parks.

Key Words and Concepts

demonstration effect

Harnessing Tourism for the
   Millennium Development
   Goals

index of tourist irritation

irridex

quality of life

social aspects of tourism

social impacts

social tourism

sociology of tourism

tourist typologies

Review Questions

1. What is the demonstration effect and in what way can it affect the quality of life at a destination?
2. Describe Doxey's irridex.
3. What is meant by the term *social tourism*? What are some examples of social tourism in Europe and the United States?
4. Why do people travel to the mountains?
5. What are the topics of the UNWTO's Millennium goals?
6. Describe the Netherlands culture and history.

Interesting Websites

Bureau International du Tourisme Social: www.bits-int.org/en/test.php?lang=2

European Commission Enterprise and Industry Tourism: http://ec.europa.eu/enterprise/sectors/tourism/index_en.htm

European Network for Accessible Tourism: www.accessibletourism.org/?1=enat.en.themes.623

European Union Federation of Youth Hostel Association: www.eufed.org/EN/home.html

Hostelling International: www.hihostels.com

World Youth Student and Educational Travel Confederation: www.wysetc.org

Internet Exercises

1. Go to the website of the Bureau International du Tourisme Social at www.bits-int.org/en/test.php?lang=2 and find the organization's mission and news.
2. Explore the website of the European Union Federation of Youth Hostel Association at www.enfed.org/EN/home.html for information on hostelling in Europe.

Apply Your Knowledge

1. What are some examples of social tourism in the U.S.?
2. Have you traveled to another country or spent time in a culture different to your own? Do you feel that it affected you? If so, how?

Suggested Activities

1. Plan a social tourism program for your community.
2. Using Doxey's Index of Tourist Irritation, assess where tourism in your community/region is on the index.

Endnotes

1. E. K. Scheuch, "Tourismus," In *die Psychologie des 20 Jahrhundrerts* (Munich: Kindler, 1988), 1089–1114, as cited in Yiorgos Apostopoulos, Stella Leivadi, and Andrew Yiannakis, eds., *The Sociology of Tourism: Theoretical and Empirical Investigations* (London: Routledge, 1996), 57.
2. J. Dumazdier, *Toward a Society of Leisure* (New York: Free Press, 1973), 129–130; G. Young, *Tourism: Blessing or Blight?* (Harmondsworth, England: Penguin, 1973), 30, as cited in Apostopoulos, Leivadi, and Yiannakis, *Sociology of Tourism*, 54.
3. Erik Cohen, "Sociology," in *Encyclopedia of Tourism*, ed. Jafar Jafari (London: Routledge, 2000), 544.
4. S. Wearing, *Volunteer Tourism: Experiences That Make a Difference* (Oxfordshire, England: CABI, 2001), as cited in Freya Higgins-Desbiolles, "More Than an 'Industry': The Forgotten Power of Tourism as a Social Force," *Tourism Management* 27, no. 6 (December 2006): 1192–1208.
5. Donald G. Reid, *Tourism, Globalization, and Development: Responsible Tourism Planning* (London: Pluto Press, 2003).
6. Ibid.
7. Jeff Wild, "Tourism and the Millennium Development Goals," *Contours* 17/18, no. 4 (January 2008): 70–76.
8. Ibid., 71
9. Ibid, 71–72.
10. Valene L. Smith, "Typology, Tourist," in *Encyclopedia of Tourism*, ed. Jafar Jafari (London: Routledge, 2000), 608.
11. E. Cohen, "Toward a Sociology of International Tourism," *Social Research* 39 (1979): 164–182, as cited in *Encyclopedia of Tourism*, ed. Jafar Jafari (London: Routledge, 2000), 608.
12. Smith, "Typology, Tourist," 608.
13. V. Smith, *Hosts and Guests: The Anthropology of Tourism* (Philadelphia: University of Pennsylvania Press, 1992), as cited in Smith, "Typology, Tourist," 608.
14. Chris Cooper, John Fletcher, Alan Fyall, David Gilbert, and Stephen Wanhill, *Tourism: Principles and Practice*, 3rd ed. (Harlow, Essex, England: Pearson, 2005), 227.
15. Al Fritsch and Kristin Johannsen, *Ecotourism in Appalachia: Marketing the Mountains* (Lexington: University of Kentucky Press, 2004).
16. Wall and Mathieson, *Tourism*, 225.
17. This draws on Cyrille Poy, "Les Atouts du Tourisme Social," *L'Humanite*, July 29, 2003.
18. Jerry McDermott, "Tourist Influx Could Destroy Machu Picchu," *Telegraph Newspaper* (London), July 11, 2007.
19. Edward Inskeep, *Tourism Planning: An Integrated and Sustainable Development Approach* (New York: Van Nostrand Reinhold, 1991), as cited in Wall and Mathieson, *Tourism*, 225.
20. E. De Kadt, *Tourism—Passport to Development?* (New York: Oxford University Press, 1979), 50, as cited in Geoffrey Wall and Alister Mathieson, *Tourism: Change, Impacts and Opportunities* (Harlow, Essex, England: Pearson, 2006), 223.
21. UNESCO, "The Effects of Tourism on Socio-cultural Values," *Annals of Tourism Research* 4 (1976): 74–105, as cited in Wall and Mathieson, *Tourism*, 223–225.
22. Ibid.
23. Intrepid Traveler: *Travel Industry Dictionary*, www.hometravelagency.com/dictionary/ltrd.html.
24. Ibid.
25. Ibid.
26. Stephen Bocher, ed., *Cultures in Contact* (New York: Pergamon, 1982), 210–212.
27. Geroge Cazes, "Social Tourism," in *Encyclopedia of Tourism*, 542.
28. Ibid.
29. Inskeep, *Tourism Planning*, p.225.
30. Ibid.
31. "Peru's Historic Machu Picchu at Risk: Too Many Tourists," *Los Angeles Times*, April 25, 2007.
32. Tourism Concern, "Vision, Mission and Principles," www.tourismconcern.org.uk/index.php?page=vision-mission-and-principles (accessed May 27, 2009).
33. Ibid.
34. Pro-Poor Tourism Partnership, "What Is Pro-Poor Tourism?" www.propoortourism.org.uk/what_is_ppt.html (accessed May 27, 2009).
35. African Pro-Poor Tourism Development Centre, "What Is Pro-Poor Tourism (PPT)?" www.propoortourism-kenya.org/what_is_propoortourism.html (accessed May 27, 2009).
36. This draws on Escape Together, "Social Tourism," http://escapetogether.com/social-tourism/ (accessed April 24, 2009).
37. http://ec.europa.eu/enterprise/tourism/major_activities/social_tourism/index_en.htm (accessed April 24, 2009.
38. Inskeep, *Tourism Planning*, 225.
39. Escape Together, "Social Tourism."
40. Ibid.
41. Inskeep, *Tourism Planning*, 225.
42. Ibid.

CHAPTER 11

Cultural and Heritage Tourism

OBJECTIVES

After reading and studying this chapter, you should be able to:

- Define cultural tourism.

- Discuss the impact of tourism on host communities.

- Explain the benefits of heritage tourism and list some of the challenges that come with it.

- Describe the four steps to a comprehensive heritage program.

GEOGRAPHY SPOTLIGHT

Nature Tourism: South Africa

The West Coast Flower Tour takes place in the Western Cape of South Africa, and costs approximately 5,335 South African rand, or $641 per person. The duration of this tour is four days, and the tour is scheduled only if there are at least 6 paying guests. This tour was created by a local tour operator in the Western Cape of South Africa who is a member of SATSA BONDED (Southern Africa Tourism Services Association), WESSA (Wildlife and Environment Society of South Africa), CTGA (Cape Tourist Guide Association), and BOTSOC (Botanical Society of South Africa). These affiliations give guests the chance to verify this operator's credentials and view testimonials before choosing to participate in the "West Coast Flower Tour." The public has a positive perception of security in South Africa, making South Africa one of the most visited countries in sub-Saharan Africa.

Over the four days of the tour, guests experience game viewing, whale watching, and bird watching and participate in a conservation project.[1]

Day 1

On the first day of the tour, guests are taken to a private nature reserve, which covers approximately 1,977 acres a mere 4 kilometers (2½ miles) from the ocean. This reserve contains both karoo-oid and sand plain fynbos vegetation, which is a phenomenal example of typical South African vegetation.

The West Coast National Park is near the city of Langebaan, South Africa. Guests visit a specific section of the national park called the Postberg Flower/Game Reserve. According to the Africa Guide website, this section of the West Coast National Park offers guests "spectacular floral displays and also game sightings."[2] In addition, this area is popular among whale watchers from June to October.

Day 2

On the second day of the tour, guests visit the organic Rooibos plantation to observe how a unique South African tea is cultivated and processed. Immediately following the tea tour, guests meet with a local vegetation expert on the Spring Flower Tour, who will discuss more of the local vegetation—sandveld and cederberg fynbos.[3]

GEOGRAPHY SPOTLIGHT *(continued)*

Courtesy of Martin Harvey, Peter Arnold, Inc.

Following the visit to the Rooibos plantation, guests are driven to the town of Clanwilliam to visit the Ramskop Nature Reserve. This reserve contains paved walkways through luscious gardens that contain more than 350 species of plants and that offer guests breathtaking views of the Cederberg Mountains and the Clanwilliam Dam.[4]

Day 3

On day 3, guests visit Vanrhynsdorp to tour the world-renowned succulent nursery. Shortly thereafter, guests travel to Nieuwoudtville and visit the Vanrhyns Pass along the way for an amazing photo opportunity. Upon arriving in Nieuwoudtville, also known as the bulb capital of the world, guests will have the privilege to come in contact with rare species of flora that are found only in South Africa. Scientists from around the world visit this city to further their research by witnessing rare species of flora. This visit takes the entire day, which gives guests the opportunity to fully appreciate the splendor of the bulb capital of the world.[5]

Day 4

On the last day of the tour, guests travel to Cape Town. While in transit, guests visit Darling, also known as "The Flower of the West Coast." According to the Darling Tourism Board, Darling is the heartbeat of the West Coast region of South Africa.[6] The town of Darling is known for the amazing array of flora. There are bulbous plants and annuals that comprise a large percentage of the town's 1,000 species of flowering plants. Before finally arriving in Cape Town, guests can walk through several private reserves along the route to the final destination.

Summary

Although the perceived security threats of sub-Saharan Africa are great, South Africa is one of the few countries in which foreigners are welcome. This is made evident by the famous golf tournaments held in South Africa and the fact that 65 percent of the country's gross domestic product is from the service sector. The raw beauty of South Africa coupled with its hospitality are treats for all environmental enthusiasts.

Endnotes

1. Africa Guide, "West Coast Flower Tour," www.africaguide.com/travel/index.php?cmd=5&pid=995 (accessed November 1, 2008).
2. Ibid.
3. Ibid.
4. Ibid.
5. Ibid.
6. Darling Tourism Board, "Darling, West Coast, South Africa," www.darlingtourism.co.za (accessed September 21, 2009).

Cultural Tourism

Cultural tourism can be defined as tourist visits "motivated wholly or in part by interest in the historical, artistic, scientific or lifestyle/heritage offerings of a community, region, group, or institution."[1] It is a recognized form of tourism that has been around for a long time and one that has gained in popularity and importance during the last decades. The older civilizations in Asia, Europe, and Latin America hold a special fascination for many Americans who appreciate the wealth of culture found in these parts of the world. Few tourists can resist being attracted to one or more aspects of culture tourism: architecture, anthropology, art, local food and beverages, music, dance, museums, scenic tours, gardens, festivals, and so on.

A study by LORD Cultural Resources entitled "Cultural Tourism and Business Opportunities for Museums and Heritage Sites" suggests that not every cultural product is willing, ready, or able to attract tourists, and not every person is interested in culture.[2] However, a key finding of this study was that there are different degrees of consumer motivation for cultural tourism, which are not always taken into account in tourism surveys.

At the center are people "greatly motivated by culture." That would involve the people who travel to a city specifically because of its theater opportunities, museums, and cultural festivals. This segment is estimated to be about 5 percent of the resident market and 15 percent of out-of-province tourists. The difference in the figures for residents and tourists is explained by the fact that the higher education/income persons who are most likely to travel also tend to be more interested in culture.

The second circle represents persons "motivated in part by culture." These are people who travel to a city because of the cultural opportunities as well as, say, to visit friends and relatives. This group accounts for about 15 percent of the resident and 30 percent of the tourist market.

The third circle, representing about 20 percent of both markets, involves people for whom culture is an "adjunct" to another motivation. That is, the main reason for choosing to visit the city might be noncultural, but while there, visitors plan to include cultural opportunities.

The outer circle involves the "accidental cultural tourist," also about 20 percent of the market. This includes people traveling to the city who do not intend to go to a cultural attraction or event but find, for example, friends or relatives they have visited take them along or a cultural opportunity is close to their hotel. In other words, attendance is not planned.

Outside the circles, representing about 40 percent of the resident market and 15 percent of tourists, are persons who would not attend a cultural attraction or event under any circumstances.

▶ Check Your Knowledge

1. Define the term *cultural tourism*.

Profile of the Cultural Tourism Market

Societal trends clearly point to increased importance of culture as a travel motivator. Who is a cultural tourist? In Canada and the United States, the data generally indicate a common pattern of characteristics of the cultural tourist[3]:

✓ Tends to be age 45 and older

✓ Is more highly educated than the general public, earns more money and spends more money and time when on vacation

✓ Tries to pack more activities into more frequent trips of shorter duration

✓ Looks for authenticity and adventure as well as meaning

✓ Has high expectations

✓ Expects and demands that the tourism industry contributes to the sustainability of communities and the natural environment

✓ Increasingly uses the Internet for information purposes

A recent U.S. poll regarding the motivating factors in travel asked the question, "What is important when planning trips?" The results were as follows:

• Understanding culture: 88 percent

• Going to a location with natural beauty: 73 percent

• Gaining a new perspective on life: 72 percent

• Visiting cultural, historical, and natural treasures: 50 percent

• Getting off the beaten track: 45 percent

These data are supported by many other sources of information, all showing that culture is dramatically increasing in importance as a travel motivator.[4]

But what do the high expectations of the cultural tourist mean for tourism entities? The bottom line is to understand just how important cultural tourism is and will be in this millennium.

Impact of Tourism on Culture

The general public and tourism experts around the globe do not seem to agree on the question of whether tourism has a positive or negative impact on culture. Take a moment to think about it. What is your opinion? Dr. Philip McKean, an anthropologist who studied the impact of tourism on cultural patterns in Bali, concluded in 1972 that the culture change brought about by tourism actually strengthened several of the folk traditions. Beginning in 1969, when a jet port was opened in Bali, tens of thousands of tourists arrived to enjoy the island and to be entertained by Balinese temple dancing performances and religious rites. They purchased handicrafts, paintings, and carvings. Interactions between tourists and the Balinese were, for the most part, structured via hotel staff and tour agencies, who may be considered "culture brokers." Although tour guides are the most common "culture broker," there are many different types of brokers. At the local level, guides and interpreters are culture brokers, but as tourism has grown from a business to an industry, others including travel agents, accommodation providers, government at all levels, and international agencies have assumed leadership.[5] In exchange for their money, the tourists were allowed to enter the mythic reality of the Balinese cosmos. They were welcomed as spectators at well-staged aesthetic events.

A lot has changed over the past four decades, and acculturation has occurred at a fast pace. An increasing number of people have taken on the Western lifestyle, discarding their traditional values and lifestyles. Popular paintings, carvings, and antiques are mass-produced, their quality steadily declining, and temples are pillaged for artifacts to satisfy naïve tourists. Religious ceremonies, dances, and traditional crafts are all being changed and in some cases subverted to fit tourist tastes. A lot of locals are profiting from tourism, but many locals have begun to curse the tourists for disrupting their native lifestyle. These are just a few of the impacts tourism has had on Bali and its rich cultural heritage.

▶ Check Your Knowledge

1. According to the U.S. poll mentioned previously, what was the top motivating factor when planning trips?
2. Who acted as cultural brokers between the tourists and Balinese?
3. What do you think has happened to the environment and residents' quality of life in Bali as a result of tourism?

Tourism and Art

The effects of tourism on the arts of developing regions have been debated, pros and cons taken into account. The impacts have been favorable in a number of

A Sedona Artist at Work
Courtesy of the Sedona Chamber of Commerce

places. Pottery making, weaving, embroidery, jewelry making, and other crafts were revived in Tunisia and Cyprus, for example. In Malta, tourism encouraged craftwork in knitwear, textiles, and glass making. Peasant music and folk dancing were revitalized, and new dances were developed. West African carving, originally closely related to ritual, was gradually disappearing until tourist purchases gave it a new stimulus. African artisans responded by developing new forms and styles based on traditional models. In the Bahamas, a couple on the island of Andros developed a style of batik printing on cotton and made it into a profitable business that sold largely to tourists. In Fiji, woodcarving was a lost art until an artist from Hawaii reintroduced woodcarving techniques so that indigenous carvers could create the works needed for a new hotel; the carvers then set up a shop on the hotel grounds where they sell their products to visitors.[6]

In general, placing local arts and crafts in hotel lobbies, guest rooms, and restaurants increases the demand for them and at the same item creates a desirable local ambiance. Inevitably, plastic objects appear in the form of, for example, shell beads made in Manila or Hong Kong and sold in Hawaii. Machinery replaces the hand in making cheap imitations, and plastic copies of art substitute for the authentic. Though many people see this development as something solely detrimental and negative, markets actually exist for both the authentic and the copies.

Several anthropologists take the view that artists in developing countries have consciously responded to the souvenir market, and in doing so they have actually in many cases improved indigenous art. New art forms have evolved and can continue to evolve. For example, Inuit art that uses ivory from Arctic animals has changed drastically in many cases from its earlier form. Although some Inuit artists market their products just as any other businesspeople do, by ascertaining what will and will not sell, the quality of their works shows in their excellence.

A number of developing nations have established state-run craft shops that tend to "authenticate" the produce and ensure its quality. The range in quality, however, is great. In Apia, Western Samoa, state-operated craft shops display all sizes and designs of tapa cloth, kava bowls, and eating utensils. The state-operated craft shop in the Acapulco Convention Center enhances the objects for sale with dramatic displays and its prestigious setting. Other craft centers, however, seem to do little but provide for middle-income functionaries.[7]

Overall, it is safe to say that tourism enhances the arts and crafts of a destination by providing new markets for artisans, often reviving a fading art or craft and fostering the development of traditional forms. In a number of instances, tourism has encouraged new art forms or adaptations of traditional ones. But the issue of all the plastic souvenirs and the imitations and copies passed off as the real thing still remains relevant, as does the issue of the new dances and "rituals" developed solely for the amusement of tourists and sold as the real thing. Are they also desirable and positive, or are they rather detrimental cultural developments and clever exploitations of gullible tourists?

Vigan City, Philippines. The entire city is a World Heritage site. These streets and houses were built about 250 years ago, during the Spanish rule of the Philippines.

ORGANIZATION PROFILE

UNESCO World Heritage Site

"Memory is vital to creativity: that holds true for individuals and for peoples, who find in their heritage—natural and cultural, tangible and intangible—the key to their identity and the source of their inspiration."

—UNESCO

A well-known name all over the world, UNESCO, which stands for United Nations Educational, Scientific and Cultural Organization, was established on November 16, 1945.[8] In short, UNESCO promotes international cooperation among its 193 member states and six associate members in the fields of education, science, culture, and communication.

In 1972, UNESCO adopted an international treaty called the Convention Concerning the Protection of the World Cultural and Natural Heritage. From that came its mission statement, seeking to "encourage the identification, protection and preservation of cultural and natural heritage around the world considered to be of outstanding value to humanity." Like most mission statements, this is quite a mouthful. In simpler terms, UNESCO's heritage program consists of work in three different areas: prevention, management, and intervention. Among many other things, the organization aims to protect the world's cultural heritage through congresses, campaigns, projects, partnerships with organizations all over the world, as well as provide and work toward protective legislation and international codes of ethics.

The UNESCO World Heritage List is probably the best-known example of the mission in action. The list contains 851 properties that have signed the previously mentioned treaty, agreeing to contribute with money and expertise to protect the world's heritage sites as well as their own national heritage. By signing, they recognize that the World Heritage sites located in their national territory belong to a common world heritage, without prejudice to national sovereignty or ownership.

World Heritage sites differ from **national heritage sites** in a couple of ways. According to UNESCO, **World Heritage sites** have "outstanding universal value" (as opposed to "just" national significance) and include each country's most outstanding examples of natural and cultural heritage.

To be listed on the World Heritage List, a country must apply to UNESCO and include a plan detailing how the site is, and will be, managed and protected. The application is then evaluated by independent advisory bodies and finally approved or declined by the World Heritage Committee in their annual meeting.

In an ideal world, a World Heritage site designation would guarantee the survival of the site in question. In reality, a variety of dangers constantly threaten these sites, including armed conflict and war, earthquakes and other natural disasters, pollution, poaching, unplanned construction, and so on. As a result of this, of the 851 World Heritage sites, 30 are currently endangered and inscribed on the World Heritage in Danger List. For example, because of mining operations being planned for outside Yellowstone National Park, the park is considered threatened by the possible off-flow of polluted water. The Everglades National Park was at one time also on the in danger list, suffering from the effects of commercial development and farming. An inscription on the World Heritage in Danger List entitled the two parks to receive particular attention and emergency conservation action to ensure their survival. Likewise, the world-famous Pyramids of Giza in Egypt were threatened by a highway project near Cairo, which would have seriously damaged the values of this important archaeological site. Negotiations with the Egyptian government resulted in a number of alternative solutions, which helped secure the site for the future.

Heritage Tourism

Tourism that respects natural and built environments, in short the heritage of the people and place, is called heritage tourism. Renewed appreciation for historical milestones, the development of heritage trails linking cultural landmarks produce new tourism services and products that can assist local economies.[9]

Tourism combined with preservation has not always been a popular match. Still, it is not unusual that the old is being cast aside, ignored, or simply replaced by the new. A famous example ultimately spurred the growth of the preservation movement—the replacement of historic Penn Station in New York with a utilitarian modern building. But tourism and preservation can work together to mutual advantage. The past decades have included an enormous growth in preservation of the world's historical and cultural heritage. As a natural by-product, heritage tourism has grown and flourished everywhere. This is in part because of people's greater interest in their roots, especially among more senior travelers. Also, it can provide travelers with unique experiences, such as getting the feel of a very particular place or time.

Heritage was for years a forgotten element in tourism planning and policy. However, with the awakening of the social conscience that has taken place during recent decades, it has now become a key element in the decision-making process in countries such as the United Kingdom. Central to the heritage issue is how irreplaceable resources are to be used by people today yet conserved for the generations of tomorrow.[10]

One of the most popular historical sites in the United States is the Alamo in Texas, a battlefield site that attracts more than 2.5 million visitors a year.[11] There are many other popular historical sites, mainly relating to the Revolutionary War and Civil War battlefields. Native American cultural sites are also significant heritage attractions. The main problem with conserving heritage is that the sheer volume of tourism may, if not properly managed, conflict with and defeat the conservation effort. Conservation and tourism need to be developed in a complementary way and in harmony.

American Express, in a unique partnership with the National Trust for Historical Preservation, has sponsored an excellent workbook, *Getting Started: How to Succeed in Heritage Tourism*. The workbook suggests that tourism and preservation are very likely to overlap. It claims that "linking tourism and preservation can do more for local economies and for tourism and preservation than promoting them separately. That's the core idea in heritage tourism: save your heritage, share it with visitors, and reap the economic benefits of tourism."[12] Indeed, some state tourism offices now help develop heritage resources, and a number of preservation organizations are marketing their sites to tourists.

The Benefits of Preservation

Why do we place so much importance on preservation? The wealth of buildings, traditions, and natural beauty that one generation leaves to the next are inherited assets. The purpose of preservation is to protect those assets for the enjoyment of present and future generations. How appealing do you think the Grand

Canyon would be if it, 20 years from now, were completely destroyed by tourism and all that it brings with it of pollution and wear and tear?

The preservation movement first gathered momentum in this country when Ann Pamela Cunningham initiated efforts to save Mount Vernon in 1853, followed by the chartering of the Mount Vernon Ladies Association in 1856 and the start of the site's restoration in 1859. A century later, the passage of the **National Historic Preservation Act of 1966** motivated many supporters to continue the early preservationists' mission of saving America's heritage resources.

Today, people are beginning to recognize the need to preserve our irreplaceable heritage as well as the direct economic benefits preservation can bring.[13] Put simply, preservation pays. A building torn down is an asset destroyed, whereas a building that is restored continues its useful life. Also, rehabilitating an existing building is often less expensive than building a new structure. A storytelling festival that perpetuates an area's oral tradition attracts listeners, and a river left wild attracts fee-paying anglers and rafters. All these examples of preservation help establish and maintain the "sense of place" that gives a community its distinct character, and we all know that a rich historic and cultural heritage attracts visitors.

The economic potential of preservation benefits cities as well as rural areas. Outside metropolitan centers, economic growth has not always been easy to build and maintain. By putting their inherited assets to work, however, small towns, groups of small towns, and even entire regions can generate new prosperity and attract other forms of economic development along with tourism.

▶ Check Your Knowledge

1. How many visitors a year does the Alamo attract?
2. What act was passed in 1966 that promoted the mission of saving America's heritage resources?

Challenges in Heritage Tourism

When a community's heritage is the substance of what it offers visitors, protecting that heritage is essential. Therefore, a major challenge in heritage tourism programs is ensuring that increased visitation does not destroy the very qualities that attract tourists in the first place. This can be a very complicated task.

Because tourism is a highly competitive, sophisticated, and fast-changing industry, it presents its own challenges. Tourism is generally a "clean" industry: no smokestacks or dangerous chemicals. But it does put demands on infrastructure—roads, airports, water supplies, and public services such as police and fire protection. It also has an impact on resources. As Morley Safer said in a *60 Minutes* segment on tourism called "Don't Leave Home," "There are 500 million of them on the move out there. By the end of the century, there'll be a billion of them. They are part of an industry that's now bigger than the oil business. 'They' are us, people, tourists, and what they—or we—are doing is beginning to destroy the very beauty we're so hell-bent on seeing."[14]

These problems, travelers increasing in number and adding stress and strain to infrastructure and heritage sites, are only the beginning, and thankfully the travel industry is already addressing them. The challenge arises not only from visitor impact, but also from visitor expectation of quality products and services. Tourism is essentially a service industry, which means that it depends on the competence of people in many different jobs and locations. Although there is no universal remedy, tourism can indeed provide an attractive form of economic development.

As a good look around almost any city or town will show, people are often tempted to provide quick-fix or "Band-Aid" solutions, for example, to cover up an old storefront inexpensively rather than restoring it. But when an area's historic and cultural assets are at the heart of its plans to develop tourism, it is essential to protect them for the long term. A good example of this is the now famous Gaslamp Quarter in San Diego, California. The restored downtown area, with its 16 blocks of beautiful Victorian architecture, is now one of San Diego's main attractions. Where else can you find a designated National Historic District doubling as an entertainment Mecca? This incredibly popular entertainment, shopping, and dining district features more than 80 of California's hottest restaurants, bars, clubs, theaters, and galleries.

However, not all stories are of success. The history of the preservation movement is a history of high hopes met, and sometimes of heartbreak. Many are saddened when irreplaceable structures are destroyed or damaged beyond repair instead of preserved and protected, as they deserve. Once a historic train station has been demolished, the visual story it could have told about the present and the past is silenced forever. A plaque pointing out that "On this site a great building once stood" can't tell that story. Equally tragic to many is the loss of traditions: a way of crafting wood or farming, of celebrating holidays or feasting on "Old World" cuisine. The preservation and continuation of traditions is important to telling the story of the people who once settled the land and to keeping the spirit of the past alive. By protecting the buildings or special places and qualities that attract visitors, an area also safeguards its future.

Finding the Fit Between Community and Tourism

Local priorities and capabilities, in other words local circumstances, determine what an area needs to do and can do in heritage tourism. Common features for programs that succeed are that they have widespread local acceptance and meet recognized local needs. They are also realistic, based on the talents of specific people as well as on specific attractions, accommodations, and sources of support and enthusiasm. One of the reasons heritage tourism is on the rise in the United States is that travelers are seeking out experiences that are distinctive, not homogenized. They want to get the feel of a very particular place or time. Heritage areas can supply that experience and benefit in the process, but only if the heritage tourism program is firmly grounded in the local environment.

▶ Check Your Knowledge

1. What is the major challenge in heritage tourism programs?

2. What are the common features for programs that succeed?

FOCUS ON

Cultural Heritage: Carnival

Michael Scantlebury

A great deal is revealed from the way a community celebrates. Some celebratory traditions date back hundreds of years. Most people enjoy a good party and very few festivals are bigger or more popular than Carnivals, whether it is Carnival in Rio de Janeiro, Trinidad, or Aruba; Mardi Gras in New Orleans; Caribana in Toronto; the Notting Hill Carnival in London; Barbados's Crop Over or New York City's Labor Day parade on Eastern Parkway. Carnivals are a time to dance in the streets to festive music, parade in costumed groups, and enjoy the company of friends.

The Western history of Carnival dates from medieval times when Catholics started a tradition of celebration ahead of the Lenten season. *Carnevale*, translated "putting away the meat," represents the last opportunity to be festive before the solemnity and fasting of Lent. This tradition spread from Italy around the world with Catholicism, although Eastern Orthodox religions also include a pre-Lent Carnival tradition.

There are probably thousands of carnivals worldwide, and they are an important marketing opportunity for increasing visitation and spending, as well as for showcasing the destination's culture. A challenge is that many carnivals take place at the same time, the two days before Ash Wednesday. Enjoying several carnivals during a single year is impossible except where the celebration takes place outside the traditional pre-Lent period.

McKercher and du Cross, in their book *Cultural Tourism*: *The Partnership between Tourism and Cultural Heritage Management* (Haworth Hospitality Press, 2002), provide a five-part typology based on the depth of experience and the importance of cultural tourism to the vacation decision-making process. This analytical framework has implications for marketing festivals and carnivals, as well as for the formulation of the visitor experience. The typology identifies the following, tourist types:

- The purposeful cultural tourist, where cultural tourism is the primary motive for visiting a destination and the individual has a deep cultural experience. This would be representative of the nationals returning home to relive the carnival experience with friends and family. The sightseeing cultural tourist, where cultural tourism is a primary or major reason for visiting a destination but the experience is shallow. This might be representative of the friends of the returning nationals who might not have the cultural connection.

- The serendipitous cultural tourist: those who do not travel for cultural reasons, but who after participating have a deep cultural experience.

- The casual cultural tourist, where culture is a weak motive for visiting a destination and the resultant experience is shallow.

- The incidental cultural tourist, where travel is not for cultural tourism reasons but nonetheless the person participates in some activities and has shallow experiences.

Whether the reason for celebration is religious or corporeal, the cultural motivation strong or weak, and the resulting experience shallow or deep, festivals are a part of the way of life of a community. They are part of the intangible cultural heritage that celebrates who we are as a community.

Source: Courtesy of Michael Scantlebury, Ph.D., Assistant Professor, Rosen College of Hospitality Management, University of Central Florida.

Four Steps to a Comprehensive Heritage Program

Groups that succeed in heritage tourism pay close attention to all parts of an integrated process. They take four basic steps:

1. Assessing the potential
2. Planning and organizing
3. Preparing, protecting, and managing
4. Marketing for success

Each of these steps gives results. The biggest payoff, however, comes when each separate action ties to the rest in a genuinely comprehensive program. The following subsections give a brief summary of each of the steps in the process that an area or destination must take to be successful in heritage tourism.

Step 1: Assessing the Potential

What will draw tourists to the area? Beaches? Huge theme parks and resorts? When assessing an area's potential, planners must not make the mistake of underestimating the drawing power of cultural resources such as art museums, theaters, or local cuisine. Partnerships between heritage sites and parks, sports facilities, as well as recreational facilities are beneficial to a community and attractive to the visitor. From a humble beginning as a bunch of storytellers swapping tales, the now named National Story Telling Festival in Jonesborough, Tennessee, has grown to attract thousands of visitors and has spun off many other profit-bringing related activities as well.[15]

Planners must keep in mind that natural resources such as local, state, and national parks do not need to be right next door to serve as a resource for a community. If a major natural resource is within a day's drive, it can bring tourists to nearby areas. In this case, scenic byways make the journey as rewarding as the destination. Another suggestion is to check out parks and sports and recreational facilities that already attract visitors. Heritage sites and events can partner with attractions such as these to keep visitors in the area longer.

Such awareness of a community and its resources may uncover hidden treasures, as was the case in Fort Scott, Kansas. In 1973, plans to tear down an old church were brought up. A resident of the community saw that the church was a valuable resource. Her efforts to halt demolition of the church initiated a prospering heritage tourism program bringing to the town nearly 100,000 visitors a year. Since the program's start, 98 percent of downtown Fort Scott has been refurbished. The fort is now a national historic site and the state highway than runs through town has been designated as the "Frontier Military Scenic Highway."[16]

Once key landmarks and destinations are chosen, community planners should prioritize the resources. A site may be the actual reason why an individual or a group will travel to a place—a destination in its own right. Tourists will add sites or events as part of the itinerary when they plan trips to a particular destination. Other visitors will learn about some sites once they are in the community and tour the site simply because they are there. But the community must also keep in mind that some sites may be important to local residents, but not attract particular interest from tourists. The purpose of the community's assessment of its potential for heritage tourism is to scout the possibilities and possible support from local organizations that can focus energies into specific projects. This way, the best service and quality can be provided to all parties involved, residents and tourists alike. Some key questions planners must answer during the assessment include these:

✓ What is the local preservation organization's view of tourism?

✓ Do local businesses support the preservation of heritage?

✓ Are people enthusiastic about developing heritage sites and willing to make a long-term financial commitment?

✓ Do organizations actively seek funds from individuals and/or companies?

Perhaps the biggest concern of the lead organization will be protecting the area's assets. Protection in this context means the full array of measures needed to protect the value of historic, cultural, and natural assets. This includes finding out what protection local governments already offer.

Step 2: Planning and Organizing

A community united can accomplish a lot; a community divided is not ready for heritage tourism. Thus, building a local consensus that supports heritage tourism is crucial. This begins by gaining support from local businesspeople including bankers, travel professionals, owners of restaurants and shops, and operators of hotels and motels. Their expertise and enthusiasm can help build a stronger foundation for a successful program. Others in the community that should be considered for help are prominent families, religious leaders, and individuals who have influence and credibility. The heritage group should seek to unite local government behind its efforts. From the government can come leadership, preservation ordinances, review boards, landmark commissions, and so on. This offers protection of the resources that attract tourists. Last, but not least, the group should seek the assistance of service organizations and local historic and preservation associations. Such groups with strong membership bases and good track records on community projects will fortify efforts of planning a heritage program.

Once the consensus comes together, the next step is to formalize the action plan. This outlines the group's mission and how they expect to carry it out. Goal by goal, and objective by objective, a good action plan specifies responsibility and accountability. The following process is a suggested model of how to construct the plan:

✓ Establish the mission.
✓ Review the assessment and determine the appropriate goals.

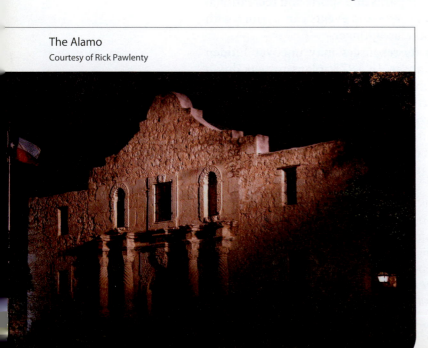

The Alamo
Courtesy of Rick Pawlenty

✓ Develop "results-oriented" objectives for each goal.

✓ List specific projects for each goal.

✓ Prepare an action plan that includes the following for each project:
  • Date of completion
  • Specific tasks to accomplish to complete the project
  • A budget and how it will be funded
  • The person responsible for the project

✓ Appoint committees with designated chairs to implement components of the action plan.

✓ Monitor progress against the timeline and mission.

✓ Plan any fund-raising efforts the group wants to undertake.

Step 3: Preparing, Protecting, and Managing

When taking this step, the community must look into the future as well as the present. As it prepares for visitors, it must make choices that will improve the community in the long-term. These choices should consider the quality of service the community provides its tourists and the lasting impression tourists take home with them. Much of the pleasure of a trip comes from how well visitors are treated. A short-tempered agent, an uninformed tour guide, a rude bus driver—these experiences are unfortunate, and often stay with the traveler the longest. The obvious goal for a community is to avoid giving tourists such bad impressions. The travel industry depends on many different people doing different jobs, so the challenge is to build community pride and understanding of the visitor's needs.

To achieve this, it may be necessary to implement a community-wide hospitality training program. For example, the State Division of Tourism for Wisconsin and the National Trust-sponsored "Celebrating Our Heritage: A Community Pride and Hospitality Training Program," a three-day seminar held at Wisconsin's four heritage tourism pilot areas. The goal was to teach participants key concepts in hospitality and encourage a better understanding of heritage tourism. When developing a training program, it is important to share with the community how the heritage program is planned to protect the area's resources, ensuring a long and productive life. The community should consider the following:

✓ Develop a comprehensive preservation plan, which gives participants a way to view and protect its historic resources overall, and not just one by one. This also helps the community to look ahead, not just react to emergencies.

✓ Use the designation of historic significance to protect historic resources. National designation occurs when resources are listed on the National Register of Historic Places. Benefits of National Register listing include the recognition of the property's significance, consideration in planning for federal or federally funded projects, eligibility for certain federal tax benefits, and qualification for federal preservation grants. The National Register provides no controls over private demolition or unsuitable alteration. Many states and municipalities also have designation programs. Federal, state, and local designation programs differ in the degree of protection they provide.

✓ Zoning, which specifies where particular land uses and densities are appropriate to keep excessive development away from sensitive historic sites.

✓ Set up a design review board to administer the guidelines that should be followed.

✓ Require demolition review so that property owners cannot abruptly tear down buildings that have historical significance.

✓ Develop a sign ordinance that regulates such matters as size, materials, illumination, and placement of signs.

✓ Set up an easement program to allow owners of historical or natural areas to receive a tax deduction by donating the development rights of their property to a tax-exempt organization.

✓ Establish a revolving loan fund to recycle the money from completed preservation projects into loans on subsequent projects.

✓ Create local incentives to encourage preservation.

✓ Integrate tourism with other forms of economic development through a growth management plan.

Step 4: Marketing for Success

Having made plans, how does the community group then get the visitors coming to the area? To draw new people and money into the community, a multiyear, many-tiered marketing plan must be developed. The goal is to reach the target market and to seize opportunities to partner with local, regional, state, or national groups. The four components that should be included in the marketing plan are these:

✓ Public relations

✓ Advertising

✓ Graphic materials

✓ Promotions

Public relations include many ventures such as short spots on radio and television to publicize sites and events. Another valuable source of public relations is documented success stories. These could include any written article or presentation featuring the community. Organizing a photo/slide library is also important and can be used for a number of projects. Setting up a speaker's bureau to respond to requests for information about the area's heritage tourism program with the names, addresses, and phone numbers of people who are willing to make public presentations is of great assistance to both the community and the visitors. Within this group should be a spokesperson to deliver important information concerning major events.

Advertising, although costly, can be very beneficial to the community in targeting audiences and attracting visitors to heritage sites. Advertising requires creating convincing messages and supporting visuals, appropriate media placement, responding to inquiries, and measuring effectiveness. When advertising, it is important to match the message with the site and the budget allotted, keeping in mind that messages do tend to get across if given frequently. Such announcements can be put in newspapers and magazines, on radio and television, and of course, on the Internet. Print advertising is generally less expensive than the electronic methods. Therefore, it is often best for heritage groups with limited budgets to start in newspapers and magazines.

"Co-op" advertising is a good way to share the costs of an ad campaign. In co-op advertising, multiple partners cooperate to produce advertisements or special sections dedicated to their area or destination. Magazines and newspapers provide special rates for advertising participants. Using co-op ads is effective, for example, when targeting a new market or entering an expensive venue such as a national magazine.

Another good idea is to develop various graphic materials communicating information about the program and its resources to potential visitors. Graphic materials bring forth to targeted audiences the image the community is trying to portray. A color scheme or unique design element (logo) that appears throughout all the graphic materials created by the area helps to define the image of the region and establishes identification for the visitor. Once a logo has been chosen it should be used widely and consistently so that it becomes closely associated with the heritage tourism program in the community.

Brochures introduce visitors to the area's attractions but can be used for other purposes as well, such as during trade shows or special events. Brochures should be displayed at key locations where they can be easily seen and picked up, for example, at visitor centers, airports, hotels, as well as historic, cultural, and natural sites. If the community is targeting a specific group, or if it wishes to promote a specific site or event, then specialized brochures should be developed. Also, a visitor and group services directory should be developed, offering information for tourists and groups about where to stay, where to eat, and what tours are available. The directory may even include suggested itineraries for groups. As with co-op advertising, this is great for promoting local businesses.

Signs should be created and placed where visitors will see them. They should be legible and informative. If possible, investing in professionally made signs is a smart move. All signs should also be made with international symbols to help guide visitors to restrooms, information centers, museums, gas stations, lodging, and dining establishments. Signs with graphic symbols such as logos help designate sites and roadways. Maps are sometimes more effective, highlighting key attractions or major features of a single attraction. These maps should be attractive, accurate, and easy to read.

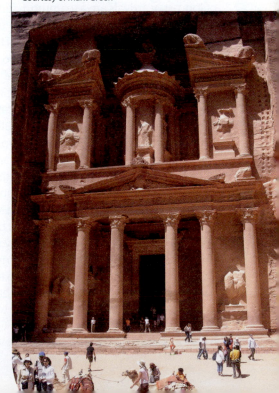

Petra Jordan
Courtesy of Mark Green

▶ Check Your Knowledge

1. What is the purpose of the community's assessment of its potential for heritage tourism?

2. How many key steps are involved in the model to construct the plan for heritage tourism?

3. Apart from the quality of service, what else should the community look into regarding its visitors?

We are not using trends in each chapter. . . . Many destinations, cities, countries, and areas are realizing the importance of cultural and heritage tourism. Some examples include the Greater Phoenix Convention and Visitors Bureau, which is working hard to bring a greater awareness of its area's diverse cultural heritage to both visitors and residents. The members of the Multi-Cultural Affairs Council (MCAC) advise and help to develop programs to increase economic opportunities for local ethnic businesses within the tourism and travel industry.[17]

In Tanzania, foreigners now have the opportunity to choose from a variety of cultural tours organized by local people through the Cultural Tourism Program.[18] Other examples include Thailand, where local development organizations and grassroots groups organize community tours that are limited to a specific number of people.[19]

CASE STUDY

Aruba's Bon Bini Festival

The year 2010 marks the 25th anniversary of Aruba's Bon Bini Festival (*Bon Bini* is the Papiamento term for welcome). Aruba is a 75-square-mile island located at 12° 30′ N, 69° 58′ W, 18 miles off the coast of Venezuela. The island has an estimated population of 103,000 persons made up of a rich cultural tapestry of ethnic groups; Amerindian, Dutch, African, Spanish, English, Hispanic, American, Filipino, East Asian, Haitian, Dominicans, and others from the Netherlands Antilles and former Dutch colonies.

Aruba records approximately 1.3 million visitors per year, 45 percent of these are cruise ship arrivals and 55 percent are long-stay or stay-over arrivals. The timeshare industry features prominently in visitor accommodation. Of the 7,500 rooms available for visitor accommodation, 40 percent are timeshare. Approximately 30 percent of long-stay arrivals are accommodated at timeshare resorts (data from the Aruba Central Bureau of Statistics).

The Bon Bini Festival takes place every Tuesday evening at Fort Zoutman in downtown Oranjestad, the capital city and chief port of Aruba. This event brings this historic Dutch fort and its Willem Tower to life. This military structure, completed in 1796, is an open-air setting for showcasing the history and culture of Aruba in music, dance, food, and handicraft. Arubans pay an admission to the festival of 5AFL, while visitors pay US$5. The event takes place from 6:30 P.M. to 8:30 P.M. with a brief intermission facilitating shopping at the handicraft booths, which feature local art, craft items, and the ever popular beads along with the ubiquitous souvenir items. Missing are the displays portraying aloe, which has been grown on the island since 1840. Aruba boasts "the best aloe in the world," which thrives in the island's dry tropical climate.

Guests can also obtain local food and drink delicacies, including Balashi, the beer of Aruba, but no Palmera Rum. Delicacies include funchi (polenta to many), rice, chicken saté with pinda sauce (peanut sauce), fish in Creole sauce, and the ever present Madam Janettes hot pepper sauce. Sweets include pan bollo (Aruban bread pudding with rum sauce), cocada (coconut aka sugar cakes), peanut and cashew cakes along with miniature pastries.

The cultural festivities commence on visitors' arrival. Guests enter the fort to the sounds of steel pan music. The steel pan, referred to as the only new musical instrument created in the twentieth century, emerged in the 1930s and 1940s from the working-class areas of Port of Spain, Trinidad. The musical art form along with Carnaval (celebrated its 55th Aruban anniversary in 2009) and calypso came to Aruba with the workers at the Lago Oil Refinery. Oil refining in Aruba dates from 1927.

The steel pan orchestra gives way to the Cah'l Orgel or Tingilingi Box. This is a crank-operated piano with its origins in 1842 in the Black Forests of Germany. It made its way to Aruba by way of Venezuela. Since 1975, there have been Cah'l Orgel competitions every November in an effort to sustain the heritage of this musical form.

CASE STUDY *(continued)*

Dance is a favorite feature of the evening. Danza, Tumba (African rhythms), Marcha, Wals (waltzes from Europe), Seu, and Carnaval mix (from the Caribbean) are all featured. The ribbon dance has a tradition similar to the English May Pole dances. But there is no bachata (South American Latin) dance hall, or reggae (Jamaican) or reggaeton (Puerto Rican). Performers are dressed in traditional costumes to highlight the festivals of the island, for example, dressing in the national colors to commemorate *Dia di Himno y Bandera*, Aruba's national anthem and Flag day. The climax of the evening, however, is the parade of the carnaval costumes as patrons are invited to join the conga line and dance their way out of the fort. Unfortunately, the fort's museum and gift shop are closed.

Coordinated by the Aruban Ministry of Culture, the objective of this festival is to offer a taste of Aruba's culture in a limited time and at a single location.

Questions

1. Who do you think is the audience for the Bon Bini Festival and what evidence is there to support your answer?
2. Would you consider Aruba's Bon Bini Festival an authentic heritage and cultural experience? Give reasons for your answer.
3. Why might some items of the heritage of the country not be included in the offerings at the festival?
4. Do you think that the festival fulfills its objective as expressed by its name? Is there an unstated expectation, and if so, what might it be?
5. How might the festival be improved?

Source: Courtesy of Michael Scantlebury, Ph.D., Assistant Professor, Rosen College of Hospitality Management, University of Central Florida.

Summary

1. The social and cultural aspects of tourism are hard to separate; they comprise the relationships between society, institutions, tourists, and host communities.
2. The past decades have seen an enormous growth in preservation of the world's historical and cultural heritage. As a natural by-product, cultural and heritage tourism has grown and flourished everywhere.
3. Tourism affects the quality of life at a destination. Yet quality of life is a highly subjective matter, and as we all know, what appeals to some people may not appeal to everyone else in the community.
4. Quality of life is affected by factors such as entertainment, infrastructure, pollution, and congestion.
5. Cultural tourism is a growing phenomenon and shows the recent trend toward travel for personal growth and enrichment. The term describes travel motivated wholly or in part by interest in history, arts, lifestyle, heritage, and so on and includes several degrees of consumer motivation, from culture being the sole reason for a visit, to tourists including cultural elements without initially planning to do so.
6. Heritage tourism is also a growing sector, fueled by an increasing interest in history and roots. It can be a great way of revitalizing and generating income for an area. However, the key to successful heritage tourism is to manage it in a way that maximizes profits/visitor enjoyment while at the same time conserving the cultural resource for future generations.

7. When planning and managing heritage tourism, there are four steps that need to be taken into account. First, the area's potential should be assessed. Next, the planning group should plan and organize the program in a way that benefits both the organization and the community. Then, they must prepare, protect, and manage the program in an appropriate way. Last, the planning group should decide on a marketing strategy that will ensure success in the long and short terms.

8. The most important trend in cultural and heritage tourism currently taking place is an increase in awareness, both from government and corporations developing programs and experiences in the area, and from educational institutions, which now often provide a whole class dedicated to cultural and heritage tourism.

9. The impact of tourism on host cultures is a much discussed topic. Whereas some claim that tourism reinforces local traditions, others argue that it is a diluter of culture.

10. Tourism affects the quality of life at a destination and the health of its native people.

Key Words and Concepts

cultural tourism
heritage tourism
national heritage site

National Historic Preservation
    Act of 1966
quality of life

World Heritage site

Review Questions

1. Who is the cultural tourist?
2. How may tourism affect the culture and art of a community?
3. What is heritage tourism? Name some benefits to the travel and tourism industry that preservation efforts have brought about.
4. What does UNESCO promote?
5. Where does the history of Carnival date from?
6. Do you agree with McKercher and du Cross's five-part typology as described by Dr. Scantlebury? Please give your reasons.
7. Describe the appeal of South Africa to a prospective tourist.

Interesting Websites

CNN: www.cnn.com
LORD Cultural Resources: www.lord.ca

National Trust for Historical Preservation: www.nationaltrust.org
UNESCO: www.unesco.org

Internet Exercises

1. Find a few countries that actually include cultural and heritage tourism as part of their nation's tourism plan.
2. Identify your nearest proposed World Heritage site and research into the length of time it has been under consideration by UNESCO. What is your community doing for it to be accepted as a World Heritage site?

Apply Your Knowledge

1. Identify a potentially attractive site for heritage tourism in or near your community and state your reasons for your selection. Now draw up a comprehensive heritage program using the steps and explanations given in the chapter. Remember, it has to be convincing and operational.

2. What challenges do you see facing cultural and heritage tourism? How would you overcome these obstacles?

Suggested Activity

Make a list of cultural tourism sites and events in your community (or one selected by your professor) and share your findings.

Endnotes

1. G. D. Lord, *The Power of Cultural Tourism* (keynote address at Wisconsin Heritage Tourism Conference, Lac du Flambeau, WI, September 17, 1999), www.lord.ca/Media/Artcl_PowerCulturalTourism-GL.pdf (accessed September 21, 2009).

2. Ted Sillerberg, *Cultural Tourism and Business Opportunities for Museums and Heritage Sites* (paper presented at Conference of School of Business, University of Victoria, "Quality Management in Urban Tourism: Balancing Business and Environment," Victoria, BC, Canada, November 1994), www.lord.ca/Media/Artcl_Ted_CultTourismBusOpps.pdf (accessed September 21, 2009).

3. Lord, *Power of Cultural Tourism.*

4. Harris Poll, as reported by the Philanthropy Nonprofit Leadership Centre, Orlando, FL, February 2008.

5. Noel B. Salzar, "Developmental Tourist vs. Development Tourism: A Case Study," in *Tourist Behavior: A Psychological Perspective*, ed. Aparna Raj (New Delhi: Kanishka Publishers, 2004), www.sas.upenn.edu/~nsalazar/DevelopmentalTourists.pdf (accessed September 21, 2009).

6. D. Lundberg, *The Tourist Business*, 6th ed. (New York: Van Nostrand Reinhold, 1995), 159.

7. Lundberg, *Tourist Business*, 161.

8. Information in this section was drawn from the UNESCO website at www.unesco.org.

9. R. Mader, "Exploring Ecotourism," Planeta.com, www.planeta.com/ecotravel/tour/definitions.html (accessed September 21, 2009).

10. Drawn from Mader, "Exploring Ecotourism."

11. Alamo, website, www.thealamo.org/ (accessed September 21, 2009).

12. Information for this section is drawn from the American Express booklet *Getting Started: How to Succeed in Heritage Tourism* produced in partnership with the National Trust for Historic Preservation. Also available at www.culturalheritagetourism.org/howToGetStarted.htm.

13. Advisory Council on Historic Preservation, "The National Historic Preservation Program: Overview," www.achp.gov/overview.html (accessed September 21, 2009).

14. "Don't Leave Home," *60 Minutes*, January 13, 1992.

15. Historic Jonesborough, website, www.jonesboroughtn.org (accessed September 21, 2009).

16. Historic Fort Scott, Kansas, website, www.fortscott.com (accessed September 21, 2009).

17. Greater Phoenix Convention and Visitors Bureau, "Multicultural Tourism," www.visitphoenix.com/meeting/index.cfm?action=multicultural&sectionID=1&subSection=333&childsection=0 (accessed September 21, 2009).

18. Tanzanian Cultural Tourism Coordination Office, website, www.earthfoot.org/guides/tctco.htm (accessed September 21, 2009).

19. Tourism Authority of Thailand, website, www.tourismthailand.se/ (accessed June 11, 2001).

CHAPTER 12

Eco-tourism

OBJECTIVES

After reading and studying this chapter, you should be able to:

- Define eco-tourism.

- Explain the characteristics of the typical eco-tourist.

- Identify some of the major eco-tourism activities and hotspots.

- Describe the scope of eco-tourism and some of the fundamental principles underlying the concept of eco-tourism.

- List the major trends currently taking place in eco-tourism as well as what is being done to encourage it.

GEOGRAPHY SPOTLIGHT

Eco-tourism: Costa Rica

Eco-tourism and Costa Rica have become synonymous: more than a quarter of Costa Rica's land has been set aside for national parks and reserves. *Eco-tourism* is the "purposeful travel to natural areas to understand the culture and natural history of the environment; taking care not to alter the integrity of the ecosystem; [and] producing economic opportunities that make the conservation of natural resources beneficial to local people."[1] Foreigners finance many Costa Rican lodges and protected areas because the locals lack the capital and knowledge to run an eco-tourism establishment. As tourism to Costa Rica becomes more popular, the country will be forced to deal with the challenge of balancing conservation demands and tourism development.

Eco-tourism in Costa Rica has not always been as popular as it is today. Deforestation issues were a major problem in the 1950s, 1960s, and 1970s. When foreign investors threatened to stop funding public projects because of the deforestation rates, the Costa Rican government decided to "[place] greater emphasis on conservation efforts."[2] In 1963, Costa Rica's first environmental protection reserve was created, and in 1969, the country's national park system was established. Although both public and private organizations have designated certain areas of protected land, one of the biggest problems the country is challenged with is illegal logging. Today, the citizens of Costa Rica are beginning to understand the potential eco-tourism has, though, and "tourism now employs half a million Costa Ricans or 17% of the population."[3]

Costa Rica "has managed to protect a larger proportion of its land than any other country in the world."[4] One of Costa Rica's most popular protected land areas is the Manuel Antonio National Park. Its relatively

GEOGRAPHY SPOTLIGHT *(continued)*

Linda Whitwam
© Dorling Kindersley

small size creates a carrying capacity of only 600 guests on weekdays and 800 on Saturdays and Sundays. While at the park, visitors can enjoy the nature trails, beaches, and wildlife viewing, which include animals such as the howler monkey, marmosets, sloths, and turtles.

One of the national parks the locals are most proud of is Monteverde Cloud Forest Reserve. Settled in 1951 by Americans, the site was originally intended for research and environmental protection. For more than 50 years, private organizations have been purchasing nearby land to include in the protected area, which today has grown to more than 14,200 hectares (more than 35,000 acres).[5] As the eco-tourism trend became more popular, so did the popularity of the park. Today, the park faces issues of overcrowding. To prevent this problem from becoming a threat to the environment, park officials raised the price of admission, trained locals from the community to give guided tours, and restricted the number of visitors allowed in the park at a time. This experiment of both eco-tourism and sustainable tourism has helped Monteverde Cloud Forest Reserve become one of Costa Rica's most successful eco-tourism destinations.

With eco-tourism becoming so popular, Costa Rica has begun to focus on sustainable tourism as well. "Sustainability, as a model of development, seeks to meet the current demands of society without compromising the rights of future generations to meet theirs."[6] The Certification for Sustainable Tourism (CST) has evolved from this concept and is benefiting Costa Rica's tourism as a "new form of competitiveness" while "[encouraging] the conservation and efficient handling of resources."[7] Previously, many "eco-tourism" destinations exploited the local environment to deal with increased numbers of tourists. Sustainability aims to prevent this from happening in the future by balancing current visitors' needs with societal and environmental concerns, as well as providing protection of land for future generations.

As the most stable country in Central America, Costa Rica's friendly and inviting locals, beautiful scenery, and eco-friendly attitude make it a popular tourism destination. From mountains to beaches, zip lining to sunbathing, big city to remote forest, family-oriented to romantic, Costa Rica has something to offer for every visitor. Although the country is still facing deforestation problems, both private and public organizations are working to protect more forests and land. The country is learning to combine eco-tourism and sustainable tourism to continue to attract visitors looking for an environmentally friendly vacation. "Costa Rica has turned to eco-tourism as its key to economic development," and with a quarter of the country's land designated as protected land, the country will likely see continued success with the increasing popularity of eco-tourism and sustainable tourism.

(continued)

GEOGRAPHY SPOTLIGHT *(continued)*

Endnotes

1. J. Dasenbrock, (2002, January). "The Pros and Cons of Eco-tourism in Costa Rica," www.american.edu/TED/costa-rica-tourism.htm (accessed February 10, 2009).

2. C. Cosgrove, "A Closer Look: Eco-tourism in Costa Rica," www.biology.duke.edu/bio217/2005/cmp8/costarica.html (accessed February 11, 2009).

3. H. Pariser, *Explore Costa Rica* (San Francisco: Manatee Press, 2007).

4. C. Baker, "The National Parks of Costa Rica," www.centralamerica.com/cr/parks/index.htm (accessed February 10, 2009).

5. Cosgrove, "A Closer Look."

6. Baker, "The National Parks of Costa Rica."

7. Ibid.

What Is Eco-tourism?

The roots of **eco-tourism** can be traced to the "responsible tourism" movement of the 1970s. This concept emerged as a reaction to the negative consequences of tourism development on natural resources, ecosystems, and cultural destinations. The movement toward responsible tourism helped spawn "environmental tourism" in the early 1980s, which in turn led to the birth of eco-tourism.

Hector Caballos-Lascurain, head of the Ecotourism Consulting program for the World Conservation Union and co-author, with Elizabeth Boo, of the book *Ecotourism: The Potential and Pitfalls*, actually coined the term in July 1983. He offers one of the most comprehensive descriptions of eco-tourism: "Environmentally responsible travel and visitation to relatively undisturbed natural areas, in order to enjoy and appreciate nature (and any accompanying cultural features—both past and present) that promotes conservation, has low negative visitor impact, and provides beneficially active socio-economic involvement of local populations."[1] The Ecotourism Society in Bennington, Vermont, suggests a simplified (and widely used) definition of eco-tourism: "Responsible travel to natural areas that conserves the environment and sustains the well-being of the host people." Dr. David Weaver, a respected eco-tourism author and scholar, defines eco-tourism as: "A form of tourism that fosters learning experiences and appreciation of the natural environment, or some component thereof, within its associated cultural context. It is managed in accordance with industry best practice to attain environmentally and socio-culturally sustainable outcomes as well as financial viability."[2] To illustrate the conceptualization of an eco-tourism system, Figure 12–1 shows a model. Notice how this is like a flower: it needs all parts of the system to harmonize to flourish.

Interactions between hosts and tourists entail more than simple transactions of money for goods or services. They also involve the exchange of expectations, stereotypes, and expressions of ethnicity and culture.[3] For example, the Infierno

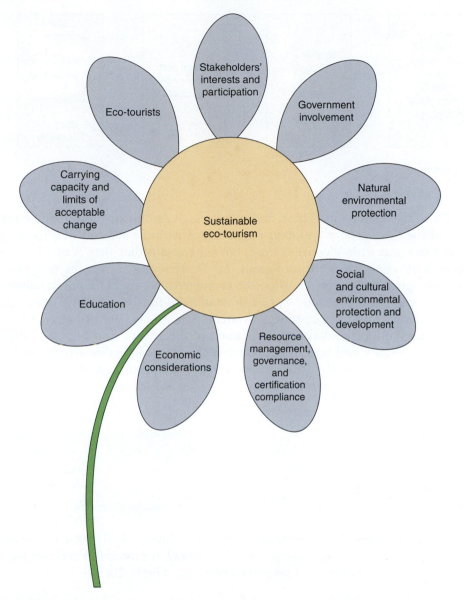

Figure 12–1 • A Model of a Sustainable Eco-tourism System

and Posada Amazonas in the province of Tambopata, Peru, is located several hours by motorized boat from the provincial capital. The community covers almost 10,000 hectares (24,700 acres) on both sides of the Tambopata River and has a mixed economy based on fishing, hunting, and gathering some horticulture. Community members travel to the market in Puerto Maldonado to sell produce and manufactured goods. Three different ethnic groups came together to form a community that signed a joint venture agreement with Rainforest Expeditions, a Peruvian eco-tourism company with the purpose of combining tourism with environmental education, research, and local sustainable development to support conservation in the areas in which they operate.[4] Over time, a lodge was built to accommodate eco-tourists and several studies were conducted on various aspects

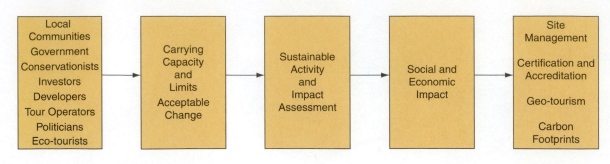

Figure 12–2 • A Framework for Eco-tourism

of life in the community. These studies examined complex issues of ethnic identity of the three groups and their relationships with the eco-tourists. Some said that there was little identity to lose, but others said that they wanted to save something about their identity from the Westernizing influences of tourism. Interestingly, it was the eco-tourists who prompted a revival of the ethnic cultures.[5]

Complementing the model of a sustainable eco-tourism system (Figure 12–1) is a framework for an eco-tourism system, which is shown in Figure 12–2. It illustrates the stakeholders and other parts of the eco-tourism system including carrying capacity and limits of acceptable change; sustainable activity and impact assessment; social and economic impact; site management, certification, geo-tourism, and carbon footprints.

PROFILE

Center for Responsible Travel (CREST)

Martha Honey

Martha Honey is co-director of the Center for Responsible Travel (CREST), which is based in Washington, D.C., and at Stanford University. Her latest book is *Ecotourism and Sustainable Development: Who Owns Paradise?* in its second edition (Island Press, 2009).

Reflections on Eco-tourism

My fascination with eco-tourism grew out of 20 years of living and working abroad as a graduate student and a journalist. I was fortunate to be based in two of the epicenters of eco-tourism—Tanzania in East Africa and Costa Rica in Central America. From these vantage points, I witnessed the struggles of poor countries to use conventional tourism as a development strategy, the difficulties of making countries saddled with poverty and political instability into successful tourism destinations, and the rise of eco-tourism as an alternative to mainstream or mass tourism. Today tourism, much of it eco-tourism, is the leading economic activity in both Tanzania and Costa Rica.

However, back in the 1970s, while I was doing my Ph.D. at the University of Dar-es-Salaam, Tanzania was very wary of tourism. There was a lively political debate in Tanzania, which had recently won independence from British colonial rule, over whether to invest in international tourism. The World Bank and other international lending agencies promoted tourism as a good development strategy for Tanzania and other economically

PROFILE (*continued*)

poor but environmentally and culturally rich countries. Indeed, Tanzania had world-class attractions—Mount Kilimanjaro, the Serengeti, Ngorongoro Crater, the island of Zanzibar, plus a remarkable founding president, a stable government, and a rich mix of cultures—all without the ethnic conflicts of Kenya, Uganda, and other neighboring countries. In this early tourism debate, many Tanzanians argued that tourism catering to wealthy foreigners was not a priority for government investment, was not a sound development strategy, and would bring social ills such as prostitution and sexually transmitted diseases.

In the end, Tanzania opted to develop a small state-owned tourism sector, centered around its northern game parks and a few Indian Ocean beach hotels. The government invested heavily in roads, airports, and other infrastructure as well as beautiful safari lodges and beach resorts. But tourism was dependent on foreign management and imports, so, as happened in many developing countries, most of the profits flowed out of Tanzania and the country gained little economically. In fact, in the late 1970s, under pressure from developing countries, the World Bank closed its tourism department and stopped funding tourism because it had not proved to be a successful development strategy. Eco-tourism was not an option—it had not yet emerged as a coherent alternative to the conventional model of tourism.

In Costa Rica, in the 1980s, the challenges were different. The region was awash with a mix of civil and Cold War conflicts. Though Costa Rica had abolished its army and was politically neutral, it was being covertly used as a base for U.S.-backed rebels ("contras") waging war against the leftist government in neighboring Nicaragua. (This eventually broke open in the Iran-contra scandal.) In this climate, international tourism was all but dead, except for a handful of hearty bird watchers. Tourism resorts and other projects proposed in the 1970s and intended to turn Costa Rica into the Cancun of Central America were shelved. This did not change until 1987, when Costa Rican President Oscar Arias won the Nobel Peace Prize as the architect of the Central American Peace Plan. With the end to the region's wars and the international acclaim brought by the Nobel Prize, tourism began to grow in Costa Rica.

By this time the concept of eco-tourism had entered the lexicon and was rapidly offering an alternative model to conventional tourism. Eco-tourism has been hailed as a "win-win" for communities, conservation, tourists, and the tourism industry: done well, eco-tourism provides tangible benefits to local communities and to conservation, is educational as well as enjoyable for the traveler, and is economically profitable. The emphasis is on small-scale, high-value, nature-based tourism that is light on the land and utilizes local people and resources. Fortunately, Costa Rica had the right ingredients to do eco-tourism well. These ingredients include, in addition to peace and political stability (from the late 1980s onward), an outstanding system of national parks, high biodiversity within a tiny country, a strong middle class capable of moving into tourism, a healthy and well-educated workforce, good infrastructure (airports, roads, electricity, etc.), and close proximity to the United States, its most important tourism market. Eco-tourism grew quickly and, by 1992, Costa Rica had been dubbed the "number one eco-tourism destination in the world."

During these two decades in East Africa and Central America, I had been a lover of travel but a close observer of the tourism industry. In the mid-1990s, after I moved back to the United States, I decided I wanted to look at this new phenomenon, eco-tourism, to see if, as they say, there was any "there there." Was it all just "greenwashing"—a marketing ploy—or did eco-tourism hold out the potential of really helping poor communities and conservation? I began as a skeptic. I took my investigative reporting skills and set off to look closely at eco-tourism in seven destinations in Africa and the Americas (Tanzania, Zanzibar, Kenya, South Africa, Costa Rica, Cuba, and the Galapagos Islands).

What I found was a much more nuanced and complex picture. I came to categorize the eco-tourism I saw in the field into three broad categories: (1) the "greenwashing" scams and shams that use green language but

(continued)

PROFILE *(continued)*

were not involved in sustainable practices; (2) eco-tourism "lite" or companies that had few generic green practices—such as giving guests the "opportunity" to not have their sheets and towels changed every day; and (3) genuine eco-tourism businesses committed to sustainable environmental and social principles and practices. Eco-tourism was therefore a mixed grill, but I became convinced that, done well, it has the power to transform the tourism industry and the way we travel.

Indeed, beginning in the 1990s, eco-tourism became the fastest growing sector of the tourism industry, typically growing three times faster than the industry as a whole. It also became increasingly important as a development tool in poor countries. In 4 out of 5 countries (more than 150), tourism is one of five top export earners, and in 60 countries it is the number one export.[6] Tourism is a principal foreign exchange earner for 83 percent of developing countries,[7] and "the only large sector of international trade in services where poor countries have consistently posted a surplus."[8] In Tanzania, for instance, wildlife tourism is the number one industry and much of it—though not all—practices eco-tourism.

Over the last 15 years, as I have worked in the field of eco-tourism, I've seen the concept deepened, broadened, and reinvented. There's been the rise of a range of like-minded terms such as *responsible travel*, *geotourism*, *pro-poor tourism*, and *sustainable tourism*, each with a slightly different focus but the same broad objectives of bringing benefits to conservation and communities. There have been important innovations, including the growth of voluntary certification programs to measure the environmental and social impacts of tourism businesses. And new concepts such as agritourism, community-based tourism, voluntourism, and travelers' philanthropy, all of which are committed to bringing more benefits to the host destinations. When, nearly four decades ago, the tourism debate took place in Tanzania, there was no alternative model. Today, we have a rich tapestry of successful experiments based on sound and sustainable principles. Collectively, eco-tourism or responsible travel is, as the motto of my organization says, "transforming the way the world travels."

Source: Courtesy of Martha Honey, Co-Director, Center for Responsible Travel (CREST), Washington, D.C. and Stanford University.

Environmental Impact of Tourism

Tourism can and does affect the environment in a number of ways. As mentioned earlier, "overvisitation" of a particular resort, attraction, or city can have an adverse impact on ecology. Natural resources may be threatened or seriously disturbed by poorly managed tourism. In the Caribbean, for example, tourist demand for seafood is the primary cause of the increasing pressure on lobster, conch, and fish populations. Tourism development also puts pressure on local resources. The superstructure (airports, convention centers, hotels, bridges, roads, railways) and the infrastructure (electric, water, sewage, communications, government services—including police and fire departments and transportation) frequently are overused in a way that they become harmful to the natural environment. Nature's delicate balance has often been disturbed by the rapid and seemingly unconstituted growth of some tourist areas. In Mexico and parts of the Mediterranean, for example, tourist demands have led to an often-disorderly urbanization of large stretches of the coastline.

Tourists also cause pollution in the form of sewage and solid waste, litter, noise, and air pollution. For residents, tourism can disrupt an otherwise blissful lifestyle. Unfortunately, these forms of tourist pollution are on the rise in many developing countries, which often lack the technological or financial capacity to handle these problems.

The big question is how to balance tourism growth in such a way as to protect the environment and residents' lifestyle and culture. The answer largely centers on partnership and cooperation within the tourism industry and between businesses, governments, and tourists. Regulation, both voluntary self-regulation and government legislation, can work in practice. A good example is Pattaya, Thailand. After years of neglect, the beach and ocean became so polluted that the tourists stayed away. This forced a collection of hoteliers, city officials, the Tourism Authority of Thailand, and a handful of tour operators to

Footprints in the sand exemplify eco-tourism because soon a wave will wipe away the footprints left by tourists.

step in. The goal was to stop sewage and waste pollution from going directly into the ocean untreated. The outcome is that the sewage treatment plants now modify the waste. The beaches and ocean are again welcoming tourists. This example illustrates the need for cooperation between central and local governments.

Governments can sponsor, with the use of tourism and other taxes, environmental studies that identify valuable fragile habitats and protect them by monitoring them. Governments have a major role to play in minimizing the environmental impact of tourism. The federal, state, and city governments can pass legislation to limit the number of tourists visiting. Generally, this is done in an indirect manner. For example, placing a height restriction on new buildings will limit the number of high-rise buildings in an area. This will in turn affect the number of hotel rooms. Governments may either increase or restrict access to destinations or attractions by manipulating air, railroad, and cruise capacity. By refusing to build or expand the access to destinations and attractions, the number of tourists will automatically be limited.

In the early 1970s, several remote areas of the world saw that tourism could be profitable; however, they did not want to destroy the exotic environment that surrounded them. One such place was Cancun, Mexico. Cancun was a prime beach location, but the number of tourists was quite low. Developers recognized Cancun's potential and drew up a master plan that placed priority on environmental protection. Unfortunately, Mexico began to experience political and economical instability. The recession caused the government and business leaders to scramble, trying to find a way to bring money into the economy—specifically, U.S. dollars. Tourism in Mexico was one of the few industries that showed signs of growth. However, in an effort to make a quick profit, Cancun's environmentally friendly attractions were sacrificed to make room for large-scale development. As a result, the few natives that were living in the assigned resort area were relocated to the mountains where they live in cardboard shacks without plumbing. The beaches surrounding Cancun are becoming cluttered with garbage, and the reef off of the coastline is damaged by ships coming into the wharf. Water treatment is insufficient and it is practically impossible to meet the growing **capacity requirement** of the tourists.

Cancun, Mexico, is not the only place to experience such disruption and environmental hardships because of tourism. We might surmise that rampant and damaging overdevelopment is present only in less developed destinations, but that is not true. Sometimes much pollution—air, water, or land pollution—and overpopulation occur in areas that are well developed.

As similar stories surface, ecologists and tourism leaders have come to realize how important it is to preserve the environment so that generations to come can continue to enjoy the earth's natural beauty. Because of this idea, most eco-tourism destinations can be found in areas with vast natural surroundings and plentiful flora and fauna. Places such as deserts, tropical rainforests, coral reefs, and ice glaciers are prime locations. Also important in eco-tourism is the presence of a culture that is different from that of the visitor. The focus of eco-tourism is to provide tourists with new knowledge about a certain natural area and the culture that is found there, along with a little bit of adventure.

Eco-tourism Foundations and Core Criteria

David Weaver, an eco-tourism expert and author of *Ecotourism* and *Sustainable Tourism*, suggests that eco-tourism entails three core criteria, namely, an emphasis on *nature-based attractions*, *learning opportunities*, and *management practices* that adhere to the principles of ecological, sociocultural, and economic sustainability.[9] Weaver adds that eco-tourism is primarily nature-based attractions and products, with associated cultural influences. Eco-tourism products can range in scope from a holistic emphasis on an entire ecosystem to an elemental focus on specific charismatic megafauna (e.g., giant pandas, quetzals, orangutans, koalas, and sandhill cranes), megaflora (e.g., redwoods, rafflesia), or megaliths (e.g., caves, volcanoes, mountains) that are largely driven by popular consumer demand.[10]

Eco-tourism offers many learning opportunities in natural and social-cultural interactions, frequently improving tourists' knowledge and enjoyment of the environment. Weaver also rightly points out that eco-tourism should be managed so that it is conducive to sustainability. Eco-tourism sites must be able to go beyond the Brundtland Commission terms and be able to assess whether sustainable eco-tourism has actually been accomplished. Managing any popular eco-tourism destination is a challenge; for example, managers of sites must deal with the deforestation in and around eco-tourism areas in Brazil and Peru. Weaver argues that the real test for a bona fide eco-tourism product is not the absence of any resulting negative impacts (which cannot be shown definitively), but rather the ongoing intent by managers to pursue sustainability outcomes in concert with best practices, preferably through a recognized accreditation protocol.[11] Better still are the proactive approaches that go beyond the status quo to a global outlook, including consideration of such issues as carbon footprints of the eco-tourism entity and the extent of greenhouse gases emitted during transportation of products for eco-tourist needs. Additionally, eco-tourism operators are strongly encouraged to plant more trees to negate the emissions they have caused.

The concept of carrying capacity—the maximum number of people that can use an area without causing an unacceptable decline in the quality of visitor experience or enjoyment[12]—and the idea that there should be limits on tourism from environmental, visitor, and community perspectives were virtually unknown only a few decades ago, but have quickly become hot topics all over the world. Geoffrey Wall, a tourism expert and author, rightly asks the questions, "What is an acceptable capacity?" and "Who should decide?"[13] Several issues must be addressed when considering carrying capacity: the acceptable number of visitors to an area, the sustainability needs of the area, the wants and needs of visitors, seasonality, access, roads, accommodations, sanitation, and foodservice.

The sustainability of eco-tourism is contingent on stakeholders recognizing the interdependent links between the four Es: *environmental* conservation, *equity*, *education*, and *economic* benefits (profits).[14] This interdependence in the tourism system means that sustainable profits will not exist in the long term without a healthy and attractive physical environment; a tranquil, stable, and equitable social environment; and an educated group of tourists and locals motivated to support measures to protect the local environment and culture.[15] Looking at it from the other perspective, the four Es also suggest that without profits, eco-tourism cannot support environmental conservation, social equity, or educational efforts.[16]

Research on a community-based eco-tourism project in Kenya revealed five factors critical to the project's success: inclusion of stakeholders, recognition of individual and mutual benefits, appointment of a legitimate convener, formulation of aims and objectives, and perception that the decisions arrived at will be implemented.[17]

Eco-tourism expert Dr. David Farrell comments, "People [including tourism officials and other interested stakeholders], no matter where and when, have found it difficult to manage resources in a sustainable way. Control does not automatically mean wise management, nor does it mean sustainable harvesting."[18]

The media have covered eco-tourism topics in depth. In addition, conferences have been held to discuss them. The World Wildlife Fund participates in the creation of an eco-tourism model. It has developed a basic planning document that offers a series of practical questions about the issues of tourism and outlines a process planners can use to write an eco-tourism strategy for an area. The WWF also contributes through various programs and publications.

The United Nations World Tourism Organization's policy is that all forms of tourism development should be sustainable. Unfortunately, that is not the case at this time. The principal characteristics that comprise eco-tourism are listed in Figure 12–3.

▶ Check Your Knowledge

1. Define eco-tourism.

2. What arguments are used pro eco-tourism and which ones are used against it?

3. What roles do governments have in minimizing the environmental impact of eco-tourism? Give examples of government action in this area.

1. Setting	It is assumed that eco-tourism takes place in some exotic, remote, undisturbed natural area. These areas are usually national parks or other protected locations reserved for such activities.
2. Activity	This includes any activity that is nondisruptive and relies on natural resources to achieve the desired experience. Activities may be light or rigorous and may include visits to historical and cultural attractions.
3. Impact	Eco-tourism should minimize negative environmental and social impacts. Visitors, locals, and tourism providers should act responsibly. Visitors should rely on local lodging, transportation, and locally made products. Conservation and preservation measures, including recycling and other methods, should be enforced.
4. Psychological Outcome	This is related to an increased awareness of environmental issues and efforts.
5. Economic Linkages	Eco-tourism is an attempt to link economic and environmental impacts, which encourages community development while protecting and preserving local resources.
6. Site Management	Eco-tourism is characterized by intensive planning for development. Strict control is needed in sensitive natural areas to prevent destruction of the community and its natural surroundings and resources. Limitations and regulations may be enforced.
7. Philosophy	Eco-tourism should not only provide visitors with adventure, but it should try to import ethics into travel experiences.

Figure 12–3 • Principal Characteristics of Eco-tourism

Bar Harbor Declaration on Eco-tourism in the United States

The Bar Harbor conference on eco-tourism was the first of its kind in the United States. It was held in Bar Harbor, Maine, and organized by the International Ecotourism Society. A part of the declaration reads as follows: "We hold that the application of ecotourism principles is helping transform the tourism industry in positive ways through the introduction and implementation of sustainable practices and incentives for conservation of destinations. Specifically, eco-tourism promotes:

- Sustainable livelihoods and tangible economic benefits to host communities;
- Protection of fragile ecosystems and natural resource-based heritage;
- Cultural diversity, including the vitality of local and indigenous communities;
- Educational experiences and opportunities for both visitors and hosts;
- Participatory, democratic, and multi-stakeholder planning, development, and operations;
- Fait trade, wages and working conditions, according to international human rights and labor norms;
- Geographic character, including a sense of place, authenticity, heritage and aesthetics.[19]

The declaration also calls on governments at the federal, state, and local levels to do a number of things like rejoin the World Tourism Organization and reestablish a national tourism office in the United States.

The International Eco-tourism Society

The International Ecotourism Society (TIES), founded in 1990, is the largest and oldest eco-tourist organization in the world dedicated to promoting and disseminating information about eco-tourism and sustainable tourism.[20] Members in more than 90 countries include tour operators, lodge owners and managers, academics, consultants, conservation professionals, governments, architects, development experts, nongovernmental organizations (NGOs), the media, and travelers. TIES provides guidelines and standards, training, technical assistance, research, and publications to foster sound eco-tourism development. TIES promotes the eco-tourism principles shown in Figure 12–4. These principles guide the actions of members and others who seek to encourage eco-tourism as a means of developing tourism in a sustainable manner.

TIES Mission and Vision

TIES promotes responsible travel to natural areas that conserves the environment and improves the well-being of local people through the following means:

- Creating an international network of individuals, institutions, and the tourism industry
- Educating tourists and tourism professionals
- Influencing the tourism industry, public institutions, and donors to integrate the principles of eco-tourism into their operations and policies

The International Eco-tourism Society (TIES) promotes the following eco-tourism principles:

- Minimize impact.
- Build environmental and cultural awareness and respect.
- Provide positive experiences for both visitors and hosts.
- Provide direct financial benefits for conservation.
- Provide financial benefits and empowerment for local people.
- Raise sensitivity to host countries' political, environmental, and social climate.

These principles guide the actions of members and others who seek to encourage eco-tourism as a means of developing tourism in a sustainable manner.

Figure 12–4 • International Ecotourism Society's Eco-tourism Principles

The size and growth of eco-tourism in the United States is worth noting. TIES states that about 13 percent of the 18.6 million U.S. outbound leisure travelers (approximately 2.4 million Americans) can be regarded as eco-tourists. In the United States, Lifestyles of Health and Sustainability (LOHAS) estimates that eco-tourism is among the fastest growing travel trends and is estimated to be a $77 billion market, representing 5 percent of the overall U.S. travel and tourism market.[21]

TIES also promotes eco-tourism certification programs, which provide important tools for distinguishing genuine eco-tourism or sustainable tourism companies, products, and services from those that are merely using *eco-* as a marketing tool to attract consumers.

Who Are Eco-tourists?

The International Ecotourism Society developed a profile of the average eco-tourist from a survey among travelers in North America.[22] The survey found that most eco-tourists were between the ages of 35 and 54 years, with variations resulting from factors such as activity and cost. There was no difference between male and female eco-tourists, although men and women preferred to participate in different activities. Whereas males tended to be more interested in specialist activities and outdoor adventure, females preferred general interest experiences. It has been assumed that eco-tourists are more highly educated than the average traveler is. The survey found this assumption to be generally true, with 82 percent being college graduates.[23]

No major differences were found between the average tourist and the eco-tourist when it came to household composition. Most of the people in the surveys live as couples. However, the survey found that more general tourists live as couples with children compared to eco-tourists, who have the tendency to live alone. When it is time to travel, fewer eco-tourists travel alone and instead travel in groups. However, whether they travel alone or in a group also depends on the type of experience and the destination. Many prefer to travel as couples, with participants from the same household or from different households. Most eco-tourists (60 percent) preferred to travel as a couple, with only 15 percent preferring to travel with their families, and 13 percent alone.[24]

The average length of each eco-tourism trip was found to be 8 to 14 days, during which a majority of travelers were willing to spend more than other tourists usually are. More precisely, most were willing to spend between $2,000 and $3,000 per trip. The length of the trip varied depending on the type of experience, the planned activities, and the destination. The survey showed that eco-tourists tend to stay longer at a location compared to general tourists, with stays ranging from two weeks to a month or longer. Just as the general tourist, most eco-tourists seem to prefer to travel during the summer months. However, a higher percentage of eco-tourists compared to general tourists were willing to travel during the

Eco-tourists Hiking Down a Trail on the Caribbean Island of Martinique
Robert Fried/robertfriedphotography.com

winter months. Eco-tourists generally are more frequent travelers than the general traveler is. The survey revealed that most eco-tourists look for (1) a wilderness setting, (2) the opportunity to view wildlife, and (3) an area in which they can participate in hiking and/or trekking. Motivating factors are mainly the opportunity to enjoy scenery and nature, as well as new places and experiences. Other things of priority include local food produced with local ingredients, friendly hospitality, as well as organized opportunities to spend time with local people.[25]

▶ Check Your Knowledge

1. What are the demographics of the typical eco-tourist?
2. What principles does the International Ecotourism Society promote? destination?

Eco-tourism Activities

What often comes to mind when people think about eco-tourism is the vision of a middle-aged couple in flannel shirts and hiking boots strolling around the wilderness with a pair of binoculars, hoping to spot a rare bird. Although a number of tourists engage in that stereotypical activity, there are many other opportunities for fun and action.

These opportunities might include a guided tour through the rain forest, witnessing the magical world under the sea, rafting roaring rapids, or participating in a cultural event. As with all tourism, the types of available activities

CORPORATE PROFILE

Ecotour Expeditions, Inc.

Courtesy of Bel Kambach, St. Cloud State University

Ecotour Expeditions operates nature trips to some of the most spectacular natural wonders of the Americas. They offer riverboat excursions in the Amazon, explorations in the Galapagos Islands, and forest lodges in Peru, Costa Rica, Brazil, and Ecuador. The business that became Ecotour Expeditions began as a lumber importing company in the 1980s. They bought lumber from sawmills in the rainforests of the Amazon and distributed it to factories and lumber outlets in the United States. By 1988, the company became aware of and convinced that rainforest conservation was one of the most important goals of the time. Therefore, in 1989 Ecotour Expeditions began to offer the first eco-tours. In the beginning, people thought that eco-tourism would never amount to more than a small corner of the travel industry. Today, Ecotour is entering its 18th year of operation.

This milestone shows the success of the idea that small nature tours could help to support local communities while protecting the environment. The growth of the eco-tourism industry is reflected in Ecotour Expeditions experiences. The first eco-tours took place in the Amazon rainforest in rugged, uncomfortable, creaky riverboats. Today the Ecotour trips take place on a comfortable, air-conditioned motor yacht. The Amazon programs retain the essential elements of an eco-tour: a small group size, minimal environmental impact, and support for conservation. In turn, the staff in the Amazon has prospered. For many crewmembers, their children are the first in their family to go to school.

Whether it is the Amazon Rainforest or the Galapagos Islands, guests on Ecoutour trips often see creatures that are missed by other travelers. This is because Ecotour does whatever they can to make it possible for guests to see wildlife. They focus on keeping the operation small. "The real interest and excitement in natural history dwells in the details." Several large companies now offer mass tourism disguised as eco-tours, but because of the size of the groups and the volume of passengers, they are unable to offer truly unique and thoughtful natural history experiences.

Source: Information gathered from the Ecotour Expeditions website: www.naturetours.com.

depend on the destination. If traveling in Norway, visitors have the opportunity to go on a whale or elk **safari**, whereas in Kenya they will encounter giraffes, or elephants, or zebras. In Brazil, they can explore the rainforest, and in the Middle East, a lush oasis.

Wildlife watching is popular in just about every location in the world. Encountering exotic animals is exciting, especially when they are in their natural environment. In less dense areas, bike tours are popular. These are more interactive, especially if the tourists take little luggage with them and opt for staying at small, locally run hotels. This also allows for participating in local cultural events, which could include watching a ceremonial dance, going to a traditional wedding, or learning how to cook the local food specialties. Actually participating in an event is even more rewarding for both the tourist and the host community.

In coastal areas, snorkeling and scuba diving are extremely popular, and available depending on the fragility of the local marine life. Boat tours and canoe rides are also commonly found on the coast and in areas adjacent to rivers, marshes, and lakes. Travelers can take an airboat ride in the Florida Everglades or a quiet canoe trip among alligators. Even better, they can experience a specialist cruise, with lectures and snorkeling, to Ecuador's Galapagos Islands, the famous site where Charles Darwin developed his theory of evolution. Opportunities are endless, and this chapter only scratches the surface of all that is out there.

Eco-tourism trips keep travelers busy and active. No matter where the destination is, there is always something to see and do. Even when there are few or no activities planned for a day, eco-tourists can find plenty to do, such as visiting local markets, taking photographs of the scenery and the people, or even laying in a hammock and enjoying what the environment has to offer.

Some important reasons why people go on eco-tourism vacations are to participate in conservation and preservation efforts, to learn about the flora and fauna of an area, and to become familiar with the culture of the host community. Bird watching is popular in many locations in the world. Being able to see exotic species of animals is exciting, especially if the chances of getting a second glimpse of the animal are almost impossible. Probably the most popular activity of an eco-tourism vacation is walking or hiking through parks and other designated areas, which provides excellent possibilities for travelers to experience the natural beauty that surrounds the host people, as well as to have a firsthand look at the host community and their lifestyle.

Photography is usually a welcomed hobby as well. Travelers encounter plenty of photo opportunities while on an eco-tourism trip. Pictures can be taken in just about every location and of just about anything that comes into view. However, if eco-tourists plan to photograph animals, they need to be very patient because wild animals tend to hide or move along rather quickly. They may also be afraid of bright lights, which is the reason why some parks and attractions prohibit flash photography. In addition, eco-tourists must be aware of the host community's norms for photographs; some cultures are against photos, and others might charge tourists for the opportunity to photograph community members.

Some eco-tourists take an eco-tourism vacation to study a specific issue or topic. For instance, eco-tourism is an excellent way to learn about a certain culture or reinforce learning of a new language. Other people take eco-tourism trips to find out more about a specific type of plant or animal life at the destination. Archaeologists and other scientists sometimes go on eco-tourism "vacations" to study the history and present culture of the area, as well as its development throughout its years of existence. Excavation projects are abundant in areas such as Tikal, Quintana Roo, Peru, Greece, Egypt, and other regions of the world that have a hidden mystery behind their culture. No matter what the destination or the activity, eco-tourism has a lot to offer the traveler and the host community.

FOCUS ON

Agritourism

Carla Barbieri

Many of my childhood memories come from my grandparents' farm. My cousins and I spent hours running between crop rows, picking eggplants (that we later didn't want to eat), petting baby rabbits, and watching the goats chew almost everything around them—even our jeans! While the farm was great entertainment for me, my grandparents intended it to be more than a hobby for their retirement. They were committed to making it profitable by growing a variety of specialty crops and raising animals. I don't know if my grandparents ever made those profits, but I had so much fun during my visits that I wanted to become a farmer!

That experience describes what is being called agritourism. That is, people visiting a farm or any other agricultural facility, such as a ranch, nursery, or production mill, for leisure or recreation. One important element of agritourism is that the setting should be a real working agricultural facility. Hence, if a developer stages a land as a farm to provide some recreational activities without having agricultural production, it is not really agritourism, but an agricultural-theme park.

Many activities fit within the agritourism concept and farmers have demonstrated extreme creativity through their recreational offerings. In the United States and Canada, the most common agritourism activities are farm tours; outdoor activities (e.g., hiking, bird watching, horse riding); special events (e.g., weddings, festivals); hayrides of all kinds (e.g., tractor rides, rubber-train tracks); recreational self-harvest (e.g., pick your own berries, cut your Christmas tree), and animal-related activities (e.g., petting zoos). Although many agritourism operations offer a variety of recreational activities aiming for a wide spectrum of visitors, there are also very specialized options. For example, dude ranches provide the authentic cowboy-life experience including cattle drives for their hosts; farms raise exotic game animals for hunting purposes; farms grow specialty herbs and provide an educational culinary experience (e.g., cooking with herbs). Other farms emphasize their multigenerational agricultural heritage, using historic barns, cottages, or chapels as bed and breakfasts, tasting rooms, or gift shops.

The variety of agritourism activities offered corresponds to different motivations driving farm visits. One common reason for visiting a farm relates to the image attached to rural and farming lifestyles. Some visitors romanticize the idea of living on a farm, raising a few animals, and growing their own food. Visiting a farm can give them that feeling for a while, especially when hands-on activities are offered. Time on the farm may also help some recall their childhood farming experiences and share those feelings with their loved ones. Other people are driven by the agricultural and local heritage preserved on farms. And more recently, agritourism is also attracting people interested in local food production.

Agritourism is more than another recreational option. It also provides several economic and personal benefits to farmers. Economic benefits include increase of farm revenues especially during nongrowing seasons, decrease of risks associated with agriculture such as crop damages caused by flood or late freezes, use maximization of farm resources, and increase of their market share and clientele, among others. Personal benefits include providing jobs for family members, capitalizing on an existing hobby or the excitement associated with being an entrepreneur. Further, agritourism can revitalize local communities by providing jobs for local people and stimulating visitors' expenditures in local restaurants and businesses.

Source: Courtesy of Carla Barbieri, Assistant Professor, Department of Parks, Recreation and Tourism, University of Missouri.

Ten Commandments on Eco-tourism

The American Society of Travel Agents (ASTA) suggests these 10 commandments for eco-tourism:

1. Respect the frailty of the earth. Unique and beautiful destinations may not be here for future generations unless all are willing to help in their preservation.

2. Patronize those (hotels, airlines, resorts, cruise lines, tour operators, and suppliers) who advance energy conservation; promote water and air quality; provide recycling; manage waste and toxic materials safely for people and the environment; practice noise abatement; encourage community involvement; and provide experienced, well-trained staff dedicated to strong principles of conservation.

3. Learn about and support conservation-oriented programs and organizations working to preserve the environment and local culture. Consider a volunteer vacation where you would volunteer to help the local community during a portion of your vacation.

4. Walk or use environmentally sound methods of transportation whenever possible.

5. Encourage drivers of public vehicles to stop engines when parked and not to idle.

6. Leave only footprints. Take only photographs. No graffiti! No litter! Do not take away "souvenirs" from historical sites and natural areas.

7. To make your travels more meaningful educate yourself about the geography, customs, manners, and cultures of the region you visit. Take time to listen to people. Encourage local conservation efforts.

8. Respect the privacy and dignity of others. Inquire before photographing people.

9. Do not buy products made from endangered plants or animals, such as ivory, tortoise shell, animal skins, and feathers.

10. Always follow designated trails. Do not disturb animals, plants, or their natural habitat.[26]

Travel is a natural right of all people and is a crucial ingredient of world peace and understanding. With this right comes responsibilities. ASTA encourages the growth of socially responsible, sustainable tourism and environmentally-friendly travel.

▶ Check Your Knowledge

1. What are the most popular activities for eco-tourists?
2. What are the most popular eco-tourism spots for archaeologists?

Important Eco-tourism Destinations

There is no definite or correct answer to the question of which eco-tourism destinations are best. Although good eco-tourism sites are too numerous and varied to list here, we try to highlight some of the most popular and interesting ones. Although North America may not be considered a top eco-tourism destination it has abundant national parks and unique and beautiful places such as the Everglades that are prime locations for a wide variety of eco-tourism and nature tourism activities.

Some of Central America's most popular eco-areas include the many tropical rainforests and sites of Mayan ruins. Belize and Costa Rica are often referred to as pioneers of eco-tourism because they began promoting large-scale tourism in the 1980s when eco-tourism first became popular. Belize and Costa Rica have many parks, beaches, and lush tropical forests that are protected by the government and prominent organizations such as the World Tourism Organization (WTO) and the United Nations Environment Programme (UNEP), allowing for greater conservation and preservation efforts to be practiced. Mundo Maya is one of the region's most successful eco-tourism projects. It is unique in that it is a joint endeavor of the countries in which Maya civilization was, and still is, found. These countries include Belize, El Salvador, Guatemala, Honduras, and parts of Mexico. Tourists can climb the massive stone pyramids, sit in one of the housing rooms, hike through the jungles, and watch for exotic birds and howler monkeys, among other animals. In some places, tourists can even see the coral reefs of the Caribbean coastline. The great thing about Mundo Maya is that the traveler can visit one area or country at a time, or enjoy a package featuring some or all countries and major attractions at once.

Costa Rica has, over the years, been a model of eco-tourism, with abundant natural wonders. The country contains 5 percent of the world's biodiversity within just 0.035 percent of the earth's surface. Also, large areas of the country are set aside as national parks, and there are plans to plant 5 million trees each year and become a carbon-neutral country by 2023.[27] Costa Rica has, in comparison with other countries, more of a range of eco-tourism offerings, from rustic to luxurious, from counterculture to indigenous culture, from spiritual to scientific, from purely Costa Rican to undeniably North American, from European to eclectic cross-cultural blends.[28]

The vast continent of South America also has a myriad of eco-tourism areas of growing popularity and importance. More tourists are finding their way into the lush jungles and down the Amazon River in Brazil, where they get to go on exciting and informative adventures with the local population of the Amazon. Ecuador is also becoming popular for eco-tourism.

One of the most popular eco-tourism destinations of all time, and indeed the one often cited as the place where eco-tourism originated, is the Galapagos Islands, located some 600 hundred miles off the coast of Ecuador. Interestingly, it was Charles Darwin who brought attention to the islands when he wrote about them in *On the Origin of Species by Means of Natural Selection*, published in 1859. Darwin noted that the wildlife with no natural predators were usually "tame," and that many of the islands had developed their own unique species of animals, birds, and plants.[29] The Galapagos Islands are home to hundreds of species of birds, mammals, reptiles, marine life, and plants. UNESCO declared the Galapagos a World Heritage site in 1978, which says a lot about its uniqueness and importance.[30]

Europe has been criticized for a lack of sustainability, but when we look away from the congested areas of, for example, London, Rome, and Paris, plenty of destinations focus on eco-tourism. In particular, tours to explore the ancient ruins, architecture, and cultures of Turkey and Greece are a popular choice. In addition, the largely untouched natural areas and distinctive culture of the Scandinavian countries are growing in recognition and importance.

Travelers who want to explore Asia can join an eco-tour to the snow-capped Himalayas in Nepal or the sultry jungles of Thailand. More places, such as Malaysia, Thailand, and the Philippines, are developing their tourism programs based on environmental conservation and protection. Looking for Shangri-la? The former hidden kingdom of the Hunza Valley in Pakistan has been opened for eco-tourism, allowing a select number of tourists to see the 700-year-old Hunza Fort and village. The project has been internationally acclaimed as an outstanding example of sustainable tourism.

More adventures await travelers in Africa, where the tourism industry, especially eco-tourism, has been growing tremendously over the past years. The most popular activity is the safari, which lets visitors get up close and personal with exotic wildlife including elephants, gazelles, lions, tigers, cheetahs, and countless others. Kenya is an important destination for safaris, as are Tanzania, South Africa, Botswana, and Malawi. Chumbe, a tiny island nature reserve off the coast of Tanzania, is another African hotspot. This eco-resort offers many activities. For example, travelers can snorkel the rare coral reef and explore the rag forest. At night, they can sleep in an ecologically self-sustaining hut, complete with solar panels, rainwater tanks, and a composting toilet.

Australia is home to an impressive variety of eco-friendly places, including the Great Barrier Reef, which is perhaps the most famous. The "Leave No Trace" program ensures that visitors act in a responsible manner. Visitors to the Great Barrier Reef can enjoy activities such as snorkeling, fishing, diving, hiking, camping, and much more with many certified eco-friendly companies.

The massive glaciers of Antarctica are subject to increasing interest and attention. These days, many regions of the world are designating their attractions as eco-tourism sites. Vacationers are becoming more adventurous and are visiting remote, exotic places. They are participating in activities that hopefully affect nature, host communities, and themselves in a positive manner.

From Yellowstone National Park in the United States to the Mayan Ruins of Tikal in Guatemala; from the Amazon River in Brazil to the vast safari lands of Kenya; from the snow-capped Himalayas in Nepal to the sultry jungles of Thailand;

Eco-tourists in Tanzania, Africa, can appreciate lions in their natural setting as well as several other animal species.
Irv Beckman © Dorling Kindersley

from the Great Barrier Reef in Australia to the massive ice glaciers in Antarctica—it seems that eco-tourism is taking place in all corners of the world. Some sort of eco-tourism activity is happening in almost every country of the world. A majority of these destinations are found in developing countries, and it seems only natural, considering that they are the home to exotic ecosystems.

▶ Check Your Knowledge

1. List the major important eco-tourism destinations around the world.
2. What countries in Africa provide great safaris?
3. What skills and attitudes are needed to be a sustainable tourist?

Eco-tourism Certification

A challenge that remains for eco-tourism concerns certification standards: who creates the standards and who enforces them? Who determines whether the many small eco-tourism businesses that say they are eco-friendly are, and if so, to what extent? One way to create an effective certification process is to examine **best practices** around the world and **benchmark** them. Yet, as David Weaver points out, "Conducting business in an environmental and socio-culturally sustainable way goes beyond what is required by government regulation."[31]

Australia's eco-certification program is widely regarded as the world leader in eco-tourism product certification. The program is managed by a committee of Eco-tourism Australia with a regular and an advanced level for eco-tourism accommodation, attractions, and tours. To encourage a broader ethos of sustainability, a nature tourism category is also provided.[32] Credibility within the industry and with communities and travelers is at the heart of the eco-certification program. This is maintained through the following:

- A rigorous assessment program including referees
- Ongoing review and updating of criteria to reflect the emerging and ongoing world's best practices
- Feedback from guests of certified operators
- Audits of operators including an on-site audit on the entire set of eco-certification criteria within approximately the first 12 months after initial certification[33]

An example of what can be achieved is Hidden Valley Cabins, northwest of Townsville, North Queensland, Australia's first fully carbon-neutral resort and tour business, which has achieved the Advanced Ecotourism Certification. This resort now generates all of its own renewable energy and has saved 78 tons of carbon emissions per year.[34]

Today, Green Globe is the only significant international certification program for travel companies and destinations.[35] Figure 12–5 shows the goals of Green Globe 21.

1. To encourage companies and destinations to join Green Globe 21 and thus show their commitment to sound environmental practice
2. To promote and explain the links between good environmental practice and good business practice
3. To highlight examples of industry best practice to both businesses and governments
4. To help sustain the quality of tourism for future generations

Figure 12–5 • Goals of Green Globe 21

Green Globe membership is open to any tourism business or community seeking certification for environmental sustainability in their operations. Industry professionals or providers can join as suppliers, provided that their products are environmentally sound. Consumers who want to be part of this growing worldwide environmental movement may join as travelers. Membership means extending businesses' involvement in the global environment concern, and it also encourages performance and strengthens brands for consumer recognition. Green Globe's newest development is the Green Globe 21 Path to sustainable tourism, a three-stage process (ABC) based on wise growth in response to consumers' growing interest in wise travel.

A company's status as a member depends on where it is on the Green Globe "ABC path." Affiliate membership is the first step on the path to sustainable tourism. Affiliate members have access to the Green Globe website, including information, tools, and opportunities for contact with other members, as well as a company marketing profile. Benchmarked membership is the second step. Here, companies/communities receive a sustainability assessment and assistance with their progress toward the next step. At this point, they also receive extended website access, more cost-reducing information, and an even greater market profile on the website. Certified members have successfully reached the third step by having their performance independently assessed and audited. They are also subject to regular re-audits to ensure that they maintain or improve sustainability performance levels. Certified members also receive a position on the Green Globe 21 website, providing them with marketing benefits.

Businesses desire certification because of concern for the environment and because of the marketing opportunities commensurate with being certified. The marketing advantages of credible certification are obvious. Consumers who are environmentally aware prefer being involved with companies that can show through independent assessment that they are addressing issues of environmental, social, and cultural responsibility. The certification removes the subjectivity of decision making for consumers, wholesalers, and suppliers. In addition, certification is likely to result in benefits including a reduction in operating costs through improved resource management and ensured compliance with present (and future) environmental legislation. A certified company continually shows its environmental concern because it is subject to re-audits.

Eco-tourism: Fad or Future?

How can we be sure that eco-tourism is not just another trend or fad that will pass as quickly as it came about? Several factors indicate that eco-tourism is here to stay. First and foremost, many organizations are concerning themselves with the issue of eco-tourism, including the respected United Nations, the initiator of the International Year of Ecotourism. The United Nations Environment Programme (UNEP) regularly hosts, sponsors, and collaborates on conferences and seminars on eco-tourism around the globe as well as publishes literature on the subject. The well-established World Tourism Organization (WTO) is the United Nations' partner in the organization of the International Year of Ecotourism and another supporter of the cause. In addition, a number of national and international organizations have been formed in support of eco-tourism. Some of these are the International Ecotourism Society (TIES) and Green Globe 21, as mentioned earlier, as well as the Ecotourism Association of Australia (EAA) and national eco-tourism associations in Honduras and Belize.

A growing trend is certification of eco-tourism destinations, attractions, accommodations, tour operators, guides, and so on. As mentioned, Green Globe 21 offers a certification program, as does the Ecotourism Association of Australia, whose Nature and Eco Certification Program aims to identify and certify genuine nature and eco-tourism operations. In addition to certification, there is a growing emphasis on developing knowledgeable eco-tourism professionals. Universities around the world have begun to offer degrees and courses in the subject. In the United States, students can study eco-tourism at several universities.

As a result of this growing awareness, more and more destinations and countries are basing their tourism master plans on the principles of eco-tourism. The Tourism Authority of Thailand (TAT) proposed in its master plan for the popular island of Koh Samui that the number of visitors be controlled so as not to exceed 950,000 people per year so that tourism does not exceed the island's carrying capacity.[36] On the other side of the world, the Association of Caribbean States has declared the Caribbean region as a sustainable tourism zone. We can only hope that more nations will follow suit.

Greenwashing

Irresponsible use of the term *eco-tourism* and destructive environmental practices have been called "greenwashing" or "eco-tourism lite." Green Globe offers a path to **sustainable tourism**, through which companies are audited, assessed, and then certified as green. However, many times members of, say, for example, the Ecotourism Society or Partners in **Responsible Tourism** only need to pay a membership fee and sign a pledge to be able to claim their operations are eco-friendly. So, serious eco-tourists must beware of greenwashing when choosing a destination. Stamped and certified or not, many destinations profit in the eco-tourism wave by designating their attractions as eco-tourism sites.

Surprisingly, countries such as Costa Rica, Ecuador, Belize, Nicaragua, and Panama serve as good examples of where greenwashing flourished. As these nations started to enjoy the benefits of a booming tourism industry that generated a "green destination" image, they experienced a negative consequence as unscrupulous developers started to abuse the image. Those developers could count on the politicians of the new government, whom they could easily seduce and corrupt with their lucrative business capital.[37]Greenwashing occurred at some of Costa Rica's most outstanding destinations. As a result, they began to show the typical symptoms of decline, such as being rejected by tour operators and tourists, who decided not to return or not to recommend the destinations because "they are not the same anymore."[38]

Few eco-tourism locations are fully established and, with the lack of role models, it is very difficult for tourism entities to know how to run such unique accommodations. Often those who plan an eco-tourism destination must use their imagination. Two examples are Mr. Selengut's Harmony and Maho Bay Camps. Selengut is a conservation-minded man, and when he purchased land in the U.S. Virgin Islands, he decided to go with the flow of nature and not the flow of the "traditional" tourism industry. All of his resorts are (he says) made of entirely recycled products and decorated with local art. But, in reality, the Maho and Concordia aren't made of recycled products; only Harmony is in eco-tents at least to some degree and decorated with Peruvian art.[39] Activities include guided tours, bird watching, botany lessons, rock climbing, mountain biking, kayaking, and more.

Each destination should develop its own master plan. What may work for one region may not work for another. Development plans must take into consideration the natural habitat of the destination, the activities and services available, and the type of eco-tourists who are the target market. Not all eco-tourists are attracted to a particular site. Thus, careful planning of the industry located at each destination must be undertaken when marketing the eco-tourism site. Demographic and psychographic studies are also useful and recommended. This information can be used to guide decisions related to product/service additions, deletions, and modifications.

Comparative master planning is key. With this type of planning, many major resort developments set the mood for hotel groups expanding internationally. This is important because many of these groups are venturing into prime eco-tourism spots. Many resorts have firsthand knowledge of the environment and culture, including the business culture of the region. In turn, the hotel groups use the resorts, including them on itineraries so as to carve a niche in international eco-tourism.

Tour operators are also essential when promoting eco-tourism packages because some eco-tourists want a tour organized for them rather than doing it all themselves. However, not all "eco"-tour operators are reliable. The best are operators or travel agents who are recognized by well-known organizations such as the International Ecotourism Society or Conservation International. Some organizations may even have their own tour operators. Many organizations have started to offer language study programs in eco-tourism destinations, which opens eco-tourism to language students and allows them to gain hands-on experience using the language in real life outside of their studies. Last but not least, colleges and universities now offer degrees in eco-tourism. Many of these schools are located in countries with developed eco-tourism programs such as Costa Rica, Canada, and Australia.

Guidelines for Eco-tourism Development

Nina Rao and K.T. Surish suggest the following guidelines for developing eco-tourism[40]:

1. Create a tourist product that is desirable and supported by an integrated infrastructure.
2. Involve all agencies, public, private and not-for-profit NGOs, and government, in tourism development.
3. Create synergy between departments and agencies that have to deliver the composite tourist product.
4. Use both the people's participation through local bodies, NGOs, and youth organizations to create greater awareness of tourism.
5. Create access for destinations off the beaten track.
6. Diversify the product with new options such as beach tourism, forests, wild life, landscapes, adventure tourism, farm tourism, and health tourism.
7. Maintain a balance between the negative and positive aspects of tourism through planning restrictions and through education of the people for conservation and development.

Although these guidelines were developed for Bangalore, they can be applied to any eco-tourism development.

Eco-tourism Standards and Compliance

After several years of eco-tourism development, the process toward rationalizing, harmonizing, and assessing the various certification schemes and building support for an accreditation body for the tourism industry began in 2000, at the first ever tourism certification workshop held at Mohonk Mountain House outside of New York City.[41] There, 45 experts from 20 countries crafted the framework for eco-tourism certification programs.[42] Costa Rica, one of the leading eco-tourism countries, has developed a government Certification for Sustainable Tourism (CST) program. The criteria are primarily performance based but also include International Organization for Standardization–like environmental management system criteria for assessing the physical plant. The criteria consist of 152 questions in the following four general categories:

- Biological and physical surroundings (including questions about emissions and waste, policies and programs, green zones, and protection of flora and fauna)
- Physical plant (including, for instance, management policies, water and energy consumption, waste management, and staff training)

- Customers (including guest facilities and instructions, management of groups, and feedback)
- Social-economic environment (including direct and indirect economic benefits, contributions to cultural development and health, and security)

Each question is weighted on a scale and a formula is used to calculate the final score in each of the four general areas. Auditing is done by a team of inspectors (auditors) with various professional specialties. First, they make an initial site visit, during which they explain the CST program, give managers a manual containing evaluation guidelines, and go over the questionnaire. Then, inspectors return a month or two later for a formal assessment, which is documented.

Geotourism

Geotourism, a term coined by NATGEO in 2008, is the cousin of eco-tourism. Geotourism is defined as tourism that sustains or enhances the geographical character of a place—its environment, culture, aesthetics, heritage, and the well-being of its residents.[43] Whereas eco-tourists are crazy about wildlife and charismatic megafauna and travel the world to see the most incredible animal migrations, geotourists are concerned with the local people and insist that they remain completely unchanged by visitors. For example, in the Kingdom of Bhutan, the king doesn't allow many visitors. Visitors are allowed to enter the kingdom only with a guide, must pay up front $250 per day, and must wear traditional dress daily.

Carbon Footprints and Carbon Offsets

A **carbon footprint** is the total greenhouse gases emitted by a person, company, event, or product. A **carbon offset** is a financial device used to lower the amount of carbon emissions. Examples of greenhouse gases include carbon dioxide ($CO2$), methane, and ozone. Carbon dioxide is the major contributor to global warming (i.e., climate change). When a car is driven, it puts off greenhouse gases. When electricity is used, it puts off greenhouse gases. In fact, most activities that use resources put off greenhouse gases, even the production of a cheeseburger! Several steps can be taken to decrease a carbon footprint, including the following:

- Recycling
- Decreasing use of plastic bags and using "green" bags
- Adjusting thermostats and water heaters to use less energy
- Only running full loads of dishes and laundry
- Eating locally
- Reducing bottled water use; filter your own

- Switching to a more fuel efficient vehicle
- Using public transportation
- Carpooling
- Paying attention to amounts of product packaging (avoiding unnecessary packaging)

A plethora of calculators are available on the Internet that calculate a carbon footprint and give suggestions on how to reduce it.

▶ **Check Your Knowledge**

1. List some of the major organizations that are concerned with the issue of eco-tourism.
2. What factors need to be considered in a country's tourism master plan?

CASE STUDY

Sustainable Tourism Planning

Lucy and Albert have inherited *Linda*, a 25-acre tract of undeveloped land within a pristine tropical forest and surrounded by beautiful landscapes. A creek running through the property provides water to many exotic wild animals, including colorful butterflies, insects and birds, different species of monkeys, wild pigs, and occasionally jaguars. The Tuckies, a small native community that has inhabited this forest for several generations, live within walking distance of Linda. Tuckies have very limited contact with Western civilization, mainly because accessing this place requires three hours of travel by river, then two hours walking through natural trails.

Lucy and Albert have decided to develop a tourism project in Linda and provide a complete "exotic" experience for small groups of tourists. They are planning to clear 10 acres of the land to build a 20-room lodge following Tuckies architectural style to blend into the surrounding landscape. They will build a one-lane road connecting the river to Linda to bring resistant building materials from a major city. Although the road will be a large expense, it will make the place more accessible for city visitors. Albert and Lucy plan to keep the Tuckies informed of their major project decisions and to involve them in different ways. For example, they will hire some Tuckies to build the lodge under the supervision of a city builder and two community members for housekeeping and guiding services. Tuckies working in the lodge will be dressed in their traditional attire to provide local authenticity.

The recreational experience at Linda will be packaged as an "all-inclusive" deal covering lodging, food, and entertainment for six days. Entertainment will include several water-based activities on the creek, including canoeing, water slides, and a wet bar; unlimited excursions to the surrounding forests, and regular visits to the Tuckies village to experience their traditional lifestyle. Lucy and Albert have decided to donate 10 percent of their annual profits to the Tuckies to show them their good will.

Given that Albert and Lucy are very concerned with sustainable development, they have hired you as a consultant to oversee their ideas and planning.

C A S E   S T U D Y *(continued)*

Questions

1. Discuss whether Linda tourism development would be sustainable considering the economic, environmental, and social dimensions of sustainability.
2. Identify and explain the following:
   a. Good practices of sustainability
   b. Issues that would affect sustainability of this project
   c. Actions to make the project (more) sustainable

Source: Courtesy of Carla Barbieri, University of Missouri.

Summary

1. Eco-tourism is defined as "responsible travel to natural areas that conserves the environment and sustains the well-being of local people." In the last few decades, there has been a major increase in interest and participation in eco-tourism.
2. Tourism, if excessive, puts a lot of pressure on local resources, superstructure, and infrastructure. It can also be harmful to local cultures and ecosystems. The responsibility for avoiding this lies with governments, involved businesses, and tourists.
3. There are many examples of government actions that have proven successful, such as placing height restrictions on buildings in an area. There are also many examples when this has failed, including the development of the popular destination Cancun, Mexico.
4. Eco-tourism has three core criteria: an emphasis on nature-based attractions, learning opportunities, and management practices.
5. The principal characteristics that comprise eco-tourism are shown in Figure 12–3.
6. The concept of carrying capacity refers to the maximum number of tourists that an area can receive before there is an unacceptable decline.
7. The average eco-tourist is 35 to 54 years old, a college graduate, traveling as a couple, and stays for 8–14 days. Furthermore, eco-tourists prefer to stay in small accommodations run by local people, and most of them are looking for wilderness settings, the opportunity to view wildlife, or an area where they can participate in hiking or trekking.
8. Popular activities for eco-tourists include hiking, scuba diving and snorkeling, photographing, and participating in conservation and preservation efforts.
9. Popular eco-tourism destinations include Belize and Costa Rica in Central America, Nepal and Thailand in Asia, Turkey and Greece in Europe, various national parks in the United States, Brazil and Ecuador in South America, Kenya and Tanzania in Africa, and the Great Barrier Reef in Australia.

10. The Bar Harbor Declaration on Eco-tourism in the United States was the first eco-tourism conference. The declaration made several recommendations on sustainable practices.
11. Important current trends in eco-tourism include extensive interest from many international associations and organizations, certification of eco-tourism destinations, more universities offering education in the subject, and increased awareness by governments, which has led to many countries basing their tourism master plans on eco-tourism principles.

Key Words and Concepts

benchmark
best practices
capacity requirement
carbon footprint

carbon offset
comparative master planning
eco-tourism

responsible tourism
safari
sustainable tourism

Review Questions

1. Who are eco-tourists? How do they differ from other tourists? How are they similar?
2. In what activities do eco-tourists participate?
3. What are the current important eco-tourism destinations? Why do you think this is? What places do you foresee being important eco-tourism destinations in the future and why? Explain your reasoning.
4. Describe agritourism.
5. What impact does tourism have on the environment? In what ways can this impact be lessened? Explain your reasoning.
6. What are the fundamental principles of eco-tourism?
7. Describe the evolution of eco-tourism in Costa Rica.
8. What recommendations did the Bar Harbor declaration make?
9. Some observers take a strong position against eco-tourism, saying that it is mostly tourism companies saying that they are eco when they are not. Argue against this position.

Interesting Websites

Center for Responsible Travel:
   www.responsibletravel.org
Global Exchange: www.globalexchange.org
Green Globe: www.greenglobe.org
The International Ecotourism Society:
   www.ecotourism.org

World Tourism Organization:
   www.world-tourism.org
World Wildlife Fund: www.wwf.org

Internet Exercises

1. What activities may eco-tourism include that are not mentioned in the book? Use your imagination and the definition of eco-tourism, do some quick research on the Internet, and see what you can come up with.

2. Go to the website of the International Ecotourism Society (www.ecotourism.org). What are the newest hot spots in eco-tourism? What are their specialties and what are they known for?

Apply Your Knowledge

Select an area or an attraction and create an eco-tourism plan.

Suggested Activity

Research a country and assess its eco-tourism offerings.

Endnotes

1. Hector Caballo-Lascurian, "Eco-tourism's 25th Anniversary," www.borneotours.com/eco-tourism.bak/ (accessed February 14, 2009).

2. David Weaver, *Eco-tourism*, 2nd ed. (Milton, Queensland, Australia: Wiley, 2008), 17.

3. Amanda Stronza, "Through a New Mirror: Reflections on Tourism and Identity in the Amazon," *Human Organization* 67, no. 3 (Fall 2008): 244.

4. Rainforest Expeditions, "Discover Peru's Finest Amazon Lodges in Peru," www.perunature.com (accessed September 21, 2009).

5. Ibid.

6. World Tourism Organization, "Tourism: A Force for Sustainable Development" (19th OSCE Economic Forum, Prague, Czech Republic, June 2, 2004).

7. Lisa Mastny, *Treading Lightly: New Paths for International Tourism,* Worldwatch Paper 159 (Washington, DC: Worldwatch Institute, December 2001), 15.

8. U.N. Council on Trade and Development, quoted in Patricia Goldstone, *Making the World Safe for Tourism* (New Haven, CT: Yale University Press, 2001), 46.

9. David Fennell and David Weaver, "The Eco-tourism Concept and Tourism-Conservation Symbiosis," *Journal of Sustainable Tourism* 13, no. 4 (2005): 373–390.

10. Ibid.

11. Ibid.

12. Geoffrey Wall, "Carrying Capacity," in *The Encyclopedia of Tourism*, ed. Jafar Jafari (London: Routledge, 2000), 72.

13. Ibid.

14. Robert B. Powell and Sam H. Ham, "Can Eco-tourism Interpretation Really Lead to Pro-Conservation Knowledge, Attitudes and Behaviour? Evidence from the Galapagos Islands," *Journal of Sustainable Tourism* 16, no. 4 (2008): 468.

15. Ibid.

16. S. Ham and B. Weiler, "Interpretation as the Centerpiece of Sustainable Wildlife Tourism," in *Sustainable Tourism: A Global Perspective*, ed. R. Harris, T. Griffen and P. Williams (Oxford: Elsevier Science, 2002), 35–44, as cited in Powell and Ham, "Can Eco-tourism Interpretation Really Lead to Pro-Conservation Knowledge, Attitudes and Behaviour?" 468.

17. Wanjohi Kibicho, "Community-Based Tourism: A Pathway to Sustainability for Japan's Protected Areas," *Journal of Sustainable Tourism* 16, no. 2 (2008): 211.

18. David A. Ferrell, "Eco-tourism and the Myth of Indigenous Stewardship," *Journal of Sustainable Tourism* 16, no. 2 (2008): 144.

19. International Eco-tourism Society, website, www.eco-tourism.org (accessed March 12, 2009).
20. Ibid.
21. Ibid.
22. Ibid.
23. Ibid.
24. Ibid.
25. Ibid.
26. American Society of Travel Agents, "Ten Commandments on Eco-Tourism," www.gdrc.org/uem/eco-tour/10-command.html (accessed March 6, 2009).
27. Martha Honey, *Eco-tourism and Sustainable Development: Who Owns Paradise?* (Washington, DC: Island Press, 2008), 161.
28. Ibid.
29. Ibid., 122.
30. United Nations Educational, Scientific and Cultural Organization, "Galapagos Islands," http://whc.unesco.org/en/list/1 (accessed November 23, 2008).
31. Weaver, *Eco-tourism*, 169.
32. Ibid.
33. Eco-tourism Australia, "Eco-tourism Certification Program," www.eco-tourism.org.au/eco_certification.asp (accessed July 4, 2009).
34. www.hiddenvalleycabins.com.au (accessed July 4, 2009).
35. Honey, *Eco-tourism and Sustainable Development*, 47.
36. Third World Network, "Eco-tourism: An Ecological and Economic Trap for Third World Countries," *The Region* 7, no. 5 (September–October 2001, www.twnside.org.sg/title/nf75.htm (accessed September 1, 2006).
37. Marco Vinicio Garcia, " 'Eco': Sustainable or Responsible: How Shall We Look at the New Paradigm of Tourism," *Contours* 17/18, no. 1 (January 2008): 134–138.
38. Ibid.
39. Personal correspondence with Dr. Martha Honey, July 10, 2009.
40. This section draws on: Martha Honey, "Protecting Eden; Setting Green Standards for the Tourism Industry," *Environment Washington* 45, no. 6 (July/August 2003), 8.
41. Ibid.
42. The Mohonk Agreement is available at www.rainforest-alliance.org/tourism/documents/mohonk.pdf.
43. Center for Sustainable Destinations, "About Geotourism," www.nationalgeographic.com/travel/sustainable/about_geotourism.html (accessed September 21, 2009).

PART 5

Operating Sectors 2

C H A P T E R 13

Tourism Distribution Organizations

OBJECTIVES

After reading and studying this chapter, you should be able to:

- Discuss the role of tourism distribution organizations.

- Describe the role of the Internet as a part of the distribution system.

- Describe the purpose of the American Society of Travel Agents (ASTA) and list its member services as well as requirements.

- Explain the functions of the Airlines Reporting Corporation (ARC).

- Discuss airfares and give examples of their complexities.

- Name the most common **computerized reservation systems**.

- Describe and identify the main types of tours, major tour operators, and wholesalers.

- Identify important current trends in the distribution of travel and tourism.

GEOGRAPHY SPOTLIGHT

Sea, Sand, and Sun Tourism: Chile

Bordered by the Atacama Desert in the north, the *pistas de esquí* in Patagonia, the Andes Mountains in the east, and a fertile central valley, Viña del Mar, Chile's premier beach destination, is located in west central Chile. Viña del Mar, often simply called Viña, was founded on December 29, 1874, by Jose Francisco Vergara Echevers and has grown into Chile's most luxurious beach retreat, attracting visitors from around the world.[1] This weekend retreat and garden residence has become a playground for the wealthy elite from Valparaíso and Santiago, and it has remained a top beach destination for Santiaguinos since its inception.[2]

Viña's peak months for tourism are December, January, and February, although Antarctic currents make swimming a chilly activity.[3] However, there are bold visitors who swim, no matter what. There are at least nine beaches that are popular with visitors to Viña including Playa Caleta Abarca, which is in the center of town, and one of the city's principal beaches. There is a cove surrounding this beach, protecting swimmers from the area's rip currents. This beach becomes crowded during the summer months because of the proximity to many of the city's main lodging establishments. Children are welcome at this beach, as evidenced by the playgrounds dotting the surrounding areas. Furthermore, a nearby discotheque offers nighttime entertainment for beachgoers. This beach has something for every visitor.

Playa Acapulco is a long strip along the coast, which is identified by its coarse sands and gentle waves. Its proximity to the center of Viña del Mar and the restaurant sector has made this beach one of Chile's

GEOGRAPHY SPOTLIGHT *(continued)*

Geoff Renner, Robert Harding World Imagery

most popular beach destinations. Playa Acapulco is entertaining to those who enjoy long walks on the beach—the best time to walk is during sunset.[5]

Playa Mirasol, which is also known as the "family hangout," includes a pedestrian walkway, complete with gardens and a handcrafts market. Because of the smooth streets around this beach, visitors may see roller skaters weaving in and out of the weekend crowds.[6]

Playa Las Salinas is a popular beach for experienced surfers, body boarders, and adventure seekers.[7] The surf is far too rough for leisurely swimming, but it is an exciting location for those looking to walk along the beach and admire the skills of surfers brave enough to battle the waters.

During the summer months, Los Marineros is filled with sun-worshipers. In the fall, winter, and spring, this beach is wonderful for strolling and fishing. There is also a playground nearby, making this a family beach. Furthermore, the beach is dotted with the Chilean Navy's antiquated artillery. Much like Playa Las Salinas, this beach is not ideal for those looking for an easy swim. Rip currents are potentially lethal to most swimmers who venture too far from the coast.[8]

Cochoa is another family-preferred beach. This beach is most popular with families that have small children. This beach is protected by a peninsula, which makes the waters calm and safe for those looking to relax in the water. Cochoa is quite popular during the summer because of convenient parking facilities, playgrounds, and a selection of restaurants across the street.[9]

Playa Amarilla was once one of the most exclusive beach communities because of the distance between it and the city center. However, an increase in public transportation has made this beach one of the most popular beaches in the Chilean Riviera. This is because of the developing urban area around the beach, the size of the beach, and its proximity to shopping and dining opportunities. This urban growth includes lodging facilities, which may now be rented at reasonable rates, drawing a considerably larger crowd.[10]

Overall, Viña del Mar is the clear choice for beachgoers throughout Chile and the world. This area is well suited for everyone from families with children to adventure seekers looking to battle the waves. Viña offers modern amenities throughout, but maintains an Old World charm. There is something for everyone in Viña del Mar, Chile.

Endnotes

1. Vina y Valpo, "About Viña del Mar, Chile," www.vinayvalpo.com/general/contact.html?client=ayr (accessed September 27, 2008).
2. Chile-Travel.com, "Viña del Mar in Chile's Central Region," www.chile-travel.com/vinamar.htm (accessed May 3, 2009).
3. Trip Advisor, "Visiting Vina del Mar, Chile," www.tripadvisor.com/Tourism-g295425-Vina_del_Mar-Vacations.html (accessed September 27, 2008).

(continued)

GEOGRAPHY SPOTLIGHT   *(continued)*

4. Wcities, "Playa Caleta Abarca," www.wcities.com/en/record/155,128519/306/record.html (accessed September 26, 2008).

5. About.com, "Vina del Mar Neighborhood Guide," http://gosouthamerica.about.com/gi/dynamic/offsite.htm?zi=1/XJ&sdn=gosouthamerica&cdn=travel&tm=548&gps=239_1357_1020_587&f=22&su=p284.9.336.ip_p531.50.336.ip_&tt=11&bt=0&bts=0&zu=http%3A//travel.yahoo.com/p-travelguide-94897-festival_de_vina_del_mar_vina_del_mar_attractions-I (accessed September 26, 2008).

6. Ibid.

7. Wanna Surf, "Las Salinas: Chile, Central Santiago," www.wannasurf.com/spot/South_America/Chile/Central_Santiago/las_salinas/index.html (accessed September 27, 2008).

8. About.com, "Vina del Mar Neighborhood Guide."

9. Ibid.

10. Ibid.

The marketing term **channels of distribution** applies to tourism. As with many other businesses, the company offering the service cannot always reach or interact with the consumer as cost effectively as when using an intermediary. For example, assume that we wanted to go on a trip to Europe. We could make lots of individual contacts with the airlines and all the hotels in the various cities, but it would likely work out to be a more expensive trip compared to a group tour organized by a tour wholesaler.

Distribution is increasingly recognized as a critical source of competitive advantage in the marketing mix.[1] According to Rosenbloom, Larsen, and Smith, the reason for this is straightforward[2]—"It has become too difficult to hold onto a competitive edge via product, pricing and promotional strategies. Yet, significant structural changes have occurred in the tourism distribution industry as **consolidation** and **vertical integration** have become more pronounced as technological change and evolving consumer preferences are driving travel patterns to more multichannel distribution with online channels."[3]

The purpose of the channels of distribution is to bring clients and providers together so that they can communicate the information necessary for making a purchase decision and then execute the process of the purchase. There are **direct and indirect channels of distribution**. Direct channels are when a product or service is sold directly to the client as with a phone call to an airline, cruise line, attraction, or hotel. An indirect channel of distribution is when the client goes through an intermediary to purchase the product or service as with a client using the Internet to book a flight. Figure 13–1 shows the travel distribution system.

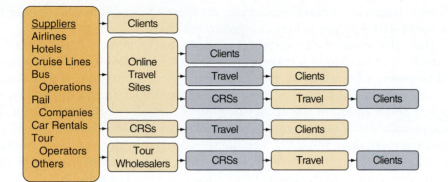

Figure 13–1 • The Travel Distribution System

Retail Travel Agents as Intermediaries in the Distribution of Travel and Tourism

Do you know the quickest way to get from Key West, Florida, to Hong Kong, China? What about the cheapest way of traveling around the world? Or the prices of and how to rent a car in London? How can you easily and painlessly find out, without having to give out your credit card number to multiple online services? The answer is as easy as it is obvious—the travel agent!

The travel agent is an important part of the **travel distribution system,** the link in a series of events that stimulate travel and make it convenient and satisfying. Ideally, the agent is a well-traveled professional who is up-to-date on schedules, accommodations, entertainment, and costs. This is not always easy because the industry is constantly changing, but it is important nonetheless. Travel agents who keep abreast of the industry and are aware of current trends are best able to meet their clients' needs. They need knowledge of the industry when attempting to locate the right product or service for a client. The travel agent acts as a consultant and sales intermediary for airlines, hotels, railroads, car rental companies, and cruise ships. Furthermore, the agent books tours and may package some tours for the agency's own account.

The travel agent is responsible to the client and, in a special relationship, to the carriers and other suppliers from which they receive a commission. Traditionally, commissions were the main source of income for travel agents. However, this changed a few years ago, and commissions from airlines, which were traditionally 10 percent of the ticket price, have now been greatly reduced or, for most airlines, canceled completely. Also, hotels are increasingly reducing or cutting commissions, which has caused a need for travel agents to seek new, creative ways of making money. The commissions paid by rail, bus, car rentals, cruises, and package tours remain about the same (10–15 percent of cost). Today, most travel agents rely on these commissions plus service fees (of about $10–$20 per ticket) charged to the client.

Does this mean the travel agent makes a lot of money? Later, we take a closer look at the life of a travel agent. The average travel agent is the owner and employee of a relatively small business. These agents have only a modest income, although the work is quite demanding. Experience, sales ability, and the size and location of the agency determine the salary of a travel agent. The median annual earnings of travel agents today is $29,210, while the top 10 percent earn more than $46,270.[4] The job is exciting, but the agent will probably never get rich. Many agents do not even enjoy such common benefits as medical or dental insurance, sick leave or vacation pay! They do, however, occasionally enjoy such perks as inexpensive travel and being able to travel widely. A typical American travel agency has annual sales of about $3–$4 million; a full-time staff of four to seven people; and a mixture of travel sales including cruises, package tours, hotel reservations, airline tickets, car rentals, and some rail tickets.

In the United States, over the past decade, the number of travel agencies has decreased from about 35,000 to approximately 20,000 travel agencies. According to the U.S Department of Labor, Bureau of Labor Statistics, the employment of travel agents is expected to experience little to no future growth. Employment of travel agents is expected to change little through 2016. Travel agents who specialize in a travel destination, type of traveler, or mode of transportation will have the best chances for success.[5] The largest agencies today are American Express, Carlson Wagonlit, and Navigant International. Thousands of people go into travel education, many with the expectation of going into the business. Some are motivated by the possibility of travel, whereas others want an income-producing sideline. The major incentives are occasional free airline tickets as well as discounts on travel, lodging, and cruises.

In today's economy, discounts are becoming commonplace. Ruthanne Terrero, editorial director of *Travel Agent* magazine, suspects deals in the marketplace will continue across the board for some time "as retailers try to navigate this muddled economic landscape."[6] She emphasizes the importance of suppliers maintaining integrity in the tough economic times: "During tough financial times, it's important that retailers and suppliers take care not to erode the integrity of their product by discounting too much. I'm hearing from travel agents that some of the cruise lines are overdoing it with what appears to be bottomless discounting. I'm surprised this is occurring because I'm sure those in question will find that it's difficult to return to more realistic pricing when the scene improves."[7]

Regardless of the economic crunch, the U.S. Department of Commerce recently announced that international visits to the United States is up 10 percent for 2008. During the first seven months of 2008, the United States welcomed 29.3 million international visitors, who spent $83.5 billion![8]

A travel agent is a businessperson that sells travel expenses. A more descriptive term would be travel *advisor* or *consultant*. Agents are entrepreneurs in the sense that they are usually in business for themselves (most work on commission) and professionals because they have the skills and training to draw on a particular body of knowledge in a meaningful way to help travelers find pleasure, convenience, and the prices and experiences they want.

A good agent is both a personal counselor and an expert in the art and science of travel. Agents not only know the advantages and disadvantages of various modes of travel, their cost, and their schedules, but in many cases they can advise customers in methods that adjust travel services to fit personality. As a professional, the agent must follow a code of ethics, which may not always favor him or her financially. For example, because travel agents' commission is usually based on what they sell, the harder they work to find travelers a lower price, the less money they actually make.

Description of the Travel Agent's or Travel Manager's Job

The successful travel agent's range of knowledge needs to be wide and constantly growing. A job description usually includes most or all of the following elements:

Travel agents can arrange trips to exotic destinations such as Bodrum, Turkey.
Courtesy of Mark Green

- Preparing individual, preplanned itineraries, personally escorted tours and group tours, and selling prepared package tours.

- Arranging for hotel, motel, or resort accommodations, meals, car rentals, sightseeing tours, transfers of passengers and luggage between terminals and hotels, and entrance to special attractions such as music festivals and the theater.

- Handling and advising on the many details involved in modern-day travel such as travel and baggage insurance, language study material, traveler's checks, auto garages, foreign currency exchange, document requirements (visas and passports), and health requirements (immunization and other inoculations).

- Using professional know-how and experience to provide information on such things as schedules of train connections, rate and quality of hotels, whether rooms have baths, and whether their rates include local taxes and gratuities. This saves the traveler from spending days or weeks making phone calls and writing letters to secure this information at considerable cost and the possibility of inaccuracy.

- Arranging reservations for special interest activities such as religious pilgrimages, sporting trips, gourmet tours, conventions, and business travel.

Dreaming up ideal vacations for clients, sending people to exotic locales, and dealing with regular clients who bring back photos and souvenirs for their agent are nice perks of the job.

▶ **Check Your Knowledge**

1. List some skills needed to succeed as a travel agent.

2. What are characteristics of a typical travel agency according to the American Society of Travel Agents?

3. Approximately how many travel agencies are there currently in the United States?

The American Society of Travel Agents

To promote travel and related activities agents formed an association. Founded in 1931 as the American Steamship and Tourist Agents' Association, the American Society of Travel Agents (ASTA) has improved and expanded with the increasing need for professional travel planning. Today, ASTA is the world's largest association of travel agents and has more than 24,000 members including travel agencies and suppliers, such as cruise lines, hotels, tours, and car rental agencies. In addition, ASTA has membership categories for students, travel schools, retail travel sellers, and others.[9] The mission statement of the organization is: "To enhance the professionalism and profitability of member agents through effective representation in industry and government affairs, education and training, and by identifying and meeting the needs of the traveling public." ASTA offers many benefits to its members, as well as to the public. Around the world the ASTA logo is a symbol of professionalism and integrity, and it is often used by media as a measure of a travel agent's reliability.[10]

The future of travel agents does not look good. They face the problems that increasingly more people choose to book trips online instead of through an agent. Use of online or e-business is spreading throughout the service industries quickly. Firms that adopt this innovative way of selling and delivering services and managing customer relationships must make technological and strategic changes. Firms in the same industry adopt e-business at different rates.[11] An even worse threat to travel agents occurred in the 1990s when the airlines cut the commissions they pay to agents, and in many cases eliminated them completely. Other sectors of the industry are following suit as are hotels, which now encourage guests to book their rooms directly through the hotel company's website. Leading industry experts predict that the worsening economic conditions will spark a spate of closures and consolidation among travel firms.[12] These obstacles have forced many agencies to charge service fees to customers, which is another incentive for customers to use free online services instead of travel agents.

Travel agencies, especially small and medium-sized companies that make up the majority, are struggling to survive, and many experts believe that a vast number will be forced out of business. These businesses have had to improve service and offer more services to their clients. They must be more flexible in their offerings to potential customers to keep up with the online competition. Peter Long, chief executive of Tui Travel, states, "For companies to be successful they need to ensure they are operating with strong financials, have flexible and diverse business models, listen to customer needs and deliver excellent customer service."[13]

Some segments still pay commissions, for example, cruise lines and tour operators; so one idea is for travel agents to focus on selling these items. Also, many people still prefer human interaction rather than computers, so agents must be personable, helpful, and a "right-hand man" as another way to keep business going. Some agents have turned to the segment of luxury clients. Other agencies have started to participate in so-called cross-border ticketing. By cooperating with agencies in countries or areas where commissions are still paid, both the domestic and the foreign agency can earn money from the non-commission-paying airlines. Agencies in, for example, Bahamas, Argentina, Mexico, and Australia are booking U.S. tickets with commission. This, of course, is not appreciated among the airlines.

▶ Check Your Knowledge

1. What different types of memberships does the American Society of Travel Agents offer?
2. What are the major benefits of ASTA membership for travel agents?

Consolidators

Travel consolidators work to make airfares more attractive to travelers, and thereby increase the number of people traveling. Consolidators sell both to travel agencies and/or directly to the public. It works like this: airlines ideally prefer to sell all their tickets at full price on their own websites, but because that does not happen, they sell blocks of discounted seats to consolidators, who in turn sell seats to the general public. Airlines discount and sell blocks of seats like this because otherwise the seats would likely remain unsold. Consolidators and the airline tickets they offer make it possible for travelers to save hundreds of dollars on one round-trip ticket.

Travel agents usually work closely with air consolidators. Linda Furry, president of United States Air Consolidation Association (USACA), states, "It's vitally important for agents to have a relationship with a trusted consolidator. This relationship is crucial when selling international air tickets and gaining access to deeply discounted airfares. Finally, an agent needs to take advantage of the high-tech booking tools that are offered by some consolidators that help agents find the best airfares."[14]

Tours

Typical travel agents book different kinds of tours. Examples include the following:

- *Special interest tours*—Special interest tours are package tours that are designed to fit the requirements of a particular group of travelers, for example, gourmets, adventure travelers, students, or art lovers. Package tours may be either escorted or unescorted. They are advertised in brochures that contain the cost, terms, and conditions of the offered package.

- *Escorted tours*—Escorted tours are all inclusive, and every detail is handled by an experienced tour director who travels with the group.

- *Foreign independent tours (FIT) and domestic independent tours (DIT)*— These more flexible tours enable the traveler to purchase an arranged package with transportation, transfers, sightseeing, hotel accommodations, and usually some meals, but the tourist does not travel with a group led by a tour director. Sightseeing excursions may or may not be arranged. The predetermined cost allows the traveler to budget most expenses in advance. The basic advantage of a package tour is convenience. Also, because the package is arranged by a specialist who buys in large volume, the suppliers— hotels, sightseeing companies, and others—are anxious to please the tour director by providing high-quality service for those who have bought the package. In addition, tour operators are usually able to offer packages at a lower price than if each service was purchased individually. (This is more completely explained in the following section on tour wholesalers.)

- *Group inclusive tours (GIT)*—A group inclusive tour is usually composed of 15 or more people traveling together who are members of a club, business organization, or other affiliated group, and who have pooled their purchasing power to realize savings, particularly on transportation. These tours are offered to almost any destination.

Tour Wholesalers

The tour business is growing rapidly and constitutes a major part of many agents' work and income. Wholesalers package tours for a country or an area, and then sell them to retail travel agents wherever possible. The wholesaler may have offices in other countries as well and sell directly to the public. If a market area does not justify setting up a complete office there, the wholesaler may arrange to be represented in that area. The best-known tour wholesalers are the Thomas Cook and American Express companies. A large percentage of all overseas tour expenditures are for tours that have been put together by fewer than 100 tour wholesalers in North America. These wholesalers negotiate directly with airlines, shipping lines, hotels, restaurants, and other travel-affiliated services and use them to assemble packages. The tours are then sold to travel agents, who, in turn, sell them to tourists.

The benefit to tourists is that they can take advantage of much lower prices for a European or Asian tour than if they were to contact the airlines and hotels directly. The wholesaler is able to negotiate big discounts based on the number of tourists they package tours for. Another advantage for tourists is that they do not really have to worry about ground transportation—how to get from the airport to the hotel—which hotel they will stay at, or where the good restaurants are: it's all planned out for them. Even airlines and motor coach operators have packages available to offer via their websites and mailings to previous passengers.

Tour Operators

Another major component of the travel industry is the one of **tour operators**. Tour operators can be local, national, or international. They are companies that arrange every aspect of a travel package. Tour operators bring together all the elements of a trip for travelers or for groups of travelers: airplane reservations and tickets, hotel reservations, ground transportation, entertainment, and more. They sell all these components together in one package. Travelers may deal directly with a tour company or may book tours through a travel agent. Package tours are advertised in the travel section of most newspapers and on websites. For a set price, airfare, ground transportation, hotel accommodation, car rental, as well as some meals, attractions, entertainment, and sightseeing are included.

Today, there is a great deal of overlapping between the services of travel agents and tour operators. Companies such as Carlson, Thomas Cook, and American Express perform both services, and many independent agencies put together their own tour packages for their customers. Among the major tour companies now operating around the world are Maupintour, DER Travel Service, Arthur Frommer Tours, Mayflower, and Chuck Olson. Many tour operators specialize in specific destinations, such as Europe, the Caribbean, or Hawaii. Tour operators offer four main types of tours:

A tour escort leading a personalized tour around an attraction.

- *Escorted tours*—A trained escort travels with the group and explains everything about the places of interest and handles all the little things that might go wrong.

- *Hosted tours*—A host resides at each destination, for example, Paris, where the host has an intimate knowledge of the city.

- *Independent tours*—A personalized tour created by the tour wholesaler or operator where the tourists travel by themselves or with family and friends.

- *Package tours*—A personalized tour including airfares and possibly ground transportation and hotel accommodations but not the full services of guides or tour directors.

The National Tour Association (NTA) is a trade organization of thousands of tourism professionals involved in the growth and development of the packaged travel industry.[15] NTA is composed of the following members:

- Tour operators who develop and sell travel packages
- Tour suppliers who provide the package components for tour operators
- Destination marketing organizations (DMOs) who promote specific destinations or regions and include national tourism organizations, state and provincial tourism offices, convention and visitors bureaus, and chambers of commerce[16]

The United States Tour Operators Association (USTOA) is another large organization of wholesale tour operators in the United States. USTOA members are companies whose tours and packages encompass the entire globe and who conduct business in the United States.[17] Services offered by tour operators vary widely and are limited only by the imagination. The tour operator buys a variety of ground services at various destinations from specialized ground-service operations. Services may include meeting clients upon their arrival at a destination. In Hawaii, for example, the tour operator is on hand to place the traditional leis around the necks of visitors, a custom that is pleasant to most. Also, the operator makes all the arrangements for transporting travelers' luggage from the airport to the hotel. According to a recent survey, USTOA companies move more than 11 million passengers annually and account for an annual sales volume of more than $9 billion.[18]

Tour operators accept complete responsibility for the tour from beginning to end. The tour covers all the expenses that the traveler would ordinarily have to pay—postage, baggage gratuities, accommodations, airfares, meals, sightseeing, and entertainment. Prices for a tour package can be anything from a couple of dollars to several thousands, and they might last anywhere from one afternoon to many months. Tour operations involve a multitude of details and demand a variety of skills, including sales, administration, strategic planning, and writing and communications skills. Employees must have the ability to visualize the step-by-step details of a complicated tour arrangement. They are constantly planning for the future and anticipating changes in markets and tour details. At times, they work under tremendous pressure.

▶ Check Your Knowledge

1. What different kinds of tours is the typical travel agent concerned with booking?

2. What are the best-known tour wholesale companies?

3. What does a tour operator do?

Corporate Travel Management

Many corporations employ travel managers or contract with a major travel company and work out details for travel guidelines. Corporations do this to keep their travel costs under control. If they allowed employees to make their own travel and hotel accommodation reservations, they would lose group and volume discounts. Acting as a kind of travel entrepreneur, the travel manager can invite agencies to submit proposals based on the company's travel needs. If a travel manager saves a company a million dollars, that money effectively goes straight to the bottom line.

Corporate travel managers create and operate travel offices within the company. They also help to establish written travel policies, work on budgeting travel and entertainment expenses, negotiate travel discounts with travel vendors, and are at the center of the travel communications network of

FOCUS ON

Corporate Travel Management

Amy Hart

Travelers very seldom think about how their travel arrangements are managed. Most understand that a travel counselor prepares the trip, but outside of that, they have little knowledge of what corporate travel managers really do on a daily basis. Why do travel agencies exist? What did they do prior to the Internet? What exactly is a corporate travel manager? Before the Internet, corporate travel managers were responsible for booking airline reservations, hotel and car reservations, and in some instances rail reservations. On occasion, they provided services for event and meeting planning.

A great deal of work went into every corporate reservation that was made by corporate travel managers. Corporate profiles contained all of the personal and business information necessary to complete each reservation. Limitations on bookings were monitored by each corporate account manager at the travel management company.

When computer reservation systems (CRS), now called global distribution systems (GDS), were placed in corporate travel sites, the job of the corporate travel manager shifted to more of an auditor of travel arrangements. Contracts were adhered to at the corporate travel management level, while travelers booked airline, car, and hotel reservations from the comfort of their offices. The freedom and flexibility it provided both the traveler and corporate travel manager was immense. This type of freedom did not eliminate corporate travel management companies, but allowed them to grow and expand their services to include financial management of corporate accounts.

Then came the ability to book travel arrangements online. Many seasoned travelers flocked to the "new" way to make travel arrangements, circumventing the corporate travel manager in many cases. Why continue using a corporate travel management company? Are travel agencies still viable with this new revolution? The last question in many cases has been answered with a resounding *no*. However, is that really the case? Many of the initial corporations that flocked to the Internet have since returned to the travel manager. Although freedom, flexibility, and ease are characteristics that travelers have stated as benefits of using the Internet, problems, lack of communication, and no personal service have been stated as reasons to return to the traditional brick-and-mortar travel management companies.

Although the Internet has provided all of us with a wealth of information regarding travel, travel professionals have been trained and educated in the field of tourism. Providing that experience and education to the traveling public is an essential element to the overall theme of customer service within the hospitality industry.

Source: Courtesy of Amy Hart, PhD (ABD), MBA, CHRM, CTC, Associate Professor, Columbus State Community College.

the corporation. One advantage of using a corporate travel department is that any discounts or commissions earned go directly back to the company, reducing the overall cost of travel (many companies have contracts with preferred airlines so that they receive a volume discount). Also, corporate travel managers usually can obtain less expensive rates on flights, hotel rooms, and other accommodations than can employees when booking online for themselves.

Incentive travel includes a number of exotic destinations, in this case Antarctica.
Courtesy of Mark Green

Incentive Travel

Incentive travel is big business. Companies such as Carlson Marketing Group and Maritz prepare incentive programs for a company's employees. If the employees meet or exceed the agreed on goals, they get a fabulous all-expenses-paid trip to an exciting destination for them and their significant others! The promise of a few days at a top resort generally motivates employees to produce, sell, or otherwise meet and exceed goals. For the travel and tourism industry, incentive travel is welcome business. The world's largest agency is American Express, followed by Carlson Wagonlit Travel, Navigant International, and Rosenbluth International.

The Society of Incentive and Travel Executives (SITE) was founded in 1973. SITE is the only international, not-for-profit, professional association devoted to the pursuit of excellence in incentives, a multi-billion-dollar global industry.[19] This organization provides educational seminars and information services to those who design, develop, promote, sell, administer, and operate motivational programs as an incentive to increase productivity in business. Currently, SITE has more than 2,100 members in 87 countries, with 35 local and regional chapters.[20]

Meeting Planners and Event Managers

Meeting planners arrange a variety of meetings, conventions, and expositions for clients in the business sector and for government and the public sector. Meeting planners represent a growing industry sector offering services to clients who do not have the expertise or time or both to plan and organize an event. They select suitable locations (city and hotel/resort) based on the client's needs—usually three cities are visited and negotiations lead to proposals from each city and hotel/resort for review and final selection. Meeting planners can also book the hotel accommodations or engage the services of a rooming agency that provides listings of hotels online in various price ranges from which clients can choose.

Meeting planners facilitate all aspects of the meeting, **conference**, or exhibition from the moment guests arrive at the destination city with airport greeting, transportation to the hotel, registration at the hotel and for the meeting or conference, and welcome reception. They also help with the selection of keynote speaker, entertainment, and meals and foodservice, and they set up city tours, events, attractions, meeting rooms, audiovisual equipment, breakout rooms for special sessions, and so on. Meeting planners develop detailed budgets for client approval and to control costs. A four-day convention can run into the millions of dollars.

Meeting Planners International (MPI) is the professional association for meeting planners. MPI includes members who are association executives (those who run an association, for example, the American Automobile Association), independent meeting planners, and suppliers who service the meetings industry. MPI has more than 24,000 members who belong to 69 chapters and clubs worldwide.[21]

The Professional Convention Management Association (PCMA) is the leading organization for meeting and event professionals. Its goal is to help members improve the effectiveness of meetings and conventions through education, training, and promotion. PCMA represents more than 6,000 meeting industry leaders including planner professionals, suppliers, faculty, and students.[22]

Convention and Visitors Bureaus and Convention Centers

Convention and visitors bureaus (CVBs) help facilitate tourist visitation—leisure and business—to destination areas by promoting the features and benefits of the area to the target markets. CVBs market their city to potential conventions and meetings by size: for example, if a city has 20,000 rooms available, it can attract small and medium-sized conventions, of which there are thousands held every year. CVBs work closely with convention centers to gain the huge economic benefits of having thousands of conventioneers spend money in the community. Conventions are planned and booked years ahead of time.

Familiarization Trips

The more travel agents travel, the better travel agents they become. Quite naturally, many agents are world travelers, taking every opportunity to visit new and different places. One of the perks of being a travel agent is the opportunity to take familiarization trips. Familiarization trips, or simply FAM trips, are often arranged for agents at little or no cost. Airlines and tourist agencies are pleased to arrange trips for agents to the areas that they represent; however, agents must have at least one year of experience at an agency to qualify for reduced-fare air travel. Many FAM trips are more business than pleasure. For example, a travel agent went on a three-day trip to Puerto Vallarta, Mexico, and had to tour 23 hotels! Also, many times these trips take place during the week, so agents are forced to take time off from work to attend.

Travel agents must know geography and culture. Every year, names and places unfamiliar to the general public suddenly become *the* destination. In recent years, the Seychelles, Bali, Phuket, Mykonos, Antalya, and Macau have all become popular. Traveling to these locales familiarizes the agent with the destinations, enabling them to better sell it.

▶ Check Your Knowledge

1. Describe some of the different elements included in the job description of a travel agent.
2. What are familiarization (FAM) trips?

Regulatory Agencies

To be able to issue tickets, travel agencies must be approved by a number of regulatory organs. The **Airlines Reporting Corporation (ARC)** is made up of domestic airlines, travel agencies, corporate travel departments, railroads,

CORPORATE PROFILE

Uniglobe Franchised Travel Agency

Tony Souter © Dorling Kindersley

Uniglobe is the world's largest single-brand retail travel franchise company, with more than 750 locations in 40 countries.[23] Its motto, "To be the best we can be. With integrity, initiative, and dependability," has proven to be a successful one, creating strong customer loyalty and brand recognition. Founded in 1995 by U. Gary Charlwood and his sons Christopher and Martin, Uniglobe was launched with an eye toward the future. They realized as early as 1998, when the airlines first started to cut their commissions, that cruising was the segment to target. This has worked out very well for Uniglobe—they are now seeking to become the largest seller of cruises on the Web.

Uniglobe's franchisees include travel agencies, home-based agents, e-commerce operations, and a call center open 24/7 to assist their customers from all over the world. Most people who have tried Uniglobe consider its customer service excellent. Examples of services provided to travelers who purchase tickets through Uniglobe include the Uniglobe 24/7 Rescue Line (which travelers can call anytime from anywhere when they have a problem, and Uniglobe promises to help), emergency foreign language translation for 140 languages, a Rescue Line for help with lost luggage, as well as corporate negotiated rates with many hotels and preferred suppliers. The new Web addition, Uniglobe Total Access, provides information on last-minute specials, customized profiles for online bookings, informative travel stories, driving directions, and travel tips to customers anytime.

Uniglobe also operates Uniglobe Main Events, which specializes in planning, managing, and operating conventions, trade shows, incentive programs, and special events. Furthermore, the organization publishes the award-winning magazine *Travel etc.*, which includes the latest in news, destinations, technology, and advice for travel professionals.

and other travel suppliers that process more than $80 billion annually through ARC's settlement system, making it the financial backbone of travel distribution.[24] The ARC is the system that processes all the transactions in the travel system. When travelers purchase a ticket, the money goes from their credit card or checking account to the airline, through Homeland Security— for airport charges—and so on, until all the appropriate payments have been made.

The regulatory bodies for international flights are the International Air Transport Association (IATA) and the International Airlines Travel Agency Network (IATAN). The IATA is an international trade body, created some 60 years ago by a group of airlines. Today, IATA represents 230 airlines and 93 percent of scheduled international air traffic.[25] Through the use of its informational and other resources, IATAN provides a link between the supplier community and the U.S. travel distribution network.[26]

The cruise conference is called the Cruise Lines International Association (CLIA). CLIA is composed of 24 of the major cruise lines in North America. It is an organization that operates pursuant to an agreement filed with the Federal Maritime Commission under the Shipping Act of 1984 and serves as

CORPORATE PROFILE (continued)

There are three different categories of Uniglobe franchisee: home-based agencies, vacation stores, and Uniglobe Cruise Centers. The major advantages of being a Uniglobe franchisee are as follows:

- Name and product recognition
- Increased buying power
- Proven systems
- Established customer loyalty

Franchisees also get benefits from the organization's marketing arrangements with carriers and other suppliers. As many others have, Uniglobe has realized that one of the most secure ways to succeed in the turbulent business of travel professionals is through alliances and strategic partnerships. The Cruise Control booking engine, developed in cooperation with Galileo, gives Uniglobe's customers access to cruise deals otherwise available only to travel professionals. This, of course, has contributed to the popularity of the site. This company is also about to launch a new reservation system for airlines, hotels, and car rental. Another strategic partnership is with Avaya Communications.

Awards given to this interesting company include the following:

- Number 3 cruise site on the Web by Gomez Associates
- Three-star (the highest possible) certification by Gomez Associates
- Listing in the "50 Essential Travel Sites" by Condé Nast Traveler
- Number 1 travel site by *Travel Weekly*

Uniglobe offers employment in a wide variety of areas, together with a new state-of-the-art benefits package.

a nongovernmental consultative organization to the International Maritime Organization, an agency of the United Nations.[27]

Finally, the National Railroad Passenger Corporation, known as Amtrak, controls rail ticketing in the continental United States. It operates nationwide and serves more than 500 destinations in 46 states. During the 2007 fiscal year, Amtrak served more than 25.8 million passengers.[28]

To get and keep an ARC or IATAN conference appointment, the travel agent must provide information concerning promotional methods, the physical setup of the agency and its location, and financial and personal data. The agency must also be bonded. Strict control of storage and use of ticket stock (blank tickets) is maintained because ticket stock is equivalent to money.

The Area Bank Settlement Plan

The **Area Bank Settlement Plan** (also called the Area Settlement Plan and Bank Settlement Plan) functions to simplify the travel agent's operations by allowing ASTA member agencies to sell and distribute tickets on the airlines' behalf. This system is administered by Airlines Reporting Corporation (ARC) to handle the processing of airline tickets, payments, and the disbursement of commissions to travel agencies.[29] Instead of purchasing and reselling inventory, the Area Settlement Plan allows agents to pass through cash and credit card payments directly to the airlines. If the customer pays with cash, the agent holds on to his or her commission, if applicable, and forwards the remainder to the airlines. If the payment is by credit card, the agent simply forwards the credit card number to the airline, which collects the money. The airline, then, through the same system remits the commission owed to the agent. Figure 13–2 illustrates the Area Bank Settlement Plan.

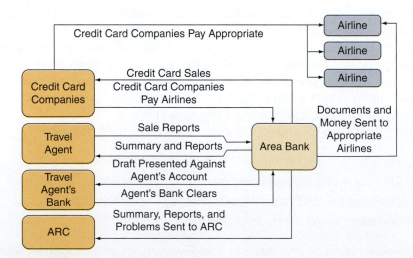

Figure 13–2 • Area Bank Settlement Plan

Air Fares

If you have ever shopped around for a flight, you probably noticed that you rarely get quoted the same price twice, even for the same flight and class. Do you know the reasons for this? Thousands of airfares are changed by the airlines each day, and it is essential for a travel agent to keep track of them. Often, one airline proclaims to have a lower rate between two cities. Within hours, other airlines competing on the same route announce that they will match the lower fare. Almost all domestic airline seats are discounted for the discretionary traveler. Most of the discount rates announced are limited to a certain number of seats on a flight, which depends on demand. If more passengers than usual book space at a given moment, the number of discount seats is cut back. If fewer seats are being sold, discount seats are added. This system is known as yield management.

Yield Management

Yield management is the umbrella term for a set of strategies that enable capacity-constrained service industries to realize optimum revenue from operations.[30] The core concept of yield management is to provide the right service to the right customer at the right time for the right price.[31] Competition has a major influence on airfares. A coast-to-coast flight served by several competing airlines can be less expensive than one crossing a single state line. Depending on location, fares may be higher on Monday, lower on Wednesday, and downright cheap on Saturday, reflecting the patterns of business travel. A requirement that a passenger remain at a destination over a Saturday night is primarily designed to get full fare from the business traveler who does not want to cut into her or his weekend at home. By being aware of these trends and flexible in travel times and dates, travelers can find some real bargains.

Classes of Fares

The fact that airfares are such a large part of the travel agents' workdays calls for a brief overview. There are three basic classes of fares: economy, business, and first class, all of which may be discounted. Price differences depend mainly on the following: sections of the plane, passenger seating space, level of attendant service, and cost of meals served—if they are served at all. First-class passengers receive the best service, seating, and amenities. On some airlines, first-class fares can be double those of economy. Business class seats are almost as expensive and are frequently used by business travelers who, because of the extra space and service, arrive more refreshed than economy travelers do. Practically all major airlines have business class, offering services, space, and amenities that are the equivalent to those offered by first class a few years earlier. First-class seating is reduced in number so that B-747s usually offer only 16 or fewer seats. Several airlines have built a reputation for first-class and business class seats. Airlines such as Singapore, Cathay Pacific, Thai, Korean, and Japan Airlines provide exceptional service to first-class and business passengers and may include limousines for airport transfers and special reservation and check-in lines.

The following list reflects some of the complexities that affect airline fares:

- *Economy*—The economy rate is higher in the peak season. On domestic flights, an extra charge is usually made for alcoholic beverages and meals in economy.

- *Excursion rates*—Excursion rates are available for trips that last 14 to 21 days and 22 to 45 days.

- *Advance purchase excursion fares (APEX)*—APEX fares are offered between selected cities within the United States, Canada, and Mexico. Tickets must be purchased 60 days in advance, and the traveler must stay at least 22 and no longer than 45 days.

- *Inclusive tours (ITs)*—A land package must be purchased along with the air travel.

- *Youth fares*—Youth fares are offered by major airlines for passengers between 12 and 21 years of age for a round trip. Seats are not confirmed until five days before departure.

- *Short-stay tour packages*—In short-stay packages, the traveler receives a number of bonus gifts and services, for instance, "Belgium with a Bonus."

- *Late-night fares*—Late-night fares are usually at least 25 percent less than day fares. Flights during the middle of the week may be less than those taken on the weekends.

▶ Check Your Knowledge

1. How does the Area Bank Settlement Plan work and who is allowed to use it?

2. What is meant by the term *yield management*?

3. What are the three basic classes of airfares?

Online Reservations

The Internet has greatly revolutionized airline reservations. Travelers can simply go online and within minutes have several quotes and often access to better deals than if they go through a travel agent. Many of the commercial online services, such as Expedia, Travelocity, America Online, Yahoo, MSN, and so on, offer a vast amount of information on traveling—from packages to fares to flight schedules. In addition, many airlines actually reward customers for booking through their company website in the form of double frequent flyer mile bonuses or other bonuses and incentives.

Travelocity is one of the world's leading online travel agencies and one of the largest travel agencies in the United States, wholly owned by Sabre Holdings Corporation. Travelocity customers can access offerings, pricing information about airlines, hotels, car rental companies, cruise lines, vacation and last-minute travel packages, and other travel-related services.[32] It has won several awards of excellence.

Global Distribution Systems

Have you ever tried to set up a complicated multiflight itinerary online all by yourself? Have you perhaps even tried to combine domestic and international flights? If so, you probably know that these are not easy tasks for most people. Many people need advice on which route to take, which airline to choose, and what times or days the flights will be least expensive. This is where travel agents come in. The information and capabilities of their **global distribution systems (GDSs)** are really awesome.

Sabre is the name of the world's number one global distribution system (GDS) and the leading provider of technology, distribution, and marketing services for the travel industry. Sabre connects its more than 50,000 travel agency members around the world and provides them with content from more than 400 airlines, approximately 76,000 hotel properties, 28 car rental

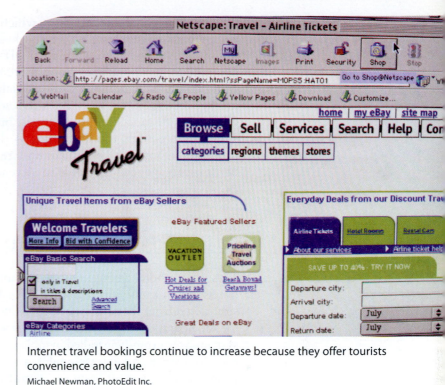

Internet travel bookings continue to increase because they offer tourists convenience and value.

Michael Newman, PhotoEdit Inc.

companies, 13 cruise lines, 35 railroads, and 220 tour operators.[33] As mentioned earlier, Sabre also owns Travelocity, one of the world's largest online travel agencies.[34] Sabre provides a variety of services for actors in the travel industry, most of them on the cutting edge of technology. Some examples include consulting, partner display and messaging, Sabre Vision, revenue management, crew management, operations control systems, and much more. Major airlines that use Sabre's services include American Airlines and Sabena, as well as British Airlines, which recently introduced Sabre's crew management program to further improve its customer service.[35]

Sabre, Travelocity, and Yahoo have formed an alliance that makes Sabre travel agents able to handle some Yahoo consumer bookings. When visiting the Yahoo website, customers have the opportunity to contact a Sabre agency for advice and bookings. Furthermore, Sabre and Yahoo cooperate in several other areas, for example, developing the broadcast services that deliver multimedia applications to Sabre agents, as well as remote training and development programs.[36]

Three other important computerized global distribution systems are Amadeus, Worldspan, and Galileo. Galileo was the first GDS to give connected agents access to vacation rental properties in the form of villas, homes, condominiums, and cottages. The arrangement, which is with Resort Condominiums International, includes more than 3,700 resorts in more than 100 countries. More agencies and GDSs are expected to follow this initiative, which greatly benefits both the agents and the vacation rental corporations.

GDSs owned by airlines play an important role in airline competition. The airlines that own the GDS have a competitive advantage because their flights are displayed on the computer first, which introduces a bias in their favor. Automated back-office systems are marketed for computerized travel agency in-house operations; these systems interface with the leased reservation systems from the airlines. The back-room system records travel sales, notes the commission, credits the agent who made the sale, completes reports, and is available for market analysis. Not only does this service conduct low-fare searches in the GDS and introduce quality controls, but it also automates the fulfillment of e-tickets and e-mails the itineraries to the travelers. By automating these three processes, many small and medium-sized agencies (which make up the majority of all travel agencies) are able to increase sales without hiring additional staff.

Hotel Reservations

Most major hotel chains are included in some computer reservation systems. The hotels assign a number of rooms for sale to a GDS, and as a room is sold, it is subtracted from the inventory. MICROS Systems provides enterprise applications for the hospitality and retail industries worldwide. More than 220,000 MICROS systems are currently installed in table and quick-service restaurants, hotels, motels, casinos, leisure and entertainment, and retail operations. MICROS also provides property management systems, central reservation systems, and customer information solutions for more than 20,000 hotels worldwide, as well as point-of-sale and loss prevention products through its subsidiary Datavantage for more than 50,000 specialty retail stores worldwide.[37]

Travelers can use toll-free telephone numbers, paid for by the hotel company, to make hotel reservations in the United States. The hotel chains are likely to spell out what is commissionable and what is not. Commissions are usually paid promptly by the hotels, once the guests have paid and departed. It can sometimes be difficult to obtain commissions for lesser-known and international hotels. For this reason, many agents prefer to work with large chains or properties with which they are familiar. Commission on meals is applicable only if clients are booked on an all-inclusive rate. To avoid paying commissions to travel agents and online booking services such as Travelocity, hotels are now trying to drive potential guests directly to their websites. Originally, when hotels were approached by online agencies, it made sense to give them the unsold inventory, but consider this: a Hilton Garden Inn with a rate of $89 would have to pay $20 to the booking service, thereby reducing its margin considerably. No longer, the owner now has the challenge of steering guests to the hotel's own or the Hilton website.

▶ Check Your Knowledge

1. Approximately what percentage of leisure travelers use the Internet to search for travel-related information?

2. What is the world's number one computer reservation system?

3. Why do travel agents usually prefer to work with large hotel chains?

CASE STUDY

Can It Ever Be 100 Percent Customer Satisfaction When Dealing with Tour Operators?

Bethany Rogers had been a travel manager of a large corporate travel management company for about 11 years. The management company primarily handled local corporate accounts, booking airline, car, and hotel reservations, but on occasion as requested would handle corporate meeting travel for current clients.

Binder Corporation, a longtime corporate account, requested that Bethany handle their annual board meeting to be located in Las Vegas, Nevada, in April. Having handled Binder Corporation's prior board meeting travel requirements, Bethany did not feel that this would be anything different, so she agreed. She gathered the information from Margo, the administrative assistant who handled all of the corporate travel at Binder Corporation. The dates, names, hotel preferences, airline preferences, meeting space requirements, meal service, and transportation to/from the airport, and any special requests for travelers that the agency did not have on file already were gathered by Bethany. One special request was that Bethany put together an escorted tour of the Las Vegas area for the spouses of the board members.

Bethany contacted Alright Tours, a tour operator in Las Vegas that she had used multiple times before, to create an eight-hour tour of Las Vegas and the surrounding area for the second day of the trip. Arrangements were presented to Binder Corporation that included a statement that there would be several hours of time spent on the bus during the tour. There would also be a significant amount of walking required when the tour reached the Hoover Dam. The itinerary for the bus tour also stated that lunch would be at a local establishment, highlighting crafts and cuisine of the area. Binder Corporation accepted the itinerary and the trip was scheduled.

A few weeks after the group returned from the trip, Bethany received the following letter from one of the spouses that went on the Las Vegas scenic tour:

Dear Mrs. Rogers,

My husband has been a long-time, valued customer of your agency. He has done nothing but brag about the great service that he has always received from the agency and the superb service he would receive while traveling. Always receiving 100 percent satisfaction, I did not expect anything less on our recent trip to Las Vegas. Well, I have to say that I did not find the trip to be 100 percent satisfactory at all. The trip with Alright Tours was just terrible. We were on a bus for 5 hours total during the 8-hour trip. At what time would you think that staying on a bus for 5 hours at anytime would be considered acceptable? I would rather have been sitting in the board meeting with my husband. At least that way we would have better seats.

The trip to Hoover Dam was OK, but I have to say if you have ever seen a big pond of water, this was the same. I was expecting to see Las Vegas in a manner that I would have felt I would not have been able to do on my own. I can call a bus company myself and arrange such a trip. It was a very long walk through the dam, up and down stairs, elevators, and the long wait in lines.

Once we left Hoover Dam, we went to a "hokey" restaurant that appeared to cater to the locals, although I cannot know that for sure, I felt as though we had stepped onto an Indian reservation and were totally out of place. I was told by the driver that this was part of the itinerary and that we were visiting a local reservation to experience the local cuisine. Bagged lunches would have been better.

The trip up and down the strip itself was ridiculous. We visited historic downtown Las Vegas, historic, really?, or just old. You tell me. We were provided with a historical overview of how Las Vegas was developed, the gangster version from what I could gather. I guess I did not really gain any new insight into Las Vegas from that trip either.

(continued)

CASE STUDY (continued)

What I am saying is that I am very disappointed with the trip. I felt as if I could have done a better job myself finding a bus to take us around the area. We can read travel guides to fill in the blanks of what we did not already know about Las Vegas, Hoover Dam, and all points in between. I want to know what you will do to provide me with the 100 percent satisfaction that my husband always raves about you and your agency. I look forward to hearing from you soon regarding this situation.

Sincerely,

Monica Ring
Unsatisfied Customer

Questions

1. What does 100 percent satisfaction mean when dealing with a tour operator? Is it the responsibility of the travel management company to provide 100 percent satisfaction?

2. What were the breaks in service, if any, mentioned in the letter presented by Mrs. Ring?

3. If you were Mrs. Rogers, would you respond to the letter? If so, how would you respond? Remember that you do not want to jeopardize the current customer relationship between Binder Corporation and the travel management company. List the breaks in service according to Mrs. Ring.

4. How should Mrs. Rogers respond to these breaks in service?

5. What responsibility exists between the travel management company, the tour bus operator, and the customer's satisfaction?

Source: Courtesy of Amy Hart, PhD (ABD), MBA, CHRM, CTC, Associate Professor, Columbus State Community College.

Summary

1. Channels of distribution bring the travel and tourism product or service to clients either directly or through intermediaries. The travel agent is an important part of travel distribution and ideally a well-trained professional who is up-to-date on schedules, fares, accommodations, entertainment, and costs.

2. Some elements included in the job description of a travel agent include preparing individual, preplanned itineraries, arranging reservations for special interest activities, and using professional know-how to provide information on such things as schedules of flight and train connections, rate and quality of hotels, and language studies.

3. Familiarization trips are usually arranged by airlines and tourist agencies to the areas they represent and are provided to travel agents at little or no cost.

4. The American Society of Travel Agents (ASTA) is the world's largest association of travel agents and has more than 20,000 members who are all committed to the special code of ethics.

5. To be able to issue tickets, the travel agency must be approved by a number of regulatory organs, including Airlines Reporting Council (ARC), Cruise Lines International Association (CLIA), and Amtrak.

6. ASTA member agencies are permitted to use the Area Settlement Plan, which allows them to sell and distribute tickets on the airlines' behalf.

7. There are three basic classes of airfares: economy, business class, and first class. At times, airlines also offer other rates such as excursion rates, advance purchase excursion fares, inclusive tour fares, youth fares, short-stay tour packages, and late-night fares. Prices also fluctuate because of changes in demand according to the practices of yield management.

8. The business of online travel agencies is growing rapidly, and most regular agencies use some kind of computerized reservation system such as Sabre, Galileo, Worldspan, or Amadeus.

9. Many large corporations establish their own travel management departments to make sure corporate policies are followed and the lowest possible fares are obtained.

10. The typical travel agent deals with four different kinds of tours: special interest tours, escorted tours, foreign and domestic independent tours, and group inclusive tours. The better-known tour wholesale companies are Thomas Cook and American Express.

11. Tour operators are companies that arrange every aspect of a travel package. Some important tour operators are Maupintour, DER Travel Service, Arthur Frommer Tours, Trafalgar Tours, Mayflower, and Chuck Olson.

12. The most influential current trend in the travel agency industry is the increasing amount of online travel services. Some other trends include mergers and acquisitions, as well as the creativity and new ways of doing business invented by travel agents as a response to the cut in commissions from airlines, hotels, and other providers.

Key Words and Concepts

Airlines Reporting Corporation
Area Bank Settlement Plan
channels of distribution
computerized reservation systems
conferences

consolidation
direct and indirect channels of distribution
global distribution systems (GDSs)

tour operators
travel distribution system
vertical integration

Review Questions

1. List some advantages and disadvantages associated with booking a trip yourself as well as using a travel agent. What do you prefer?

2. Why is it important for a travel agent to be up-to-date with current events, trends, and happenings?

3. What are familiarization trips, and why do they take place?

4. What is the purpose or mission statement of American Society of Travel Agents (ASTA), and approximately how many members does this organization have?

5. Name some of the major conferences (regulatory bodies) that an agency must be approved by to issue airline and rail tickets.

6. What is the Area Bank Settlement Plan and who has access to it?

7. Explain the concept of yield management.

8. List and describe the three basic classes of airfares and the differences between them. Also, name at least three other types of airfares.

9. Discuss the advantages associated with having a corporate travel management department or a corporate travel manager.

10. Which beach would you go to at Viña del Mar, Chile?

11. What do you think of the benefits and drawbacks of travel managers versus the Internet?

Interesting Websites

Airlines Reporting Corporation: www.arccorp.com

American Society of Travel Agents (ASTA): www.astanet.com

Expedia Travel: www.expedia.com

International Air Transport Association (IATA): www.iata.org

International Airlines Travel Agency Network (IATAN): www.iatan.org

Maritz Inc.: www.maritz.com

National Tour Association: www.ntaonline.com

Orbitz Travel: www.orbitz.com

Travel Industry Association of America: www.tia.org

Travelocity: www.travelocity.com

United States Tour Operators Association: www.ustoa.com

Uniglobe: www.uniglobetravel.com

Internet Exercises

1. Surf the websites of some of the tour companies mentioned in this chapter. Find and list at least three different tours that interest you, their destinations, durations, and prices.

2. Go to an online travel agency or website of your choice. Search for airfares between New York and Orlando or Chicago and Las Vegas from 6 A.M. to 9 P.M. When are the cheapest fares offered? Check again the next day. Are the fares offered the same? If not, how much is the difference and why?

Apply Your Knowledge

1. If you were president of a large corporation would you:
   a. Employ a travel manager or contract with an outside agency for all your travel and lodging needs?
   b. Simply publish strict reimbursement policies?
   Provide reasons for your response.

2. Why is yield management so important and what does it accomplish?

Suggested Activity

Investigate airfares for a visit to your favorite destination starting 260 days out then 130 days, then 61 days, then 31 days, then 15 days, and then 7 days, and record the price differentials. Share your results with your classmates.

Endnotes

1. Douglas G. Pearce and Mei Taniguchi, "Channel Performance in Multichannel Tourism Distribution Systems," *Journal of Travel Research* 46, no. 3 (2008): 256.

2. B. Rosenbloom, T. Larsen, and B. Smith, "The Effectiveness of Upstream Influence Attempts in High and Low Context Export Marketing Channels," *Journal of Marketing Channels* 11, no. 4 (2004): 3–19, as cited in Pearce and Taniguchi, "Channel Performance," 256.

3. Laurel Reid and Douglas G. Pearce, "Distribution Channels for New Zealand Outbound Tourism," *International Journal of Tourism Research* 10, no. 6 (2008): 577.

4. U.S. Department of Labor Bureau of Labor Statistics, "Travel Agents," in *Occupational Outlook Handbook, 2008–09 Edition*, www.bls.gov/oco/ocos124.htm (accessed September 21, 2009).

5. Ibid.

6. Ruthanne Terrero, "Maintaining Marketing Integrity in Tough Times," *Travel Agent* 333, no. 10 (November 2008): 14.

7. Ibid.

8. "Agents Report Blue Christmas," *Travel Agent* 333, no. 10 (November 2008): 4.

9. American Society of Travel Agents website. www.asta.org/about/index.cfm?navItemNumber=502. December, 2008.

10. American Society of Travel Agents, "About ASTA," www.asta.org/about/index.cfm (accessed September 21, 2009).

11. S. Wang and W. Cheung, "E-Business Adoption by Travel Agencies: Prime Candidates for Mobile e-Business," *International Journal of Electronic Commerce* 8, no. 3 (2004): 65–78.

12. Tricia Holly-Davis, "Experts Forecast Casualties," *Travel and Trade Gazette* no. 2842 (November 2008): 22.

13. Ibid.

14. George Dooley, "Air Consolidators: Lower Capacity and Higher Fares Make Agents Need for Trusted Consolidator Even More Crucial," *Travel Agent* 333, no. 3 (August 2008): 56.

15. National Tour Association, www.ntaonline.com/ (accessed December 2008).

16. Drawn from the National Tour Association, www.ntaonline.com (accessed December 2008).

17. United States Tour Operators Association, "Who We Are," www.ustoa.com/whoweare.cfm (accessed September 21, 2009).

18. Ibid.

19. Society of Incentive and Travel Executives, www.conventions.net/marketplace/industry_associations-c33/society_of_incentive_travel_executives-a786.asp (accessed December 2008).

20. Ibid.

21. Meeting Professionals International, "Facts and Figures," www.mpiweb.org/cms/mpiweb/mpicontent .aspx?id=18992 (accessed September 21, 2009).

22. Professional Convention Management Association, "About PCMA," www.pcma.org/Header_Pages/About .htm (accessed September 21, 2009).

23. Information gathered from Uniglobe Travel International, website, www.uniglobetravel.com (accessed September 21, 2009).

24. Airlines Reporting Corporation, "About Us," www.arccorp.com/aboutus/index.jsp (accessed September 21, 2009).

25. International Air Transport Association, "About Us," www.iata.org/about/accessed September 21, 2009).

26. International Airlines Travel Agency Network, "About Us," www.iatan.org/iatan/about/mission.htm (accessed September 21, 2009).

27. Cruise Lines International Association, "About CLIA," www.cruising.org/about.cfm (accessed September 21, 2009).

28. Amtrak, "Amtrak National Facts," www.amtrak.com/ servlet/ContentServer?pagename=Amtrak/am2Copy/ Title_Image_Copy_Page&c=am2Copy&cid=1081442 674300&ssid=542 (accessed September 21, 2009).

29. Travel Industry Dictionary, "Area Settlement Plan," www.hometravelagency.com/dictionary/ area-settlement-plan.html (accessed September 21, 2009).

30. Glenn Withiam, "Yield Management," Cornell University School of Hotel Administration, Center for Hospitality Research, www.hotelschool.cornell.edu/ research/chr/pubs/reports/abstract-13622.html (accessed September 21, 2009).

31. Ibid.

32. Travelocity, "Our Brands: Travelocity," www .sabre-holdings.com/ourBrands/travelocity.html (accessed September 21, 2009).

33. Sabre Holdings, "Our Brands: Sabre Travel Network," www.sabre-holdings.com/ourBrands/travelNetwork .html (accessed September 21, 2009).

34. Ibid.

35. Sabre Airline Solutions, *Ascend*, www.sabreairlinesolutions.com/ascend/ (September 21, 2009).

36. News Release: Sabre and Yahoo! Announce Multi-Year Strategic Alliance to Leverage Power of Their Extensive Travel Industry and Consumer Networks.

37. Micros, "About Us," www.micros.com/AboutUs/ (September 21, 2009).

CHAPTER 14

Transportation

OBJECTIVES

After reading and studying this chapter, you should be able to:

- Describe the development of the cruise industry and the key players in it.
- Describe the importance of the rail history.
- Discuss the present and future of high-speed and high-tech trains.
- Explain the importance of the automobile in the American society.
- List some major historic and scenic drives throughout the United States.
- List different bus services and some of the major players in the business.
- Explain the concept of airways and the jet stream.
- Discuss the hub and spoke concept.
- Identify the components of airline profit and loss.
- Identify trends in the transportation industry.

GEOGRAPHY SPOTLIGHT

Adventure Tourism: Croatia

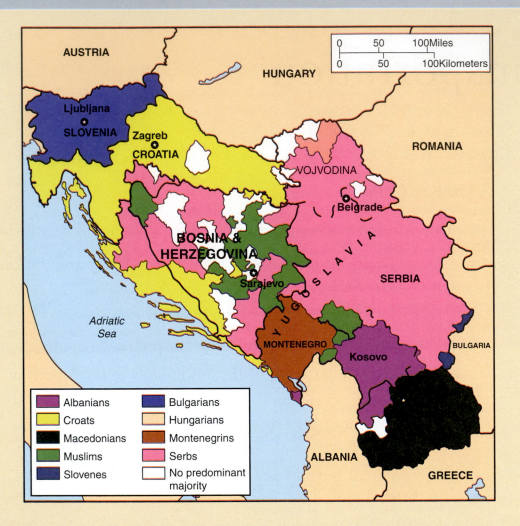

As a part of former Yugoslavia, Croatia has been establishing itself as a tourist destination since declaring its independence in 1991. In 2008, after only 17 years of independence, Croatia welcomed more than 9 million tourists.[1] The popularity of the country continues to increase as the country advertises its wide variety of tourism destinations. In a country that is smaller than West Virginia, tourists can experience sun-sea-sand activities, see cultural and heritage sites, and visit eco-friendly natural areas.[2]

Croatia offers tourists "endless breathtaking beaches, clear blue seas, and miles of unspoiled Croatian coastline."[3] With more than 1,185 islands throughout the country, tourists can participate in activities including sunbathing, sailing, scuba diving, and sea kayaking. One of Croatia's islands, Hvar, "has on average 2,718 hours of sunshine per year."[4] For tourists looking for nontraditional accommodations, several companies

GEOGRAPHY SPOTLIGHT *(continued)*

Tony Souter © Dorling Kindersley

charter private yachts, which can be used to explore the coastline. Whether seeing the country from land or sea, the beautiful beaches of Croatia attract many tourists each year for a seaside vacation.

Tourists wanting to escape from the beaches and discover the interior of the country will not be disappointed. Croatia has cultural attractions that have existed since the third century. The country also boasts six UNESCO World Heritage sites. One of the World Heritage sites, the Basilica of Euphrasius in Porec, consists of Christian religious monuments that were created in the sixth century. It is the "most complete surviving complex of its type."[5] Dubrovnik, a popular tourist destination, "is the most magnificent and well preserved fortified city in the world."[6] The walls, which are as high as 25 meters (82 feet) and as wide as 6 meters (19 feet), have helped protect the city since the sixth century.[7] Less than a hundred miles from Dubrovnik is Split; here, the ruins of Diocletian's Palace remain. Also a UNESCO World Heritage site, the ruins feature the elaborate palace of the Roman Emperor Diocletian.[8] Built in the third century, its importance to European heritage is significant "because of its level of preservation."[9]

Another type of UNESCO World Heritage site is Plitvicka Jereza (Plitvice Lakes); national parks such as Plitvice Lakes are becoming increasingly popular in the eco-tourism trend. Croatia has eight national parks and "almost 10 percent of the country is protected as part of a national park or preserve."[10] Plitvice Lakes consists of 16 small lakes. While in the park, tourists can see waterfalls and wildlife that may include brown bears. Adventure-seeking tourists can find a variety of thrilling activities in Croatia's national parks such as white water rafting, rock climbing, and hiking. Croatia's national parks are "areas around Croatia with exceptional ecological, cultural, historical, aesthetical, tourist, and educational characteristics."[11]

Tourism in Croatia will continue to grow and develop as tourists hear about the impressive sun-sea-sand destinations, cultural attractions, and natural beauty of the country. Tourists will be "amazed to find so much history, so much beauty, and so many perfect holiday destinations in such a small country."[12] The land and attractions have fascinated people since the third century; now, less than two decades after declaring its independence, Croatia is proving it can attract tourists from around the world to come and experience "the Jewel of the Adriatic."[13]

Endnotes

1. Croatian Bureau of Statistics, "Tourism—Cumulative Data—Jan –Aug, 2008," SeeNews, www.seenews.com/_c/SaveAs.php?Id=120722&Type=2 (accessed May 4, 2009).

2. Central Intelligence Agency, "Croatia," in *World Factbook*, https://www.cia.gov/library/publications/the-world-factbook/geos/hr.html (accessed May 4, 2009).

3. Croatia-Official.com, website, www.croatia-official.com/index.html (accessed May 4, 2009).

(continued)

GEOGRAPHY SPOTLIGHT *(continued)*

4. About Croatia, website, http://about-croatia.com/ (accessed May 4, 2009).

5. Croatian Tourist Guide, http://croatiantouristguide.com/index.htm (accessed May 4, 2009).

6. About Croatia, website.

7. Ibid.

8. T. Marasovic, "Diocletian's Palace," 1994, http://w3.mrki.info/split/diokl.html (accessed May 4, 2009).

9. Ibid.

10. Croatian Tourist Guide.

11. Ibid.

12. About Croatia, website.

13. Croatia-Official.com, website.

Changes in the technology of travel have had widespread implications for society. In the United States, rail travel influenced the building of towns and cities, caused hotels to be built near rail depots, and opened up the West. Likewise, auto travel produced the motel and a network of highways, while the commercial jet created destination resorts in formerly remote and exotic locations, made the rental car business a necessity, and changed the way we look at geography. Cruising has made several exotic destinations within reach of millions of passengers who may enjoy cruises of various durations in places such as the Caribbean or Mediterranean. Although long-distance travel has always been fairly comfortable for the wealthy, it was not until the development of the railroad in the 1830s that travel became comfortable and cheap enough to be within the reach of a large percentage of the population.

By the 1920s, the automobile and the bus began to replace the position of the railroad as the leading means of transportation and have since been the dominant modes of transportation for short-distance travel.

The choice of travel mode rests on the individuals' preference, budget, and time available. If cost is an issue, the bus is often a good choice. Auto travel is the most convenient for short distances and less expensive per person when the car is full. The train can be great in densely trafficked areas, whereas the airplane is the obvious choice for longer distances.

Probably the biggest decision factor in choosing a mode of transportation is the reason for travel: is it for pleasure or business? Can the travelers take their time, or do they need to rush to their destination and rush back? Given the choice, people who can afford it usually choose speed and convenience over cost. Increases in gasoline prices have had only limited long-term effects on the extent to which people use their cars, and the same can be said of air travel. When fuel rises in cost, more attention is generally paid to the efficiency of transportation instead of a reduction in travel time.

Cruising

Cruising . . . the mere word conjures up images of lazy days by the pool, romantic evenings with fine dining, entertainment, moonlight promenades, and exciting excursions at distant exotic ports. Does this sound like a dream? It doesn't have to be! The best part of the story is that in recent years, cruising has become increasingly varied and affordable, giving virtually everyone the opportunity to share the experience. As we see later in the chapter, more people are making their dream of a cruise a reality, and the overwhelming majority are completely enthralled with the experience.

More than 200 cruise lines offer a variety of wonderful vacations, from the "Fun Ships" of Carnival, to the "Love Boat," to freighters that carry only a few passengers. Travelers associate a certain romance with cruising to exotic locations and being pampered all day. Being on a cruise ship is like being on a floating resort. Accommodations range from luxurious suites to cabins that are even smaller than most jail cells or faculty offices. Attractions and distractions range from early morning workouts to fabulous meals, with nightlife consisting of dancing, cabarets, and sometimes gambling. Day life might involve relaxation, visits to the spa or beauty parlor—or both—organized games, or simply reclining in a deck chair by the pool reading a novel. Nonstop entertainment includes language lessons, charm classes, port-of-call briefings, cooking, dances, bridge, table tennis, shuffleboard, and more.

Cruise Industry Development

Cruising has not always been a popular vacation choice. For centuries, a seaworthy vessel was simply considered a mode of transportation, especially for those who inhabited coastal communities on oceans, rivers, and lakes. Even after Columbus's historic voyage in 1492, cruising the high seas was only a way to establish new colonies and bring glory to your country. Ship travel was uncomfortable and unsanitary—a far cry from the luxury lines that sail today. For some unfortunate few, however, it was a necessity. Until about the 1830s, the principal reasons for undertaking water travel were immigration, trade, and war. Ship travel developed from the first cruise ships to an important part of the world's largest industry.

The First Cruise Ships

The Peninsula and Oriental Steam Navigation Company (P&O) is recognized as the inventor of cruising. Their first cruises in 1844 sailed from Britain to Spain and Portugal.[1] By 1880, one of P&O's ships had been upgraded to the status of a cruising yacht, and it sailed around the world.[2] The first American cruise ship didn't set sail until 1867. The *Quaker City* left port from New York City and traveled to Europe and the Middle East.[3] However, passengers aboard the P&O cruise line and the *Quaker City* represented a very small minority in transatlantic travel. Most ocean travel still consisted of poor immigrants looking for a better life overseas.

In the early 1900s, more passengers took to the sea. By this time, wealthy landowners and merchants also felt the need to travel by sea, which resulted in the eventual evolution of luxurious ocean liners. The elite were fitted into first-class accommodations, while other passengers were crowded into unsanitary conditions and cramped living quarters. This aspect of sea travel was well portrayed in Hollywood's blockbuster hit movie *Titanic*.

The original *Titanic* was one of three new ships built in the early 1900s by the White Star Line in an effort to compete against Cunard, the world-famous luxury cruise line. White Star's goals were to make its new ships—the *Olympic*, *Titanic*, and *Britannic*—the quietest, most luxurious, and most stable ships afloat. This was made possible, in part, because White Star installed only as many lifeboats as maritime regulations called for (enough to carry half the people aboard).[4] In 1911, the *Olympic* made its maiden voyage. It was a huge success, so its sister ship, the *Titanic*, made its first trip one year later on April 10, 1912. It carried 2,225 passengers, most of whom traveled in second and third class. On April 15, the *Titanic* collided with an iceberg, and we know the rest of the story. The poorer passengers were locked below deck while the first-class passengers boarded lifeboats. Only 705 passengers survived, and Captain Smith, who is blamed for the *Titanic* disaster, went down with the ship. The only good thing that came out of the accident was the realization of the need to increase safety regulations—particularly, for ships to carry sufficient lifeboats.[5]

World War I dramatically changed the ship travel industry. Many factors played a part in this, including changes in U. S. immigration policies and the new attraction that travel to Europe came to hold for the Americans. All in all, cruising became the fashionable thing to do, leading to an increase in the number of cruise ships built and operated. Despite a slight decline during World War II, the popularity of cruising continued and transatlantic passenger cruises reached an all-time high in 1957. Later, passenger numbers declined temporarily with the increasing popularity of air travel. Today, most cruises are Caribbean or Mediterranean cruises that stress the ease of being aboard. Ports of call are only a side note. Transatlantic and around-the-world voyages are rare, but cruises are still available to all parts of the world. Technological advances in ship engines were a reason for the increase in the size of cruise ships and their speed.

Interestingly, the airplane, which caused the demise of most transoceanic passenger service, actually helped stimulate the cruise business. In fact, as early as the 1950s, most of the passengers on some Mediterranean-based cruise ships arrived at the **embarkation** point by plane. These **air–cruise packages** made cruising an option for millions of potential new passengers, and to this date they are still a popular means for inland passengers to make their way to the coast. For many years, the packages meant savings for the cruise passenger. This trend has turned, however, as cruise lines have found themselves at odds with the airlines, to the point where it sometimes may be cheaper for customers to make their own travel arrangements.

Cruising Today

Today, cruising is on the rise. The cruise business is reported to be a $35.7 billion industry.[6] The major cruise lines continually launch new cruise ships. In the past decade, embarkations from North American ports have increased, and currently there are no signs that this growth will stop. The past couple of years have resulted in a port expansion program for the United States cruise industry.

The cruise industry has experienced a steady growth over the last 10 years. Cruise lines are spending billions on new and refurbished ships, all with the intention of adding capacity. Yet significant growth opportunities still exist for the industry. With only about 10 percent of the potential cruise market tapped and with an estimated market of millions, the cruise industry has a bright future. For the 2010 season, it is estimated that approximately 12.62 million passengers worldwide will be cruising.[7] The state of Florida will account for 56 percent of all U.S. embarkations.[8]

Portofino, Italy, one of the many exotic places that cruise ships visit around the world.
Courtesy of Mark Green

Key Players in the Cruise Industry

The three key players in the cruise industry are Carnival, Royal Caribbean Cruises, and Norwegian Cruise Line. Carnival Cruise Lines is the most successful financially, netting about 20 percent of global sales. It targets adults between the ages of 25 and 54 years and expects to attract close to 3 million passengers with its awesome atriums and around-the-clock activities. Its largest income, other than the fare itself, is from beverage service. Casino income is also high, and its casinos are the largest afloat. Carnival hopes that passengers will enjoy buying drinks and putting quarters, or preferably dollars, into the shipboard slot machines and playing at the gaming tables. It also hopes passengers do not mind their small cabins because the activities on the ship can occupy all their waking hours. Carnival Corporation & PLC has a portfolio of 12 cruise brands, including Carnival Cruise Lines, Princess Cruises (Princess), Costa Cruises (Costa), Holland America Line, P&O Cruises, AIDA Cruises (AIDA), Cunard Line (Cunard), P&O Cruises Australia, Ocean Village, Swan Hellenic, Seabourn Cruise Line (Seabourn), and Windstar Cruises (Windstar).[9]

The second largest cruise line is Royal Caribbean Cruises, which operates two cruise brands, Royal Caribbean International and Celebrity Cruises.[10] Combined, the two cruise brands carry more than 3 million passengers a year, and because of increasing demand, the company has introduced four more ships. Royal Caribbean Cruises targets passengers who are in their 40s with a relatively high income and welcomes families.[11]

The third largest is Star Cruises, which now operates Norwegian Cruise Line (NCL). Star Cruises received "The Leading Cruise Line in Asia-Pacific" award. Star Cruises Limited continues to grow with new ships coming. The cruise line currently employs what it calls the "freestyle cruising" concept, in which everyone is allowed to dress as they wish and eat when and where they like. NCL operates

The Pride of America, *The Pride of Aloha*, and *The Pride of Hawaii* in the Hawaiian islands, mostly on seven-day cruises around the islands and one cruise to and from California.[12]

The Cruise Market

Who goes cruising? Cruising is now more affordable than ever and appeals to a broad market—from silver-haired seniors to young couples getting married or families celebrating an occasion. The growth of cruising has been phenomenal, with passenger demand exceeding capacity (ships). According to the **Cruise Line Industry Association (CLIA)**, the average cruise passenger is 50 years old, married (78 percent), has no children in the household (65 percent), and a household income of $79,000. However, cruisers are not a homogeneous group and they take a wide variety of vacations of which cruising is but one kind. They usually travel with family members, in particular their spouse (65 percent). Despite the rising popularity of singles cruises, only 2 percent of cruisers travel alone.[13]

Most of the cruise market is for trips of seven days or fewer, regardless of the fact that cruise passengers spend more per day on short cruises than on longer ones. While the average age of the short-cruise passenger gets younger each year, the middle-aged passengers prefer to take cruises of two to three weeks in length, and the around-the-world cruise is usually for older adults, who have the leisure time and the income available for such a long trip. However, people of all ages find that if they work hard enough during the year, they can save enough money to take one week out of the year on board a cruise ship. They see the ship as a relaxing and safe venture where they don't need to plan any activities. Passengers can enjoy afternoon naps or tea, gambling, sunbathing, and participating in a number of shows and events offered on board.

About 10 million passengers take a cruise each year and many passengers are remarkably loyal to their particular cruise line and even to a ship; as many as half of the passengers on a cruise may be repeat guests. Rates vary from a starting point of about $100 per person per day on Carnival Cruise Lines to $800 on the Radisson Diamond. Rates typically are quoted per diem (per day) and are cruise-only figures based on double occupancy. Beverages, gaming, spa treatments, and shore excursions are extra.

Types of Cruises

Cruises can be categorized as follows:

Regional Cruises—Regional cruises are the most popular and sail in the Caribbean, the Mediterranean, and to a lesser extent, the Baltic Sea and other small seas. The majority of cruise lines offer regional cruises, and many specialize in one area, such as the Caribbean, or switch between the Mediterranean during summer and the Caribbean during winter.

Coastal Cruises—Coastal cruises are offered in northern Europe, the United States, and Mexico. Significantly smaller than the average floating resort, they sail closer to land, seeking out areas not accessible to larger ships. This way, the passenger gets to see more than a destination's main ports.

River Cruises—River cruise ships have a friendly atmosphere, which offsets the fact that they are often lacking in size and luxury. The newer, more modern vessels often have the feel of a small hotel, with features like public rooms, a large dining room, three to four decks, air-conditioning, an observation lounge, a bar, heated pool, sauna, gym, massage therapists, and salons. Cabins are small but comfortable, and meals are of high quality. River cruises are not only found in Europe, however. Russia, China (the Yangtze), Egypt (the Nile), Australia (River Murray), and the United States (the Mississippi) are some other exciting destinations.

World Cruises—For those with time and money to spare, a world cruise is the ultimate opportunity to see the world in style. These cruises generally last from three to six months and are for many people the travel experience of a lifetime. The accommodations are luxurious, the food is delicious, the entertainment is great, and passengers get the best of sightseeing and excursions. However, world cruises can be very expensive, sometimes up to $3,000 per day per person, with suites costing up to $300,000. Some ships, however, are more reasonable. Ukrainian vessels, for instance, sometimes charge less than $100 a day per person, and that's including gratuities! There is also the option of booking just a part of the trip on a ship.

For such long cruises, planning and preparation are vital. World cruise ships must be totally self-sufficient, and fuel, foods, and other supplies must last between ports. Once the ship has left the port, it may not see land for several weeks. Therefore, there is a large storeroom where all sorts of odds and ends and spare parts are stowed, just in case. Cruise entertainment is also an issue and includes hundreds of entertainers, lecturers, musicians, and bands who must be booked a year in advance.

Crossings—The term crossing implies sailing across the North Atlantic Ocean either to or from the Americas, although it can take place across any major ocean. The five-day Europe–America crossing is seen by most people as romantic and magical, reminiscent of the pilgrims' hazardous voyages, or maybe one of the great ocean liners of the past. Only one ship offers regular crossing service, Cunard's *Queen Mary 2*. Other cruise ships sometimes offer crossings as one-way trips to make a profit while repositioning their vessels. In spring, they sail from the Caribbean to the Mediterranean to catch the European summer season and vice versa in the fall. These crossings may last anywhere from one to two weeks.

Specialty and Theme Cruises—For those who wish to enjoy the relaxing and luxurious life aboard a cruise ship while at the same time expanding their knowledge, countless theme cruise options are available. These are often culture-rich, off-the-beaten-path itineraries built around passengers' special interests and hobbies, and they are high on enrichment and adventure. The target customers are the experienced cruisers who are looking for something more than the conventional cruise experience.

Popular themes over the past couple of years have been nature, art, theater, literature, history and heritage, all kinds of music, sports and fitness, food and wine, education, and lifestyle. Other cultural and enrichment trends are destination-intensive cruises, eco-tourism and natural history, enrichment seminars and demonstrations, special performances by artists and musicians, even singles and gay and lesbian cruises—if you can think of it, it probably exists!

CORPORATE PROFILE

Carnival Cruise Lines

Geri Engberg, Geri Engberg Photography

The name Carnival Cruise Lines is a good indication of what the company is all about. Festive yet casual, and affordable to all, Carnival is the company that brings *fun* to cruising. Starting in 1972 with only one ship named the *Mardi Gras*, entrepreneur Ted Arison realized his vision of making cruising available to the wider population and not to only the very rich. Fifteen years later, Carnival had, with seven ships in service, become the first cruise line to advertise on network TV (1984), earned its distinction as "Most Popular Cruise Line in the World," carried more passengers than any other cruise line, and undertook its initial public offering on Wall Street to raise capital for expansion.[14]

So, how is the situation today? Not surprisingly, Carnival is still the largest and most popular cruise line in the world. Carnival Cruise Lines is only one part of the huge Carnival Corporation. Carnival also operates Holland America and Windstar and has interest in Cunard Line, Costa Cruises, and Seabourn. A merger with P&O Princess Cruises PLC (now called Carnival PLC) made the company even larger. Carnival Corporation and Carnival PLC function as a single economic entity through contractual agreements between two separate legal entities. Together, these brands operate 77 ships totaling more than 128,000 lower berths. Carnival Corporation & PLC also operates the leading tour companies in Alaska and the Canadian Yukon, Holland America Tours, and Princess Tours.

What is it like to cruise with Carnival? The key word is *fun*, fun for all ages. What sets Carnival apart from the competition is its commitment to enhance all aspects of the vacation experience and stay ahead of the industry, as expressed by the phrase "Today's Carnival." All ships have a diverse and always improving selection of amenities, activities, and facilities. Each vessel has at least three swimming pools, a full casino, duty-free shopping, the feature "Nautica Spa" health club, Internet cafes, and a complimentary "Camp Carnival" children's program, top rated in the industry. Some ships even have a wedding chapel! Activities span every age group's interests and include multigenerational games for the whole family to enjoy. Entertainment ranges from Las Vegas–style shows to high-tech revues with the latest in video projections, laser techniques, and pyrotechnics; comedy shows; big band music; and much more. Shore excursions offer the traditional city tours and nature walks as well as kayaking, scuba diving, and "flightseeing" for the more active cruiser. As if this wasn't enough, Carnival has excellent foodservice, ranging from elegant multicourse meals to casual bistros for alternative dinner services, specialty areas, and 24-hour pizzerias and room service.[15]

Carnival is the only cruise line (at the time of writing) to offer a Vacation Guarantee. Confident that passengers will have a great time, Carnival offers a refund and a chance to disembark should they for some

CORPORATE PROFILE *(continued)*

reason not be satisfied with the cruise experience. For first-time cruisers, this gives a sense of assurance and increases their likelihood of trying a cruise despite any doubts they might have.[16]

Carnival's list of awards is practically endless. Some of the more prestigious awards include the following[17]:

- For the past two years, the "Fun Ships" of Carnival Cruise Lines have been voted the number one cruise choice in *Southern Living Magazine*'s annual readers' poll.

- For the past four years, Carnival's group reservations and sales service departments were named the "best of the best" by *Cruise One*, a national travel consortium that comprises some of the top travel agencies in the United States and Canada.

- Carnival received the "Gold Award of Excellence" based on the responses of more than 2,000 *American Express Travel Network* company owners and representatives who were asked to rank various components of service, including sales assistance, reservations, product, and an overall evaluation of the company.

- For three years in a row, Carnival received Cruise Line of the Year, Best Group Department, and Best District Sales Managers awards based on a survey of more than 700 National Association of Cruise-Oriented Agencies (NACOA) members who were asked to rate cruise operators in a variety of service- and marketing-related categories.

Just when we thought that was it, Carnival continues to expand. The recently launched cruise ships include the launch of Carnival *Freedom* in 2007. This will be the line's fifth 110,000-ton vessel. There is also an as-yet-unnamed 112,000-ton vessel—which will be the largest "Fun Ship" ever constructed.

Traveling by Train

Coast to coast, the United States has a lot of land to cross, with a fair share of mountains, plains, canyons, forests, deserts, and rivers. Moving goods or people from state to state back in the "old days" was extremely difficult and inconvenient, and most modern people wouldn't even consider crossing the country under the conditions back then. The solution to travel hassles, the railroad, was a huge breakthrough that changed the whole nation and made possible what we see today. Rail travel is a part of our nation's mythology, an icon of progress. The train made travel possible for almost everyone. Long-distance travel became both cheaper and faster than the horse and ship. The vast rail networks across North America, Asia, Australia, Africa, and Europe made the train station a central part of many communities. Naturally, entrepreneurs soon built hotels conveniently close to train stations.

Although highly important for many years, the popularity of rail travel started to decline in the 1920s. People stopped using the train for two main reasons: the bus and automobile, and later the airplane. By 1960, airplanes had taken over much of the long-distance travel market, further reducing the importance of the train. Facing a possible collapse of passenger rail services, Congress passed the Rail Passenger Service Act in 1970 (amended in 2001). Shortly after, the National Railroad Passenger Corporation began as a semipublic corporation established to operate intercity passenger trains, a move in the direction of seminationalization of U.S. railroads. The corporation is known today as Amtrak.

Rail Travel Abroad

While the United States tries to rejuvenate rail travel under the direction of Amtrak, rail service in other parts of the industrialized world is far ahead. Taking the train makes good sense in densely populated areas such as those in western Europe, and high-speed networks are already well developed, often drawing most of the traffic that formerly went by air. One famous example is the Eurostar, which connects the United Kingdom with mainland Europe via the 31-mile long underwater Channel Tunnel. France's **TGV trains** (Tres Grande Vitesse) are serving more than 150 cities in France and beyond, and they travel at about 186 miles per hour (although they have the capacity of running at 250 mph). The TGV's most spectacular feature is the smoothness of the ride; passengers say it is like sitting in an armchair at home. Because of their importance, all trains—high-speed or not—run frequently and on time.

The first spectacular rail accomplishment after World War II was Japan's **Shinkansen**, also called the Bullet Train system, which began operations right before the 1964 Olympics in Japan. The Bullet Trains now make the 550-mile run between Tokyo and Osaka in just over 2 hours, which certainly is better than the former time of 18 hours. Furthermore, the ride is so smooth that a passenger can set a full coffee cup on the windowsill and not spill a drop. In the more than 40 years since opening, the Shinkansen network has carried billions of passengers without a single major accident. The Shinkansen network boasts not only high speed (up to 300 kilometers per hour—the equivalent of almost 187 miles per hour), but also high frequency. For example, at least six trains per hour (not per day!) operate between Tokyo and Shin-Osaka Stations during daytime hours.[18]

In Europe, 17 nations banded together to offer visitors unlimited first-class rail service for a reduced price on the famous **Eurail** pass. The Eurail pass is sold only outside of Europe.[19] Pass holders can choose to travel in only 1 country, a few countries, or in all 17.[20] Great Britain has its own reduced fare ticket, BritRail, which can be booked by using one of the major airline reservation systems or on the BritRail website. In other parts of the world, Australia offers the

The Colosseum, Rome, Italy, is a popular place to visit for many people on a Eurail pass.

Britta Jaschinski © Dorling Kindersley

Austrail pass, India the Indrail pass, Canada the Canrail Pass, and Canada and the United States offer the North American Rail Pass, to name but a few.

Does the Train Have a Future?

For long trips, flying is obviously a lot faster than train travel. Therefore, long-distance train service is generally used mainly by those who don't want to fly and those who enjoy train travel as an experience in itself. But, as in the case of Amtrak, rail travel may make a comeback in the United States. As airports and roads become more congested, the price of airfares rise, and parking becomes a rare luxury, a train ride becomes more appealing. With the necessary improvements and the development of high-speed links, trains may become more time efficient, too.

Magnetic levitation, or maglevs, have arrived. Not aliens from outer space, but superfast trains suspended in the air and propelled by magnetic force. Maglevs can travel at speeds of more than 300 miles per hour, lifted off the ground on a cushion formed by magnetic forces and pulled forward by magnets.[21] They also run more quietly and smoothly and can climb steeper grades than conventional trains can. Maglevs require fewer personnel to operate, run at a lower cost than similar transportation, and are more energy efficient.

The maglev concept was first developed at Massachusetts Institute of Technology (MIT), and research and development has been ongoing in the United States, Germany, Britain, and Japan for decades. Plans were made in Germany to put Europe's first long maglev line in service by 2005, but the German government canceled plans because of the excessive cost of construction of a line that would only marginally improve the current high-speed service between Berlin and Hamburg. China, on the other hand, does not seem to worry about the steep cost of the maglev. The city of Shanghai has chosen to build a 20-mile maglev link connecting the new Pu Dong International Airport to Shanghai's business district. If successful, an 800-mile link will be installed from Shanghai to Beijing.[22]

In the United States, several proposed projects are under serious consideration. The Pennsylvania Project is in cooperation with Maglev, Inc., and envisions a 47-mile network linking Greensburg, Monroeville, and Pittsburgh International Airport. A competitor is a 40-mile maglev line running from Baltimore to Washington, D.C.

Is the maglev really feasible? Opponents of the idea claim that the maglev is far too expensive to be worth the investment, considering that current high-speed trains can travel at speeds exceeding 200 miles per hour if given the right conditions. Others point out the lack of design standards and manufacturers of components or spare parts, as well as the lack of tools to estimate system reliability. Although they are fast, maglevs have the capacity to travel only less than half the speed of aircraft. This means that to keep operating there is a need for cheaper tickets, fast boarding, and convenient locations for customers. That said, the automobile was also dismissed in its early days, and look what happened there! One option is proposed by Sandia National Laboratories in Albuquerque, whose Seraphim trains would be on wheels and pushed forward by magnetic propulsion. These trains would reach speeds up to 125 miles per hour all while saving power, retaining the maglev's ability to climb steep hills, and running quietly.

Another interesting recent trend in rail travel is theme packages. The Orient Express offers adventurous tourists rail travel to several destinations in Europe and Asia, such as Mandalay (Burma/Myanmar), through the Alps to Venice, or through Thailand, Malaysia, and Singapore. The American Orient Express runs between Washington, D.C., and Los Angeles or New Orleans. During the trip, passengers sleep in luxury cabins, enjoy fine dining in the restaurant car, and kick back in the club car and the observation car. These packages make rail travel a lot more than just a means of transportation—it is the actual experience.

▶ Check Your Knowledge

1. What is a TGV?
2. Where does the Shinkansen operate?

Traveling by Car on the Roads and Highways

The importance of the automobile in the United States is obvious, and we can be fairly sure that this will not change in the future. Not only is it of vital importance to the U.S. economy, but traveling by car is also the most common mode of transportation for tourists in the United States.

Road trips are a must for most Americans, college students, families, and retirees alike. Travel by car is by far the largest of all segments in the ground transportation sector of the travel and tourism industry. Therefore, is it no wonder that the highways and byways play such important roles in tourism. So, what are the advantages of auto travel? In many cases, cars bring people to places that are otherwise inaccessible. Mountain resorts, ski destinations, dude ranches, and remote spas are just a few examples. This generates millions of dollars, and in certain places the local economy depends almost completely on the auto tourist.

The United States has an expansive network of roads and highways, making auto travel a convenient way for tourists to experience the country. The following subsections discuss the U.S. interstate system, the world-famous **Route 66**, and some of the other scenic byways that help an ever-increasing number of road-trippers to explore the United States. The interstates allow people to travel quickly and conveniently across the country. Traveling by auto enables tourists to plan an itinerary and stop at many places along the way to view historical, cultural, theme park, and other types of attractions. Many leisure auto travelers are adventurous people who are not afraid to travel on their own. The interstate system, although not always exactly beautiful and scenic, serves as a quick and easy route that can be navigated by virtually anyone.

Route 66 and Other Great Drives

RVers and leisure motorists can still travel the "Main Street of America," also known as Route 66. The route is currently 2,448 miles long, crosses 8 states and 3 time zones, and stretches from Chicago, Illinois, in the heart of the Midwest to Santa Monica, California.[23] Along the way, it cuts through Illinois, Missouri, Kansas, Oklahoma, Texas, New Mexico, Arizona, and California. The original route was commissioned in 1926 and was the United States' first transcontinental highway. The road is sometimes called the "Highway of Hope" because in its early years many people fled rural life in the Midwest for the perceived riches of California. Its presence used to spur thousands of people to take to the road, and it still does.

Twisters Café, Williams, Arizona, One of Many Memorabilia Stops on Route 66
Alan Keohane © Dorling Kindersley

Route 66 is still the most famous in the States and attracts many tourists every year. Route 66 was decommissioned in 1985. By then, it had been replaced by the quicker and more efficient interstate highway system. Because many people opted for the convenience of the interstates, Route 66 was neglected. As a result, the towns that spanned along Route 66 faded away with the setting of the sun. Without tourist dollars to support their economies, many people closed shop and headed elsewhere. Those who have stayed have faced tough times. Today there is, however, an increase in the number of Route 66 devotees and seekers of nostalgia. The combination of history, culture, scenic views, and the fact that it might be the most famous stretch of American highway make it an excellent choice for a road trip.

Other **scenic trips** also interest motor tourists: the Wiregrass Trail (Georgia), the Blue Ridge Parkway (the Appalachian Mountains), the Natchez Trace (Mississippi, Alabama, and Tennessee), the Pacific Coast Highway (the West Coast), and the Klondike Trail (Canada).

▶ Check Your Knowledge

1. What are the major advantages of car travel over other means of transportation?

2. Between what cities does Route 66 stretch?

Automobile Associations

People who have a car, and especially those who do road trips, might find it a good idea to join an automobile association. Two important associations are the U.S. American Automobile Association (AAA) and the Canadian Automobile Association (CAA). Both set important standards in the industry and lobby political parties to enforce stricter automobile safety laws on behalf of motorists. However, the reason most people join is because of the roadside services offered. If a motorist should get stuck in the middle of nowhere, car broken down, it could be a potential budget buster. Members of an auto association enjoy benefits ranging from roadside first-aid repairs, to battery boosts, fuel delivery, lockout service, flat tire service, extrication, free towing (for up to seven miles), and emergency financial assistance. AAA also offers insurance, travel counseling and ticketing, hotel discounts, international driver's licenses, and tour packages.

Rental Cars

Some 5,000 car rental companies operate in the United States. Waiting at nearly every sizable airport in the world are several highly competitive car rental agencies, a significant segment of the travel and tourism business. About 75 percent of their sales take place at airport counters that are leased from the airport, the cost of which is passed on to the customer.

The larger companies do 50 percent or more of their business with large corporate accounts, accounts that receive sizable discounts. The hurried business traveler is likely to rent a car, speed out of the airport, do his or her business in a day or two, return the car to the airport, and hop on a plane to return to home base. The pleasure traveler, however, is more likely to rent a small car for a week or more. This group constitutes about 30 percent of the rental car market.

The five big rent-a-car agencies in the United States are Enterprise, Hertz, Avis, National, and Budget. Most rental car companies have undergone several changes in ownership, being bought and sold like a commodity, with huge profits made and large debts acquired. High turnover among employees is common. Avis, for example, was at one time, unusual in being employee-owned (but also heavily in debt).

Car rental companies have a number of practices that don't exactly encourage repeat customers, such as excess charges for dropping off a car at a different place from where it was picked up, or for failing to refill the gas tank before returning the car. Their advertising often fails to specify extra costs, such as insurance, charges for being under a certain age, taxes, and so forth. This way, the incredible $19 per day deal can easily become a much larger number. Pressuring or "persuading" customers to buy collision insurance is a criticized practice because many customers are, without knowing it, covered by their own car insurance. A great part of the industry's revenue comes from insurance sales, which is mostly profit for the rental car companies. Further, travelers who take advantage of express drop-off service often find that their credit card bill has add-ons that they did not anticipate.

► Check Your Knowledge

1. What are the two most important automobile associations in North America?

2. What services and benefits do these organizations offer?

Traveling by Coach

Though maybe not the most obvious choice, coach travel still provides a great transportation opportunity, no matter whether passengers just want to go to work, to the local mall, or to criss-cross the whole country. It is a huge industry with many employees, corporations, and passengers involved. Great deals on bus passes can be had as well as return and one-way tickets for many routes.

A Greyhound bus can take travelers to a number of interesting destinations.
© Dorling Kindersley

The Role of the Coach

Although the scheduled coach routes aren't as competitive as scheduled services for airlines, they still play an important role in the travel and tourism industry, especially with regard to their charter and tour services. Some coach operators even offer services such as destination management, incentive programs, as well as planning of meetings, events, and conferences. A couple of companies to check out are Canadian Tours International, Trailways, Greyhound, Gray Line World-wide, and Contiki Tours.

The two major reasons passengers select the coach over other modes of travel are convenience and economy. Many passengers are either adventurous college students from the United States and abroad or older adults, both with limited funds but plenty of time. Most people don't choose coach travel for long trips, however, because a flight is much quicker and often just as economical. But in places such as the heavily populated Northeast corridor, regular bus service between most sizable communities in New England and New York often makes it easier and safer for travelers to ride the bus than to drive their cars into the city. Anyone who has experienced New York's traffic will probably agree.

Another reason why coaches are popular is that they allow the leisure traveler to sit back, relax, enjoy the scenery, and as the advertisement says "leave the driving to us." In addition, they are hassle free and provide an opportunity to make new friends and stop anywhere along the way. Long-distance buses offer a variety of amenities similar to an airplane, with an extra benefit of door-to-door service! Buses travel to almost any community, small and large, bringing with them tourist dollars and thus a boost to local economies.

Types of Coach Services

In addition to routes between towns and cities, coach travel includes local route service; charter, tour, and special services; commuter service; airport service; and urban and rapid transit service. The largest and most recognized of all of the specialized travel services is Gray Line. Founded in 1910, Gray Line is a franchise operation based in Colorado. The company assembles package tours and customized tours, arranges rail and air transfers, and even plans meeting and convention services. Its major service, however, is sightseeing trips by coach. When a traveler arrives at a destination and wishes to see the town and the major tourist attractions, Gray Line is usually ready to serve. Its trips are widely diversified, and destinations are anywhere from Paris, France; to Panama City, Panama; Beirut, Lebanon; Jakarta, Indonesia; to Melbourne, Australia.

▶ Check Your Knowledge

1. What are the two most common reasons for selecting the bus over other means of traveling?

2. Which is the largest and most recognized of all the specialized bus travel services?

Coach Associations

There are several coach associations in the United States and Canada; here we introduce two of the largest ones. The American Bus Association (ABA) was founded in 1926 and is a trade association of the intercity bus industry in the United States and Canada. A couple of its most important functions are to facilitate relationships between the North American motor coach industry and all related segments of the travel and supplier industry, as well as to create awareness of the motor coach industry among consumers in North America (United States, Canada, and Mexico) and communicate publicly on important issues such as coach and highway safety.[24]

ABA sponsors several programs including the Certified Travel Industry Specialist Program and the George T. Snyder Jr. Scholarship Program. It also prints *Destinations Magazine* and the *ABA Motorcoach Marketer*. ABA's total membership is more than 3,200 members, approximately 950 of which are motor coach and tour companies. The National Motorcoach Network (NMN) includes an extensive number of charter and tour affiliates. The network has an established nationwide reservations center and publishes *Byways Magazine* to help consumers plan their leisure vacations. It also works to promote safety among its affiliate members.

FOCUS ON

Air Travel

Janet Zinck

Today, hopping on an airplane is something people do on a regular basis. You can jump on the Internet or make a call to your travel agent, and be on a flight in a few hours to any corner of the world. Airfares change in a minute, multiple airlines compete for travel to most destinations, and people know that they must do their research to find the best possible fare. I must tell you that this amazes me because I have literally watched the way we get around by air transform in my lifetime. I don't consider myself old, although you may feel very differently about that, but this airline world as you know it is a rather young industry.

It isn't that airlines did not exist back in the 1960s when I was in grade school, but I didn't know of any kid my age who had flown on an airplane back at that time. If I had asked a classroom of students to raise their hands if they had ridden on a commercial plane, I doubt a hand would have gone up. Consider the contrast to a classroom of children today. More hands would go up than not.

Although planes were taking people internationally and long haul back in the 1960s, the idea of travel by jet was in its infancy. Most Americans had not yet experienced the magic of airline travel. Flying was such a novelty, I can recall a time when American Airlines offered a sightseeing flight out of the Rochester Airport to expose people to the flying experience. At that time, it cost about $25, and passengers were buckled in to experience the excitement of the airport, a jet, takeoff, and landing. My brother entered a contest on a local radio station and won two seats on this sightseeing flight. He brought me along, and we flew a leisurely flight path out of the Rochester, New York, airport, circling over Syracuse and then again over Buffalo, and then returned home. I can remember seeing Niagara Falls out the airplane window. I thought this was the thrill of a lifetime, and my friends were in total awe! I was intrigued by the stewardesses (which is what they were called back then) as they walked around the plane in their airline uniforms, all young and attractive women, serving beverages and snacks.

This was the defining moment in my life when I knew I wanted to work for an airline. I felt the excitement of this new industry and wanted to be part of it. Can you even imagine a time when the airlines had to encourage people to come to the airport and get on a plane so that they could see what an airplane actually looked like? Can you even imagine a time when airlines had to actively market the flying experience to an audience predominantly made up of nonflyers? Those were also the days when individuals would hop in their family car on a weekend evening and visit the observation deck at the airport. It was a thrill to see an actual airplane close up and personal, and to watch them take off and land.

As the general public became more and more intrigued by airplanes, the United States government also began to realize that airline travel was growing at a rapid pace and deemed it necessary to create a separate government agency to manage this growth. The Civil Aeronautics Authority was created to oversee and promote this new airline business in the United States. The government wanted to make sure it grew in a sane and controllable manner. It also wanted to make sure that airlines entering into this "flying" business were profitable, and that the consumer purchasing the product would be safe.

The airline industry in the 1960s and 1970s was not the cut-throat competitive industry that you know today. In fact, it was very civil and noncompetitive. To go into the airline business, a prospective company needed to approach the government to obtain its "blessing" to become an authentic airline business. Once the company was granted permission to be an airline, it needed to seek permission for the route it wanted to fly. The government had to approve what cities the company could offer service between; airlines couldn't

(continued)

just decide they wanted to fly from New York City to San Francisco. The government needed to determine whether there was a need for service to those areas, and it needed to make sure this airline would not interfere with another airline's ability to be profitable. If two airlines were permitted to fly the same route, it was because there was enough business for both airlines to survive. If one airline charged $100 for that route, the other airline would have to charge the same. If an airline wanted to change its flight schedules, fares, or add routes, permission would again need to be granted by the government. Similar to the childhood game "mother may I," the government, not the airline, had the final say. The Civil Aeronautics Authority not only granted permission to fly between certain cities, but also needed to give permission if an airline wanted to eliminate service on a certain route.

Everything changed in 1978 when deregulation was signed into law. The logic behind deregulation was that in the United States, people should be able to go into business and make their own decisions. The success or failure of their companies should be in their hands, not the government's. Deregulation removed government control over fares, routes, and market entry of new airlines for commercial aviation. Airlines could now decide where to fly, what to charge, and make their own decisions for the first time. A new airline chaos had been created.

There have been positives and negatives to deregulation. It is a much more complicated airline world. Fares are totally unpredictable and confusing. Now a client can call a travel agent or a customer can go on a website and pull up information on flights. Travelers must weed through multiple airlines that service this route, numerous fares with rules and regulations galore, and within two minutes, the fare they were looking at is no longer there. An airline might be in business today and bankrupt tomorrow. But, on the other hand, airlines fly more places and offer more affordable fares than ever before. They have created ways to do business smarter. Airlines now fly customers through connecting cities to utilize their fleets more efficiently and they have developed partnerships with smaller carriers to help create a more affordable product. Airlines are finding it more and more difficult to realize an affordable product, but the consumer certainly has realized a much more affordable product. Flying is now something almost everyone can take advantage of.

Source: Courtesy of Janet Zinck, Monroe Community College.

Air Transportation

Now that we know more about ground transportation, let us take a closer look at a major area of business: air transportation. As a student of tourism, you know that the development of air travel is closely linked to the growth of the travel and tourism industry. In the short space of 70 years, it has brought the world together. Air travel has made it possible to build great resorts on remote islands; it has fostered multinational enterprises and broadened the horizons of hundreds of millions of people. Without the airplane, many resort destinations would have been virtually impossible to build. The number of international travelers would be far fewer because of the time, money, and difficulty involved in travel. The airplane makes travel easier and more convenient because even the most remote location is just a few hours away by plane and reasonable airfares make it possible for many more people to take advantage of this.

Air transport has become an integral factor in the travel and tourism industry. Hotels, car rental agencies, and even cruise lines depend heavily on airplanes for profits. For instance, lower airfares result in more passengers, and hence a larger occupancy at hotels. Whole towns and cities can and do benefit from this same concept. This leads to better public facilities, better schools, and even less taxes. This section describes the air transportation industry from its birth in the early part of the twentieth century to its current use, its impact on society, and proposed advances in the future.

How many people travel by airplane? By 2012, total passenger traffic between the United States and the rest of the world is projected to reach 1 billion flights annually. The expansion of the airline industry was tremendous in the 1990s, and even though many U.S. airlines are currently facing financial problems, the number of flights is almost back to pre–September 11 levels, and the industry growth is expected to continue in the future, with additional security measures both in the airports and on board.

The most popular of the Boeing jets are the 747-400, the 737 new generation series, including the 737-900, the 777 series, and the new Business Jet. Airbus has also introduced a number of jets, including the A300/310, A320, the A330/340/350 family, and the A380.[25] The A380, Airbus's response to Boeing's Jumbo Jet, is expected to become one of the most successful planes ever built. Being a full-sized double-decker (not only with a small upper floor as is the case with the Boeing 747), it has the capacity to carry almost twice as many passengers as the Boeing 747 and still use less fuel. The A380 has recently been introduced to the market. The A380 burns 17 percent less fuel per seat than today's largest aircraft. This is one of the most significant steps forward in reducing aircraft fuel burn and resultant emissions in four decades. Low fuel burn means lower carbon dioxide emissions.[26]

In response to the overwhelming preference of airlines around the world, and the need for efficiency, Boeing has developed the 787 Dreamliner Series, a family of superefficient planes. The planes will carry between 210 and 330 passengers and (depending on the plane) will have a range of up to 8,500 nautical miles. The planes will use 20 percent less fuel for comparable missions than today's similarly sized airplane. It will also travel at speeds similar to today's fastest wide-bodied aircraft.[27]

The interior of the cockpit of a jumbo jet showing the flight deck controls and pilot and co-pilot seats.
Richard Leeney © Dorling Kindersley

▶ Check Your Knowledge

1. How many passenger flights are expected between the United States and the rest of the world by 2012?

2. What did deregulation do for the airline industry and its passengers?

Highways in the Sky

How can it be that with so many flights in the same areas, planes don't crash into each other every day? Well, the answer is that commercial airliners are subject to many regulations. Jets fly along **airways** just as cars drive on highways. Jet Eighty, for example, is a major aerial artery across the central part of the United States. Airways do not necessarily connect cities. Instead, they follow radio beams emitted from navigation stations 200 to 300 miles apart. Except for deviations caused by weather conditions, pilots follow these sky tracks from station to station. More important, perhaps, are international rules designed to keep airplanes well apart from each other. Planes generally must be at least 1,000 feet above or below one another, and 10 miles on either side. At takeoff, planes are separated by time intervals of one minute when going in different directions, and two minutes when going in the same direction.

In the sky, commercial aircraft fly at altitudes between 18,000 and 75,000 feet. The air space between 45,000 and 75,000 feet is reserved for the **supersonic jets**. Subsonic jets fly at about 30,000 to 40,000 feet, where the thinner air of the higher altitudes offers less resistance to the plane and reduces the amount of fuel needed. The lowest layer is used by turboprop and propeller-driven aircraft. Below 18,000 feet and outside established airways, pilots generally fly on a "see and be seen" basis without radar guidance. Passengers in a plane coming in for a landing at night will notice lines of white stroboscopic lights. These are sequence flashers that aid the pilot in marking the runway centerline. The red approach lights indicate an "undershoot zone," an unobstructed runway section some 1,000 feet long in which pilots should not land.

Effect of the Jet Stream

Do you ever wonder why it takes about half an hour longer to fly from the East Coast to the West Coast than to fly west to east? It is because there are winds resembling huge streams circling the hemisphere, usually at altitudes of 30,000 to 40,000 feet. These **jet streams** are established when cold polar air meets hot air from the tropical regions. They generally flow from west to east, but may flow north to south. Airline pilots can ride these streams when flying east, which makes the trip shorter, but must fly against the current when traveling west. Picture a swimmer in a river swimming upstream. The force of the current pushes the person back, which makes it take longer to get where he or she is going.

Routing

How do pilots find their way on these invisible highways? Is there an airline version of Mapquest where they can plot in where they are and where they want to go, and get directions? Believe it or not, there is! For long flights, computers are used to project the fastest and most fuel-efficient routes. This is important because fuel costs make up about 25 percent of the total operating costs. The altitudes for most efficient flight are also projected. It was once believed that the highest possible altitude was best, but a jet loaded with fuel burns excessive amounts in the climb. Therefore, the climb upward is taken in steps. The plane becomes lighter as more fuel is consumed, and then the plane is taken higher up. On takeoff alone, a B-747 burns 185 gallons of fuel a minute. On a long flight, such as the 6,000-mile trip from New York to Tokyo, fuel can initially account for as much as half the weight of the plane (about 50,000 gallons of kerosene).

Long-distance flights follow routes different from what would be expected by looking at the usual map of a flat world. Weather and traffic conditions help determine the best route. Flights from Los Angeles to London, for example, may go diagonally across the United States or fly north to Winnipeg, across Canada, over Greenland and Iceland, and then southeast to London. Thank goodness for computers!

The Hub and Spoke Concept

The major airlines link their routes together through a **hub and spoke system**, selecting one or more hub cities, into and out of which most of their flights radiate. By linking flights at the hubs and tightly coordinating flight schedules, the airline can offer service that is more frequent and attract more passengers. The airlines have set up 120 U.S. hubs, among them, 12 **fortress hubs**, in which one airline controls 75 percent or more of all passenger boardings, thus an airport chosen as a hub by a particular airline is usually dominated by that airline. The airlines that dominate a hub often raise fares for the local passengers who are flying short distances. The dominant airlines control most of the gates and terminal facilities, making it difficult for competing airlines to gain entry into the airport. With less competition, the carriers are able to charge higher fares, and the market will be forced to pay them. For longer flights however, fares are often much more competitive. This is valuable information for a travel agent trying to get his or her client the best possible price. For instance, if a client does not need to land in a major city, rural airports will be less expensive.

Although the hub-and-spoke concept promotes airline efficiency and provides for rapid change of planes, it has some disadvantages. In bad weather, flights tend to back up and passengers miss their connections. Atlanta's Hartsfield Airport, a hub for Delta Airlines, has become notorious for overcrowding, long delays in departures, lost luggage, and angry passengers. As someone once put it, "Even to get from heaven to hell you have to transfer in Atlanta." In less congested hubs, such as Kansas City and Memphis, the hub-and-spoke concept works to the airline's and the passenger's advantage. Less baggage is lost, and the passenger can easily make a connection at a nearby gate.

Air transit points or gateway cities around the world are a variation of the hub-and-spoke concept. Airports become transit points because of their geographical location and their importance to large populations and concentrations of wealth and power. London, Paris, Amsterdam, Frankfurt, Copenhagen, Madrid, and Rome are important European transit points. In Southeast Asia the major gateway cities are Hong Kong, Singapore, Tokyo, Bangkok; in Canada, the airports serving Vancouver, Toronto, and Montreal are major transit points.

▶ Check Your Knowledge

1. What is a jet stream and how do jet streams affect flight times?

2. Define the concepts of hubs and fortress hubs.

3. Name some major hubs in the United States.

Airports Around the World

The busiest airports are like giant waiting rooms for people in transit. According to the Airport Council International, the world's 10 busiest airports are as shown in Figure 14–1.

Most of the transatlantic flights from North America terminate in Europe, usually London, Paris, Copenhagen, Frankfurt, Amsterdam, Lisbon, Rome, or Madrid. In the Middle East, the major air centers are Istanbul, Turkey; Jeddah, Saudi Arabia; Dubai, United Arab Emirates; and Tel Aviv, Israel. Africa as well has several major airports: Nairobi and Kenya in the east, and in the west, large terminals in the Ivory Coast and Senegal. The major airports in South Africa are at Johannesburg and Cape Town. In Asia, Tokyo is the major air center for Japan, and Seoul is the same for South Korea. China has large airports in Beijing, Hong Kong, and Shanghai, which are large trading and tourist centers; Indonesia has Jakarta, and Singapore is a major hub for the Far East. Flights from the United States to New Zealand and Australia usually pass through Honolulu or Papeete, Tahiti, and sometimes Nadi, Fiji. The major airports in New Zealand are at Auckland and Wellington, while those in Australia are at Sydney, Perth, and Melbourne.

Most large cities in the Western world are not only air transit points but also tourist centers that attract both pleasure and business travelers. In the United States, New York, Miami, San Francisco, and Los Angeles are examples of tourist centers. In Europe, London, Paris, Copenhagen, Rome, and Vienna are centers of tourism as well as centers of culture, government, and business. Mexico City, Caracas, and Rio

1. Atlanta's Hartsfield-Jackson
2. Chicago's O'Hare
3. London's Heathrow
4. Tokyo's Haneda
5. Los Angeles International
6. Dallas/Ft. Worth International
7. Paris's Charles de Gaulle
8. Frankfurt International
9. Beijing International
10. Denver International

Figure 14–1 • The World's Top 10 Busiest Airports

Source: Airport Council International, "Statistics Highlight," www.airports.org/cda/aci_common/display/main/aci_content07_c.jsp?zn=aci&cp=1-5_666_2 (accessed September 23, 2009).

de Janeiro are major travel and transit centers in Latin America, while Tokyo, Bangkok, and Singapore stand out as tourist centers in Asia. Yet size alone does not create tourist appeal. Places such as Mumbai, Sao Paulo, Calcutta, and Jakarta have huge populations, but arouse little tourist interest. Climate, environment, and development are just a few of the factors that can have an influence on tourism.

▶ Check Your Knowledge

1. What are the three busiest airports in the world?
2. What are the major airports in Europe; the Middle East; Southeast Asia; and Australia/New Zealand?

International Airline Organizations

Two international organizations based in Montreal are concerned with airline coordination and safety: the International Civil Aviation Organization (ICAO) and the International Air Transport Association (IATA). ICAO is an association of national governments, whereas IATA is an association of airlines. ICAO, an intergovernmental regulatory agency, concentrates on air navigation and air transport with regard to safety and coordination of air services.[28] It is funded by governments, with the largest share coming from the United States.

IATA, on the other hand, has a different interest. In the past, a principal purpose of IATA was to get member airlines to agree voluntarily on airfares for international flights. Members generally live up to the agreements, which have kept airfares higher than would have occurred in open competition. IATA's mission is to represent, lead, and serve the airline industry. Its members comprise more than 240 airlines—the world's leading passenger and cargo airlines among them—representing 94 percent of scheduled international air traffic.[29] IATA focuses on several "freedoms," or rights of the air, and over the years, three unofficial freedoms have been added to the list. Still, it is important to note that not all of the freedoms have been completely accepted worldwide. The eight freedoms are shown in Figure 14–2.

In 1946, the United States and the United Kingdom negotiated a bilateral agreement known as the Bermuda Principles. The Bermuda agreement incorporates the spirit of the Flying Freedoms and is the model for all subsequent agreements. The Helsinki Accord of 1975 is a general statement declaring tourism a positive force, one that should be encouraged and facilitated. The Helsinki Accord acknowledges the contribution of international tourism in the development of mutual understanding between people and recognizes its value in promoting economic and social well-being.

International landings and other flight agreements are used as diplomatic and economic bargaining chips. No nation wants a travel deficit (greater foreign expenditures for travel than income from foreign travelers). One way to increase national tourism income is to gain as many advantages as possible for the national carriers and limit the advantages of foreign carriers.

- *First Freedom*—The right of an airline to overfly one country to get to another.
- *Second Freedom*—The right of an airline to land in another country for a technical stopover (fuel, maintenance, etc.) but not to pick up or drop off traffic (passengers or cargo).
- *Third Freedom*—The right of an airline registered in country X to drop off traffic from country X to country Y.
- *Fourth Freedom*—The right of an airline registered in country X to carry traffic back to country X from country Y.
- *Fifth Freedom*—The right of an airline registered in country X to collect traffic in country Y and fly on to country Z, as long as the flight either originates or terminates in country X.
- *Sixth Freedom*—The right of an airline registered in country X to carry traffic to a gateway (a point in country X) and then abroad. The traffic has neither its origins nor its ultimate destination in country X.
- *Seventh Freedom*—The right of an airline registered in country X to operate entirely outside of country X in carrying traffic between two other countries.
- *Eighth Freedom*—The right of an airline registered in country X to carry traffic between any two points in the same foreign country.

Figure 14–2 • The Eight Freedoms of the Air

▶ Check Your Knowledge

1. What are the main purposes of ICAO and IATA?
2. Think of two examples of how nations increase tourism income by gaining advantages for their national air carriers.

Airline Safety

Safety and technical oversight of commercial aviation is under the jurisdiction of the Federal Aviation Administration (FAA), an agency of the Department of Transportation (DOT). It is to this agency that service complaints are directed.

The FAA concentrates on passenger safety, aircraft certification to meet safety standards, pilot licensing, and air traffic control. The FAA also investigates aircraft accidents along with the National Transportation Safety Board (NTSB) and sets standards for the design and building of new aircraft and equipment.[30] Its primary concern is to direct air traffic in the federal airway system, which covers 350,000 miles. Aircraft flying above 18,000 feet are constantly monitored by ground-based radar, and air traffic controllers direct air traffic into and out of commercial U.S. airports.

Airfares

Deregulation and more efficient operations have reduced airfares drastically. The average ticket price has dropped in comparison to other consumer costs. Airfares are set to serve two broad markets, the business traveler and the leisure traveler. Business travelers usually have few options in scheduling their trips. They need to go and return at specific times. Standard airfares are quoted for the business traveler; whereas discount fares attract the discretionary traveler. The difference between the two can be huge. Fares for two seats, side by side, may vary as much as several hundred dollars, depending on the discount or special fare being paid by the passengers.

Discounted fares are usually highly restrictive: the traveler must go and return as specified. Penalties for not following the schedule can be high. This two-tier system of pricing puts the burden of the fare on the business traveler, who usually accepts the premium charge out of necessity and the fact that the trip is tax deductible. Originally intended for the individual business traveler, airlines courted these highly profitable customers with frequent flyer bonuses in the form of free trips and other rewards. For several years now, this practice has been extended to the leisure traveler as well.

Airfare distortion is also caused by **cabotage**, which restricts foreign airlines from engaging in passenger service within a country. For example, when Singapore Airlines stops in Hawaii for refueling on its way to and from the United States, it is not allowed to drop off or pick up passengers between Hawaii and the continental United States. If foreign airlines were given passenger service within the country, airfares would be more competitive. On the international scale, fares are not only determined by distance but by national interest, bilateral and multilateral negotiations, and competition.

Overbooking and Bumping

Airlines legitimately overbook the number of passengers on a flight for a very good reason. A certain percentage of the passengers who have booked seats do not appear (they are called "no shows"). The percentage normally varies from 2 to 33 percent. Some travelers book more than one flight, and then fail to cancel flights not taken. Bad weather, time of day, traffic conditions, and late connections are other reasons for no shows, and the airline response is to overbook so as not to lose revenue.

Oftentimes, more passengers show up than there are seats available, and some passengers are **bumped**. If they have a confirmed reservation and arrive at the departure gate at least 10 minutes before the scheduled departure time for domestic flights, they are entitled to compensation. Airlines often offer money to confirmed passengers, or credit for future travel on that airline, to take a later flight that is not filled. This happens to the extent that some people actually hope and volunteer to be bumped! If you could get a $400 voucher toward another ticket for flying two hours later than planned, wouldn't you do it?

Deregulation and Profits

For 40 years, from 1939 to the late 1970s, the airline industry was highly controlled and protected by government with protected routes, profits, employees, and management. The major airlines even had a mutual-aid pact, an arrangement by which colleagues grounded by strikes were compensated by other pact members. The deregulation brought about major changes in the number of airlines, which quickly jumped from 22 to more than 80. New airlines often employed enthusiastic nonunion personnel; in some cases pilots worked for a third of the union salaries. Some acted as ticket agents and baggage handlers, and then climbed aboard to fly the plane. These new airlines could underprice their competitors' fares because of lower labor costs and more enthusiastic and productive employees.

Most of the new airlines failed to survive, however. Starting in the late 1980s, a huge consolidation of major airlines has taken place as airlines have bought other airlines. The main reason for airline failure was and is undercapitalization. Existing airlines have more capital backing, which enables them to underprice the new airlines for extended periods. In other cases, the new entrepreneurs misread the market. In reality, however, there were not enough potential customers to sustain so many new airlines.

Some of these low-cost airlines remain profitable even today, with profits and market shares increasing faster than those of the traditional airlines. With their much lower ticket prices, the low-cost airlines provide both a great opportunity for budget-conscious travelers and a major threat to the traditional, older airlines.

Reregulation?

Deregulation of the airline industry in 1978 was followed by years of falling prices; it increased the number of cheap travel options and produced strong industry competition. So, why might the airlines be looking at *re*-regulation? After deregulation, the airlines racked up large financial debts in an attempt to finance expansion. Competition became intense, leading to the bankruptcy of some major and several smaller carriers, as well as the layoff of thousands of airline employees. Airline workers faced pay cuts (for example, a senior pilot was paid $250,000 for a few flights a month), increased hours, a cut in vacation days, increased out-of-pocket medical expenses, and a no-strike clause. All this and increasing fuel, medical, and pension benefits make the airline industry a very tough one in which to compete.

Some people maintain that the airline industry must be nationalized and run as a public utility, that the well-being of passengers and employees cannot be sacrificed in pursuit of greater profits. Another argument is that major carriers often offer consumers significant discounts in an effort to drive smaller companies out of the market. Consumers, on the other hand, greatly benefited from the increased competition and the lower airfares that came with it.

Deregulation of the airlines led to more airlines, more flights, discounted fares, and an explosion in the number of domestic passengers. To remain competitive, the airlines cut salaries and the number of people in a cabin crew. The consequences of that action were in many cases less service and more passenger complaints. This situation has two sides, however. On the one hand, airline employees get paid less and even risk losing their jobs in a merger. On the other hand, passengers benefit through lower prices, although sacrificing the in-flight service and the meal that used to be an integral part of flying in the past. Which do we prefer, cheaper flights or better service?

▶ Check Your Knowledge

1. What are the most important costs for airlines?
2. What are the major arguments pro and con for reregulation of the airline industry?

CAREER INFORMATION

Those interested in pursuing a career in the cruise industry might be surprised at the variety of jobs to choose between. The first decision you need to make is whether you would like to work on land or at sea. Land-based jobs are much like those of any tour operator, in areas such as administration, sales, reservations, marketing/public relations, human resources, accounting, finance, customer service, and so on. Jobs onboard a cruise ship are a bit different, ranging from food and beverage, catering, hotel, and concierge type jobs, to entertainment and activities, through to all the traditional shipboard jobs needed to keep the vessel safely afloat.

No two ships are alike. Each has its own personality and character. The nationality of the ship's officers and staff contributes greatly to the ship's ambiance. For example, the ships under the Holland America flag have Dutch officers and Indonesian/Filipino crew, and those belonging to the Epirotiki flag have Greek officers and crew. Most cruise ships sail under foreign flags and were built abroad for the following reasons:

- U.S. labor costs for ships, officers, and crew are too high to compete in the world market.
- U.S. ships are not permitted to operate casino-type gambling.
- Many foreign shipyards are government subsidized to keep workers employed, thereby lowering construction costs.

In addition, cruise ships sail under foreign flags (called flags of convenience) because registering these ships in countries such as Panama, the Bahamas, and Liberia means fewer and more lax regulations and little or no taxation.

Employment opportunities for Americans are mainly in sales, marketing, and other U.S. shore-based activities, such as reservations and supplies. On board, Americans sometimes occupy certain positions such as cruise director and purser. The reasons that few Americans work onboard cruise ships are that the ships are at sea for months at a time with just a few hours in port. The hours are long and the conditions for crew are not likely to be acceptable to most Americans. No, you don't get your own cabin! Still interested? One good place to start your search is the website www.cruiseshipjob.com. There you can browse the qualifications needed, the job descriptions, and the salary ranges for all positions in the industry.

Cruise ships have a limited number of high-ranking onboard positions such as cruise director and hotel manager. Most ships also have foreign crews because they can avoid American laws on issues such as overtime. As mentioned earlier, there are numerous onshore careers in marketing and sales, human resources, accounting, and finance. Cruise directors arrange all the onboard activities and entertainment. This sounds exciting, and it is so long as you're organized and can work under pressure. The career path to a cruise director begins with a position as an activities staff member or a sports and fitness specialist. Then, after a year or more at each of these positions, promotion to a supervisor in one department and then other departments occurs, leading to becoming an assistant cruise director.

Because the cruise industry is one of the fastest growing sectors in the world it comes as no surprise that the job prospects are good. It is estimated that 5 to 10 ships are being built each year. This creates a big increase in the number of employment opportunities that are offered yearly. As mentioned earlier, employment opportunities for Americans are mainly in sales, marketing, and U.S. shore-based activities (i.e., reservations and supplies). There are also positions such as cruise director, purser, chief steward, and hotel manager. Employment opportunities are also available in the other areas of transportation such as the airline, auto rental, and motor coach industries.

CASE STUDY

Delays

You are the chaperone of 25 college-aged students. You are departing Buffalo, New York, and will be flying to Orlando, Florida, where you will transfer to your cruise ship for the next four days. All the students arrive on time at the prearranged meeting place and check in with the airline. They have been advised that they are allowed to check one bag and that there will be a charge for that bag. They have also been advised on security regulations and weight restrictions. All goes well, and you sigh with relief once you take a head count and the flight takes off out of the Buffalo airport.

While connecting in Baltimore, Maryland, however, it becomes evident that the aircraft your group is scheduled to fly on to Orlando is experiencing a mechanical delay. The students can see the mechanics busy working on the aircraft, and the gate agent is unsure of how long this delay will actually take. The 50-minute scheduled connection is now approaching two hours in duration. It is now 10:45 A.M., and you are becoming increasingly concerned. You know that the actual flying time between Baltimore and Orlando is approximately 2 hours and 15 minutes. You also know that once the airplane is flight ready, it will take at least a half hour to board the aircraft. You also know that Orlando is an extremely large airport and that it takes a minimum of 30 minutes once the airplane lands in Orlando to deplane the passengers, to transfer from the arriving gate area to the baggage area, and for bags to actually arrive at the turnstiles. In addition, it is a minimum drive time of 45 minutes to the pier. All passengers must be at the pier by 3 P.M. or they will not be permitted to board the ship.

Questions

1. At 10:45 A.M., it is unclear how much longer this plane will be delayed. What actions might you take as the leader of this group? What are some of the alternatives you might consider at this point?

2. If you could get some of the passengers on another flight, what decisions would you have to make regarding baggage, splitting the group up, and so forth? Would you travel with the students who will arrive in Orlando first or stay with the group that will arrive later? Why?

3. If the airline is able to fix the problem and depart, what would you do if when you arrive in Orlando, you have only 50 minutes to get to the ship? Will you wait for the baggage? Will you go to the ship without the baggage? How will you calm down your students, who will be extremely upset if they are not able to wait for the baggage? How will you handle this situation with the airline? How will you handle this situation with the cruise line?

Source: Courtesy of Janet Zinck, Monroe Community College.

Summary

1. The U.S. railroad was developed mainly because of the need to move goods and people from one region of the country to another.
2. By the 1960s, the car and the bus had taken over most of the travel market, and the decline of the railway was a fact.
3. The Rail Passenger Service Act (1970) facilitated the creation of the organization now known as Amtrak, which seminationalized the U.S. railroad.
4. Trains are more widely used in other parts of the world, especially in Europe, where high-speed networks make it easy and convenient to take the train.
5. Travel by car is the largest segment in the ground transportation sector of the travel and tourism industry, bringing motorists to places that otherwise would have been inaccessible.
6. Historic Route 66 is perhaps the most famous highway in the United States.
7. Automobile associations are of great help to motorists, providing roadside assistance such as free towing, setting industry standards, and lobbying on behalf of their members. They also offer ticketing, international driver's licenses, travel counseling, and research on travel patterns and impacts.
8. Although losing customers to the car and airplane, buses still play an important role in the travel and tourism industry.
9. The American Bus Association (ABA) is a trade association of the intercity bus industry in the United States and Canada. The National Motorcoach Network has more than 75 charter and tour companies in its member base.
10. The development of air travel is closely linked to the success of the travel and tourism industry, and vice versa. The airplane makes travel easier and low airfares make it possible for everyone to travel. Hotels, car rental agencies, and even cruise lines depend heavily on airline passengers for revenue.
11. Commercial airliners fly along airways just as cars drive on highways. International rules are designed to keep airplanes well apart from each other during takeoff, flight, and landing.
12. A hub-and-spoke system is used by major airlines to link their routes together through one or more hub cities, into and out of which most of their flights radiate.
13. The two major international organizations are the International Civil Aviation Organization (ICAO) and the International Air Transport Association (IATA). IATA focuses on several "freedoms," or rights of the air, which it hopes will be adopted by all countries.
14. The Federal Aviation Administration (FAA) oversees safety and technical aspects of commercial aviation.
15. Airlines overbook flights because of the high percentage of passengers who do not appear even though they have made a booking. When more passengers show up than there are seats available, some passengers are bumped.
16. Air miles and travel reward programs have flourished, creating a sense of loyalty between the airline and the customer.

Key Words and Concepts

air–cruise packages
airways
bumping
cabotage
Cruise Line Industry
   Association (CLIA)

embarkation
Eurail
fortress hub
hub and spoke system
jet stream
magnetic levitation or maglevs

Route 66
scenic trip
Shinkansen
supersonic jet
TGV trains

Review Questions

1. Changes in the technology of travel have had widespread implications for society. Give at least three historical examples that support this statement.
2. What was the dominant mode of transportation before the 1920s? How did that change after the 1920s?
3. Travelers today can choose between car, train, bus, ship, and plane. Name some advantages and disadvantages to using each mode of transportation.
4. Do you think that train travel has a future in the United States? Please explain your answer.
5. How has the automobile changed the American way of life?
6. How do you see the future importance of the bus in the tourism industry? Use current examples to back your answer.
7. How has the development of air travel affected the tourism industry?
8. What was the effect of World War II on the airline industry?
9. What do we mean by "highways in the sky"?
10. How would you explain the concept of routing?
11. What is the hub-and-spoke concept? Name some advantages and disadvantages of the hub-and-spoke system.
12. Why do airlines overbook their flights? What happens if more passengers turn up than there are seats available?
13. What does Croatia offer tourists?
14. Which companies does Carnival Cruise Lines own?
15. Compare and contrast pre-deregulation and after deregulation of the airline industry.

Interesting Websites

American Automobile Association (AAA): www.csaa.com/home

Department of Transportation: www.dot.gov

Federal Aviation Administration: www.faa.gov

International Civil Aviation Association: www.icao.org

National Transportation Safety Board: www.ntsb.gov

Trailways: www.trailways.com

Internet Exercises

1. Go to the websites of some of the companies that sell Eurail passes. Plan your own trip to Europe. What kind of pass would you buy, for how long, and for what zone/s? At what price?
2. Check out the homepages of the major U.S. bus corporations. If you want to do an exotic trip, what packages do they offer, where to, and at what price?
3. How large actually are the difference in prices of flight tickets? Choose a route that you are interested in and check different airlines, times, and so forth. How much does the cheapest ticket you found cost? What about the most expensive?

Apply Your Knowledge

1. Why do you think cars are so important in the United States compared to other Western countries?
2. What are the major airlines today in the United States? Internationally?
3. Which do you think has the greatest potential: traditional "high-service" airlines or low-cost ones? Why? Discuss the different advantages and disadvantages.

Suggested Activity

Select your ideal vacation and cost it out so that you might receive it as a graduation gift.

Endnotes

1. P&O Cruises, website, www.pocruises.com/pocruising/company- history.aspx (accessed September 22, 2009).
2. Ibid.
3. Bob Dickinson and Andy Vladimir, *Selling the Sea* (New York: Wiley, 1997), 3.
4. William H. Miller, Jr., "A History of Luxury Cruising," *Seabourn Club Herald*, Spring 1996.
5. Ibid.
6. Cruise Lines International Association, *The Cruise Industry: A $35.7 Billion Partner in U.S. Economic Growth*, http://staging.cruising.org/Press/research/2006.CLIA.EconomicSummary.pdf (accessed September 21, 2009).
7. Michael Verikios, "Cruise Industry Experiences an Unprecedented Growth," *International Travel Daily News*, February 13, 2007, www.traveldailynews.com/pages/show_page/20532 (accessed September 21, 2009).
8. Cruise Lines International Association, *The Cruise Industry*.
9. Carnival Corporation & PLC, "Investor Relations," http://phx.corporate-ir.net/ phoenix.zhtml?c=140690&p=irol-index (accessed September 21, 2009).
10. Celebrity Cruises, "Company Profile," www.celebritycruises. com/aboutceleb/heroSingleTxt.do;jsessionid=00006Asx31D_v0QtYXJHDk47ebq:12hdebebp?pagename=company_profile&cS=SIDENAV (accessed September 21, 2009).
11. Royal Caribbean International, "Fact Sheet," www.royalcaribbean.com/content/pdf/RCI_Fast_Facts.pdf (accessed September 21, 2009).
12. Star Cruises, "About Us," www.starcruises.com/About/index.html (accessed September 21, 2009).
13. Cruise Lines International Association, "Cruise Industry Overview," www.cruising.org/press/overview%202006/9.cfm (accessed September 21, 2009).
14. Carnival Cruise Lines, "Virtual Press Kit," www.carnival.com/CMS/Articles/history_virtual2.aspx (accessed September 21, 2009).
15. Carnival Cruise Lines, *Carnival Capers*, www.carnival.com/cms/Images/Onboard_Experience/sample_capers07.pdf (accessed September 21, 2009).
16. Carnival Cruise Lines, www.carnival.com/CMS/static_templates/vacation-guarantee.aspx (accessed September 21, 2009).
17. Carnival Cruise Lines, awards, www.carnival.com/CMS/Static_Templates/Awards.aspx (accessed September 21, 2009).
18. Japan Railways Group, "Shinkansen (Bullet Train)," www.japanrail.com/JR_ shinkansen.html (accessed September 21, 2009).
19. Eurail, "Our Company: About Eurail.com," www.eurail.com/eurail_company (accessed September 21, 2009).
20. Eurail, website, www.eurail.com (accessed September 21, 2009).
21. U.S. Department of Transportation, Research and Innovative Technology Administration, "Final Report on the National Maglev Initiative," http://ntl.bts.gov/DOCS/TNM.html (accessed September 21, 2009).
22. Ibid.
23. Legends of America, "Route U.S. 66," www.legendsofamerica.com/66-Facts.html (accessed September 21, 2009).
24. American Bus Association, "About ABA," www.buses.org/aboutaba (accessed September 21, 2009).
25. Airbus, www.airbus.com/en/presscentre/ (accessed September 21, 2009).
26. Airbus, "A380 Family," www.airbus.com/en/aircraftfamilies/a380/index2.html (accessed September 21, 2009).
27. Boeing, "Boeing 787 Dreamliner Will Provide New Solutions for Airlines, Passengers," www.boeing.com/commercial/787family/background.html (accessed September 21, 2009).
28. International Civil Aviation Organization, "Strategic Objectives of ICAO," www.icao.int/icao/en/strategic_objectives.htm (accessed September 21, 2009).
29. International Civil Aviation Organization, "Mission," www.iata.org/about/mission (accessed September 21, 2009).
30. Federal Aviation Administration, "Our Mission," www.faa.gov/about/mission/ (accessed September 21, 2009).

CHAPTER 15

Lodging and Restaurants

OBJECTIVES

After reading and studying this chapter, you should be able to:

- Describe the characteristics and classifications of the lodging industry.

- Explain the importance of the lodging and restaurant sectors of the travel and tourism industry.

- Outline the different types and characteristics of hotels, resorts, motels, and related accommodations.

- Describe the different types and characteristics of restaurants.

- List the classifications of restaurants.

GEOGRAPHY SPOTLIGHT

Adventure Tourism: Malaysia

Teeming with life and with new experiences for travelers around each turn, the island of Borneo offers visitors an unparalleled adventure in a completely unique environment. A long-standing war zone over ownership of the pristine natural landscape of Borneo, the territory is currently claimed by Indonesia, Brunei, and Malaysia. Separated from China by the South China Sea, the island of Borneo, as well as the country of Malaysia, abounds with multiculturalism, incorporating aspects of Chinese, Indian, and Malay culture in harmony with the abundant natural surroundings.[1]

One of Malaysia's geographical gems for tourists is the vast underground system of caves. Most of the caves are hidden in the rainforests and mangroves and are some of the largest in the world. The Gunung Mulu National Park is located on the island of Borneo, which is home to a few of the most popular and easily accessible caves. According to Tourism Malaysia, several of the caves are archaeological sites where some artifacts date back 40,000 years while others contain ancient rock paintings and burial grounds.[2] Although many of the caves have been explored by explorers and topographers, there are still a few that have never been explored—offering a great opportunity for adventurous travelers to experience pristine and untouched surroundings. Cave guides can be contracted through the Malaysian Nature Society at the park office, and they offer guided expeditions that usually range from a few hours to overnight trips.

GEOGRAPHY SPOTLIGHT *(continued)*

Nigel Hicks © Dorling Kindersley

For those who prefer aboveground vistas, the Mulu Canopy Skywalk stands as the world's longest tree-based walkway at 1,600 feet in length! Gunung Mulu National Park is a United Nations Educational, Scientific and Cultural Organization (UNESCO) World Heritage area and is protected by the National Park Authority.[3] Open in 2005, this treetop walkway covers more than 50 hectares (123 acres) and visitors can walk along galvanized iron walkways suspended 20-plus (60 feet) meters above the jungle floor.

For sea exploration, Tourism Malaysia states that Borneo is "one of the leading dive destinations of the world with one of the richest marine environments in the Indo-Pacific Basin."[4] The best dive sites around Malaysia include diverse underwater environments such as sloping reefs, coral blocks, wall dives, deep dives, drift dives, and wreck dives. Labuan Island is located off the northwest coast of Borneo and is surrounded by four World War II shipwreck dive sites.

After exhausting the activities on Borneo, travelers can complete their trip by visiting Kuala Lumpur, the capital of Malaysia. Located on the mainland, this metropolitan city is home to some of the world's tallest buildings. This, of course, is an invitation for the extreme sport athletes and spectators of BASE jumping. BASE stands for building, antenna, span, and earth, which describes the four sites that jumpers leap from.[5]

A few miles outside of the city center is Taman Pertanian. This park and reserve is home to SkyTrex Adventure, "Malaysia's first organized outdoor 'eco-recreational cum educational' activity."[6] SkyTrex Adventure offers a wild and unique adventure for its visitors. The facility is similar to that of an obstacle course located in the canopy of the forest. Though this may sound like the typical zip line tour, SkyTrex goes beyond that, challenging participants to swing, climb, crawl, and glide through different obstacles as high as 75 feet. Kayaking, fishing, and paintball activities are also available throughout the property.

From the top of the world's tallest buildings to the bottom of the deepest caves, Malaysia and its section of the island of Borneo offer unparalleled exploration and excitement for the most adventurous of travelers. Adventurers can experience all Malaysia has to offer.

Endnotes

1. Tourism Malaysia, website. www.tourismmalaysia.gov.my/ (accessed April 5, 2009).
2. Ibid.
3. Ibid.
4. Ibid.
5. Menara Kuala Lumpur, "KL Tower International Jump Malaysia," www.kltowerjump.com/main.html (accessed September 22, 2009).
6. SkyTrex Adventures, "About the Park: Where the Fun in the Forest Never Ends!" http://skytrex-adventure.com (accessed April 6, 2009).

Lodging

Tourist travel implies at least one night away from home in hotels, resorts, motels, and related accommodations. Travel and tourism as we know it today could not exist without them. In almost any part of the world, overnight accommodations are available for public rental. Much of travel hinges on the quality and availability of an area's hotels. A developing country, no matter how poor or remote—Nepal, the Philippines, Bolivia, or Kenya—usually has at least one first-class hotel. There are close to 16 million hotel and motel rooms worldwide, approximately 4 million of which are in the United States.[1]

Hotels support, participate in, and extend trade and convention centers, government centers, entertainment centers, and theme parks. New York, Chicago, Los Angeles, Atlanta, and Boston are examples of trade centers; Washington, D.C., and the state or provincial capitals are examples of government centers. In cities and resort destinations, hotels and the activities taking place in them constitute a large part of the cultural landscape. Hotels say a lot about a city, help define it, provide character, add or detract from its reputation, and constitute a considerable part of its architectural profile. What would New York City be without its luxury hotels? What would Orlando, Florida, be without its 116,902 plus guestrooms?[2] Paris would not be Paris if it lacked luxury and other hotels. Honolulu would not be Honolulu if it lacked its fleet of hotels facing onto Waikiki Beach. Singapore's rise to financial eminence was also influenced by the construction of luxury hotels. Resorts are popular accommodations for tourists because they offer a range of facilities that appeal to guests on vacation. Casino hotels and resorts are in Las Vegas and Atlantic City, on the Mississippi River and on Indian reservations.

The kinds of accommodations offered to pleasure travelers are an integral part of the travel experience. Some travelers want only luxury hotels; the reputation of the place is a reflection of the traveler's self-image. Other travelers, who want to meet the local people and learn their culture, seek out the bed-and-breakfast inn in Charleston, South Carolina, or spend a week at a dude ranch in Wyoming. Tourists traveling by automobile mostly want convenience, accommodations that are close to the highway to make for a quick getaway in the morning.

The tremendous growth of conventions and meetings has prompted the construction of many convention hotels, several with more than 1,000 rooms, built to serve convention groups. Conference-center hotels are specialized properties built in response to the training and meeting needs of corporations and associations.

Resort condominiums, made possible because of rising middle-class incomes, spawned the new business of **vacation ownership** and fractional ownership by which condo owners have the exclusive ownership of the unit for weekly blocks of time.

Types of Accommodations

Depending on budget and taste, travelers have a variety of accommodations to choose from: the New York hotel room with a view of the brick wall of the next building! Or, sleeping in a six-foot capsule (with television) in Tokyo, or staying at a secluded Caribbean resort or a mega casino resort in Las Vegas.

Young hikers are delighted to have a place to spread their sleeping bags and find cold and sometimes hot water in a youth hostel, for which they will pay only a few dollars. The nonprofit Hostelling International has 4,000 hostels in more than 60 countries.[3]

The economy traveler may be pleased with minimum motel accommodations at a Motel 6 for about $40 a night.[4] Rooms sold for $6 a day when this motel chain started. The traveler with a family may find a Holiday Inn, or similar hotel, with its swimming pool and a moderately priced restaurant, highly satisfactory at about $130 a night.[5] Affluent travelers may spend $950 a night at the Four Seasons George V in Paris,[6] while the traveler who wants complete luxury and a taste of status will be happy to spend $650 per night living like a lord, with a lord, in one of England's stately homes: for tax purposes, some of the British aristocracy are obliged to rent out rooms in their mansions to bring in additional revenue. Another interesting and reasonably priced form of accommodation is the bed and breakfast inn where, for about $30 a night and up, visitors can stay in a room in a private house where the owner knows the area and places of interest.

Resorts are generally end destinations situated in exotic locations and offer a range of activities from water sports—sailing, para-sailing, scuba diving, snorkeling—to beach activities. Resorts located in ski areas offer both active and passive winter and summer sporting activities. Resorts offer a more relaxed setting, and guests usually stay longer than they stay at other hotels. Room types at various properties match the needs of guests and are described in the next section.

Hotel Types

Several terms have been used to describe and classify lodging facilities in the United States and other countries. Smith Travel Research uses the following classifications for the lodging industry: luxury—Ritz-Carlton; upper upscale—Embassy Suites; upscale—Hilton Garden Inn; midscale with food and beverage—Quality Inn; midscale without food and beverage—Hampton Inn; economy—Homestead.[7]

Resorts

Resorts offer tourists and convention guests an attractive array of active and passive activities. As mentioned, many resorts are situated in exotic locations such as Hawaii, Florida, California, Virginia, South Carolina, and many exotic international destinations such as Bali, Indonesia, where there is a combination of a good climate and often a beach or golf course, or both.

Resorts offer leisuretime and pleasurable as well as business opportunities through a variety of recreational activities such as golf, tennis, and skiing. Resorts guests tend to stay a few days longer than guests at other types of hotels stay—up to a week or two is normal. They are also a kind of "captured clientele" because it is often difficult for guests to travel too far from the resort. Resorts tend to exude a more relaxing atmosphere compared to regular hotels. Guests often expect to be pampered, and those who are will often return year after year.

Mega Resorts

A few years ago, the size and the complexity of large resort properties rose to a new dimension when several mega resorts were built in Hawaii. Known also as destination resorts, they are of a size and scope not previously seen. This was made possible by the investment of billions of Japanese yen. Today, the swimming pools are immense, embellished with islands, water slides, fountains, and waterfalls. The Waikoloa Beach Resort on the big island of Hawaii (managed by Hyatt) has a concrete swimming pool that covers almost three-quarters of an acre; sand for the beach was imported from another island.

Destination resort hotels are invariably located on or near a scenic beach or in the mountains. The Westin Kauai purchased all of the production of a Chinese marble quarry. The $360 million Hyatt Waikoloa offers guests a choice of transport from lobby to guest room: walk down a sweeping, columned staircase, or ride a monorail to one of three guestroom towers.

What makes these new properties distinctive are their immense size and the variety of attractions they offer. The Westin Kauai has a large collection of oriental art and 500 landscaped acres through which run a mile of canals that guests can explore in outrigger canoes or motor launches, passing a shoreline populated with monkeys, zebras, wallabies, llamas, and other animals.

▶ Check Your Knowledge

1. Outline the different types of tourist accommodation.
2. What are some of the main characteristics of a resort?

Gaming Entertainment Resorts

Places such as the Principality of Monaco, the tiny independent state on the French Mediterranean coast, Biarritz on the French west coast, and Baden in Germany were known for casino gambling prior to the twentieth century. Las Vegas, Reno, and Atlantic City are products of a relaxed view toward gambling in the United States; Las Vegas was built when casino gambling was legalized in 1931.

Although relatively few in number, gaming entertainment resorts play a significant role in the financial success of a few hotel companies. The idea of extravaganza entertainment and huge luxury hotels built around casinos is an American idea. Today, there are several casino resorts in Las Vegas, among them are Wynn; the Bellagio; New York, New York; MGM Grand; the Mirage; the Venetian; and the Luxor. It is interesting to note that a good percentage of Hilton's and other hotel companies' profits come from gaming in Las Vegas.

Island Resorts

Island resorts are great attractions for travelers. They can be found on each continent of the world (with the exception of Antartica). Some of the loveliest resorts are located in Bermuda, the Bahamas, the Hawaiian Islands, and the islands of the South Pacific, isolated in the middle of the ocean. For example, Barbados is a year-round warm weather destination with sandy beaches. Other island resorts are cold-water islands with beach activities in season, such as Nantucket or Martha's Vineyard. Island resorts provide excellent dramatic vistas, imaginative pools, and interesting sightseeing. Island resorts must be built only where superstructure (airports, cruise terminals) and infrastructure (roads, rail, water, electricity, and sewage) can accommodate the resort. The island must have enough water, dependable electricity, paved roads, and efficient transportation.

All-Inclusives

The term *all-inclusive* refers to resorts that pattern themselves after Club Med. They provide meals and free access to water attractions and entertainment activities for one flat price. The all-inclusives expanded on the island of Jamaica during a time of political unrest. Because guests stayed in the hotels day in and day out, the hotels were prompted to create more features to keep their guests busy, happy, and safe within the grounds of the prop-

Resorts in the Popular Destination of Cancun, Mexico
Corbis RF

erty. The concept of the all-inclusive caught on. It is proliferating in more destinations, appealing to more markets, and producing more innovations.

Airport Hotels

Airport hotels are generally not actually on airport property, although a few are, such as the Tampa airport Marriott. Most are within a 15-minute taxi or courtesy shuttle ride to the airport. For example, the twin Hyatts at the Dallas–Fort Worth Airport are within walking distance of the terminal and have enough amenities to qualify as mini resorts.

The advantage of airport hotels is their location, particularly those located in major gateway cities and at hub airports. Their relationship to the city, the availability and cost of public transportation, and the financial investment in building and operating the property are other advantages.

Hotel Chains

In the mid-1900s, numerous hotels owned by individuals or companies united to form chains. Elsworth Statler, who opened his first hotel in 1901 and charged $1.50 a night with the slogan "a bed and a bath for a dollar and a half," started the first great hotel chain. Statler died in 1928 and the chain was eventually sold to Hilton in 1954 for $111 million, the largest property transaction in the world at that time. Hotel chains gained greater presence and recognition in the market. Propriety chains sprouted as a result. Some hotel companies actually owned the hotels they built, but today they avoid that large capital expenditure by having others own the property for which they now have a management contract to operate. Major chains such as Marriott International manage more than 2,000 properties.

It is believed that a chain can operate more efficiently and less expensively than most independent hotels. All hotels in a chain use the same name, and some operate in many countries. Holiday Inns (now a part of InterContinental Hotels Group, one of the largest lodging enterprises in the world) grew by the strategy of franchising. Kemmons Wilson, a developer, had a disappointing experience while on a family vacation when he had to pay for an extra room for his children. Therefore, Wilson decided to build a moderately priced family-style hotel. Each room was comfortably sized and had two double beds; this enabled children to stay free in their parents' room.[8] The Holiday Inn concept became popular and Wilson began franchising them.

Throughout the years, remarkable improvements have been made in the operations of hotel chains. In the 1950s, for instance, only a few leading companies, including InterContinental Hotels, Hilton International, and Sheraton, had tapped into the international hotel market. By the 1970s, major chains had clearly established their plans for international growth. Today, they have reached more countries than ever. Starwood, for example, now operates the St. Regis, the Luxury Collection, Westin, W Hotels, Sheraton, and Four Points. Starwood operates 275,000 rooms in 897 hotels and resorts in 100 countries, in the Caribbean, Mexico, Central and South America, Europe, the Middle East, Africa, Asia, and the Pacific.[9]

There are two main ways to decide which is the largest hotel chain: by the number of rooms, and by the number of hotels. The largest hotel chain, with 465,000 rooms in 5,700 properties and with 995 under construction, is Choice Hotels International.[10] The name reflects the chain's variety of product segments. It includes several segments under its corporate umbrella: Econo Lodge and Sleep Inns; luxury budget—Rodeway Inns, Suburban Extended Stay Hotels, Main Stay Suites, and Comfort Inns; midpriced—Comfort Suites, Quality Inns and Hotels, Cumbria Suites, and Quality Suites; and upscale—Clarion Hotels and Resorts, Clarion Carriage House Inns and Suites. Choice Hotel conducts business in 35 countries on 5 continents with most operating as franchises.[11]

► Check Your Knowledge

1. What infrastructure do island resorts need for successful operation?

2. How did Holiday Inn hotels begin?

Hotel Development and Ownership

Franchising and management contracts are the two main driving forces in development and operation in the hotel business. After the potential of franchising caught on, there was no stopping American ingenuity. In about half a century, the hotel business was changed forever, and here is how it happened.[12]

Franchises

Franchising hotels in the United States began in 1935, when Howard Deering Johnson started franchising motels.[13] Franchising is a system used by numerous hotel chains where properties can use the same name and design but are operated and owned by different companies. One good example is Wyndham—one of the world's largest franchise hotel companies. In the Wyndham system, an individual, a partnership, a small corporation, or a group of investors buys the right to own and operate a hotel in a chain for a certain numbers of years, usually 25 or 30. The owner can operate the business after paying the chain an initial fee plus part of the hotel's annual income and about $6.00 for each room booked via the franchisor's central reservations system; in return, the owner can use the chain's reservation system and well-known name and reputation. This arrangement is extremely valuable to both parties. The per-room franchise fee is a bargain price compared to the $20 per room charged for rooms booked by Hotels.com or a similar Web reservations company.

The franchisor's primary concern is to preserve its good name in all ways, so it provides support in marketing, management, operating procedures, and training to franchisees. Franchising spreads the costs of promotion, advertising, and reservation systems among all properties. Franchises are the most common form of chain ownership.

A brief look at the history of franchising tells us that although this segment of the lodging industry began in 1935, it did not really take root until the late 1950s and 1960s. Hoteliers adopted franchising as a way to grow without having to invest substantial capital. The construction of hotels requires a lot of capital. The development of franchising led to the rapid expansion of hotel and motel companies.

Management Contract

Large companies purchase a hotel or hotel chain as a part of their portfolio (large companies may own office buildings, a hotel, and other investments—they diversify in this way to spread financial risk over several investments) but arrange a contract for the hotel to be operated by a hotel company. This arrangement proves to be beneficial to both parties: the owner of the hotel supplies the physical structure, and the hotel management company supplies the hotel management expertise. All the major hotel chains operate management contract businesses. They like them because they do not need to use their capital to build hotels; rather, they concentrate on operating them.

The **management contract** was actually conceptualized in the 1950s. It opened the opportunity for chains based in the United States to grow overseas. It helped them establish hotels in countries where foreign ownership laws and political instabilities deterred ownership by outside companies. Overseas developers who are satisfied with the skills and expertise of the U.S. chains began to invest in properties and to contract U.S. companies to operate them. The management contract usually allows for the hotel company to manage the property for a period of 5, 10, or 20 years. For this, the company receives a management fee, often a percentage of gross and/or net operating profit, usually about 2 to 4.5 percent of gross revenues. Lower fees in the 2 percent range are more prevalent today, with an increase in the incentive fee based on profitability. Some contracts begin at 2 percent for the first year, rise to 2.5 the second, and 3.5 the third and stay there for the remainder of the contract.[14] Today, many contracts are for a percentage of total sales and a percentage of operating profit.

▶ Check Your Knowledge

1. Describe hotel franchising.
2. What is a management contract?

FOCUS ON

The Concept of Overbooking in the Hotel Industry

Neha Singh

The hospitality industry is characterized by relatively fixed capacity, the ability to segment markets, perishable products, products sold in advance, and fluctuating demand. Rooms form one of the major products offered by the hotel industry, contributing revenue directly to the hotels' bottom-line profits. Rooms are hotels' perishable product, and thus, hotels have been trying hard for years to maximize room revenue by using overbooking policies. Overbooking ensures that the potentially unsold rooms are filled. The hotels practice overbooking by accepting reservations for more than their available capacity to overcome the shortcomings of canceled reservations or no-shows (guests who fail to arrive and without notice). Thus, overbooking in hotels refers to the practice of accepting reservations in excess of the number of guests who can be accommodated.

Overbooking doesn't happen all the time, but it does happen. Sometimes it's inadvertent. Hotels will sometimes be fully booked, and then run into a problem with some maintenance issues such as faulty air-conditioning, a leaky faucet, or other problems that force them to take those rooms out of their inventory for the day. But other times, hotels overbook on purpose to protect themselves from any potential loss of business from last-minute cancellations and no-shows.

If no rooms are available to guests who have reservations, they are "walked," a term that means they're provided with accommodations at another hotel. This practice is used by hotels in conjunction with other yield management techniques for profit maximization. When overbooking happens, hotels usually are ready to give guests upgrades for their next visit, extra points in frequency programs, fruit baskets, and free nights at another property. Still, walking is an inconvenience to both hotels and the guest.

Every hotel company has its own policies on overbooking depending on its historical data and perception of revenue optimization. Even though hotels have been using overbooking techniques to increase revenue, there are costs involved with the practice. There has been a growing concern in the industry about the expense of earning this revenue. Not only has it been raising ethical concerns about being able to guarantee a product to customers and then not delivering as promised, but also of the costs attached to walking guests to other hotels. The costs are far more than they seem in the long term. There is also a possibility of lost patronage and lost future room revenue that the hotels need to think about.

Just as each hotel company sets its own policies on overbooking, hotels also have their own kind of compensations offered to their walked guests for the inconvenience. And sometimes, these expenses outweigh benefits, leading to decrease in revenue earned. Thus, the hospitality industry is critically evaluating the concept of overbooking to better understand the benefits and costs attached to the practice.

Source: Courtesy of Neha Singh, PhD, Assistant Professor, the Collins College of Hospitality Management, California State Polytechnic University (Cal Poly Pomona).

Hotel Ratings

The hotel industry offers several types of lodging types and amenities to cater to the needs of specific market segments. To give tourists some help in decision making, hotel rating systems have been devised. In North America, there are two rating systems: the Mobil Travel Guide's Star Awards system ranks accommodations on a scale of 1 to 5, where 1 means that the room is clean and comfortable, and 5 means that the property offers an exceptionally distinctive luxury environment with superlative, personalized service.[15] The American Automobile Association (AAA) rates hotels in the United States, Canada, Mexico, and the Caribbean. Hotels do not pay to be included in the ratings but can apply for a rating. To become AAA Approved, the hotel must first meet 27 basic requirements, covering comfort, cleanliness, and safety.[16] If the hotel is approved, AAA sends out anonymous raters to evaluate the hotel and assign a diamond rating from 1 to 5 based on the criteria listed in Figure 15–1. At present count, about 32,000 hotels are AAA Diamond rated.[17]

One Diamond

These establishments typically appeal to the budget-minded traveler. They provide essential, no-frills accommodations. They meet the basic requirements pertaining to comfort, cleanliness, and hospitality.

Two Diamond

These establishments appeal to the traveler seeking more than the basic accommodations. There are modest enhancements to the overall physical attributes, design elements, and amenities of the facility typically at a moderate price.

Three Diamond

These establishments appeal to the traveler with comprehensive needs. Properties are multifaceted with a distinguished style, including marked upgrades in the quality of physical attributes, amenities, and level of comfort provided.

Four Diamond

These establishments are upscale in all areas. Accommodations are progressively more refined and stylish. The physical attributes reflect an obvious enhanced level of quality throughout. The fundamental hallmarks at this level include an extensive array of amenities combined with a high degree of hospitality, service, and attention to detail.

Five Diamond

These establishments reflect the characteristics of the ultimate in luxury and sophistication. Accommodations are first class. The physical attributes are extraordinary in every manner. The fundamental hallmarks at this level are to meticulously serve and exceed all guest expectations while maintaining an impeccable standard of excellence. Many personalized services and amenities enhance an unmatched level of comfort.

Figure 15–1 • AAA Hotel Diamond Rating
Source: Courtesy of American Automobile Association

Location and Pricing

Hotel location and room location have direct impact on the price of the room. A deluxe resort hotel overlooking a magnificent beach can command higher room rates compared to a resort hotel on a major highway five miles away from the same beach. Rooms are even more costly if the hotel monopolizes the whole area. In cities, hotels that are adjacent to commercial centers, sightseeing attractions, and fashionable shopping arcades are more expensive than are rooms in properties found on the outskirts of the same city.

It is interesting to know that the location of the room in the hotel's area has an effect on the room's price; this is particularly true of resort hotels. Rooms with the best views, usually on the upper floors, are the highest-priced rooms. Most rooms located farthest from busy and noisy public areas such as restaurants, swimming pools, and discotheques also command higher prices.

Season and Length of Stay

Room rates also depend on the season of the year. Almost every resort has its own high, low, and shoulder seasons, usually based on weather changes. For example, in ski resort areas summer rates are considerably lower than winter rates. Resorts in the Caribbean, Florida, Mexico, and Hawaii have their high season from November to April and during school vacation periods. European properties, on the other hand, have high seasons during Easter and the summer—particularly August. In Europe, employees are usually given four to six weeks of vacation from work.

In contrast, a center-city hotel aims for year-round high **occupancy, room rates,** and **revpar** (revenue per available room). Along with the season of the year, such hotels have to contend with day-of-the-week fluctuations. For example, business is heaviest during the week, making the hotel's occupancy higher at that time. However, city hotels need to attract leisure traveler business by designing weekend packages for groups, conventions, and individual travelers.

Corporate, Convention, and Group Rates

Discounts are available to members attending conventions and meetings or traveling as members of a group. These discounts are generally about 20–30 percent below the **rack rate** (the top/full room rate). The group's meeting planner, tour operator, or travel agent can negotiate with the hotel management using the concept of "run-of-the-house" and limited to the dates of the actual meeting or convention. Corporate rates require guests to be associated with an approved corporation. Almost anybody can check into a hotel, ask for a corporate rate, show some form of company identification, and get a discounted rate. An actual corporate rate is specific to a corporation and is arranged by the corporation's travel manager.

Taxes and Service Charges

Sometimes guests are shocked upon receiving their bills. Additional charges in the form of taxes (called Transient Occupancy tax or bed tax) are added to the bill and vary depending on the destination. Generally, taxes range from 8 percent up to 16.25 percent, plus $2 Javitz Center and $3 state taxes in New York. Other additional charges such as the service charge are called gratuities (tips) for the hotel staff, plus a 2 percent special surcharge for energy and security. In the Bahamas, hotels also assess a pool charge!

Yield Management

Yield management simply follows the economic concept of supply and demand. The more demand there is for a product or service, the higher the price charged. Yield managers study the history of booking curves, prices, trends, competitive conditions, and other variables. They assign prices to rooms according to these variables throughout the year. Today, yield management systems can assign rates for each night based on anticipated and known demand.

Yield management is made possible by computer systems and is a critical component of revenue management, the maximizing of revenue for each available room. The concept, which was borrowed from the airlines, is formulated to maximize total revenue through planning, implementation, and control of systems and procedures. Yield management is used when the hotel has overcapacity—too few rooms and too many guests (so, the room rates are automatically raised on rooms); or as the supply shrinks, the price goes up.

Yield management benefits those who make reservations 90 days out with more attractive rates than if the same reservation were to be made just a few days prior to the guest's arrival. So, guests who want to stay at a hotel next week will likely pay more than they would if they had made the reservation several weeks in advance. However, when demand is low, there is an oversupply of rooms.

▶ Check Your Knowledge

1. Describe yield management.
2. What does the price of a hotel room depend on?

Alternative Forms of Lodging and Accommodation

Aside from hotels and motels, other members of the lodging industry include paradors, pensions, resort condominiums, youth hostels, elder hostels, time shares, health spas, holistic learning centers, and private hotels.

Paradors

Paradors are old buildings that have been converted into hostels by the government and that are run by a national tourism office. They may be an old convent, monastery, school, castle, fortress, or other similar building. Famous paradors are found in Spain, Portugal, Ireland, England, France, and Germany where historical buildings are given new life. Paradors offer reasonable prices with full meal plans. They appeal to tourists who long for the romantic ambiance of the past.

Pensions

A pension is a large home that was turned into a guesthouse. Pensions offer food and lodging. Meals are generally served at a specific time from a planned menu. Pensions are popular with travelers especially in Europe and Latin America because of the casual family atmosphere they offer. Their excellent cuisine and unique décor also capture the attention of guests. They are often but not always less costly than a hotel of the same quality.

Resort Condominiums

Resort condominiums are alternatives to hotel accommodations in Florida, Hawaii, Colorado, and other famous vacation areas. Condominiums are individually owned residential units under common management within multiunit properties. They are frequently used by the owners for vacation and then rented throughout the rest of the year. Condominiums offer apartment-style accommodations, with kitchen facilities and recreational amenities either on site or nearby.

Vacation Ownership

Vacation ownership started in the French Alps in the late 1960s. Since then, it has become one of the fastest growing accommodation segments of the travel and tourism industry. *Vacation ownership* is the polite way of saying time share. With vacation ownership, a person purchases a unit such as a condominium for blocks of time, normally weeks. Henry Silverman of Cendant, who owns the Indianapolis, Indiana-based Resort Condominiums International (RCI), says that a *time share* is a two-bedroom suite that is owned, rather than a hotel room that is rented for a transient night. A *vacation club*, on the other hand, is a travel-and-use product. People do not buy a particular week(s) at a certain resort; rather, they purchase points, which entitle them to the club's vacation benefits. This has an advantage of being flexible, plus the point system works well with marketing programs, such as those that reward frequent flyers.[18]

Marriott Vacation Club International, the Walt Disney Company, Hilton Hotels, Hyatt Hotels, Inter-Continental, and even Four Seasons all use their brand power to capture an opportunity in vacation ownership. RCI estimates that only about 3 percent of U.S. households own vacation ownership. RCI estimates that this figure could rise to 10 percent in the next decade for households with income of more than $50,000. It is not surprising that hotel corporations are finding this a lucrative business.

RCI's Vacation Ownership has grown to about 3.4 million family memberships.[19] Members are allowed to exchange vacations with other locations. Globally, RCI operates approximately 4,000 properties in more than 100 countries.[20] Vacationers from countries around the world are turning to vacation ownership resorts as their preferred travel destination. North America is the global leader, with about half of the resorts. Europe has about 25 percent of the market, and the remainder is mostly spread over Latin America and Asia.

In the United States, there can be some tax advantages to vacation ownership. The reason for purchasing most frequently cited by owners is the high standards of quality accommodations and services at resorts and the flexibility to exchange vacation resorts. Cost effectiveness is also an important factor in the decision-making process.

Youth Hostels

As the name implies, youth hostels' target market is students. Travelers are provided with overnight lodgings at rock bottom prices. Hostels provide only basic facilities—guests have to provide their own bedding, share a communal washroom, and prepare their own meals. Despite these conditions, youth hostels are popular because the lower prices are suitable for students and other travelers with limited budgets.

Bed and Breakfast Inns

Bed and breakfast inns are most popular throughout the British Isles and Europe, and the idea has been adopted in the United States. Bed and breakfast inns (B&Bs), as the name implies, offer a comfortable room, a full breakfast, and a shared or private bathroom. There are many different styles of B&Bs with prices ranging from about $30 to $300 or more per night. B&Bs may be quaint cottages with white picket fences, tiny and homey, with two or three rooms available. Or they may be sprawling, ranch-style homes in the Rockies; multistoried town homes in large cities; farms; adobe villas; log cabins; lighthouses; or stately mansions. The variety is part of the thrill, romance, and charm of the B&B experience.[21]

An English Tudor Bed and Breakfast in Lavenham, Suffolk, England
Rob Reichenfeld © Dorling Kindersley

► Check Your Knowledge

1. What is a parador?
2. What is a vacation club?

Restaurants

Food is essential for sustaining life. Restaurants not only provide tourists and travelers with nourishment, but they also make important contributions to travelers' social well-being. Dining is an experience, whether it is for pleasure or business, and the great variety of restaurants provides tourists with plenty of choices. The dining experience allows patrons to use all of their senses: taste, smell, sight, hearing, and touch may be used to enjoy the ambiance, food, and service. Today there are more than 945,000 restaurants with 13 million employees, or 9 percent of the U.S. workforce,[22] making restaurants the largest employer outside of government. The restaurant industry's share of the food dollar has risen to 47.5 percent. On a typical day more than 130 million people in the United States are guests in restaurants and foodservice operations.[23]

The restaurant industry is made up of two distinct groups: **independent restaurants**, as in Lettuce in New York, and **chain restaurants**, as in TGI Friday's or **franchise restaurants**, as in KFC. There are also several subgroupings of restaurants:

- *Full Service*—These are restaurants that cook to order more than 12 entrées. Full-service restaurants may be either ethnic, chain, or independently operated.

- *Quick Service*—These restaurants, also known as fast-food restaurants, can specialize in a type of fast food: hamburger/sandwich, taco, burrito, pizza, falafel, hot dog, and others.

- *Fine Dining*—Fine-dining establishments include upscale independent restaurants such as Charlie Trotter in Chicago, Daniel in New York, and steak houses such as Flemings and Ruth Chris.

- *Ethnic*—These restaurants offer the fare of a specific region: Caribbean, Chinese, Mexican, Italian, Greek, Thai, and more.

- *Theme*—Theme restaurants are built around a concept. They usually emphasize fun and fantasy, glamorize or romanticize an activity such as sports or travel, or celebrate an era in time such as the good ole days or the Hollywood of yesterday.[24]

- *Celebrity*—These are restaurants owned or partly owned by a celebrity, who usually makes token appearances from time to time. A few movie stars, singers, and sports figures are celebrity restaurant owners.

Independent Restaurants, Chains, and Franchises

The main difference between an independent (indy) restaurant and a chain-operated one is that the independent restaurant is able to develop its own theme, menu, décor, and service, whereas, with a chain restaurant, those aspects are already decided at the corporate office.

Franchise restaurants are part of a large chain where the original owner and/or company may own a number of restaurants (stores) while several more may be franchised. As with other franchise operations, the concept originator and the original operator may, after successfully establishing and operating a few restaurants, decide to franchise the concept. Franchising ensures a more rapid growth using other people's money, which, in turn, means greater market penetration and potentially greater profits.

There are more franchised restaurants in the quick-service restaurant (QSR) segment than there are in other segments. Among the better-known franchise restaurants are McDonald's, Burger King, Wendy's, Taco Bell, Subway, Pizza Hut, Domino's Pizza, KFC, and Kenny Roger's.

Franchisees pay an initial fee and a percentage of sales for marketing, sales, advertising, and general support. In return, they receive the benefits of a proven concept, assistance in location selection, training, manuals, systems for food preparation and operations, and promotional materials. But it is still expensive to become a franchisee—a simple deli-like store can cost $15,000 and the franchisee must lease the restaurant space, make the alterations, and purchase the fixtures, furnishings, and equipment (FF&E) necessary to open as a restaurant.

Quick-Service Restaurants

For those in a hurry, fast food restaurants, or quick-service restaurants (QSRs), offer food served quickly in pleasant, clean spaces with few frills and very limited service. QSRs rely on heavy traffic and large sales volume to make a profit. They are consequently located in heavy traffic areas such as city centers, malls, and densely populated suburbs.

QSRs offer limited menus featuring items such as hamburgers, chicken, fries, hot dogs, tacos, burritos, gyros, and teriyaki bowls. Guests order their food at the counter, above which menu items, including combinations, are usually illuminated. Offering a simplified menu and limited service enables operators to minimize costs while "attempting" to offer appetizing food.

Full-Service Restaurants

A full-service restaurant is one where a selection of menu items—a minimum of 12 entrées—are all cooked to order. Most of the food is prepared in the restaurant kitchen from "scratch" using fresh and raw ingredients. Full-service restaurants can be casual or formal, and may be further categorized in any of the already-mentioned categories.

A Riverside Restaurant in San Antonio's River-Walk Area, San Antonio, Texas
Paul Franklin © Dorling Kindersley Media Library

Full-service restaurants generally offer a high level of service. Upon arrival, the host greets guests, escorts them to their table, and hands out menus. Captains and food servers offer assistance in menu selection and describe various menu items, including daily specials. Bussers assist by laying tables with cutlery and glassware, pouring water, and clearing plates.

▶ Check Your Knowledge

1. How many restaurants are there in the United States?
2. What is the difference between an independent restaurant and a chain-operated one?
3. What do full-service restaurants offer?

Fine Dining

Fine dining restaurants are at the luxury end of the full-service segment. Most cities have a fine dining restaurant. In a city like New York, obviously there are several such as Daniel, Four Seasons, and Le Cirque. In Chicago, there is Le Perroquet; Maison Robert is in Boston. In Philadelphia, there is Le Bec-Fin; in San Francisco, L'Etoile/La Bourgogne; and in Los Angeles, Campanile, among others.

Many fine dining establishments have French names because French cuisine has greatly influenced American food. Fine dining restaurants charge higher prices because of the increased costs associated with upscale locations, decorations, and higher food and labor costs. Together, the elements of location, ambiance, food quality, and service create memorable dining experiences.

Hamburgers and Pizza

The hamburger is the most popular and frequently ordered restaurant food item. Popularized by Ray Kroc, who in the 1950s was actually a soda fountain salesman. He received a call for two soda machines from two brothers who ran a restaurant in California called McDonald's. When Ray Kroc received the order, he was interested to find out why they ordered two soda machines (restaurants usually ordered just one). When he went out to the McDonald Brothers' restaurant he saw the simple menu and systems that they had established that enabled them to serve more people more quickly than at any other restaurant Kroc had ever seen. He later persuaded the McDonald Brothers to allow him to franchise their restaurant, and billions of burgers later, the success of the franchises can be summed up as the result of strict adherence to quality, speed, cleanliness, service, and value.

The main hamburger chains such as McDonald's, Burger King, Wendy's, and Hardee's often provide first employment opportunities for teenagers. However, the restaurant industry is far more than flipping burgers. The complexity of restaurant operations increases with the sophistication of concept.

The appeal of pizza is that it is also a quick and convenient food item. For a few dollars, it is possible to feed a family a tasty meal. Most QSRs, however, are not known for serving balanced, nutritious meals. The pizza segment of the industry is composed of four major and several other corporations. Pizza Hut, Domino's, Godfather's, and Little Caesar's are the larger chains, and each has a feature for which it has become known. For example, Pizza Hut has stuffed-crust pizza and delivers. Dominos, which pioneered the home delivery of pizza, now features the Ultimate Deep Dish pizza and a Pesto Crust Pizza, with 12 toppings to choose from.

Chicken and Steak Restaurants

Restaurants featuring chicken items on the menu are popular and reasonably priced and provide an alternative to hamburgers and pizza in the QSR segment. KFC (which interestingly changed its name to KFC because Kentucky *Fried* Chicken was not so appealing to the more health-conscious public) is the market leader and has introduced items such as tender roast to appeal to those who avoid fried foods. Other operators such as Kenny Rogers Roasters offer marinated, flame-broiled chicken and rotisserie chicken.

In recent years, the steak house segment has undergone a revival. During the 1980s, beef was not considered a healthy food and consumption declined. However, in the 1990s as if in tandem with a buoyant economy, beef restaurants made a comeback. Not only did the upscale restaurants such as Ruth Chris, Morton's, and Charthouse continue to thrive, but also newcomers such as Outback Steakhouse and its upscale brand Fleming's joined the segment. Operators of steak restaurants do not expect people to eat red meat every day. They are happy if their regular and occasional guests visit them two or three times a month.

Seafood/Fish

The seafood restaurant segment is no different from others in that there are chains and independent restaurant operators. Red Lobster and Bonefish Grill are the leading chains and as such have the advantages of purchasing in large quantities, which means quantity discounts. Seafood and fish menu items have increased in popularity in the past few years. No doubt a more health-conscious public has caused this.

Family Restaurants

The evolution of family restaurants is patterned after the "coffee style" restaurant. A large segment of these restaurants are individually or family operated. Target locations of family restaurants are places with easy access to the suburbs. Most are designed to be an informal setting, and they offer simple menu items suitable to all members of families. Some of these restaurants offer alcoholic beverages, which mostly consist of beer, wine, and perhaps a cocktail special. Guests are well attended, too. Usually, there is a hostess/cashier standing near the entrance to greet and usher guests while food servers take orders and bring the plated food from the kitchen. Incorporating salad and dessert bars is a new concept of some family restaurants as a way to offer more food items and augment the average check.

A variety of restaurant types—in this photo, a family restaurant—offer a selection of menus to tourists.
Peter Bennett, Ambient Images

Ethnic Restaurants

Most ethnic restaurants are independently owned and operated. They aim to provide something new and a pleasant experience to the adventurous diner or a taste of home for those of the same ethnic background as the restaurant.

Traditional ethnic restaurants surfaced to cater to the taste of immigrant groups—Italian, Caribbean, Chinese, and so on. Mexican restaurants are noted for their fast growth in terms of popularity and demand in the United States. Mexican food has a heavy representation in the southwestern states, although, because of near market saturation, the chains are spreading east.

Casual Dining

The name casual dining implies relaxation, and this segment usually includes restaurants with several characteristics: they can be chain or independent, ethnic, or theme. Hard Rock Cafe, Friday's, Ruby Tuesday, the Olive Garden, Applebee's, Houston's, and Red Lobster are good examples of casual dining.

A variety of restaurant chains call themselves *dinner house restaurants.* Some of them could even fit into the theme category. Over the past few years, the trend in dinner house restaurants has been toward more casual dining. This trend merely reflects the mood of society. Dinner house restaurants have become fun places to let off steam.

Any dinner house restaurant that has a casual, eclectic décor may promote a theme. Chart House Restaurant, for example, is a steak and seafood chain that has a nautical theme. Friday's is an American bistro dinner house with a full menu and a décor of bric-a-brac that contributes to the fun atmosphere. Friday's is a chain that has been in operation for more than 30 years, so the concept has stood the test of time.

Theme Restaurants

Many theme restaurants combine sophistication with a specialty. They generally serve a limited menu but aim to "wow" guests with the total experience. Of the many popular theme restaurants two stand out. The first highlights the nostalgia of the 1950s, as done in the T-Bird and Corvette Diners. These restaurants serve all-American food such as meat loaf in a fun atmosphere that is a throwback to the seemingly more carefree 1950s. The food servers appear in short polka-dot skirts with gym shoes and bobby socks, and they usually are chewing bubble gum. If a guest fills up on the main course and declines the nondessert offerings, he is likely to receive an off-beat reply from the server like, "Thank God, because my feet are killing me."

The second popular category of theme restaurants is the dinner house restaurants. Among the better-known national and regional chains are TGI Friday's, Houlihan's, and Applebee's. These are casual American bistro-type restaurants that combine a lively atmosphere created in part by assorted bric-a-brac to decorate the various ledges and walls. These restaurants have remained popular over the past 40 years. In prime locations, they can do extremely well.

The ability of theme restaurants to provide a total experience and a social setting is their main attraction. They achieve this through decoration and atmosphere and by offering a limited menu that blends with the theme.

Celebrity Restaurants

Recently, celebrity-owned restaurants have gained popularity. Some celebrities, such as Alice Waters, Wolfgang Puck, Charlie Trotter, Mario Batali, and Bobby Flay, come from a culinary background, whereas others, such as Naomi Campbell, Claudia Schiffer, and Elle Macpherson (owners of the fashion cafe) do not. A number of sports celebrities also own restaurants. Among them are Michael Jordan, Dan Marino, Walter Payton, Junior Seau, and Wayne Gretzky.

Television and movie stars have also gotten in on the act. Oprah Winfrey was part owner of the Eccentric in Chicago for a number of years. Dustin Hoffman and Henry Winkler are investors in Campanile, a popular Los Angeles restaurant; Dive, in Century City (Los Angeles), is owned by Steven Spielberg; House of Blues, by Denzel Washington and Dan Ackroyd. Musicians Kenny Rogers and Gloria Estefan are also restaurant owners. Kevin Costner owns Clubhouse; Matt Damon and Ben Affleck own the Continental; Jennifer Lopez owns Madre's; and Eva Longoria owns Beso. Celebrity restaurants generally have extra zing—a winning combination of design, atmosphere, food, and perhaps the thrill of an occasional visit by the owner(s).

Cost

Restaurants are relatively easy to set up if the owners have a few thousand dollars and are prepared to work hard. However, few realize just how much work they can be. It is best for prospective restaurant owners to do a business plan detailing the concept, who the guests will be, and how many meals will be served each meal period. Once a good approximation of total sales (comprising food, beverage, and other revenue) is arrived at, then all the expenses can be deducted in the form of a **projected income statement**. Controllable costs include salaries and wages, employee benefits, direct operating expenses, music and entertainment, marketing and promotions, energy and utilities, administrative and general, and repairs and maintenance. Figure 15–2 shows a projected income statement for an independent restaurant.

	Budgeted	Actual Amount	Percentage	Variance + (−)	Last Period	Same Period Last Year
Sales						
Food						
Beverage						
Others						
Total sales		_____	100			
Cost of Sales						
Food						
Beverage						
Others						
Total cost of sales		_____				
Gross profit		_____				
Controllable Expenses						
Salaries and wages						
Employee benefits						
Direct operating expenses[a]						
Music and entertainment						
Marketing						
Energy and utility						
Administrative and general						
Repairs and maintenance						
Total controllable expenses		_____				
Rent and other occupation costs						
Income before interest, depreciation, and taxes						
Interest						
Depreciation						
Net income before taxes						
Income taxes		_____				
Net Income		_____				

[a] Phone, insurance, legal, accounting, paper. glass, china , linens, office supplies, landscaping, cleaning supplies. etc.

Figure 15–2 • An Income Statement for a Restaurant

Source: Walker, John R., *Introduction to Hospitality Management*, 3rd, © 2010. Electronically reproduced by permission of Pearson Education, Inc., Upper Saddle River, New Jersey.

▶ **Check Your Knowledge**

1. Describe what sets theme restaurants apart from others.
2. What do controllable costs include?
3. How do restaurant owners come to an approximation of total sales?

CASE STUDY

Overbooked Hotel

Jackie Ma has accepted the position of a front desk agent at a five-star business hotel. She arrives for her first day 15 minutes before her evening shift starts, hoping that she can take a detailed handover from the previous shift's agents. She is excited to join one of the busiest properties in the city that is known for their customer service.

On entering the back office for the front desk department, Jackie finds everyone panicking and running around to find rooms to allocate for the 3 P.M. check-ins. The shift manager is busy taking a handover of all the guests who are waiting for clean rooms. A front desk agent is calling the Housekeeping department to get an update on clean rooms. Another front desk agent is explaining to a guest trying to check-in that the hotel had 100 percent occupancy the night before and the rooms are not ready yet. All Jackie can see is chaos and guests angry at the front desk agents. She quietly sits down, waiting to get the attention from the shift manager. After waiting for 15 minutes, the shift manager finally looks at her. The manager says, "So, you are the new front desk agent joining us?"

"Yes," Jackie replies.

"Have you ever worked at the front desk before because we are short-staffed and help is needed?" asks the manager. Jackie is scared and finally replies that she has never worked at the front desk before, to which the manager sighs. "We are overbooked today, so we will have to walk guests to other hotels," the manager says to Jackie. "We are going to be very busy today. We have no time for training. Just go to the front desk and try and help the other agents as much as you can," the manager continues.

Jackie is surprised and disappointed. She walks out to the front desk and notices all front desk agents dealing with guests. She stands to a side, waiting to offer help to the front desk agents and wondering what she has got herself into. She hears one of the agents explain to the guest who is trying to check in that there is no room available for his guaranteed reservation. She sees the guest get angry and frustrated at the front desk agent. "Oh, when will this day end?" thinks Jackie.

Questions

1. What is overbooking?
2. What was wrong with the preceding situation?
3. What steps can the manager take today so that in the future, things could be smoother?

Source: Courtesy of Neha Singh, PhD, California State Polytechnic University (Cal Poly Pomona).

Summary

1. Travel implies the use of hotels, resorts, motels, and related accommodations. Travel and tourism as we know it today could not exist without them.
2. Depending on budget and taste, travelers can choose from a variety of accommodations.
3. Several terms have been used in describing and classifying lodging facilities in the United States and other countries. Commonly used terms include *hotel, resort hotel, inn, all suites,* and *motel.*
4. Hotels' management structures vary: independent ownership, chain membership, a franchise operation of the chain, or operated by a management contract.
5. Yield management simply follows the economic concept of supply and demand. The more demand there is for a product or service, the higher the price.
6. Aside from hotels and motels, other members of the lodging industry include the following: paradors, pensions, resort condominiums, youth hostels, time shares, health spas, holistic learning centers, and private hotels.
7. Today there are more than 945,000 restaurants with 13 million employees (making it the largest employer outside of government).
8. The main categories of restaurants are fine dining, specialty, independent, and chain. Further distinctions can be made: quick-service, ethnic, dinner house, and casual. In general, most restaurants fall into more than one category.

Key Words and Concepts

chain restaurant
franchise restaurant
independent restaurant
management contracts

occupancy
projected income statement
rack rate
revpar

room rate
vacation ownership

Review Questions

1. What are the advantages of (a) management contracts, and (b) franchising? Discuss their impacts on the development of the hotel industry.
2. Explain how hotels cater to the needs of business and leisure travelers in regard to the following concepts: (a) resorts, and (b) airport hotels.
3. Explain what vacation ownership is. What are the different types of time-share programs available for purchase?
4. How are restaurants classified?
5. Explain why there is no single definition of the various classifications of restaurants; give examples.
6. What does Malaysia offer tourists?
7. Do you agree with hotels overbooking? Why or why not?

Interesting Websites

HotelJobs.com: www.hoteljobs.com

Hotels magazine: www.hotelsmag.com

National Restaurant Association: www.restaurant.org

National Restaurant Association Educational Foundation: www.nraef.org/

Restaurant Careers bulletin board: www.restaurant-careers.com

Internet Exercises

1. Organization: Hilton Hotels
   Website: www.hilton.com
   Summary: Hilton Hotels Corporation and Hilton International, a subsidiary of Hilton Group PLC, have a worldwide alliance to market Hilton. Hilton is recognized as one of the world's best-known hotel brands. Collectively, Hilton offers more than 2,500 hotels in more than 50 countries, truly a major player in the hospitality industry.
   a. What are the different hotel brands that can be franchised through Hilton Hotels Corporation?
   b. What are your views on Hilton's portfolio?

2. Organization: *Hotels* magazine
   Website: www.hotelsmag.com

   Summary: *Hotels* magazine is a publication that offers vast amounts of information on the hospitality industry with up-to-date industry news, corporate trends, and nationwide developments. What are some of the top headlines currently being reported in the industry?

3. Organization: Charlie Trotter's Restaurant
   Website: http://charlietrotters.com/restaurant
   Summary: Charlie Trotter is regarded as one of the finest chefs in the world. Chef Trotter's restaurant has received numerous awards, yet Chef Trotter is seeking new opportunities. What are Chef Trotter's recent activities?

Apply Your Knowledge

1. From a career perspective, what are the advantages and disadvantages of each type of hotel?

2. In groups, evaluate a restaurant and write out a list of weaknesses. Use the headings outlined in the restaurant section of this chapter. Then, for each of the weaknesses, decide on which actions you would take to exceed guest expectations.

Suggested Activities

1. Identify which kind of hotel you would like to work at and give reasons why.

2. Think of your favorite restaurant and write down all the things you like about it. Compare your answers with the other members of your class.

Endnotes

1. Personal correspondence with The International Hotel and Restaurant Association, October 7, 2009.
2. Cynthia Pio-Gray, Orlando Convention and Visitors Bureau, March 18, 2009.
3. Hostelling International USA, website, www.hiusa.org (accessed March 18, 2009).
4. Motel 6, website, www.motel6.com (accessed March 18, 2009).
5. www.ichotelsgroup.com/h/d/6c/1/en/availsearch? errorURL=/h/d/6c/1/en/advancedsearch&availCheck Caching=n&_requestid=210605 (accessed March 18, 2009).
6. Four Seasons Hotel and Resort, "George V, Paris," www.fourseasons.com/paris (accessed March 18, 2009).
7. Personal correspondence with Kim Heslinuses of Smith Travel Research, March 17, 2009.
8. John R. Walker, *Introduction to Hospitality*, 5th ed. (Upper Saddle River, NJ: Pearson, 2009), 88.
9. Starwood Hotels & Resorts Worldwide, www .starwoodhotels.com/corporate/company_info.html.
10. Choice Hotels International, website, www .choicehotels.com (accessed March 18, 2009).
11. Ibid.
12. John R. Walker, *Introduction to Hospitality Management*, 3rd ed. (Upper Saddle River, NJ: Pearson, 2009), 88.
13. State of Wisconsin Department of Financial Institutions, "A Brief History," www.wdfi.org/fi/securities/franchise/ history.htm (accessed March 15, 2009).
14. Personal conversation with Bruce Goodwin, former vice president of Pannell Kerr Forster, January 11, 2009.
15. HowStuffWorks.com, "Rating Criteria: Lodging," http://static.howstuffworks.com/pdf/lodging-criteria-12-2008.pdf (accessed March 25, 2009).
16. AAA, "Guide to AAA Ratings," http://hotelsabout .com/od/hotelratingsystems/a/aaa_ratings.htm (accessed March 18, 2009).
17. Ibid.
18. Mike Malley, "Timeshare Synergies," *Hotel and Motel Management* 212, no. 5 (March 17, 1997): 18.
19. Group RCI, "Vacation Exchange," www.grouprci.com/ about/vacation_exchange/index.cfm (accessed September 22, 2009).
20. Ibid.
21. TravelASSIST MAGAZINE, "What Is a Bed and Breakfast inn?" www.travelassist.com/mag/a88.html (accessed September 22, 2009).
22. National Restaurant Association, website, www .restaurant.org (accessed March 19, 2009).
23. www.restaurant.org/research/ind_glance.cfm (accessed March 19, 2009).
24. John R. Walker, *The Restaurant: From Concept to Operation*, 5th ed. (New York: Wiley, 2008), 42.

CHAPTER 16

Tourism in the Future

OBJECTIVES

After reading and studying this chapter, you should be able to:

- Identify contributing factors that influence the future of travel.

- Discuss the role government plays in the future of tourism.

- Evaluate trends that have a positive influence on the future of travel.

- Identify trends that may inhibit travel.

GEOGRAPHY SPOTLIGHT

Remote Tourism: Central Asia

By familiarizing themselves with the history of a potential travel destination, travelers come to better understand and appreciate the various characteristics of a specific area. With an understanding of Kyrgyzstan's extensive history, travelers can discover the reasoning behind much of the country's multicultural influences and the importance of the remote destinations on this journey.

Several civilizations have had the opportunity to influence the country's landscape throughout the centuries. Fortunately, the ruins of the settlements created by the myriad conquerors remain. Furthermore, Kyrgyzstan escaped heavy Soviet industrialization by being designated as a specialized agricultural supplier for the rest of the Soviet Union, leaving much of the countryside relatively untouched.[1] On a journey in Kyrgyzstan, guests can survey the area by air and take a field excursion to the Krasnorechenskoe archaeological site in the Chu River Valley (the lost cities), visit the Ala-Archa Canyon, and hike around Lake Issyk-Kul.

The aerial survey and field excursions enable guests to view the "Lost Cities" of Kyrgyzstan. The first city is known as Krasnaia Rechka, or Navekat. Guests fly over and eventually visit the remains of a Buddhist temple, a Kharakhanid palace, and Buddhist and Nestorian Christian cemeteries.[2] According to the Lost Nomads Travel Agency, Navekat's ruins are associated with the medieval town of Navekat, which was established as a Sogdian merchants' stopover on the Great Silk Road circa AD 4–9.[3]

GEOGRAPHY SPOTLIGHT *(continued)*

James Strachan, Robert Harding World Imagery

The next Lost City guests encounter is Balasagun. Guests journey to the Burana Tower, located in a town that was built in the tenth century.[4] The word *Burana* comes from the Turkic word *munara*, meaning minaret. The Burana Tower was built in the eleventh century and reached a height of 135 feet. Earthquakes in the fifteenth century reduced the tower to a height of 73.5 feet.[5] Surrounding the tower are stone figures called "balbals." These stones were placed in the area between the sixth and tenth centuries. The legend of these balbals is as follows:

> Predecessors of the modern Kyrgyz people made a hill over the tomb of the noble people of their tribe and set a statue, which faced east. Thus, the dead person was materialized in granite and became the patron of the whole tribe. That is why the statues made by local sculptors were provided with many features inherent in living members of the tribe and at the same time were referred to as spirits capable of performing miracles.[6]

The Ala-Archa Canyon is located at the highest part of the Kyrgyz Ridge, which is famous for its "eternal snow-stretching plot," which extends approximately 125 miles.[7] The name of the Ala-Archa National Park means "many-colored juniper," which suggests the incredible amount of trees visitors can see. Some of the incredible peaks around the canyon include Dvurogaya (2.7 miles), Korona (2.9 miles), Baylyanbaish (3.01 miles), and the highest peak of the Kyrgyz Ridge—Semenov-Tian-Shansky (3.02 miles).[8]

Finally, guests can hike around Lake Issyk-Kul. Lake Issyk-Kul lies 1 mile above sea level and has an area of 2,396.15 square miles (111 miles long and 37 miles wide), making it the second largest alpine lake in the world after Lake Titicaca in South America.[9] One-hundred and thirty-four rivers flow into Lake Issyk-Kul. This allows all of the minerals from the rivers to settle at the bottom of the lake, which visitors can see through the crystal clear waters. Furthermore, archaeologists have discovered the ancient city of Chigu that was once the capital of Usuni State during the second century BC, which also served as the trade center for the Tian Shan on the Silk Road.[10] Balbal statues surround the lake.[11]

For lodging, guests can stay in the great outdoors for the entire journey. Because this journey takes place in such a remote setting, staying in a commercialized hotel would defeat the purpose. Tents, sleeping bags, and other outdoor gear are necessary for guests who want to experience some of the most remote locations in Central Asia.

This journey to remote locations in Kyrgyzstan is for history lovers, nature lovers, those at home in solitude, and those who thoroughly enjoy being adventurous. Kyrgyzstan offers a mix of history, culture, and untouched nature that is difficult, if not impossible, to find anywhere else in the world. During their visit, travelers can begin to understand and appreciate the unmatched beauty found in Kyrgyzstan.

(continued)

GEOGRAPHY SPOTLIGHT *(continued)*

Endnotes

1. Library of Congress, "Country Profile: Kyrgyzstan," January 2007, http://lcweb2.loc.gov/frd/cs/profiles/Kyrgyzstan.pdf (accessed November 11, 2008).

2. Horizon Travel, "Kyrgyzstan," www.horizon.elcat.kg/english/intro.html (accessed November 11, 2008).

3. Lost Nomads, "Lost Cities over the Chu River Valley; Flight over Nanekar," http://lostnomads.com/en/lost_cities (accessed November 11, 2008).

4. Horizon Travel, "Kyrgyzstan."

5. Ibid.

6. Svetlana's Brides, "The Balbals Appear at Midnight," 2003, www.svetlanasbrides.com/kyrgyzstan/balbals/balbals.htm (accessed November 11, 2008).

7. www.centralasiatravel.com/kyrgyzstan.html (accessed November 11, 2008).

8. Ibid.

9. Ibid.

10. Ibid.

11. Horizon Travel, "Kyrgyzstan."

Predicting the Future of Tourism

In the future, tourism is likely to continue the course it takes in the present, where it is one of the fasting growing interrelated industry groupings. The United Nations World Tourism Organization (UNWTO) forecasts that by 2020 there will be 1.6 billion international arrivals. Of these worldwide arrivals, 1.2 billion will be intraregional and 378 million will be long-haul travelers.[1] The total tourist arrivals by region show that by 2020 the top three receiving regions will be Europe (717 million tourists), East Asia and the Pacific (397 million), and the Americas (282 million), followed by Africa, the Middle East, and South Asia.[2]

We must begin to consider the number of additional tourists in and from China and India who have or will soon have the economic ability to travel. Humans seem to have a natural curiosity about how and where others live. Tourism in the future will be influenced by several factors. In the following sections, we take a closer look at some of these influences.

Demand Influences and Issues

Demand factors include consumer behavior and preferences. Associated with **demand factors** are demographics, for example, age and socioeconomic status. Nearly 70 million Americans, the baby boomers, are beginning to retire and thus have more time and the desire to travel. Another demand issue is the continued splintering of **tourism niche** (specialized) markets, for instance, nature tourism in the form of bird watching. Demand will be further influenced by an enormous increase in outbound tourism from China and India. When another 500 million tourists begin to travel, capacity control will become a major issue. Mass tourism will grow to accommodate the numbers, but so too will customizations resulting from the increased demands of tourists who want something different from the masses.

Supply-Side Influences and Issues

The supply side of tourism will continue to modify and change product offerings, placing greater emphasis on environmental protection while providing the tourism experiences that consumers want. In many emerging markets, the quality of tourism services must improve before these destinations become popular mainstream tourism destinations. Tourism's supply side will provide greater fulfillment to tourists by making available more experiences that tourists want, from space tourism to medical and volunteer tourism.

Capacity Control and Impact

Capacity control refers to the ability of a destination to receive and care for the needs of tourists by attempting to limit the number of tourists permitted to visit the destination to within the destination's capacity. Some major destinations already experience too many tourists; some places (such as many Caribbean islands) completely rely on tourist dollars, so a balance must be struck between limiting the number of tourists to preserve the integrity of the destination and its ability to satisfy guest needs and welcoming tourism for its economic and social benefits. Consider Notre Dame Cathedral in Paris as well as the many other attractions in Paris and other cities that must restrict the number of tourists visiting them. Impacts are environmental, social, and economic and can have negative outcomes at the destination and in its community.

The Environment

A number of environmental issues will affect tourism in the future. The travel, lodging, and foodservice sectors have begun to address and rectify their contributions to global warming, but more needs to be done for these industries to become carbon neutral. Tourism can affect whole ecosystems; for example, too much visitation to an ecologically sensitive area can do irreparable damage.

Climate change may elevate sea levels, leading to the destruction or loss of some low-lying destinations, such as Venice, Italy, and coastal regions of the Maldives and Seychelles Islands.

Governments and the private sector must work together to promote more responsible travel and tourism. The travel sector will continue to develop alternative fuels; for example, airlines are aiming for a 50 percent reduction in carbon emissions by 2050.[3] At the 2009 G8 Summit, world leaders agreed to join a global effort to achieve 50 percent reduction in global emissions by 2050 and to a goal of 80 percent or more reduction by developed countries by that date.[4]

Eco-tourism will likely grow because consumers now expect more sustainable vacation experiences. Issues of certification and compliance in environmental sustainability will gain in importance as both consumers and providers seek environmental aesthetics and environmental auditing. Environmental best practices of some industry leaders will become models for others to follow in their environmental management systems.

Destination Management

Destination management can include land use planning, business permits and zoning controls, environmental and other regulations, business association initiatives, and a host of other techniques used to shape the development and daily operation of tourism-related activities.[5] Tourism executives are struggling to manage change and find it increasingly difficult to determine the impact environmental forces are likely to have on destinations.[6] Destinations will find it more difficult to "manage" the competing forces of tourism development and carrying capacity, plus there will be an increased desire of tourists for destinations to develop tourism in a sustainable manner. Most destination organizations have amended their traditional business models to keep pace with the evolution of new technologies, emerging innovative advertising strategies, changes in the consumer market, and growing global competition.[7]

Managing destination demand will be a challenge for future tourism officials here in Sorrento on the Amalfi coast, Italy.
Demetrio Carrasco © Dorling Kindersley

Information Technology

E-tourism has evolved from a trend to a mainstream business reality, creating opportunities as well as challenges for both practitioners and researchers in the area.[8] Information technology will improve rapidly to help facilitate tourism and tourists.

Access to information will greatly improve—even in remote places. Tourists will be able to see the websites for more destinations and resorts and gather the information they need to make informed decisions. Technology will also help improve the travel experience. Citizens of more countries will be able to visit other countries without visas because the Visa Waiver Program will increase in size.

Technology will improve the tourism experience, offering travelers greater ease in booking travel and accommodations through a greater, seamless connectivity of systems. The Internet makes information easily accessible to the consumer. This reduces the complexities of purchasing, marketing, and distribution.[9] However, more options (and increasing price competition) make it harder for individual companies to capture and keep loyal customers.

Transportation will likely be a challenge. Airports are already congested, airplanes full, and service levels on the decline. The online tourism market has put more demand on these existing distribution systems. These systems must gain the ability to swiftly adapt to the changing market to stay competitive.

Through information technology, people can become "virtual tourists" and "visit" destinations without leaving their homes. They can also gain valuable information about destinations to contemplate whether they would like to visit them in the future. Technological improvements will help the Department of Homeland Security scrutinize visitors to the United States through the use of machine-readable passports and visas with biometric data, including fingerprints and a digital image of the person's face. Frequent travelers can opt for pre-screening so that they can bypass lineups and use the express lanes at airports.

Economic Change

Given the current global economic situation, only a modest growth in tourism is likely in the next few years. Tourists from developed countries will continue to drive tourism by visiting other developed countries and developing countries. By virtue of their economic development, countries such as China, India, Brazil, and Russia will contribute millions more potential tourists to the industry.

So, where will all these new tourists travel? The United States, Canada, Mexico, many European countries, and several Asian countries will see an increase in international visitors. The citizens of eastern European countries will, as their nations' economies improve, gain the ability to travel, but until that time these countries are likely to receive more tourists because they offer good value and a different experience. Tourism in the expanded European Union will likely increase as more tourists have the means and inclination to travel to see other European countries.

Government Promotion

Given that travel and tourism has an enormous impact on the world economy, it is no surprise that it is receiving increasing attention from local, state, provincial, and federal governments. Tourism is perceived as a viable means to stimulate sluggish economies. This concept is covered in more detail in the next section.

▶ **Check Your Knowledge**

1. How many international arrivals are expected by 2020?
2. Define *demand influences*.
3. What effect will information technology have on the future of travel?

Government Involvement in Tourism

When private tourism and travel-related companies develop and expand, the world's governments also benefit greatly in the form of increased collected taxes and other income. As a result, an array of government entities promotes tourism directly and indirectly. On the national level are the national tourist offices (NTOs). In the United States, the NTO is the **Office of Travel and Tourism Industries (OTTI)**, which is an official government organization.

Many states and provinces also advertise travel or help fund travel promotion efforts. They do this with money raised from taxes and from contributions donated by corporations involved with tourism. Large portions of government money are allocated to the budgets of convention and visitor bureaus, whose main functions are to attract conventions, expositions, groups, and leisure travelers to the area served by the bureau, and thereby stimulate the local economy.

The U.S. federal government views tourism as a possible means for developing the economies of states such as Kentucky and West Virginia. The **Economic Development Administration** has underwritten millions of dollars worth of resort developments for parks in those states and has set aside even more money to foster tourism on Native American lands. States where tourism is a major industry, such as California, New York, Nevada, Colorado, Wyoming, Texas, Illinois, Arizona, and Florida, are well aware of the value of the tourist dollar.

Many areas turn to tourism as the only realistic way of raising themselves from the poverty level. The tourist dollar, if it is maintained, is more valuable to a local economy than the local dollar generated and spent within the economy. This is because tourist money is money that is "new" from outside the economy, triggering rounds of additional spending. Much of the tourist dollar is allocated to services involved with construction and operation of vacation facilities.

The U.S. government over the years has become more serious about tourism, which has lead to the creation of the Tourism Policy Council. This is, according to then Secretary of Commerce Ron Brown, in recognition of tourism's "explosive potential." The council works with the private sector as well as state and local governments to "ensure that the national interest in tourism is fully considered in federal decision-making affecting tourism development." The council coordinates national policies and programs relating to international travel and tourism, recreation, and national heritage resources.[10] However, the funding allocated to tourism does not truly indicate the economic power of the industry. Most likely in the future, tourism taxes will not be reinvested in the industry; instead, they will be used to fund education and other unrelated services that rely heavily on public financial support.[11]

Prospects for Future Travel

The future looks bright for the tourism industry and it is expected to grow, but what factors are causing this growth? Is there anything holding it back? In this section, we look at factors that make the tourism industry grow, as well as factors that hinder its growth.

Trends That Favor Tourism

Trends that favor travel include rising disposable incomes, increased number of retired persons, greater mobility, greater discretionary time, smaller families and changing roles, a higher divorce rate and many singles, smaller living spaces, increased education, travel simplifications, shifts in values, and interest in new places. Rising income and more leisure time are two of the main contributors to the increase in leisure travel taking place in the United States. Following is a closer look at these factors.

Rising Disposable Income

Overall, more money means more tourism. In the United States and other developed countries, there are a large number of double-income families. According to the U.S. Travel Association, 67 percent of travelers are employed full or part time. The mean annual household income of travelers is $70,200.[12] Moreover, the world is experiencing a redistribution of income as some countries are rapidly developing. Segments of the population in these resource-rich and emerging nations, especially China and India, are now receiving incomes that make travel and tourism a possibility for an increasingly larger number of their population. As soon as the current recession is over, there will likely be considerable pent up demand for tourism.

Greater Discretionary Time

It is likely that millions of Americans will be retiring soon and many of them will have lots of discretionary time and want to be tourists. The workweek has shrunk considerably since two generations ago from more than 50 hours to currently 40 hours per week. In addition, some European governments mandate 25 paid vacation days for all workers. This means that many Europeans have a total of six weeks of vacation.

Changing Family Structure

American and European birthrates have declined sharply, giving adults more free time away from family responsibilities. Sexual equality and shifts in household roles and composition favor more travel. At the same time, divorce rates are rising. Still, according to the U.S. Travel Association, 70 percent of U.S. travelers are married, 16 percent are single or never married, and 14 percent are divorced. Approximately 36 percent of travelers have children in the household.[13]

▶ Check Your Knowledge

1. What is the role of the Tourism Policy Council?
2. What are two of the main contributors to the increase in leisure travel taking place in the United States?
3. According to the U.S. Travel Association, what percentage of travelers are employed?

FOCUS ON

Career Prospects

Alan Seidman

There's never been a better time to be a future travel and tourism professional. As our world continues to get smaller and long-distance transportation gets safer, people of all ages and from all regions will be on the move. Even now businessmen and women use airports as mobile offices, cruise lines proliferate as droves of new passengers take to the seas, and families ride around the country in new, energy-efficient, high-speed trains. And for all these travelers, there will be the need for someone to advise and assist them.

Most experts predict a huge leap in tourism as baby boomers retire and leverage their good health and energy into years filled with travel. Many, driven by intellectual curiosity, will flock to museums, galleries, and events throughout the world. They will want to stay in hotels that provide both comfort and convenience and will be willing to spend whatever necessary to acquire these benefits. The travel/tourism professional will be needed to help plan their travel needs.

The Millennial generation is mobile and curious and also yearns to travel. Although they may not have the disposable income of baby boomers, they will have scores of faraway friends met through online social networking sites. Lack of money will not stop them from seeking out adventure or keep them from exploring new lands. Once again, the travel/tourism professional will be needed to assist them.

Furthermore, we can expect an increase in travel by people with disabilities. Tourism-related services will provide more services for travelers with special needs. Even now, accommodations are provided for travelers who require special beds, wheelchairs, or even dialysis machines. The continued growth in health-related support services will make it easier for people with disabilities to travel.

There is no doubt, however, that the industry has changed. The role of the travel agent has lessened considerably as more people use the Internet to research and book their travel plans, but more people are necessary to staff airports, ports of call, and car rental companies. Entrepreneurs will be needed to develop tours and shore excursions that will meet the needs of this next wave of travelers.

Flexibility will be key because these professionals may be asked to move halfway around the world at a moment's notice. Those who are fluent in a variety of languages will be in high demand. Understanding diversity is also a requirement, and those who enjoy interacting with people from all over the world will be valuable assets to this growing industry.

College students everywhere should take notice. The travel/tourism industry is growing and will need lots of creative, high-energy people to serve as the next generation of leaders. There has never been a better time to be a travel/tourism professional.

Source: Courtesy of Alan Seidman, College Chair, the Hospitality College, Johnson & Wales University–North Miami.

Increased Numbers of Retired Persons

Many people are retiring at an earlier age than before, and about 70 million Americans will be reaching retirement age in the next few years. Extensive pension plans are available for many, guaranteeing an income. In addition, life expectancy continues to rise as a result of increasing health consciousness and more people engaging in planned exercise. Thus, many retired people today have the ability, the desire, and the energy to travel. In addition, transportation discounts for senior citizens are already widespread in Europe and are growing in the United States. Currently, 14 percent of all U.S. travelers are retired, and the number is on the rise![14]

Change in Living Conditions

Higher costs of homebuilding have increased apartment and condominium living. Smaller living spaces stimulate the need to "get away from it all." At the beginning of the last century, only 15 percent of the world's population lived in cities; now that figure is much higher. Cities are growing, and the urban lifestyle often includes traveling. People have become more accustomed to making moves required by their careers and to traveling in general. With the increase in Internet technology, more and more people are taking control of their own travel plans. There is also an increase in telecommuters, who are able to work from any location.

Education and Shift in Values

As millions attend colleges and universities, people tend to think more in global terms and become interested in foreign cultures. According to the U.S. Travel Association, 39 percent of travelers have a college degree, including 17 percent with graduate work started or completed.[15]

A shift in values is currently taking place. Possession of such things as expensive cars, houses, clothes, and jewels now has less appeal for some than they had in the past. For many people, doing something, or taking part in something, has assumed more importance than the material possessions they have. Millionaires may live in relatively modest condominiums, wear blue jeans, and drive old cars. The luster of travel, however, shines ever brighter. Television and movies enlarge the travel perspective, creating interest in places never before considered as travel destinations. The spread of technology is also making the once-desolate locations more appealing to travelers. President Barack Obama's election victory has triggered a surge in "roots" tourism to destinations such as Kenya, Hawaii, and Indonesia.[16]

Travel Simplification: The Package Tour

Travel packaging has been significant in the industry ever since Thomas Cook shepherded his first tour groups around England. Tour packages, in which everything is planned, arranged, and included for one price, are usually more popular with the less adventurous person looking for simplicity in booking.

Factors That Inhibit Travel

What is the destination of your dreams? Have you been there yet? If not, what are the reasons why you have not been able to go? Whether you would like to take off to a place in the United States, South America, Africa, Asia, Australia, or Europe, there are several possible reasons why you have not, cannot, or would not go right now. Factors that inhibit travel include uncontrollable issues such as economic uncertainty, recession, and political unrest. In addition, such things as travel hassles, lack of security, health hazards, and the aspect of distance and money may make people think twice before taking a trip. Let us look at some of them.

Uncontrollable Issues

Economic uncertainty, recession, political unrest and terrorism, and excessive labor costs in transportation are some of the factors that inhibit travel. These are hard to deal with because they are largely out of the control of the managers of travel companies. It's a fuzzy concept and nearly impossible to quantify, but consumer confidence may play the biggest role in the financial future of domestic tourism.[17]

Travel Hassles and Security

Travel hassles, on the other hand, such as baggage problems, delays, overbooking, and jammed airport terminals, are factors that may inhibit someone from taking a trip but are within the area of control of tourism company managers. Lack of security in public places, hotels, and travel centers may cause people to prefer remaining in the security of their own homes. Certain areas may acquire the reputation of being dangerous, for various reasons, and thus become less desirable travel destinations. Along with the lack of security, some people may not travel because of the hassle of too much security. Traveling by air in the United States requires passengers to abide by a list of rules as well as pass through security checkpoints, remove their shoes as they pass through security, limit the volume of liquids that they can transport, and avoid bringing prohibited items onto the plane, and the list goes on.

FOCUS ON

Industry Trends: Space Tourism

Courtesy Bel Kambach

For a mere $200,000, you can secure your seat on the most coveted adventure of the future. Book now and join the ranks of the 250 Virgin Galactic non-NASA astronauts who will venture into space soon.

Reservations have only just begun to be taken, and a deposit of $20,000 will secure your spot on this incredible, once-in-a-lifetime voyage of discovery. Many businesspeople are cashing in on this newest craze as space tourism becomes the latest phenomenon in the travel and tourism industry, where wealthy adventurers are spending up to $20 million for a chance to travel in Low Earth Orbit (LEO) and beyond.

The possibility of space exploration opened up for us mere mortals when California multimillionaire Dennis Tito became the world's first private-pay space traveler. In April 2001, Tito, the founder of Wilshire Associates and former Jet Propulsion Laboratory (JPL) scientist, spent $20 million to hitch a ride on a Russian Soyuz capsule launched by Space

FOCUS ON (*continued*)

Adventures, Ltd., that had successfully flown six private citizens to the International Space Station (ISS). The Russian Soyuz TM-32 transported Tito to the Space Station, where he spent a week. In 2002, South African millionaire Mark Shuttleworth followed Tito as the second person to embark on space tourism, also spending approximately $20 million to travel aboard a Russian Soyuz TM-34.

They were followed by 40-year-old, Iranian-born U.S. citizen Anousheh Ansari, who became the first woman to travel in space and the fourth overall to make the trip from Russia to the ISS. She traveled onboard the Russian Soyuz TMA-9 spacecraft, which launched September 9, 2006, from Kazakhstan's Baikonur Cosmodrome. Ansari, along with her family, was the largest multi-million-dollar donor to the X-Prize for space tourism, and, for her generosity, the Anasari X-Prize was named after her.

Most of us would argue that John Glenn in 1962 was the first official extraterrestrial tourist, but others may discount that claim because Glenn was a nonpaying participant in the flight.

Virgin Galactic

Virgin Galactic will become the world's first Spaceline, giving us all the groundbreaking opportunity to become nonprofessional astronauts. Virgin Galactic owns and will operate its privately built spaceships, modeled on the remarkable, history-making *SpaceShipOne*. Virgin's vast experience in aviation, adventure, luxury travel, and cutting-edge design combined with the unique technology developed by Burt Rutan will ensure an unforgettable experience unlike any other available to humankind. These spaceships will allow affordable suborbital space tourism for the first time in the history of the universe. Virgin's diverse experience will be vital in contributing to the design of the spaceship, the smooth operation of the spaceline, and creating the experience of a lifetime.

Who's behind Virgin Galactic?

Sir Richard Branson, owner of Virgin Atlantic Airways, which has become the second largest long-haul international airline operating out of Gatwick and Heathrow, is the brains behind Virgin Galactic. Billionaire Branson is known for his legendary contributions to this industry.

Expensive Travel? Think Again

If you think space tourism is so expensive that nobody will want to go or that nobody would want to go anyway, then think again. There is already a waiting list of travelers to be launched into Low Earth Orbit both aboard the ISS and Virgin Galactic. Space tourism, like Dubai, has been criticized tremendously as being "playgrounds for the filthy rich." And although there may be some truth to this now, the vision for the future is to make space tourism affordable and available to the general public in a few years. However, like anything new, it will start out expensive and attract rich people who have a spirit of adventure, so they'll get there first. But fundamentally the goal is to make it affordable for regular people to get into orbit.

Don't Hold Your Breath Waiting to Become a NASA Astronaut

Many people still think that to go into space you need to become a government-employed astronaut. Unfortunately, the chance of that happening is small, simply because the astronaut program is extremely competitive. Astronauts are few and far between, and there's little prospect of many more being employed. So, the closest we can get to becoming an official astronaut is to pay $800 to spend a weekend at NASA's Space Camp.

(*continued*)

Many in the "space community" find the idea of a million people per year going into space almost inconceivable. Yet people in aviation find such a figure almost inconceivably small—it's less than 1/1,000th of the 1 billion passengers carried on scheduled airline flights each year. Clearly not an unrealistic target!

Start Saving for Your Ticket!

Far more people will travel to space as tourists than as astronauts, and the first thing they must do to get there is to start saving. The initially high price for a roundtrip flight to Low Earth Orbit is estimated to decrease over time. The target of the Space Tourism Study Program of the Japanese Rocket Society is to bring the price down to about 1 million yen (US$10,000) on a turnover of about 1 million passengers per year. However, the demand is expected to be very high, like everything new in the early stages, plus because people are fascinated by space—the Smithsonian Air and Space Museum has the distinction of being the world's most visited museums.

You Don't Have to Be Young—But It Can Help!

In Arnold Schwarzenegger's movie *Total Recall*, space tourism was a central theme. It won't be long before young travelers want to revisit films like this. These orbital flights will involve some preflight medical checks. Early indicators show that the required medical assessment will be simple and unrestrictive and that the vast majority of people who want to fly will be able to.

Experiencing Zero-G Thrills

Just the experience of viewing Earth from space could transform people's attitudes. Floating in a completely weightless environment for days and being able to see the night sky like never before can make anyone appreciate the true majesty of the universe and the fragility of Earth.

Experiencing zero-G (no gravity) may be the main attraction of space travel. Whereas the experience is quite stimulating for some, for others it can be disturbing and nauseating. A privileged few have experienced a similar sensation onboard NASA's aircraft known as the "Vomit Comet" that is used for cosmonaut training. Zero gravity will undoubtedly be fun, particularly for adventurous souls.

Prior to blasting off into space, space tourists will be acquainted with the spacecraft and conditions they will experience once inside. Travelers must be ready to deal with zero gravity and weightlessness beyond an altitude of 60 or 80 miles. Traveling to the vast frontier may be exhilarating, and tourists must be physically and mentally ready to accept the challenges.

Three days of preflight preparation, including bonding and training onsite at the spaceport, are planned. Learning how to make the most of time in zero-G and tips on how to be most comfortable in macrogravity will form an integral part of travel preparation.

How Safe Will It Be?

As a result of the unique technology developed by Burt Rutan's Scaled Composites now exclusively licensed to Virgin, the spacecraft design overcomes many of the safety and cost issues that had previously made space travel the preserve of the privileged few. To prepare tourists for space travel, corporations have been given the go signal by the Federal Aviation Administration (FAA) to conduct zero-gravity or weightless flights for people who want to experience the sensation of floating in space. The goal is to ensure that all passengers can fly safely.

Let's Not Forget Environmental Impact

Almost every astronaut you read about is an environmentalist. The fact is that the hostile vacuum of space makes it hard to do damage beyond leaving debris behind. Polluting space may be difficult. One of the great

F O C U S   O N   *(continued)*

things here is that Virgin Galactic could be completely solar-powered. In September 2006, Sir Richard Branson declared that all future proceeds from the Virgin Group will go into transportation renewable energy initiatives. He further announced a $25 million prize to encourage the development of a viable technology that can remove anthropogenic atmospheric greenhouse gases. His foundation is also putting significant effort into Virgin Unite, which focuses on entrepreneurial approaches to social and environmental issues. And this is only some of the good news we want to hear in this industry.

Although many of the people involved in space activities today really can't see that space tourism is going to take off, or will even be a popular pursuit, space future is eminent. The fact is people want to go there and in large numbers. The technology exists already, it just needs to be put together in the right system. That's all this industry needs—ready and willing travelers and a feasible service. It's going to happen and it is going to happen sooner than we think—it's about time!

If you were bitten by the travel bug when you were young and have always dreamed of going beyond the confines of Earth, that possibility may exist sooner than we all thought. We'll have to wait a few years to book our flight, though, as all the details are being worked out. Until then, keep reading this book! And of course, keep dreaming of getting those red socks and astronaut wings from Virgin Galactic!

Space Tourism Web Sites

- Kennedy Space Center: www.kennedyspacecenter.com/groups-camp-kennedy-space-center.aspx
- NASA: What Is the Vomit Comet? www.nasa.gov/audience/forstudents/brainbites/nonflash/bb_home_vomitcomet.html

  For just under $3,000, the zero-G experience will be a full-day program under the instruction of a veteran astronaut
- NASA: John Herschel Glenn, Jr., Biographical Data www.jsc.nasa.gov/Bios/htmlbios/glenn-j.html
- NASA: Franklin Chang-Dìaz: Biographical Data www.jsc.nasa.gov/Bios/htmlbios/chang.html
- Smithsonian: National Air and Space Museum www.nasm.si.edu

  Maintains the largest collection of historic air and spacecraft in the world
- Space Adventures: www.spaceadventures.com

  How to belong to the exclusive and elite network of space enthusiasts and explorers
- Space-Tourism: www.space-tourism.ws
- Virgin Galactic: www.virgingalactic.com
- Virgin Galactic: Accredited Space Agents: www.virgingalactic.com/htmlsite/asa.php

Source: Courtesy of Bel Kambach, St. Cloud State University, Minnesota.

Health Issues

With an increase in international travelers, the risk of infectious diseases being spread worldwide also increases. Health hazards such as malaria and HIV will certainly keep a portion of potential visitors away from certain destinations. For instance, HIV and AIDS more heavily affect sub-Saharan Africa than any other region of the world. An estimated 22 million people were living with HIV at the end of 2007, and approximately 1.9 million additional people were infected with HIV during that year.[18] AIDS has orphaned more than 11 million children.[19] These are not the only health issues travelers must be aware of in the African region. Other concerns include the following:

- *Malaria*—A serious and potentially fatal disease caused by protozoan parasites. Usually people catch malaria by being bitten by an infected female *Anopheles* mosquito.

- *Bird Flu (avian influenza)*—This infection is caused by a particular variety of avian influenza virus. The virus is found in wild birds and is easily passed to domestic birds raised for food (chicken, ducks, etc.).

- *Schistosomiasis (more commonly known as bilharzia)*—Caused by parasitic worms. Infection occurs when skin comes into contact with contaminated fresh water. Fresh water becomes contaminated through infected humans defecating or urinating in the water.

- *Dengue Fever (also known as breakbone fever)*—Caused by a virus that is spread by infected mosquitoes. In 2009, the Centers for Disease Control and Prevention posted a dengue outbreak notice for tropical and subtropical regions.[20]

- *Putzi Fly (myiasis)*—Infection occurs when humans come into contact with Putzi fly eggs. Usually the eggs are on hanging clothing and are hatched once they come into contact with human skin. The larvae then burrow into the skin, creating boil-like sores as they develop into a fully grown maggot. Easily removed once identified.

- *African Trypanosomiasis (sleeping sickness)*—Occurs when a person is bitten by an infected tsetse fly. Tsetse flies are found only in Africa. This disease is fatal if left untreated.

- *Rabies*—Fatal viral disease caused by the bite of infected animals. Found also in raccoons in temperate climates.

- *Yellow Fever*—A virus transmitted through the bite of an infected mosquito. Effects range in severity from a self-limited febrile illness to severe hepatitis and hemorrhagic fever.[21]

- *Tuberculosis (TB)*—A bacterial infection caused by *Mycobacterium tuberculosis*. TB spreads through the air when an infected person coughs, sneezes, or talks. Left untreated TB can be deadly.[22]

- *Cholera*—An acute, diarrheal illness caused by infection of the intestine with the bacterium *Vibrio cholerae*. A person may get cholera through drinking water or eating cholera bacterium–contaminated food. In an epidemic, the source of the contamination is usually the feces of an infected person.[23]

- *Swine Flu (H1N1 virus)*—A contagious respiratory disease caused by a new type of influenza virus not seen in humans before 2008. It is spread primarily from person to person through coughing or sneezing.[24]

This is just a selection of health hazards—the list goes on. The best thing travelers can do before traveling is to be aware. They can check travel warnings, get vaccinated, and be cautious!

▶ Check Your Knowledge

1. What percentage of the world's population lives in cities?
2. What is meant by a "shift in values"?
3. In 2007, how many people were living with HIV in sub-Saharan Africa?

Instant Communication and Technology

Instant communication is another factor that somewhat inhibits travel because fax machines, teleconferencing, and the Internet partially eliminate the need for business travel. According to the U.S. Travel Association, business travel accounts for approximately 25 percent of U.S. domestic trips.[25] Combined business and pleasure trips account for 9 percent.[26] So, a total of 34 percent of travel is business related—more than one-third of all travel! If use of technology eliminates some business travel, it has a large impact.

In addition, the increasing number of retiring baby boomers will have to put forth the effort to keep up with technology because it played a very limited role, if any, in their youth.[27] Travel and tourism organizations should be aware of their clients' differing needs and technological comfort zones.

Cost and Location

Finally, the price and distance of a trip can also be major reasons people either postpone the trip or put it off completely. With the economic downturn, consumers are spending less, which makes it less likely they will book a trip to a distant or expensive location. With the price of oil fluctuating and climbing, airlines (along with most other travel providers) are charging more for their services. As the demand for their services becomes less, they will be forced to lower their prices. The current recession, record unemployment levels, the financial crisis, and the loss of people's retirement savings are deterrents to tourism; however, there are still a number of people traveling and the numbers will increase as the economic environment improves.

CASE STUDY

Middletown Airport

Middletown Airport is a medium-sized airport located in the Southeast. For several years, city leaders have been trying to increase airline usage and capacity by increasing the length of the runways, adding new terminals, and providing more terminal services for passengers. Their hope is that a larger airport will not only increase revenue, but increase passenger volume, which will result in an increase in tourism revenue to the surrounding area.

Unfortunately, Middletown discovered that airport expansion is a difficult process. The biggest obstacle is resistance from the surrounding community, which opposes the expansion. Many Middletown residents

(continued)

CASE STUDY (continued)

believe a bigger airport will result in increased traffic, noise, and air pollution. So far, they have successfully been able to delay expansion through a well-organized, grassroots opposition. The city leaders, however, are strongly in favor of airport expansion and are determined to override the efforts of the community.

The city leaders plan on holding meetings with the local community in which they will present their case for airport expansion. They feel that once they present the full spectrum of economic opportunities, the opposition will be won over.

Questions

1. How would the airport benefit by increasing the size of the runways?
2. Give specific examples of how a bigger airport will increase tourism revenues.
3. Given your responses to the preceding questions, do you feel the Middletown community should drop its protest?
4. If the airport expansion moves forward as planned, what might be some of the capacity control issues that Middletown would have to face?

Source: Courtesy of Alan Seidman, Johnson & Wales University.

CASE STUDY

Tourism Development Coordinator

You have been appointed the tourism development coordinator for your city. One of your first duties is to evaluate the current state of the tourism industry in the city. Your duties include ensuring that tourism in the community is sustainable. You decide to use the triple bottom line (TBL) concept (whereby you want a balance of social, economic, and environmental sustainability) as your theoretical guide. The challenge with the TBL concept is that it is difficult to measure.

Questions

1. Even if you can measure individual concepts (like economic impact), how then do you know if the tourism is really sustainable?
2. How do you go about measuring and monitoring your community for TBL?

Source: Wayne Smith, College of Charleston.

Summary

1. The United Nations World Tourism Organization forecasts that in 2020 there will be 1.6 billion international arrivals.
2. Demand influences and issues such as consumer behavior and preferences affect tourism.
3. Associated with demand factors are demographics. The baby boomers are aging and some 70 million Americans are beginning to retire and thus have more time and the desire to travel.
4. The supply side of tourism will continue to modify and change product offerings and place greater emphasis on environmental protection while providing the tourism experiences that consumers want.
5. Capacity control refers to the ability of a destination to receive and care for the needs of tourists within the limits of sustainability.
6. Destination management can include land use planning, business permits and zoning controls, environmental and other regulations, business association initiatives, and a host of other techniques to shape the development and daily operation of tourism-related activities.
7. Information technology will improve to help facilitate tourism and tourists. However, it will lead to less business travel.
8. Countries such as the United States, Canada, and Mexico will experience an increase in international visitors. As the economy improves in other countries, such as India and China, more people will become tourists; but until then, these regions will receive more tourists.
9. When private tourism and travel-related companies develop and expand, the world's governments also benefit greatly in the form of increased taxes collected and other income.
10. An array of government entities promotes travel.
11. Trends that favor travel include rising disposable incomes, increased number of retired persons, greater mobility, and greater discretionary time.
12. Factors that inhibit travel include economic uncertainty, recession, political unrest, and excessive labor costs in public transportation.
13. Other inhibiting factors include things such as travel hassles, lack of security, health hazards, and the costs of travel in terms of time and money.

Key Words and Concepts

capacity control
demand factors
destination management

Economic Development
    Administration

Office of Travel and Tourism
    Industries (OTTI)
tourism niche

Review Questions

1. What is destination management?
2. What are the benefits of the increase in information technology on the future of tourism?
3. What are the drawbacks of the increase in information technology on the future of tourism?
4. Discuss two trends that favor tourism.
5. Discuss two trends that inhibit tourism.
6. What does Kyrgyzstan offer tourists?
7. Do you agree with Alan Seidman and other experts who suggest that in the future there will be a huge leap in tourism? Why or why not?
8. Discuss governments role in tourism.
9. What is Virgin Galactic?

Interesting Websites

Office of Travel and Tourism Industries:
http://tinet.ita.doc.gov/

Travel and Tourism Research Association: www
.ttra.com

United Nations World Tourism Organization:
www.world-tourism.org

Internet Exercises

1. Go to the Transportation Security
   Administration website at www.tsa.gov.
   a. Search the home page for the TSA Week at
      a Glance.
   b. How many passengers were arrested due to
      suspicious behavior or fraudulent travel
      documents?
   c. How many firearms were found at security
      checkpoints?
   d. How many artfully concealed prohibited
      items were found at checkpoints?
   e. How many incidents involved a checkpoint
      closure, terminal evacuation, or sterile area
      breaches?

Apply Your Knowledge

1. Discuss the top two factors that may inhibit
   you from visiting a location where you would
   otherwise like to vacation.
2. Is travel simplification through a package tour
   something that interests you?
   a. If so, what factors of the package most
      appeal to you?
   b. If not, what type of travel booking do you
      prefer? Why?

Suggested Activity

Make a plan for the next 20 years of tourism in your area.

Endnotes

1. United Nations World Tourism Organization,
   "Tourism 2020 Vision," www.world-tourism.org/facts/
   2020.html (accessed January 6, 2009).
2. Ibid.
3. International Air Transport Association, "G8 Supports
   Global Sectoral Approach for Aviation—Encourages
   Government–Business Partnership on Environment,"
   www.iata.org/pressroom/pr/2009-07-09-01.htm
   (accessed July 20, 2009).
4. CNN, "G8 Leaders Have Ambitious Environmental
   Goals," www.cnn.com/2009/WORLD/europe/07/
   08/g8.summit/index.html?eref=rss_latest (accessed
   July 20, 2009).
5. Sustainable Tourism Gateway, "Tourism Destination
   Management," www.gdrc.org/uem/eco-tour/
   destination-mgmt.html (accessed January 6, 2009).

6. H. Pechlaner and M. Fuchs, "Towards New Skill Requirements for Destination Organizations: An Exploratory Study," *Tourism Analysis* 7, no. 1 (2002): 43–53.

7. S. Formica and T. Kothari, "Strategic Destination Planning: Analyzing the Future of Tourism," *Journal of Travel Research* 46 (2008): 355, http://jtr.sagepub .com/cgi/content/abstract/46/4/355 (accessed January 14, 2009).

8. A. Papathanassis and D. Buhalis, "Exploring the Information and Communication Technologies Revolution and Visioning the Future of Tourism, Travel, and Hospitality Industries," *International Journal of Tourism Research* 9 (2007): 385–387.

9. Ibid.

10. ITA Office of Travel and Tourism Industries, http://tinet.ita.doc.gov/policy/tpc.html?ti_cart_cookie= 20001020.165310.01992 (accessed August 2, 2006).

11. Formica and Kothari, "Strategic Destination Planning," 355.

12. U.S. Travel Association, "U.S. Travel market Overview—Demographics," www.tia.org/ researchpubs/us_overview_demographics.html (accessed January 6, 2009).

13. Ibid.

14. Ibid.

15. Ibid.

16. "'Obamania' Tourism Sweeps the World," *Canadian Travel Press* 41, no. 11 (December 2008): 3–23.

17. Ibid. 3.

18. AVERT: Averting HIV and AIDS, "HIV and AIDS in Africa," www.avert.org/aafrica.htm (accessed January 6, 2009).

19. UNAIDS, "2008 Report on the Global AIDS Epidemic," www.unaids.org/en/KnowledgeCentre/ HIVData/GlobalReport/2008/ (accessed January 2, 2009).

20. Centers for Disease Control and Prevention, "Outbreak Notice: Update: Dengue, Tropical and Subtropical Regions," wwwn.cdc.gov/travel/ contentDengueTropicalSubTropical.aspx (accessed January 9, 2009).

21. Centers for Disease Control and Prevention, "Yellow Fever," www.cdc.gov/ncidod/dvbid/yellowfever/index .htm (accessed January 9, 2009).

22. Medline Plus, "Tuberculosis," www.nlm.nih.gov/ medlineplus/tuberculosis.html (accessed January 9, 2009).

23. Centers for Disease Control and Prevention, "Cholera," www.cdc.gov/nczved/dfbmd/ disease_listing/cholera_gi.html (accessed January 9, 2009).

24. University of California, San Francisco, "FAQ on H1N1 Influenza A (Swine Flu)," http://today.ucsf.edu/ attachments/faq-on-hini-influenza-a-swine-flu (accessed September 23, 2009).

25. U.S. Travel Association, "U.S. Travel Market Overview—Travel Volumes and Trends," www.tia.org/ researchpubs/us_overview_volumes_trends.html (accessed January 6, 2009).

26. Ibid.

27. Formica and Kothari, "Strategic Destination Planning," 355.

Glossary

Adventure travelers   Tourists seeking active and challenging activities to add something extra to their vacation.

Advertising   Communication about a product in different types of media.

Agenda 21   A comprehensive program of action adopted in 1992 by 182 governments at the United Nations conference on Environment and Development known as the Earth Summit. It provided a blueprint for securing the sustainable future of the planet into the twenty-first century.

Air–cruise package   A travel package that combines the booking of airfare and cruise price.

Airlines Reporting Corporation   A corporation made up of domestic airlines, travel agencies, corporate travel departments, railroads, and other travel suppliers who process more than $80 billion annually through ARC's settlement system, making it the financial backbone of travel distribution.

Airways   Routes along which jets fly, similar to cars on a highway. Pilots follow these sky tracks from station to station.

American Automobile Association (AAA)   One of the largest membership organizations in the world. AAA offers its members an array of savings and useful services.

Americans with Disabilities Act of 1990   Addresses access for people with disabilities throughout most or all aspects of life in the United States, including employment, government services, and many others.

Analytical research   Also commonly referred to as *explanatory research*, builds upon descriptive research by seeking to uncover causation.

Applied research   *See* normative research.

Area Bank Settlement Plan   A system that allows American Society of Travel Agents members to sell and distribute tickets on the airlines' behalf.

Association   A group of individuals or organizations, generally self-governing, that represents an industry. Its purpose is to promote its agenda by lobbying, marketing, educating, and providing various member services.

Attractions   Places that tend to draw people to a certain area.

Benchmark   Identification and comparison of products, services, and practices by a business, which then attempts to improve its own performance to match or surpass its competitors.

Best practices   Practices recognized as being the best in the industry. These practices are then benchmarked for emulation.

Better than the competition   A market positioning approach used when the product marketed is similar to that of the competition. Better can be obtained in many ways, including lower price or higher quality.

Brand   *See* brand identity.

Brand identity   Unique elements that identify a product and set it apart from the products of other producers or service providers.

Brand loyalty   A situation where customers buy a product repeatedly, even if competitors' products are cheaper or the subjects of heavy advertising.

Bumping   Occurs when more passengers show up for a flight than there are seats available, and some get transferred to another flight.

Business travel   Taking a trip for business.

Cabotage   Restricts foreign airlines from engaging in passenger service within a country.

Capacity control   The ability of a destination to receive and care for the needs of tourists within the limits of sustainability.

Capacity requirement   What a destination needs to supply all the tourists visiting, for example, water, sewage, and transportation.

Carbon footprint   The total greenhouse gases emitted by a person, company, event, or product.

Carbon offset   A financial instrument aimed at a reduction in greenhouse gas emissions. Renewable energy projects are the most common source of carbon offsets.

Career path   The pattern a person's career can take, including the various positions that person might have over time.

Carrying capacity   Limits on tourism from environmental, visitor, and community perspectives.

Causation The act of causing something to happen.

Chain restaurant A restaurant that shares a brand with similar restaurants and central management; usually these have standardized business methods and practices.

Chambers of commerce Associations that provide forums for the discussion of general business topics including tourism.

Channels of distribution See direct and indirect channels of distribution.

Closed-ended question A question that can be answered finitely. These include dichotomous (yes/no), scaled (excellent, good, fair, poor), and multiple-choice questions.

Comparative master planning Planning that includes comparison to other plans for the purpose of improving the plan being developed.

Comparative pricing approach Assessing what prices similar operations are charging for the same or similar service/product. In other words, fitting expenses and profit margin within a predetermined price.

Computerized reservation systems The instrument used by travel agents to simplify the reservation of complicated, multiflight itineraries.

Conference Regulatory bodies that set standards travel agencies have to meet to be appointed to act as sales agents for the air carriers.

Confounding variables Variables in experimental studies that are hard to separate from the independent variable and dependent variable. They can have influences on the variables of interest that the experimenter has not accounted for.

Consolidation The act of combining into an integral whole.

Consumer needs The difference between the state of a person and his or her desired state.

Continuous loyalty Continued faithfulness or commitment.

Convention A large business or professional meeting.

Convention and visitors bureau (CVB) An organization that aims to attract people to a specific area and keep them coming back.

Convention center A large structure in which conventions and exhibitions can be held, the purpose of which is to attract more convention groups, conferences, and trade shows to a particular area.

Core indicators Indicators that provide relevant information that can contribute to better decision making and, consequently, a more sustainable future for the tourism industry. Core indicators may be applied to all destinations.

Cost-benefit analysis (ratio) The benefits of tourism divided by the costs.

Cost-plus pricing approach A pricing approach that accounts for all costs and allocates an amount for profit before the selling price is determined.

Cruise Line Industry Association (CLIA) World's largest cruise association, composed of 24 of the major cruise lines serving North America; operates pursuant to an agreement filed with the Federal Maritime Commission under the Shipping Act of 1984 and serves as a nongovernmental consultative organization to the International Maritime Organization, an agency of the United Nations.

Cultural tourism Tourist visits motivated wholly or in part by interest in the historical, artistic, scientific, or lifestyle/heritage offerings of a community, region, group, or institution.

Customer groups A group of customers who have important demographic factors in common.

Demand See law of demand.

Demand-backward pricing A pricing method in which the price is set at a level that will ensure that the required quantity of the product or service is sold.

Demand curve Illustrates the law of demand; the demand curve's downward slope indicates the inverse relationship between price and demand, meaning that when one factor increases, the other decreases, and vice versa.

Demand factors Include factors such as consumer behavior, preferences, and demographics (see also demographic factors).

Demand side The side of tourism that concerns tourist motivation.

Demographic factors Factors such as age, gender, income, social class/occupation, family structure, lifestyle/interests, and ethnicity that can be used to divide the market into segments.

Demographics Consumer characteristics such as gender, age, civil status, education level, ethnic background, place of residence, income; these are good indicators of what the tourist needs and expects from a vacation.

Demonstration effect Situations where someone else sees another person doing a particular thing, and, as a result wants to do or have the same thing for himself or herself.

Density indicator Measures potential levels of overuse of the natural resource in question.

Dependent variable (DV) In research, the dependent variable is the variable measured to see if there is a change. The change is dependent on the independent variable.

Descriptive research Also commonly referred to as statistical research, aims to answer the questions who, what, where, when, and why? It is used when researchers want to describe the characteristics of a population or phenomenon.

Destination management May include land use planning, business permits and zoning controls, environmental and other regulations, business association initiatives, and a host of other techniques to shape the development and daily operation of tourism-related activities.

Destination-specific indicators Indicators that provide relevant information that can contribute to better decision making and, consequently, a more sustainable future for the tourism industry. Destination-specific indicators can be applied to particular ecosystems or types of tourism at a particular site, location, or destination.

Dichotomous Divided or dividing into two separate and identifiable parts.

Different from the competition approach A market positioning approach in which a company introduces a product that is different from and better than all current ones on the market.

Direct and indirect channels of distribution Direct channels are when a product or service is sold directly to the client, as with a phone call to an airline, cruise line, attraction, or hotel. Indirect channels are when the client goes through an intermediary to purchase the product or service, as when a client uses the Internet to book a flight.

Economic development With the increase in tourism revenue and foreign exchange earnings, per person income and tax revenues increase as well, which can be reinvested and contribute to economic growth.

Economic Development Administration An administration established under the Public Works and Economic Development Act of 1965, as amended, to generate jobs, help retain existing jobs, and stimulate industrial and commercial growth in economically distressed areas of the United States.

Economics The efficient utilization (such as consumption), distribution, and production of scarce resources (goods and services) to satisfy human wants.

Ecosystem-specific indicators Indicators that provide relevant information that can contribute to better decision making and, consequently, a more sustainable future for the tourism industry. Ecosystem-specific indicators can be applied to coastal areas, parks and protected areas, or mountainous areas.

Eco-tourism Responsible travel to natural areas that conserves the environment and sustains the well-being of local people.

Education and training The objective is to increase awareness of the industry's contribution to job creation, enhance career and employment opportunities, and develop professional skills in the industry through improved public and private sector coordination of education and training program.

Embarkation Entering or boarding a ship.

Employment growth Increasing demand for workers and availability of job positions.

Environmental policy The objective of preserving natural, historical, and cultural resources for future generations, and expanding urban and rural economic development opportunities through a national strategy of fostering environmental and cultural tourism.

Equilibrium The product price at which the quantity demanded equals the quantity supplied.

Eurail A train pass for travel in European countries during a limited time.

Event tourism The systematic planning, development, and marketing of festivals and special events as tourist attractions, development catalysts, and image builders for attractions and destination areas.

Experimental method Method of research that examines cause-and-effect relationships under controlled conditions. This involves the researcher setting up a test, or experiment, to simulate what happens in the real world.

Explanatory research The ideal type of research used when a problem can be sensed, but is not yet clearly defined.

Exposition An exhibit designed to interpret or explain a specific topic.

Extent of tourism growth Tourism growth stimulates economies, but its impact on local communities, their heritage, and the environment has to be monitored.

Extraneous variables *See* confounding variable.

Factual surveys Surveys that are concrete in the questions they ask. Answers are based on fact alone; no interpretation or opinion is expressed.

Fair A gathering of buyers and sellers for trade, pleasure, or for educational purposes.

Familiarization (FAM) trips Trips arranged for travel agents at little or no cost by airlines and tourist agencies to areas they represent.

Festival A time of celebration; may be of religious or cultural significance with entertainment.

Focus groups Groups of approximately 6 to 12 prescreened respondents. The interviewer then asks focused questions about the topic being investigated.

Foodservice Making, transporting, and serving or dispensing prepared foods.

Fortress hub An airport hub where one airline controls 75 percent or more of all passenger boardings.

Franchise restaurant (1) The authorization given by one company to another to sell its unique products and services; (2) the name of the business format or product being franchised.

Gambling The act of playing for stakes in hopes of winning.

Geographic concentration A concentration of businesses or other entities or populations within a particular geographic area. The concentration is expected to have economic and social advantages.

Global distribution system (GDS) System that connects travel agency members around the world and provides them with content from airlines, hotel properties, car rental companies, cruise lines, railroads, and tour operators.

Global positioning system A car navigation system that enables the driver to receive road directions via cell phone, a screen, or a voice device and to find their destination easily and conveniently anywhere in the world.

Goal A projected state of affairs that a person or a system plans or intends to achieve.

Green Globe A worldwide benchmarking and certification program developed by the World Travel and Tourism Council as an outcome of Agenda 21 recommendations.

Guest loyalty Guests who come back time after time to the same service provider.

Harnessing Tourism for the Millennium Development Goals The United Nations World Tourism Organization (UNWTO) issued this declaration recognizing the economic benefits to the tourism providers and recreational and educational benefits to the consumers; it also stated that tourism has the potential to be destructive of human rights, social and cultural values, and local environments without necessarily benefitting those suffering most.

Heritage The identification, protection, conservation, and transmission to future generations of the world's cultural and natural heritage.

Heritage tourism A branch of the tourism industry concerned with preserving the natural, cultural, and built environments of an area.

Hub-and-spoke system The system in which airlines link their routes together, at a central hub airport, to offer more frequent service and attract more passengers.

Hybrid vehicles A cross between a small adaptable gasoline- or diesel-powered engine and an electric motor, substantially reducing emissions.

Hypothesis A prediction about future behaviors that is derived from observations and theories.

Import propensity The percentage or part of the tourist dollar that leaves the local economy; represents a leak from the destination area.

Imports Tourism imports take place when citizens of a country buy foreign goods and services and hence bring them into their country.

Incentive A management tool used to reward employees for achieving goals or outstanding behavior.

Incentive market   Incentive travel programs for corporate employees to reward them for reaching specific targets (the incentive market).

Incentive travel   A management tool offering rewards to staff, consumers, and dealers; rewards normally include an all-inclusive travel package for the employee and his or her spouse.

Independent restaurant   Also known as an "indy," a restaurant individually owned and not affiliated with a chain or franchise.

Independent variable (IV)   In research, the independent variable is manipulated by the researcher in some way to see if the manipulation has an effect on the dependent variable.

Index of tourist irritation   *See* irridex.

Industry sectors   Groupings of industry into sectors such as air transportation or the cruise industry; or lodging, restaurants, attractions, and so forth.

Infrastructure   The hotels, shopping plazas, restaurants, and convention centers of a certain area.

Intangible   Incapable of being perceived. Not definite or clear.

Integration   To make into a whole or make part of a whole.

International Association of Convention and Visitors Bureaus (IACVB)   The world's largest association of convention and visitor bureaus (CVBs).

Interpretative surveys   Surveys that ask respondents to answer why they chose a particular course.

Interrelated businesses   Enterprises that are connected with each other in such a way as to facilitate the seamless integration of services offered to the traveling public.

Irridex   Index covering five levels of reaction on the part of the host community toward tourism: euphoria, apathy, annoyance, antagonism, and acceptance.

Jet stream   Winds resembling huge streams circling the hemisphere, usually at altitudes of 30,000 to 40,000 feet. They are established when cold polar air comes into contact with hot air from the tropical regions.

Labor intensity   Relates how many employees it takes per customer to deliver a product or service; generally low in manufacturing companies and high in businesses with direct customer contact, such as restaurants and hotels.

Law of demand   Indicates that if the price of a good or service increases while other prices stay the same, consumers have a tendency to substitute that good or service with a cheaper one.

Law of supply   Indicates that if the price of a good or service increases while other prices stay the same, producers tend to produce a greater quantity of that good or service.

Learning organizations   Are dedicated to the continuous improvement of the service process by closely monitoring every step of the service experience and constantly motivating and educating employees.

Leisure   Free time in which a person can chose what to do.

Leisure travel   Taking a trip for the purpose of leisure; includes travel for recreation, visiting friends and relatives, history and culture, attractions, entertainment, cruising, and sightseeing.

Life cycle   The sequence in the life span of a business experience, beginning with the birth (or introduction), followed by growth and maturity, and ending with decline.

Limits of acceptable change   Allied with the concept of carrying capacity. A term used to define how far a destination should (and is able to) go to attract guests.

Load factor   The percentage of seats filled on all flights, including planes flown empty to be in position for the next day's schedule.

Long-term planning   Also known as *strategic planning*. Planning for needs that need to be met in the long term.

Macroeconomics   The study of the economy as a whole, totaling direct and indirect tourism income.

Magnetic levitation or maglevs   Superfast trains suspended off the ground on a cushion formed by magnetic forces and pulled forward by magnets.

Management contracts   Contracts that usually allow a hotel company to manage a property owned by others for a period of 5, 10, or 20 years.

Man-made attractions   Attractions developed by humans (example: theme parks).

Market conditions   Measures of the potential of a product in a foreign country.

Market opportunities   Newly identified need, want, or demand trend that is not being addressed by the competitors.

Market positioning   The process of determining and influencing customers' perception of the product or service marketed.

Market power   The ability to influence price.

Market segment   *See* target market.

Market segmentation   The process of dividing the market into segments, profiling the segments, analyzing the segments, and formulating a strategy for each segment.

Market share   The percentage of the total sales of a given type of product or service.

Market size   The size of the market.

Market trend   Trends that help to unveil the economic impact of tourism, occupancy trends, and general consumer behavior.

Marketing   The process of planning and executing the conception, pricing, promotion, and distribution of ideas, goods, and services to create exchanges that satisfy individual or organizational objectives.

Marketing management   The process of marketing a product with the four tools of product, price, place, and promotion.

Marketing orientation   The philosophy of understanding what guests want and need, developing products and services that best meet their needs, and communicating with them to generate awareness, interest, and purchase.

Meeting   An assembly or gathering of people, as for a business, social, or religious purpose.

Meeting planner   A person who plans, coordinates, and executes meetings.

Meetings, incentive travel, conventions, and exhibitions (MICE)   In the hospitality industry, an acronym for meetings, incentive travel, conventions, and exhibitions.

Microeconomics   The study of individual units in an economy, including restaurants, airlines, cruise lines, hotels, motels, attractions, gaming, and other tourism entertainment.

Multiplier effect   When money entering an economy is spent and respent in the area, stimulating economic growth.

National heritage site   According to United Nations Educational, Scientific and Cultural Organization (UNESCO), sites that have national significance (as opposed to World Heritage sites, which have universal value).

National Historic Preservation Act of 1966   An act that motivated preservationists toward their mission of saving America's heritage resources.

National park   Generally, a large natural place that has a wide variety of attributes, sometimes including significant historic assets. Hunting, mining, and consumptive activities are not authorized in national parks.

National Register of Historic Places   The United States' official list of districts, sites, buildings, structures, and objects worthy of preservation. The National Park Service maintains properties.

National Tourism Policy Act of 1981   This act redefined the national interest in tourism and created the United States Travel and Tourism Administration (USTTA), replacing the United States Travel Service as the nation's government tourism office.

National Tourist Office (NTO)   An organization designed to promote travel and tourism to and within the country it represents.

Natural attractions   Attractions developed by nature (example: beaches and mountains).

Normative research   Also known as applied research. It aims to uncover the facts and seeks to provide recommendations for future improvements.

Observational method   Also called naturalistic observation; involves examining the constructs of interest in real-world conditions.

Occupancy   Period of time during which someone rents or otherwise occupies certain land or premises.

Office of Travel and Tourism Industries (OTTI)   The United States' national tourism office for research and policy issues. As part of the U.S. Department of Commerce, International Trade Administration, OTTI is mandated to develop, collect, and report the necessary statistical and market research on international travel to facilitate and guide planning in the public and private sectors.

Open-ended question   A question that enables respondents to provide responses of their own free will.

Operational definition A clear, concise, and completely detailed question.

Opinion surveys Surveys that ask respondents questions regarding what they think about particular topics.

Opportunity cost The cost associated with not choosing the best alternative.

Personal selling Promotional method where there is direct contact between the customer and a sales representative from a company.

Pilgrimage Another word for religious travel.

Planning *See* tourism planning.

Predictive research Aims to make a prediction about an occurrence of something happening in the future.

Primary data The original data collected for the specific purpose of solving (in this case) tourism related research issues.

Professional traveler A person for whom traveling has become a way of life.

Projected income statement A statement of the projected profitability of the business over the time frame covered by the plan.

Public relations Activities aimed at creating a positive image of a company among shareholders, customers, and the government.

Qualitative methods Research based on individual, often subjective, analysis.

Quality of life As it pertains to tourism, the negative and positive impacts tourism has on the people of a particular destination.

Quantitative methods Research based on some quantity or number rather than on some quality.

Rack rate The top or full rate.

Religious travel Travel to satisfy one's religious convictions and/or fulfill one's curiosity about a particular faith or practice.

Representative sample A group used in research that reflects the characteristics of the general population to be studied.

Research and statistics Measuring the economic activity of different segments in the tourism and travel industry to evaluate their impact on the economy, which helps identify problems and their causes, trends, market changes, and customer preferences.

Responsible tourism Another word for eco-tourism or adventure tourism.

Revenue management *See* yield management.

Revpar The revenue per available room in a hotel.

Room rate The rate charged daily for a hotel room.

Route 66 A historic highway that goes from Chicago, Illinois, through eight states to end in Santa Monica, California. This route is also called "The Highway of Hope."

Safari Wildlife watching in Africa that lets visitors get up close and personal with exotic species such as elephants, gazelles, lions, and cheetahs.

Sales promotion Activities aimed at giving consumers or retailers an extra incentive to buy the product or service.

Scarcity The inability to satisfy all our wants.

Scenic trip A road or part of a stretch of road that offers spectacular views.

School-to-work programs Programs that combine school and work during the same period of time, which helps students learn skills and gain knowledge to qualify for a full-time job in the near future.

Seasonality The peaks and valleys of demand for a destination and its facilities.

Secondary data Data that were collected for another purpose than the one for which they are currently being used.

Semistructured interviews Interviews that allow the interviewer to adapt follow-up questions according to the respondent's answers. There is a schedule to be followed, but this is simply to ensure that all topics of interest are covered.

Shinkansen Also referred to as the Bullet Train system; a Japanese train system that started in time for the 1964 Olympics in Japan.

Short-term plans Also known as tactile or operational plans. Plans to meet short-term needs.

Site-specific indicators Indicators that provide relevant information that can contribute to better decision making and, consequently, a more sustainable future for the tourism industry. Site-specific indicators are developed for one specific site.

Site stress Stress on the tourism site caused by overuse.

Social aspects of tourism Tourism motivations, roles and social relations of tourists, the structure and dynamics of the tourism system and of touristic institutions, the nature of attractions and their representations, and the impact of tourism on host societies.

Social impacts The positive and negative impacts tourism has on a particular destination. Examples include revival of the arts and increased crime.

Social, military, educational, religious, and fraternal groups (SMERF) A market segment for the sales of banqueting rooms and meeting facilities.

Social tourism A concept implying at least a partial subsidy of the travel itself or of the destination experience.

Socioeconomic groups Groups of people with similar social and economic standing.

Sociology of tourism The study of human social behavior, especially the study of the origins, organization, institutions, and development of human society as it pertains to tourism.

Statistical research *See* descriptive research.

Strategic planning Long-range planning that steers an organization towards its goals and mission accomplishment.

Strategies Plans of action designed to achieve a particular goal.

Structured interviews The least flexible of the interview types. Very orderly and include prearranged interview questions. In addition, they often use codes for responses.

Supersonic jet An airplane that flies at supersonic speeds. The only supersonic plane ever used for civil aviation is (or was) the *Concorde*, which cruises at a speed of 1,458 miles per hour.

Superstructure The airports, bridges, roads, and railways of a certain area.

Supply *See* law of supply.

Supply curve Illustrates the law of supply; the supply curve's upward slope indicates a direct relationship between price and demand, meaning that when one factor increases, the other increases as well.

Supply side The sectors of the tourism industry that take care of tourist needs.

Survey method Gathering information about human populations by asking questions of respondents.

Sustainable approach Plans that avoid environmental and sociocultural degradation. Involves setting strict guidelines that help protect the community for future generations, such as visitation volume limits.

Sustainable development The optimal use of natural and cultural resources for national development on an equitable and self-sustaining basis, and in harmony with the environment.

Sustainable tourism Tourism that satisfies current demands without compromising the needs of future generations.

SWOT analysis A tool commonly used for marketing strategy purposes, consisting of investigation of strengths, weaknesses, opportunities, and threats.

System of National Accounts (SNA) National accounts as part of an overall system.

Systems approach Planning process that views tourism as a complete and integrated system.

Tactical or operational planning Plans generally created for up to approximately one year that fit into the strategic plans.

Target market The consumer or business groups that hold the highest profit potential for a product or service.

Technology In the tourism and travel industry, the objective is to increase the use of new and emerging technologies that work more efficiently in terms of time and costs and that can enhance the visitor experience. Changes in technology also change the way the travel and tourism industry operates.

Telephone survey A survey method in which the interviewer (or computer) simply reads questions over the telephone to the respondent from a questionnaire and records the person's answers into a computer database as they are provided.

TGV trains (trains à grande vitesse) High-tech/high-speed trains originating in France.

Theory An explanation of a phenomenon based on careful and precise observations.

Tour operators Companies that arrange every aspect of a travel package on a local, national, or international level.

Tourism Travel for recreation or the promotion and arrangement of such travel.

Tourism Industries, U.S. Department of Commerce Office of Travel and Tourism Industries (OTTI) An organization that collects, analyzes, and disseminates international travel and tourism statistics for the U.S. Travel and Tourism Statistical System.

Tourism industry sector Subsets of the tourism industry whose components share similar characteristics. Sector analysis separates and shows the major components of tourism in the U.S. economy, including the production of tourism commodities (goods and services purchased), the supply and consumption of tourism commodities, tourism (purchasing) demand by type of commodity and type of visitor, tourism gross domestic product, and tourism employment.

Tourism master plan A plan developed by a government to achieve its country's goals regarding tourism.

Tourism niche Specialty travel forms of tourism.

Tourism planning Similar to "regular" business planning. Sets the perimeters of the proposed project of development. The process of planning is typically done in seven steps including goal setting, researching, data collecting, analyzing, developing, implementing, and monitoring.

Tourism policy A plan or course of action of a government, political party, or business related to tourism that is designed to influence and determine decisions, actions, and other matters with a goal in mind. Its primary purpose is to establish tourism as a foundation for peace and prosperity and as a means to improve quality of life by realizing the benefits of tourism for destinations.

Tourism and satellite accounts (TSA) A system developed to measure travelers' purchases of different products and services.

Tourist A person who takes trips away from home of 100 miles or more and who stays at least one night away from home.

Tourist dollar Money spent by foreign tourists in a country. The tourist dollar is valued higher than money coming from within the country because it comes fresh into the economy and often triggers rounds of additional spending.

Tourist typologies Classifications of tourists reflecting the diversity of individual motivations, styles, interests, and values over time.

Trade liberalization The reduction or elimination of barriers to trade in services between countries, such as reducing high taxes imposed on foreign firms and decreasing the amount of documentation necessary for doing business in other countries. May lead to unified quality standards for similar services provided by different countries, improved market transparency, and competition.

Transient Occupancy Tax (TOT) A local tax levied on hotel accommodations.

Transportation Any means used to move goods or people from one area to another. Usually includes automobile, ship, rail, and air transport.

Transportation infrastructure A system combining the facilities, equipment, and organizations needed to make an area's transportation system function and available to the traveling public, such as roadways, signage, gas stations, railways, airports, shuttle services, taxis, buses, cars, limousines, trains, aerial tramways, subways, airplanes, harbors, ships, and cruise ships.

Travel and Tourism Research Association (TTRA) An international network of more than 800 travel and tourism research and marketing professionals who advocate standards, quality research, and marketing information to the industry.

Travel chain The series of events that stimulate travel and make it convenient and satisfying.

Travel distribution system System that connects travel agents and agencies with travel service providers and provides them with content from airlines, hotel properties, car rental companies, cruise lines, railroads, and tour operators.

Travel Industry Association (TIA) A nonprofit trade organization that represents and speaks for the common interests of the U.S. travel industry.

United Nations World Tourism Organization (UNTWO) The leading international organization in the field of tourism that serves as a global forum for tourism policy issues and a practical source of tourism know-how.

U.S. Travel Data Center (USTDC) The research division of the Travel Industry Association (TIA).

Unstructured interviews Also called *nondirectional;* interviews that have no prearranged format. The interviewer may have a general set of probe topics to pursue but is not confined to or required to ask about them.

Use intensity indicator *See* density indicator.

Vacation ownership The opportunity for consumers to purchase fully furnished vacation accommodations in a variety of forms, such as for use in weekly intervals or in a points-based system, for a percentage of the cost of full ownership.

Validity Production of the desired results correctly deduced from a premise. In research validity, the degree to which evidence and theory support the interpretations of test scores. Validity is also a part of research design referring to the degree to which a study supports the intended conclusion drawn from the results.

Vertical integration Ownership of or linkage with suppliers of raw materials or airlines owning hotels.

Visa Waiver Program (VWP) A program created by the U.S. Congress that provides access for international visitors from, currently, 34 low-risk countries to visit the United States for up to 90 days without having to obtain a visa.

Visitor facilitation Improving customer service and reducing entry barriers to the country for visitors through facilitative policies and procedures at the nation's borders and ports of entry; designed to improve the visitor's experience of gaining access to and arriving in the country.

Visitor safety and security Establishment of policies and procedures that enhance visitor safety and security.

World Heritage site According to United Nations Educational, Scientific and Cultural Organization (UNESCO), sites that have been found to have "outstanding universal value" (as opposed to just national significance), and include each country's most outstanding examples of natural and cultural heritage.

World Travel and Tourism Council (WTTC) An international organization of travel industry executives promoting travel and tourism worldwide.

Yield management Practice of analyzing past reservation patterns, seat rates, cancelations, and no-shows in an attempt to maximize profits and seat rates and to set the most competitive room rates.

Index

Part Opener and Chapter Opener Photo Credits

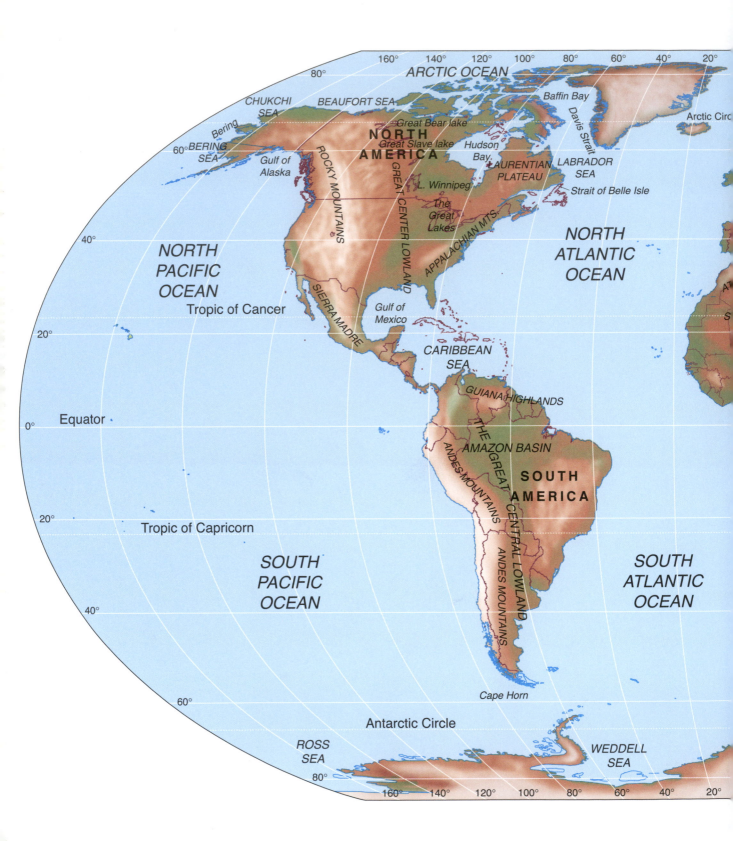

ARCTIC OCEAN

CHUKCHI
SEA

BEAUFORT SEA

Baffin Bay

Arctic Circ

Great Bear lake

NORTH
AMERICA

Hudson
Bay

Great Slave lake

Bering

BERING
SEA

Gulf of
Alaska

ROCKY MOUNTAINS

GREAT CENTER LOWLAND

L. Winnipeg

The
Great
Lakes

LAURENTIAN
PLATEAU

LABRADOR
SEA

APPALACHIAN MTS.

Davis Strait

Strait of Belle Isle

NORTH
ATLANTIC
OCEAN

NORTH
PACIFIC
OCEAN

Tropic of Cancer

SIERRA MADRE

Gulf of
Mexico

CARIBBEAN
SEA

GUIANA HIGHLANDS

Equator

ANDES MOUNTAINS

THE
AMAZON BASIN

THE GREAT CENTRAL LOWLAND

SOUTH
AMERICA

AT
S

Tropic of Capricorn

SOUTH
PACIFIC
OCEAN

ANDES MOUNTAINS

SOUTH
ATLANTIC
OCEAN

Cape Horn

Antarctic Circle

ROSS
SEA

WEDDELL
SEA